PRAISE FOR CUBA

"Ada Ferrer's *Cuba* is a remarkable work of history. Covering more than five centuries and much of the Atlantic world, *Cuba* is also deeply thoughtful and highly personal in a way that truly enriches it. Imaginatively conceived and beautifully written, *Cuba* tells complex human stories in riveting ways and challenges our understanding of an island whose history has shaped—and will continue to shape—the Americas. *Cuba* is *An American History* in the fullest sense."   —STEVEN HAHN,
Pulitzer Prize–winning author of *A Nation Under Our Feet*

"An encompassing look back at Cuba, from before the arrival of Columbus to the present day . . . A moving chronicle of the relationship between the United States and Cuba and what that's meant for both sides."
—*FORBES*

"A riveting, nuanced, and insightful narrative told through a multitude of personalities—from the well-known to those whose names have been lost to history. Here is the saga of Cuba presented in all the complexity it deserves: an *American* story that is inseparable from that of the United States. This clear-eyed chronicle will forever change your perspective on the historic relationship between the two countries and upend much of the history you thought you knew. Ada Ferrer is a gift, a scholar with the subtle prose of a novelist and the heart to chronicle a history that is both personal and epic. *Cuba* is an absolutely essential read."   —ANA MENÉNDEZ,
Florida International University,
author of *In Cuba I Was a German Shepherd*

"*Cuba* focuses on the equivocal relationship of the two countries, and presents it convincingly as symbiotic. . . . Exemplary . . . [full of] lively insights and lucid prose . . . By being equally severe with Cuban leaders and US leaders, Ms. Ferrer achieves an honorable objective: pleasing nobody by being just."   —*THE WALL STREET JOURNAL*

MORE PRAISE FOR *CUBA*

"This monumental new book represents another formidable piece of original scholarship. It is written, moreover, in an admirably paced narrative style, which, one suspects, will earn it pride of place among the published histories of Cuba."

—Jon Lee Anderson, *Foreign Affairs*

"Offers a fresh look at the long and complicated relationship between Cuba and its larger neighbor to the north, upending long-held conceptions and untangling myth from reality."

—*USA Today*

"With singular mastery and insight, Ada Ferrer reconstructs the intertwined histories of Cuba and the United States. It is an intimate and timely story of conflict and misunderstandings, but also of opportunities and possibilities."

—Alejandro de la Fuente, Afro-Latin American Research Institute, Harvard University

"Ada Ferrer makes Cuba's American history come to life. Whatever you may think of the politics around Cuba, its rich and complex history and that of its people is told here in a thoughtful and compelling way, with revealing detail, deep research, and beautiful writing."

—Soledad O'Brien, host of *Matter of Fact with Soledad O'Brien* and coauthor of *Latino in America* and *The Next Big Story*

"To explore the history of Cuba is to explore the history of the United States. . . . Ferrer is an exceptionally thorough guide of the fifteenth century onward, careful to keep her readers' attention with interesting characters, new insights on historical events, and dramatic yet accessible writing. This new history of Cuba shows how connected all of our countries' histories really are."

—*BookPage*, "Best Books of 2021" (starred review)

"Ada Ferrer has written a sweeping, beautiful, and indispensable history of an endlessly fascinating country. *Cuba* captures the breadth and emotion of the story of a small country that has been at the center of so many major events shaping our world."

—Ben Rhodes, author of *After the Fall: Being American in the World We've Made*

"Ferrer has produced an English-language history of Cuba remarkable not only for being comprehensive, but also eminently readable. . . . Ferrer delves into deep background that students of contemporary history may have never before encountered."

—*Booklist* (starred review)

"A fluid, consistently informative history of the long, inextricable link between Cuba and the US, well rendered by a veteran Cuban American historian . . . Ferrer is an endlessly knowledgeable guide. . . . She is especially good in delineating how a distinct Cuban identity was forged over the centuries. A wonderfully nuanced history of the island nation and its often troubled dealings with its gigantic and voracious neighbor."

—*Kirkus Reviews* (starred review)

"So near and yet so far. We think we know Cuba but this book reveals that we have never grasped its epic and frequently tragic history. Ada Ferrer offers us the penetrating perspective of someone who is neither the complete insider nor the complete outsider, but who cares passionately about Cuba and its confounding entanglement with the United States."

—Lynn Hunt, author of *History: Why It Matters*

"In clear and elegant prose, Ada Ferrer, a leading historian of Cuba, vividly brings to life the history of Cuba. I now have an unequivocal answer to those who ask me to recommend a book that will introduce them to the island nation, as well as a clear choice when selecting a text that will engage my students in the dramatic story of Cuba."

—Lisandro Pérez, author of the award-winning *Sugar, Cigars, and Revolution: The Making of Cuban New York*

"A captivating history of Cuba, highly recommended for general readers and specialists alike."

—*Library Journal*

"With deft prose and a subtle sensibility, Ada Ferrer narrates the intimate, intertwined histories of the United States and its island neighbor Cuba. Antonio Maceo, José Martí, and others sought to transform the Spanish colony into a cross-racial republic, while thwarting US intrusion into the larger Americas. But powerful outsiders have presumed the right to shape events on the island, and found domestic allies willing to assist. As Ferrer's delicate stories of ordinary people unfold alongside the doings of visionaries and politicians on both sides of the Straits of Florida, she wonders: Could there eventually emerge a mutual respect that might save our respective rulers from folly?"

—Rebecca J. Scott, author of *Degrees of Freedom: Louisiana and Cuba after Slavery*

ALSO BY ADA FERRER

Insurgent Cuba: Race, Nation, and Revolution, 1868–1898

Freedom's Mirror: Cuba and Haiti in the Age of Revolution

CUBA

AN AMERICAN HISTORY

ADA FERRER

SCRIBNER

New York   London   Toronto   Sydney   New Delhi

Scribner
An Imprint of Simon & Schuster, Inc.
1230 Avenue of the Americas
New York, NY 10020

First Scribner trade paperback edition June 2022

SCRIBNER and design are registered trademarks of The Gale Group, Inc., used under license by Simon & Schuster, Inc., the publisher of this work.

For information about special discounts for bulk purchases, please contact Simon & Schuster Special Sales at 1-866-506-1949 or business@simonandschuster.com.

The Simon & Schuster Speakers Bureau can bring authors to your live event. For more information or to book an event, contact the Simon & Schuster Speakers Bureau at 1-866-248-3049 or visit our website at www.simonspeakers.com.

Interior design by Wendy Blum

Manufactured in Italy

1   3   5   7   9   10   8   6   4   2

Library of Congress Cataloging-in-Publication Data
Names: Ferrer, Ada, author.
Title: Cuba : an American history / Ada Ferrer.
Description: First Scribner hardcover edition. | New York ; London :
Scribner, 2021. | Includes bibliographical references and index.
Identifiers: LCCN 2021020533 (print) | LCCN 2021020534 (ebook) |
ISBN 9781501154553 (hardcover) | ISBN 9781501154577 (ebook)
Subjects: LCSH: Cuba—History. | Cuba—Foreign relations—United States. |
United States—Foreign relations—Cuba.
Classification: LCC F1776 .F397 2021 (print) | LCC F1776 (ebook) | DDC 972.91—dc23
LC record available at https://lccn.loc.gov/2021020533
LC ebook record available at https://lccn.loc.gov/2021020534

ISBN 978-1-5011-5455-3
ISBN 978-1-5011-5456-0 (pbk)
ISBN 978-1-5011-5457-7 (ebook)

For my father, Ramón Ferrer, *siempre presente*

To the memory of:
My mother, Adelaida Ferrer (1926–2020), whom I adored
My half brothers, Hipólito Cabrera (1953–2020)
and Juan José González (1946–2009), both left behind
My aunt, Ada Fernández (1930–2017), who welcomed me back

For my sister, Aixa, born here, and for Nailah, her daughter
For my husband, Gregg, and my daughters, Alina and Lucía, with all my love.
In more ways than one, this is their story, too.

CONTENTS

CONTENTS

CONTENTS

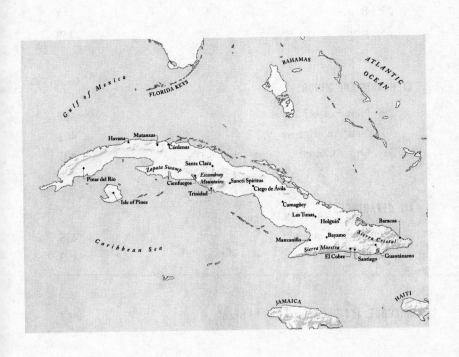

CUBA

Prologue

THERE AND HERE

*C*uba: An American History tells the story of a tropical island that sits between the Atlantic Ocean and the Caribbean Sea, not far from the United States. It is a history of more than half a millennium, from before the arrival of Christopher Columbus to the death of Fidel Castro and beyond. Yet, for a history so sweeping in scope, this is also a deeply personal book.

I was born in Havana between the Bay of Pigs invasion of 1961 and the Cuban Missile Crisis of 1962. My father was in New York, having left the island a few months earlier. My mother went into labor alone and hailed herself a cab to Workers' Maternity. The hospital's name fit the moment; Cuba was, after all, in the throes of a radical revolution, avowedly socialist and stridently anti-imperialist. Yet the hospital had been built two decades earlier under the rule of Fulgencio Batista, the very dictator Castro unseated in 1959. Monumental in size and style, the hospital won architecture awards when it was built. Its most emblematic feature towers over the main entrance, a soaring ceramic statue of a mother and child created by Teodoro Ramos Blanco, a Black sculptor who was among Cuba's most renowned artists. That morning in June 1962, my mother paused and looked up at the statue as if in prayer before entering the hospital to give birth. Ten months later, she left Cuba, statuesque in her heels and with me an infant in her arms.

We left the house at six in the evening. My nine-year-old brother was outside playing with friends, and she had not told him that we were leaving without him. His father, her first husband, would not grant permission for him to go. At the airport, a woman in uniform put her fingers to my earlobes to feel the tiny gold-post earrings, as if about to take them, and then changed her mind. On arriving in Mexico, my mother had to rely on the kindness of a stranger to make it into the city. When we got to Jim Crow Miami a few months later, my mother

1

encountered an old acquaintance helping officials assign newcomers to hotels. In the United States, my mother might have been regarded as Black, though in Cuba she was not. Her old friend assigned us to a white hotel. Arriving at the airport in New York a few days later, I opened my arms to my waiting father, as if I already knew him. These and other stories were my inherited memory of our departure from Cuba and our arrival in the United States.

After some initial moving around—Harlem, Brooklyn, Miami—we settled in West New York, New Jersey, a working-class community that was predominantly Cuban. On Saturdays, I wrote letters to my brother and grandmother in Cuba. On Sundays, I listened to our priest pray for the release of political prisoners on the island. Every September 8, I walked in the procession for Cuba's patron saint, La Caridad del Cobre, or the Virgin of Charity, marching past buildings painted with anti-Castro graffiti. After work, my mother sometimes cried about people still back home—her son, in particular. An absent presence, a present absence, Cuba was impossible to escape.

Eventually I stopped trying and decided instead that I needed to understand it. To the stories I had heard for so long, I began adding my own questions. My parents had not lost property or income to the revolution, so why had they left? Why had their brothers and sisters mostly stayed? Does a revolution change people? Does migration? Who had my brother become, and who would I be if we had stayed? Alongside the phantasmagorical Cuba that surrounded me, I began conjuring my own.

Then in 1990, I returned to Cuba for the first time. I visited the people we had left behind—those still living. I listened to their stories and studied their old pictures. I traveled to the countryside where my parents were born, each in a different part of the island. I even went to Workers' Maternity and took photographs of Teodoro Ramos Blanco's sculpture of a mother and child. I made Cuba mine. In fact, I made it my life's work. Immersing myself in its libraries and archives, I began a decades-long process of reconstructing the island's past, and my own, from a seemingly bottomless source of frayed old documents. Sometimes the ink on their pages literally became powder in my hands; occasionally I paused at the sight of the shaky Xs—actually crosses—that took the place of signatures for people unable to write. And in the process of trying to summon up Cuba's past, I came to regard it anew. I learned to see it from within and without, refusing the binary interpretations imposed from on high in Washington and Havana and Miami. I began translating Cuba for Americans and the United States for Cubans. Then I used all that to see myself, my family, and my own home—the United States—with different eyes.

THERE AND HERE

This book is one result of that effort, a product of more than thirty years of work and of a lifetime of shifting perspectives between the country where I was born and the country where I made my life. It is at once a history I inherited and a history I have fashioned out of many possible ones. It is, in other words, what I have made of my sometimes heavy inheritance.

THE HISTORY OF CUBA LENDS itself to monumental and epic tellings. It is a story of violent conquest and occupation; of conspiracies against slavery and colonialism; of revolutions attempted, victorious, and undone. Epic, however, is often the preferred narrative of nation-states. So in telling this history, I have tried to heed the late Howard Zinn's admonition to not let history become the memory of states. I have also remembered Leo Tolstoy's advice in his second epilogue to *War and Peace* to not focus our histories merely on monarchs and writers, but rather to tell "the history of the life of the peoples," as he called it.[1] So, in this history of Cuba, kings and presidents, revolutionaries and dictators share space with many others. Some are human versions of historic men and women to whom monuments have been built. Other people—whether those taking up arms in a revolution or sewing to the light of glowworms in a slave hut or building a raft to take to sea—appear here without names, for those have not always survived in the historical record. They, too, serve as guides through this history, for they, too, move the stories of war and peace and life in these pages.

There is, however, another major force in the history of Cuba—not as important as its own people, but critical nonetheless. The United States. More than a history of Cuba, then, this book is also a history of Cuba in relation to the United States, a history of the sometimes intimate, sometimes explosive, always uneven relationship between the two countries. That is one reason I have titled the book *Cuba: An American History.*

The connections between Cuba and the United States stretch back over centuries and run in both directions. Few Americans have likely considered the significance of Cuba for the United States. During the American Revolution, Cubans raised funds in support of Washington's army, and soldiers from Cuba fought against the British in North America and the Caribbean. As the thirteen colonies lost access to other British possessions, the Spanish colony of Cuba became a vital trading partner. In fact, Havana's storehouse of coveted silver currency helped finance the new nation's first central bank. Later, after Florida and Texas became states of the Union in 1845, propertied southerners—and even some northerners—looked to Cuba as a potential new slave state or two, as a way to buttress the power of slavery and its economy.

In 1898, the United States intervened militarily in Cuba and declared war on Spain. With that intervention, the United States turned what had been a thirty-year movement for Cuban independence into the conflict that history usually remembers as the Spanish-American War. The end of some four hundred years of Spanish rule was ritually observed at noon on January 1, 1899, with the synchronized lowering of every Spanish flag on the island. But the flag raised in its place was not a Cuban flag but an American one. With that began a full-fledged military occupation that ended four years later, only after Cuban leaders, under enormous pressure, agreed to grant the US government the right of intervention in Cuba. If the events of 1898 were fateful for Cuba, they also helped produce two consequential developments in the United States: first, the reconciliation of the white South and North after decades of disunion and, second, the emergence of the United States as an imperial power on the world stage.

For more than a century, the role of the United States in Cuban independence has been the subject of disagreement—a shared history viewed in radically divergent terms. Historically, American statesmen have tended to view US intervention in 1898 as an illustration of American benevolence. The United States had rallied to the cause of a neighbor's independence and declared war to achieve it. In this version of history, Cuban independence was a gift of the Americans, and for that Cubans owed them a debt of gratitude. In Cuba, however, 1898 represents something entirely different: more theft than gift. There, 1898 was the moment when the United States swept in at the end of a war the Cubans had already almost won, claimed victory, and proceeded to rule over Cuba as a de facto colonial power. *Cuba Does Not Owe Its Independence to the United States* read the title of an important book published in Havana in 1950.[2]

Alongside that American presumption and Cuban resentment, however, existed dense networks of human contact forged over decades by people of all kinds in both countries. Cuba's flag was designed and flown for the first time by Cuban exiles in the United States. The first pro-independence Cuban newspaper was published in Philadelphia, and the first national novel was written in New York. Cuba's most famous patriot and writer, José Martí, spent more of his adult life in the United States than in Cuba, and the largest memorial service for Cuba's most important war hero, Antonio Maceo, was held at Cooper Union in New York. Cubans traveled to the United States to study at Harvard and Tuskegee, to shop in Miami, to play baseball in the American Negro Leagues, to escape dictators, and to view the famous falls at Niagara. Americans traveled in the other direction: to drink during Prohibition in the States, to buy land and cigars, to convert people to Protestantism, to forge networks of Black solidarity, to honeymoon and to fish, to hear jazz and get abortions. Americans listened to Cuban music, and Cubans watched American movies. Americans bought Cuban sugar; Cubans bought American appliances. Actually, Cubans bought just about everything (except sugar) from the United States.

Then all that changed. Not overnight, exactly, but almost. When Fidel Castro was organizing and fighting his revolution against Fulgencio Batista, few could have foreseen the drastic realignment about to take place. But within two years of the revolutionary seizure of power in January 1959, the two countries would be at veritable war. The new Cuban government nationalized US properties, and Cubans staged a mock funeral, complete with coffins bearing the names of Esso, United Fruit, and so on. Crowds overturned the American eagle atop the monument to the *Maine*, the ship that launched the Spanish-American War and US intervention. They knocked down part of the monument to the island's first president, Tomás Estrada Palma, who was once also a naturalized US citizen. Visiting the site today, one would find only the statue's shoes atop the original pedestal. The history of American empire—and its repudiation—is written into the very streetscapes of Havana.

Soon the two countries closed their embassies and forbade travel. In 1961, American forces composed of Cuban exiles invaded, only to be captured and eventually returned to the United States in exchange for medicine and baby food. At the height of the Cold War, Cuba, long a client state of the United States, became the staunch ally of that government's avowed enemy, the Soviet Union. Now Cuban sugar went to the Soviet Union, and oil and machinery that would have once come from the United States came from there as well. In October 1962, for the first time in its history, the mainland United States faced nuclear warheads pointed in its direction from within striking distance. Battle lines had not only been drawn, but also barricaded and mined.

The exigencies of the Cold War meant that for decades Americans generally understood Cuba primarily as a small—if dangerously proximate—satellite of the Soviet Union. Yet, its role in that global conflict notwithstanding, the Revolution of 1959 cannot be understood only within a Cold War framework. The Cuban Revolution was not one thing; it changed over time in goals and methods. Before taking power, it was emphatically not communist, nor particularly anti-American. Cubans did not support the movement against strongman Fulgencio Batista because they desired to live under socialism or at near war with the United States. Yet the revolution produced both outcomes in relatively quick succession. What explains how that happened, and what would follow, is less the context of the Cold War than the revolution's relationship to history. Understanding that history—fascinating on its own terms and intriguing in its thorny entanglements with the United States—is therefore vital. Indeed, to overcome the ingrained enmities of more than half a century in both countries, a clear-eyed reckoning with the past, with history, is the first step forward.

HISTORY, HOWEVER, ALWAYS LOOKS DIFFERENT depending on where one stands. This book takes that observation as a point of departure. It is a history of Cuba that functions *also* as a kind of history of the United States. It is a shadow history, a necessarily selective, incomplete history of the United States reimagined from Cuban ground and Cuban waters. From that vantage point, America looks different. Indeed, it is not even America, a name that Cubans—like many others across the world—use to name not the United States, but the two continents and the islands of the Western Hemisphere. It is a name that, in theory, belongs as much to Cuba (or Mexico, Argentina, and Canada) as it does to the United States. That is another reason this book is called *Cuba: An American History*, to unsettle expectations about what America is and is not. Cuban history, meanwhile, can be many things. One of those is a mirror to the history of the United States. In this history of Cuba, then, US readers can see their own country refracted through the eyes of another, from the outside in, much as I have lived and understood both Cuba and the United States most of my life.

Part I

DISPATCHES FROM THE FIRST AMERICA

A woodcut illustration from the 1494 publication of Christopher Columbus's report of his arrival in the New World.

Chapter 1

HEAVEN AND HELL

The history of Cuba begins where American history begins. *History*, of course, has more than one meaning. It refers to events of the past—war and peace, scientific breakthroughs and mass migrations, the collapse of a civilization, the liberation of a people. But *history* also refers to the stories that people tell about those pasts. History in the first sense refers to what happened; in the second, to what is said to have happened. Cuban history begins as American history does in the second sense of the word: history as narrative, as one telling of many possible ones, invariably grander and necessarily smaller than the other kind of history—history as it is lived.[1]

For both Cuba and the United States, this second kind of history—history-as-narrative—often begins in 1492 with the epic miscalculation of a Genoese navigator Americans know as Christopher Columbus. In its day, Columbus's gaffe was a perfectly reasonable one. He had studied navigational maps and treatises of both his contemporaries and the ancients; he had sailed on Portuguese ships to Iceland and West Africa. He understood—as had the Greeks and Muslims long before and most Europeans in his own time—that the world was not flat. And he used that knowledge and experience to make a deceptively simple argument. From Europe, the best way to reach the East was to sail west.

In an age when every European explorer was racing to find new trade routes to Asia, Columbus approached several European monarchs to propose his westerly route. The king of Portugal said no. King Ferdinand and Queen Isabella of Spain twice rejected the proposal. Eventually, after his third attempt, they decided to let him try. The year was 1492. The Spanish monarchs had just waged the final, victorious campaign of the Christian Reconquest, ending seven hundred years of Muslim control on the Iberian Peninsula. The majestic city of Granada, the last Muslim stronghold, fell to the Catholic kings on January 2, 1492. Columbus was there that day. He saw the royal banners of Ferdinand and Isabella flying atop the towers of the Alhambra, and he watched as the Muslim king knelt to kiss their royal hands. Columbus was still in the city later that month when Ferdinand and Isabella ordered Jewish residents of their kingdoms to convert to Christianity, leave voluntarily, or face expulsion. Thus did Columbus witness the final victory of a militant and intolerant religiosity. In fact, he was its beneficiary, for it was only with that war over that the Catholic monarchs acceded to Columbus's unusual venture.

On Friday, August 3, 1492, just three days after the deadline for the Jews of Spain to leave and a half hour before sunrise, Columbus set sail. He bore the title the king and queen had conferred on him: High Admiral of the Ocean Sea and Viceroy and Governor for life of all the islands and continents he might discover. As befitting a man of that rank, he peered out at the horizon with confidence. Wealthy, thriving Asia awaited him, just on the other side of a sea he was sure he could cross "in a few days with a fair wind."[2]

Two months and nine days later, on October 12, 1492, Columbus and his weary sailors made landfall on a small island. Convinced he was somewhere in Asia, which Europeans of the time called India, he asked two captains to "bear faithful testimony that he, in the presence of all, had taken . . . possession of the said island for the King and for the Queen his Lords."[3] Columbus directed a secretary to come ashore with him and consign the event to writing, and therefore to history. Nothing anyone wrote, not even Columbus's own journal, survived in its original form. The people who watched from shore—henceforth known to Europeans as Indians because of Columbus's error—wrote nothing at all. Even had the first survived and the second existed, no writing produced in that moment could have conveyed the momentousness those events would later acquire. Columbus and his men had arrived in another world—new to them, ancient to the people already there. With that arrival began not history itself, but one of the most important chapters of it ever written.

THE STORY OF COLUMBUS'S ARRIVAL in the so-called New World is completely familiar to readers in the United States and has been for centuries. One of the country's early national anthems was called "Hail, Columbia," the title referring, of course, to Columbus. Cities and towns across the young country took Columbus's name. In the nation's capital, the District of Columbia, a painting called the *Landing of Columbus* has graced the Rotunda of the Capitol Building since the 1850s. The date of that landing remains today a national holiday. Generations of American schoolchildren have learned the story of Columbus, usually only a little after learning to read. That they often forget most of the details can be gleaned from the recent experience of a park ranger at the national monument at Plymouth Rock, the site of the first landing of the *Mayflower* pilgrims. The park ranger once explained that the most common questions she fields from visitors have to do with the famous Genoese sailor. "Was this where Columbus first landed?" they often ask her. Confused, many ask why the historical marker at the site says 1620 and not 1492.[4] Columbus begins US history not only in this kind of popular conception, but also in much of the nation's written history, from the very first ones ever published in the early decades of the nineteenth century to the 2018 book *These Truths: A History of the United States*, by Harvard professor and *New Yorker* writer Jill Lepore.[5]

For decades, historians and activists have pointed out at least two glaring problems with the Columbus myth as history. They focus on the violence unleashed by Columbus's arrival—the long and tragic history of genocide and Native dispossession it inaugurated. Here, Columbus is no hero at all. In 2020, activists across the United States targeted monuments dedicated to his memory—tying ropes around his statue and pulling it down in Minneapolis, beheading one in Boston, setting another aflame in Richmond and then plunging it into a lake. Activists and historians point out another simple fact: namely, that Columbus did not discover America. The people of the lands on which he arrived in 1492 already knew they were there. The hemisphere had a population significantly larger than Europe's and cities that rivaled Europe's in size. Its people had political systems, agriculture, science, their own sense of history, their own origin stories set in pasts long before Columbus. This critical and accurate appraisal of the Columbus myth applies not just to the United States, but to Cuba and all the Americas.

Yet there is a further distortion that arises from making Columbus the beginning of US history specifically. In a casual conversation with a Connecticut businessman waiting to board a flight in Havana's airport, I mentioned writing a book on the history of Cuba from Columbus to the present. His question was sincere: Did Columbus discover Cuba, too? I hesitated before responding, feeling a little like the park ranger at Plymouth Rock. He did land in Cuba, I said, forgoing the word *discover*. But he never set foot anywhere on what we now call the United States. The businessman looked at me in disbelief. It was a simple, indisputable fact received like a revelation: Columbus never came to this America.

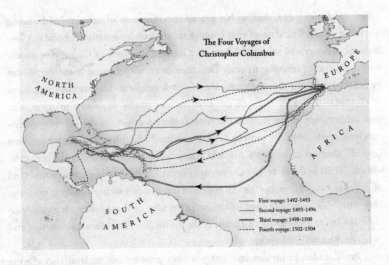

The Four Voyages of
Christopher Columbus

First voyage: 1492-1493
Second voyage: 1493-1496
Third voyage: 1498-1500
Fourth voyage: 1502-1504

How is it that a history that did not even occur on the North American continent came to serve as the obligatory origin point of US history? There are, after all, other possibilities—even for those people who insist on beginning with the arrival of Europeans: Leif Erikson and the Vikings in 1000, for example, or John Cabot in 1497, Jamestown in 1607, or Plymouth Rock in 1620, to name the most obvious. Scholars sometimes maintain that a newly independent United States, searching for an origin story not indebted to Great Britain (its erstwhile mother country), pivoted to embrace Christopher Columbus and 1492. Then the renarration stuck.⁶

Yet Columbus was convenient for another reason as well. The conception of US history as originating in 1492 emerged precisely as the new country's leaders began developing policies of territorial expansion. As early as 1786, Thomas Jefferson had prophesied that Spain's empire would collapse, and he expressed his wish for the United States to acquire it "peice by peice [sic]."⁷ By the 1820s and 1830s, Jefferson's casually stated desire had become a matter of national policy. The 1820s saw the enunciation of the Monroe Doctrine, which sought to limit the reach of Europe in newly independent Latin America, leaving the continent open to the growing power of the United States. The 1840s saw the emergence of Manifest Destiny, the idea that the United States was meant to extend through Indian and Spanish territories all the way to the continent's Pacific Coast. The lands of the collapsing Spanish Empire, an empire set in motion by Columbus's voyage of 1492, were now squarely in the sights of

American leaders. George Bancroft, the author of one of the very first histories of the United States, was one of those politicians. As secretary of the navy and acting secretary of war, his actions would further US expansion into once-Spanish Texas and California during the administration of James Polk, himself also a strong advocate of US expansionism and one of several presidents to propose purchasing Cuba from Spain.

When early US historians such as Bancroft nudged Columbus, a man who never set foot in the lands of the United States, into the first chapter of a new national saga, they essentially seized a foreign history to make it theirs, some of them fully expecting that the lands on which that history had unfolded would soon be theirs, too. Today, Americans recognize the basic story of Columbus, often unmindful of the fact that it unfolded in another America. If Columbus begins US history as written, that is partly because, consciously or unconsciously, imperial ambitions have shaped US history from the beginning, too. And Cuba—where Columbus did land—is a critical presence in that American history.

IN 1492, COLUMBUS FIRST MADE landfall not in Cuba, but on the easternmost island of the Bahamas. He immediately claimed it for Spain and christened it San Salvador, though the people already there had always called it Guanahani. Meeting them for the first time, Columbus concluded that they would make good servants and convert easily to Christianity. They rowed out to the Spanish ships in canoes, which Columbus and his men had never seen before, bearing skeins of cotton thread, parrots, darts, and things so numerous and small that he declared they would be too tedious to recount. Columbus had other things in mind. "I was attentive and took trouble to ascertain if there was gold . . . and by signs I was able to make out that to the south . . . there was a king who had great cups full." The next day, taking several Native people to serve as guides, Columbus left Guanahani and continued his journey. He did not sail past any island without taking possession of it, something he did by merely saying it was so. To each, he gave a name, even though they already had names.[8]

On October 28, Columbus arrived at an island he thought looked larger than all those around it. He was right. At more than 42,000 square miles, it boasted 3,700 miles of coastline, most of it on the northern and southern coasts. The distance between its eastern- and westernmost points—some 750 miles—would be roughly equal to that between New York City and Savannah, Georgia. Some say that the island's very long, narrow shape gives it the appearance of an alligator, one of its own native species.

Columbus landed on the island's northeastern coast. It was, he said aloud, "the most beautiful that eyes have seen." He spotted dogs that did not bark, unknown fruits wonderful to taste, land that was high like Sicily, mountains with peaks like beautiful mosques, and air that was scented and sweet at night. Though the people of the place called the island Cuba or Cubanacán, Columbus insisted that it was Cipangu, the name Marco Polo had given to Japan, a land awash in great riches. Unfortunately for Columbus, Cuba had no teeming cities, no golden-roofed palaces; it had no silver and no obvious sources of bountiful gold.[9]

Eventually, out of deference to that stubborn reality, Columbus did two things. First, he modified his original assumption. Cuba was not Cipangu, but Cathay, or mainland China. (Columbus died more than a decade later, still never having come to terms with the fact that Cuba was simply Cuba.) Second, when the island disappointed him, he did what many continue to do to this day: he left. Thirty-eight days after his arrival, he sailed away in search of more land and more gold. Undeterred, he wrote to his royal patrons as if that were no setback at all. He emphasized other forms of wealth: natural beauty and pliable Indians whose souls might be easily saved. With a confidence that came from a few weeks of exploration, he promised thriving cultivation in cotton, which could be sold in the cities of the "Gran Can, which will be discovered without doubt, and many others ruled over by other lords, who will be pleased to serve" the king and queen of Spain.[10]

From Cuba, Columbus headed east to another island. The people of Cuba called it Bohío or Baneque; the people of that island called it Ayiti, or land of high mountains. The Spanish would call it simply Española (in English, Hispaniola), home today to both Haiti and the Dominican Republic. On December 25, 1492, a few weeks after his arrival, one of his ships ran aground. Columbus established Europe's first permanent settlement in the New World at the site. He called it Navidad, Christmas. A few weeks later, leaving forty men and the damaged vessel there, he departed for Spain with samples of gold, six Natives, and exciting discoveries to report.

Columbus told of the lands he had claimed for Spain—not necessarily as he found them, but embellished, as he wished them to be. Everywhere he went, people honored him as a hero. He rode on horseback next to the king, and men hurried to volunteer for his next voyage. For Columbus and the Spanish monarchs, the goal of the second expedition was to establish a permanent Spanish presence in what they thought was the heart of Asia and to use it as a base for trade, exploration, and conquest. When Columbus set sail this time, he was at the head of an expedition with seventeen ships and a contingent of about 1,500 men. There was a mapmaker, a doctor, and not one woman. While several priests joined the expedition hoping to bring their god to the Natives, most of the passengers hoped for more earthly rewards, namely gold. On that voyage, Columbus also carried sugarcane cuttings. He had no way of knowing then that sugar would have a far greater impact in the Caribbean islands than either God or gold.

When the expedition arrived in Hispaniola in November 1493, a new reality greeted them. On disembarking, the eager arrivals found Christian clothing strewn near the coast and the bodies of Spaniards decomposing under light brush. Locals explained that the settlers had angered their immediate neighbors by murdering some men and taking five women each "to minister to [their] pleasure." Leaving behind the scenes of carnage, Columbus sailed on and founded a new settlement, La Isabela, named in honor of his queen. He put his brother in charge and left almost immediately to do what he liked best: to sail and explore and, hopefully, to find gold. He returned to Cuba and explored the island's southern coast. Sailing by the eastern portions of that coast, he would have seen mountains that rose abruptly to heights of thousands of feet; farther west on the southern coast, he would have noted the marshland and mangrove islands that dominate the landscape. From there he continued his explorations, landing in Jamaica for the first time. But fast surmising that the best chance of gold lay in Hispaniola, which he now likened to the biblical lands of Sheba, he returned there and assumed his position as governor.[11]

It was in Hispaniola that the first phase of European conquest and colonization of the Americas unfolded in earnest. Trouble there began immediately. Internal rivalries cleaved the community of Spanish settlers. While some of those conflicts centered on the authority of Columbus, most derived from the fact that every settler seemed to want more—more gold and more people to work it. The disputes among the Spanish were trifling compared to the suffering inflicted upon the Native people of the island. To command their labor, Spaniards removed men from their villages and transported them to mines far from home to work without respite. Relations with Native people soured quickly, sometimes erupting into open warfare. Between the unforgiving work, malnutrition, war, and disease, the population decline was catastrophic. According to estimates, more than eight of every ten Native persons died by 1500, less than a decade into the conquest. By 1530, the Indigenous population of Hispaniola had declined by about 96 percent.[12] With the labor supply dwindling even faster than the gold, colonists embarked on slaving missions to nearby islands, stealing people from the Bahamas, Cuba, and elsewhere to staff the mines they hoped would make them rich. When that was not enough to sustain the settlers, they set their sights on nearby islands.

IT WAS THEN THAT THE conquest and colonization of Cuba began in earnest. In 1511, Diego de Velázquez, who had accompanied Columbus on his second voyage, founded the first Spanish settlement on the island and became its governor. The Indigenous name for the place was Baracoa; Velázquez called it Nuestra Señora de la Asunción. But the original name stuck, and the Spanish and everyone else continued to call it Baracoa, the name it bears today. The settlement was near the tip of the island, facing east into the Caribbean. From the mountains that rose behind it, a person could see Hispaniola just about fifty miles across a sea passage navigable by Native canoes.

Native people traversed those waters frequently, to trade and fish, to share news, to flee their new bearded masters. As Spanish enslavement of Natives in Hispaniola began destroying lives and communities, some escaped across those waters to Cuba. So, when the Spanish first arrived in Baracoa, there were people there who already knew about Europeans and what they had done in Hispaniola.

One of them was a man named Hatuey, a nobleman and chief from Hispaniola, who led his followers to Cuba to elude the conquerors. The story of Hatuey's last stand has survived because Bartolomé de Las Casas, onetime colonist turned priest, included it in his searing condemnation of the Spanish conquest, *A Short Account of the Destruction of the Indies*, which the English eagerly translated with titles such as *Spanish Cruelties* and *The Tears of Indians*.[13] Las Casas's conscientious objection to conquest, his passionate voice, and the moralizing character of his account sometimes give his stories the feel of parable. That is the case with his telling of Hatuey's history. But if he perhaps embellished for the sake of narrative, the basic outline of his account—the violence of the conquest, the pain and resistance of the conquered—is undeniable.

Las Casas tells us that, once in Cuba, Hatuey gathered his people on the banks of a river and addressed them. "You already know that it is said the Christians are coming here; and you have experience of how they have treated . . . those people of Hayti; they come to do the same here." Why do the Spanish do this, he asked his listeners, who speculated that it was out of cruelty and wickedness. No, Hatuey insisted, "not alone for this [reason], but because they have a

God whom they greatly adore and love; and to make us adore Him they strive to subjugate us and take our lives." Hatuey gestured to a basket of gold and intoned, "Behold here is the God of the Christians." To get rid of the newcomers they had to get rid of the gold, Hatuey concluded. Then he threw the basket into the river.[14]

The Spanish came nonetheless. Initially, Hatuey and his followers resisted. Soon, however, the invaders captured and condemned him to burn at the stake. Before the sentence was carried out, a Spanish priest gave Hatuey the opportunity to convert to Christianity and thus save his soul and ascend to heaven. Hatuey asked whether Christians went to heaven. When the friar answered that the good ones did, Hatuey at once answered that he preferred hell, "so as not to be where Spaniards were."[15] That may have been the first political speech recorded on Cuban soil. But it did nothing to avert Hatuey's fiery death, nor to save Native people from the catastrophe already befalling them.

HATUEY AND HIS PEOPLE CAME to be known as Taínos, though what they called themselves in 1492 or 1511, we do not know. Taínos lived in the four largest islands of the Caribbean (Hispaniola, Puerto Rico, Cuba, and Jamaica), as well as in the Bahamas. In Cuba, the Taínos were not the only Indigenous group, but they were by far the most numerous, and they bore the first brunt of European conquest. They had settled in Cuba at least five hundred years before, and by the time of Columbus's arrival, they numbered between one and two hundred thousand souls. The bulk of this population was concentrated in the eastern and central parts of the island, where they lived in villages, sometimes with hundreds of residents and a leader called a *cacique*. Their modest thatched-roof homes—*bohíos*—looked much like the typical rural dwellings that dot parts of the Cuban countryside to this day. Rather than slash and burn their fields, they developed a sophisticated system of agriculture, heaping up the soil in mounds several feet high and more feet wide. Called *conucos*, the mounded fields improved drainage, checked erosion, and were particularly suited to growing root vegetables such as cassava (*yuca*), a staple of the Taíno and, eventually, the Cuban diet. The *conuco* system, wrote one scholar, was "an imitation by man of tropical nature, a many-storied cultural vegetation, producing at all levels, from tubers underground through the understory of pigeon peas . . . a second story of cacao and bananas, to a canopy of fruit trees and palms . . . an assemblage [that] makes full use of light, moisture, and soil." Three centuries after the Spanish conquest, a version of the *co-nuco* was still in use—not by the Taínos (of whom by then there were relatively few) but by enslaved Africans, who had come to represent a large share of the island's population and its main generator of wealth.[16]

The Taíno planted tobacco separately, smoked it, chewed it, and introduced it to Europeans, who had never seen it before. They played *güiros* and maracas, musical instruments that are still played today across Latin America and the Caribbean. Women prayed to Attabeira, the spirit guardian of female fertility, for a safe childbirth. Taíno youths played elaborate ball games using rubber balls. The Spaniards, who had never before encountered rubber and had no verb for what rubber did, struggled to describe what they were seeing: "These balls ... even if they are only let slip from the hand to the ground, they rise much further than they started, and they make a jump, and then another and another, and many more." Taíno words for things like hurricanes and sharks, unknown in Spain before 1492, are the words still used today across the Spanish-speaking world: *huracán, tiburón*.[17]

The Spaniards of Cuba occasionally recorded observations of this sort. But, for the most part, they were less concerned with the culture of Taíno people than with making fortunes off their backs. To rule the Taíno, the Spanish used the same means they had developed in Hispaniola. In both places (and later across Mexico and South America), the foundation of early colonial rule was a system called *encomienda*. Under its provisions, the Spanish governor assigned each local ruler (*cacique*) with all the people of his village to a Spanish settler, now an *encomendero*. Some *encomenderos* received perhaps three hundred Natives; a few received more; some just forty or sixty. The *cacique* was then responsible for sending groups of laborers to the mines for months at a time to harvest gold for the *encomendero*. When those workers returned (or died), others went.[18]

The Spanish Crown hoped that the *encomienda* would yield a better result in Cuba than in Hispaniola, where both gold and Natives had diminished rapidly. Wanting to avoid the same fate in his new territory, the king asked officials to draft a set of laws in 1512, just as Spaniards began settling Cuba. The new legislation was meant to curb Spanish abuses and ensure the smooth functioning and longevity of this unprecedented endeavor. The laws, for example, forbade *encomenderos* from punishing Natives with whips or clubs or from calling them dogs.[19]

Another law from this period required conquerors to read a prepared script as they first entered villages. Known as the *requerimiento*, the 1513 document informed Natives of a "chain of command from God to pope to king to conquerors." It also required Native leaders to recognize papal and royal authority and to surrender their lands and persons without resistance. To those who acceded, the document promised:

> Their highnesses and we in their name, shall receive you in all love and charity, and shall leave you, your wives, and your children and your lands, free without servitude ... and they shall not compel you to turn Christians, unless you yourselves, when informed of the truth, should wish to be converted.

To those who rejected the conquerors' demands, however, the *requerimiento* promised a different fate:

> With the help of God, we shall powerfully enter into your country, and shall make war against you ... and shall subject you to the yoke and obedience of the Church and of their highnesses; we shall take you and your wives and your children, and shall make slaves of them ... and we shall take away your goods, and shall do you all the mischief and damage that we can ... [and] the deaths and losses which shall accrue from this are your fault and not that of their highnesses or ours.[20]

Written on the eve of the founding of Spain's first permanent settlement in Cuba, the *requerimiento* theoretically guided the beginnings of European colonization there. The king admonished Velázquez, the governor of Cuba, to refrain from relying too much on war against Native people and urged him to perform the *requerimiento*. Even at the time, however, some observers recognized the absurdity of the document. It was read in Spanish to people with no knowledge of the language. Some chroniclers said it was read to trees and empty huts, residents already having fled in terror. Other commentators doubted whether anyone bothered to read it at all.[21]

WITH THESE CONTRADICTORY AMBITIONS, THE Spanish conquered and settled Cuba. In just four years, Velázquez established seven towns: Baracoa, Bayamo, Santiago, Trinidad, Camagüey, Sancti Spíritus, and Havana. Initially, for the Spanish at least, the new towns prospered. In each, Velázquez appointed councilmen, judges, sheriffs, and notaries. He ordered the planting of crops and the building of churches, gold mines, and a smelting plant to process ore. The labor for all of it was performed by Taínos.[22]

By law, *encomienda* required that in exchange for that labor, the *encomendero* feed, clothe, Christianize his charges, and not overwork them. Between theory and practice, however, there was a chasm. The *encomenderos* could not feed their charges, because their charges were actually feeding them, using their own labor and knowledge to grow the food on which everyone depended. Generally, the *encomienda* system wreaked havoc on Taíno communities. Most of the gold in Cuba was far from existing villages. When the Spanish mobilized people to work it, they took them far from their homes and their livelihoods. Without sources of food near the mines, hunger exacerbated the hardship of overwork. The Spanish confiscated food from villages to feed the workers, but the supply was never sufficient, and the extraction left the villages more susceptible to hunger.

Under these conditions, it is not surprising that people resisted. Hatuey—the man who preferred Hell to sharing Heaven with the Christians—was among the first and most famous. But resistance did not end with him. Two Taíno chiefs who claimed to have supernatural powers (immunity to Spanish weapons and the ability to see and know everything that transpired anywhere on the island) were captured and killed in 1528. Another named Guamá led anti-Spanish movements for years, until he was killed in the early 1530s.[23] Many others, whose names have not survived in the historical record, ran away or resisted by other means.

The combination of overwork, famine, and war would have been sufficient to cause significant loss of life. But Indigenous people across the Americas also faced a rash of diseases completely new to them—smallpox, measles, yaws, and influenza, against which they had no immunity. Periodic epidemics ravaged a population already severely compromised. According to one estimate, a Native population of about one hundred thousand in 1511 dwindled to less than five thousand by 1550. An unknown number died by their own hands. One Spaniard testified that in some areas more than half the Indigenous population had killed themselves. When the same man found three boys ill from eating dirt—potentially a form of suicide—he "had their penises and testicles cut off . . . made them eat them soaked in dirt, and afterwards he had [the boys] burned" to death. He never considered, or maybe never cared, that trying to deter suicide through torture might simply result in more suicide. In a few decades, the Indigenous population in Cuba declined by perhaps as much as 95 percent.[24]

Desperate for more people to rule over and make work for them, the settlers began fanning out to other shores. In 1516, an expedition to an island off the coast of the Yucatán Peninsula returned with 20,000 pesos' worth of gold—fully one-fifth of what was amassed in Cuba in an entire year. Another expedition in 1517 landed in Mexico and returned to Cuba with two Natives and tales of lands blessed with precious minerals and Indigenous populations not in decline. News of that discovery "set the Christians mad with desire to possess the country they described."[25]

In February 1519, another expedition left Cuba for Yucatán. Its leader was the *encomendero* Hernán Cortés, who had aspirations to wealth greater than what Cuba offered. He embarked illegally, in defiance of the governor, with whom he was in a long-standing dispute. In April 1519, he landed his forces, claimed Mexico for Spain, and began his march into the heart of the Aztec empire. From there he sent word abroad that anyone who wished to come conquer and settle in the newly discovered lands would be paid in gold, silver, and jewels, and they would be granted *encomiendas* as soon as the country was pacified.[26] For men who had come to the New World seeking fortune and reinvention, the prospect of more gold and more Natives was too tempting to forgo.

Thus began the conquerors' exodus from Cuba. Hatuey, the island's first anti-Spanish warrior, had been correct. The bearded white men did follow the gold. In the same way that Spaniards had poured into Cuba a few years earlier, they now poured out, in pursuit of riches and glory elsewhere. Between 1517 and 1520, some two thousand Spaniards left the island; between 1520 and 1540, Cuba lost about another 80 percent of its Spanish population. To halt the exodus and not cede territory already claimed for Spain, the king made leaving Cuba punishable by loss of both property and life. But there weren't enough officials on hand to enforce the order, and the Spaniards continued to leave for Mexico. After the 1530s, they departed for the fabulous Inca empire of South America, or for Florida, "a continent of which nothing was known and everything anticipated."[27]

CALL IT THE CURSE OF an island. Land was tangibly finite. So, too, seemed opportunity. Many of those who could leave, left. The capital city of Santiago was reduced to thirty Spanish households; Trinidad was deserted; Baracoa, the island's first European settlement, was reduced to "the shadow . . . of a rural hamlet." A 1544 count of the population across the island tallied just 122 Spanish heads of household, about 900 free Native people, and some 700 enslaved souls. These numbers, however, did not take account of small Native communities that survived by remaining hidden and uncounted by the Spanish. Equally important, the 700 people held in slavery included not only Natives, but also Africans, who had begun arriving through the nascent transatlantic slave trade, to which we will turn a little later.[28]

Not every Spaniard left, of course, and not every Indigenous person died. A few Native communities quietly rebuilt. People had children and grandchildren, sometimes of mixed Spanish, Taíno, or African ancestry. Today in Cuba, a small number of people proudly claim Taíno identity. In a recent genetic study, 35 percent of the women sampled descended from an Amerindian woman.[29] And Cubans, often without realizing it, regularly use things that the Taínos bequeathed to them: from tobacco to hammocks to a host of everyday words whose origins recall a time long before Columbus.

But, in the 1520s or 1530s, had it been possible to fly a hot-air balloon over the island, that legacy would not yet have been apparent. Instead, our pilot would have observed a few scattered towns and settlements of modest structures and few people—ghostly, resilient places where survivors remembered the multitudes of people lost. All around the island, our pilot would have seen beautiful, lush forests. Coming down a little lower, she might have noticed all the pigs, tens of thousands of them. Brought to the New World by the conquerors, they flourished and multiplied in the tropical landscape, devouring crops, and, in the absence of substantial human settlement, becoming masters of the land and, many years later, Cuba's favorite meal.

Chapter 2

KEY TO THE INDIES

From the moment of their arrival in the New World, Spanish explorers and conquerors began elbowing for legacy. Juan Ponce de León had not been the luckiest or most accomplished among them. Briefly governor of Puerto Rico, he lost that title because of a rivalry with the Columbus family. Perhaps in recompense, the king authorized him to explore lands to the north, claim them for the Crown, and rule them as governor for life. In 1513, eager to make his mark, he set sail at the head of a convoy of three ships for an island known as Bimini, famed, according to some accounts, for its gold and, according to others, for its Fountain of Youth.[1]

Ponce de León found two other things instead. The first was a great peninsula he named Florida. He did not think to name the second, stranger thing he encountered: a current more powerful than the wind, like a warm, rushing river in the middle of the sea. It formed in the Gulf of Mexico (not yet named) and reached maximum speed in the straits between Cuba, Florida, and the Bahamas. At its most powerful point, which Ponce de León called the Cape of Currents, he lost one of his ships for several days, even though the weather was clear. Unbeknownst to his sailors, the current continued north, parallel to the coast of North America, which the Spanish did not yet realize was a continent. Eventually, it turned east and out into the Atlantic Ocean, which the men of the age called simply the Ocean Sea, believing there to be but one ocean in all the universe.[2]

More than two centuries later, Benjamin Franklin would encounter the same current at a more northern point. He studied it, interviewing New England whalers and reading navigation accounts of the ancients. Then he mapped it and named it the Gulf Stream. But in 1513, the powerful current was just one more mystery of nature in an age that provided many.

23

CUBA

The pilot who navigated the lead ship in the 1513 voyage that first encountered the Gulf Stream was Antón de Alaminos, a man with a knack for being in the right place and near the right people at the right time. A few years after his voyage with Ponce de León, he was the lead pilot of the expedition that sailed from Cuba to Mexico under the command of Hernán Cortés. A few months later, Cortés dispatched him to Spain carrying the first news of Mexico's conquest and the first substantial shipment of New World treasure. Cortés, who had left Cuba in defiance of the island's governor, warned Alaminos to avoid the island on his voyage. But the master sailor recalled the strange, powerful current he had encountered with Ponce de León, and he knew what his route would be. He sailed into the Gulf of Mexico, north around the western tip of Cuba to Havana.

In August 1519, however, Havana was not yet Havana. The Spanish settlement that bore that name was still on the island's southern coast, plagued by mosquitos and readying to relocate to the site where it sits today. So, Alaminos arrived at the small settlement on the northern coast a few months before Havana itself officially did. That suited him just fine. Given Cortés's enmity with Cuba's governor, Alaminos was not looking to make a formal call at port, nor, possibly, to land in jail. He wanted only provisions and to locate the strange current he remembered from before. The Cuban governor, however, had his spies, and from them he learned of Alaminos's visit. When Alaminos set sail for Spain, people gathered to watch, and they wondered at the unusual course his ship took, a course, they said, unknown and dangerous. Why, the governor later pondered, did Alaminos, who was "so skilled in seafaring ways," take "a route by which no one ever sails"?[3] But Alaminos knew something that others had not yet figured out: the place where Havana was about to move sat almost within sight of the extraordinary current he had discovered only a few years earlier. He used that current now to propel himself—and the treasure he carried—north and then east with the winds, all the way to Spain.

FOR ALMOST THREE CENTURIES, SPANISH treasure fleets carrying dizzying amounts of gold and silver would follow that same route. The great quantities of precious minerals in Mexico and Peru, and the existence in both places of massive Native empires capable of providing the labor to mine them, soon transformed Spain into the wealthiest and most powerful place on earth. And the discovery of the Gulf Stream that guided the treasure ships to Spain turned Havana into the "Key to the New World."

24

As Spain's fortunes soared, other European states paid keen attention, wondering how they, too, might reap the rewards of the New World. England and France began commissioning sea captains to attack Spanish vessels as they returned to Europe loaded with gold and silver. The Mediterranean Sea filled with pirates, corsairs, and privateers. It did not take long for them to realize that Spain's treasure was significantly more vulnerable in the Caribbean, where the Spanish had fewer forts and ships, and fewer soldiers and sailors.

Havana, where Spanish ships usually stopped to restock and rest before the long journey across the Atlantic, was especially vulnerable. A small hamlet and not yet the capital of the colony, it had but a few dozen Spanish households in 1538, the year of its first known pirate attack. Little information has survived about that assault, but whatever happened, it prompted the Spanish Crown to order the construction of the island's first fortress.[4]

The Spanish governor who oversaw its construction was a woman. Isabel (or Inés) de Bobadilla arrived in Havana in 1538 with her husband, Hernando de Soto, a conqueror recently returned from Peru having collected part of the gold ransom for the Inca king executed by Francisco Pizarro. The Spanish king appointed de Soto governor of Cuba and charged him with organizing an expedition to conquer Florida, which the Spanish knew about but had not yet begun to colonize. Less than a year after his arrival, he left Cuba with six hundred men, designating his wife as his replacement. Four years later, he died on the western banks of the Mississippi River, never having returned to Cuba or to his wife.

Old Cuban myth casts Inés de Bobadilla as heartbroken by the departure of her husband. Today, a bronze statue of a woman, which legend claims is her, sits in a weathervane atop the city's oldest surviving fortress. For centuries, the statue has been a symbol of Havana. High above the city, she scans the horizon looking north toward Florida for all eternity, "always turning toward the wind that will bring her missing husband home."[5] In real life, however, she was almost certainly too busy to pine. Governor of an increasingly important city at a dangerous time, she protected her territory from pirate attacks and oversaw the construction of the new fortress. On the side, she owned several sugar mills near Cojímar, a village just east of Havana that Americans would later know as the setting for Ernest Hemingway's *The Old Man and the Sea*.

CUBA

SHORTLY AFTER INÉS DE BOBADILLA'S rule, the Spanish Crown made a decision that transformed the fate of Havana. By order of the king, all vessels making the journey from Spain to the New World would travel in groups of no less than ten 100-ton vessels accompanied by an armed ship, hence the term *armada*. For the return voyage to Spain, vessels were required to assemble in Havana and then cross the Atlantic together. In 1551, the year Spain introduced its famous armed galleons, an armada of over thirty ships wintered in Havana. Small, exposed, and unprepared, the city suddenly found itself the warehouse for the globe's greatest treasure.[6]

Life in Havana revolved around the yearly arrival of the treasure fleets. Before they arrived, innkeepers cleaned, tidied, and readied for the advent of fleet season. Outside the city, farmers grew the food that would later feed the sailors. They raised large numbers of pigs and used the meat—cut and dried under the sun—to provision the ships and their crews. In the 1550s and 1560s, the average stays of the ships loaded with Mexican treasure was almost two months; the ones from South America stayed about forty days. Sometimes as many as sixty vessels with thousands of sailors and crew converged on the city. While the ships were in port, the erstwhile sleepy hamlet hummed with life. Taverns, which outnumbered the city's year-round households, did a brisk business. Innkeepers made their yearly earnings in those two months. Having learned some of the ways of the island's Native inhabitants, they rented out hammocks to visitors. To help pass the time, and perhaps to frontload pleasure in a way that might allow its memory to sustain them on the long journey ahead, sailors sought hard drink, games of chance, and human companionship of one kind or another. They saw to practical matters as well: they repaired their ships and purchased supplies for the Atlantic crossing. Some sought notaries "to organize their earthly affairs before sailing through an ocean populated by unknown beasts and by well-known pirates, all of them enemies of His Catholic Majesty."[7]

In many ways, Havana became a version of what it would remain for centuries to come: a place oriented outward. Its economy depended on precious minerals from other Spanish territories of the New World and on goods and markets from many corners of the globe. Increasingly, Havana would become the site of a secular, commercially oriented, cosmopolitan culture. But day-to-day in the early sixteenth century, people lived that culture by looking out to sea. Everyone—guards stationed atop fortresses, the governor in his residence, ordinary people walking near the water's edge—eagerly searched the horizon for the dependable source of manna of every year: ships laden with gold and silver and manned by men eager to partake of (and pay for) everything that Havana had to offer.

THERE WAS, HOWEVER, A MAJOR problem: if wealth came from outside, so, too, might the forces that could violently destroy it. The City Council complained repeatedly to the king about how easy it would be for enemies to seize the port and how great would be the damage to the Crown were that to happen. "God forbid," they added for good measure. They lamented that the town had but thirty heads of household, many of them aged and infirm, incapable of resisting a foreign attack, ready only to perish should one come.[8] The city depended on the outside world for its survival. But residents also knew that as the rest of Europe increasingly challenged Spain's ascendancy, the city's potential annihilation might also arrive from the outside, on those ships visible on the horizon.

At about sunrise on July 10, 1555, the guard posted at the lookout on the headland across the bay from the city saw a caravel and raised a flag in signal. When the ship sailed past the port, heading west, observers knew this was no ordinary ship. The governor sent two men on horseback to follow the vessel along the shoreline. What they saw sent them racing back to warn everyone: the ship had anchored and landed two boatfuls of well-armed men. They numbered about two hundred, and in neat formation they were marching to Havana over land. As many had feared, the city was unprepared for an attack. Within a half hour of their arrival, the invaders burned down the gates of the recently constructed fortress, took two dozen prisoners, and hoisted their flag over the fort. "It all happened so quickly that it seemed the stuff of dreams," recounted one witness.[9]

The leader of the attack was the French pirate Jacques de Sores. Nicknamed the Exterminating Angel, he had cut his teeth as captain under the notorious one-legged pirate known as Peg Leg. Like most French pirates, Sores was a Protestant. Perhaps for that reason he enjoyed negotiating Havana's ransom with a Catholic priest and demanding the substantial sum of thirty thousand pesos. When the priest came back with a counteroffer significantly lower, Sores replied, "I thought only France had lunatics." Unless he received the ransom, he warned, he would "raze the earth."[10]

The city did not have the ransom to pay, so on July 28, Sores ordered all Havana burned to the ground. The fortress built under the rule of Inés de Bobadilla was so badly damaged it was rendered unusable. Only three buildings survived the assault: a hospital, a church, and the house where the pirates had holed up. Sores's men went into churches and desecrated them. From the robes of priests, they made cloaks and capes. They stole chalices and a monstrance. They stabbed a wooden sculpture of the Virgin Mary and disrobed another. They dismembered a statue of Jesus on the cross and burned the crucifix. The pirates attacked the countryside as well. Near Cojímar, they burned farms and took more prisoners, among them six enslaved Africans for whom Sores demanded another ransom. Residents refused to pay, and the Africans—whose names the chroniclers did not bother to record—were hanged outside the pirates' headquarters and left there for all to see. Then on August 5, 1555, under a full moon, Sores and his men set sail with their ransom of 2,200 pesos and a gold chain, leaving Havana "no better than the Greeks left Troy," according to one account.[11]

Sores's attack made clear to the Spanish Crown that Havana was too easy a target. And because Havana was the seasonal warehouse for all of Spain's New World treasure, Havana's weakness rendered the whole empire vulnerable. By the 1580s, the waters of the Caribbean were said to be "caked with corsairs" and as "full of French as Rochelle."[12] The English, too, refused to recognize Spain's monopoly over the Americas. English privateers attacked Spanish cities and ships wherever they found them—in Asia (where Spain ruled over the Philippines), off Peru on the Pacific coast of South America, and all around the islands and coasts of the greater Caribbean. In wartime, the English government licensed as many as one hundred privateers a year to attack Spanish shipping.[13]

To counter such threats, Madrid strengthened its defensive policies. It started appointing military men—as opposed to lawyers—as governors of the island. It sent expeditions to attack French outposts in Florida and to reassert Spain's ostensibly God-given right to the hemisphere, established by a papal bull in 1494. The king ordered the construction of a new and massive fort—the Castillo de la Real Fuerza (atop which today stands the statue that legend describes as Inés de Bobadilla). Soon after, he ordered the construction of two new forts, one on each side of the bay. The fort of San Salvador, facing the mouth of the harbor, was completed in 1600. The Castle of the Three Wise Men, which sits atop the promontory across the harbor, was partially functional by 1594 and finished in 1630. All would be staffed by a permanent garrison and funded by Mexican silver.[14]

Havana, famed "key to the Indies," was the most fortified city of the New World. The four-pointed fortress of La Fuerza dominates this map of Havana drawn sometime after 1567. A boom between the smaller fortifications on either side of the bay impeded the entry of unauthorized ships.

Together, the massive new structures proclaimed the strength of Spain's empire. This was the new Havana. A famed Italian philosopher in 1591 referred to it as "the key, not only to this island, but of the whole new world." Fittingly, when King Philip II of Spain granted Havana its own coat of arms in 1592, the image was of three fortress towers topped by a golden key.[15]

LIKE VIRTUALLY ALL NEW WORLD wealth, Havana's had an underside: African slavery. African captives had been arriving in Cuba since the beginning of Spanish rule, accompanying Columbus and then successive waves of Spanish settlers. Voyages directly from Africa to Cuba did not begin until 1526, when two ships arrived from the West African coast with 115 captives. The first recorded voyage to Havana occurred in 1572. Others followed, and by the first decade of the seventeenth century, Africans would represent almost half of Havana's population.[16]

Their labor was visible everywhere. In the countryside, Africans and their descendants produced the food that fed the city, its soldiers, and its transient fleets. A loan from the Crown helped establish almost twenty new sugar mills in the early seventeenth century, all of which used slave labor.[17] In Havana, enslaved Africans built the forts meant to make Havana impregnable. African men extracted, chopped, carved, and chiseled large stones; they felled trees and dug ditches for the fortifications. Some had learned blacksmithing in Africa and now worked making cannonballs and chains for the forts. Enslaved women performed other kinds of labor, cooking, cleaning, and doing laundry for soldiers and sailors. Some rented out rooms, or charged for sex. In the city, enslaved people had more opportunities to hire themselves out to others, an arrangement that allowed them to retain a portion of the cash they earned for their masters. They used that cash for myriad things: a hen to supplement their diet, a Sunday skirt, or even a slave of their own.

Early slavery in Cuba was governed by the thirteenth-century legal treatises known as the *Siete Partidas*. In theory, these laws offered the enslaved access to legal practices unknown in British North America. Enslaved people in Cuba could denounce abuses of their masters, and those denunciations might result in their transfer to another, ostensibly less abusive, master. Slaves could also purchase freedom on installment, whether their own or that of loved ones—children, partners, siblings, parents. Legal avenues to freedom, combined with the opportunities afforded by a vibrant mercantile economy, meant that the population of free people of color increased dramatically. By 1610, about 8 percent of *habaneros* were free people of color. By 1774, the year of the first census in Cuba, they represented more than 40 percent of the island's population of color. Throughout this period and beyond, they would play a major role in the course of Cuban history.[18]

That the enslaved in Cuba (and elsewhere in Spanish America) had recourse to legal institutions such as self-purchase might at first suggest that slavery in those places was milder, or more flexible, than that which came to prevail in British North America or, later, in the United States.[19] But limited rights in theory rarely equated to rights in practice. Take the question of corporal punishment. Spain's medieval law of slavery placed strict limits on it, yet slaveholders practiced it with impunity. The pervasiveness and severity of punishment was such that authorities had to step in. The island's first municipal laws, published in 1573, stated that masters were abusing their slaves by "whipping them . . . and stuffing them with different types of resin and burning them, and other cruelties from which they die." To discourage that behavior, the law announced that masters would be subject to the confiscation of those they mistreated and to other unspecified punishments. Yet the confiscations rarely happened.[20]

Another practice that gives the lie to the theory of a mild, benevolent slavery was one pursued by the enslaved themselves, who sought amelioration of their condition or freedom itself by running away from slavery. Fugitives sometimes

headed to settlements in nearby hills (Havana, unlike eastern Cuba, had no mountains to serve as shelter). They might hide in the city and hope to blend in among
the growing population of free and freed Blacks. Men tried to make it to the ships
in the harbor and find work and passage on vessels headed somewhere else. Flight
from slavery was common enough that the same municipal ordinance that sought
to punish slaveholders for cruelty also offered payment to people who captured
runaways.[21]

IN THIS SIXTEENTH-CENTURY WORLD OF pirates, fortress builders,
and fugitives, some enduring outlines of Cuban history began to take shape. One
was the overwhelming power of Havana in relation to the rest of the island. As the
new capital boomed, the old capital of Santiago survived largely by recourse to con-
traband. Sometimes several years would pass before the arrival of a Spanish vessel.
Neglected by Spain, the people of eastern Cuba looked sometimes to Havana, but
more often to the Caribbean—to the region's growing numbers of French, Dutch,
and English eager to buy and sell them goods. These were not random or sporadic
encounters, but part of a vibrant system of illegal trade. Havana flourished, observes
one historian, "as a result of the official presence, in defense of colonial policy; the
east flourished as a result of the official absence, in defiance of colonial policy."[22] In
either case, whether in Havana or Santiago, another outline comes into focus—that
of an island whose people, of necessity, looked outward beyond its shores, from
whence could come either salvation and deliverance, or invasion and destruction.

Chapter 3

COPPER VIRGIN

Almost five hundred miles east of Havana, much closer to where Columbus first landed on the island of Cuba, green mountains dotted with tall palms rise abruptly more than six thousand feet above sea level. These are prodigious, bounteous mountains. During the conquest, they served as refuge for Taínos fleeing Spain's invasion; later, they shielded Africans escaping from slavery. In the nineteenth century, they sheltered bearded patriots waging wars of independence against the once-conquering Spanish. In the twentieth, they sustained other unshaven revolutionaries soon to challenge the supremacy of a newer imperial power, the United States.

In the seventeenth century, with Havana the depot for New World treasure, the mountains were bountiful in a different way. They were laden with rich deposits of copper ore. At the time, copper was in high demand for important commodities: the oil lamps that lit the altars at which the faithful prayed, the church bells by which people of the early modern world measured their days, the weapons with which men took each other's lives. The copper mined in the mountains of eastern Cuba supplied artillery foundries in Havana, where the mineral was fashioned into cannons for new fortifications meant to fend off the likes of other Jacques de Sores.

High in the copper mountains of eastern Cuba was a small settlement with a historical significance that far outweighed its size. It was founded in 1599, almost a decade before the founding of Jamestown, Virginia, the first British settlement in North America. Christened with the cumbersome name of Royal Mines of Santiago del Prado, it soon became known by the simpler title of El Cobre (the copper), which is the name it bears today. Down the steep mountain slopes from the mines toward the Atlantic Ocean was a flat and fertile expanse of land where Native people and enslaved Africans planted cassava, corn, and plantains, and where they tended cows, pigs, and chickens. On the coast to the north, they collected salt. The crops they harvested and the meat they dried, preserved, and seasoned with that salt fed the enslaved men and women who mined the copper.[1]

One day, probably in September 1612, two Indigenous brothers named Rodrigo and Juan de Hoyos and a ten-year-old enslaved boy called Juan Moreno set out from that settlement with orders to bring back salt from the coast of the bay of Nipe. It was hurricane season, and bad weather forced the men to shelter overnight near a place known as Cayo Francés (probably after the French pirates who always threatened). Early the next morning, with the sea unusually still, the trio headed out in search of salt.

Instead, they encountered a divinity. In the water, the men spied a white object floating in the distance. Juan Moreno, the young Black boy, described the discovery some seventy-five years later as an old man.[2]

> Drawing nearer it looked to them like a bird and even closer, the
> Indians said that it looked like a Girl. And in this discussion, they
> got closer and recognized and saw the Image of Our Lady the
> Holy Virgin with a child in her arms standing over a small plank.

One of the men leaned out over the edge of the canoe and used his hat to scoop up their unusual find. The statue was small, some four inches tall. The wood on which she stood had "big letters ... and they said I am the Virgin of Charity. And they were astonished that although her garments were made of cloth they were not wet."

When the three returned home with the effigy of the Virgin, everyone marveled. A few people quickly made a rustic altar and decorated it with branches, leaves, and flowers. The local overseer charged an enslaved African, Antonio Angola—so named for the African region of his birth—to alert authorities in El Cobre. There the administrator of the copper mines ordered that a shrine be built, and he sent a lamp (made of copper) to be placed at the altar, commanding that its flame remain always lit.[3]

But mysterious things happened. More than once, the Virgin disappeared from her altar in the middle of the night and reappeared in the morning with her clothes wet. Some suspected that Rodrigo de Hoyos, one of the two brothers who had found her at sea, was hiding her. Taínos often hid religious objects—*cemís*—in rivers to protect them from enemies. Some witnesses claimed to have overheard him saying that the Virgin was his and that the whites could not have her. But even after authorities tied up Rodrigo at night to prevent him from hiding the statue, she still disappeared. Worried, authorities decided that the Virgin should be taken to the city of Santiago, where she could be properly guarded and honored. The statue left for Santiago in a grand procession, escorted by royal soldiers, accompanied by music and volleys of rifle salutes. According to one account, when the group reached the fork in the road that divided the paths to Santiago and the mining settlement of El Cobre, the procession took the path to El Cobre instead of the intended one to Santiago—a sign, said some, of the will of God, or of hers.[4]

El Cobre—made up mostly of enslaved Africans—thus became the Virgin's home. Local authorities ordered the construction of an altar for her in the parish church. There, too, reports of her miracles took flight. She was said to save and heal people, the oil in her lamp to replenish itself mysteriously. As had happened earlier, she took to disappearing at night, sometimes for days at a time. According to one legend, a young girl named Apolonia was walking in the mountains looking for her mother, an enslaved woman working in the mines, when, on top of a rock high on a hill, she found the missing Virgin. The recurring disappearances led people to conclude that the Virgin needed a chapel, a place where she wanted to be. So the priest celebrated a mass in which parishioners prayed for guidance in selecting a site for the shrine. That night, says another legend, three lights appeared atop the mountains, emanating from the very place where the young Apolonia had found the Virgin. The same lights were said to appear the following night. The choice seemed clear. It was at this site, high in the copper mountains, that the first permanent shrine to the Virgin of Charity was built in 1617.[5] Thus began a five-hundred-year history of devotion and mythmaking that would turn the Virgin of Charity—La Caridad—into Cuba's patron saint and one of the island's most enduring cultural symbols. Today her story is known by all Cubans, whether they live in Santiago, Havana, Miami, or New York.

THERE IS, HOWEVER, ANOTHER STORY of the copper Virgin that has largely disappeared from popular memory. Unlike the tale of her miraculous appearance, it is a story of the *material* world in which the Virgin's cult took root and flourished. It is the history of a singular community of enslaved men and women in the mining village of El Cobre.

The people of El Cobre—*cobreros*—were devotees of the Virgin of Charity; they saw her as their patroness and protector. Over the years, the community, composed of both enslaved and free people of color, raised funds to build and repair her altars and sanctuaries, and they honored her with processions, prayers, and promises. They asked for her divine intercession, for her help in the quest for salvation in the next world and in their struggle for liberation in this one.

El Cobre was a prosperous mining venture. Its copper was smelted locally, five hundred miles away in Havana, and across the Atlantic Ocean in Seville and Lisbon. In the second half of the seventeenth century, however, the mines ground to a standstill. The owners had mismanaged them, and pirates swarming the coasts made it almost impossible to transport the copper to its destinations. But what spelled disaster for the mine owners was a blessing for the miners. As copper production declined, the community of El Cobre thrived. Left to their own devices, enslaved and free *cobreros* worked for their own sustenance and benefit. Most of the men cultivated the land; the women engaged in surface, alluvial mining for copper. They sold the copper, once smelted, for bells, lamps, and other decorative pieces rather than for cannons. With their efforts and their earnings, many purchased their own or their family members' freedom. The slaves of El Cobre, said one contemporary observer, "have been naturalized by Liberty."[6]

Such matters, however, were not on the minds of authorities in Madrid when, in 1670, they confiscated the unprofitable mines. The only thing of real value left on the land was the enslaved labor force of 271 men, women, and children. And the king's plan was to sell them. Rumors about their impending sale rocked the community that had lived as virtually free for decades. In 1677, when the *cobreros* learned that authorities were about to undertake an official inspection, presumably to begin the process of selling them, one hundred of them, armed with sticks and clubs, marched higher into the mountains. Among their leaders was Juan Moreno, the very man who at age ten had witnessed the Virgin's miraculous apparition at sea and who in his thirties had served as guardian of her hermitage. Now in his seventies, he was the leader of the *cobreros*.[7]

From the mountains, Juan Moreno spoke for his community, which was composed, he said, of "humble blacks, slaves of His Majesty Our King and Lord." They lived in peace, raised their families, worked in the copper mines, and helped build the church. A local official had recently said that the slaves of El Cobre were "not like the others; they are the king's. They have a regard for words." In 1677, Moreno used that regard for words to entreat the king to "grant us the mercy of remaining in our *pueblo*, paying our tribute in whatever manner is decided while we find [the means] to [purchase] our freedom." Moreno's petition referred to his people as a *pueblo*, a juridical term denoting a corporate entity with rights and obligations. By using it, Moreno made the case that their community was a legitimate political unit. And when he referred to its members' desire to purchase their own freedom, he was invoking a long-standing right established in Spanish law. Moreno knew what he was doing.[8]

The petition worked. Town criers across the region read aloud a new decree promising on behalf of His Majesty that no one would be sold or taken from the community. The *cobreros* returned to their homes in El Cobre to live as a *pueblo* and as slaves of the king of Spain working toward their freedom. They converted empty or abandoned lands into their own small de facto farms and built new homes around the parish church, the heart of this most unusual *pueblo*. Whether they attributed their victory to the Virgin of Charity's intercession, we do not know. But that same decade, with their own funds, they began constructing a new church for her. They built a new altar and honored her with a new lamp—now silver, rather than copper.[9]

The *cobreros'* victory, however, did not put an end to struggles over their rights and freedoms. In the decades that followed, the community clashed repeatedly with local governors and mine administrators. In 1708–09, the governor attempted to disarm them. In the 1710s–20s, the government reduced the amount of land available to them. In 1731, the governor decreed that all the "discontented" slaves would be taken out of the village and sold as slaves. Fed up with what they saw as infringements on their rights, most of the *cobreros* rose up in rebellion. They chased away the few officials in town and together marched higher into the mountains. On the way, they stopped at the Virgin's sanctuary to take her effigy with them. "They said it was theirs and that she was their remedy." The rebellion proved worthwhile. The king reprimanded the governor and commanded that El Cobre's royal slaves be treated well and without oppression.[10]

Still, the reprieve was temporary, as local officials continually challenged the *cobreros'* prerogatives. By 1780, this near-permanent standoff was poised to end and deliver a thrashing defeat to the people of El Cobre. The Spanish Crown, eager to revive (and tax) the Cuban copper industry, surrendered the mines and the surrounding land to private owners, the descendants of the original sixteenth-century proprietors. The royal slaves would be sold in Santiago, Havana, and even as far away as Jamaica and Cartagena. Some of the *cobreros* working on the fortifications in Santiago heard the news and rushed to warn their companions. Hundreds of *cobreros* together made for the mountains in rebellion.

At the same time, the *cobreros* pursued legal avenues of protest. They sent a representative to Madrid, Gregorio Cosme Osorio, a free man of color born in El Cobre, married to an enslaved woman also born there. Cosme presented the community's petition to the Crown. Like Juan Moreno's more than a century earlier, the petition spoke of their dedication and loyalty to their king and church. For almost two decades, Cosme remained in Madrid making the case for his community. He received letters from his neighbors back home telling of the abuses of the new mine owners, who sent agents to take the *cobreros'* money, clothes, and jewelry; they tied up and flogged men and boys, and stole their animals.[11] One *cobrero* wrote to Cosme on behalf of the entire community, urging him to make haste with his mission:

> Brother, hurry up by God, because the new masters are destroying us. They treat us like capital enemies, with inhumane punishments. I would tell you more but there is no pen capable of expressing them. Don't forget Our Lady of Charity ... whom I trust will help you succeed.[12]

Eventually, the king listened, and on April 7, 1800, he ordered that henceforth every *cobrero* would be free. They would receive parcels of land that could not be sold, divided, or taken away. Any lands vacated would be granted to other *cobreros*. In March 1801, the royal decree of freedom was ceremoniously read aloud in the Sanctuary of the Virgin of Charity, with all the community present.[13] Their liberty came almost a full century before the end of slavery in Cuba. A miracle? Perhaps. But the achievement of freedom for this unusual *pueblo* was above all the result of less mysterious, more earthly forces: a powerful sense of community that nurtured a century and a half of legal and extralegal struggles for freedom and rights.

FROM AN OBSCURE LOCAL SYMBOL in the remote mountains of eastern Cuba, the Virgin of Charity would eventually become one of the most important cultural symbols of the nation as it emerged from four hundred years of Spanish rule. In due time, we will examine the Cuban struggle for independence. Here, however, it is worth pointing out that when the first independence war began in 1868, its leader hoisted a flag made from the canopy that had adorned the altar of the Virgin of Charity in his family's chapel. Cuban rebels pinned her medallion to their undergarments; sometimes they borrowed her statue from churches to take into battle. Then, after independence was won, veterans of the wars against Spain successfully petitioned the Vatican to recognize the Virgin as a saint and the patroness of the Republic of Cuba.[14]

Over time, however, the story of the Virgin's apparition changed. She grew lighter in complexion. The three persons to whom she had first appeared also changed. From two Indians and a Black slave, her discoverers became Native, Black, and white, representing the three cultures that served as the basis for Cuban nationhood. The names of the three men were altered as well; they became the three Juans—three Johns, or three Cuban "everymen." The Black Juan—the enslaved ten-year-old boy from El Cobre, who as an old man had petitioned the king of Spain on behalf of his community and later provided the only known surviving account of the Virgin's apparition—became indistinguishable from the others, in name at least. He was not entirely forgotten, but almost—just like the community of *cobreros* to which he belonged.

Yet history as lived is always a layered proposition, far richer and more human than the myth that sometimes goes in its guise. However dominant the whitewashed myth of Cuba's patron saint, the other part of the story—the struggles of the *cobreros* for their freedom—did survive. After the *cobreros*' victory, enslaved people in other parts of the island invoked their example. We want freedom like the *cobreros* said some of the enslaved who rebelled in Cuba in 1811. For decades, the mountains sheltered runaways from slavery, which continued to exist in Cuba until 1886. Descendants of the Black *cobreros* who won their freedom in 1800 fought for a different freedom later in that century, helping to win Cuban independence in 1898. Today, in El Cobre the traces of those and other struggles linger on barely under the surface. They repose quietly in the offerings left for the Virgin in her sanctuary—a medal, a crutch, a bullet offered by someone who survived a war, say. They whisper in the things inscribed in her book of autographs— "Blessed Virgin, please protect the liberty of Cuba," wrote a man named Sixto Vasconcelos on January 11, 1903.[15] They echo off the looming monument built in 1997 high on the slopes of El Cobre to honor the thousands of runaways from slavery, *cobreros* among them, who tried to make other histories on land much older than Columbus.

A View of the Franciscan Church & Convent in the City of Havana, taken from the Alcalde's House in Granby Square.

In the eighteenth century, Havana was the third largest city in the New World and larger than any city in Britain's thirteen North American colonies. This 1768 engraving shows the Convent of San Francisco de Asís, built in 1738 and located near the city's port.

Part II

A COLONY WORTH A KINGDOM

Chapter 4

HAVANA FOR FLORIDA

Today, the Castle of the Three Wise Men in Havana is perhaps the country's most iconic landmark. Better known by the name of the Morro (a generic word for the high promontory on which it sits), its fortress and lighthouse stand watch over a city that in the eighteenth century was the third largest in the Americas—smaller than Mexico City and Lima, grander and richer than any in Britain's thirteen North American colonies. A thousand ships could anchor without confusion in its harbor, and its shipbuilding yard was the largest anywhere in the New World. The city boasted elegant buildings made of stone and almost a dozen churches, many decked with lamps, candlesticks, and ornaments of gold and silver. In a Caribbean Sea dotted with cash-strapped island colonies, silver coins flowed so freely in Havana that one British merchant likened it to the lands of the biblical King Solomon.[1]

Havana was also the most fortified city in the New World. In addition to the Morro, two other large fortresses—the Castillo de la Real Fuerza and San Salvador de la Punta—guarded the entrance to the harbor. To the east and west, along the island's north coast, thick-walled towers impeded coastal landings and blocked access to rivers that might lead enemies to Havana by a different route. A massive stone and mortar wall five feet thick and more than thirty feet high protected the heart of the city. Together these fortifications seemed to guarantee destruction to any potential invader. And, indeed, in the many years since the pirate attack of 1555, most were deterred from trying. Havana was invincible, "the inviolate symbol of Spain's sovereignty in the west."[2]

The Seven Years' War threatened to change that. Sometimes known as the French and Indian War, it began in 1756 as a conflict between Britain and France over disputed territory in North America. While the war had drawn in many

European states as allies of one or another camp, Spain had managed to remain on the margins for most of the war. In August 1761, however, the French and Spanish kings signed a "family compact," so called because the men represented two branches of the Bourbon dynasty. The agreement publicly obligated the two signatories to stand with each other in conflicts with the British. In response to the agreement, Britain declared war on Spain on January 4, 1762. Immediately, Madrid sent word to Havana, but accident (or design) intervened. The British captured the ship carrying the letters, and the news never made it to Cuba, though rumors of a conflict did soon start to circulate.[3]

So, on Sunday morning, June 6, 1762, no one in the beautiful, fortified city that every European king wanted for his own knew with any certainty that their government was at war—not even the man who stood guard atop the Morro looking out to sea. That morning he spotted something unusual: more than two hundred British vessels approaching from the windward side, headed straight toward the city of Havana. Immediately he sent for the governor, Juan de Prado. Prado was on his way to Mass, but he rushed across the bay to assess the potential danger. As he peered through the telescope atop the lighthouse, he seemed more annoyed than impressed. It was just a commercial convoy, he determined, perhaps larger than usual because Britain and France were at war. There was no cause for alarm.[4]

Prado sailed back across the harbor to resume his Sunday routine. But he found the city in pandemonium. Havana denizens had spotted the British flotilla and assumed the worst. Church bells were ringing out alarms; people were flooding the Plaza de Armas to prepare. For the second time that morning, the governor became annoyed. Everyone was overreacting, he thought. When the ships cruised past the entrance to the harbor, his coolheadedness seemed vindicated.[5]

Prado's relief, however, was short-lived. The ships sailed a few miles east of the city and then just stopped. Increasingly sure that the vessels meant to attack, the governor summoned all the troops in the capital—naval forces, regular Spanish troops, paid and volunteer militias, free Black and mulatto battalions. He called on slaveholders to send their enslaved to the city to help defend it. Urgent appeals for soldiers and volunteers also went out across the island. Still, with no sure knowledge of the war between Spain and England, many hoped for an explanation that would render all those preparations moot.[6]

THE MEN ABOARD THE BRITISH ships, however, were merely waiting out high winds and surf before launching their attack. Perhaps sensing the apprehension of his men as they looked ashore toward the city long deemed invincible, George Keppel, who was the Earl of Albemarle and commander in chief of the campaign, gathered his captains and gave a speech unsurprising for its time. "Courage, my lads," he exhorted, "we shall soon be as rich as Jews, Havana is paved with gold which the lubberly Dons have gathered for us, and the Admiral has just given us leave to take yonder town with all its treasures." Then the men drank to victory.[7]

The next morning, June 7, dawned with calm seas. Admiral Pocock, the commander of the expedition's naval forces, raced to the mouth of the harbor with twelve ships. With the Spanish readying to repel them there, the much larger part of the expedition under Albemarle began disembarking about six miles east of the capital. "In one hour and without opposition or the loss of one man, the whole army was landed." Then they began the slow march overland, their destination: the impregnable Morro fortress. By June 11, they had established a redoubt at the place known as La Cabaña, a rough, hilly area east of the Morro. There, "tortured by the heat of the tropical sun," they began building artillery batteries to pound the Morro and its garrison into quick submission.[8]

The Spanish, recovering from their initial surprise, worked feverishly to deter the invaders. From the Morro, they fired on British columns coming from the east under Albemarle. At La Chorrera, where the smaller of the two British forces threatened from the west, Havana's Black militia offered fierce resistance. In the city itself, Governor Prado ordered that women, children, and everyone not able to pick up a gun or machete evacuate the city immediately. Nuns in habits began trekking through terrain made almost impassable by recent rains, hiding sacramental ornaments in the folds of their robes to keep them from falling into British (and Protestant) hands. Prado ordered the burning of neighborhoods just outside the city walls to deny their refuge to the enemy. The people who lived there would take up arms or work in defense; if they were unable to do that, they were commanded to leave the city. Fearing that the British might offer freedom to slaves who joined them, Prado preemptively decreed that any enslaved person who defended the city would be given freedom, and he announced that locals would be given a cash reward for every British soldier they captured and turned over to authorities. Finally, he also ordered the sinking of three Spanish warships at the entrance to the harbor. The sunken vessels, together with the protective boom chain between the fortresses of the Morro and the Punta, were to prevent the invading naval forces from entering the harbor.[9]

The British, however, boasted two advantages that no such measures could eliminate: ships and men. Albemarle had arrived with thirty warships and more than two hundred transport and support vessels, while Havana had a fleet of only eighteen warships, four of them out of commission. The invasion forces numbered about ten thousand sailors, twelve thousand soldiers, two thousand slaves, and six hundred free Black militiamen. The Spanish could muster only a modest fighting force: about twenty-three hundred from the regular army and a larger force of close to five thousand from the volunteer militias.[10]

Everything seemed to be going Britain's way. Albemarle threatened from the east with the bulk of the invading force and readied an attack on the Morro. Pocock's forces prepared to squeeze the Spanish from the west. This was, without a doubt, an auspicious start to the most daring, ambitious campaign of the whole Seven Years' War. It would have taken a miracle to save the place the English called "the Havannah."

WARS, THOUGH, HAVE A WAY of reversing advantages and imposing suffering on everyone involved. A month into the siege, a British officer complained that the endeavor was proving "to be tuffer work, and the Spaniards more resolute than was at first imagined."[11] And as the Spanish forces resisted, the conflict ceased to be a naval siege and became a war of attrition on land.

While the British vastly outnumbered the Spanish, a determined foe can still wreak considerable damage. Among the enemies most determined to defeat the British were local men of color. Some were members of the free Black and mulatto militias, men who asserted both their legal freedom and their right to honor and dignity through military service. Others were enslaved men motivated by the governor's promise of freedom for their service. On June 26, a group of thirteen such men stationed at the Morro marched out to repel an advance team of fourteen British soldiers heading their way. Machetes in hand, they killed one and took seven prisoners. The governor awarded them immediate freedom. With that as precedent, the number of slaves volunteering for service grew by the day, and a new fighting unit was created to accommodate them. On June 29, a group of enslaved men took forty-seven prisoners, captured three flags, and killed a captain; on July 13, Black fighters took four hundred British prisoners; on July 18, another group killed an artillery captain and took eighteen British prisoners. Freedom was mighty motivation, indeed.[12]

Of the enslaved men who waged battle against the British we know little. Sometimes their names survived precisely because they didn't: Antonio Poveda killed by rifle shot on July 2; Antonio Agustín by a bomb fragment on July 4; Pedro by cannon shot on July 7. They died in battle, and their names survived because the king offered to compensate their masters for their value as chattel. But even when the names of Black fighters did not survive, stories of their exploits did. Half a century later, José Antonio Aponte, a free Black carpenter and the grandson of one of the Black militiamen who defended Havana against the British, painted pictures precisely of scenes like this, of Black troops taking British men prisoner, of military encampments guarded by Black soldiers. Indeed, Aponte would use those pictures to recruit Black men to a major conspiracy against slavery.[13]

In 1762, the British faced other formidable enemies—ones that required no training at all: climate and disease. While rains had poured on the city immediately before the siege, weeks of extreme heat and no rain after their arrival made the day-to-day work of the siege excruciating. Provisions ran out quickly, and the men had no regular access to fresh water. As they tried to build batteries on the Cabaña hill to attack the Morro, the baked soil broke the points of their tools. The heat and dryness (and fire from weapons on both sides) were such that in the middle of the night on July 3–4, the British forces awoke to find that all the batteries they had constructed were ablaze. In one hour, more than two weeks' worth of work by some six hundred men—work that might have allowed them to take the Morro in a matter of days—was almost entirely destroyed.[14] In a diary entry written on July 4, a British officer acknowledged that the men were growing fatigued. "The disappointment of the Morro's not being reduced so speedily as at first they were made to hope," he added, "helped to depress [their] spirits."[15]

Disease depressed their spirits, too. The Spanish called it *vómito negro*—black vomit—because the blood in the vomit of the sick made it appear black in color. The English used a different color to name it: yellow fever, because the liver damage it caused turned the sufferer's skin yellow. At the time, it was among the very deadliest of infectious diseases, aided in its spread by institutions such as the slave trade and warfare, both of which moved hundreds of thousands of people across continents and islands.

The first of British deserters arrived on the Spanish side just four days after their landing, announcing that men had started falling ill. One British officer wrote: "The carrion crows of the country kept constantly hovering over the graves which rather hid than buried the dead, and frequently scratched away the scanty earth, leaving in every mangled corpse a spectacle of unspeakable loathsomeness and terror to those who, by being engaged in the same enterprise, were exposed to the same fate." British desperation was such that Albemarle was soon contemplating ending the siege, taking his men to recover or die elsewhere, and leaving Havana untaken, invincible after all.[16]

That was what the Spanish hoped for, certainly. If they could prolong the battle, they might compel the British to desist.[17] Unfortunately for them, they were subject to the same weather as the British, and they, too, experienced the scourge of yellow fever. In fact, they had been suffering from it since 1760, when an epidemic began ravaging the city and surrounding area. Now it was much worse and the stakes infinitely higher.[18]

Death was everywhere: in the city under siege, in the fortresses that protected it, in the waters that surrounded it. On June 16, Prado announced that anyone caught committing even the slightest theft would be immediately hanged without trial. The governor was true to his word. Every day, people were executed—for robbery, for providing intelligence to the enemy, for selling them supplies, sometimes for violent assaults. Bodies hanging from scaffolds became part of the landscape of the besieged capital. The governor ordered that all dogs in the city be killed—from hunger they would howl through the night—and it was done immediately. At the closing of many battles came the ritual flag of truce. Then the Spanish marched in among their enemies to retrieve their dead and bury them. Men on both sides of the war sometimes sought escape from the carnage by jumping into the water and then drowned. On some days, the harbor was crowded with their floating corpses.[19] The two parties were locked in a violent, destructive waiting game. Unable to counter the British, Prado hoped for a passive victory, delivered not by military might but by yellow fever and hurricane season. Albemarle, meanwhile, wavered between contemplating retreat and praying that their slow, tortured advance on the Morro would bear fruit while enough of them were still alive to occupy the city.

IT WAS THEN, MORE THAN seven weeks into the siege, that British reinforcements arrived from New York City. From the start, King George had known that taking Havana would be no easy task and that North American forces would be necessary. Most colonists, however, were reluctant to serve in the Caribbean, where tropical diseases were almost as deadly as foreign armies. So, the Crown was willing to do some enticing. King George authorized Albemarle to offer the provincials, as they were then called, "any further Douceurs . . . and to take special care that they be treated with all such proper attention and humanity."[20]

In the end, organizing the North American portion of the expedition required less *douceur* than simple deception. Jeffrey Amherst, commander of the British Army in North America, wrote to the governors of New York, Connecticut, New Jersey, and Rhode Island, asking them to produce the requisite number of volunteers. He promised that the men would have every indulgence, that they would not be fatigued by the long marches of past campaigns, and that they would return home quickly. Amherst mentioned nothing about Cuba, even though he knew that Havana was their destination. Perhaps because he was so purposely vague, or because of swirling rumors of a Caribbean campaign, the colonial assembly in New York asked for assurances that the men would be employed only on the North American continent. Amherst prevaricated: "Their destination must remain a secret for the present as I am not at liberty to divulge it."[21]

Once the men arrived in New York, it did not take long for everyone to figure out their destination. The largest number of men (about one thousand) were from Connecticut. Major General Phineas Lyman and Lieutenant Colonel Israel Putnam, later a Revolutionary War hero, served at the head of the forces. The men they commanded were mostly farmers and sons of farmers. Among them was seventeen-year old Levi Redfield, who volunteered for service eager to fight the French in North America. Now he sat aboard one of eleven ships in New York Harbor with thousands of volunteers such as himself, forbidden from going ashore for fear of desertion once the men realized that they were bound for Cuba.[22]

Their arrival in Havana on July 28 cheered and heartened the weary Brits. Maybe now they could finally storm the Morro. Between the British encampment on the Cabaña and the Morro fortress lay a great ditch cut in the solid rock, fifty-six feet wide and sixty-three feet deep. British engineers had decided that their best chance to take the Morro was to sink a deep shaft into the rock, run mines in it, and then detonate them. The explosions would throw a great mass of rocks into the gulf and thus make it possible for British troops to storm the fortress by foot. The contingent from New York arrived just in time to finish that work.[23]

At two o'clock in the afternoon on July 30, the British exploded the mines. Rock flew everywhere, filling the ditch and immediately killing the Spanish sentries and grenadiers. Then the British, led by the 3rd Regiment of Royal Americans, stormed the fortress. The Spanish tried resisting the attack, but to no avail. Their commander, Luis Velasco, fell mortally wounded. A crusty fifty-year-old sailor who had spent thirty-five years at sea, he had resisted the British for forty-five days. When he fell, the others surrendered the fort. More than five hundred men on the Spanish side were killed, wounded, or captured that day, and the rest escaped by boat to Havana or drowned trying. By 5 p.m., the British flag was raised over the fort.[24] After a siege of seven weeks and five days, the unconquerable Morro had finally fallen.

The rest was just a matter of time, and not much time at that. With the Spanish defeated at the Morro, the British were free to attack Havana from all sides. Thirty Americans were put to work building platforms so that the guns of the Morro could assault the Spanish fort across the bay. The artillery fire was relentless, stopping only briefly to allow for the hasty burial of the Morro's old commander Luis Velasco. As more troops arrived from New York, they built more batteries, and the fire kept intensifying. On August 10, Albemarle sent a letter to the Spanish governor. Surrender, he said, and avoid the total destruction of the city. Prado refused. At daybreak on August 11, all the British batteries opened fire: forty-three pieces of cannon and eight mortars. One by one, the remaining Spanish positions were silenced, and by two in the afternoon, the Spanish had surrendered the city.[25] Havana—Key to the New World—was now British territory, part of the same empire as the thirteen colonies.

EVERYWHERE, THE BRITISH CELEBRATED. IN London, the Duke of Cumberland wrote to Albemarle, "You have made me the happiest man existing." He was so happy, in fact, that when he saw Albemarle's elderly mother at a party, he almost kissed her, in public, in the drawing room. From Philadelphia, Ben Franklin wrote to a friend congratulating him on the taking of Havana; it would help guarantee favorable terms of peace in the war just ended, provided "John Bull does not get drunk with victory, double his fists and bid all the world kiss his Arse." In Boston, a public sermon in honor of the victory was frank in a different way: "We have an account of great Sums of Money already found, from which our Forces, under the General Lord Albemarle and Admiral Pocock we hope will reap a rich Reward of their great Toils and Valour."[26]

As conqueror of Havana, Albemarle was hoping for the same thing. He held court immediately on entering the city as victor and installing himself as governor. Prominent Havana residents came to see him. According to a story later told to the king of Spain, one visitor presented him a *guacamaya*—a colorful red macaw then native to Cuba and now extinct. Albemarle was not impressed. "He didn't want birds," he said, "he wanted silver." Another visitor collected contributions from local sugar mill owners and presented him with a gift of a large quantity of sugar. Again, the new British governor balked. "An innkeeper in England has more wealth," he complained. "He deserved ten times as much!"[27] Whether or not these particular stories were true—they were relayed to the king by Albemarle's fiercest detractor—there is no denying that the men who conquered the city profited handsomely: almost £123,000 each for Albemarle and Pocock, with smaller amounts distributed by rank all the way down to ordinary soldiers and sailors, who received just over £3 and £4, respectively.[28]

For many British, perhaps especially ordinary soldiers and sailors, the payment may have seemed unequal to the hardship suffered. Even after the siege was over, the men kept dying. Albemarle lost three thousand men to disease in the two months *after* Spain's surrender. The North American recruits, who had arrived in Havana as the yellow fever epidemic peaked, had the highest mortality rates among the British forces. They were sent back to New York, as the king had promised. But on the ships, they continued to die. Levi Redfield, the Connecticut teenager who volunteered for service, saw his brother and twenty-one others die on the journey home. Not only did many return home sick and grieving, but many were also "in a dissatisfied frame of mind." They had suffered much, and their recompense, they thought, was meager.[29]

Albemarle, meanwhile, stayed in Havana and reaped his monetary rewards. Whatever his profit, victory had also made him governor of Havana and all its people. Now technically Spanish subjects of his British Majesty, they were free to practice Catholicism, just as they were allowed to preserve all their property intact. By agreement, Havana's City Council continued to operate and to run the day-to-day work of government. Albemarle appointed his lieutenant governor and other officials from within its ranks. He banned British soldiers from visiting bars to avoid potential contretemps with the locals, and he held elaborate weekly soirées. Sparsely attended at first, they soon became the talk of the town. There, British officers and merchants dined and drank with members of Havana's most prominent families. The daughters of planters and merchants danced with British officers; some struck up courtships, and some of those courtships even inspired ditties.[30]

WHILE IT IS HARD TO imagine that as loyal Spanish subjects, Havana's wealthy residents would have wished for a British victory, now that one had come, they rushed to make it work in their favor. For them, more than anything else, that meant developing a sugar industry.

Today, sugar is so ordinary, so unremarkable that it is hard to grasp the unbridled enthusiasm it provoked among Havana's elite. Once a luxury for aristocrats, it was fast becoming a staple in the diets of poor and working people in

Europe and North America. Sugar added sweetness—and calories—to bitter tea and coffee, two other tropical products on the rise. As the Industrial Revolution took root, sugar, combined with tea or coffee, sometimes served as substitutes for food—proletarian hunger killers, in the words of anthropologist Sidney Mintz.[31]

Sugar's transformation from the treat of kings to a product of mass consumption also changed the history of the New World and Africa. It resulted in the deforestation of vast amounts of land in the Western Hemisphere and the repeopling of places where the original population had been largely decimated by conquest. Because sugar required massive amounts of labor, it was the major impetus to the transatlantic slave trade. Roughly two-thirds of the almost eleven million Africans forcibly landed in the New World ended up working in sugar.

Produced in massive quantities, sugar was immensely profitable. And at the time of the siege of Havana, the British knew this perhaps better than anyone else. England's first experiment with the crop was in Barbados, an island just fourteen by twenty-one miles wide. The combination of European sugarcane, land largely emptied of its Native population, and the importation and labor of hundreds of thousands of Africans—an estimated 350,000 between just 1625 and 1750—made the small island Britain's most profitable colony at the time. As the soil became depleted, the British re-created the model elsewhere. By the time of the siege of Havana in 1762, Jamaica had supplanted Barbados as the brightest jewel of the empire, having received more than 513,000 African captives, most of them aboard British slavers.[32]

Havana's hinterland, by contrast, had fewer than a hundred sugar mills, with a total of perhaps some four thousand slaves—thoroughly unimpressive compared to British Jamaica.[33] But the men who owned those mills and held those people in slavery knew well who Havana's new conqueror was. It was Britain, whose Caribbean colonies produced much of the world's sugar and whose ships carried a majority of the African captives sold in the Americas. Suddenly under British rule, those Cuban planters quickly concluded that it was their turn now. They would use the occupation to reap the great rewards of sugar for themselves.

British policy in Cuba helped them do just that. Albemarle immediately abolished Spanish taxes. British merchants (including those from the thirteen colonies) descended on Havana. More than seven hundred private British vessels arrived during the occupation (compared to under twenty the entire year before). Traders came to purchase Cuban tobacco, hides, meat, tortoiseshells, lumber, and, of course, sugar. Among them were men like William Bedlow, first postmaster of New York City and part of the Bedlow family for whom the Statue of Liberty's island was named. North American merchants arrived to sell their products as well: flour, cloth, sugar-making equipment, even beaver hats, which had become all the rage in Havana, despite the climate. One Spanish official complained that the quantity of North American goods arriving in Havana was so large that it would take years to consume it all.[34]

But what Cuban sugar planters most craved was a very different kind of commodity: human beings. Planters had already been advocating an expansion of the slave trade, believing that access to cheap labor would propel them to greater prosperity. At the time, the British were the main players in the lucrative business of the transatlantic slave trade. And British traders knew two things about Havana: there was an untapped market for African captives, and buyers had ready cash in silver.

According to one source, a British slave ship was already in the harbor waiting for Spain's capitulation to become final. As soon as it did, the ship coasted into port and began selling its human cargo. To run the occupation-era slave trade to Cuba, Albemarle selected John Kennion, a Liverpool merchant, who as part owner of ten slave ships had amassed enough money to buy his own sugar plantations in Jamaica. Albemarle gave him an exclusive license to import African captives. Among Kennion's clients were some of the most prominent people in the city, men like Laureano Chacón, a municipal official who had only recently led men in battle against the British invaders, and Sebastian Peñalver, who served as Albemarle's lieutenant governor in the occupation. All told, the British appeared to have introduced about thirty-two hundred African captives to Havana in the ten months of occupation. To help put that in perspective, it is useful to recall that, before the occupation, the number of enslaved workers in the sugar mills ringing Havana numbered about four thousand. In other words, in less than a year, the British expanded the size of Havana's enslaved population by about 80 percent. With more enslaved laborers, and with obstacles to trade removed, the sugar industry soared.[35]

It is perhaps for this reason—the impetus to sugar and slavery—that the British occupation of Havana is often accorded enormous importance in Cuban history. The British occupation did not create Cuba's sugar industry, but it did give it a commanding boost. It was a harbinger of a new Cuba—and a lasting one. The island's reliance on sugar as the basis of its economy would expand significantly in the decades after British rule; indeed, it would endure for more than two centuries.

———

AS PEOPLE IN HAVANA WERE adjusting to the occupation, European monarchs were negotiating a treaty to end the Seven Years' War. Everyone wondered what would happen to the city long regarded as the key to the Indies. The Spanish desperately wanted it back; the British were divided. Jamaican planters, who had a huge influence in Parliament, were not keen for competition from Cuba. British statesman William Pitt, who had long lobbied for taking Havana, thought that Britain should absolutely hold it. When he heard that the preliminary treaty surrendered it, he left his sickbed and appeared before the House of Commons. In a speech of more than three hours, he fumed against a treaty that "obscured all the glories of the war [and] surrendered the dearest interests of the nation."[36]

As Pitt feared, under the 1763 Treaty of Paris, Britain gave up Havana. In exchange, Spain ceded Florida—the first time, but certainly not the last, that the fates of glorious Havana and swampy Florida became entangled. Spaniards in Florida packed up and sailed to Havana. In their place arrived new settlers, mostly North Americans from colder colonies. Among them were men who had taken part in the expedition against Havana and who a few years later would join a revolution against the British.[37]

In Havana, British rule ended thirteen months after the Morro guard first spotted Albemarle's two hundred ships on the horizon. On July 4, 1763, a new Spanish governor, the Count of Ricla, arrived to retake possession of one of Spain's oldest colonies. His troops marched into the city, into the Morro citadel where so many had lost their lives a year earlier, and into every fortress and guard post in the city and its surroundings. At each one, the British flag was lowered and a Spanish one raised in its place. Food and drink flowed; parties lasted around the clock. On the third day, the new governor summoned every enslaved person who had fought on Spain's behalf and had not yet been granted freedom. So many came that it took the governor more than two weeks to hear their cases. He freed at least 156, posting their names publicly, so that there would be no confusion over their status.[38]

Shortly after his arrival, Ricla also began a major fortification project on the Cabaña hill. Had a fortress existed there before, the British siege might well have had a different outcome. When the new fort was finally finished in 1774 and the king of Spain was notified, he asked for his telescope. The Havana fortress had cost so much and taken so long to build, he said, that surely it would be visible from Spain.[39]

The story of the telescope is likely apocryphal, but had the king been able to see across the Iberian Peninsula and the Atlantic Ocean, he would have observed a Havana different in degree rather than in kind from the one Albemarle had invaded in 1762. Massive fortresses guarded the impressive city. Four thousand regular troops and some six thousand militia members drilled in city streets every Sunday, their presence giving the city the air of a grand urban barracks. In the wide, deep harbor that the whole world celebrated, he would have noticed more ships, many entering with African captives, others leaving with tobacco, woods, hides, and sugar. In fact, by the time the Cabaña fortress was finished, sugar exports were already at around ten thousand tons a year, more than five times greater than before the British siege. Even the most powerful telescope, however, would not have allowed him to see that the standing army there was now predominantly Cuban- rather than Spanish-born. He could not have seen that the bricks used in his expensive new fortress came from Virginia and New York. Nor could he have detected that many of the merchants swarming the port spoke English with the accents of Baltimore and Boston, New York and Charleston.[40]

Chapter 5

MOST FAVORED NATION

On January 12, 1776, a visitor arrived in Havana: Fichacgé of the Uchiz Nation—chief of twenty-nine Indian towns on Florida lands that had earlier belonged to his people, later to Spain, and, since the 1763 Treaty of Paris, to Britain. The visitor arrived with deer pelts and horses, and he offered his protection to the fishermen who came from Cuba to fish off the Florida coast. In exchange, his people wanted clothing, tools, and boats—Indian canoes were not really designed to transport horses. He wanted something else, too: Spain's help in making war on British colonists who were encroaching on their land. Delegations such as Fichacgé's were common in Havana; Creek emissaries from Georgia and Alabama had made nineteen such visits between 1763 and 1776. On this occasion, Havana's governor gave Fichacgé of the Uchiz Nation his customary three-part answer. Please, could they stop showing up in Havana uninvited; he had no authority to grant the things requested; finally, he could offer no help against the British, as the two countries were at peace.[1] The Seven Years' War and the siege of Havana were fresh enough in everyone's memory to make the thought of provoking Britain an uneasy proposition.

This was 1776, however, and invitations to anger the British were everywhere. On July 4 of that year, colonists from Georgia to New Hampshire proclaimed independence from their mother country. The leaders of that effort—men such as George Washington of Virginia and Ben Franklin of Philadelphia—understood the same truth that Fichacgé of Uchiz did: war required allies, preferably ones with deep pockets and powerful navies.

To seek out such allies for the American Revolution, the recently established Continental Congress sent emissaries to Paris. The best known was Ben Franklin, who wore a coonskin cap instead of a powdered wig and seemed to Parisians the embodiment of a new age. Franklin's colleague Arthur Lee, a Virginia physician turned lawyer and diplomat, was less popular. His detractors described him as having "an unpleasant stiffness in conversation, a family homeliness of feature, an ill natured asperity of manners, and a selfishness very ill adapted to his present exalted situation." Even Lee's allies complained that he could not "easily govern his temper." Apparently a jealous man, he resented the popularity of Benjamin Franklin. An impatient man, he fretted that the French were too slow in providing aid. He knew, as well, that it was only the joint support of France and Spain that would "give the fullest alarm" to Britain. Convinced of the wisdom of his logic and waiting for approval from no one, Lee embarked on a perilous journey across the Pyrenees to reach the Court of Spain, uninvited and unannounced. This was what some would later call "guerrilla diplomacy."[2]

When the king in Madrid heard that Lee was on his way to see him, he balked. Madrid was a small, landlocked capital, full of British spies. The American, he decided, would not be received. By the time word of the king's refusal reached Paris, however, Lee was already on his way. Spanish officials sent letters to every obvious stopping point on the route from the French border to Madrid. Whoever found him was to notify authorities and to keep him from continuing on to the capital. The king's representatives would come to him instead. Lee, the letter said, might be using a false name, but he would be easy to spot nonetheless: he spoke no Spanish and had absolutely no knowledge of the country. Surely he would stand out.

An official of the royal mails easily spotted the American at a tavern in Burgos, some 150 miles north of Madrid, and asked him to await the arrival of Spain's minister of state, the Marquis de Grimaldi, who was fluent in Spanish and French, and Diego de Gardoqui, a Basque merchant who was fluent in English and had extensive trading experience in North America. Lee, the representative of a government that no one yet recognized and that was still far from defeating Britain, seemed eager to observe some of the rituals of international diplomacy. So, when the three men sat down for their important conversation on Spain's possible support for the American Revolution, Lee insisted that they all speak French. There was just one problem: Lee's French was exceedingly poor. Grimaldi tried speaking slowly, but Lee couldn't form responses in the language he insisted everyone speak. In this halting, frustrating conversation in three languages, Lee finally conveyed his message: the fate of the revolution rested with the Bourbon monarchs. Without the assistance of *both* France and Spain, the colonists could never win.[3]

It was probably lucky for Lee and the Americans that the Spanish had already decided to help, even before that awkward meeting. The Spanish promised to open a line of credit for the Continental Congress at a bank in Holland. They offered supplies, immediately dispatching three thousand barrels of gunpowder and blankets for the American troops. They authorized the transfer of Mexican silver through Havana to the revolutionaries. Finally, they extended assistance in the form of trade. Henceforth, the merchants and vessels of the American Revolution would be welcomed in Havana as "a most favored nation."[4]

DESPITE THE INAUSPICIOUS BEGINNING OF the American Revolution's overtures to the Spanish-speaking world, Spain—the New World's oldest colonial power—opted to support the hemisphere's first anticolonial movement. For the revolutionaries, the promise of Spanish aid and access to trade in Havana was a major triumph. Spanish currency—the famous silver pieces of eight—was the preferred coinage not only in the thirteen colonies, but also across much of the globe. Havana received a regular subsidy of Mexican silver to cover the island's military and administrative expenditures. The government there usually had a substantial supply on hand. Spain's support and its promise of access to Havana thus guaranteed the revolutionaries access to the most valuable money in the world.

For Spain, however, the decision to aid the American colonists was not a simple one. On the one hand, Britain was Spain's traditional enemy. For more than a century, it had challenged Spain's claims to territory in both the old and new worlds. The recent and humiliating defeat in the Seven Years' War was a fresh memory. The North American rebellion, then, presented an opportunity to retaliate and to regain territory lost to Britain—Florida, certainly, and maybe even Jamaica or Gibraltar.

On the other hand, the Spanish had powerful reasons not to help the Americans. Spain held territory contiguous to the rebellious colonies. To side with the revolutionaries was to invite a British attack, and Spain stood to lose a lot: the lower Mississippi Valley, Cuba, Puerto Rico, Santo Domingo. Moreover, as a monarchy with its own American colonies to safeguard, Spain was not easily inclined to embrace Americans fighting for independence from a European king. Would that not set a dangerous precedent? Might not Spain's own colonists attempt something similar? Who were these British colonists anyway? Should they win, what would stop them from expanding into Spanish or once-Spanish territory in the Louisianas, Floridas, and beyond?

So, even as Spanish leaders promised assistance, they hedged their bets and turned to that time-tested practice in the diplomatic arsenal of states: spying. Because Havana already had significant commercial links with the thirteen colonies, authorities in Madrid instructed its governor to use those links to gather information on the North American revolutionaries. Havana's governor chose a merchant named Juan de Miralles for the task. Born in Spain, Miralles had lived in Havana since 1740 and spoke fluent English. He was also a slave trader with ties to North American merchants doing business in Cuba. He had served as the official representative of the outfit that held the slave trade monopoly in Havana. The company's representative in Philadelphia was Robert Morris, delegate to the Continental Congress. Miralles thus had an almost automatic entrée to the highest echelons of the American Revolution. He prepared a new will, and on December 31, 1777, he set sail from Havana, ready to execute his mission.[5]

Pretending to have encountered trouble with his vessel en route to Spain, Miralles landed in Charleston, South Carolina, early in the new year. His performance exceeded all expectations. A massive fire in the city's business district on January 15 gave Miralles the opportunity to play the role of benefactor. He lent the state of South Carolina a hefty sum to help with relief efforts. The city's most distinguished residents invited him into their homes. Whenever it made sense, Miralles mentioned his desire to propose to the Continental Congress an expansion of trade between Havana and the thirteen colonies. Receptive, the governor arranged for him to travel northward with delegates returning to session after the holidays, and he gave Miralles letters to take to Henry Laurens, a Charleston merchant and slave trader then serving as president of the Continental Congress.[6]

Miralles "travelled in style, with five mounts so that his horse would always be fresh." All along the way, he was welcomed by some of the American Revolution's most important figures. He visited the headquarters of George Washington in Middlebrook, New Jersey. Eager to win Spanish recognition of American independence, Washington lavished great attention on him. Designating the day's signs and countersigns, he made one of them "Don Juan" for Miralles himself. The Americans staged a review of the troops and a mock battle for him. Decked in a suit of crimson and aiguillettes of gold, Miralles marched in a parade with the revolutionary leaders: Washington on "his bright bay with the grace of a perfect horseman," and "the slender and erect Colonel Hamilton, with his distinguished presence and aristocratic bearing."[7]

Miralles had a front seat for the heady days of the American Revolution. Soon after that first visit to Washington's headquarters, Miralles accompanied the Continental Congress on its triumphant entry into Philadelphia in June 1778, when the British withdrew from the city for the last time. He participated in the city's first Fourth of July celebrations, rented a house on Third Street, and dined weekly with Continental Congress president Henry Laurens, who called him a man of "honorable deportment" and "personal merit." Miralles had Christmas dinner with George and Martha Washington and cohosted a New Year's Eve banquet for them and seventy other guests.[8] His closest associate in Philadelphia was Robert Morris, merchant, slave trader, and the man who came to be known as the financier of the American Revolution. Together they established what one historian calls "a private shipping channel" between Havana and Philadelphia. After Congress lifted its embargo on the export of flour, they sent thousands of barrels, which always commanded a high price in Havana, payable, of course, in the famed and coveted Spanish pieces of eight.[9]

Miralles was busy in Philadelphia, conducting business, visiting new statesmen, and socializing. But he was also on a political mission. In that capacity, he exerted pressure on both the Spanish and American governments. Communicating regularly to officials in Madrid and Havana, Miralles extolled the virtues of the men who would come to be known as the Founding Fathers. He insisted that they could win the war, that they were worthy, and that the Spanish could work with them. It was his sincere hope that Spain make an alliance with them and declare war on the British. The king ultimately agreed.

From the Americans, meanwhile, Miralles sought an important concession on behalf of Madrid: North American recognition of Spain's right to reclaim Florida. Meeting with members of Congress, Miralles stressed that this was a small price to pay for Spain's help. In addition, Spain, which was then master of Louisiana and the port of New Orleans, was also promising to grant the new country free navigation of the Mississippi River "into and from the sea." The Continental Congress voted on September 17, 1779. Some delegates—already imagining Florida as part of their new Union—voted against the proposal. But a majority, George Washington among them, believed that they needed Spain's help to defeat Britain, and they voted to recognize its claim to Florida. To celebrate the deepening of the two countries' alliance, Miralles sent Washington a hundred-pound sea tortoise.[10]

American revolutionaries could now count on greater Spanish naval and financial assistance; Britain, meanwhile, would face another powerful threat and distraction. Miralles wrote to Washington that a thousand regular troops had left Havana for New Orleans to attack the British in the lower Mississippi; another group was soon to embark for Pensacola. A Spanish attack there, Washington believed, would draw the British away from South Carolina and Georgia. With renewed confidence, he predicted "this formidable junction of the House of Bourbon will not fail of establishing the Independance [sic] of America in a short time."[11]

Washington's predictions notwithstanding, victory did not come quickly. The winter of 1780 was the most trying of all the war. At Washington's camp in Morristown, New Jersey, thirty miles from the British in New York, troops suffered through the worst snowstorms in living memory. Even inside their tents, men with single blankets—and sometimes without—were "buried like sheep under the snow."[12] It was still cold on April 19, when Miralles arrived in Washington's camp for an extended visit. Four days later, suffering a high fever, he summoned Alexander Hamilton and a few friends to his bedside to compose a new will, naming as executors his secretary, Francisco Rendón, and his business partner Robert Morris. Surrounded by his new friends, Miralles died a few days later on April 28. Hamilton arranged the funeral, consulting with the Spanish secretary to make sure everything was done in proper Catholic form. Morris and Washington walked as chief mourners, along with other army officers and members of Congress, in a funeral procession that extended for more than a mile. Miralles was laid out "in a scarlet suit embroidered with rich gold lace, a three-cornered gold-laced hat, . . . large diamond shoe and knee-buckles, a profusion of diamond rings decorated the fingers, and from a superb gold watch set with diamonds, several rich seals were suspended." He was laid out so richly that a guard was placed at the grave, lest the soldiers "be tempted to dig for hidden treasure." The next day, Washington wrote to Havana with the news: "I the more sincerely sympathize with you in the loss of so estimable a friend, as ever since his residence with us, I have been happy in ranking him among the number of mine. It must however be some consolation to his connexions to know that in this Country he has been universally esteemed and [his death] will be universally regretted."[13]

THOUGH MIRALLES DID NOT LIVE to see it, Cuba continued to provide important assistance in the final phases of the American Revolution. Trade between the island and the thirteen colonies flourished in the early 1780s. With some twelve thousand extra soldiers and sailors in Havana during the war, officials eagerly welcomed American vessels. Between 1780 and 1781, the amount of flour entering Cuba from the thirteen colonies increased an astounding 668 percent. The trade was important on its own, but it was also a major source of silver currency for the American Revolution and, increasingly, for the Bank of North America, the new republic's first central bank.[14]

Spain's war against Britain provided another advantage to the Americans. Under the leadership of Bernardo Gálvez, and with support in money and troops from Cuba, the Spanish captured important territory from the British: Baton Rouge, Natchez, Mobile, and Pensacola. The Americans welcomed these developments because they weakened their enemy and drew British resources away from the war against them.

Even in the most important theaters of war in the thirteen colonies, Spanish and Cuban assistance could make all the difference. The famous battle of Yorktown in October 1781, for example, was financed in large part by Cuban funds arriving at a critical moment. At the time, Washington's troops were penniless and demoralized. There was money neither to pay nor feed them, and major mutinies had already broken out several times that year. The French troops fighting alongside the Americans under the Comte de Rochambeau were also suffering and out of money. Washington pinned his hopes on the arrival of the French naval officer the Comte de Grasse with funds and reinforcements. De Grasse was trying to collect funds in Saint-Domingue (today Haiti), then the richest European colony in the world. He appealed for money from sugar planters and merchants, posted printed notices on street corners, and offered bills of exchange redeemable at profitable rates. Those efforts notwithstanding, he was unable to raise even the bare minimum required.[15]

At that impasse, Spanish emissary Francisco Saavedra—whom some called a "roving troubleshooter"—arrived in Saint-Domingue. Saavedra convinced the Frenchman to sail to Havana, where there was almost always silver at hand. Unfortunately, when they arrived on August 15, the treasury was empty. A large shipment of money had just sailed for Spain, and the silver due from Mexico had not yet arrived. So Saavedra and the governor of Havana appealed to city residents directly, making "known the urgency of the case, so that each man would give what he could." Some say that women in Havana offered their jewels to the cause. Within six hours of their arrival in the city, Saavedra and de Grasse had the money they needed. De Grasse sailed at midnight with 500,000 pesos in silver.[16]

When de Grasse's fleet arrived in Virginia, all was jubilation. One French diarist among Rochambeau's men wrote, "We saw in the distance, General Washington shaking his hat and a white handkerchief, and showing signs of great joy." The always serene Washington embraced Rochambeau with visible emotion and announced the good news to his troops. "No circumstances cou'd possibly have happened more opportunely in point of time," wrote Washington. Then he added an important detail: "The Commanding Officers of Corps are to cause abstracts to be immediately made for a month's pay." The Cuban money was divided between Washington's troops and Rochambeau's. In the middle of the night, a floor in the house where the money was stored caved in from the weight of the silver. One historian refers to the funds as "the bottom dollars upon which the edifice of American independence was raised." The Americans won at Yorktown, the decisive battle of the American Revolution.[17]

AFTER THAT VICTORY, THE BRITISH and Americans entered final negotiations for Britain's recognition of the independence of its former colonies. The Spanish government, which had not yet achieved its own goals for the war, was not ready for that outcome. Unable to reconquer Jamaica, the king ordered an attack on the Bahamas. He hoped, at the very least, to recover the islands where Columbus had first set foot in the New World. The troops sailed from Havana on ships that included American privateers. The Cuban forces included Havana's Black militia—the men who had defended the city against the British in 1762, and also their sons and grandsons. Among them was José Antonio Aponte, grandson of a Black captain in the 1762 campaign, and soon to become a revolutionary figure in his own right. That, too—the fact that North American independence might make other colonial revolutions imaginable—also explains Spain's hesitation in recognizing the new American republic.

In more ways than one, the new republic became a source of "grief and fear" for Europe's oldest colonial power. As one Spanish statesman predicted, the United States might have been born a "pygmy," but soon it would be a giant, an "irresistible colossus" bent on territorial expansion. The Spanish government also worried about the economic and commercial implications of US independence. Already, the ties between Cuba and North America were formidable. What would happen now that the former British colonies were no longer tied to the British Empire and its Caribbean colonies? The Spanish already knew the answer. At the very least, the new country would be a rival for the profits of its colonies, Cuba prime among them.[18]

In August 1782, officials in Madrid wrote to Havana to inform them that foreign ships should no longer be welcomed. But Havana authorities ignored the directive. To turn away the flour and other foodstuffs arriving from North America was to risk starvation in a city still housing a wartime garrison. It was not until May 1783, after months of speculation and rumor about an impending change, that Havana's governor ordered all foreign ships in the harbor to expedite their business and leave. Henceforth, all foreign ships would be turned away.[19]

The decree, translated into English, appeared in gazettes from Charleston, South Carolina, to Newport, Rhode Island. It caused immediate and "widespread vexation," because the new country's traders would be unable to "get from any other port the quantity of cash they take out of Havana."[20] Americans lobbied Spain's representative in Philadelphia to allow the Cuban trade to continue. An anonymous appeal, likely penned by Robert Morris, argued that "if Spain would permit the free introduction of American Products into its islands, such would be the abundance which would reign in them that . . . they would quickly enrich themselves and consequently they would enrich the Nation to which they belong." Spain had no cause to fear that its possessions "may wish to be independent."[21]

The government in Madrid, however, was not convinced, and in February 1784, it issued a more draconian decree. All North Americans still in the city were to leave immediately. Soldiers patrolled streets, searched houses, and arrested foreigners in public. Spanish officials pulled up the anchor of one ship and escorted it out of the harbor. In spite of the expulsions, some traders stayed on illegally, hopeful that the tide would turn in their favor.[22]

They were right. In 1789, the Spanish government instituted a major economic reform in its colonies. It abolished a long-standing monopoly arrangement in the slave trade, allowing individual foreigners to sell African captives in its ports for the first time. Americans began arriving in Havana once more, now to sell human beings. And in the holds of the ships, they smuggled flour and other goods as well. Soon the start of new revolutions in France and Saint-Domingue enveloped the Atlantic world in war. To avoid starvation, Cuban officials welcomed US ships once more. A few years later, the Spanish consul in Philadelphia lamented the situation in Havana: "The ports with true trading privileges are not in Spain but rather here; and it appears that citizens of the United States hold exclusive trading rights with Cuba."[23] In practice, if not always in law, the newly independent republic was fast becoming Cuba's "most favored nation." Miralles, had he been alive, might have marveled at the realization—perhaps in glee as a Cuban merchant anticipating great profits, perhaps in apprehension as a Spanish commissioner dreading the growing dominance of the United States. Among the Uchiz and other Native people who had once sought Spanish protection from Britain's erstwhile colonists, apprehension regarding the new republic was surely paramount, and with good reason.

Chapter 6

SUGAR'S REVOLUTION

In 1788, when the Havana City Council needed a man to represent its interests to the king of Spain, it settled on a lawyer named Francisco Arango. Thin and elegant, he wore his dark hair short, combed forward toward his eyes. A scion of a family that had been in Cuba almost as long as Spain had, Arango was among the wealthiest men on the island. His sugar mill, *La Ninfa*, the Nymph, would soon rank as the island's largest and, with a labor force of 350 enslaved, among the largest and most modern in the world.[1]

Almost immediately on arriving in Madrid, Arango submitted his first petition to the king on behalf of the government in Havana. It was a proposal for the expansion of the slave trade. A successful sugar planter, he believed that the fastest means to develop that industry was to increase the number of African captives available for purchase. For centuries, the Crown had been granting successive companies an exclusive license to import Africans to its ports, a monopoly that left the supply inadequate and the prices high. Arango's first task, then, was to propose a free trade in unfree people. The king acceded, decreeing that for a two-year trial period, any Spaniard—and foreigners under stricter parameters—could introduce captive Africans in his colonies. The law's impact was decisive. In the two years that the policy was in effect, the number of captives entering Havana more than tripled, from less than two thousand a year to almost seven thousand.[2] Not since the British occupation of Havana in 1762–63 had there been such an increase, and the new numbers dwarfed even those.

The frenzy was such that the new Spanish governor, Luis de Las Casas, rushed to participate. On his arrival in Havana in 1790, the planters welcomed him with a gift: his very own sugar plantation, complete with slaves and machinery. They called it *Amistad*—Friendship. The island's governor was now one of them. He took to the enterprise, and the following year, he purchased a second plantation. To observe the law in technicality rather than in spirit, he registered the properties under the names of friends and associates. He also took advantage of the expanding slave trade. When slave ships arrived in the harbor, he went himself or sent his agents to the warehouses to have first pick from among the new arrivals. The Spanish governor thus became one more, very powerful sugar planter. Even in the collusion of Spanish officials, Cuban planters seemed poised to get everything they had ever wanted.[3]

Back in Madrid, the king and the Council of State were scheduled to meet on November 21, 1791, to decide whether to renew the open slave trade beyond its two-year term or to revert to the old monopoly arrangements so despised by Arango and his wealthy countrymen. Everyone expected the open policy to be extended. But on the eve of that meeting, entirely unexpected news arrived in Madrid. Three months earlier, fifty miles from the island of Cuba, in the French colony of Saint-Domingue (Haiti), slaves had risen in rebellion. Numbering in the thousands, the rebels had torched two hundred plantations, killed three hundred white residents, and then taken to the mountains. That rebellion would grow into the world-historical event we know as the Haitian Revolution. Within a month, the rebels numbered in the tens of thousands, and the property destroyed amounted to more than a thousand sugar and coffee farms. By August 1793, in the hopes of pacifying and retaining the colony, local authorities began decreeing the abolition of slavery. Then, in February 1794, the revolutionary government in Paris ended slavery in all French territories, declaring that "all men living in the colonies, without distinction of color, were French citizens." A decade later, the Black citizens of Saint-Domingue declared themselves free not only from slavery, but also from French rule. On January 1, 1804, the independent nation of Haiti was proclaimed—the second independent nation in the hemisphere, and the only one ever founded by former slaves and without slavery.

All this had happened in what had been the world's largest producer of sugar and coffee, the most profitable colony anywhere on earth, the place everyone called the pearl of the Antilles, before they gave that name to Cuba. Reading news of the early rebellion, Arango did not have to know how the story ended—he would have been incapable of imagining it—in order to worry. Would cautious statesmen in Madrid—men who controlled the fate of Cuba—tremble at the news? Would they imagine that the same destiny awaited Cuba? Might that fear prevent them from renewing the open slave trade—the key to the growth and expansion Cuban planters so craved?

In less than a day Arango penned a treatise on the uprising in Saint-Domingue. An ocean away from unfolding events, Arango wrote with a confidence that came from calculation rather than evidence: What was happening in the French colony could never happen in Cuba. He sympathized with the planters of Saint-Domingue, but their misfortune was also Spain's—and Cuba's—opportunity. Spain, he insisted, needed to pursue "advantage and preponderance over the French." Rather than something to fear, the upheaval in the neighboring colony was something to welcome—decisively, gratefully, almost as if heaven-sent.[4]

Authorities in Madrid listened. They renewed the open slave trade policy and invited Arango to submit a proposal on how to develop Cuban agriculture more fully. This second treatise—one of the most cited documents in the history of colonial Cuba—was a methodical plea for the accelerated expansion of sugar and slavery. That expansion would make Cuba, one of Spain's earliest colonies, finally "equal in value to a Kingdom," in the words of one French writer. As if compiling a wish list, Arango proposed policy after policy: to expand the already thriving slave trade, to exempt planters from taxes, to allow freer trade for Cuban sugar and other products. The massive rebellion in Saint-Domingue made *this* the moment to act. With prophetic voice, Arango proclaimed: "The hour of our happiness has arrived."[5]

HAPPINESS, OF COURSE, IS ALWAYS a relative measure. The sugar boom that made men like Arango so prosperous depended above all on the brutal exploitation of multitudes of men and women held as slaves. Between 1790 and 1820, more than 270,000 Africans were forcibly embarked for Cuba. That is more than ten times the number that arrived in Cuba over the previous three centuries of Spanish rule. It was in this period that Cuba's Black population surpassed the white for the first time. The census of 1774 classified over 56 percent of the population as white. By 1817, it had diminished to 43.4 percent. In areas dense with sugar plantations, the demographic change was even more dramatic. In Güines, where both Arango and the Spanish governor of Cuba owned their sugar mills, the white population declined from about 75 percent to less than 10 percent. This shift in the racial composition occurred alongside a dramatic increase in the island's overall population, which grew more than 220 percent between 1774 and 1817.[6]

The city of Havana doubled in size, becoming the capital of a vibrant "sugar revolution." The number of mills on its outskirts grew exponentially. To provide fuel for the mills' machinery, humans felled the forests. Soon the boom began outgrowing Havana, reaching west to Trinidad and Matanzas. On a fundamental level, Cuba's sugar revolution consolidated an economic system based overwhelmingly on the export of a single crop, produced on large plantations by a fast-growing number of enslaved Africans. Sugar was king, and, by 1830, the island of Cuba was producing more of it than any other place on earth.

Historians readily detect such patterns in hindsight. But even people living at the time were able to discern the change with their own eyes. Imagine someone living or working in the area of Old Havana that abutted the wharves. They would have observed more ships in the harbor and watched more captives being unloaded. They would have walked by new warehouses, built to hold the African men, women, and children arriving in chains and soon to be auctioned in those very buildings.[7]

Enslaved workers on plantations, meanwhile, lived the expansion of slavery body and soul. As more land was turned to sugar, slaves often lost access to their *conucos*, the garden plots that still bore the centuries-old name once used by the Native Taínos. With the loss of those provision grounds, even basic sustenance became more precarious. As the demand for labor intensified, more Africans arrived to be "seasoned." Planters had few qualms about working them to death—literally. With the slave trade now open to all, workers could be replaced easily. As the wife of a Boston merchant touring the island's sugar plantations remarked, "It is a rare thing to see an old Negro" in Cuba.[8]

The work was brutal. Even before the cane could be planted, workers had to chop down forests and clear fields. In the fall, they dug trenches over hundreds of acres to accommodate the cane cuttings, which they then tended for months. The harvest began in January, when the sucrose content of the cane was at its highest point. Harvest time was the most grueling of all. At sunrise, companies of men and women headed out to the fields to cut cane—tall, thick stalks that swayed with whatever breeze there might be. Two swings of the machete cut away the leaves; a third stroke cut the stalk close to the ground, where the plant was yellow and at its thickest. To keep the pace brisk, slave drivers cracked whips over the heads of the people bent over the cane. Oxcarts trailed the cane cutters through the fields. One group of workers filled the carts; another delivered the cane to the mill. Initially powered by oxen and later by steam engine, the mill was where enslaved workers fed the thick stalks manually, one by one into rollers that squeezed out the juice. Then still other workers transported that juice to the boiling house.

The boiling house was just what it sounds like—a structure where the cane juice was boiled in a succession of large copper vats. Slaves stood over the open pans skimming away impurities, using giant ladles to transfer the bubbling liquid to other pans. With each successive boiling, the juice lost more of its waste and water content, eventually becoming granulated sugar. After the sugar was cooled and air dried, workers packed it into cone-shaped receptacles to drain. When they opened the molds a few weeks later, the sugar inside was divided into three categories—the white sugar on top; yellow in the middle; moist brown sugar at the bottom. The yellow and brown went to buyers who would refine it further in other countries. The white was sold for direct consumption. The substance that drained out of the bottom of the container was sold abroad for use in the manufacture of rum. [9]

The description of the labor process and the technology that sustained it, however, cannot really convey what the work was like: the extreme heat, the sickening smell, the relentlessness of the toil, the pain in people's bodies. Because the sucrose content of the cane begins to spoil almost immediately after it is cut, there was never a break in the rhythm. During the day, the "monotonous chants of the gangs filling the wagons or the trough" rang out uninterrupted. The mills, meanwhile, operated around the clock, the cauldron men shouting out instructions to the stokers. Everywhere were scenes of "condensed and determined labor." The fatigue and the pace made accidents all too common—fingers sliced, hands crushed, arms lost to the machinery. At night in their quarters, exhausted, before shutting their eyes for a few hours of sleep, the enslaved might pray or talk or make love, the faint light of glowworms serving them as candles. But whatever respite the enslaved carved out of their days or nights did not change the fact that these plantations, like their counterparts across the US South, were forced labor camps. [10]

As the demand for work intensified, so too did corporal punishment. In 1806, enslaved workers from the booming sugar region of Güines testified about the escalation and ubiquitousness of physical punishment and torture, speaking for companions who no longer could. They mentioned Rafael, who died as a result of a punishment that in Jamaica was called Derby's dose, in which slaves were made to eat the excrement of other slaves; María del Rosario, who was locked in a henhouse and pecked to death; Pedro Carabalí, beaten to death with a stick and thrown in a fire; and an unnamed seven-year-old boy who died as a result of unspecified punishment. Witnessing and experiencing such brutality sometimes drove the enslaved to plot rebellions against slavery. "Compañeros," said one of the leaders, "you already know ... the subjection and punishment that the whites give us." The time had come to act; it was time to kill them. During the investigation into that conspiracy, authorities asked another leader what had driven them to plot their rebellion. He answered with a weary frankness: they had wanted "to ease the burden of their enslavement."[11]

In making the case for the expansion of sugar and slavery in Cuba in the wake of the Haitian Revolution, Francisco Arango had announced that the hour of happiness had arrived. The testimony of the enslaved allows us to glimpse Arango's happiness through the eyes of the men and women whose suffering made it possible.

THE FACT THAT SUGAR AND slavery took root in Cuba in the shadow of the Haitian Revolution (1791–1804) shaped the experience and vision of both masters and the enslaved. Ships from revolutionary Saint-Domingue arrived in Cuba with people seeking refuge. In just six months in 1803, more than eighteen thousand arrived in the old eastern capital of Santiago, nearly doubling the city's population. Almost every one of these refugees arrived bearing firsthand accounts of the Haitian Revolution. With such talk becoming ubiquitous, many white residents of Cuba began to wonder if their own island might follow in the same path as Haiti. Cuba's first woman novelist, Gertrudis Gómez de Avellaneda, later recalled that her father regularly predicted for Cuba a fate like Haiti's—"seized by the blacks"—and he constantly implored her mother to leave with him for Spain. Such sentiments were not exceptional. White residents of the island imagined signs of insolence and peril everywhere—a hushed conversation, a confident gait, even in a glance.[12]

In fact, fear of the Haitian Revolution played an important role in the island's history. The Age of Revolution convulsed the world, as first the American and then the French and Haitian revolutions threw into question the underpinnings of social and political life across both hemispheres. When, in 1808, Napoleon Bonaparte kidnapped the king of Spain and put his own brother on the Spanish throne, cities across Latin America began forming independent juntas to rule in the absence of their king. Even if those juntas emerged initially out of loyalty to the Crown, they established the dangerous precedent of home rule. By 1826, after more than a decade and a half of war and revolution unevenly spread across Spanish America, all but Cuba and Puerto Rico had won their independence. In this context, prominent Cubans weighed their options. Francisco Arango, Havana's old representative to the Spanish court, briefly entertained the idea of forming an independent junta to rule in the absence of the king (and surely to usher in more of the kinds of economic reforms the planters had always sought). But those efforts were halfhearted and went nowhere. So as revolution swept first through Haiti and then through Spanish America, the island of Cuba remained more or less quiescent.

Why? One answer is that the Cuban elite, fearful of the potential social upheaval that might accompany an armed bid for independence, opted to stick with Spain. In the words of one foreign sugar planter on the island, Cuban elites "knew without a doubt that any movement would lead them to their ruin, and they feared exposing themselves to the fate suffered by the unfortunate victims of [Haiti]."[13] In this view, apprehension—not loyalty or love—kept Cuba Spanish.

Fear, however, was not the only factor; greed was important, too. A new class of Cuban sugar barons had just come into its own, and many were reluctant to endanger their newfound status and wealth with an uncertain strike for independence. They eschewed political revolution and remained loyal to Spain. Then they leveraged that loyalty to extract ever greater concessions from Madrid and to guarantee their own ascendancy. They lived in stately homes in the city and palatial estates in the countryside, both decorated in the French style. Their sugar mills boasted the most modern machinery, all imported. They traveled, attended the theater, commissioned their own portraits, and went for evening rides in their fancy horse-drawn carriages. They lived like masters of their worlds. And at all costs, they would avoid the destruction that had swept Saint-Domingue and that was now engulfing, in a different manner, much of Spanish America.

BUT WHAT OF THE MANY Africans and their descendants held as slaves in Cuba? On the one hand, they were living the entrenchment of slavery firsthand, feeling its effects viscerally. Yet at the same time, they were also hearing news of the Haitian Revolution and of people such as themselves making war against their masters and against slavery. That news fired their imagination and their sense of possibility. In fact, in the period and aftermath of the Haitian Revolution, Black conspiracies and rebellions were uncovered at fairly regular intervals across the island: twice in 1795, again in 1796, at least five times in 1798, then in 1802, 1803, 1805, and 1806, twice in 1809, half a dozen times in 1811–12. The list goes on.[14] It was as if slavery itself were a kind of permanent standoff, a war averted only by another kind of violence, another kind of terror.

In the investigations into these incidents, authorities usually forced the accused to recount the conversations they had among themselves as they plotted their rebellions. That testimony allows us to listen in on conversations full of unexpected things. Thus, two enslaved conspirators born in Africa spoke about the success of the Haitians and wondered what had contributed to it. The same kind of faith, said one, that had motivated Charlemagne and his twelve peers during the reconquest of Christian Europe from the Muslims. Sometimes would-be rebels sought models closer to home. They invoked the example of the *cobreros*—the men and women near the mines of El Cobre and the shrine of the Virgin of Charity, who had resisted for centuries and secured their freedom in 1800. Above all, they dwelled on Haiti's example, discussing time and again the feats of Haitian leaders. They spoke of Toussaint Louverture—former slave and the most famous figure of the revolution, the man so powerful that Napoleon eventually imprisoned him in a cold, dank jail cell in the Jura Mountains on France's Swiss border. They talked of Jean-François—a former slave who became an important early leader of the revolution and who allied with Spain in fighting against the French Republic. Across Cuba, from east to west, during and following the Haitian Revolution, enslaved people shared their admiration and respect for Black people who they said had "taken the land" and become "masters of themselves."

Of all the conspiracies and rebellions in Cuba in this period, the most fascinating is one that came to light in 1812. Its leaders were mostly free Black men who allied with enslaved people to end the institution of slavery. In an epoch that saw upheaval all across the hemisphere, this movement was perhaps the closest Havana came to revolution. On March 14, 1812, a free Black man named Juan Barbier, who authorities said was from Charleston, South Carolina, left Havana for its outskirts. Barbier, however, was traveling as someone else, having assumed the name and identity of Jean-François, a Black Haitian general well known and admired among enslaved and free people of color in Cuba. That night in Havana, Barbier wore a blue uniform adorned with gold buttons. He arrived with two companions at a sugar plantation, gathered the workforce, and read to them in French from a document he insisted was an order from his king to lead them in a war against slavery. (In fact, the document was a printed advertisement for William Young Birch, publisher and stationer in Philadelphia.) Then he led the slaves to a second plantation, Peñas Altas, where they set fires and killed five white people, including two children. At the third plantation, the rebels were defeated.

In the weeks and months that followed, Spanish authorities captured and punished more than fifty rebels and suspects in Havana alone, publicly executing and displaying the remains of fourteen of them. Jean-François/Barbier was hanged, his head severed and put on a stake at the entrance to the plantation where a few weeks earlier he had arrived heralding freedom and revolution.[15]

Had the rebellion not been thwarted, the events of March 14, 1812, would have been but the opening move in a powerful, ambitious revolution. The conspirators had intended to burn down other plantations and mobilize their enslaved labor forces. In the capital, they had planned attacks on the city's fortresses and armories to seize weapons with which to arm the hundreds of recruits they claimed to have ready. Leaders had dictated a public proclamation and nailed it to the door of the governor's palace. They had flags and standards ready to post at the camps they hoped to establish. Their networks stretched from plantations to the heart of the capital city, and, according to some contemporary accounts, as far east as Santiago, perhaps even to some foreign locations. All this labor and planning was directed to one end: freedom for the slaves.

The mastermind of this would-be revolution was a free Black carpenter named José Antonio Aponte. We have met him and his grandfather already, if only in passing. His grandfather had served in the city's Black battalion and defended Havana against the British invasion of 1762. The younger Aponte, the leader of the 1812 conspiracy, was himself a veteran of Havana's Black militia and had fought against the British in the Bahamas during the American Revolution. Now in 1812, Aponte plotted to attack the city and install a government that would end slavery and, with it, the power of planters and colonial officials.

When the Havana police searched Aponte's house during the investigation, they found an odd collection of documents and artifacts—published laws on the Black militia; fabric for the flags and standards of the rebellion; images of the Virgin Mary, George Washington, and Haiti's King Henri Christophe. They found volume three of *Don Quixote*, guides to the cities of Havana and Rome, grammar handbooks, art manuals, and a compendium of the history of the world. And hidden deep inside a trunk full of clothes, authorities found a pine box with a sliding top. Inside was another book, created by Aponte himself. Like the other items confiscated from his house, the book's contents were a confounding mix of materials and images—hand-drawn pictures and maps, scenes or words cut out from fans and prints and pasted onto the pages of the book. Represented were Greek goddesses and Black saints, Ethiopian kings and European popes, Havana and the heavens. In one picture, Aponte had drawn the house of Francisco Arango, Havana's onetime representative in Madrid and a principal architect of Cuba's sugar revolution. In another, Aponte portrayed himself as king.[16]

As he plotted, Aponte had shown the book to his co-conspirators, explaining some of its images as a way to help prepare for their revolution. He showed them the pictures he had drawn of Spanish military camps during the British siege of Havana in order to demonstrate where they should place their flags and sentries in the impending battle. He showed them pictures of Black armies defeating white ones, perhaps to give them hope that their project had a chance. He showed them images of important Black men—priests, diplomats, generals, kings—to illustrate a world in which men such as themselves wielded state power. He showed them the book, in other words, to prove to them that another world was possible.

For the governors of a colonial society dependent on slavery, Aponte's book and conspiracy represented the gravest form of subversion. Over the course of three long days, Aponte was forced to explain his book image by image before authorities. A few weeks later, they condemned him to death and, on April 9, 1812, hanged him before a crowd. His head was severed from his body and placed on a pike in a cage, about a block and a half from his house, at a major crossroads on the route from the city to the sugar plantations. There it remained, a gruesome warning for all to see. To those who might harbor intentions akin to Aponte's, the governor vowed that he had the resources "to annihilate them in a single moment."[17] Then, sometime after the execution—no one knows when—Aponte's unusual book of paintings disappeared, and no one, it seems, has seen it since. All that remains of it are the descriptions he was compelled to give at trial.

Aponte's violent end and the loss of the book notwithstanding, his story and figure continued to resonate long after his execution. For some, his name became synonymous with danger. The saying "más malo que Aponte"—worse, or more evil, than Aponte—was popular by the 1840s and remained in use a century later. Other Cubans, however, drew inspiration from his example. In the 1940s, a group of veterans of the Cuban War of Independence (1895–98) and Republican sympathizers of the Spanish Civil War (1936–39) successfully lobbied for the Havana street that bore the name of the governor who ordered Aponte's execution—Someruelos—to be renamed Aponte. (A friend in Havana tells me, however, that she has seen a recent electric bill for an apartment on that street that still bears the name of the old Spanish governor). A bronze plaque in honor of Aponte and his companions was placed there in the 1940s, though it was stolen in more recent times. Among Black communities in Havana, his memory was kept alive from generation to generation. Afro-Cuban historian José Luciano Franco recalled that in the 1960s, stories of Aponte's accomplishments—including his participation in the American Revolution—were well known in popular neighborhoods. In the 1970s and 1980s, a Cuban American priest of Santería in the Bronx shared stories with his followers about Aponte as guide and teacher, and he kept an image said to be of Aponte on his altar. In 2017, an international exhibit titled *Visionary Aponte: Art and Black Freedom* invited contemporary artists from Cuba, the United States, and the Caribbean to reinterpret Aponte's missing book of paintings for the present. It opened in Miami in 2017, and in 2019 traveled to Cuba, where it was enthusiastically received.

But in Aponte's own era and that of his children and grandchildren, it was not his vision that carried the day, but rather its antithesis: the vision of Francisco Arango, the sugar planter who saw the intensification of slavery as happiness itself. Aponte's antislavery kingdom did not come to pass. Arango's sugar revolution soared. Plantations kept growing in number and size, taking over more land and more forests, and consuming more and more African lives. What had been a society with slaves became instead a slave society, one in which the system of slavery left its mark on everything from political to social to economic to cultural life. In the process, the island of Cuba became not only a colony "equal in value to a Kingdom," but also, increasingly, the apple of the eye of a young United States.

STEAM SAWMILL
on the
NEW-HOPE SUGAR ESTATE — CUBA

The proprietor of the New Hope Sugar Estate was Senator James DeWolf of Rhode Island, one of many US citizens who owned plantations in nineteenth-century Cuba. DeWolf's manager, George Howe, drew the sugar mill on a page in his diary.

Part III

AN EMPIRE FOR SLAVERY

Chapter 7

ADAMS'S APPLE

On Sunday, April 7, 1822, Senator James DeWolf paid an urgent evening visit to Secretary of State John Quincy Adams. DeWolf was a new senator from Rhode Island and also one of the wealthiest men in the United States, with business interests from New England to Russia. He had made his fortune as a textile manufacturer and merchant; he also owned a rum distillery and a bank. A very significant part of his fortune, however, derived from the transatlantic slave trade. In fact, DeWolf was among the most notorious slave traders in the country. Announcing his election to the Senate, one Pennsylvania newspaper ventured that *Wolf* was "certainly an appropriate name for a man-stealer." In a well-publicized case years earlier, he had been tried for the murder of a captive woman on the slave ship *Polly*, which he both owned and captained. Sailing from Africa's Gold Coast to Cuba with 142 Africans, he had murdered the woman himself. He gagged and bound her to a chair, and then (without touching her, because he believed her to have smallpox) he hoisted her overboard to her death. Whatever problems he encountered on that journey, nothing deterred him from making others. Indeed, DeWolf's vessels made at least forty-four slaving voyages between 1790 and the end of the legal transatlantic trade to the United States in 1808. Even after it became illegal, DeWolf continued buying and selling human beings. Of all the slaving voyages undertaken on DeWolf's ships, well over half went to Cuba, landing more than two thousand Africans there. DeWolf kept some of the captives for himself, for use on the three sugar and coffee plantations he personally owned on the island. The Rhode Island senator did so much business in Cuba that he even became a naturalized Spanish citizen.[1]

It was Cuba that was on DeWolf's mind when he barged in on Secretary of State Adams that Sunday night. DeWolf had it on excellent authority that the

British were planning to take possession of Cuba within the month. Great Britain, once the greatest slave-trading power in the world, was by then a major force against the slave trade (though it would cling to slavery in its own Caribbean colonies until 1834). In 1807, it had illegalized the transatlantic slave trade to its territories and by its citizens. Its navy captured slaving vessels on the high seas, and its statesmen negotiated treaties with foreign powers to end the trade everywhere. A British takeover of Cuba would mean the immediate end of DeWolf's slave-trading business, on which his Cuban plantations relied. The senator had ample reason then for apprehension, and he pleaded with Adams to block British designs on Cuba.

Adams, however, did not put too much stock in the new senator's urgency. It was DeWolf's timing, rather than the warning itself, that he dismissed. Adams was as interested as DeWolf in keeping Cuba out of the hands of other powers: Britain, France, and now also the newly independent nations of Latin America. At the time, the Mexican government was pondering an invasion of Cuba to liberate it from Spain and annex it to Mexico. The island's geographic location, argued Mexican statesmen, made it their natural appendage—"a great warehouse and shipyard created by nature for [our] use." Just look at a map for proof, urged one official.[2]

For Cuba—situated at the gateway of the Gulf of Mexico and for centuries regarded as Key to the New World—geography was destiny. In the first decades of the nineteenth century, no one believed that more than the leaders of the United States. Since its founding, they had conjured imaginary maps of the hemisphere that redrew the actual existing boundaries of their republic. For Thomas Jefferson the ideal map of the United States included Cuba. As he wrote in 1809, "I would immediately erect a column on the Southernmost limit of Cuba & inscribe on it a *Ne plus ultra* as to us in that direction. We should then have only to include the North [Canada] in our confederacy . . . and we should have such an empire for liberty as she has never surveyed since the creation."[3] Already in 1809, the slaveholding Jefferson prophesied an American empire that encompassed an American Cuba.

Talk of expansion into Cuba was so well known that Spanish diplomats believed that actual maps and plans already existed. With each passing day, warned one Spaniard in 1812, "the ambitious ideas of this republic increase . . . . a map has already been prepared . . . which includes within these limits the island of Cuba, as a natural possession" of the United States.[4] The US acquisition of Florida from Spain in 1821 only fed speculation about US designs on Cuba.

As Adams himself wrote, using language strikingly similar to that of Mexican officials:

> These islands, from their local position, are natural append-ages to the North American continent; and one of them, Cuba, almost within sight of our shores, from a multitude of consid-erations has become an object of transcendent importance to the political and commercial interests of our Union. [It has] an importance in the sum of our national interests, with which that of no other foreign territory can be compared, and lit-tle inferior to that which binds the different members of this Union together.... Such indeed are, between the interests of that island, and of this country ... [that] it is scarcely possible to resist the conviction that the annexation of Cuba to our federal republic will be indispensable to the continuance and integrity of the Union itself.... [5]

Two centuries later, that position seems strange. But in the early 1820s—a generation and a half after the American Revolution, less than a decade after the end of the War of 1812, with the boundaries of the United States quickly expanding south and westward—the acquisition of Cuba represented a logi-cal next move. At the time, New Orleans, where the Mississippi River flowed into the Gulf of Mexico, was on its way to becoming a major US port for agricultural goods headed to the eastern seaboard, Europe, and Latin America. However much had changed since the Spanish conquest of the New World, Cuba still sat between the Gulf of Mexico and both the eastern seaboard of the United States and the Atlantic Ocean. That position granted whatever state controlled Cuba enormous power over the United States. A government there could ostensibly deny safe passage to the thousands of ships leaving New Or-leans with all the cotton and other products produced across the vast expanse of land that was the Mississippi basin—1.2 million square miles and more than 40 percent of the continental United States.[6] Cuba's master, then, had the potential to cripple American commerce. For the statesmen of the early nineteenth century, there was no room for doubt: to guarantee the success and permanence of the young American republic, the acquisition of Cuba was, as Adams had said, "indispensable."

Cuba's location at the crossroads of the Atlantic Ocean and the Gulf of Mexico piqued the interest of early American statesmen, who realized that whoever controlled Cuba could potentially cripple US commerce.

For Adams, it was not only a matter of commerce and geography, but also of physics. He finished his thoughts on the natural connection between the United States and Cuba with a prediction and a metaphor that many Cubans today can paraphrase from memory. He wrote:

> [T]here are laws of political as well as of physical gravitation; and if an apple severed by the tempest from its native tree cannot choose but fall to the ground, Cuba, forcibly disjoined from its own un-natural connection with Spain, and incapable of self-support, can gravitate only towards the North American Union, which by the same law of nature cannot cast her off from its bosom.[7]

For Adams, as for most of his fellow statesmen, the question was not *whether*—but *when*—Cuba would become part of the United States. An American Cuba was inevitable, a consequence of the most elemental law of nature: gravity.

LAWS OF NATURE, HOWEVER, CAN try human patience. They tempt people to try and prod them along, to foolishly imagine that they can accelerate the pull of gravity. In this case, those who tried were not only American, but also Cuban. Beginning in 1822, and then on and off over the following decades, a powerful sector of wealthy, ambitious Cubans saw in a formal association with the United States the answer to everything that troubled them.

Why—as almost every territory of the Americas was winning its independence—would Cuban elites seek to attach themselves to the United States, a country with a different language, culture, and religion? Their logic was simple. The wealthiest and most powerful Cubans were slaveholders. They worried that the road to independence—whether initiated by a foreign invasion or nourished on Cuban soil—would inevitably lead to the mobilization of slaves, the abolition of slavery, and, in short order, "the ascendancy of the blacks," as they called it. "The existence of slavery in Cuba," calculated a minister in Madrid, "was worth an army of 100,000 men." The Spanish governor on the island agreed: "Even though there are many who wish not to depend on Spain, the moment they look at the Blacks, they do not dare pursue that [course]." Simply put, slavery—both its profits and the prospect of its violent destruction—deterred wealthy creoles from striking for independence on their own.[8]

Yet even as they rejected Cuban independence, planters also worried about remaining Spanish. In 1817, Spain had signed a treaty with Great Britain to end the slave trade to all Spanish possessions starting in 1820. By 1822, about the time the slave-trading Senator DeWolf called on John Quincy Adams, the thriving and now-illegal slave trade to Cuba was under British assault. Cuban planters had little confidence that, in the face of mounting British pressure, Spain would be able to defend the slave trade and slavery in Cuba. If independence threatened to end slavery by revolution, the continuation of Spanish rule threatened to end it by diplomacy.

Enter the United States. In 1807, it had banned the international slave trade to its territory, penalizing captains who engaged in it, though liberating none of the captives they carried. In spite of the ban, it remained a booming slave economy, arguably the most important remaining slave power on earth. It also already had a major share of Cuba's export trade. In 1817, the king of Spain had authorized free trade between the island and the United States, as a way to keep creole elites happy and dissuaded from pursuing independence. By 1820–21, more than 60 percent of the sugar, 40 percent of the coffee, and 90 percent of the cigars imported into the United States came from Cuba. Indeed, the value of Cuban imports to the United States was surpassed only by the value of those from industrializing Britain.[9] On both sides of the Florida Straits, moneyed, powerful men wondered: Wouldn't it make sense, then, to formalize and expand the island's connection to the United States?

In September 1822, a mysterious Cuban named Bernabé Sánchez showed up in Washington, DC, to ask precisely that question. There on behalf of "several respectable and influential Cubans," he presented no credentials. But access was different then, and President James Monroe welcomed him to the White House. Sánchez said he had urgent news: a Cuban conspiracy against Spanish rule was imminent. Its real purpose, however, was not independence. Instead, the plotters wanted to break with Spain and immediately pursue annexation to the United States, not as a territory like Florida, but as a full state of the union, like Maine (1820) and Missouri (1821). The Cuban visitor was there to assess President Monroe's support for their plan.[10]

Monroe listened with interest and convened his cabinet to discuss the merits of the proposal. That the cabinet was enthusiastic comes as no surprise. South Carolina native John C. Calhoun, then secretary of war and soon to become the South's foremost proslavery ideologue, was among the most eager supporters of Cuban annexation. The youngest man in the room, he claimed to speak not only on his own authority, but also that of Thomas Jefferson, who had told him just two years earlier that the United States should "at the first possible opportunity" acquire Cuba. While Calhoun agreed, he also worried that taking the island might lead the United States into a costly, perhaps disastrous war with Spain and Britain. The discussion continued into the following week.[11]

Ultimately, the cabinet decided not to pursue the annexation of Cuba—for the moment. President Monroe informed Sánchez that the United States was unable to undertake the proposed annexation because of its friendship with Spain. Unofficially, however, he instructed Sánchez to obtain more information on the current state of Cuba and, in particular, on the strength of annexationist sentiment there. "More information upon all this would be necessary before we could take a step of any kind in an affair of deeper importance and greater magnitude than had occurred since the establishment of our Independence."[12]

Monroe also asked American agents in Cuba to gather their own intelligence on the question. Their reports strengthened the hand of those arguing for annexation. One agent assured the president that Cubans were determined to resist the transfer of the island to Great Britain. The power of Britain's campaign against the slave trade and the fact that Blacks constituted the majority of the population in Cuba (57 percent) led the island's white residents to regard the prospect of becoming British territory as tantamount to the end of slavery and the establishment of a Black republic. Monroe's agents contrasted Cuban antipathy to British rule with the apparent eagerness for the island's incorporation into the United States. One important source of that enthusiasm came from the belief that the Americans had both the will and the power to protect slavery. According to one agent, two-thirds of the white inhabitants of Cuba favored annexation to the United States as "the only security against foreign dominion and domestic insurrection." Neither the American agents nor President Monroe and his cabinet stopped to consider the irony of Cuban creoles opting for US statehood as an alternative to "foreign dominion." For the moment, the island would remain Spanish and that, Monroe decided, suited the Americans fine. So long as nothing changed, American interests in Cuba were safe.[13]

NO SOONER HAD MONROE MADE that decision than something major changed. In April 1823, the French invaded Spain to defeat a liberal revolution that had taken power in 1820. Convinced that it was liberal reform that had propelled the loss of Spain's empire, the newly reinstalled king dissolved the legislature and revoked the liberal constitution. Absolutism was restored.

News of the French invasion of the Spanish peninsula prompted heated discussion in Monroe's administration. Cabinet members speculated that Britain might use the upheaval to lay its hands on Cuba. Calhoun—as a southerner and the secretary of war—overcame his earlier caution: if Britain made a move on Cuba, he said, war was a reasonable option. Another cabinet member recommended, instead, that the United States urge the Cubans to declare their independence. John Quincy Adams, who admitted he could be "a gloomy misanthropist," intervened with characteristic skepticism. The Cubans, he pronounced confidently, would be incapable of holding on to independence, should they even manage to acquire it. As for Britain, the United States could not prevent it from taking Cuba if it so chose. The conversation grew heated. Some wanted to call Congress in for a special session; Adams brushed off the suggestion as absurd. That night, he ended his diary entry with a short note to himself: "Memorandum—to be cool on this subject." Even with a cool outlook, however, American statesmen kept returning to two distinct and unwelcome possibilities: that Cubans would achieve their own independence or that the British would somehow acquire the island. In either case, they thought, Cuba would be lost to the United States.[14]

In preventing the first of those outcomes—independence—the Americans had a powerful ally in the island's new Spanish governor: Francisco Dionisio Vives. He was sent by the king immediately after the restoration of absolutism in Spain, to rule Cuba in the same spirit. Madrid had recently tolerated reform in Cuba partly in the interest of using the island as an operations center against independence movements in South America. Now, with those colonies lost to Spain, the calculus had changed. The new governor arrived on the island in 1823, just in time to crush a Masonic conspiracy that had sought to declare independence and establish a sovereign republic named Cubanacán, one of the island's names from the time before Columbus. In the aftermath of the conspiracy, Madrid outlawed Masonic lodges and banned the importation of all books that disparaged church or king or that advocated independence or rebellion. In 1825, the Crown established the Comisión Militar, a military court that superseded traditional mechanisms of justice and that, in its first seven years alone, tried more than six hundred defendants. Finally, the king granted the governor *facultades omnímodas*, which translates roughly as "absolute authority," equivalent to "all the powers which by royal decree are conceded to the governors of cities in a state of siege." These included the power to replace officials at will, to banish anyone he considered suspicious, to confiscate property, and to suspend the execution of any royal orders he deemed inappropriate or dangerous. The decree—which remained in place for more than fifty years—severely limited Cubans' rights under the law and gave the governor and his successors almost absolute power. As if to flaunt its iron-fisted hold on the island, Madrid conferred a new honorific title on Cuba: "siempre fiel," or ever faithful. The phrase would be stamped atop official state documents in Cuba until the end of Spanish rule more than seventy years later.[15]

The restoration of absolutism and the hardening of colonial rule created deep unease in Cuba. Initially, some antigovernment plots surfaced. In addition to the 1823 Masonic plot, there were minor conspiracies in the 1820s, led mostly by men with little financial stake in slavery and sometimes with the participation of free people of color. The year 1825 also saw a rebellion involving African-born slaves on coffee plantations in Matanzas, the same region where Senator James DeWolf and other Americans owned plantations. All these movements—whether against Spain or against slavery, or both—went nowhere. There was simply no space on the island to mount a credible challenge to Spain.[16]

It is not surprising, then, that the most impassioned pleas for independence came from Cubans in exile, where the implications of organizing politically were less mortal. Félix Varela was a thin, bespectacled priest and philosophy professor in Havana, with many disciples among the city's lettered youth. In 1821, during liberal rule in Spain, he was elected as Havana's delegate to the Spanish legislature, where he advocated for Cuban self-rule. When the king restored absolutism, Varela escaped to the United States, living briefly in Philadelphia and then New York for more than twenty-five years. There, he worked on a Spanish translation of Thomas Jefferson's *Manual of Parliamentary Procedure*, was invited to participate in discussions about the founding of New York University, and published what is widely regarded as Cuba's first pro-independence newspaper and the United States' first Spanish-language newspaper. In its pages, he openly advocated for separation from Spain. For that, the Spanish king ordered his assassination.

If Varela was powerful as the voice of Cuban independence in exile, he was also an immigrant in New York. On Mott Street in downtown Manhattan, he founded the Church of the Immigrant (later renamed the Church of the Transfiguration), where priests and parishioners included Spaniards, Irish, Austrians, Italians, and others. He helped establish the Asylum for the Relief of the Children of Poor Widows, and during New York's cholera epidemic of 1832, he provided spiritual guidance at city hospitals. Today, Varela remains well known among Catholic leaders in New York, and in 1997, the US Postal Service issued a stamp in his honor. Older Cubans still speak of him as the man, the saying goes, "who taught Cubans to think."[17] Yet while Varela is considered an early exponent of Cuban nationhood, he spent most of his life in exile in the United States. In Cuba itself, the bespectacled priest could do little.

On the island, the Spanish counted on the expansive powers that authorized Governor Vives to mete out an unforgiving repression and on an army that, with the independence wars in South America lost, could now concentrate almost entirely on safeguarding Cuba. The US government understood the governor's power in Cuba and its chilling effect on political agitation. And it was grateful. In the words of John Quincy Adams, Vives endeavored to "tranquilize and conciliate the submission" of Cuba. Consequently, the United States "heard nothing further of intended insurrection in Cuba during the remainder of Mr. Monroe's administration, and the whole of mine."[18] For the moment anyway, Cubans could not strike for independence.

CUBA

THE AMERICANS WERE SIGNIFICANTLY MORE worried about British designs on Cuba. The British, anxious that the Americans would make their own move on the island, reciprocated the concern. It was the British who blinked first. In October 1823, James Monroe received a proposal from the British foreign minister inviting the United States to join Britain in pledging, first, that neither country would attempt to seize Spain's current or former colonies and, second, that neither country would countenance such seizure from any other power.

Thomas Jefferson wrote from retirement in Monticello that the questions raised by the British proposal were "the most momentous which [have] ever been offered to my contemplation since that of independance that made us a nation." For Jefferson, the principal question was this: "Do we wish to acquire to our own Confederacy any one or more of the Spanish provinces?" His answer was yes, and Cuba. "I candidly confess that I have ever looked on Cuba as the most interesting addition which could ever be made to our system of states." Together with Florida—just acquired from Spain—it would give the United States control over the Gulf of Mexico "... as well as all those whose waters flow into it." Given that there was little chance of Cuba becoming British—Cubans "being averse to her"—Jefferson came to a conclusion that echoed Adams's apple-falling-from-a-tree analogy. It might be "better then to lie still, in readiness to receive that interesting incorporation when solicited by herself. For certainly," he concluded, the island "is exactly what is wanting to round our power as a nation, to the point of it's [sic] utmost interest." Cuba "would fill up the measure of our political well-being."[19]

For his part, the austere, calculating Adams agreed with Jefferson. He understood that Spain was not ever going to reconquer its former colonies in South America. Adams, who liked to prognosticate political futures with colorful metaphors, declared that the chances of that were no greater than of Chimborazo (a famous Andean mountain peak) sinking beneath the ocean. Assuming Latin America's independence from Spain was assured, the British on their own would oppose any interference there by another European power. So, the proposed joint pledge would really accomplish nothing regarding the recently (or soon-to-be) independent countries of Latin America. But it would significantly tie the United States' hands with regard to Cuba. All the information available to Adams suggested that the Cubans would never stand for British rule. If that was unlikely to happen anyway, then why forgo the possibility of making Cuba American sometime down the road?[20] After all, Washington had already received at least one request for annexation from

Cubans themselves. While the time was not yet propitious, Cuba's annexation to the United States was simply a matter of time, he believed—as inevitable as a ripe apple falling from a tree.

With Adams leading the way, the Monroe administration decided to enunciate its own policy unilaterally. Monroe announced it on December 2, 1823, in his annual message to Congress. The policy, which came to be known as the Monroe Doctrine, stipulated that the Western Hemisphere was henceforth closed to European colonization. He declared, "the American continents, by the free and independent condition which they have assumed and maintain, are henceforth not to be considered as subjects for future colonization by any European powers." Regarding the remaining colonies of Europe in the Americas—Cuba, for instance—the United States pledged nonintervention and expected the same from all of Europe. Spain's former colonies in Latin America were too preoccupied with founding new nations to mount risky expeditions to Cuba. (And, just in case, the United States separately exerted pressure against that possibility, as well.) More important, the Monroe Doctrine kept Great Britain—at once the globe's greatest naval power and the world's new crusader against the slave trade—out of Latin America.[21]

The Monroe Doctrine thus allowed the United States to wait things out as "the laws of political gravitation" inevitably separated Cuba from Spain and propelled her into the American Union. It preserved Cuba for an American future. And in the present, it safeguarded an already emerging system that bound the US economy to Cuban slavery.

GRADUALLY SINCE AMERICAN INDEPENDENCE, AND more decisively after Spain's 1817 concession of free trade to the Cubans, the economies of the United States and Cuba were becoming intricately entangled. By the eve of the Monroe Doctrine, the North American republic was Cuba's principal trading partner, far outpacing even Spain. For the United States, meanwhile, the island consistently ranked as one of the country's top three trading partners. The deepening of these trade ties was premised above all on the expansion of sugar and slavery in Cuba. As its economy increasingly turned to sugar, the island looked to the United States to import everything from luxury goods (because ever-richer planters developed ever-richer tastes), to basic foodstuffs (because land was more profitable if it grew sugarcane), to industrial machinery (because it was necessary to turn the cane into sugar).[22]

If US businesses helped supply the machinery that powered Cuban sugar production, they also helped supply the people who did most of the labor. The United States had prohibited its citizens from selling human beings in foreign countries in 1800, and it outlawed the transatlantic slave trade to US territory in 1807. Spain, by a treaty signed with Britain, ended the slave trade to Cuba in 1820 (and then again in 1835, because the first ban was so ineffectual). Yet the vast majority of Africans brought to the island through the transatlantic slave trade arrived *after* the trade to Cuba became illegal. Indeed, of all the Africans forcibly transported there over three and a half centuries, more than 70 percent arrived after Spain illegalized the trade in 1820.[23]

Americans were deeply implicated in that illegal commerce. In the late 1830s, the number of US-flagged ships involved in the slave trade to and from Cuba nearly doubled, and US-built ships accounted for an estimated 63 percent of captives introduced in Cuba. Many of the vessels were Baltimore clippers insured by New York companies. They set out not only from southern ports, but also from New York, Boston, Baltimore, Bristol, Rhode Island, and New Bedford, Massachusetts. They made the crossing to West Africa, where they purchased men, women, and children, often dealing with American agents resident there. They crossed the ocean in the opposite direction, loaded with hundreds of captive Africans, and landed in Havana, Matanzas, Cárdenas, Trinidad, and elsewhere in Cuba (or Brazil) and sold people at profit margins that made everyone—save the captives—rich. Instead of policing the illegal trade, the US consul in Havana helped run it. He charged a fee to help people flout the law; indeed, he purchased his very own Cuban plantation with his earnings. James DeWolf, even as US senator and well after the trade was illegal, continued to carry human cargo aboard his ships and to sell them in Cuba. Americans reinvested the hefty profits from all this in financial firms, banks, insurance companies, and manufacturing ventures from Charleston and New Orleans in the South to the towns and cities of the "Deep North"—to use the phrase of a DeWolf descendant.[24]

Some US industries were tied directly to Cuban ones. Cigar manufacturing in New York, for instance, was a growing business and one that depended on the importation of Cuban tobacco. Distilling and manufacturing rum from Cuban molasses made the fortunes of families such as the DeWolfs. Sugar refineries in New York purchased raw brown sugar from Cuba, processed it into refined white sugar, and then sold it at a significant profit in the domestic market and even for export abroad. That all Cuban sugar was slave-grown meant that fluctuations in the wholesale price of US-refined sugar correlated almost perfectly with fluctuations in the price of slaves in Cuba. Meanwhile, Spain had no sugar refineries at all.[25]

US merchants often had agents in Cuba. They were already used to dealing with cotton planters in places like Georgia and Alabama. They dealt with Cuban sugar barons in the same way, advancing credit on the next year's crop. Planters used the credit to purchase African captives and machinery for their mills. When the crop disappointed, American merchants might end up as partial—or full—owners of Cuban sugar plantations. American merchants also purchased plantations independently, as a way to invest in a booming business or to diversify their holdings. Sometimes the profits from slave-grown Cuban sugar appeared in unexpected places—for example, as a modest monthly stipend sent back home to, say, the St. Michael's Episcopal Church in Bristol, Rhode Island, hometown of the DeWolf family.[26] A much greater percentage of sugar profits, however, were invested in US industries such as coal, iron, manufacturing, railroads, banking, and so on. Moses Taylor, a New York sugar broker, made his early fortune in what everyone called "the Cuba trade" and then invested it in banking and industry. Within a few decades, he was president of the National City Bank of New York, precursor to Citibank. When he died in 1882, his estate was worth at least $35 million, the equivalent of perhaps $1.3 billion in 2020.[27]

In recent years, it has become commonplace to point out that slavery—as the beating heart of an economic system that linked the US North and South—built capitalism. But neither slavery nor capitalism was ever circumscribed by national boundaries. Slave-grown cotton from the US South fed the textile mills and factories of the Industrial Revolution in England and the US North. Slave-grown sugar from Cuba helped kill the hunger of their workers, and its profits fueled the growth of American industries. Cuba—its sugar, its slavery, its slave trade—is part of the history of American capitalism.

The United States was implicated in the bedrock of the Cuban economy, which was slavery. If that was evident in the prices of sugar and slaves, or in the activities of New York merchant houses, it was also evident on the ground in Cuba, in cane fields and manor houses and slave quarters, sometimes even in the relations between masters and the men and women they held in bondage.

James DeWolf, the slave trader and senator from Rhode Island who pleaded with John Quincy Adams to protect US interests in Cuba, had three plantations in Cuba. Family members by blood and marriage owned another three. New England men supervised the clearing of forests for the construction of the mills; they managed the production and sale of sugar; they bought and sold people; they separated families and meted out punishments.[28] "The first Negro I struck was this evening for laughing at prayers," recalled the new American manager of one of DeWolf's plantations. The manager's diary confirms that the man he hit that night was indeed only the first of many. DeWolf's nephew, who managed another plantation, allowed neighboring slaveholders to use the DeWolfs' stocks—the wooden torture instrument—to punish their own slaves.[29]

The region of Matanzas, which served as home to James DeWolf's largest plantation, New Hope, was ground zero of the Cuban sugar boom in this period. That boom had begun in Havana in the 1790s, and as land and forests disappeared, it slowly spread eastward. Matanzas, about sixty miles from Havana on the island's northern coast, was one important hub of that growth. It was "crowded with Americans," reported one observer. According to one British official writing in 1839, US citizens had recently purchased or established "not less than 40 plantations" in the area. East of Matanzas lay the city of Cárdenas. It attracted so many American residents and property owners that by mid-century it had earned the moniker "the American City." More than 90 percent of its trade was with the United States. Every autumn, American engineers descended on the Matanzas-Cárdenas area to prepare the mills and tend to the US-made machines during the five-month harvest. The railroad that took the sugar from the plantations to the ports of Matanzas and Cárdenas was American. At those ports, about half the ships present at any given moment were also American. From the slave ships in the harbor, to the workers stooped over the cane, to the machines in the mills, to the railroads heading to port, to the agents trading the product—American citizens were involved in every part of Cuba's slave regime.[30]

IT WAS THIS EMERGING SYSTEM that the Monroe Doctrine protected and enabled. While the policy attempted to limit European power in all of Latin America, it played a very specific role with respect to Cuba. By seeking to shield the island from the influence and power of Britain—the world's greatest naval power turned crusader against the slave trade—it bolstered slavery and safeguarded a whole range of US investments there. The Monroe Doctrine, simply put, protected Americans' stake in Cuba.

The Monroe Doctrine also stacked the deck—not just against a potential British takeover of Cuba, but also against the possibility of a Cuban takeover of Cuba. The sugar revolution that had begun at the turn of the nineteenth century created a powerful incentive for Cuban elites to protect the status quo, even as so many other colonies around them became independent nations. Under the sway of the Monroe Doctrine, Cuba's sugar revolution became also an American business. And the power of the United States—its government and its capitalists—became one more barricade against change. Cuba's political status would hold. Britain and Europe would stay out; a weakened Spain would ostensibly retain control. Americans would continue to invest and profit. And when the time came—as it surely would, John Quincy Adams had said—the ripe apple of Cuba would fall from the tree and into that other America's eager embrace.

Chapter 8

TORTURE PLOTS

When men like James Monroe or John Quincy Adams fretted about British designs on Cuba or homegrown independence plots, they calculated the stakes and plotted their moves at a distance. Inevitably, they missed some of the drama in the unfolding story—the ways in which an unlikely alliance, a seemingly unremarkable person, a chance encounter, or an intimate family history might act upon their grand design for Cuba.

In Havana in 1809, a Spanish ballerina named Concepción, beautiful by all accounts, gave birth to a boy. The baby's father, Diego, was a man of color—in the lexicon of the age, a quadroon, or mixed-race and a quarter African. He worked as a barber at the city's main theater, where he met and wooed the ballerina. In a slave society that paid strict attention to racial hierarchies, giving birth to a non-white child was perhaps the most scandalous thing a white woman could do. It was perhaps for that reason that, eighteen days after the birth, the young mother placed the infant in the city's main orphanage. He was baptized the next day as Diego Gabriel de la Concepción, a name that combined the father's name with the mother's. For a last name, the orphanage gave him Valdés, the name of the priest who had founded the institution more than a hundred years earlier and the last name given to all the children deposited there.

The boy's natural father seemed not to have shared the mother's shame and took the child to his own mother and aunts to be raised. The boy, whom they called Gabriel, grew up in humble conditions, first in Havana and later in Matanzas. He earned a living by various means. He worked at a carpentry shop and at the studio of a famous Black painter; he made tortoiseshell combs and set type at a print shop. But one of his principal ways of earning money, and the one he enjoyed the most, was writing. Having learned to read and write only at the age

97

of ten, he took to it with passion and was soon composing, improvising, and performing poems for money at weddings, baptisms, and other festive gatherings. He signed his poems Plácido, the name of the protagonist in one of his favorite books, a French novel recently translated into Spanish. It is by that name that history remembers the young Black poet of illegitimate birth.

No one in Cuba published as many poems as he did—close to seven hundred in just ten years. Plácido's poetry, combined with the fact that he was free and a man of color, brought him to the attention of all kinds of important people. By his early twenties, he began moving in literary circles. His contemporaries considered him a romantic poet, inspired by the likes of Blake, Wordsworth, and Coleridge. Others later described him as an early exponent of *criollista*, or indigenist poetry, which glorified local customs and exalted the island's first inhabitants, the men and women who had greeted Columbus so long ago. Some of Plácido's poems treated political questions. In one, a caged canary waits for the opportunity to free itself; in another, "a tree of liberty" makes a rebel of anyone who drinks water from the stream at its base.[1]

In 1843, Plácido's modest fame brought him into the vortex of rebellion and conspiracy that swept through Matanzas, the rich sugar region where the late US senator James DeWolf had owned several plantations. Twice, authorities arrested Plácido on suspicion of playing a major role in antislavery movements. The first time, he was imprisoned for six months. The second time, dozens of witnesses identified him as "the president of the principal gatherings, recruiter, instigator, and one of the first agents" of a conspiracy meant to end slavery and declare independence in Cuba. Early the morning of June 28, 1844, in a central square in the city of Matanzas, before a crowd that included the US consul, a government firing squad took his life.[2]

PLÁCIDO'S PATH TO THAT VIOLENT end was paved with the good intentions, regrets, and the betrayal of another Cuban poet and writer, the white Domingo del Monte. Del Monte, like Plácido, wrote poetry in the romantic style and also published literary criticism and political essays. He had tried unsuccessfully to found a Cuban Academy of Literature (Spanish authorities would not allow it), and he had studied under Félix Varela, before the priest relocated to New York and began tending to the spiritual needs of immigrants. Del Monte was widely respected, a man of standing and influence. As the island's most important literary patron, he commissioned and published the only known autobiographical account of slavery in Cuba, written by the formerly enslaved Juan Francisco Manzano. The poet Plácido moved in the same circles.[3]

As is often the case with cultural elites, Del Monte was also part of Havana's economic elite. He married into one of the richest families on the island, the Aldamas. The family's home in Havana was one of the city's most luxurious residences, a splendid neoclassical palace that was the first major structure built outside the city walls. (Today it sits in center city.) It had the first flush toilet on the island, before any had made it to Spain. The workers who built the palace were enslaved Africans, and when they rose up to protest their work conditions, seven were killed and another ten wounded. The family patriarch, meanwhile, was a prominent advocate of annexing Cuba to the United States and a founding member of the Junta Cubana, the main organization pushing for an American purchase of the island. The family owned five plantations and held hundreds of people in slavery. Del Monte himself owned a nine-hundred-acre plantation and held one hundred souls in slavery. A man of letters surrounded by wealth, del Monte was ambivalent about his privilege. So, while his family members grew their fortunes in slaves and sugar, while they plotted annexation to the United States, the young del Monte appeared to have been scheming with British abolitionists and Black revolutionaries.[4]

Among Del Monte's collaborators was David Turnbull, a Scotsman and one of the most adventurous antislavery writers and diplomats of his time. In the late 1830s, Turnbull had written a scathing critique of Cuban slavery that masqueraded as a travelogue. When, in 1840, the British government appointed him as its consul in Havana, the Spanish raised loud objections. Turnbull ignored them, maybe even relished them. Instead of proceeding cautiously, he made his presence known everywhere. He complained vociferously against illegal slave trading and brought infractions before a new joint Spanish-British court established for that purpose. He made himself so notorious that to avoid arrest, perhaps even assassination, he moved onto a British vessel in the harbor where freed captives from illegal slavers were temporarily housed. Even more provocative was Turnbull's active involvement in ambitious plots to revolutionize the island and end slavery. He made contacts among liberal creoles interested in reform and possibly open to abolition, and he established strong ties to free men of color to plot against Spain and slavery. Cuban planters wanted him executed. The Spanish governor merely expelled him.[5]

Turnbull's deputy was Francis Ross Cocking, perhaps as ardent an abolitionist as his boss. Cocking continued to work on the project allegedly masterminded by the Scotsman. He met regularly with a group of men he called his "white committee." No membership list has ever been found, but we can assume that Del Monte, a leading reformer who had already worked closely with Turnbull, would have been a prominent member. At the same time, Cocking met with what he called his "colored committee," which, again if such a list existed, would certainly have featured the poet Plácido among its leaders. With Cocking coordinating the work of both committees, the conspirators settled on a plan. The two groups would work together and publish a declaration of Cuban independence. Enslaved people who joined the movement would be rewarded with their freedom, and masters would be compensated for their lost property. (No one considered compensating former slaves for their labor.) Once independence was achieved, the victors would seek British assistance and protection in civil and political rights "for all classes and colours of men" in Cuba.[6]

Almost immediately, members of the so-called white committee started having second thoughts. Was it wise to arm slaves? Once that happened, would it be possible to control the course of events? Members of the "colored committee," meanwhile, took the plan to heart and began working immediately to make it a reality. They deputized agents to fan into the countryside and ready a revolt. Realizing that white support for the movement was evaporating and Black support intensifying, Cocking tried to get his allies among the free people of color to postpone the rebellion. But they were already too invested. They "had Agents traveling all over the Island [and] had raised a spirit of revolt which it was not easy to prevent from breaking out." They were, Cocking continued, "ready to risk their lives and all they possess in an attempt to gain for themselves and their still more degraded brethren, that Liberty . . . which as men they deserve to enjoy."[7]

Black enthusiasm significantly quelled the already dwindling cooperation of the white committee. Del Monte, who was, recall, the son-in-law of a wealthy planter-annexationist, then did something thoroughly unsurprising: he turned to the United States. Alexander Everett, special diplomatic agent on the island, had been meeting with and courting prominent creoles to the cause of annexation. A diplomat and a man of letters, he had struck up a friendship with Del Monte. Everett had even asked Del Monte to write a book-length history of Cuba, one that would tell that history as a way to make an argument for the island's annexation to the United States.[8]

With the conspiracy dangerously unravelling in November 1842, Del Monte wrote to Everett to confess his misgivings and to warn of imminent violence and destruction. He reported that British abolitionists on the island had been secretly plotting a rebellion. They had offered independence and protection to Cubans on the condition that they join with people of color and declare the abolition of slavery. Del Monte worried that the inevitable outcome of the project would be the establishment of a "black military republic" similar to Haiti and synonymous for him with the destruction of the island. He worried about his own personal fate, too. He begged Everett not to reveal his identity as informant to anyone. "I have believed it my duty not to conceal this [conspiracy] from you, even though I fear, as I write these words, for the loss of my life." Nothing happened to Del Monte. Soon after penning that letter, he took his family on an American holiday, then traveled to Paris, soon resettled in Spain, and never returned to Cuba.[9] His prediction of a major slave rebellion, however, did soon prove correct.

IN MARCH 1843, FOUR MONTHS after Del Monte's warning to US officials, a stretch of the Matanzas countryside was up in flames. "The men working the night shift heard it first," historian Aisha Finch tells us. It was the height of the harvest season, and they were feeding cane into the machines, tending fires, and stirring the boiling cane juice in the pans. The men and women who worked the fields had risen up, and the mill workers soon joined them. They set fire to the sugarcane and the buildings, stole raw hides to use as shields, and killed several Black overseers and an American engineer who worked in the mill. From that plantation, Alcancía, the group marched "in military order, clad in their holiday colors," to the next plantation, and then another, and another. Enslaved men working on the new railroad also joined the rebellion. Armed with machetes, they attacked at least one plantation and freed slaves being held in the stocks. All told, between five hundred and one thousand slaves rebelled. Every slave rebellion in modern history, save the Haitian Revolution, has been defeated, and this one was no different. Over two days, soldiers and volunteers captured, dispersed, and killed the rebels.[10]

Charleston doctor John Wurdemann, who was visiting the area, noted the state of deep anxiety in the countryside immediately following the rebellion. Whites—Cuban and foreign—looked at slaves and people of color and saw in the smallest gesture or glance traces of the thwarted rebellion or, worse, of ones yet to come. Enslaved people, meanwhile, felt terrorized, under suspicion, vulnerable to accusations made even on whims. The battle against the rebel slaves was brutal. Many were killed; many others hid in the woods. To avoid a violent death at the hands of soldiers or executioners, some committed suicide. Wurdemann wrote, "So resolute, indeed, were they in destroying themselves, that standing under the branches to which the vines clung, they twisted them around their necks, and then, raising their feet from the ground, suffocated themselves." On a single tree, he wrote, "more than twenty were found thus suspended." Sometimes they placed African religious artifacts at the base of the trees from which they hanged themselves.[11]

Even with all that death and violence, smaller rebellions and plots continued to sprout across Matanzas and Cárdenas. Then, in November 1843, what has come down in history as the largest Cuban slave rebellion of all time erupted on a sugar plantation called Triunvirato, or Triumvirate. Carlota Lucumí, born in Africa (her last name an ethnonym indicating that she was from somewhere in the Bight of Benin), raised her machete against the overseer's daughter and led her fellow enslaved in battle. With the plantation in flames, they marched to neighboring Acana. There Fermina Lucumí (from the same African region as Carlota) led the fight, taking the rebels to the masters' house and pointing out the rooms where people might be hiding. But both Fermina and Carlota were captured and killed. Carlota died in battle. Fermina, meanwhile, was executed by firing squad, her body thrown into a fire and burned until almost nothing remained.[12]

A month after Carlota's and Fermina's rebellion, yet another conspiracy surfaced on the sugar estate named Santísima Trinidad, eighteen hundred acres in size and famously picturesque. The owner, Esteban Santa Cruz de Oviedo, was a notorious figure—a wealthy planter and proprietor of several plantations, known for his abusive behavior. On the same estate where the alleged conspiracy was discovered, he ran the most important slave breeding factory in all the island. He himself was said to have fathered at least twenty-six children by enslaved women he raped. When he heard of a major new rebellion planned for Christmas Day, he notified authorities, who deputized him to begin investigating. He immediately executed sixteen slaves and imprisoned more than one hundred. That was only the beginning. Authorities arrested enslaved men and women from over 230 plantations. On single plantations hundreds were imprisoned in the stocks as suspects in the movement.[13]

ULTIMATELY, THE REBELLIONS AND CONSPIRACIES of 1843–44 and the widespread repression that followed came to be known simply as La Escalera, or the Ladder.[14] The name derived from the torture to which suspects were subjected in the course of the investigation. A New York lawyer visiting Cuba described how the accused were taken to a room which had been white-washed, and whose sides were besmeared with blood and small pieces of flesh, from the wretches who had preceded them....There stood a bloody ladder, where the accused were tied, with their heads downward, and whether free or slave, if they would not avow what the [interrogator] insinuated, were whipped to death....They were scourged with leather straps, having at the end a small destructive button, made of fine wire....Their deaths were made to appear, by certificates from physicians, as having been caused by diarrhea.

A single officer whipped forty-two free and fifty-four enslaved people of color to their deaths. Thomas Rodney, US consul in Matanzas, explained an obvious (if still too often forgotten) truth: the "exquisite torture" suffered by the accused caused them to say whatever would halt the nightmare. No wonder then that the year 1844 came to be known as the Year of the Lash.[15]

In Washington, where statesmen clung to their dreams of dominion over Cuba, people watched closely. Congressmen wrote to the president to report rumors of plots they heard from Spanish and Cuban friends. From Wisconsin to Washington and New York to New Orleans, newspapers followed the events. "Melancholy intelligence of another insurrection," read one headline. The president ordered three warships to Havana Harbor, to keep an eye on external threats from the British and internal ones from slaves and free people of color—the very same threats that the US government had been monitoring since the days of Monroe and Adams.[16]

Other Americans watched on the front lines—as owners of plantations, as masters who held as property men and women who rebelled or who were punished, as engineers in sugarhouses put to the torch, and, in a few rare cases, as victims of the rebels. María Gowen Brooks, a New England poet, wrote one of her most famous poems, "Ode to the Departed with a View to the Heavens," sitting on a plantation in Matanzas in 1844. The poem, she explained, "was conceived and partly executed in the midst of a death such as had not for many years been known in the island of Cuba." (Curiously, she had composed her other famous poem *Zophiel* in Matanzas in the aftermath of another slave rebellion in 1825.[17]) Seven people held as slaves by Thomas Phinney, a direct descendant of the *Mayflower* pilgrims, died under the lash, and another was tried and executed as one of the leaders of the 1844 conspiracy. Phinney described the ladder punishment in detail and then wondered, "Good God! is it the nineteenth Century that we live? or the palmy days of the Inquisition once more returned?"[18]

In the end, some three thousand people died—by execution, torture, fighting, suicide, and diseases incurred in jail. Many others were banished or just disappeared. In the city of Matanzas, it seemed as if almost every free person of color was targeted. At least 38 were executed, 743 imprisoned, and 433 banished. Under the "total powers" instituted by Spain in Cuba in 1823, the property of all those executed and banished reverted to the government. One of Cuba's earliest and most important musicians, the Black violinist, double bass player, and band director Claudio Brindis de Salas, was arrested and banished. Years later, when he returned to Matanzas and tried to reorganize his orchestra, he found that almost all his band members had been executed. As the US consul in Matanzas observed, the repression of 1844 was like a harvest picked "to the last grain." His counterpart in Havana, monitoring events at a distance from the scenes of subjection, stayed laser focused on a different possibility: that a slave revolution in Cuba might spread to the US South. And from that premise, he concluded that "no punishment can be too severe" in order to preserve what he saw as the "salutary institution" of slavery.[19]

Among those executed on the morning of June 28, 1844, was the poet Plácido, son of the Spanish ballerina and the Black barber. Named in the testimony of thirty-two witnesses, he emerged as a ubiquitous presence in the conspiracy, attending meetings, delegating responsibilities, linking the world of city and plantation, of free people and enslaved. One US newspaper identified him as "a mulatto poet, said to be very clever . . . [who] was to be known as Emperor Plácido I," had the conspiracy unfolded as planned. The US consul who witnessed his execution described the poet's final moments. Plácido "sustained himself like a man and died true game, the first fire he received three balls but did not kill him." He sang out "fire!" and "goodbye world" and then crumbled under a fresh hail of bullets. From Plácido, the state confiscated nothing; he had nothing for them to take. Instead, he left a poem, composed shortly before his execution. He titled it "Plea to God"—"King of kings, God of my grandparents," to whom he proclaimed his innocence.[20]

A FEW MONTHS AFTER PLÁCIDO'S execution, on October 5, 1844, the day of his patron saint, an enormous hurricane ravaged Matanzas and the countryside of the Escalera conspiracy. Plantations and villages were leveled; ships sank in the harbor; and people murmured about the mulatto poet, divine retribution, and the coming of end times. "All is apparently tranquil here," reported one British correspondent in 1844, "but it is the tranquility of terror."[21]

To this day, no one is absolutely certain of Plácido's guilt or innocence. Some doubt the very existence of any conspiracy in December 1843, the one betrayed on the slave breeder's plantation and which unleashed the worst repression. Some scholars argue that the planter overreacted and that the Spanish government simply stepped in to take advantage. Looking to secure its future in Cuba, it unleashed a brutal repression that devastated the class of free people of color—upwardly mobile and sympathetic to both British abolitionism and independence from Spain. Among the enslaved, meanwhile, the spectacle of violent repression offered, in the words of the Spanish governor, a reason to "desist from so alarming an idea." The violence and upheaval also served as deterrent to white creoles contemplating an independence struggle on Cuban ground. The stakes, the Spanish had just demonstrated, were gargantuan and the outcome for white creoles possibly deadly. By demonstrating that, however, the Spanish government inadvertently increased the appeal of annexation to the United States—the surest solution for those who wanted the surest protection for slavery.

Chapter 9

DREAMS OF DOMINION

It was the worst inauguration in the history of the United States. The new president looked despondent as he stood alone to take his oath of office. His eleven-year-old son had died in a train accident two months earlier. His wife, now the first lady, refused to attend the inauguration. She was angry at her husband for having accepted the nomination, and she was suffering from severe depression after having witnessed their son's death. Maybe as a concession to her, maybe because of his own pain, the president had canceled the traditional inaugural ball. Even the weather refused to cooperate. As he delivered his inaugural address, a heavy snow began to fall. We do not know, then, with how much energy or conviction the new president delivered the most saber-rattling words of his speech: "The policy of my Administration will not be controlled by any timid forebodings of evil from expansion. Indeed . . . our attitude as a nation and our position on the globe render the acquisition of certain possessions . . . eminently important for our protection." Everyone knew he was talking about Cuba.[1]

It wasn't just the weather and family travails that weighed on President Franklin Pierce that cold inauguration morning in March 1853. For the first time in the history of the republic, Americans had organized a counterinauguration, a parade of unemployed workers expressing their opposition to the new administration. Divisions over slavery and uncertainty over the future of the American Union cast a long shadow over the inauguration, as well. Newly elected Pierce, a northerner, had appealed to southerners because he rejected the abolition of slavery and advocated territorial expansion. His vice president was William Rufus King, a wealthy cotton planter from Alabama, whose family held some five hundred people in slavery. King was seen as a moderate in those times: a fierce defender of slavery who also excoriated the militant slaveholders flirting with secession. In 1853, then, the combination of northern Pierce and southern King was supposed to embody moderation on the era's most pressing questions.

But because this was the worst inauguration in living memory, it somehow made sense that the vice president was not present to embody moderation or anything else. He was instead a world away, on a palatial sugar estate in rural Cuba, exhausted from the campaign and dying of tuberculosis.

VICE PRESIDENT KING HAD TRAVELED to Cuba on the advice of his doctor to recuperate in the salutary airs of its countryside. In fact, many Americans in the nineteenth century were undertaking similar trips, almost all of them making stops at sugar plantations. "To visit Cuba and not see a sugar estate," remarked a visitor, "is to read Hamlet, leaving out the Prince of Denmark's speeches."[2] Like King, a subset of those tourists chose Cuba for medical reasons, journeying to the island's interior to cure all kinds of ailments, from arthritis to gout to tuberculosis. Doctors published guidebooks, magazines recommended itineraries, American-owned hotels catered to the ailing, and convalescents shared advice on how to get well in Cuba. For tuberculosis, doctors recommended something called the sugar cure, which consisted of spending time in an active sugar mill, where the heat and vapors from the boiling sugar were supposed to work their wonder.

King fittingly chose to take the sugar cure in Matanzas, the still-booming center of sugar production that was home to many American-owned plantations. John Wurdemann, the Charleston doctor who had described the suicides by hanging in the aftermath of the 1843–44 rebellions in the region, thought it was the ideal place to recover from illness and reinvigorate the system—its countryside graced by "continuous fields of sugar-cane carpeting the soil for miles with a lively pea-green, over which hundreds of tall palms waved their dark verdure." It was there that King established himself, on the Ariadne plantation, owned by a Saint-Domingue native by way of Charleston. The many American travelers who visited the Ariadne loved it. The air, the beauty, the pace of life (for those people not forced to work), all made it "the most pleasant spring residence on the island"—the perfect place to recuperate one's health.[3]

January, February, and March, the months that King spent on the Ariadne, were peak harvest season. And even in the beautiful valleys of Matanzas, taking the sugar cure was anything but pleasant. Every afternoon, King sat in the boiling house for hours, surrounded by enslaved men and women working around the clock. He would have seen them bringing in cane from the fields, feeding the stalks into grinders of the mill, stoking the fires, stirring boiling cane juice in the pans. We do not know if the spectacle of forced labor he saw before him at the Ariadne would have moved him at all. He was, after all, a defender of slavery and a slaveholder. Engulfed by the choking smell of sugar being processed, perhaps King felt the rise of nausea. But he bore that and the heat, because he was there to elude death.[4]

In King's case—as in most—sugar did not cure him. Too sick to make it back to Washington for the inauguration, King requested authorization from Congress to be sworn into office on foreign territory. So, on March 24, with twelve witnesses and two US consuls present, he took his oath of office on the Ariadne sugar plantation in Matanzas. The ceremony took place at the highest point on the estate, a three-hundred-foot peak that offered a view over the endless fields that Americans always described so effusively. It was a Thursday in harvest season, so those fields would have been busy with men and women bending over to cut the tall stalks of sugarcane, and the boiling house chimneys would have spewed their smoke uninterrupted. King, by that point, was too frail to stand unassisted, but two Americans helped him to his feet. Then, with his hand on the Bible, he repeated the oath that made him vice president of the United States. His sister and niece looked on. Absent was his longtime companion, James Buchanan, the man with whom he had lived in Washington, DC, for the last thirteen years. The two had been so inseparable that people referred to them as Miss Nancy and Aunt Fancy. Those days, however, were long gone. Exhausted from his brief and unprecedented swearing in, King accepted everyone's congratulations and retired to rest. All, including King, knew that he would die in a matter of weeks, if not days. It was a strange sight, reported one observer, "to see an old man, on the very verge of the grave, clothed with honors which he cared not for, and invested with authority which he could never exercise."[5] Less than two weeks later, secure in the knowledge that he would soon die and preferring to do so in his beloved Alabama, King returned to his own plantation of King's Bend on April 17. He died the next day.

THE STORY OF THE INAUGURATION of an American vice president in Cuba is unexpected. Yet the spectacle of an Alabama slaveholder taking office as vice president of the United States in the heart of Cuban sugar country laid bare a fundamental truth: King's homes in Alabama and Washington, DC, and King's improvised sanitarium in Matanzas were part of one system. It was a system that had linked American wealth to Cuban sugar and Cuban slavery since at least the 1820s. By the time of King's Cuban inauguration in 1853, it had fully matured.

A cornerstone of the system was the illegal transatlantic slave trade to Cuba, which boomed after 1850, when the trade to Brazil ended, leaving Cuba as the single American market for African captives. In the 1850s and 1860s, approximately 164,000 enslaved Africans landed in Cuba. Americans were major players in that trade. By then, almost 90 percent of the slave ships that landed in Cuba were built in the United States. They had American financing, American papers, and American flags to protect them from British inspection and seizure on the high seas. The trade, of course, was illegal. But people, northerners included, broke the law because the profits could be enormous. In the late 1850s, one Florida senator reported that US ships sailing to Angola could buy Africans for about $70 and then sell them in Cuba for almost $1,200. In the summer of 1854, James Smith captained a ship from New York to Ambriz (in present-day Angola) on the west coast of Africa, where he loaded 655 captives, buying a five-year-old boy at $7.50 for his own speculation. When he arrived in Cuba, his ship unloaded 500 Africans, the other 155 having perished en route. In 1861, the "notorious spinster" Mary J. Watson was tried and found guilty for sponsoring another New York–Africa–Cuba voyage that carried more than 500 captives. And in 1862, Nathaniel Gordon was tried and executed for another voyage on the same route.[6] Even on the eve of the US Civil War, the slave trade was also a northern business.

Cubans, too, were an integral part of the illegal slave trade. A pyramid of subterfuge and corruption implicated all levels of society, from slave traders and planters to local police, lighthouse keepers, fishermen, and even priests. Ships built in places like Cohasset, Massachusetts, or Baltimore, Maryland, or Providence, Rhode Island, set out for the African coast. A few months later, they arrived in Cuba with human cargo. In some cases, the crews might set fire to their vessels; doing so destroyed evidence of their crime while barely making a dent in their profits. On clear nights, the fires were visible for miles around. Yet the men in charge of guarding the coast did not see them. They were paid not to. For a fee, others averted their eyes as well: the seamen who used their small boats to ferry the hundreds of African men, women, and children from the ships' hold; the petty traders and muleteers who arrived with clothes to cover up the captives' nakedness; the guides who marched the emaciated and barefoot captives inland to sugar plantations, directing them across sharp reefs referred to locally as "dog's teeth" or "inferno's knife"; the priests who performed hasty mass baptisms and produced papers that made it seem like the Africans had all been born in Cuba, rather than brought there in violation of all the laws and treaties that made the transatlantic slave trade illegal. Every single one of those people was implicated, and each of them charged a fee. José Martí, today the foremost icon of Cuban patriotism on both sides of the Florida Straits, witnessed one of those landings when he was nine years old and remembered it vividly enough to compose a poem about it as an adult—verse XXX (30) of his *Versos sencillos*.[7]

We can be absolutely sure that among the enslaved workers cutting and carting cane into the building where Vice President William Rufus King was taking his sugar cure were men and women who had arrived in Cuba precisely in this fashion. And King very likely knew it. His taking the oath of office on an American-owned sugar plantation in Cuba exemplified the power of a system that linked planters, slave traders, and investors from New York to Charleston to the African coast to Havana, Matanzas, and the green cane fields of the island's interior.

That an American vice president took his oath of office on a Cuban sugar plantation was fitting in another way as well. King had won on a ticket committed to making Cuba American. In the victory parade the day after the election, supporters had carried banners announcing "Pierce and Cuba." And in his inauguration speech, Pierce had promised "no more timidity" about foreign acquisitions and territorial expansion. Having Vice President King take his oath of office in Cuba, then, marked the island as imminent American territory.

AMERICAN STATESMEN HAD BEEN DREAMING about making Cuba American for decades. Jefferson had begun fantasizing about it at the dawn of the nineteenth century. In the 1820s, James Monroe and John Quincy Adams had given it serious consideration. The Monroe Doctrine emerged precisely out of such deliberations. But it was in the years after the Escalera upheavals of 1843–44 and leading up to King's unusual inauguration that the drive to annex Cuba to the United States grew more frenzied—and plausible—than ever.

When the United States annexed Texas in 1845, many Americans fully expected that Cuba would be next. As the famed abolitionist Frederick Douglass lamented, "The history of Cuba may be read in [the] past history of Texas." From other, more powerful quarters, however, came determined calls for the acquisition of Cuba. Secretary of State James Buchanan, Vice President King's old friend, seemed to rub his hands in anticipation. "Cuba is already ours. I feel it in my fingers' ends," he wrote in 1849. In Washington, a "Buy Cuba" lobby exploded onto the political scene, led by Jane McManus Cazneau, a New Yorker earlier prominent in Texas annexationist circles and increasingly invested in the acquisition of Cuba. President James Polk was more than happy to do his part, sending emissaries to Spain with an offer of up to $100 million for the purchase of Cuba.[8]

It would be grievously incorrect, however, to associate the drive to annex Cuba to the United States only with American expansionists. In fact, annexation was a major force in Cuban politics, as well. Wealthy sugar planters saw incorporation into the United States as their salvation—their bulwark against British abolitionists and the likes of the poet Plácido and hundreds of thousands of Cuban slaves. Joining the American Union—as a slave state, or two, or three—would guarantee the future of slavery in Cuba. Exile organizations in New York—with strong financial ties both to Cuban sugar and American merchants—lobbied hard for the annexation of Cuba to the United States. In fact, they were the ones who provided the funds that Polk offered to Spain as payment for Cuba.[9]

The Spanish government's refusal to sell Cuba to the United States—"sooner than see the Island transferred to any power, they would prefer seeing it sunk in the Ocean"—dissuaded neither American expansionists nor Cuban annexationists. In fact, it gave the upper hand to the most militant among them: the filibusterers. Whatever association the term now has with Senate practice, back then it referred to the launching of ostensibly private expeditions against other nations. In this case, it involved expeditions to Cuba designed to secure immediate independence from Spain, to be followed very soon after by annexation to the United States, as had recently happened in Texas.[10]

The major figure on the Cuban side of the filibustering craze was Narciso López. The Venezuelan-born López had served in Spain's army against the independence movements there and relocated to Cuba after South American independence. In Cuba, he was appointed president of the Military Commission, the military court that tried allegedly political crimes. In that capacity, he had presided over the first trials in the Escalera conspiracies of 1843–44, ordering the execution of several men of color. By the end of that decade, López was a private citizen, eager to work with Americans to preserve slavery in Cuba and to make a fortune in the meanwhile. Among his American allies, the most enthusiastic and powerful were men such as John C. Calhoun, Monroe's old secretary of war, former vice president, and then US senator for South Carolina; John Quitman, governor of Mississippi; Virginian Robert E. Lee, a decorated veteran of the Mexican-American War and later a general in the Confederate Army; and Jefferson Davis, US senator from Mississippi and later president of the Confederate States of America.

With their support, López organized three filibustering expeditions to Cuba. The majority of the recruits—the foot soldiers of the invading force—were southern veterans of the recently ended Mexican-American War. For them, the experience of taking Texas from Mexico now served as a model for taking Cuba from Spain. López promised them $8 a month, a bonus of $1,000, and 160 acres of land in Cuba, if the expedition succeeded.[11]

The first one, in 1849, never made it to the island, prevented from doing so by US federal agents. When the second expedition sailed to Cuba in 1850, the *New York Sun* flew a newly designed Cuban flag from atop its headquarters in Manhattan. The flag was red, white, and blue, with five stripes and one star—the star of Cuba soon to join the thirty then present on the American flag. It was the first time a Cuban flag was ever flown, and it was flown in New York to signal Cuba's impending incorporation into the United States. Despite that history, it remains Cuba's flag today, its annexationist origins curiously absent. In New Orleans, where many of the preparations for the second expedition took place, the *New Orleans Delta* published López's proclamation pronouncing that "the star of Cuba ... will emerge beautiful and shining, on being admitted with glory into the splendid North American constellation, where destiny leads it." Destiny led the expedition to another failure. After landing in Cárdenas, the Spanish fell on the invaders almost immediately, and the group beat a hasty retreat by sea. Two failures, however, were not enough to dissuade eager annexationists.[12]

In preparation for the third expedition in 1851, annexationist activity across the South reached a fever pitch. Troops trained openly for the invasion and paraded on city streets. In Georgia, the governor equipped recruits with weapons from the state arsenal. In Arkansas, someone established a military school designed specifically for filibusterers. Observing and reporting on all this activity, abolitionist Frederick Douglass compared the mood to that which had existed just before the annexation of Texas. "Then as now," he wrote, "the rotten-end of this Republic was literally alive with sympathizers with the rebels [filibusterers], and, as usual, Liberty was the watchword and disguise of the freebooters, pirates, and plunderers." The prediction that Cuba would soon be American had been around for decades; in 1851, many white southerners wanted to make it true in a matter of weeks.[13]

On August 3, López set sail from New Orleans with more than four hundred men, almost all of them American. His second in command was William Crittenden, the blond, blue-eyed nephew of the US attorney general. Stopping in Key West before sailing to Cuba, López and his companions heard that all of western

Cuba was in rebellion, and they hurried to get there. But the news was a trap, a fake story planted by the Spanish to entice the expedition to somewhere near Havana. When it landed, the Spanish were waiting. Crittenden was captured first with about fifty men. The Spanish made them kneel in groups of six, their backs to the firing squad. When it was Crittenden's turn, he allegedly refused and spoke words later reproduced all over the United States: "An American kneels only to his God and always faces his enemy." López himself survived that first encounter, but with no prospects for reinforcements, the expedition's future was bleak. Hiding in the hills, he ended up having to eat his own horse, roasted with corn and plantains. Authorities captured and then quickly tried and condemned him. Just before his execution, he shouted, "My death will not change the destiny of Cuba!" Then he was garroted to death before a crowd.[14]

News of the executions—particularly Crittenden's—produced an uproar in the South. In New Orleans, where so much of the preparation for the expedition had happened, angry mobs attacked the property of resident Spaniards and called for vengeance, and with it—still, again—the seizure of Cuba. "American blood has been shed," exhorted one Louisiana paper. "Our brethren must be avenged! Cuba must be seized!" A popular new banjo song issued its own call to arms: "The spirits of fifty murdered Americans are crying for de whole Yankee nation to go on, / Straight off to Havanna their blood to avenge." As the Alamo was to the acquisition of Texas, so "the massacre at Havana" must lead to the taking of Cuba.[15]

IT WAS WITH THAT FAILURE in recent and vivid memory that Franklin Pierce and William Rufus King were elected president and vice president of the United States in 1852. And it was Cuba that Pierce invoked during his snowy inauguration when he promised "the acquisition of certain possessions." Failed expeditions were a thing of the past; under his watch, Cuba would finally become US territory.

That pledge went the way of most campaign promises. A few months after the death of Vice President King, the Spanish appointed a new governor for the island. Immediately on assuming his post, Juan Pezuela alarmed the entrenched slaveholding interests of both Cuba and the United States. He reestablished the free Black and mulatto militias, which had ceased to exist in the aftermath of the Escalera conspiracy a decade earlier. More alarming to Cuban and US planters was Pezuela's vow to eliminate the illegal slave trade and to punish officials and proprietors who disobeyed. One of his proclamations allowed authorities to enter and search plantations to ensure that all enslaved workers had entered the island legally. Slaves for whom masters could not show legal provenance would be subject to confiscation. The slave trade to Cuba had been illegal for decades. That meant that by the time the governor issued his decree in 1854, the vast majority of enslaved people in Cuba had been brought to the island illegally and would thus be subject to confiscation and liberation. The new governor did not abolish slavery, but he knew—and American and Cuban slave interests knew—that the enforcement of his decrees could soon end it in practice. For that reason, he earned the nickname "Captain General of Abolition." Planters and their allies in both countries denounced what they called "the Africanization of Cuba." Meanwhile, enslaved and free people of color, who saw in the governor an ally, referred to him as "titi Juan," or "Papa Juan, the Patron of Liberty and Equality."[16]

Cuban planters complained to Madrid, and, with more cunning, they sought out the Americans. Wouldn't annexation to the United States right now be a good thing? Cuban annexationists in exile in the United States joined the chorus, requesting meetings with President Pierce and lobbying highly placed officials across the US government. Ambrosio José Gonzales—second in command during one of Narciso López's failed expeditions—made the appeal plainly: "Shall [the US] consent to have . . . sixty miles from her Southern border, on the path of her coasting trade, across the isthmian routes that command her Pacific and eastern commerce, a colony . . . of wild, untutored and ferocious Africans . . . ?"[17]

Southern planters and politicians, for their part, needed no nudge. John Quitman, former governor of Mississippi, who owned land and people in that state as well as in Louisiana and Texas, exemplified the militant planter-statesmen of the moment. Since July 1853, and with President Pierce's support, he had been organizing a new filibustering expedition to liberate Cuba from Spain and annex it to the United States as a slave state. To wait any longer, thought Quitman, was to foreclose the possibility of acquiring Cuba before the Spanish ended slavery there. "Our destiny is intertwined with that of Cuba. If slave institutions perish there, they will perish here," he wrote in 1854. And what would be the point of annexation then?[18]

Campaign promises notwithstanding, Pierce had grown timid. He still wanted Cuba, without a doubt. But he preferred to purchase it, rather than invade it, and he worried that Quitman's adventure would only anger the Spanish and derail his plan. He issued a proclamation outlawing the formation of "private enterprises of a hostile character" against foreign countries. He met privately with Quitman and succeeded in getting the Mississippian to desist. Separately, Pierce pursued his plan to purchase Cuba. He had reason for hope. Spain was in severe financial straits in that moment, and a distracted Britain was sparring with Russia over power in the Middle East. Unfortunately for Pierce, the delegate he selected for the task of negotiating the purchase with Spain—Louisiana planter and slaveholder Pierre Soulé—went rogue. He leaked to the press the contents of a document known as the Ostend Manifesto, which made an argument by then thoroughly familiar. The Union, it insisted, "can never enjoy repose, nor possess reliable security, as long as Cuba is not embraced within its boundaries." Like many earlier proposals, it advocated the US purchase of Cuba. That was hardly surprising. What made the new document so controversial was its insistence that, should Spain decline to sell Cuba, the United States would be justified in wresting it away. One version of the document bore the belligerent—and surely too candid—subtitle: "If you can't buy Cuba, steal it." The leaked document starkly revealed that the US government would be willing to go to war to preserve slavery in Cuba.[19] Jefferson's empire for liberty, it seems, was really an empire for slavery.

News of the Ostend Manifesto arrived in Washington at the same time as the passage of the Kansas-Nebraska Act. The act made the fate of slavery in the new American territories contingent on (white male) popular sovereignty and thus effectively revoked the Missouri Compromise, which for decades had limited the extension of slavery across the continent. Pierce and the Democrats had just expended all their political capital in support of expanding slavery in North America. Most northern congressmen were now immovable: they were not going to allow the president to take the country to war to acquire yet more territory for slavery. "There was a time," announced one northern newspaper, "when the North would have consented to annex Cuba, but the Nebraska wrong has rendered annexation forever impossible."[20] The Democrats lost the House in the elections of 1854. Permanently damaged by the Kansas-Nebraska Act and the failure to annex Cuba, Pierce lost his own party's nomination in 1856 to James Buchanan, longtime companion of late vice president William Rufus King.

At Buchanan's inauguration, unlike Pierce's, there was no snow, and there were no protests. Buchanan's speech, like Pierce's before him, invoked Cuba without naming it: "No nation will have a right to interfere or to complain if in the progress of events we shall still further extend our possessions," he pronounced. Everyone knew he was talking about Cuba. Almost immediately after the ceremony, a mysterious sickness descended on the city's largest hotel and struck many of the guests who had arrived for the inauguration. Called the National Hotel Disease, it claimed the life of John Quitman, former slaveholding governor of Mississippi and would-be invader of Cuba.[21]

Chapter 10

CIVIL WAR JOURNEYS

In the halls of a fancy French boarding school in New York City in the 1830s, two young boys became friends. One was Cuban, the other an American with a French-sounding name: Beauregard. Decades later, P. G. T. Beauregard would become the first brigadier general of the Confederate Army. The Cuban, Ambrosio José Gonzales (the Americans called him Gonzie), was descended from a wealthy planter family in Matanzas, not too far from where William Rufus King was inaugurated as US vice president. As an adult, Gonzales had been shot twice in the leg when he accompanied Narciso López on his second failed expedition to free Cuba and then annex it to the United States. A decade after that, with Beauregard himself, Gonzales joined another lost cause: the Confederate States of America. He helped arm the rebels, selling LeMat revolvers and the patented Maynard Breech Loading Rifle—the "secessionist gun" in the parlance of the day. Later he became a colonel in the Confederate Army and chief of artillery for South Carolina, Georgia, and Florida. In Confederate-held Charleston, he was known as a music enthusiast and would sometimes play and sing during evening gatherings, ending always with the Marseillaise. In 1863, Gonzales defended the city against Union forces, receiving written thanks from his old friend Beauregard. Then in April 1865, both men surrendered. Southern secession, like Cuban annexation, had failed.[1]

In another American school, a Catholic school run by the Sisters of Charity in New Orleans, seven-year-old Loreta Velázquez daydreamed about the exploits of one of her ancestors, Spanish conquistador Diego Velázquez, the first European governor of Cuba. Loreta knew in her bones that women could be heroes, too. So she also daydreamed about Joan of Arc, the French peasant girl turned military hero and saint. In the privacy of her bedroom, the young Loreta dressed like a man, practiced walking like one before a mirror, and craved the chance to make her mark. At the age of fourteen, she secretly married a Texan, escaped with him to St. Louis, and then lived in a handful of frontier posts in the ever-expanding United States. When her husband died shortly after the start of the Civil War, Loreta disguised herself as a man and joined the Confederate Army. She called herself Henry Buford and participated in the battles of Bull Run and Shiloh. When her identity as a woman was discovered, she offered her services as a spy.[2]

Loreta Velázquez and Ambrosio Gonzales were not the only two Cubans fighting for the South in the US Civil War. In fact, some seventy Cubans served in the Confederate Army. A smaller number served the Union. Francisco Fernández Cavada, for example, became a colonel in a Philadelphia regiment. An excellent artist, he used to ride hot-air balloons over Confederate territory and sketch enemy camps. He was captured at the Battle of Gettysburg and spent nine months in a Confederate prison.[3]

THE CIVIL WAR WAS A conflict over the future of slavery in the United States, but powerful southerners had long believed that preserving slavery in the South was also about preserving it in Cuba. They feared that abolition followed by the establishment of a majority-Black republic on the island would doom white supremacy on their own home ground. For abolitionists, meanwhile, challenging and destroying slavery at home was also about destroying it abroad. As historian Gregory Downs tells us, "The Civil War was fought over the future of slavery inside *and* outside the United States."

In Cuba, meanwhile, the greatest and most transcendental questions of the nineteenth century had revolved around two issues: slavery and the island's political future. Would Cuba remain Spanish? Would it become part of Britain or the United States? Or would it strike out on its own? With the fate of US slavery and the American republic itself now in the balance, Cubans believed that the island's future was intertwined with the outcome of the American Civil War. Understandably, then, they paid attention, and they picked sides.

Enslaved people, unsurprisingly, rooted for the North. According to two US consuls on the island, they coined a new song, the chorus of which went "Onward, Lincoln, onward! You are our hope." In port cities, Blacks were said to hasten to the wharves to hear the latest news of "the redeemer of their race." Lincoln, in fact, had a substantial following on the island. His assassination in April 1865 produced "an unparalleled demonstration of grief." In some cities, men and women mourned in public, wearing black ribbons with pictures of the slain president. José Martí, then just twelve years old, wore a hemp bracelet as a sign of mourning and also as a protest against slavery.[4]

Though the North was popular in Cuba, the Confederacy seemed to have the more powerful adherents. The Spanish government had formally adopted a policy of neutrality, but it recognized both sides as "belligerents." By so doing, it gave the South the status of legitimate challenger to US authority. The Confederate States of America mobilized almost immediately to take advantage of that, appointing a special agent to represent them. Charles Helm, who had once served as US consul in Havana, was heartened by the welcome he received in the Cuban capital. "I find a large majority of the population of Havana zealously advocating our cause and am informed that the same feeling extends throughout the island," he reported. At one point, he was even offered "a company of Cubans, armed, fully equipped, and paid" to join the war for the Confederacy.[5]

On Helm's second full day in Havana, he met for over an hour with the island's governor. Helm reported to his superiors in the Confederate capital of Richmond that the meeting was warm and encouraging. The governor could not receive him as an official representative of the Confederacy. But he encouraged Helm to visit as a "private individual" and to continue the "friendly relations" the two men had enjoyed when he was the US consul. The governor also gave Helm assurances that Confederate ships would be received in Cuban ports. He was true to his word. "The Confederate flag flies honored and respected in all the ports of the island," reported Helm a few months later. One southern newspaper rejoiced that the admission of Confederate ships in Cuba represented "a practical recognition of the independence of the Confederate States."[6]

In 1862 alone, some one hundred Confederate vessels docked in Cuban ports. For those ships to make it there required besting the Union's naval blockade along the Atlantic or Gulf coasts. From New Orleans, Mobile, and elsewhere, Confederate "blockade runners" went back and forth to Cuba. They arrived for repairs, safe haven, and to engage in trade. They sold cotton and collected funds to support the Confederacy. A wartime trade in weapons allowed Confederate ships in Cuba to procure rifles, gunpowder, cartridges, bayonets, shells—anything that might help them take Union lives and defend their own. Blockade runners also traded in other things, for both necessity and profit: tobacco, coffee, salt. They purchased Cuban rum at seventeen cents a gallon and then sold it in Florida for twenty-five dollars. One Charleston man, a druggist, built a wartime business importing leeches from Cuba.[7]

A much more sinister traffic also existed. As the institution of slavery crumbled in the southern states, some slaveholders tried to avert financial loss by shipping the people they claimed as property to Cuba—sometimes to safeguard them there as chattel, other times to sell them. The practice was so well known that Cuba was used as a threat against southern slaves (and even free people of color): acquiesce to the demand in question or be shipped to Cuba. Sometimes, as planters fled ahead of the Union's advance, they took their slaves with them, hoping to make it to Texas and from there to Cuba. In 1862, Union forces captured one such group, "four hundred wagons large." Abolitionists argued that Cuba had become a depot for enslaved people kidnapped from the US South. One American woman visiting a Matanzas plantation during the war was surprised to find that most of the enslaved on the estate spoke English. Technically, their entry as slaves would have violated Spanish law, but authorities on the island were not interested in enforcing such restrictions. They preferred to protect slavery, and, de facto at least, they sided with the slaveholding South.[8]

But the Spanish government was also wary. Almost since the independence of the thirteen colonies, Madrid had agonized about American designs on the island—with good reason. The Spanish also realized that, of late, most American attempts to acquire Cuba had roots precisely in the South. US officials from the North conveniently reminded Spanish ones that every filibustering expedition against Cuba had been organized in and launched from the southern states. To counter that argument, Confederate agents were blunt about the past and pragmatic about the future. Yes, it was true that the South—like the North—had once conspired to control Cuba. The North had done so "for the profits of its commerce," the South "to make three new States of it" in order to balance the power of the North in what southerners called "the Federal Senate." But an independent Confederacy would no longer need new territories to balance out the North. It would have its own legislature fully composed of slave states. After a southern victory, Spain and the Confederate States of America would be the best of allies, their bond sealed by their joint commitment to slavery.[9]

THINGS, OF COURSE, TURNED OUT otherwise. In April 1865, Confederate forces surrendered to the United States. One Cuban historian has argued that tacit Spanish support from Cuba allowed the South to fight longer and under better conditions than it would otherwise have.[10] Perhaps. But that did not change the outcome: the South had seceded, fought a war, and lost; legal slavery no longer existed in the United States. The southern dream of annexing Cuba had also died. Southern advocates of annexation saw no point to that now: Why annex Cuba to free its slaves?

Yet even in their loss, southerners found Cuba useful. Almost immediately after their defeat, high-ranking Confederates began descending on the island. In the short term, most sought to avoid punishment and futures they perceived as deeply humiliating. Twelve years after Vice President William Rufus King had traveled to Cuba in the hopes of saving his life, the man who had been his successor as vice president of the United States did exactly the same thing. On June 11, 1865, John C. Breckinridge arrived on a seventeen-foot open boat with a skimpy sail and four oars. He was by then not only a former US vice president, but also a former senator charged with treason and the secretary of war of the just-defeated Confederate States of America. Worried that he would hang, he made for Cuba. Breckinridge was only the first in a prominent group to do so. Another was former secretary of state for the Confederacy Judah Benjamin, who, as the only one who spoke Spanish among them, was much in demand. The men arrived defeated and devastated, and their bodies and faces showed it. When Breckinridge sent a picture to his wife in Canada, she was shocked at his appearance: gaunt, worn, sunburned.[11]

Cuba revived them. Trusten Polk, former governor of Missouri and Confederate colonel and judge, was moved by the beauty of Havana. It was "a magnificent panorama . . . the most beautiful and fairy-like scene I had ever beheld." Another Confederate extolled the island's fertile and boundless wealth. With the sting of defeat but not disapproval, he added that all of it was dependent on slave labor. Almost all of the Confederates stayed at the Hotel Cubano, a sunny, five-story hotel on Calle Teniente Rey in Old Havana. Owned by southerner Sarah Greer Brewer, it was the Confederates' headquarters in the Cuban capital. When a Confederate arrived and booked a room somewhere else, the others would go retrieve him and resettle him at the Cubano. Former Confederate president Jefferson Davis stayed there more than once and would saunter over to the Hotel Inglaterra—still in operation today—to sip champagne with colleagues or occasionally with his wife, to talk politics, ponder the future, and perhaps to rewrite the past, if only in fantasy. Cubans sympathetic to their cause and to slavery often gave them effusive welcomes. In Cárdenas, the so-called American city, a Cuban planter rode thirty miles on horseback to make the acquaintance of the visiting and defeated Confederate politicians.[12]

It wasn't just Confederate officials who went to Cuba. As the Confederacy's defeat in the Civil War became clear, some southern planters tried to find new homes in places where slavery still existed. One group settled (briefly) in Brazil, where they established a colony and called themselves the Confederados. Others went to Cuba, to plantations they already owned or to ones newly purchased. Seeking to re-create the slaveholding society they had lost in the South, they continued to hold human beings as property and to enjoy the privileges of mastery.

Eliza McHatton Ripley was among those southern refugees. She fled Baton Rouge with her family in 1862, ahead of Union forces. They tried taking the people they claimed as slaves to Texas, hoping to get them out of the United States and thus retain them as property. But most of them deserted to the Union army along the way. After a brief stay in Mexico, the Ripleys traveled to Cuba and purchased a one-thousand-acre plantation in Matanzas. Tall palm trees lined a path a third of a mile long to a whitewashed single-story house for the new owners. They called the estate Desengaño, or disillusionment. Forced to give up slavery in the United States, the family continued to hold sixty-five people as property in Cuba. One of them was a man named Zell, who had made the journey with them from Baton Rouge, a man who had just missed the freedom granted by Lincoln's Emancipation Proclamation a few months after their departure. For him the name of the plantation might have had a bitter resonance.[13]

Almost every Confederate veteran who visited the island spent time at Desengaño being lavishly feted. While these visitors might have felt heartened by the familiarity of plantation routines, there was much that would have been unfamiliar, too. In particular, visitors were amazed at the presence of Chinese laborers. In the decades before Eliza Ripley's arrival in Cuba, the Spanish government had imported tens of thousands of Chinese men as contract workers. The government and planters saw them as an antidote to the high price of African captives, and to the ever-present specter of abolition. By the mid-1870s, almost 125,000 Chinese had landed in Cuba. Tricked or kidnapped in Macao, Hong Kong, Canton, Shanghai, and elsewhere, they were transported to Cuba, often on US-owned ships, and bound for eight years to work on Cuban plantations. The workforce on Ripley's plantation was composed of both enslaved Africans and Chinese contract workers. She used Chinese men as domestics, a fact that startled American guests on the plantation. While Chinese workers were already in the United States building the transcontinental railroad, Ripley had no personal experience to draw on to command them. She observed them, hypothesized on their character, tested the limits of their obedience, even of their hunger. It was hunger that provoked them one morning to descend on the plantation house, throw stones at the overseer, and shout their refusal to work. After Spanish authorities subdued them, the officer in charge ordered that the rebels' long ponytails be cut off. "How quickly they wilted! How cowed they looked!" Ripley wrote.[14]

Her glee at that particular victory notwithstanding, Ripley and other southerners in Cuba soon realized that their efforts to re-create southern slaveholding society in Cuba could never boast the success they wanted. Everything was different now—their old homes, their new ones, and the relationship between the two. Southern interest in Cuba had always depended on slavery—acquiring Cuba was a way to shore up and expand slavery in the United States. That particular dream of dominion was now moot, and both in the United States and Cuba, long-familiar talk of annexation seemed to fade away.

Slavery, the system that had lured southerners to Cuba after its defeat in the United States, felt almost as tenuous on the island as it had back home in the days before the Civil War. By 1868, the slave trade from Africa to Cuba had finally been halted. Chinese contract workers had helped alleviate the shortages, but that trade too was increasingly threatened. Reports of their systematic mistreatment led Chinese authorities to send a commission to Cuba. It interviewed more than one thousand Chinese and confirmed widespread instances of abuse—beatings, illegal extensions of contracts, withholding of food, rest, and wages—abuse so pervasive that it led to a scourge of suicide. An interviewee named Lin A-Pang reported that he had seen some twenty men die, "by hanging themselves and by jumping into wells and sugar cauldrons." In response to the shocking report, the Chinese government cut off the trade entirely in 1874.[15]

By then, Eliza Ripley was gone. In 1872, soon after the death of her husband, she returned to the United States. It wasn't just the personal loss or the problems with labor that had driven her away. A new war had begun, this time in Cuba—a war for independence from Spain. For Ripley, American plantation mistress in Cuba, the calculus was simple: it was time to go home. Zell, the enslaved man who had arrived with her in Cuba from Louisiana, stayed behind with his wife and children, as a witness to the rise of a new Cuba, soon without slavery, and, only a little later, without Spanish rule.[16]

The military struggle for Cuban independence was waged by a popular multiracial fighting force known as the Liberation Army. Members of that army are photographed here crossing a river sometime during the War of Independence from 1895 to 1898.

Part IV

¡CUBA LIBRE!

Chapter 11

SLAVE, SOLDIER, CITIZEN

On October 10, 1868, a sugar planter and slaveholder named Carlos Manuel de Céspedes rose up and proclaimed the end of Spain's rule in Cuba. That morning, he gathered all the enslaved people on his plantation and granted them their freedom. "You are as free," he told them, "as I am." Then, addressing them as "citizens," he invited them to help "conquer the liberty and independence" of Cuba. The rebellion's first significant triumph was the taking of Bayamo, one of the island's oldest European settlements. To consecrate the victory, Céspedes led his men into the town's cathedral and marched up to the altar so that the priest could bless the flag of a new Cuba. It was red, white, and blue, but it was not the filibusterers' flag that had flown over the *New York Sun* in 1850. Céspedes had his flag sewn with fabric taken from his family's altar to the Virgin of Charity, the brown virgin who had appeared to an enslaved boy and his two Native companions more than three centuries earlier. Thus began the first Cuban War of Independence—with the leadership of an aristocratic sugar planter, the participation of enslaved people, and the blessing of the island's favorite saint.[1]

When the island's Spanish governor first learned of the rebellion, he was unfazed. He reassured authorities in Madrid that he had "more than enough forces to destroy [it] in a matter of days."[2] He badly miscalculated. Twelve more Spanish governors would rule the island before it ended a decade later—hence its name, the Ten Years' War.

In the first few years of the war, military advantage shifted back and forth between the contending parties, as Cuban rebels—the Liberation Army—fought a guerrilla war against Spanish forces. In addition to their army, the rebels also established a government, a republic-in-arms, with a president and legislature. As one would expect of any ten-year conflict, it was a brutal affair. It decimated much of eastern Cuba, where most of the fighting happened. While we have no reliable evidence on the number of people who died in the conflict, the destruction was terrible. In Bayamo, the first rebel stronghold, residents burned the historic city almost to the ground just before the Spanish army marched in to take it from the Cubans. Rural destruction was even worse. In war-torn Camagüey, just one of 110 sugar mills remained standing and producing sugar by the end of the war. Of more than four thousand farmhouses in the same region, only about one hundred survived. People, homes, farms, and animals disappeared in ten years of war. And by 1878, much of what remained was scarred. Bullet holes in trees, shells of old buildings, and other physical remains of warfare became semipermanent landmarks, later pointed out to newcomers by witnesses to the war.[3]

The war wrought more than physical devastation. It also destroyed institutions. And of these the most important was slavery. The rebels destroyed it partly by design and partly as the revolution assumed its own logic. Given the history of nineteenth-century Cuba, how could it have been otherwise? For decades, Cuban planters had spurned independence in the interest of protecting slavery and white rule. The profits from slave-grown sugar convinced them to opt for continuity rather than rupture. The prospect that an independence struggle would mobilize the enslaved had done the same. By 1868, however, the world was a different place. Slavery in the United States was dead. The illegal transatlantic slave trade had ended, and the prospect of protecting the institution of slavery in Cuba was almost nil. That the war of 1868 began with a slaveholder renouncing his human property and inviting them to join the cause of independence revealed how much had changed. It also portended that the very foundations of Cuban society were about to be shaken to the core.

CÉSPEDES LAUNCHED THE WAR BY freeing his own slaves. However powerful symbolically, that was an individual act of liberation, a master freeing his chattel voluntarily. When Céspedes issued the revolution's first public manifesto that same day, he expressed only a *desire* for general emancipation—one that would compensate slaveholders and become effective only when the war was over and the Cubans had won. To Céspedes and his companions—slaveholders-turned-revolutionaries—the proposal seemed prudent. In the promise of a gradual (and indemnified) emancipation, slaveholders heard that no immediate financial loss would occur. Meanwhile, the enslaved heard that a rebellion had started and that, should the rebels win, they would all be free. The plan, then, had the obvious tactical advantage of appealing to both slaves and masters.

This cautious balancing act became one of the first casualties of the war. Spanish authorities observed this right away. "I have no doubt," wrote the governor, "that the instigators of the uprising ... conceived of something limited ... but the fact is that shortly after their uprising, they began to burn sugar mills and take the slaves as free people, ... arousing with their conduct the spirit of the people of color." Céspedes himself began to worry that the war was outpacing his plan for gradual abolition. Just days into the conflict, he promised that the rebel army would respect all property, including human property. Before the month was out, he expressly forbade officers from accepting any slaves into their ranks without his own authorization or that of their masters. Then, two weeks later, he decreed that any person raiding farms to incite the enslaved to rebellion would be tried and sentenced to death if found guilty.[4]

These measures, however, were futile. The problem for leaders was not just that insurgents kept recruiting slaves. It was also that the enslaved did not need prodding to strike for freedom. On their own, they began appearing at rebel camps and offering their services. One enslaved man named Pedro de la Torre arrived at a rebel encampment professing "his desire to sustain the Holy Cause." Another named José Manuel from a coffee farm near El Cobre escaped from his farm and traveled to neighboring ones with copies of rebel proclamations in order to recruit more people such as himself. Rosa Castellanos, the enslaved daughter of Africans, joined the war with her husband, also enslaved. She became widely known as Rosa la Bayamesa (Rosa from Bayamo) and received praise from the movement's most prominent leaders for both her nursing and her fighting.[5]

Two months into the war, rebel leaders realized that the question of abolition could not be deferred. On December 27, 1868, Céspedes decreed that all slaves belonging to the enemy would be freed and their owners not compensated. Slaveholders who supported the independence movement and willingly "presented" their slaves to the rebels would receive compensation, and their slaves would receive their freedom. It was a limited emancipation, accessible only to a fraction of the island's enslaved and, in many cases, valid only with the consent of those who still saw themselves as their masters.

But that guarded decree changed everything. Thousands of enslaved people rushed to join the rebel forces. Writing a week later, Céspedes boasted that former slaves now "marched in companies giving cries of long live Liberty and [long live] the whites of Cuba, who [only] yesterday had governed them with the harshness of the whip, and who today treat them as brothers and grant them the title of free men." For Céspedes, it was a perfect display of worthiness. On one side, he saw magnanimous masters who granted the enslaved not only freedom but also an invitation to history. On the other side, he saw former slaves, grateful and unwavering in their loyalty to onetime masters and the nation they were creating together.[6] Had Céspedes been able to, he might have chosen to stop time at that very moment, to give permanence to that instance of mutual satisfaction. Instead with every passing week, the questions of slavery, race, and their relation to national independence became only more volatile. Modest promises of eventual freedom drew an ever-increasing number of enslaved to the cause; their participation then pushed leaders to do more about abolition.

When, a few months later in April 1869, the rebellion's civilian leaders drafted a constitution for the republic-in-arms, nothing less than full emancipation was viable. Article 24 declared that "all inhabitants of the republic are entirely free." Article 25 specified that "all citizens of the republic are considered soldiers of the Liberation Army." Enslaved workers were now soldiers and citizens of a new republic.[7]

As the independence movement mobilized the enslaved, it also introduced a new language of citizenship that explicitly exalted racial equality. Rebel proclamations could make heady pronouncements for a slave society. "All men are our brothers, whatever the color of their skin," started one. Another announced: "Every Cuban (white or black for we are all equal).... Everyone without distinctions of color, age or sex, can serve ... Liberty." How different were these assertions from the earlier conviction that enslaved and free people of color were an impediment to nationhood. The independence movement adopted a language of race-blind citizenship. Enslaved people heard the rebels' new language, captured it, used it. They called themselves (and each other) citizens, and they publicly professed their patriotism. On gaining their personal freedom, some even changed their last names to Cuba.[8]

IF THE WAR OPENED UP freedom and citizenship to the enslaved, it also gave free men of color access to positions of leadership. Afro-Cuban leaders began emerging almost immediately. The most famous and celebrated was Antonio Maceo. Before the war, he lived on his family's farm about twelve miles north of the city of Santiago. He had grown up listening to his father read the novels of Alexander Dumas and biographies of Haiti's Toussaint Louverture and South America's Simón Bolívar. The twenty-three-year-old Maceo joined the rebellion as an ordinary soldier just two days after it started. After only one battle, he was promoted to sergeant. Many other promotions followed: by the end of the first month of war he was a lieutenant; he was promoted twice in January 1869. In 1873, he became General Maceo. By then, his renown was so great that the king of Spain condemned him to death, if only the Spanish could get their hands on him.[9]

Maceo's ascent through the ranks of the Liberation Army was riddled with controversy, however. In 1873, geography exacerbated the polemic. That year, Máximo Gómez, who despite being from the Dominican Republic was one of the highest-ranking officers in the rebel army, proposed that Antonio Maceo lead a massive invasion of western Cuba. Until then, the war had not spread to the west, where large, modern sugar plantations dominated the countryside. In eastern Cuba, which served as the base for the rebellion, sugar was a smaller industry. The mill owned by Céspedes, for example, ranked a very low 1,113 of 1,365 in annual sugar production among those operating across the island in 1860. Eastern plant-ers were also much less reliant on enslaved labor than their western counterparts. While in sugar boom territories of western Cuba enslaved people often outnum-bered whites, in the specific areas where the eastern rebellion began and flour-ished, the enslaved population was generally under 10 percent.[10] Those geographic and economic differences go a long way to explaining why, from the start of the rebellion, planters such as Céspedes supported revolution and favored abolition while those from the west did not.

To divide east and west in wartime, the Spanish government built a massive fortified trench traversing the island from north to south. Built with the labor of enslaved and Chinese contract workers, the *trocha* was the largest fortification in all the Americas. The Spanish intended it to serve as an invincible barrier between the war zones of eastern Cuba and the rest of the island. Máximo Gómez, how-ever, believed that Antonio Maceo at the head of five hundred men could cross the line, break out of the east, and fight his way westward, maybe even as far as Havana. On the way, Maceo would seize territory carpeted with sugarcane, dotted with sugar mills, and in 1873 still a bastion of racial slavery.

The civilian leaders of the movement listened to Gómez's proposal for the invasion, and they worried. They did not question Maceo's military ability. They anguished over something else: the wisdom of sending a man of color at the head of a significantly Black army to make war and free slaves in the Cuba of large plantations and majority Black populations. Maceo's ascent had already given rise to rumors that he sought to convert Cuba into a Black republic and declare himself its leader. Maceo's opponents used the same, ready bogeyman that Spanish and US officials had always used against Cuban independence: the specter of "race war" and "another Haiti." "Do we liberate ourselves only to share the fate of Haiti and Santo Domingo?" asked one.[11] Maceo's opponents prevailed, and he never led a westward invasion during the Ten Years' War.

FIGHTING CONTINUED, BUT THE REBELS were unable to extend their presence over greater territory or to keep up the intense pressure of the early war. One Spanish official explained that by mid-decade, the conflict was less like a regular war or a decisive challenge and more like the struggle of Florida Seminoles against US authorities. Rebel leaders sometimes conceded the point. In 1877, Máximo Gómez wrote in his diary that the year had been the "most dismal" of the war that "it would be very difficult to direct the revolution on a sure path of victory." Even the most ardent among the Cuban forces were war- and bone-weary.[12]

By the end of that most dismal of years, the Spanish governor, knowing victory was close at hand, suspended hostilities and established a neutral zone in Camagüey to facilitate peace talks. On February 8, 1878, the rebel legislature, prohibited by its own laws from negotiating with Spain, dissolved itself and appointed a commission to work out a peace agreement. Two days later, at a place called Zanjón, the committee accepted Spain's proposal for peace. The Pact of Zanjón did not recognize Cuban independence, but it pardoned insurgents, allowed for the creation of political parties, and recognized the freedom of slaves and Chinese contract workers who had fought in the war. One by one, Cuban forces began surrendering. Insurgents moving around the countryside changed their response to the habitual "Halt, who goes there?" from "Cuba" to "Peace."[13]

Antonio Maceo, however, wanted nothing to do with a pact that granted neither the independence of Cuba nor the abolition of slavery. He called a meeting of the remaining troops. Among them were many Black officers who had risen through the ranks over the last ten years. Maceo was forceful, calling the agreement dishonorable and humiliating. But he was also clear about its consequences: with peace secured elsewhere, Spanish forces would now be free to come at them with all their might.

Maceo also requested a personal interview with the Spanish governor of Cuba. On receiving the invitation for a meeting, the governor was hopeful that Maceo was ready to surrender, or at least to negotiate. Instead, Maceo informed him that he would yield only after Spain granted freedom to all the slaves living in Cuba. The governor refused, so Maceo pledged to continue the war. The meeting between Maceo and the Spanish governor is well-traveled territory in Cuban history. Known as the Protest of Baraguá, it has come to represent the principle of no surrender. More than a century later, in the early 1990s, after the fall of the Berlin Wall and the dissolution of the Soviet Union, billboards across the island announced that Cuba itself was an "eternal Baraguá." As Eastern Europe surrendered to capitalism, the signs implied, Cuba would continue the fight. The billboards did not mention that despite his noble and fiery intentions, Maceo had no choice but to lay down his weapons soon after that defiant protest. He had few troops remaining; they had been fighting for ten years, and victory was out of the question. On May 10, 1878, under orders from the president of the still-nonexistent republic, Maceo left Cuba for Jamaica, never having formally surrendered.[14]

PEACE, HOWEVER, IS NOT A good name for what followed. Too much remained unsettled. There now seemed to be two nodes of Cuban leadership: the men at Zanjón, who had accepted peace under Spain over independence and abolition; and those with Maceo at Baraguá, who had called for the continuation of war until independence and full emancipation were achieved. The two nodes continued to collaborate, but tensions persisted. Now with most of the leadership in exile and peace at hand, the question of who would speak and act for the Cuban cause assumed pressing proportions. Who were the rightful leaders of Cuban independence: The men who presumed to have the juridical power to negotiate peace in February or the men who presumed to have the moral authority to reject that peace in March?

If questions loomed about the movement's future, there were other, more urgent questions on the ground in Cuba. The peace pact of 1878 had freed those slaves who had fought in the war, but left in slavery those who had remained loyal. The treaty thus created new and greater incentives for the enslaved to ally with would-be rebels. Spanish officials were soon reporting that the enslaved were engaging in "passive resistance to work and refus[ing] to obey their owners and overseers. They want their freedom like the *convenidos*," the name given to those freed by the peace agreement. One Black rebel officer of the war just ended reported that "the blacks [were] impatient" and wanted to rise up. Everyone, everywhere, he said, spoke "*sotto voce* of the imminent uprising."[15]

Little wonder, then, that peace was short-lived. In August 1879, just eighteen months after the end of the Ten Years' War, a second war of independence began. Even its name suggests its fate: the Little War, or Guerra Chiquita. It was so short, in fact, that many people sometimes forget that it happened at all. But if its military importance seems secondary, it reveals perfectly, in condensed form, the problems at the heart of the movement for Cuban independence, indeed at the heart of Cuban history for much of the nineteenth century.

THE NEW WAR WAS IN many ways a continuation of the one just ended. The setting was the same: eastern Cuba. The means were the same: guerrilla warfare. So, too, were the goals: abolition and independence. But there was one important difference. Simply put, the new uprising was blacker than the first. Enslaved people, who had seen their old companions freed for participating in the last war, welcomed the arrival of another chance for freedom. Some burned cane fields, chanting "No freedom, no cane!" In the first two months of the rebellion, authorities estimated that five thousand enslaved fled their workplaces. At the level of leadership, as well, the description of the rebellion as blacker is apt. Many elite white insurgents of the first war, now members of the newly established Liberal Party, preferred, for the moment, to pursue peaceful avenues of activism. They condemned the new war effort, casting it as unfeasible and dangerous. The withdrawal of elite white support became even more significant because it occurred alongside the mass mobilization of slaves and former slaves. It also left more room for the rise of Black insurgent leaders. The two principal military commanders of the new war were José Maceo (brother of Antonio) and Guillermo Moncada, a Black carpenter born to free parents. Both men were veterans of the Ten Years' War and the Protest of Baraguá.[16]

The label of "blacker," however, was more than a description. At the time, it was also an argument. As soon as the rebellion began, Spanish officials insisted that it consisted "entirely of people of color," and constituted "only the prelude to race war." In order to ensure that a majority of people believed that, Spanish authorities engineered appearances to make the war fit the label they gave it. The Spanish governor of the province was quite explicit about the strategy: "We must remove all white characteristics from the rebellion and reduce it to the colored element," he wrote. "That way it will count on less sympathy and support." He tampered with lists of captured insurgents, removing white names to make the movement seem overwhelmingly Black. When he secured the surrender of a prominent white officer, as a condition for pardon he made the officer publicly affirm that he had surrendered because the movement's leaders wanted "a race war."[17]

The Spanish manipulated reality to make the rebellion seem blacker, and the more they did that, the blacker the rebellion became. Afro-Cuban leaders protested vehemently. Guillermo Moncada called the Spanish "petty assassins" who "falsified judgments and deformed facts" to characterize Cuba's "holy cause" as a "race war."[18] But such objections were to no avail. The Spanish continued the policy, and the policy continued to work. Potential white combatants hesitated to join; others surrendered, and the rebellion faltered.

In June 1880, realizing there was no hope for success, José Maceo and Guillermo Moncada entered into peace negotiations with the governor. As the talks progressed, the governor learned that Calixto García, a white general and veteran of the Ten Years' War, had just arrived on the island from a brief exile in New York, ready to assume command of all the rebel forces. The governor immediately realized that he stood to lose what had thus far "kept a large part of the people on [Spain's] side, namely the race war, which whites feared." During the negotiations with Moncada and José Maceo, he kept the Black leaders isolated, and both surrendered without ever learning of the white general's arrival. The governor then used that surrender as further proof that the insurrection was a race war. Why else would its two most prominent leaders—both men of color—refuse to recognize the leadership of the white García? Without the support of Maceo and Moncada, García's expedition quickly failed.[19] The second independence war was over, its defeat due in no small part to Spain's wily use of race as a powerful tactic of counterinsurgency. For now, at least, Cuba would remain Spanish.

BY THE END OF THE Little War, however, the other goal of the independence movement had been achieved. Slavery was abolished everywhere across the island. The two wars just ended had gone a long way in making the institution unsustainable. Rebels had freed and mobilized enslaved people; they had also let loose a language of equality and freedom that reverberated everywhere. In 1870, in an effort to minimize the revolution's appeal to the enslaved, the Spanish government began to decree its own cautious policies, outlawing the whip, for example, and enacting a free womb law that granted freedom to all children henceforth born to enslaved mothers. No more children would be born into slavery in Cuba. The treaty that ended the first war in 1878 gave freedom to sixteen thousand slaves who had fought in the war. Then in February 1880, with the Little War still raging in the east and little prospect of reversing the tide of history, the Spanish government abolished slavery in Cuba.

Full freedom, however, was not granted immediately. Instead, slavery gave way to an apprenticeship system, called the *patronato*, which was to last for eight years. The 1880 law of abolition did not compensate owners for their financial loss, but by guaranteeing them the labor of their former slaves as apprentices for eight years, the law served the purpose of indemnification. The enslaved, meanwhile, received no compensation at all for their lifetimes of labor, done by force and for free. The decree also established that apprentices could petition for their freedom through self-purchase or denunciations of their masters' failure to live up to the provisions of the law. Many rushed to do so. In 1886, with only 25,381 apprentices remaining throughout the island, the colonial government declared the abolition of the apprenticeship system—two years ahead of schedule and almost four hundred years after Spain's arrival in Cuba.[20]

Decades later, an elderly African-born man named Genaro Lucumí and his wife, Irene, both formerly enslaved, sometimes gathered neighborhood children— my own mother among them—to tell stories. He recounted tales of fighting in Antonio Maceo's independence army; she recalled buying her freedom in the final years of slavery. Even in their Sunday stories, the struggles for freedom from slavery and freedom for Cuba were part of the same epic.

Chapter 12

A REVOLUTION FOR
THE WORLD

Interviewed for the *New York Herald* in October 1880, eight months after Spain's abolition of slavery and three months after he reluctantly surrendered in the Little War, General Calixto García tackled an unexpected question. Wasn't Cuban independence a foregone conclusion? García grew pensive. Perhaps he furrowed his brow, which bore a deep scar from a bullet wound he had inflicted upon himself in 1874, attempting suicide to avoid capture by the Spanish. He replied candidly: independence was "by no means an easy enterprise." The principal obstacle, he said, was white anxiety. "[Among] the whites . . . some [were] eternally wavering on account of the risks of the enterprise, and others hesitating out of a fear of a servile war with the negroes and mulattoes if Cuba became free."[1] While García's words were meant to explain the recent defeat of the Cuban cause, they also revealed something about the momentous challenge that lay ahead. To succeed, the independence movement would have to change the way people thought about race.

To change assumptions about race, however, was—and remains—a daunting task. Cubans were still living through the end of racial slavery. Next door was the United States, where Jim Crow laws were systematically inscribing segregation and inequality, and where racial violence was approaching its brutal nadir. Everywhere, a burgeoning field of racial "science" seemed to give racism the cover of expertise. It was in that unpropitious context that Cuba's independence movement had to undermine the era's central claims of racial knowledge. Remarkably, and against the prevailing assumptions of their age, leaders insisted that the very idea of race was an invention, the work of powerful groups who conjured "textbook races" to justify expansion and empire. Looking at Cuba specifically, they roundly rejected old arguments that the island's past of racial slavery incapacitated it for nationhood. In vehement opposition to that axiom, they wrote of a nation forged by Blacks and whites who fought together—*as* Cubans *for* Cuba. In this view, the nation was born explicitly, almost literally, of racial unity.

This idea crystalized quite clearly and powerfully at this precise juncture, in the peace that came after the failed independence wars of 1868–80, and as activists prepared for what they hoped would be a final, triumphant struggle. Today, this notion of a Cuban identity that transcends race remains one of the two most important pillars of Cuban nationalism—the word *nationalism* referring here to pro-independence sentiment. Predictably, the other pillar of that nationalism emphasizes the pervasiveness of US designs on the island.

IRONICALLY, IT WAS PRECISELY IN the financial capital of US empire that the vision that helped Cuba triumph over Spain had its greatest author and spokesman: José Martí. He was the figure who most powerfully voiced the notion of a racially transcendent Cuban nationality. Today, Martí statues and busts are ubiquitous across Cuba and Miami. His likeness graces sites farther afield, too: a New Jersey pedestal less than a mile away from where Aaron Burr killed Alexander Hamilton; the Artists' Gate entrance to New York's Central Park; plazas and buildings from Delhi to Manila and Sydney to Kingston.

We have encountered Martí a few times already—as a boy witnessing the illegal unloading of a slave ship on Cuban shores, as a teenager mourning the death of Abraham Lincoln. Born in Havana in 1853 to Spanish parents, by the age of sixteen, he was publishing a pro-independence newspaper during the Ten Years' War and jailed for his efforts. Sentenced to six years' hard labor in the whites-only work unit, he was issued a number (113) and a loose gray uniform; he wore an iron shackle on his right ankle tied to a heavy chain around his waist. In 1871, because of his deteriorating physical condition, authorities released him from his original sentence and banished him to Spain. He spent three years there, completing his university education and writing his first major work, *El presidio politico en Cuba*, or "Political Prison in Cuba." "These pages should be known by no other name than infinite pain," began his account of his imprisonment and forced labor in a Havana stone quarry.[2]

After Spain, Martí moved around: Paris for a time; New York very briefly (twelve days), Mexico for two years, then Guatemala, where he worked as a university professor of literature, among other things. In 1878, when Spain pardoned those imprisoned during the Ten Years' War, Martí returned to Cuba. His stay lasted only about a year. Shortly after the start of the Little War in 1879, Spanish officials arrested him preemptively and sentenced him to hard labor in a Spanish penal colony in North Africa. Sent first to Spain, Martí escaped and sailed to refuge in New York City.[3]

So, in 1880, at the age of almost twenty-seven, the peripatetic Martí became one more immigrant in the great American metropolis. He started out in Manhattan and moved to Brooklyn. He worked as a file clerk for a time, served as New York consul for several Latin American nations, and translated US literature into Spanish. Every morning he took the ferry to Manhattan and strode to his cold walk-up office on Front Street. A gifted speaker, he was invited to give public lectures at meeting halls across Manhattan, among them the long-gone Tammany Hall on 14th Street and Hardman Hall on lower Fifth Avenue, very near the old offices of Charles Scribner's Sons.

However busy all that work kept him, Martí's main occupation in New York was writing—essays, a serialized novel, a play, and, above all, poetry and journalism. He wrote for many publications, including the *New York Sun* and the *Revista Ilustrada de Nueva York*. (Since the days of Cuban immigrant priest Félix Varela, there were US periodicals published in Spanish.) For several Latin American newspapers, Martí wrote of his impressions of New York and the United States, describing episodes as disparate as a commemoration of the revolutionary siege of Yorktown, a Mississippi River flood, the passage of the Chinese Exclusion Act, a graduation ceremony at Vassar College, and a memorial event at Cooper Union on the death of Karl Marx. He wrote about immigrants arriving at Castle Garden in Battery Park—440,000 in one year. They were, he wrote, "living poetry" and "an army of peace." That, he ventured, was "the secret to the prosperity of the United States: they have opened their arms." His chronicles of New York are at once fine journalism and a testament of daily life in what he called "a city of cities." As most New Yorkers do, Martí grew both to love and hate the city. New York, he said, was like "death by a thousand cuts." Yet, when he left it to go anywhere other than Cuba, he felt like he was losing a part of himself.[4]

Martí wrote with special feeling about violence in the United States—against immigrants, labor leaders, Native and African Americans. In 1892, for instance, he described the public lynching of a Black man accused of offending a white woman: "The ladies waved their handkerchiefs, the men waved their hats. Mrs. Jewell [the man's accuser] reached the tree [where the man was tied], lit a match, twice touched the lit match to the [petroleum-soaked] jacket of the black man, who did not speak, and the black man went up in flames, in the presence of five thousand souls."[5] In an American republic whose institutions he admired, this happened—not the work of one political leader, or a single villain, but of five thousand men and women who went to church, voted for their town council members, kissed their children good night, and watched a man be burned alive.

Martí's experience of living in the United States made him confront that republic. He recorded some of his initial reactions in short handwritten notes. "One lives in the United States," he wrote, "as if under a hail of blows. These people speak as if they were brandishing fists before your eyes." In one undated fragment, he described a lecturer speaking "with pride of the American Union, alluding of course to his North America, without thinking that there might be another America." It was to him a revelation: that the place he—and, in fact, much of the world—called "the United States" was in the United States itself called instead "America." We can almost imagine Martí bristling every time people said America and meant the United States, "without thinking that there might be another America."[6]

This other America Martí referred to passingly in that fragment became one of the central organizing principles of his work. He came to call it not "another America," but "Our America." He gave that title to an essay he wrote in New York and published in Mexico in 1891. It eventually became his most famous, most anthologized work. The essay, which never mentioned Cuba, was an ode to Latin American unity. It was also a warning. "The hour is near when [our America] will be approached by an enterprising and forceful nation that will demand intimate relations with her, though it does not know her and disdains her. . . . The disdain of the formidable neighbor who does not know her," he wrote, "is our America's greatest danger, and it is urgent—for the day of the visit is near."[7] The formidable neighbor was, of course, the United States.

FOR ALMOST FIFTEEN YEARS, MARTÍ lived in New York and wrote prolifically. Yet his greatest concern that whole time was Cuban independence. In 1892, he founded a newspaper called *Patria* and a political party he named the Cuban Revolutionary Party, both devoted to that cause. He collaborated closely with other important figures of the movement: Antonio Maceo and Máximo Gómez, the presumed military leaders of the coming struggle; Tomás Estrada Palma, former president of the Republic in Arms. Martí also worked with and raised funds from Cuban tobacco workers—many of whom were men and women of color, some in Brooklyn (where cigar factories proliferated by the 1880s), as well as in Florida.

One of Martí's closest associates in New York was Rafael Serra, a former tobacco worker turned journalist and teacher. Born free and Black in Havana, Serra was already a teacher when he arrived in New York in 1880. Later that decade he founded an association, La Liga (or the League), devoted to the advancement of Black workers from Cuba and Puerto Rico. Located off Washington Square Park in Greenwich Village, the association ran a night school, where Martí taught class every Thursday evening.[8]

Whether teaching in the night school for Black workers, writing for the pages of *Patria*, or meeting with like-minded activists, Martí worked tirelessly in pursuit of Cuban independence. Beyond trying to organize the next war, he was also thinking deeply about the peace that would follow, about how to create a just and worthy republic. "A republic for all," was what he called it.

A central feature of Martí's imagined republic was a deep racial harmony and transcendence. "Men," he wrote, "have no special rights simply because they belong to one race or another. When you say *men*, you have already imbued them with all their rights." If Martí believed that as a general proposition, he also believed that, in Cuba, the independence movement was itself forging that truth. Already, the first war had converted slaves into soldiers and citizens of an aspiring republic. Black and white men had become one community, in his view. They had died together on the battlefield, their souls rising to the heavens in a permanent embrace. "There will never be a race war in Cuba," he insisted fervently. Against skeptics and worriers, Martí posited powerful images of a nation premised on racial unity: a new kind of republic that would not be white or Black, but simply Cuban.[9]

This was the Cuba that Martí imagined from New York. In fact, living in the United States helped convince him that Cuba's future as an independent republic required nothing less. As he witnessed the color line in the United States grow more and more rigid and the consequences for crossing that line become more and more lethal, Martí grasped the depth of the injustice all around him. And with that knowledge, he was able to see his own Cuba with new eyes. It was that juxtaposition that made him realize how potentially distinct and mighty was the movement being made in Cuba. By mobilizing and uniting former slaves and former masters, Blacks and whites, Cuban independence would be something novel, something profoundly good. It could be a model for the hemisphere, perhaps for all the world.

As he sat in New York thinking about Cuba's future, he also thought about "our America," and the powerful neighbor who disdained her. And those ruminations, too, led him to see Cuban independence as a global force. If Cubans could resist the power of the United States, the new republic would be a check on its expansion into the other America, his America. In this way, as well, his Cuba would be a blessing for the hemisphere.

Ultimately, then, Martí believed that Cuban independence, if truly successful, would do two things for the world. First, it would serve as a brake on US expansion. Second, it would be an example to the world of a new kind of republic—one that stood opposed to the racial and ethnic violence then so readily on display in the United States. As a paragon of racial justice, as a check on US empire, the Cuban Revolution would be a revolution for the world.

BY THE START OF 1895, Martí and his fellow travelers were prepared to make that revolution real. On the morning of January 31, 1895, convinced that he needed to be part of that war, to fight and write from within it, Martí boarded a steamship and left New York, his city of cities, for the last time.

It is fitting that en route to making Cuba free, Martí traveled to the island of Hispaniola, site of Spain's first colony in the New World and home to Haiti and the Dominican Republic. At the border town of Montecristi, Martí reunited with General Máximo Gómez. There Martí wrote (and both men signed) a proclamation announcing Cuba's War of Independence to the world. Cuba, it said, would be a free and prosperous archipelago at the crossroads of the world, a boon to all mankind. About two weeks later, on April 11, 1895, Martí and Gómez landed on a deserted coast near Guantánamo. The war, which had begun on February 24, was now in full swing in eastern Cuba, the same region that had been home to the first and second wars of independence.[10]

In the United States, people watched closely. A long-standing interest in Cuba—and the ever-growing significance of US investments there—focused American attention on the political fate of the island. In the first three months of war, Cuba made the front page of US newspapers at least seven thousand times. The *New York Herald* sent a special correspondent, George Bryson, to interview the rebel leaders in the countryside. After marching for days, he arrived at Martí and Gómez's camp late the evening of May 2, as the men were settling in for a dinner of bread and cheese. The reporter offered the leaders the chance to make their case from the pages of a major US newspaper. Martí saw the value of the endeavor and worked with Bryson until 3 a.m. that night and then again all of the following day.[11]

In their long conversations, the *Herald* correspondent relayed many pieces of disturbing news—about a "Yankee syndicate" working with "rapacious white Spaniards" to establish a "toehold" in Cuba, and about "men of the legal ilk" plotting some kind of transfer of power from Spain to the United States. None of this surprised Martí. Writing to a close friend in Mexico a few weeks later, he said that he grasped clearly the enormity of the challenge before him and his compatriots. He wrote:

> Every day now I am in danger of giving my life for my country and my duty . . . in order to prevent, by the timely independence of Cuba, the United States from extending its hold across the Antilles and falling with all the greater force on the lands of *our America*. . . . I lived in the monster, and I know its entrails—and my sling is the sling of David.[12]

Martí never finished the letter. He started a sentence, "There are affections of such delicate honesty. . . ." Then something interrupted him. The next day, he was killed in battle. Ironically, it was on the day of his death that the *New York Herald* published the proclamation he had given to the reporter. "Cuban Leaders to the *Herald*," announced the headline, on page one, May 19, 1895.

MARTÍ'S DEATH CAME JUST THREE months into a war that proved much longer than anyone wanted. For the revolutionaries, the high point of the war was the invasion of the west, a massive, fighting march from the mountains and valleys of eastern Cuba all the way to the island's westernmost point. The leaders of the Liberation Army had been plotting such an invasion ever since the first war, but it was not until late 1895 that they succeeded. The insurgents marched westward in two massive columns—one led by the army's commander in chief, Máximo Gómez; another by General Antonio Maceo, already known as the Bronze Titan. A third, smaller column led by General Quintín Bandera, a prominent Black hero of the Ten Years' War and the Little War, marched closer to the island's southern coast. Together, they crossed over the fortified line Spain had built to contain them. And then they kept going, marching west across the central province of Santa Clara, through Matanzas and rural Havana, all rich with sugarcane.

A member of the invading army observed that, as they marched through towns and farms on their path, "everyone said in a single voice: here comes Maceo, here comes Máximo Gómez . . . and here comes Quintín Banderas at the head of the blacks with nose rings." Even before the rebel army's arrival, people in western Cuba had heard the rumors about Black troops sporting nose rings, and some wondered. It might be true—eastern Cuba was far away, its customs possibly different. But the notion of Black rebels with nose rings also sounded like a government lie. José Herrera (nickname Mangoché), a fifteen-year-old sugar plantation worker in Havana province and the grandson of an African-born midwife, debated the issue at length with his friends. Unable to contain his curiosity, one of them journeyed east from Havana to get a glimpse of the invading army before they arrived. He came back with an authoritative, eyewitness answer: he had seen the rebels, and they did not wear nose rings.[13]

As the Liberation Army approached, people craned their necks to see the notorious insurgents for the first time and to judge for themselves. Thousands of men on horseback came at thunderous speeds. The earth loosened by the horses' hooves covered them—their skin, their hair, their beards—in red dust. People leaned out their doors and porches to cheer them on with loud cries of "long live Máximo Gómez, Antonio Maceo, and Cuba libre." But the Spanish and their allies had so long impugned the character and motives of the Cubans, that one rebel officer thought the "wide-open eyes of woman and children [also] concealed or covered the fear or terror that we caused them, and upon looking us over they searched in our faces—since they did not see the nose rings that the Spanish said we carried—for signs of something horrible and ferocious . . . and they were astonished to find none."[14] The arrival of the Liberation Army in western Cuba was for people there a moment of reckoning, in which long-held assumptions and emerging ideas about race and nation were affirmed, denied, modified, all in the act of seeing rebels without nose rings.

On sugar plantations, the insurgents' arrival was a moment of reckoning in another way as well. Slavery was nine years dead. But freedom itself was up for grabs. Across plantations on the invading army's path, workers joined the rebels in droves. Some were young Black men, born free to enslaved women in the waning days of slavery in the heart of sugar country. Others were former slaves. For both, joining the Liberation Army was a way not just to help make Cuba free, but a way to give meaning to their own freedom. Most could not read or write, so there are few war diaries or memoirs that recount their experiences. In fact, only two are known to exist. One was authored by Mangoché, who had debated with his friends about nose rings; the other was written by Ricardo Batrell, who at age fifteen joined the rebel army when it arrived at the plantation where he cut cane. It was the very same Matanzas plantation that in 1843–44 had been at the center of the Escalera rebellions and conspiracies, when Black men and women had been tied to ladders to extract confessions.[15]

Like Batrell and Mangoché, there were thousands of these new recruits, swelling the ranks of the Liberation Army. By the time it arrived in Cienfuegos, just west of the island's midpoint, rebel numbers had doubled. Insurgent forces rang in the year of 1896 within sight of Havana. In the capital city, students, writers, and aspiring professionals spent hours at the café of the Hotel Inglaterra (at the same café where defeated Confederates had nursed their woes), singing the praises of Maceo and making plans to join the fight. By that point, however, the rebel army had gotten so big that it was having to turn away recruits. From Havana's countryside, part of the army continued west all the way to Mantua, the westernmost town of the island's westernmost province.[16]

All told, over ninety days and seventy-eight marches, the rebel army covered more than a thousand miles and fought twenty-seven major battles. An early one was witnessed by Winston Churchill, who arrived in Cuba in awe: "Here was a scene of vital action. . . . Here was a place where something would certainly happen. Here I might leave my bones." He almost did, when the horse behind him was felled by a bullet fired by the Cubans. That skirmish paled in comparison to the whole endeavor. Strong from one end of the island to the other, the independence fighters now posed the deadliest threat ever to Spain's four-hundred-year rule in Cuba.[17]

MILITARY CAMPAIGNS ALWAYS HAVE HIGH points, moments perched on the cusp of victory. The insurgents' invasion of the west was such a moment. But something can be imminent for only so long before momentum stalls and victory slips away. In this case, that happened, too.

In January 1896, the government in Madrid appointed a new governor of Cuba: Valeriano Weyler. A week after his arrival, he began a ruthless campaign of counterinsurgency. His most famous policy was "reconcentration"—a precursor term for much more notorious and brutal concentration camps elsewhere in the twentieth century. Weyler ordered all people living in the countryside (or small unfortified towns) to move to designated Spanish-held areas, where they would be unable to help the rebels. He then sent troops into the country to destroy remaining crops, houses, and animals—anything that might offer sustenance or shelter to the rebels. No provisions were made for feeding and housing the hundreds of thousands of Cubans thus reconcentrated. Within two months, newspapers around the world were reporting the obvious consequences—hunger, disease, and death. Historians now estimate that perhaps some 170,000 people—one-tenth of the island's population—died. People called Weyler "the Butcher." A popular poem in Havana described him as having "the look of a reptile, the body of a dwarf, the instinct of a jackal, a soul like mud." In the United States, newspapers dwelled on the suffering of the *reconcentrados*, publishing pictures of emaciated children and the mass graves of Cubans who had succumbed. The coverage was almost obsessive and helped launch what came to be called "yellow journalism"—a new wave of sensationalized news with bold, alarmist headlines.[18]

Whatever the world's opinions of Weyler, the Spanish government placed in him all its hopes of retaining Cuba. Madrid sent him reinforcements and set aside questions about the morality or efficacy of his policies. Weyler escalated engagements with the enemy and ordered the killing of wounded, captured, or surrendered combatants. He built a second fortified line west of Havana from the northern coast to the southern. Its purpose was to trap Maceo and his troops in the far western province of Pinar del Río and attack them with the new reinforcements concentrated around the capital. Total war had come to Havana's doorstep.

Maceo, however, was defiant. When the Spanish bragged of their new fortified trench, Maceo declared it inconsequential. If he had crossed trenches on his way west, he announced, he could cross them whenever he decided to go east. When the Spanish reported false news of Maceo's death, he broadcast his presence by making a devastating circle around Havana. When the Spanish declared the western province of Pinar del Río pacified, he marched back to demonstrate that it wasn't. Maceo's renown grew—in Cuba, in Spain, Europe, and the United States.

Renown, however, does not guarantee victory. Weyler and the Spanish vowed that when they killed Maceo, they would make a broom with his beard. Among Cubans, Maceo was widely respected and loved, but old and long-standing tensions sometimes vexed his leadership. Civilian leaders complained that Maceo handed out promotions without their approval. For his part, Maceo grumbled that the civilian government was too slow to send him war materials and played favorites among officers. He was not among their favorites, he implied. The tension between the two branches of the movement—civil and military—was in part a question of political theory: What should the relationship between civilian and military authority be in the new nation? But the fact that the army was significantly Black and the civilian wing of the movement largely white also gave those tensions a distinctly racial cast.[19]

Maceo did his best to ignore it. But Máximo Gómez, by then back in the east-central province of Camagüey, which was also the headquarters of the rebel government, had to confront it every day. When that government wrote a law that required him to submit the army's "operational plans" for its approval, Gómez wrote to Maceo for help. He implored him to return to the east so they could confront the government together. The very survival of the revolution, said Gómez, required Maceo's presence in Camagüey. So Maceo readied to cross the island once more, this time from west to east.[20]

Maceo and a small group of his men left Pinar del Río and entered the province of Havana. The march aggravated an old battle wound—his twenty-fourth, sustained six months earlier when a bullet shattered a bone in his lower leg. On December 7, 1896, Maceo was resting on a hammock at an improvised camp in an abandoned sugar mill. His chief of staff, who had been writing a chronicle of the war at Maceo's side for over a year, was reading aloud from his description of one of Maceo's most daring battles, when they heard real gunfire. A bullet struck Maceo's face. Another bullet, the fatal one, hit his chest. The men around him tried to save him. Máximo Gómez's son was among them; then he, too, was wounded mortally, and the rest of the men were forced to flee, unable to take their fallen with them. Spanish soldiers stripped the bodies of their clothes and valuables. Not realizing they had just killed the famous Antonio Maceo and the son of the almost-as-famous Máximo Gómez, they left the bodies. For that reason, no one made a broom of Maceo's beard.[21]

Rumors of Maceo's death spread like wildfire. Many hoped that he would do as he had always done and disprove the news with some daring military feat. Yet even without confirmation, people feared the worst. "A halo of painful bitterness hangs over everyone," wrote Máximo Gómez's chief of staff. When Gómez received confirmation of the deaths, he declared ten days of mourning. Soldiers and generals cried. Even New York mourned. Cuban sympathizers in the city organized a procession that ended with a service in Maceo's honor at Cooper Union. So many attended that the crowd spilled out of the building onto Cooper Square.

The Senate Foreign Relations Committee called for an investigation into the manner of the general's death. Across the United States, African Americans, who were already praising Maceo as one of the century's greatest heroes, began giving his name to their sons, though they pronounced it *May-see-oh*, with the accent on the first syllable. Maceo Antonio Richmond, born in Iowa to a homemaker and a foundry worker on March 15, 1897, was one of the first.[22]

THE CUBAN INDEPENDENCE STRUGGLE HAD lost two of its principal figures: José Martí and Antonio Maceo. Yet Spain seemed no closer to victory. In October 1897, a new government came to power in Madrid determined to end the war in Cuba. It removed the hated Weyler and began offering concessions and pardons to Cubans. In November, it announced its intention to grant the island political and economic autonomy effective January 1, 1898. Under the plan, Cuban men, regardless of property or literacy, would elect a parliament with control over all domestic affairs, including trade, agriculture, industry, education, and so on. Madrid, meanwhile, would retain control over military, legal, and diplomatic matters.

Would these new concessions and the weariness with war be enough to produce peace before independence, as had happened in the first two wars? Unlikely, decided rebel leaders. Just in case, they outlawed discussions about accommodation under Spain and vowed trial and execution to anyone who violated the law. They issued public proclamations condemning the idea of peace without independence: "The names of our champions who have fallen and those of the 150,000 defenseless Cubans pitilessly murdered by General Weyler would condemn us from Heaven if we were to [negotiate] with Spain" on the basis of anything other than absolute independence for Cuba.[23]

Many loyal Spaniards hated autonomy as well. For the most conservative among them, it was a sign of weakness. On January 1, 1898, some marched through the streets of Havana, shouting "Death to Autonomy!" and "Long Live Weyler!" Because the United States had been urging Spain to grant autonomy to Cuba as a way to restore order to the island (and thus protect US investments and trade there), the protestors also attacked the offices of the US consul. In response, the United States stationed the battleship *Maine* in Havana harbor. It was a friendly visit, said Washington, but also a robust deterrent to any further attempts on Americans or their property in Cuba.[24]

Most people on the island did not believe that Madrid could hold on to

Cuba, no matter the number of concessions. Some among them—landholders and merchants, Spaniards, and those Cubans who had not particularly favored independence—worried what that would mean. And they wondered if some kind of US rule might not be preferable to independence. In February, leading Spaniards in Havana established a commission to approach the United States. "The Mother country cannot protect us. . . . If left to the insurgents our property is lost. Therefore, we want the United States to save us." According to US diplomats in Havana, "Cuban planters and Spanish property holders are now satisfied that the island must soon slip from Spain's grasp, and would welcome immediate American intervention."[25]

This had been José Martí's gravest worry, the outcome of the war that he most feared. He had expressed it in the unfinished letter he wrote the day before his death, when he excoriated those who always preferred "that there be a master, Yankee or Spaniard." That was why Martí fought, not just for independence, as he had written in that letter, but also, recall, "to prevent, by the timely independence of Cuba, the United States from extending its hold . . . and falling with all the greater force on the lands of *our America*."[26]

ALMOST THREE YEARS AFTER MARTÍ penned that letter and died in battle, the Cubans were on the verge of victory. In January 1898, Máximo Gómez predicted it would come before year's end—the first time, he said, he dared make a prediction that specific. Cuban leaders planned their final assault, certain that Spain's defeat was imminent. The US government knew this, too. In a confidential memorandum, the US assistant secretary of state explained that "Spain's struggle in Cuba has become absolutely hopeless. . . . Spain is exhausted financially and physically, while the Cubans are stronger."[27]

If that truth buoyed the Cubans, it deeply worried their powerful neighbor to the north. Since the days of Jefferson in the 1790s, Adams and Monroe in the 1820s, Polk in the 1840s, and Pierce and Buchanan in the 1850s, almost every presidential administration in Washington had imagined Cuba as eventual US territory. Unable to accomplish that outright, they had settled for it belonging to a weak Spain. Never could it belong to anyone else, not even to the Cubans, whom they saw as incapable of maintaining their independence anyway. Now, in early 1898, Cubans seemed on the cusp of victory. It remained to be seen, however, whether Martí's prediction about the United States swooping in would materialize.

Then at 9:40 p.m. on Tuesday, February 15, 1898, the *Maine* exploded in Havana harbor, killing at least 260 US sailors. To this day, Spaniards and Cubans believe that the United States planned the explosion themselves as a pretext for declaring war on Spain and making themselves masters of Cuba. Americans blamed Spain from the outset. The front page of the *Washington Evening Times* announced, "Blown up by Spain . . . Two Hundred and Fifty American Sailors the Food of Sharks." The clamor for war was instantaneous. Even before the sinking of the *Maine*, calls for war were already popular among an American public attuned to vivid and lurid press reports of Cuban civilians dying in reconcentration camps. After the sinking of the *Maine*, the calls became thunderous. The *New York Journal* printed a special million-copy run calling on the United States to declare war on Spain. The same newspaper boys that Martí had written about years earlier shouted the calls to war from street corners. "War Talk in the Senate," they cried; "Spain's Time is Short."[28]

Newly elected president William McKinley preferred to protect US interests in Cuba without war if possible. One month after the sinking of the *Maine*, McKinley instructed his ambassador to Spain to make an offer to purchase Cuba. It would be a way for Spain to resolve the conflict without the humiliation of defeat in war—either by the Cuban rebels or by American forces. But Madrid was not yet prepared to give up the island voluntarily. The United States then attempted to negotiate a peace between Spain and the Cuban rebels. In response to American pressure, Spain called a cease-fire. But the Cubans refused to lay down their arms. Leaders wrote to McKinley, "Nothing you could propose would be so beneficial to Spain and so detrimental to Cuba as an armistice. If an armistice is carried out in good faith, it means the dissolution and disintegration of the Cuban army." And why would that army dissolve itself without having achieved independence? Now, "more than ever before, the war must continue in full force," proclaimed Máximo Gómez.[29]

The failure of the armistice proposal and continuing pressure from Congress and the American public to intervene on behalf of the Cubans seemed to make the call to war irresistible. On April 11, 1898, McKinley requested authority from Congress to declare war on Spain. Colorado senator Henry Teller successfully introduced an article to the joint resolution authorizing the war. Known as the Teller Amendment, it disavowed any "intention to exercise sovereignty, jurisdiction, or control over said island except for pacification thereof." It also asserted that when pacification was accomplished, the United States would "leave the government and control of the island to its people." With that, the United States declared war on Spain on April 20, 1898.[30]

The Americans were headed to Cuba, to fight against Spain and to help Cubans secure their independence. The Cubans, however, were already close to victory. Everyone—including members of McKinley's administration—knew it. American intervention in 1898, then, was not to help Cubans achieve a victory over Spain. That was forthcoming, anyway. American intervention was meant precisely to block it.

The United States intervened in Cuba's War of Independence by declaring war on Spain in 1898. For Americans, the Spanish-American War represented an opportunity for national reconciliation after the Civil War. In this staged photo taken by St. Louis photographer and Civil War veteran Fitz W. Guerin circa 1898, the Union and Confederacy unite for the freedom of Cuba, pictured as a young white girl breaking the chains that bind her.

Part V

AMERICAN INTERREGNUM

Chapter 13

A WAR RENAMED

On April 23, 1898, two days before Congress declared war on Spain, President William McKinley issued a call for 125,000 volunteers. The last time Americans had mobilized for war was the Civil War, when they enlisted to combat each other. For four years they had fought, killed, and died in what remains to this day the war with the most US casualties. In 1898, the circumstances could not have been more different. American soldiers would fight for four months rather than four years. And unlike the Civil War, in the new war there was minimal fighting by Americans. US battle deaths (across all the theaters of war) numbered under four hundred. Finally, if the crux of the Civil War had been disunion, the men who fought against Spain in 1898 seemed to represent a fresh American union—"the boys who wore the blue and the boys who wore the gray" now united as brothers by one overarching purpose: to defeat the tyranny of oldest Europe. The war, writes historian Greg Grandin, was "alchemic. It transformed the 'Lost Cause' of the Confederacy—the preservation of slavery—into humanity's cause for world freedom."[1]

Even before the sinking of the *Maine*, Theodore (Teddy) Roosevelt, then assistant secretary of the navy, had called himself "a quietly rampant 'Cuba Libre' man." He preached "with all the fervor and zeal [he] possessed, [Americans'] duty to intervene in Cuba, and to take this opportunity of driving the Spaniard from the Western World." He knew in his gut that if and when that war came, he would fight. He was gratified, then, that on the very day Congress declared war on Spain, the US secretary of war asked him to lead a volunteer regiment of "frontiersmen possessing special qualifications as horsemen and marksmen"—"'Cow boys,' so called." The volunteers would soon be known as the Rough Riders. Roosevelt resigned his post as assistant secretary of the navy and boarded a train from Washington, DC, to San

Antonio, Texas, where he met his close friend Leonard Wood, an army surgeon who was to lead the regiment of Rough Riders alongside him and who in short order would become governor of Cuba.[2]

The men of the Rough Riders were all different sorts: miners and actors, attorneys and carpenters, lawmen and outlaws. In a story—often repeated, never verified—one fugitive from the law found himself volunteering before the very officer who had been hot on his trail. Expecting to be arrested, he was instead pardoned on the spot: "I didn't come for you," said the marshal. "I'm here to fight under Roosevelt same as you are. . . . I haven't any enemies now but Spaniards." The Rough Riders came from across the country. Some were friends and acquaintances of Roosevelt's from Harvard and Manhattan—among them a champion yachtsman, a famous steeplechase rider, and more than one veteran of Harvard football. Other volunteers were immigrants from East Coast cities—Irish and Polish Catholics and Eastern European Jews.[3]

The majority of the Rough Riders, however, were young men from New Mexico, Arizona, Oklahoma, and so-called Indian Territories, none of them states at the time. Many were "Hispanos." They were not immigrants, but rather descendants of Spaniards who had colonized the region centuries earlier, long before it became US territory. New Mexico governor Miguel Otero reported that they were eager to go to war on behalf of Cuba and the United States, and that their bilingualism might prove a boon for US troops. Among the Hispanos was the captain of Troop F, Maximiliano Luna—an insurance agent, former sheriff, and Republican member of New Mexico's legislature. Luna's "people," wrote Roosevelt, "had been on the Rio Grande before my forefathers came to the mouth of the Hudson or [Leonard] Wood's landed at Plymouth."[4]

The Rough Riders trained in the dusty Southwest. They sported new khaki uniforms, cooler than the traditional wool, and they brandished machetes just like the ones carried by Cuban insurgents (conveniently manufactured in Hartford, Connecticut). They boarded trains adorned with large banners calling everyone to "Remember the *Maine*" and headed to San Antonio. The city boasted a major fort and an arsenal, was surrounded by horse country, and sat close to the ports of the Gulf of Mexico. San Antonio was also home to the Alamo, which provided an uncanny congruence. Remember the Alamo was now Remember the *Maine*. Texas was now part of the United States; might Cuba soon be as well? As the volunteers waited to leave San Antonio for war, the parallels surely resonated.

A WAR RENAMED

FOR MANY OF THE ROUGH Riders, the war represented an opportunity—a chance to show their worth as men and as Americans. Captain Luna of Troop F insisted on serving to "prove that his people were as loyal Americans as any others." Whether immigrants, Hispanos, Anglo cowboys, or Harvard poets, enthusiasm for the war and eagerness to volunteer for the fight was proof positive of their worthiness as representatives of US military and moral power. Whatever their origins, the Rough Riders shared some version of that conviction.[5]

African Americans, however, were barred from joining Roosevelt's troops. They served in the war, anyway, and in large numbers—as volunteers in the "immune regiments" (volunteer units composed of men falsely believed to be immune to tropical disease) and as members of one of four Black regiments of the US army. Whether they served as professional soldiers or volunteers, many believed that the war was an opportunity to prove their merit as men and as Americans. For them, however, that reasoning resulted from a history very different than that of new immigrants or longtime residents of the American Southwest. In the immediate aftermath of the Civil War, Reconstruction in the South had promised to deliver the profoundest transformations. Across the former Confederate states, new constitutions extended equal rights and protections to all citizens without distinction of color. The conventions that drafted the new state constitutions included dozens of Black delegates, and the constitutions themselves passed because former slaves and other men of color exercised the right to vote. The Fourteenth Amendment to the US Constitution, ratified in 1868, enshrined those gains in the fundamental law of the land, declaring that all native-born people were full citizens of the United States. It was these changes that gave Reconstruction revolutionary import.

Yet—as Cubans were just about to find out—no revolution escapes the perils by which the past encroaches on the future. In the years leading up to US intervention in Cuba in 1898, a violent reversal of Reconstruction had unfolded across the US South. New state constitutions curtailed rights secured by African Americans, and successive restrictions on the exercise of the franchise by citizens of color decimated voting rolls. In Louisiana, for instance, there were almost 130,000 Black voters in the 1880s, but the provisions of a new state constitution in 1898 shrank that number to just over 5,300 by 1900. This story of disenfranchisement was accompanied by another one, more (or differently) brutal: lynching, the ritualized and extrajudicial executions often performed before approving white crowds.[6]

It was in this context that Black men considered their position on the war of 1898. Many were eager to serve and exercise what they saw as a sacred duty of citizenship in order to secure its equally sacred rights and guarantees. Yet from the start, the mobilization of Black troops for the war in Cuba highlighted the limits of Black citizenship in turn-of-the-century United States. In 1898, there were four Black units in the regular army, all (despite the grumbling of soldiers) under the command of white officers. Veterans of wars against Native Americans and cattle rustlers, African American troops were popularly known as Buffalo Soldiers. In spring 1898, just as the Rough Riders did, they boarded trains headed for Tampa. As they crossed the Great Plains, people cheered them. Black soldiers pulled off buttons from their uniforms and tossed them to the crowd as souvenirs. But as the trains entered the South, the mood changed, and the stares of the crowd grew hostile.[7]

Tampa, the point of embarkation for US forces headed to Cuba, was home to a vibrant, politically active, and multiracial community of Cubans, many of them cigar workers. Cuban revolutionary clubs there had routinely hosted Martí and raised funds for the independence struggle. But Tampa was also a southern city, and since 1885, it had been subject to Florida's segregation laws. In Ybor City, the neighborhood where most Cuban émigrés lived and worked, Cubans had managed to resist the strict dichotomies of Jim Crow. Now the sudden presence of American troops—white and Black—strained an already fragile arrangement. White soldiers insulted local Afro-Cubans. African American soldiers pitched their tents as instructed, but white residents in the area balked at their presence and its challenge to segregation. When Black men tried visiting saloons and stores, shopkeepers chased them out. Then, the night before the troops were to embark for Cuba, violence erupted. A group of drunken white volunteers from Ohio used a two-year-old Black child as target practice. They grabbed him from his mother and bounced him around while the men tried to get their shots as close to the boy as possible without hitting him. They took turns holding back the screaming mother. The man who won the perverse game managed to skim the boy's shirt without drawing blood. When African American soldiers heard about it, they set out to punish the offenders. In the confrontations that followed, at least twenty-seven Black soldiers and three white ones were seriously wounded. Local reports said the streets of Tampa "ran red with Negro blood."[8]

Chaplain George Prioleau, born to enslaved parents in Charleston, witnessed all this and publicly raised questions that many other African Americans were already asking. He wrote, "You talk about freedom, liberty . . . about fighting and freeing poor Cuba and of Spain's brutality. . . . Is America any better than Spain? Has she not subjects in her very midst who are murdered daily without trial of judge or jury?"[9] Other African Americans predicted that their service in the war would never result in full citizenship at home. Indeed, some worried that the intervention of the United States in Cuba, rather than advancing the cause of African Americans, could serve instead to spread Jim Crow segregation and racial violence to Cuba.[10]

Soon after after the Tampa melée, the troops embarked for Cuba. In one way, the outcome of the war was already certain. No one expected Spain to win. But other mysteries loomed large. What would happen when an ever more rigid racial system in the United States encountered in Cuba a popular multiracial mobilization that had consciously challenged racial injustice? And, bluntly, as José Martí had asked a few years earlier, once the Americans arrived, would anyone be able to make them leave?

ON JUNE 22, 1898, AMERICAN forces landed on the beaches of Daiquirí, located between Santiago and Guantánamo. With the arrival of those men, Cuba's War of Independence became new again. If most observers were already predicting a Spanish defeat, the US declaration of war against Spain permitted everyone the luxury of forecasting that that defeat was now certainly only a matter of extremely little time.

This newfound certitude changed the Cuban War of Independence and the Cuban army that waged it. Since February 1895 (and before that during the Ten Years' War and the Little War), the struggle for independence had been waged by a profoundly diverse fighting force: former slaves and former masters, peasants and lawyers, workers and doctors. Perhaps some 40 percent of the commissioned officers in the Liberation Army were men of color. Among rank-and-file soldiers and noncommissioned officers, the number—though unknown—was surely much higher. In fact, the bulk of Cuba's Liberation Army was composed of humble men—"rustic men" and "sons of the people," to quote the Black general Quintín Bandera.[11]

In spring of 1898, the arrival of US forces and the imminence of Spain's defeat produced streams of very different recruits to the Cuban army. An avalanche was what one observer called the wave of new enlistments. So many men joined the Liberation Army in the eleventh hour that old insurgents invented nicknames for them. In Pinar del Río, they were known as the blockaded ones (because they joined only after the US naval blockade); in Santiago, as the reluctant ones (because they volunteered so late); in Camagüey, as the burnt-tails (because they had to have fires lit under them to join). In several other parts of the island, they earned the cleverest nickname of all: the sunflowers, because they turned always to where the sun was shining. It was not their numbers, however, that changed the army. It was their origins. Of all the rural workers who joined the Cuban Liberation Army, a majority joined *before* the sinking of the *Maine*. Yet among recruits with more elite professions, more joined *after* that date. The new recruits were "sons of distinguished families," "decently dressed and well equipped," said longer-standing insurgents. A good number arrived from exile in the United States. Many were professionals; they spoke English; some were even naturalized US citizens.[12]

That this avalanche of new recruits materialized at the end of the war gave it a significance even beyond its numbers. Over thirty years of independence struggle, the rebel army had eroded social distinctions. Black men marched alongside—and also ahead of—white ones. But with peace at hand and with the most vocal advocates of that vision—Martí and Maceo—gone, the prospect of continuing to level social hierarchies took on different implications. In February 1898, Máximo Gómez, as commander of the entire rebel army, asked his principal officers to recommend people for promotions to commissioned ranks. With his request, he issued a warning: make the recommendations with the most diligent scrutiny, "so as not to find ourselves surrounded later by officers with whom we would have no idea what to do." Calixto García, commander of the rebel army in eastern Cuba, agreed. Only men deemed honorable and civilized deserved to end the war in positions of power. In confidence, he stressed to another colleague that Cuban leaders would "have to find new men soon for certain positions in which we cannot retain those currently in place." His conclusion was akin to a wink: "You, as a professional man, a cultured man" will surely understand.[13]

Across the island, old-timers witnessed the sudden appearance of new commanders. One young man by the last name of Figueredo arrived from exile and was promoted to first lieutenant in August 1898, after only three months in the army. Like him, there were many others: men who arrived almost at the end of the war, said one observer, "to take all the glory for themselves." Ricardo Batrell, a Black sugar worker from Matanzas who had joined during the insurgent invasion of western Cuba, called the latecomers "false stars"; they "falsified the history of the Liberation Army."[14]

To soldiers like Batrell, who had been in the war for years, the last-minute promotion of newcomers began to feel more and more like their own displacement. Take the case of Silverio Sánchez Figueras, a Black veteran of the first two independence wars. Shortly after Maceo's death, Sánchez began a long process of petitioning the rebel government for formal recognition of the promotions granted to him by Maceo, as well as for the concession of a new promotion he thought he amply deserved. After several requests were denied (or ignored), he wrote to the rebel government's secretary of war about "something observed, of much murmuring about the existence of privileged races to whom ranks are given without merit." Other Black officers were demoted outright. In March 1898, Martín Duen, a man "dark as ebony," a cook before the war and commander of a regiment in Matanzas, lost his post to the son of a distinguished local family. Duen continued to serve dutifully until the formal end of hostilities, but, in spirit at least, the real war had ended for him when he was stripped of his command. The last entry in his war diary is a transcription of the letter from his former superior asking him for "patriotism and subordination" in accepting his demotion.[15] If war had mobilized humble people, imminent peace seemed to require their relegation.

In the final months of war, then, two processes converged. Independence leaders, focused on the question of who would end the war in positions of power, began promoting particular kinds of men—not so humble and not so rustic. At the same time, US intervention produced a new pool of fresh recruits—a pool with a relatively high selection of the kinds of urban, educated men who now seemed so desirable to anxious white leaders thinking about the exercise of political power in peacetime.

CUBAN LEADERS—AND THEIR FOLLOWERS—had other, very momentous things to worry about, as well. Namely, the United States. Initial suspicions about US motives had subsided somewhat with the passage of the Teller Amendment to the joint resolution authorizing war against Spain. The amendment disavowed any US intention to exercise sovereignty over Cuba and claimed to recognize that such sovereignty resided only in the Cuban people. Still, when the United States defeated Spain in July, people wondered what would happen with all those American troops in Cuba. Indeed, even after Spain conceded defeat, American servicemen kept arriving. Cubans watched attentively. And they read every action and every statement as a sign: the flying of an American flag instead of a Cuban one; a US official's literal erasure of the seal of the Republic of Cuba on stationery. Calixto García furrowed his scarred forehead and explained, "We are in a tremendous haze, with the bleakest of futures, because of our complete lack of knowledge about the plans of the American government regarding this country." Amidst all the uncertainty, Cuban leaders were sure of one thing: that the US government had granted to itself the power to decide Cuba's destiny. "We are," said Máximo Gómez, "before a Tribunal, and the Tribunal is formed by the Americans." That fact required that every Cuban guard appearances, remain peaceful, and respect people and property. "Only in this way," Gómez urged, could Cubans "prove to the world that [they had] full right in desiring to be free and independent."[16]

But that assumption took something very important for granted. It presupposed that US leaders—trained for decades to presume that Cubans were unfit for independence—would be willing to change their minds. Some Americans dismissed the idea out of hand: "Self government!" exclaimed General William Shafter, commander of US forces in Cuba and veteran of the Union army in the Civil War. "Why, these people are no more fit for self-government than gunpowder is for hell."[17]

When American troops defeated Spanish ones and occupied the city of Santiago on July 1, 1898, Cuban forces were forbidden from entering the city. Two weeks later, US and Spanish officials met in Santiago to negotiate a preliminary peace agreement. Captain Maximiliano Luna, the bilingual New Mexican Rough Rider, was there to translate. But no Cuban was invited to attend. One insurgent expressed his disappointment with an analogy to US history: "We feel as the patriots under Washington would have felt had [they] captured New York and the French prohibited the entry of the Americans and their flag." To the astonishment of Cuban observers, US officers protected Spanish bureaucrats, granting them authority to remain in their positions. And though it was Spain that lost the war, it was Cuban soldiers—not Spanish ones—who were being asked to lay down their arms. Unable to congregate or celebrate in Santiago or Havana, insurgents found other ways to mark their victory. Some made pilgrimages to the shrine of the Caridad del Cobre, the island's beloved copper virgin, to recognize her in their victory and to ask for her blessing in whatever political future awaited.[18]

On July 17, 1898, Calixto García, as head of the Cuban Liberation Army's eastern division, wrote to the US general in command of the city of Santiago. The letter captures perfectly the dismay and incomprehension felt by many Cubans in the moment of Spain's defeat. It is worth quoting at length:

> The city of Santiago surrendered to the American army, and news of that important event was given to me by persons entirely foreign to your staff. I have not been honored with a single word from yourself informing me about the negotiations for peace or

the terms of the capitulation by the Spaniards. The important ceremony of the surrender of the Spanish army and the taking possession of the city by yourself took place later on, and I only knew of both events by public reports.

I was neither honored, sir, with a kind word from you inviting me or any officer of my staff to represent the Cuban army on that memorable occasion.

A rumor, too absurd to be believed, General, describes the reason of your measure and of the orders forbidding my army to enter Santiago for fear of massacres and revenge against the Spaniards. Allow me, sir, to protest against even the shadow of such an idea. We are not savages ignoring the rules of civilized warfare. We are a poor, ragged army as ragged and poor as was the army of your forefathers in their noble war for independence, but like the heroes of Saratoga and Yorktown, we respect our cause too deeply to disgrace it with barbarism and cowardice.

It is not clear that Shafter bothered to respond to García's complaint. [19]

IN DECEMBER 1898, REPRESENTATIVES OF Spain and the United States met in Paris to sign the treaty that sealed the end of Spanish rule in Cuba. Again, Cubans were denied a seat at the table. The Treaty of Paris granted the United States control of four Spanish territories: Philippines, Guam, Puerto Rico, and Cuba, none of which were represented at the negotiations. By agreement, Spain's rule over all of them would lapse at year's end. [20]

In Cuba, at exactly noon, on January 1, 1899, every Spanish flag came down. The main ceremony was in Havana, at the Morro lighthouse that had guarded the entrance to the city for centuries, succumbing only once in the fateful British siege of 1762. For the second time in history, the Spanish flag over the Morro came down, replaced this time by a new flag—red, white, and blue, with five stripes and forty-five stars. A "distinguished American senator" present for the ceremony pointed to the US flag and quietly voiced a prediction: "That flag will never come down in this Island." Absent that day were the soldiers of the Liberation Army; US authorities had forbidden their presence in the capital city for the formal transfer of power. Also absent was the highest-ranking commander of the Cuban Liberation Army, Máximo Gómez, a sixty-two-year-old father who had lost his son and many of his closest friends fighting for Cuban independence. Gómez refused to attend the flag raising. "Ours is the Cuban flag, the one for which so many tears and so much blood have been shed."[21]

To Gómez and many others, nothing made sense. The decades-long struggle for Cuban independence had ended in the defeat of Spain. But as if by sleight of hand, someone had shifted the ground from under them, switched the very war in which that defeat had happened. The Cuban War of Independence—the third war in thirty years—seemed suddenly irrelevant, supplanted (like the Black officers suddenly demoted in favor of newcomers) by the Spanish-American War. That was the new name for the war, a name in which Cuba deserved not even a mention. In the struggle between Cuba and Spain, then, it was the United States that emerged victorious.

Chapter 14

ISLAND OCCUPIED

As the Spanish government evacuated the island of Cuba after four hundred years of rule, it took its soldiers, its ships, and its papers. The Spanish were prolific record keepers, so there were mountains of documents to transport. When the workers responsible for the move grew tired of going up and down the stairs of the building where the records were stored, they began throwing tied bundles of documents out the windows to carts waiting below. Many landed on the ground, or they fell off the wagons as they drove away. The workers who stayed behind gathered them up. The documents were random, from many periods and many different departments of government. No one could figure out where they belonged. Eventually they became the nucleus of a single collection in the National Archives of the Republic of Cuba, where I first heard this story. The name of the collection—inadvertently born that day in 1899 as the Spanish relocated their record of rule—is Miscellany of Files, an apt title for an assemblage of documents that fit no existing category. Today, its contents are listed in a twenty-eight-tome index typed on thin onionskin paper, which in some volumes has turned to dust, literally.[1]

The story of that mess of papers—the raw material of history—is a fitting metaphor for the profound ambiguity that marked the moment. After thirty years of armed and unarmed struggle for independence, the island was no longer Spanish. But what was Cuba besides that? For decades, a statue of Spain's Queen Isabel II had stood in Havana's Central Park. But times were new now, and Cubans had to determine whose likeness should replace hers. One popular Cuban magazine solicited opinions from its readers. The photograph on that issue's cover said it all: an empty pedestal topped by a question mark.[2]

CUBA

PART OF WHAT MADE EVERYTHING so uncertain was the presence of a US military government of occupation. Before intervening, the United States had publicly disavowed any intention of exercising sovereignty over Cuba. It had promised that pacification would be followed immediately by the withdrawal of US forces and the establishment of a fully sovereign Republic of Cuba, with its own constitution and elected government. It was, however, the US military government that would decide when the island was pacified enough to end the occupation.

For the moment, then, the United States ruled Cuba. American officials issued military and civil orders that functioned as the law of the land. They wrote Cuban budgets; they appointed mayors and department secretaries. They established asylums for the *reconcentrados*, as well as for widows and orphans of the war. To rid the island of yellow fever, Americans worked with Cuban doctor Carlos Finlay, the first person to discover that the disease was transmitted by mosquitos. To feed the hungry and begin reconstruction, they required people to clean streets and build roads and paid them in rations. The aftermath of a destructive war came with heavy labor.

However important that work, the United States saw a different task as the key to pacification: figuring out what to do with the Liberation Army. It consisted of about fifty thousand men—armed and now mostly unemployed (because the countryside had been so thoroughly devastated by war). In the Philippines, also acquired by the United States in 1898, the US occupation was facing a major

SPECIAL COMMISSIONER ROBERT P. PORTER ARRANGING WITH GENERAL GOMEZ AT REMEDIOS FOR THE DISBANDMENT OF THE CUBAN ARMY—Drawn from Life by T. Dart Walker

The US military government of occupation prioritized disbanding Cuba's Liberation Army, a popular, multiracial fighting force of about fifty thousand men. General Máximo Gómez, head of that army, is shown here seated at the edge of his chair, discussing the disbandment with American authorities.

rebellion by the Philippine forces that had been fighting for independence from Spain. To avoid the hint of anything similar in Cuba, the Americans were eager to disband and disarm Cuba's once-rebel army.

The dissolution of the Cuban Liberation Army took three months, ending in late summer 1899. Cuban soldiers reported to authorities, gave their names and ranks for the roster, and surrendered their weapons (to Cuban mayors, because they refused to hand them over to Americans). In exchange, the soldiers received seventy-five dollars to return to homes and farms that often no longer existed, to a countryside wild and untended. In place of the popular, multiracial army that had fought for independence, the occupation government eventually created the Rural Guard, charged primarily with protecting property. US authorities selected its officers from among those they regarded as "the best classes of veterans." Members had to have enough money to purchase their own horses, and, once accepted, they swore allegiance to the US occupation government. The *New York Times* noted how well dressed and organized the Rural Guard was, how different from the "motley assemblage" that had composed Cuba's Liberation Army.[3] For the occupation government, that was precisely the point.

With the most urgent relief work completed and the rebel army disbanded, Cuba was arguably pacified. The island, said one Cuban provincial governor and future president, "is ready and able to govern itself."[4] Did this mean that the conditions for withdrawal specified by the Teller Amendment had been met? Did it mean that the Americans would now leave?

Speculation on that question exploded. In the United States, the newly established Anti-Imperialist League called for an end to the occupation. Prominent progressive figures loudly echoed the call: social reformer Jane Addams, socialist Eugene V. Debs, labor leader Samuel Gompers, Black civil rights leader Booker T. Washington. In Cuba itself, rumors that the Americans planned on making their occupation permanent elicited ardent appeals for full and immediate independence. A newly established association of veterans of the Liberation Army wrote directly to President McKinley; Cuban mayors across the island did the same. Then, from November 29 to December 7, 1899, rallies and protest meetings sprang up in Cuban cities; people carried banners emblazoned with mottos such as "Cuba Libre" and "Independence or Death." A US Senate subcommittee visited the island and returned to Washington reporting that "all classes in Cuba ... are looking to the establishment of an independent government, a Cuban Republic." Cuba was pacified, prevailing opinion said. It was time for the US government to make clear its plan to leave.[5]

That did not happen. A year into the occupation, US authorities changed their watchword from pacification to self-government. The Americans would leave not when the island was pacified, said US officials publicly, but when Cubans proved that they were up to the task of governing themselves. No one bothered to specify what would constitute that proof, but everyone understood that the US government would serve as judge.

As 1899 and the century came to a close, a new American governor took command of Cuba: General Leonard Wood, descendant of the *Mayflower* pilgrims, onetime surgeon turned warrior, and recent commander (with Teddy Roosevelt) of the Rough Riders. In 1898, he had won a medal for his participation in the US Army's last battle against Apache leader Geronimo. At forty, Wood was tall and muscular, with skin so fair and hair so blond that some people likened him to a Viking. In his own words, his job was "to prepare the people of Cuba for self-government."[6] And if capacity for self-government was the requisite for US withdrawal, then it was he whom Cubans needed to convince. He was the one who approved all decisions. "Frankly," he reminded them, "this is a *military* occupation."[7]

Wood embraced his new role as if he had been waiting for it all his life. As the highest authority in Cuba, he pursued ambitious policies that targeted everything from culture to politics to the economy. Ultimately, the changes instituted under his rule sought to subordinate Cuban interests and to redefine them for the benefit of the United States. In that way, Wood's policies were often a concrete, tangible manifestation of American dreams of dominion that long predated—and had long sought to delay—Cuban independence.

LET US BEGIN WITH WHAT may seem like the least likely subject of reform for a decorated American general: public schools. Education was one of Wood's cherished projects in Cuba. When he took the reins of government in December 1899, the entire island had just over three hundred public schools. Nine months later, there were more than thirty-three hundred free, mandatory, coeducational schools for children ages six through fourteen. Wood's office received many inquiries from young Americans eager to help staff those schools. All were refused. Instead, occupation authorities hired Cubans and gave them salaries comparable or higher than those of teachers in the United States. Indeed, Wood devoted almost a quarter of the island's budget to public education. He considered the expenditure amply justified. As one contemporary observer noted, "Education will act as a medium, a neutral inoffensive agent which may reach the people by a different power than that of armed control. It will continue to operate even though our presence be withdrawn."[8] New US-designed schools would help "Americanize" the Cuban population by indirect, unobjectionable means. They would function, in other words, as an instrument of soft American power.

A Board of Superintendents of Schools, chaired by an American, decided what topics would be taught and how, when, and for how long. Students learned US history alongside Cuban. They memorized the names of every US president, and they learned English—in theory at least. Particular attention was given to what US educators called moral and civic instruction. To that end, the occupation implemented a program of "school cities." Originally devised for US schools in places with high numbers of immigrant children, the program sought "to teach citizenship by practical means and to raise its quality to the highest standard." Under the school city plan, each school functioned as a model state, governed by a constitution called the "Charter of the School City."[9]

American educators and officials, however, tweaked the program when they took it to Cuba, writing an appendix to the charter specifically for Cuban teachers. It began with a lesson in political philosophy: human beings everywhere possessed a natural tendency toward monarchy. In Spanish America, the lesson continued, those monarchical figures were not kings, but rather "hot-headed orators with machetes and guns." Cuba now had the opportunity to become a democratic republic, but only if it was able to defeat that natural human tendency. That was a challenge of enormous proportions, warned the appendix; "it takes decades for this and centuries for this."[10] Here was the lesson Americans wanted Cubans to learn: independence should never be hurried. The charter appendix made that case to the teachers, and teachers would then convey it to their students. But a charter was just a charter, an appendix just an appendix. Officials knew that it would take much more for teachers, much less students, to internalize that lesson.

Of all the plans devised to accomplish this, the most compelling arose during a meeting between the American superintendent of Cuban schools and a prominent American businessman in Havana. Both were Harvard men, and Harvard was at the heart of their plan. They proposed to send 1,450 Cuban teachers to study there in the summer of 1900. The plan captured everyone's imagination. Wood, with his ambitious plans for Cuban education and himself a Harvard graduate, loved it. Harvard president Charles Eliot shared Wood's enthusiasm. Cuban children were the Cuban citizens of tomorrow, he said, and "how can we work on the Cuban children better than through the Cuban teachers?" The university raised $75,000, an amount that exceeded the estimated cost of the program. Harvard students volunteered their dorm rooms (but emphatically not their beds or linens) for the male teachers; local residents agreed to host the women in their homes. One American observer claimed that when the Cubans learned about the program "such a wave of excitement swept over the island as can only be imagined by those who fully understand the Latin temperament." The "universal cry" among teachers was "We want to go to Harvard!"[11]

They went—1,273 of them. About two-thirds of the teachers were women. That so many women, some as young as fourteen, would travel to a foreign country unchaperoned and in the relatively close company of men had at first seemed inconceivable. Marveling at the fact that parents allowed their daughters to participate, one US official mused that that may have been "the greatest moral victory ever won in any country." The Cuban teachers overran summertime Cambridge. They were everywhere, wearing identification pins featuring both the Cuban and US flags. Shop owners posted all signs in Spanish; a Catholic Club took over rooms named after famous Protestants; a huge banner reading "Cuba Libre!" floated on the white granite façade of University Hall. One observer commented, "I don't know how useful it is, but it's majestic, and you don't inquire into the use of majestic things."[12]

But the American architects of the program had expectations well beyond spectacle. Cuba's school superintendent explained the aims in lofty terms. "I want these Cuban men and women . . . to see Plymouth Rock and Bunker Hill, and to know what these things mean to us, so that when they return to their own country they may tell the story of the great results of republican self government." Ideally, however, they would return to Cuba spreading another message as well: that the attainment of a self-governing republic was a very slow process. Just as the School City Charter had counseled patience, so, too, did the administrators and teachers at Harvard. The university's president explained to his faculty that he expected the Cubans "to see what has come of the steady, slow development of civil, political, social and industrial liberty through eight generations of men. . . . [Americans] have been patient and slow in the development of their own institutions. There is a great lesson here for the Cuban teachers." The professor who taught them US history took the same approach, stressing always "the slowness of development that has characterized the growth of our national institutions." The Cubans cut his class.[13]

Indeed, Cuban teachers routinely displayed their opposition to anything other than absolute and immediate independence. They took the lessons about American exceptionalism and used them to make their own case. "We Cubans feel profound gratitude for Americans, and our gratitude will be much greater the day our Cuba is independent," wrote one teacher. "Upon seeing this great and powerful people and on remembering what they did for my country, I feel love; and I trust that they will keep their honored word—Cuba for the Cubans, free and independent," wrote another.[14]

Whatever the Cuban teachers learned at Harvard, they rejected the lesson American officials most wanted them to accept. They would not serve as conduits for a message that told Cubans to wait indefinitely for independence. For that and other reasons, the project of using education as a subtle, indirect means to Americanize Cubans—and to convince them to forestall immediate independence—failed.

WHILE EDUCATION MAY HAVE BEEN Wood's pet project in Cuba, he devoted considerable and sustained attention to economic policy. Changes in that arena proved easier to implant, and their very real effects remained palpable long after Wood was gone. Plainly put, the economic policies of the US occupation put obstacles in the way of the Cubans' ability to recover financially from the war, while removing obstacles to US investment.

The independence war of 1895–98 had devastated the Cuban countryside. Of approximately 1,100 sugar mills operating on the island in 1894, only 207 had survived the war. Almost everywhere, agriculture had suffered. Crops were burned, machinery destroyed, livestock killed or lost. Cubans asked US occupation officials to provide credit to farmers trying to restore or establish farms. Doing so would help rebuild the countryside and provide employment to members of the recently disbanded Liberation Army. Despite those appeals, the occupation government refused to grant credit—a clear sign that a landscape dotted with modest Cuban-owned farms was not what the US government envisioned in the island's future.[15] US officials also rejected Cuban proposals to expel Spaniards or expropriate their land, as had been done in the United States with British loyalists after the American Revolution. Finally, the treaty that ended the Spanish-American War established a US-Spanish Treaty Claims Commission, charged with compensating owners for damages incurred during the independence war. But only US citizens were eligible to file claims. Cuban owners would have no such recourse. Together, those policies stacked the deck against Cuban landowners, particularly those without significant resources.

At the same time, Governor Wood facilitated the acquisition of Cuban land by American investors. In 1899, the occupation authorities in Cuba had declared a temporary moratorium on the collection of debt, thereby protecting people from losing their land in the immediate postwar period. But in 1901, Wood lifted the moratorium, allowing creditors to claim mortgaged properties if outstanding debts were not paid. Because of the destruction wrought by the war, balances on mortgages were often significantly higher than the actual value of the land. In most cases, landowners were unable to pay them. The result was a massive wave of dispossession and bankruptcy. Referring to the effect of his policy on Cuban sugar mill owners, Wood was blunt: "There is no hope of this class of people getting out of the hole."[16]

Other occupation policies had similar effects. Civil Order 62 tackled what US officials referred to as "the mess" of Spanish land titles. By mess they meant the system of large communal landholdings prevalent, in particular, in eastern Cuba. Under that system, individual owners held claims—known as *pesos de posesión*—to a portion of larger communal tracts of land originally granted by Spain, sometimes centuries earlier. But those individual claims did not specify a particular and demarcated piece of property. Instead, they established "a right in the land, to some of it somewhere within the boundaries" of the larger communal tract. Over generations, owners had transferred, sold, and divided the *pesos de posesión*. But the boundaries of the large communal land grant never changed, only the percentage of it that corresponded to any given person. The land was never surveyed, and boundaries were measured by things like the distance traveled by the sound of a conch shell horn. When American officials tried to understand and describe it, they spoke of chaos and confusion. Still, they understood enough to know that such a system stood in the way of the kind of development they wanted for Cuba.[17]

A Cuban commission established to study the communal lands informed US occupation officials that this system was the bedrock of agrarian society in parts of the island. For three or four generations, people had been distributing their titles among themselves, and for many, that access to land was all that guaranteed "the decorous support of a family." The commission cautioned against implementing any policy that would destroy those long-held claims without "distribution of the soil among the cultivators."[18]

American officials ignored the recommendation and issued Civil Order 62 instead. The order allowed people to hire lawyers and land surveyors to determine the boundaries of a tract of communal land. Officials then examined all the individual claims held for portions of that land, determined their legitimacy, and issued new land titles more in keeping with US notions of property. By design, the order made it easy for people with access to lawyers and cash to acquire such land and nearly impossible for Cuban smallholders without that access to retain it. Other things not formally part of the law added to the burdens of existing titleholders. For example, the fact that the war had destroyed so much meant that old titles— no matter how vague or imprecise—did not always exist. In addition to paying surveyors and attorneys, potential buyers often paid off the local officials whose job it was to determine the legitimacy of older claims on communal land. As one manager on a large estate later conceded, the legal proceedings that broke up communal estates were "notoriously crooked—without exception."[19]

Order 62 thus destroyed the island's old land tenure system and created in its place a booming market in Cuban land. It accomplished by other means what the US federal government had been doing for more than a century in North America, as it used land surveys, legislation, and outright violence to create new realms of speculation on former Native, Spanish, and Mexican lands. In Cuba, that feat was accomplished by Civil Order 62, which laid the groundwork for the emergence of modern corporate development in the countryside. Indeed, the character of the land regime that the US occupation helped put in place would endure for decades, until the revolution that came to power with Fidel Castro in 1959 set out to destroy it.

LAUNCHING CUBAN POLITICAL LIFE IN a manner that met US approval was another major focus for the island's occupation government. But unlike the economic and land policies, the debates over Cuba's political future generated impassioned debate in both the United States and Cuba.

One of the first tasks Governor Wood had to address in this regard was determining the character of elections. The first elections in post-Spanish Cuba were slated for June 1900 to elect municipal authorities. The US government in Cuba thus needed to decide essential questions: Who had the right to vote? Who could run for office? Wood wanted a limited franchise available only to men who could prove either property ownership or literacy. But Cubans balked. They pointed out that Wood's system would deny the vote to tens of thousands of men who had fought for independence from Spain. That may well have been Wood's intention, but Cuban pressure forced him to compromise. The electoral law of April 1900 granted the vote to men over the age of twenty-one who met one of three conditions: $250 in property, literacy, or service in the Cuban Liberation Army.

The first elections were held in June. Had they been marred by violence, the

Americans could have used them as proof that Cubans were not ready for self-government. But, by all accounts, the election was peaceful. The results, however, displeased US officials. Across the island, victories went to what Wood called "the extreme and revolutionary element," by which he meant the most vocal advocates of an immediate US evacuation. Members of the victorious Cuban National Party telegrammed President McKinley, saying they were confidently awaiting his prompt decision to comply with the Teller Amendment and leave Cuba for the Cubans.[20]

A month after the municipal elections, the military government announced elections for delegates to a Constitutional Convention. The framing of a constitution was a pivotal step in the process of founding a new republic. But the initial enthusiasm and relief that greeted the announcement turned into suspicion when the text of the order was published and Cubans read it carefully. American instructions stated that in addition to drafting a constitution, the convention would also adopt it, something that ordinarily would fall to the people of the country. The instructions further stated that the Constitutional Convention would "agree with the Government of the United States upon relations to exist between that Government and the Government of Cuba."[21]

The call was ominous. Cubans had expected that it would be their newly established government—duly elected and sovereign—that would determine the island's relationship to the United States. The new American proposal, if followed, would mean that a small Constitutional Convention, rather than a free and independent government, would decide what relationship Cuba wanted with the United States. It would do so with the US military still occupying the island, and the decision would be given permanent form in the republic's founding constitution. Again Cubans mobilized. Political parties organized protest rallies; citizens sent telegrams to McKinley. The seventy-two-year-old Salvador Cisneros Betancourt, a veteran of the Ten Years' War and the War of Independence, published an impassioned appeal to the American people on behalf of Cuba. It made no sense, he said, to ask the Constitutional Convention to consider the question of US-Cuban relations. That was not a constitutional question. The decision regarding what relations to pursue with the United States would be determined by the government of Cuba, once it was elected and established. In fact, he believed that the US occupation of Cuba needed to end before the Constitutional Convention.[22]

As with voting requirements, the US government saw itself bound to revise its initial plan. The convention would draft and adopt the constitution, and once that process was complete, as a separate issue, it would give an opinion on US–Cuban relations. Viewing this concession as a setback and worried about the defeat of his favored candidates at the polls, Wood decided to travel across the island before the election of the delegates to the Constitutional Convention. Everywhere he went, he made not-so-subtle threats. If Cubans elected "a lot of political jumping jacks as delegates they must not expect their work will be received very seriously." What he meant by not having that work taken seriously was clarified in a separate warning: "Bear in mind that no Constitution which does not provide a stable government will be accepted by the United States."[23] There it was, laid bare. The Cubans would soon meet to frame a constitution, but its adoption could not happen without the approval of the US government. And without that adoption and approval, the US military occupation of Cuba would not end.

Wood's admonitions notwithstanding, the election for the members of the convention resulted in the victory of the most fervent "independence now" factions. In Wood's words, voters elected "some of the worst agitators and political rascals in Cuba." Among them, he said, were "about ten absolutely first class men and about fifteen men of doubtful qualifications and about six of the worst rascals and fakirs in Cuba."[24]

THE CONSTITUTIONAL CONVENTION BEGAN ITS deliberations on November 5, 1900. Wood opened the proceedings, wished its members well, and left. Over almost three months, the delegates considered the questions one would expect— the boundaries of national territory, the structure of government, the rights of citizens. In the end, they produced a document, similar in many respects to the US Constitution, though the Cuban one, unlike the American, included universal manhood suffrage from the beginning.

Wood, who always questioned Cubans' capacity for self-government, was uncharacteristically impressed by the constitution. "I do not fully agree with the wisdom of some of the provisions of this constitution," he wrote, "but it provides for a republican form of government; it was adopted after long and patient consideration and discussion; it represents the views of the delegates elected by the people of Cuba; and it contains no features which would justify the assertion that a government organized under it will not be one to which the United States may properly transfer the obligations for the protection of life and property."[25]

Wood wrote that in Havana, but it was not what power holders in Washington wanted to hear. In fact, Senator Orville Platt, who chaired that body's Committee on Relations with Cuba, had been working behind the scenes to prevent a straightforward adoption of a Cuban Constitution. His rationale was simple: Cubans owed their independence to the United States. Gratitude was in order. And it was up to the United States to decide what form that gratitude would take. He wrote:

> [T]his nation secured freedom for Cuba....That fact gives the United States certain rights and privileges in Cuba....For instance, Congress may, I think, declare upon what terms and conditions military occupation of Cuba shall cease, and in doing that might express its opinion as to what necessary guarantees of our future relations should be embodied in its Constitution.[26]

He referred to the Cuban Constitution, not the American one. And Platt wanted the new constitution to grant the United States the right of intervention in Cuba and the cession of land for an American naval base.

Wood had been in Cuba long enough to predict the Cubans' response to such proposals. Rather than call the convention members into his office to tell them, he invited them to accompany him on a crocodile hunting trip. He gave them the news of the US position on a train headed into the great swamp just west of the Bay of Pigs. One can easily imagine the distress and disbelief on the faces of the delegates as they heard Platt's conditions. The worst was confirmed when they received the US proposals in writing on the very day that the delegates of the convention signed the constitution, dampening what might otherwise have been a more celebratory occasion. The old Salvador Cisneros Betancourt refused to agree to anything proposed by the Americans. In fact, he objected even to sending a copy of the constitution to Washington. "Cuba is now independent," he insisted, "and I can see no reason for sending this Constitution to the United States for acceptance. The United States government has no right to pass upon it."[27]

The Cuban delegates rejected Platt's conditions and submitted their own counterproposals. Nowhere among them was the right of the United States to intervene in Cuba. They did, however, state that Cuba would never allow its territory to be used for operations against the United States or any foreign power, a proposal that in theory should have allayed American concerns, had they really been primarily about a third country using Cuba against them.[28]

Whatever care Cuban delegates put into framing their proposal, the US government simply ignored them. Just days later, on February 25, 1901, Senator Platt introduced a resolution as an amendment to the army appropriations bill. Known as the Platt Amendment, it looked to history and completely rewrote it. It stated, incorrectly, that the joint resolution that had authorized war in 1898 obligated the United States to leave Cuba only after the Cubans established a government under a constitution that explicitly defined "the future relations of the United States with Cuba." The joint resolution, however, said no such thing. Instead, it had promised to leave Cuba to the Cubans once the island was pacified. Over three years of occupation, US officials transformed that original benchmark into a new and more nebulous requirement that Cubans prove their capacity for self-government. Now Washington was converting that threshold into a much clearer one: Cuban capacity for self-government could be proven only through acceptance of the Platt Amendment.

And what did the amendment establish? Not outright colonialism, but something close to it—an American prerogative to exercise permanent, indirect rule in Cuba. Among other things, the eight articles of the Platt Amendment limited the Cuban government's ability to sign treaties with third nations or to incur debt on its own. It set aside Cuban territory for American use as naval bases and coaling stations. The third article, the one Cubans most despised, gave the United States the right to intervene militarily in Cuba, uninvited.

The Cubans were incredulous, and furious. In Havana and across the island, they organized protest rallies and torchlight processions. Almost with one voice, Cubans spoke out forcefully against the Platt Amendment. The response among the convention delegates was the same: dismay and indignation. The most forceful statement came from delegate Juan Gualberto Gómez, born in 1854 to enslaved parents who had purchased his freedom right before his birth. In the 1880s and 1890s, Gómez had been a journalist and close associate of José Martí, as well as a prominent activist for Cuban independence and Black civil rights. Now as a member of the Constitutional Convention, Gómez penned a long treatise repudiating the assumptions and claims of the Platt Amendment. He devoted particular attention to Article 3, which granted the United States the right of intervention under multiple guises: to preserve Cuban independence; to maintain an orderly government; to protect life, liberty, and property. Gómez discredited each of those justifications. To preserve Cuban independence? Surely the Cubans were more interested in that than the Americans. "For Americans to reserve the right to determine when independence was under threat and thereby when they should intervene to protect it, is to give them the keys to our house." Similarly, granting the United States the right to intervene for the purpose of maintaining an orderly government would give Washington control of the country's internal political life. By what logic, he asked, should the Americans have a greater right to determine when a Cuban government was adequate than Cubans themselves did? Regarding US intervention for the sake of the protection of life and property, that was unnecessary, said Gómez, as that is the first duty of every government. If the ultimate power of that protection fell to the United States, the Cuban government, by definition, would be born impotent, a government in name only, in a republic that would not deserve that title.[29]

The convention as a whole adopted the same position. A vote on April 6 rejected the Platt Amendment 24 to 2. A group of convention delegates traveled to Washington to meet with McKinley and US secretary of war Elihu Root. Root presented a revisionist history, in which the United States had always championed Cuban independence—even though since the 1820s, the United States had pursued policies specifically designed to ensure that Cuba remained Spanish until such a time as the US could make it American. Root insisted that the Platt Amendment was merely an updating of the Monroe Doctrine of 1823, as if this would serve as consolation to the Cubans. The situation was becoming increasingly clear: either the Cubans accepted the Platt Amendment, or they accepted the continuation of US military rule. In fact, the Americans said so explicitly. Root told Wood to make the Cubans see that "they never can have any further government in Cuba, except the intervening Government of the United States, until they have acted." And by acted, he meant accepted the Platt Amendment.[30]

On June 12, 1901, seeing no other plausible option, the convention delegates voted 16 to 11 to accept the Platt Amendment and incorporate it into the Constitution of the Republic of Cuba as an appendix. Among those who voted against it were Juan Gualberto Gómez, author of the recent treatise, and the venerable Salvador Cisneros Betancourt. Some who voted in favor explained that they had done so because it was the only way to establish a Cuban republic, the only way to put an end to the US military occupation. But everyone surely remembered the recent words of Juan Gualberto Gómez, who had argued that under the Platt Amendment, the island "would only have a fiction of a government." Even Leonard Wood essentially admitted the same thing when he wrote to Teddy Roosevelt on October 28, 1901: "There is, of course, little or no real independence left Cuba under the Platt Amendment."[31] Ultimate power, ultimate sovereignty would rest with the US government.

ISLAND OCCUPIED

HOWEVER MUCH CUBANS RESENTED THE Platt Amendment—and most resented it deeply—there is a way in which it signified a partial failure of US designs for Cuba. Wood's early conviction—that Cuba could be ruled subtly and indirectly through the influence of Americanized "better classes"—had proved unfeasible. Those people had not won at the polls. Instead, Cuban men—including many members of the now-defunct Liberation Army—had consistently elected candidates who sought an end to US occupation and the establishment of a sovereign republic. Cuban teachers, who Wood hoped would mold a new generation of pliant, pro-American citizens, refused to play that role. To the dismay of Washington, a majority of Cubans had preferred to press for full and immediate independence. In that context, the Platt Amendment was a guarantee—an effective and portentous one—that the new Cuban Republic would pursue policies not at odds with US interests. The instrument of the guarantee was the US military, now authorized to occupy and govern Cuba should Washington deem that necessary. It was only with that right established that the United States was ready to leave Cuba to the Cubans—more or less.

After Cuba became independent in 1902, the United States exerted considerably economic, cultural, and political influence on the island. In the 1920s, the Cuban capital of Havana was receiving about ninety thousand American tourists a year and importing almost five thousand American cars. A group poses in a Studebaker in front of the majestic Presidential Palace, built in 1920 and today the site of the Museum of the Revolution.

Part VI

STRANGE REPUBLIC

Chapter 15

EMPIRE OF SUGAR

At five minutes before noon on May 20, 1902, in the old Spanish Palace of the Captains-General, Leonard Wood entered the great hall from the left, and the new president of Cuba, Tomás Estrada Palma, entered from the right. They met in the middle, shook hands, and Wood relinquished the reins of government to Estrada Palma. Cuba had a president, and he was Cuban.[1] Born under the sign of the Platt Amendment, the new Cuban Republic was not what most Cubans had envisioned during their struggle for independence. But it was the only republic they had. So they celebrated. Crowds thronged the newly inaugurated Malecón, Havana's now iconic seawall and promenade, to watch the raising of the Cuban flag over the Morro. Temporary arches on prominent street corners had pictures of Maceo and Martí and of women representing liberty and Cuba. There were banquets and poetry readings, and when evening descended, people gathered to watch fireworks. Amidst the fanfare, people may have walked home that night confident, buoyant. Maybe their strangely born republic would thrive. After the

Tomás Estrada Palma and his cabinet in 1902 in the old Palace of the Captains-General. The photograph, in stereograph format, gave viewers using a stereoscope the impression of "entering" the meeting.

parties ended, as citizens of the new republic settled into life after the evacuation of the US occupation government, the ground felt at once solid and shifting. They had arrived at the other side of a line, at the boundary of a new era. Independence. Would it be theirs to build?

THE NEW GOVERNMENT GOT TO work as if there was no question that it was. President Tomás Estrada Palma was almost seventy, the former president of the Cuban Republic in Arms, close collaborator of José Martí in New York, a converted Quaker, and a onetime naturalized citizen of the United States. The Congress, full of leading veterans of the war just ended, prepared to legislate. All the lawmakers were men; several were Afro-Cuban. One of the first and most important matters to come before the new Cuban government was determining its commercial relationship with the United States. The Platt Amendment, which had codified the political relationship between the two countries, was nonnegotiable. But, encouraged by occupation officials, Cuban statesmen believed that their acceptance of the Platt Amendment entitled them to some concessions from the United States in other areas. The concession they most wanted was preferential access to the largest economy in the world.

The result of those efforts was a treaty of commercial reciprocity, signed in Havana in 1902 and ratified by both countries in 1903. The treaty cut tariffs on US products entering Cuba and reduced by a hefty 20 percent the tariffs on Cuban sugar entering the United States. At the time, Cuban leaders saw it as a major victory: they had just nudged their way into a much larger share of the rapidly expanding US market for sugar. In 1899, the average American consumed 63 pounds of sugar a year; on the eve of World War I, they were eating 81 pounds each.[2] Now Cuba would supply most of it. With a permanent market guaranteed and with profits set to expand because of the lower tariffs, the Cuban sugar industry seemed poised on the brink of a new prosperity. And with sugar the bedrock of the national economy, that prosperity might be Cuba's, as well. That, anyway, was what members of the new Cuban government hoped.

What their calculations did not fully consider was that the Cuban sugar industry was becoming less Cuban all the time. The policies of the US occupation had made land plentiful and cheap, and US citizens and corporations were the main beneficiaries. Estimates of the proportion of US-owned land varied greatly—anywhere from one-third to one-thirtieth. By 1907, foreigners owned an estimated 60 percent of all rural property in Cuba. Resident Spaniards owned another 15 percent, which left only a quarter of rural property under Cuban ownership. The number is so staggering it bears repeating in slightly different terms: less than a decade after independence, perhaps three-quarters of Cuban territory belonged to foreigners, a significant portion to Americans. In some regions, the proportion was even higher; in the central region of Sancti Spíritus, for instance, Americans owned about seven-eighths of rural land. The direction of things was so very clear that Manuel Sanguily, storied veteran of the wars of independence and among the fiercest critics of the Platt Amendment at the Constitutional Convention, drafted a law for the Cuban Senate's consideration in 1903. Article 1 was unequivocal: "From this date it is strictly forbidden to make any contract or agreement by which property is transferred to foreigners." It never even reached debate. Similar proposals in 1909 and 1919 suffered the same fate.[3]

In some cases, US companies purchased land, divided it up, and sold it as individual parcels to American buyers. They touted the fertility of the soil, the perpetual sun, and the US government's guarantee of property and stable government in Cuba. An outfit in New York purchased 180,000 acres in this manner; a Los Angeles company acquired 150,000; one in Pittsburgh snagged 135,000. The Cuba Land, Loan and Title Guarantee Company of Chicago purchased a huge tract on what had recently been the communal landholding of Majibacoa, a Taíno name. The Chicago firm renamed it after a different Native people, the Omaha of the US Midwest. The company parceled the land and recruited American settlers, giving families free plots of ten acres to entice them to Cuba. In exchange, families were required to build houses, fence the property, pay a ten-dollar tax for an English-language school, provide one day's labor per month on a road to the nearest Cuban town, and plant 2.5 acres in citrus crops in the first year. The new town of Omaja—the *j* in Spanish sounds like the *h* in English—soon resembled a midwestern community in the tropics. It had a Protestant church, Bible study groups, church bake sales, social clubs, and youth dances. By 1903, there were thirty-seven such American "colonies" in Cuba; ten years later there were sixty-four; by 1920, about eighty. La Gloria, the largest of them, had at its height one thousand residents.[4]

Despite the fad of American towns in Cuba, by far the most important result of the rise of US land ownership at the turn of the twentieth century was the sweeping Americanization of the sugar industry. The industry had changed significantly from a century before. Back when US senator James DeWolf owned several Cuban estates, or when Vice President William Rufus King took his oath of office on the peak of a Matanzas plantation, sugar properties combined large tracts of acreage for cane with a mill complex where the raw cane was processed. Beginning in the 1870s, however, advances in technology pushed out mill owners who could not afford to modernize. The destruction of three independence wars eliminated still others. Remaining owners invested in new technology and swallowed up the land of those who had failed. Over the last three decades of the nineteenth century, then, the sugar industry had become increasingly centralized. Of about 2,000 mills in 1860, only 207 remained by 1899. The concentration of land continued after the US occupation, with just 163 mills operating in 1929.[5]

Before independence, modern sugar plantations had been concentrated, for the most part, in western and central Cuba. That changed dramatically under the US occupation. It was in the east that the wars had done the most damage to agriculture. In addition, modern sugar production had not yet penetrated the region. So it was there, in the provinces of Oriente and Camagüey, that most of the new US investment in sugar would focus. Relying on laws enacted by the US occupation, American sugar companies purchased hundreds of thousands of acres of land and transformed them from dense hardwood forests into massive sugar enterprises. Just one of those companies, the United Fruit Company, which came to control vast expanses of land across Central America, the Caribbean, and parts of South America, purchased two hundred thousand acres.[6] It was to these new establishments that most of the profits guaranteed by the 1903 reciprocity treaty would accrue.

THE NEW AMERICAN PROPERTIES WERE enterprises of gargantuan proportions. The center of their operations was the large, modern mill, in Spanish the *central*, in English sometimes the central factory. It was there that workers and machines transformed sugarcane into raw sugar and then into processed sugar. Shiny machines with sometimes strange names—shakers, choppers, crushers, shredders, centrifuges, green-pulp burners, multi-effect evaporators—did the work that enslaved people had done for centuries. The profits were in the processing, so owners strove to acquire a lot of raw sugar at low prices. They rented some of their lands to farmers (*colonos*) to plant and harvest cane, which by contract could be sold only to the mill owners. To work other lands not rented out, the mill owners imported cheap, seasonal labor from Haiti and islands of the British Caribbean. In sugar boom years, up to fifty-eight thousand workers arrived for the season from Haiti and Jamaica. The companies built barracks to house them. In fact, they built whole company towns around the sugar mill. To some observers, these US-owned central factories—with the town and workers' barracks that adjoined them and the vast expanses of cane fields that stretched in all directions—were like foreign kingdoms occupying more and more Cuban territory.[7]

Annual Sugar Production in Bags*

- 700,000-900,000
- 500,000-700,000
- 300,000-500,000

Top-Producing Sugar *Centrales* in Cuba, 1925

1. Delicias	11. Punta Alegre
2. Morón	12. Boston
3. Chaparra	13. Violeta
4. Manatí	14. Francisco
5. Baraguá	15. Jatibonico
6. Cupey	16. Jagüeyal
7. Cunagua	17. Elia
8. Jaronú	18. Florida
9. Preston	19. Gómez Mena
10. Stewart	20. Jobabo

*1 bag = 325 pounds

Of the twenty most productive sugar *centrales* in Cuba in 1925, only one (Gómez Mena) was Cuban. Nineteen were US-owned, all of them in the provinces of Camagüey and Oriente, which were opened to modern sugar production following Cuban independence. The railroad system, built to facilitate the transport of sugar to ports, expanded in the east, as well.

Of all the American mills established in Cuba in the early twentieth century, Chaparra was the largest. It began with Texas Republican congressman Robert Hawley. Hawley was a sugar broker in Galveston, Texas, and the owner of a sugar refinery in Louisiana. In 1899, he joined forces with a group of New York investors and traveled to Cuba in search of profitable opportunities. Hawley's contact in Havana was Mario García Menocal. Some of Menocal's ancestors were part of the titled nobility who had arrived in Cuba in the seventeenth century and received land grants from the Spanish Crown. In the much more recent past, Menocal had studied engineering in the United States. He had served as a general in Cuba's Liberation Army, stationed for much of the war precisely in the areas now being opened to US investment. When Hawley traveled to Cuba in 1899, the "ideally competent and bilingual" Menocal was already working for the US occupation. He had established and headed the Havana police and served briefly as inspector of public works. But Menocal had his sights aimed higher, and in more ways than one.[8]

Menocal convinced the Texas congressman to buy, among other things, an old sugar mill called Chaparra and the sixty-six thousand acres of virgin forest that surrounded it. Located on Cuba's northeastern coast, it was in a region Menocal knew well, having traveled it extensively as an officer in Cuba's Liberation Army. Hawley hired Menocal to survey the land and to oversee the establishment of a new sugar mill there. With Hawley as its president, a capital stock of $1 million, and its headquarters on Wall Street, the Chaparra Sugar Company was incorporated in October 1899.[9]

Near the same stretch of coast that Columbus explored on his first voyage to the New World, the trees came down. Dense forest became immense fields of sugarcane. "Mammoth Sugar Plant to Be Established in Cuba," announced one US newspaper. It was so mammoth that it was "without precedent in the history of Cuba and probably the entire world." This was not the first time an American politician owned sugar property in Cuba, but nothing had ever approached this scale. The enterprise was the largest ever in Cuban history. It boasted the first twelve-roller mill on the island and an initial capacity of two hundred thousand bags (forty thousand tons), or 10 percent of the island's entire sugar crop in 1900. When the company purchased an adjoining mill, Delicias, in 1910 and began running the two as a single unit, the property became the largest sugar estate anywhere in the world.[10] By the 1910s, Chaparra's company town consisted of almost six hundred homes, a combination of modest houses and elegant chalets. It boasted wide avenues, a hotel, as many as ten schools, three movie theaters, a Masonic lodge, a dry cleaner, a dentist, a pharmacy, a post office, a company hospital, even a YMCA. Chaparra issued currency—tokens—that could be used in stores on its property. But with a shortage of Cuban coin, the tokens became the practical equivalent of Cuban tender, routinely used across eastern Cuba and even as far west as Matanzas. Because it imported workers from neighboring islands, Chaparra determined the patterns of migration and the composition of the area's population. Because it rented lands to farmers, it determined what people could plant, where, and when. Chaparra's control, in other words, was felt in ways big and small.[11]

The mill was American, but Mario Menocal ran it as general manager. He chose the site; he oversaw the clearing of the land, designed the mill, and supervised its construction. He named Cubans—many of them fellow or subordinate officers in the Cuban Liberation Army—as heads of various departments in the mill, and he distributed cane farms to them, as well as to each of his six brothers. He also donated a tract of Chaparra land as a permanent station for a unit of Cuba's Rural Guard, created by the US occupation government to protect rural property.[12] A few years later, a Spanish journalist visited the mill and heard rumors of brutal, even fatal punishments meted on workers. But no one would speak openly or with specifics. Staying at Chaparra's hotel overnight, she lay awake listening to someone in the distance singing an unsettling song:

Tumba la caña,	Cut the cane,
Anda ligero;	Step light;
Corre, que viene Menocal	Hurry, here comes Menocal
Sonando el cuero.	Cracking the whip.[13]

As one Cuban historian later wrote, "Each *central* situated in the bowels of our countryside consolidates the entire economic system of its region and dominates it politically and economically. . . . And against them, neither the law nor any protest is practical."[14]

CHAPARRA MAY HAVE BEEN THE largest of the American sugar mills in Cuba, but it was really just one of a piece. In 1905, US-owned mills in Cuba produced about 21 percent of the island's annual sugar crop. The trend accelerated over subsequent decades. By 1926, seventy-five US-owned mills produced 63 percent of the annual Cuban sugar harvest. Together, these mills represented an American sugar kingdom in Cuba. Not surprisingly, then, the largest share of Cuban sugar exported to the United States was produced on US-owned property. The 1903 reciprocity treaty with the United States had guaranteed Cuban sugar producers a major portion of the American market and reduced tariffs on Cuban sugar imported to the United States. Two decades into independence, its impact was crystal clear: the profits of Cuba's principal export accrued overwhelmingly to US companies.[15]

The reciprocity treaty had also reduced tariffs on US products entering Cuba. Cheap goods manufactured in the United States flooded the market, which made it nearly impossible for fledgling Cuban enterprises to compete. Across the island, 357 Cuban-owned manufacturers closed their doors. The reciprocity treaty thus made it difficult for the government to diversify and industrialize the national economy. Because it deterred new industries and made old ones less likely to survive, the treaty sealed the island's dependence on sugar. Monoculture was here to stay.[16]

For some Cubans, the most pragmatic guarantee of economic advancement and opportunity consisted in serving as "junior partners" to American capital. Such partners were everywhere. Take the example of José Lacret. A veteran of the independence wars, he was elected to the Constitutional Convention of 1900. He had supported universal manhood suffrage against American attempts to limit it, and he had also vehemently opposed the Platt Amendment. He called the day of its passage "a day of mourning." Yet by 1902, he was a real estate consultant for Americans interested in investing in Cuba. Advertising in Havana's English-language newspaper, the *Havana Post*, he offered to use his "practical knowledge of the entire island" to assist in "buying and selling farms and plantations, mining properties, native timber, and all kinds of leases."[17]

Increasingly, those who worked with US investors also held positions in Cuban governments. The overseer for a US-owned estate in Puerto Padre in Oriente province served on the town's council; the mayor of Guantánamo worked for twenty-five years at an American mill there; the president of the Cuban House of Representatives and a senator both sat on the board of directors for the New York–based Cuba Cane; another senator was senior counsel for United Fruit in Cuba. In Banes, home to a United Fruit sugar mill, the company paid no taxes, and the town's mayor was also the mill's lawyer. And the ambitious general manager of Chaparra, Mario Menocal—the Menocal of the whip—became president in 1912, not of Chaparra, but of Cuba.[18]

IN THIS LARGE CORNER OF the Cuban countryside, then, American sugar companies were king. They used local allies to subvert or bend the law—to avoid taxes, say, or to punish workers with impunity. But even with Cuban help—with senators on their payroll or presidents on their board—the US companies knew that, ultimately, it was someone else who had their backs. The final arbiters were in Washington, DC. It was to them that US investors could appeal for everything from gunboats to patrol their coasts to carte blanche to import cheap labor. Under the shadow of the Platt Amendment of 1901, their prerogative was guaranteed. Under the Reciprocity Treaty of 1903, so, too, were their profits. Another treaty of 1903 further guaranteed the interests of US landowners in eastern Cuba. The Permanent Treaty of that year gave the United States forty-five square miles of territory stretching up from both sides of a large bay named Guantánamo, home to this day of the US naval base that Washington has long called Gitmo. Rent was a paltry $2,000 a year; no end date was specified. So, now, in addition to everything else—easy access to Cuban land, favorable trade guarantees, the protection of the US-created Rural Guard—American landowners had the US military firmly ensconced, within easy distance. For US investors, this strange Cuban Republic suited just fine.

Chapter 16

CITY OF DREAMS

No country is one thing. In Havana, worlds away from the American sugar mills of eastern Cuba, a girl named Renée Méndez Capote was born with the new century. She was conceived, she later wrote, around the time that a small group of elected men were meeting in Havana to draft a constitution for the soon-to-be Republic of Cuba. Her father presided over the deliberations and became senator in 1902 and Cuba's vice president in 1904. Because her family ran in those circles, as a little girl she knew many of the republic's early politicians. President Tomás Estrada Palma knew her by name. Senate president Manuel Sanguily, independence war veteran and Platt Amendment critic, was familiar enough to tease her for being distracted. He had tea in her company every week at the home of Puerto Rican poet Lola Rodríguez de Tío, a "modern" woman who wore her hair short, always with earrings. Lola allowed little Renée to attend the literary salons she hosted in her home. It was there that Renée saw a virtuoso piano performance by a boy not much older than her, child prodigy Ernesto Lecuona, considered to this day one of Cuba's most accomplished pianists and composers. Conversation at the salons was more frequent than live music, however, and Renée sat quietly and listened as the adults argued about politics and literature and life. Sometimes the hostess would despair about her home island of Puerto Rico, still under direct US rule, and Manuel Sanguily would place his hand on her shoulder in a gesture of solidarity. All this the young Renée watched, absorbing the feeling, the ideas, the comings and goings of singular characters and the excitement of a new century in the booming capital of a new republic.[1]

A new energy—a modern energy—was visible all around her. Across the city, avenues named after kings now bore the names of independence heroes. A new bandstand stood outside the city's oldest Spanish fortress at La Punta. Modern parks began replacing old colonial plazas as favorite haunts of city denizens. An amusement park in the style of Coney Island opened in 1906 and was the subject of the first film ever shot in Cuba. The faces of the young women in white hats sliding down tall, twisty slides glowed with the thrill of things unknown. The Malecón grew in popularity with its wide boulevard for the automobiles then appearing across the city—more than four thousand of them by 1910. New electric streetcars ambled down Havana streets by their own power. Some sixty thousand passengers rode them daily. The most popular trolley line connected Old Havana to El Vedado, once on the capital's outskirts, now a flourishing, desirable neighborhood.[2]

Renée knew the neighborhoods on either side of the streetcar line well for a girl of her class in that age. The salon of her beloved mentor Lola Rodríguez de Tío was in Old Havana, in a house on Aguiar Street. She also visited Old Havana regularly to accompany her mother to an elegant dressmaker's shop on O'Reilly Street, where she first came to appreciate the "treasure of a pretty dress." From there, they went to Old Havana's best ice cream shop. Even with a carriage, they walked and walked, always returning home to Vedado late and tired.[3]

There were other parts of Old Havana a girl like her would have never frequented, prime among them the working-class neighborhood of San Isidro, in the corner of the old city near the port and the old arsenal turned national archives. San Isidro was home to the tolerance zone, a euphemism for the prostitution district. The twelve-block area bustled with vice and with people there to profit from or partake in it. Ancillary businesses grew up around the bordellos: live sex shows, pornographic nickelodeon parlors, music bars, gambling dens. Street vendors hawked their food and wares. Census data recorded more than 700 prostitutes living in 338 brothels in the city. A majority were white and Cuban-born, but there were women of all colors and many nationalities selling their services. The French prostitutes were said to have introduced oral sex to the business in Havana. To compete, Cuban and Spanish ones introduced the option of adding a dog to their service (apparently to lick the client's genitals during the sex act). Havana's prostitution district became famous internationally, as far away as Paris and New York.[4]

The small neighborhood had its king, for that was what everyone called him—King Yarini, whose real name was Alberto Yarini y Ponce de León. His father descended from long-ago Italian immigrants, his mother from an old patrician family of unknown relation to the original seeker of the Fountain of Youth. The family was well-to-do and respected, the men all doctors and dentists. The name of one graces to this day a salon in the city's Calixto García General Hospital. No member of this distinguished family ever understood the vocation of the son everyone called King Yarini.[5]

Yarini ran the neighborhood and much of its sex trade. Nobody knows how many women worked for him while he reigned over San Isidro, but he lived with some of them a block from the street that gave the neighborhood its name. Local lore calls Yarini beloved and charismatic. He was only five foot six in height, but thin, well dressed, handsome, and always perfumed. He walked around the neighborhood with a bodyguard and two purebred Saint Bernards.[6]

He was also a politician, a local ward boss for Cuba's Conservative Party, the very party over which the young Renée's father presided. Some considered Yarini something of a patriotic hero himself. He was too young to have fought in the wars against Spain. But since independence, he had become famous for standing up for Cubans against foreigners. In 1908, sitting at an elegant café on Prado Avenue with friends, he overheard some American men disparaging Cubans for their racial laxness, for the fact that at a place as nice as that café, Blacks and whites could mix so casually. Yarini, who spoke English and who was sitting with a Black general of the War of Independence, took offense. When it was time to leave, he let his friends go ahead and confronted the Americans. How dare they disrespect a hero? The men were unrepentant, and Yarini attacked them physically, breaking the nose of one who turned out to be chargé d'affaires in the US embassy. The Americans pressed charges, but local politicians conveniently made them disappear.[7]

Two years later, Yarini was dead, killed in a violent showdown with a French rival in the sex trade. His funeral was fit for a king. The hearse was drawn by eight plumed horses draped in finery; four wagonloads of flowers and wreaths followed. More than a hundred carriages and a procession of thousands—some say up to ten thousand—marched with the coffin. Among the mourners were high-level politicians, heroes of the independence wars, doctors and lawyers, stevedores, carpenters, musicians, actresses, and, yes, the women who sold sex in San Isidro. Ribbons on the funeral wreaths bore the names of some of them. The wreath from the local party committee he had presided over read "To our unforgettable President, the Conservative Committee of San Isidro."[8]

A hero's sendoff for Yarini angered American observers—not the ones who frequented the neighborhood's bordellos, but observers farther afield. One newspaper in Oklahoma considered Yarini's funeral the height of Cuban arrogance and ingratitude:

American blood was spilled in order that Cuba might be relieved from bondage. Never have the Cuban people appeared sincerely grateful for having been aided by this country in escaping the dominion of a tyrant....As an insult to Americans, the Cuban people the other day made a tremendous demonstration of sympathy and respect at the funeral of Alberto Yarini, notorious leader of the Cuban white slave traders. This villain had been the idol of the Cubanese as the chief exponent of Havana anti-Americanism since his assault on ... [the] charge d'affaires of the United States legation in [1908]. Cuban newspapers laud Yarini as an illustrious patriot.[9]

Among the people attending Yarini's funeral was, quite likely, Domingo Méndez Capote, president of the Conservative Party that Yarini represented and father of the spirited little girl Renée.

RENÉE BELONGED NOT TO THE world of Yarini's San Isidro but to that on the other end of the new streetcar line: El Vedado. Abutting the ocean, not far from where the famed French pirate Jacques de Sores had invaded the city in 1555, the area had been sealed off from development for most of the colonial period—hence its name *vedado*, or forbidden. While some construction began in the late nineteenth century, it did not really take off until independence, when moneyed people began building mansions there, tired of the overcrowding of Old Havana. It soon became home to prominent well-to-do officers of the old Liberation Army, to the aspiring young politicians of the new republic, as well as to American residents of the city.

Unlike the old Havana of narrow streets lined with buildings that came right up to the sidewalk, Vedado was modern. Its layout was ordered and rational, with streets organized as a simple grid. Parallel to the seacoast ran odd-numbered streets; perpendicular to those and running uphill from the Malecón were lettered streets followed by even-numbered ones. Vedado was a garden city with wide, verdant avenues. Trees, as stately as the neighborhood mansions, grew branches that reached down to take root in the ground. A young Dulce María Loynaz, like Renée a would-be writer and the daughter of a general from the independence wars, described the beauty of her new house on 19th and E, surrounded by "a leafy garden filled with begonias, jasmines, rare lilac-hued dahlias, honeysuckles, vines of blue and white and red, and sturdy trees." There were even white peacocks, she said. Renée recalled all the bats and owls. To her, the garden city growing up all around her was marvelous. One day, she woke up and on her block was a tent city of people she called gypsies. They set up shop, and all was frenetic activity. The men shoed horses; the women told fortunes; a bear danced. Then, a few days later, they left and set up shop somewhere else, but she never knew where.[10]

As Renée imbibed Vedado's sense of wonder and possibility, she noticed other things as well—mundane, sometimes troubling things that adults tended to explain away with a one-word answer: politics. She noticed the preponderance of Spaniards, for one. They owned most of the retail shops (with some exceptions, including Chinese storekeepers and Afro-Cuban women dressmakers). She noticed that many policemen were also Spanish. It was an astute observation for a young girl—one borne out by data that would have been unavailable to her. More than four hundred thousand Spaniards immigrated to Cuba between 1902 and 1916. Vanquished in the recent war, Spain became a major source of migrants to the territory it had just lost. Spanish immigrants joined the workforce of almost every expanding sector of the economy. They represented about 90 percent of the island's miners; they displaced Afro-Cubans as servants; they owned about half the cigar factories in the city. In small numbers (twenty), Spaniards even joined the new republican government, where they outnumbered Afro-Cubans, of whom there were only nine. Little wonder, then, that the prominence of Spaniards in post-independence Cuba stood out to young Renée. But her father, a well-heeled conservative politician, would probably not have discussed any of this with her.[11]

If social convention had made it possible for a worker to hold political conversations with an employer's young daughter, one man in her household would surely have raised the issue. The man was Evaristo Estenoz, a master builder who in 1904–05 designed and oversaw the construction of Renée's parents' house and that of their next-door neighbors. Renée remembered Estenoz as an elegant man, with greenish eyes and curly hair. He always dressed in white and wore a Panama hat. He used the long pinky nail on his left hand to tap the ash off the end of his cigar. She described him as "mulatto," because his father was white, his mother Black.[12] In the United States, the one-drop rule would have rendered him Black. But Cuba did not have a one-drop rule.

Estenoz was a veteran of the Liberation Army. Originally from eastern Cuba, he moved to Havana at the end of the war. In 1899, as head of the bricklayers' union, he led the first major workers' strike after Spanish rule and won for the strikers the right to an eight-hour workday. While Estenoz agitated for the rights of workers, he did the same for the rights of Afro-Cubans. During the US occupation, many white Cuban leaders had urged their Black compatriots not to make demands for fear that it would prolong the American presence. With the United States no longer exercising direct rule over Cuba, Estenoz and other Black veterans wanted to enjoy the full rights of citizenship they felt they had amply earned—Afro-Cuban men, after all, had constituted the majority of independence fighters. On May 25, 1902, just five days after the end of the US occupation, they formed an organization of Black veterans. In June, delegations from the group met twice with Cuban president Estrada Palma to make their case for greater representation and guarantees of equality before the law. Estenoz among them, they complained that Black veterans were routinely passed over for state jobs, whether in the federal government or municipal police forces, which were largely white. To create the republic they had all fought for together, Black veterans explained to the president, required guaranteeing the rights of Cubans of color and combatting racial discrimination. Estrada Palma dismissed their entreaties as inconvenient. When the men insisted, he told them that by demanding Black rights, they were being racist.[13]

Estenoz was not deterred. He continued advocating for the rights of Afro-Cubans—writing in newspapers, attending meetings with other Black veterans and activists. He combined his activism with the demands of making a living. He shared a house with his wife in Old Havana, less than a ten-minute walk from where the infamous Alberto Yarini was assassinated. It was there that his wife, Juana, operated a fancy French clothing and hat boutique. The whole time, he worked as a master builder, constructing homes for prominent white veterans in Vedado, homes like that of Renée Méndez Capote's family, which he finished in the spring of 1905.[14]

It was perhaps with the earnings from that job that Estenoz booked passage to New York that summer. He traveled with Martí's old collaborator, the Black politician, educator, and writer Rafael Serra. According to the Black press in the United States, Estenoz made the trip to observe the condition of African Americans. He met with prominent Black businessmen and intellectuals, including the Puerto-Rican born Arthur (Arturo) Schomburg, founder of the Negro Society for Historical Research, of which Estenoz became a corresponding member and which later grew into what is now the New York Public Library's Schomburg Center for Research in Black Culture, located in Harlem.[15]

We know little of Estenoz's 1905 New York trip beyond that. But just a few months after his return to Cuba, Estenoz emerged as one of the leaders in a conspiracy to topple Tomás Estrada Palma, who was standing for election to a second term. It was the first presidential election since the US occupation, and hence the first in the history of the Cuban Republic. While Estrada Palma had been elected to the presidency the first time without a party affiliation, now he ran on the Moderate Party ticket (formerly known as the Conservative Party). His vice president was Domingo Méndez Capote, father of Renée. Against him ran José Miguel Gómez, a veteran of the War of Independence representing the Liberal Party, which was actively and successfully courting the Black vote.

The campaign season was punctuated almost daily with accusations of fraud, corruption, and abuse. Moderate Party leaders fired civil servants, even school-teachers, who were not allied with their party. Two months before the election, 150,000 fictitious names were found on electoral rolls. A leader from the opposing Liberal Party was assassinated in Cienfuegos. In this context, on the eve of an election many believed would be fraudulent, Estenoz participated in a rebellion against the government. Rebels amassed weapons with which to engage the Rural Guard in the countryside near Havana; the police claimed that another group in the city was to assassinate the president himself. They were quickly arrested, and the election proceeded as expected. Tomás Estrada Palma won, but the victory meant little. The Liberals had widely boycotted the elections. Its candidate for president, fearing for his life, had fled to New York weeks before. From there, he called on the United States to intervene under the provisions of the Platt Amendment.[16]

That was the thing Americans were about to learn about the Platt Amendment: with the United States legally obligated to intervene to preserve life and property, opponents and aspirants to power did not necessarily have to defeat sitting governments. If they posed a credible enough threat of trouble, rumors of possible intervention exploded. One US senator had predicted this danger earlier. "Suppose they have an election. One party or the other will be defeated. The party that is out is apt to complain, and with this kind of a provision, it seems to me . . . by making trouble and creating difficulties, they would make a condition that would lead to an intervention of the United States to put the successful party out."[17]

The stirrings of 1905, however, were much more than that. A generation of

Cubans who had fought for and supported independence from Spain were disappointed with the results. The US occupation had been part of that disappointment. But many expected that with the end of US military rule in 1902, the government would fulfill the republic's promise. That had not happened. Instead, Cubans lost property to American buyers and jobs to Spanish immigrants. Afro-Cuban men, who had made up of the bulk of Cuba's Liberation Army, felt the sting of that more deeply than most. They complained that the government for which they had fought passed them over for civil service jobs. All around them, they encountered doors closed to their advancement.

Master builder Evaristo Estenoz, veteran of the Liberation Army and member of the Association of Veterans of Color, was among those willing to call the government to task. Though he was jailed for his participation in the election-eve rebellion, he and his companions were pardoned by Estrada Palma on May 19, 1906, the day before the latter's inauguration as second-term president of Cuba and also the eleventh anniversary of José Martí's death. But Estenoz and other Black veterans were not done with their fight. Soon after their pardon, they joined a new Liberal Party rebellion against the president. The rebels established what they called the Constitutional Army. Filled with veterans of the old Liberation Army, it was up to 80 percent Black, according to some estimates. One of its principal leaders was Quintín Bandera, Black general and veteran of three independence wars, the man who in 1895 along with Antonio Maceo and Máximo Gómez had led Cuban forces during the western invasion, the man whose troops had been rumored to wear nose rings.[18]

Bandera exemplified the disappointment that followed independence for many former revolutionaries. After the war and the US occupation, he was unable to find suitable employment. He lobbied the government for a position, but never received one. His livelihood was so insecure that he sent out form letters soliciting assistance; his friends and associates organized a fundraiser for him in Havana's Payret theater. He once stormed the Senate while it was in session to condemn the treatment against him, a war hero. When he requested the post of Havana police chief, the government offered him that of door attendant in the Senate building. At one point, he distributed soap samples to laundresses. The famous Cuban soap company, Candado, printed his photograph on their advertisements, and under it the words, "I am a son of the people." At one point, necessity forced him to work as a garbage collector. To make a point and to turn his humiliation against his detractors, he collected garbage wearing his general's uniform.[19]

General Quintín Bandera

So, when a new Liberal Party revolt started in August 1906, Bandera took command of one of the rebel units, and master builder Evaristo Estenoz quickly joined him. Despite some successes in the countryside east of Havana, within a week of rising up, Bandera knew the cause was lost. He offered his surrender in exchange for safe passage out of the country. At a farm outside the city, he waited for the government's response. When troops appeared in the middle of the night, he felt confident that his request was being granted and stood up to greet the soldiers. The look on their faces revealed to him that their purpose was otherwise. The seventy-three-year-old Bandera reminded the young soldiers that he had been fighting for Cuba for decades. That did not deter them. On orders of their government, they shot him. Then they attacked him with machetes and shot him some more. His body was unceremoniously tossed in a wagon and brought to the capital. Outside the morgue, in Neptuno Park, a large crowd, mostly Black, gathered and watched in heavy silence. His mutilated body, missing his left ear, was displayed to the public. When his widow appealed for his remains so that she could bury him properly, President Estrada Palma refused. Bandera's crude coffin was placed in a cart usually used to carry coal, without a flag, and without the military honors due his rank. It was then taken to Colón Cemetery and buried in a rudimentary grave. In the 1940s, a monument to him was built in a tiny park in Central Havana. But to this day, the descendants of Quintín Bandera decry his treatment in life, death, and national memory. His house in Havana is today almost a ruin, despite entreaties from his family and from Black activists for the government to do something to preserve it and his memory.[20]

By the time of Bandera's assassination, the Liberal rebellion against the government had spread to every province. Most veterans of the War of Independence were swept up on one side or another. Mario Menocal, the general manager of the Chaparra Sugar Company and a leader of the main veterans' association, tried to intervene and mediate between the president and the rebels, to no avail. And everywhere—especially from land and business owners—were cries for the United States to intervene under Article 3 of the Platt Amendment.

IN WASHINGTON, OLD ROUGH RIDER Teddy Roosevelt, now president, was in a snit. "I am so angry with that infernal little Cuban republic that I would like to wipe its people off the face of the earth." Roosevelt sent the US secretary of war and the assistant secretary of state to Havana to mediate between the two parties, but they made no progress. Three days later, US naval forces landed in Santiago. A week after that, the Cuban president tendered the resignation of his entire administration and handed over the treasury to the two Americans. US secretary of war William H. Taft (who would become the next president of the United States) became temporary governor. And ten days later, he appointed his own successor, Charles Magoon, recent governor of the US Panama Canal Zone, now the new governor of the Republic of Cuba.[21]

The 1906 occupation solved the immediate conflict between Cuba's two political parties, the turmoil of a contested election, and the rebellion against its illegitimate victors. But it left other, more substantial problems unresolved. The first was the glaring contradiction of the Platt Amendment. The obligation of the United States to intervene in Cuba to preserve order and property left each country at the mercy of the other. Cubans had always to consider the position of the United States on any given policy; the US government, meanwhile, feared Cubans could manipulate them into intervening to defeat internal opponents. Second, the conflicts that produced the second intervention were rooted in a deep dissatisfaction among the people who had actually made Cuban independence. They took pride in their service in the wars against Spain, but they decried the lack of opportunity for them in postindependence Cuba. This sense of grievance was felt with particular power by Afro-Cuban veterans of the war—men precisely like Quintín Bandera and Evaristo Estenoz. US intervention would never be the solution to that particular problem.

The new American occupation lasted three years. Havana continued to boom; Renée Méndez Capote's Vedado grew in stature and elegance. In the countryside, Americans—whether as individuals or as heads of corporations—continued to purchase land. In 1908, before the occupation ended, new elections were called. The Liberals won overwhelmingly, and independence war veteran José Miguel Gómez became president. Then the Americans left; a majority of people hoped it was for good. But the Platt Amendment remained, and that meant no one could know for sure. The test would come soon enough.

Chapter 17

FRATRICIDE

On May 18, 1910, people in Havana looked across the bay at the Morro lighthouse and thought the world was ending. There, "standing still [and] threatening to slash out with its tail," was Halley's Comet. The famed comet made appearances near Earth about every seventy-five years. But in 1910, it was to come especially close; in fact, this time, the planet would pass straight through Halley's tail. Apocalyptic predictions abounded. The gasses in the tail, opined some, would permeate the earth's atmosphere and destroy all life on the planet. And there it was, nearly touching the tip of their beloved lighthouse, visible to all *habaneros* who dared cast their glance upward. "People cried from fright," a famous Havana actress later recalled. Pharmacies ran out of sedatives and smelling salts; some people died of heart attacks. In Pinar del Río in western Cuba, an accident detonated a box of dynamite in an armory, resulting in about 50 deaths and more than 150 wounded. Convinced that the explosion had been somehow caused by the comet's gasses, people took to the streets running and screaming.[1]

In eastern Cuba, the predictions about Halley's Comet fused with another, more familiar fear to create a much more destructive panic. At the center of that story was master builder Evaristo Estenoz, the elegant man with the white Panama hat who built fancy houses in Vedado. A veteran of the independence war, labor strikes, and the 1906 Liberal Revolt, Estenoz founded the Partido Independiente de Color, or the Independent Party of Color (PIC), in 1908. The new party fielded candidates in elections (without much success), and it published a weekly, and later daily, newspaper out of Estenoz's home in Old Havana. Its first declaration of principles explained the party's goals: "a harmonious nationality, as Martí had envisioned and for which Maceo . . . and a whole illustrious pleiad of Cuban blacks spilled their blood." The party's platform demanded reforms specifically in the service of racial justice, including an end to discrimination and equal access to public jobs. It also called for the expansion of free compulsory education, the abolition of the death penalty, and the distribution of land to Cubans. "Cuba for the Cubans," vowed the first issue of the newspaper.[2]

By 1910, the PIC, by its own (perhaps exaggerated) count, boasted 150 branches across the island and some 60,000 members, among them 15,000 veterans of the War of Independence, including 12 generals and 30 colonels. The organization's growing strength worried the Liberal Party, which until then had been the prime beneficiary of the island's substantial Black vote. In and beyond the Liberal Party, others fretted that the PIC's explicit racial appeal would fracture national unity. As a result of both concerns, in 1910, the Cuban legislature prohibited the formation of political parties that limited membership by race. The senator who authored the law was himself a man of color: Martín Morúa Delgado. Other Afro-Cuban legislators—they numbered about 15 percent in the Senate and the House—similarly rejected the idea of a Black party. They thought it would be roundly repudiated by many Cubans, and they argued that the struggle for equal rights was better served by working within established institutions. Support for the proposed law illegalizing race-based parties was almost unanimous.[3]

In an effort to defeat the bill before it became law, the PIC mobilized across the island. Estenoz launched an ambitious speaking tour; hundreds went to hear him. He told audiences that he was continuing the struggle of Antonio Maceo. At almost every opportunity, Estenoz and other leaders argued that they wanted only equality and justice, not—as detractors claimed—preponderance over whites. "Peace," he said, "is our terrain, and the vote, our [weapon]."[4]

His explanations notwithstanding, on May 4, 1910, as Halley's Comet approached the skies over Cuba, Estenoz's Independent Party of Color became illegal. Leaders organized peaceful protests across the island. But all seemed to fall on deaf ears. The government arrested party activists, including Estenoz, and sent troops to areas that seemed particularly vulnerable. In some, the presence of soldiers heightened alarm; their absence in others did as well. Some white officials in eastern Cuba predicted that PIC activists would take advantage of the arrival of Halley's Comet to "kill all the whites." They said one Black leader had even taken to calling himself "Halley." In Santiago, the governor sent frantic letters to Havana predicting that Estenoz and his men were about to "cut off a few heads." In El Cobre, newspapers claimed that members of the Black party had sworn before the Virgin of Charity to exterminate the whites. In Guantánamo, whites were said not to sleep on the night of the comet's passing, expecting to be attacked in their beds. And in the fishing village of Caimanera, just north of Guantánamo's naval base, white residents fled in fear, rowed out to neighboring islets, braving the caiman alligators that gave the place its name, and camped overnight.[5] The precautions, of course, were wholly unnecessary. Near pandemonium notwithstanding, the twin destructions—by comet or race war—never happened.

STILL, WE MIGHT SAY THAT the something approaching a race war did come—just two years late and not in the way most prognosticators had imagined. Though the PIC had been outlawed in 1910, it continued to mobilize and lobby for the reversal of that law so that it could field candidates in elections. With few results for those efforts, the party decided to organize a nationwide armed protest against the Morúa Law. Set for May 20, 1912, it would coincide with the tenth anniversary of the Cuban Republic. Estenoz, with Pedro Ivonet, fellow veteran of the War of Independence and a leader in the party, chose as the principal site for the protest the eastern province of Oriente, the birthplace of Cuba's independence struggle and also the province where Afro-Cubans represented 44 percent of the electorate, the largest anywhere on the island. The purpose of the protest was not rebellion, but rather a disciplined demonstration of Black strength in an election year. Estenoz insisted that he stood by the promise of a Cuba built on racial fraternity. But the recent history of the republic had led him to believe that to make that promise real and effective, Black activists had to confront Cuba's very real and effective racial discrimination. Ultimately, the hope of PIC leaders was that a significant show of force on independence day might prompt President José Miguel Gómez—a Liberal who had made past alliances with Black officeholders and voters—to rescind the Morúa Law and legalize the PIC before the elections of 1912. Such shows of force were standard political fare, but sometimes—as had happened in 1906—they could lead to armed conflict and US intervention. What happened this time shocked almost everyone.[6]

As soon as the protest was announced, detractors gave it old, familiar labels. "The Racist Revolution," read one headline. "This is a racist uprising, an uprising of blacks," declared another article. Newspapers made it sound as if all of Oriente was on fire, and the rest of the island soon to be. They claimed the leaders were not just Black, but Haitian. They reported false rumors of horrific rapes of white women by Black rebels. Estenoz tried to counter these portrayals, giving interviews to the press and stating unequivocally, "we do not rob or accost women, much less assassinate whites.... [The idea] that this is a race war is false."[7] But the die was cast. The press reports helped create the momentum for a wave of anti-Black repression that would shatter the notion of a fraternal republic.

Whatever the role of the press, it was the government of Cuba that orchestrated the violent and merciless repression that took root in 1912. On May 21, President Gómez began dispatching troops and sending weapons to eastern Cuba. Two days later, the government asked for civilian volunteers to join the military campaign. Throughout the island, writes historian Aline Helg, "thousands of whites organized themselves into local 'self-defense' militias and volunteered to go fight in Oriente." Among the volunteers were many veterans of the Liberation Army. One white former aide-de-camp to Antonio Maceo organized a volunteer militia of five hundred men and left Havana for Oriente aboard a ship named *Patria*. Independence war veteran Mario García Menocal—general manager of the US-owned Chaparra sugar estate and the Conservative Party's candidate for president in 1912—offered to lead three thousand volunteers to crush the Black movement. The man who played the largest role in the repression, General José de Jesús Monteagudo, was an independence veteran as well. On May 27, he sailed for Oriente with twelve hundred men to command the operation against the PIC protest. More than four thousand regular soldiers, Rural Guards, and volunteers were already there, ready to join the campaign when he arrived.[8]

In Washington, President William Howard Taft was watching and wondering if the Platt Amendment would require yet another intervention.[9] Eastern Cuba was home to much of the recent US investment in Cuba—not only the massive sugar mills, but also railroads and mines. There were also dozens of American "colonies" with hundreds of US citizens living in the area. No one was entirely surprised, then, when on May 24, the Taft administration announced it would be sending warships and 750 marines to Guantánamo to protect US property and US citizens in eastern Cuba. On June 5, it sent four warships and 450 marines. US authorities called the deployment merely "preventive"—not a harbinger of intervention, but rather an attempt to provide protection so that no intervention would become necessary.[10]

President Gómez was furious. He complained to Washington that there was no need for intervention; he had everything under control. The fact that he had to prove to the United States that the so-called "negro rebellion" was under control gave Gómez more incentive to escalate repression against the protestors. The presence of American troops protecting US property also freed the Cuban forces to fall with all their might on the vastly outnumbered and mostly unarmed rebels.[11]

FRATRICIDE

THE MILITARY CAMPAIGN AGAINST THE Black independents gave no quarter. Reports circulated about mass and indiscriminate killings. The mayor of Guantánamo, an independence war veteran, killed fifty presumed rebels. On May 31, General Carlos Mendieta—another veteran of the Liberation Army, as well as a future (provisional) president of Cuba—invited journalists to view the efficiency of the army's new machine guns during a simulated attack on a rebel camp. In reality, the alleged camp was not a camp at all, but a small rural settlement—noncombatants, in other words. The Cuban army gunned down about 150 people there that day. Across the region, army units and volunteer militias treated almost every person of color as suspect. It was widely reported that when the soldiers encountered Black peasants in the countryside, they assumed they were rebels and shot them summarily. Witnesses remarked that the countryside was soon dotted with Black corpses. Victims died in myriad ways—shot in battle or point blank. Some were cut down by machete. In one instance, white volunteers entered a town carrying the ears of alleged Black rebels. Other times, Black men were hanged from trees. One newspaper headline asked "Has Mister Lynch Arrived?"—a reference to the prevalence of lynching in the United States.[12]

To say the Cuban government's response to the PIC movement was not proportional to the threat is a grave understatement. The PIC protest, in fact, was relatively small and did little to threaten property or persons. By conservative estimates, three hundred protestors participated in the May 20 demonstration in eastern Cuba. The majority of them were unarmed; many had just finished working the seasonal sugar harvest and joined the protest with "only their work machetes and their hammocks." Facing violence and with no chance of success, they largely tried to retreat into the mountains. There they were reported to steal some horses, as well as merchandise from rural stores. On May 31, they carried out a few acts of sabotage. On June 1, some defeated a small group of Rural Guards and took control of the town of La Maya, where Afro-Cubans were in the majority. But at that point, the protestors were fighting against the government's scorched-earth policies. Repression preceded actual rebellion.[13]

Of course, the characterization of the conflict as a story of white against Black does not always hold. There were many Black Cubans who did not join or support the protest, whether for ideological reasons or out of fear of precisely the kind of repression they were now witnessing all around them. Still, it is difficult to avoid the conclusion that less than two weeks after it had started, the government's military campaign in Oriente had devolved into something close to a race war. Almost all the government forces used for the campaign were white. Similarly, the victims were almost all Black. So the repression, in practice, consisted of mostly armed white men targeting mostly unarmed Black ones.[14]

On June 5, the government suspended constitutional guarantees in eastern Cuba. Now, said one observer, the army could "kill Negroes without the courts mixing in the matter." The violence and brutality of the repression escalated further. Even General Monteagudo, commander of the government operation, conceded that the campaign had become mere butchery.[15] A day after the suspension of constitutional guarantees, President Gómez issued a proclamation to the people of Cuba. One might assume it was an attempt to restore calm, an appeal for an end to the violence. It was instead a call to arms. Again, he labeled the PIC movement as a race war and the Cuban government's campaign against it as a struggle for civilization itself. He called for more volunteers to help fight against a "ferocious savagery . . . beyond the bounds of human civilization." The enemy was not even human anymore.[16]

Evaristo Estenoz responded by writing his own proclamation to the people of Cuba. It, too, was a call to arms—but against the government's brutal campaign against them. He emphasized that the protestors had not wanted to fight. They did so now, he said, "with regret and sadness" to defeat "iniquity and oppression . . . in this land that is ours also, because in it we have been born, we have watered its soil with our sweat for four centuries, and with our blood abundantly in its epic struggles for freedom." Blacks in slavery and then Blacks as independence fighters had made Cuba. Now they demanded their place in the republic. Throughout the proclamation, Estenoz presented himself and the movement not as a threat to civilization but as its embodiment. It was their enemies who were acting with "savage selfishness." The document was not only a defense of his actions and of his race, but an appeal for the Cuba he had once thought possible. He closed with a direct rebuttal of the president's proclamation: "We want everyone to know: this is not a race war."[17]

Estenoz never had the chance to distribute or publish the manifesto. Fleeing from pursuers on June 13, he left it behind. An army captain found it and sent it to his superiors. Then it was published in several Cuban newspapers. On June 27, just days after its publication, Evaristo Estenoz—once master builder in elegant Vedado—was dead, shot at point-blank range in front of fifty of his men. Cuban soldiers brought Estenoz's body into the city of Santiago. Shortly after the autopsy, two doctors and a group of white army officers posed for a photograph standing behind Estenoz's naked body on a table. His torso appears mutilated, his flesh sewn back together. His face is not visible to the camera, for his head was placed facing the other direction. A doctor holds Estenoz's head in his hands to signal the large bullet hole on the back. The photograph was published in newspapers across the country; someone even made commemorative postcards with the gruesome image. Estenoz's body—naked, mutilated, covered with flies—was transported to Santiago and displayed in public in front of the army barracks named after Guillermo Moncada, a Black hero of all three independence wars against Spain. Observers noted the somber mood among Afro-Cubans in the city. Then Estenoz was buried in a common grave with no headstone, in order to prevent the site from becoming one of pilgrimage.[18]

Estenoz was just one among the many casualties of 1912. Official Cuban sources put the number of dead among the rebels at two thousand. US citizens living in the area, as well as some PIC members who survived, estimated that the number was between five and six thousand. One recent Cuban scholar put the death count at three thousand. Despite all the dead, the government confiscated fewer than a hundred revolvers and a few dozen shotguns, rifles, and machetes. Most of the people killed by the government were unarmed, after all. The official count of those killed on the government side, meanwhile, was sixteen. Among them were eight Afro-Cuban soldiers murdered by their companions in arms.[19]

THE STORY OF 1912 IS an ugly one, as stories of racial violence always are. Indeed, it may be the ugliest chapter in the history of the Cuban Republic. Thousands of citizens—mostly Black and unarmed—were murdered by their white compatriots. The charge of "race war" was a familiar one in Cuba. Historically, the term was meant to invoke the specter of Black violence against whites; just as fear of race war tended to suggest white fear of that violence. Yet, here, as perhaps in most cases, the violence was that of the state and the white civilians it deputized. And whatever fear white citizens felt in the midst of the race war rumors, it would have paled in intensity, and certainly in reasonableness, when compared to Black fear of white violence.

However uncomfortable a basic retelling of that story may be, it is made even more so when we consider it in light of the independence movement that preceded it. That movement had extolled the principle of racial equality. The instrument of its victory had been a Liberation Army that was thoroughly multiracial and in which Black men had ascended through the ranks to hold positions of power. In José Martí's vision, the effort had been a revolution of love, in which the white man marched not only alongside the Black, but sometimes willingly and respectfully behind him. On its face, the violence of 1912 was a repudiation of those principles.

What made the violence of 1912 ugliest of all, however, was that participants on either side of the divide were often the very men who had fought together in that struggle for an inclusive republic. Once comrades in a multiracial army that proudly voiced antiracist principles, they now faced off in a battle precisely over the meaning and limits of that vision. When Black veterans mobilized as Black Cubans to demand rights, to decry discrimination, to expose the government's failure to live up to the once-shared ideal of an antiracist republic, white veterans accused *them* of being dangerously divisive, of repudiating the principles on which the republic was founded. That interpretation made white repression politically feasible in that moment. Yet it was the naked brutality of the events of 1912 that threw into question the very foundations on which Cuban independence had been fought and won. It gave the lie to the vision of a Cuba somehow above or beyond racism. It is in part for that reason that the history of 1912 remains, to this day, one of the most challenging and controversial topics of historical conversation on the island.

IN THE IMMEDIATE AFTERMATH OF the events, people did talk about it. Because the violence had been perpetrated by the Liberal Party, its opponents used the horrific episode to argue against incumbents. Indeed, it was partly in response to those events that President José Miguel Gómez—who would be forever haunted politically by 1912—lost that year's election to Mario García Menocal, independence veteran and once general manager of the mammoth US-owned sugar estate of Chaparra. A little more than two decades after Cubans defeated the architect of the 1912 massacre at the polls, the government erected a massive and luxurious monument to him in Havana. It sits today at the intersection of two major Vedado streets, 23rd and Avenue of the Presidents. No one constructed a monument to Estenoz.

After 1912, Black politicians, activists, and intellectuals had to be especially careful. The events of that year made it difficult to point out racial discrimination concretely and nearly impossible to imagine a new mobilization along racial lines. A decade after independence, then, the multiracial movement that had extolled the ideal of a republic for all was deeply fractured—a casualty not of war, but of a flawed peace forged under the shadow of US power.

Perhaps it was the profound disappointment with that reality that, on September 24, 1915, put two aging Black generals at the head of a contingent of two thousand men, all veterans of the Liberation Army. They filed out of the city of Santiago on horseback, treading over land that had seen the brutal horror of 1912. But the men were not all Black; they belonged to every race and every political party. Nor were the men going into battle. Instead, their destination was the old sanctuary to the Virgin of Charity atop the mountains of El Cobre. The leaders of the procession carried with them a copy of a petition that Cuban veterans had sent to the Vatican. It asked the Holy See to recognize their beloved virgin as the patron saint of the Republic of Cuba.[20] She was the brown virgin who four centuries earlier had appeared to two Native men and a young African boy. In more recent tellings of the story, one of the Native men had become white, so that the story of her appearance—to an Indian, an African, and a Spaniard—aptly personified the historical roots of the Cuban nation.

This was the way Cubans were supposed to talk about race—a multiracial contingent of patriots championing a multiracial symbol of a harmonious Cuba. What might it have meant for the Black members of the procession to participate in that event? Many had directly witnessed unspeakable racial violence just three years earlier. At the very least, that experience would have made them doubt the existence of the Cuba their march and their petition exemplified. But if most would have doubted its actual existence, many also would have believed in the principle. Perhaps, then, the effort to make the brown virgin the patron saint of all Cubans was a prayer for that principle to hold and to somehow become more real. The unspeakable horror of 1912 notwithstanding, Black Cubans continued to mobilize, seek office, publish newspapers, organize strikes, and found organizations, all in the service of realizing their vision of a Cuban republic for all.

Chapter 18

BOOM, CRASH, AWAKE

On April 7, 1917, Cuban president Mario Menocal declared war on Germany. The declaration came one day after Woodrow Wilson's and three years into World War I. The battleship *Patria*—the same one that had carried soldiers and volunteers to eastern Cuba to put down Black political protest—left Havana Harbor carrying men from "the best families in Cuba." They were headed to Galveston and San Antonio to train as war pilots and mechanics and then set off for the French front as the *escadrille cubaine.*[1] By the time they were ready to go, the war was over. Cuba's entry into World War I ended up being purely symbolic.

Yet World War I wrought significant transformations there. As war turned Europe's sugar beet fields into battlefields, Cuban sugar was in even higher demand than usual. Profits were great even with wartime price controls. Once the war ended and controls were lifted, profits soared. The harvest of 1919–20 was almost magical. At its start, the price for sugar on the world market was 7.28 cents a pound, a figure that already exceeded the industry's target. By the end of the harvest, just six months later, the price had skyrocketed to 22.51 cents a pound. In the end, that one harvest brought in about $1 billion—more than all the harvests from 1900 to 1914 combined. It was the biggest boom in all of Cuban history— "dream-like," said observers, more like a movie than real life. People called it the era of the fat cows or, more elegantly, the dance of the millions.[2]

Using sugar's exceedingly high price to make their calculations, people borrowed, bought, and speculated. But as quickly as it began, the bottom fell out. And all those mill owners who had borrowed against the price of sugar months earlier suddenly found themselves bankrupt. Sugar mills defaulted on loans; then banks failed. Twenty Cuban banks with 334 branches closed. American banks, which had the backing of their parent companies in the United States, survived. Indeed, they flourished as the new crisis and its attendant defaults brought more and more properties under their control. One-quarter of Cuban sugar mills passed to New York's City Bank, and by 1922, fully two-thirds of the sugar harvest was produced by US-owned or -controlled companies.[3]

US dominance of the Cuban economy was not entirely new. Policies put in place during the first military occupation had facilitated the transfer of land to foreign owners at the expense of Cuban ones. But the changes wrought by World War I and its aftermath accelerated that process and rendered US power in Cuba that much more entrenched.

US economic influence was not only powerful, it was persistent. It could shape the way Cubans lived, how they ate, how they traveled, how they worked, how they enjoyed themselves, even how they looked. At a moment when mass production was on the rise in the United States, Cuba represented an easy, accessible market. In 1914, the value of US imports was $69 million; in 1920, at the height of the sugar boom, it soared to $404 million. Among those imports were products indispensable to Cuba's export economy: advanced machinery that increased the output of sugar factories and equipment for the expanding railroads and highways that crisscrossed the island. But US exports to Cuba were more ubiquitous than that—from ready-to-wear fashion to simple household appliances, cigarettes to radios, telephones to elevators, toilets to automobiles. Cars, perhaps more than any other import, seemed to symbolize a new era. They had first arrived on the island in 1899, with the end of Spanish rule. By 1919, reported one foreign journalist, Cuba had more automobiles per capita than any country in the world. The observation was more impressionistic than accurate. In fact, Cuba had the third-highest rate of car ownership per capita of Latin America (after Argentina and Mexico), and Havana had a rate similar to New York City's. Most of those cars—4,722 of the 5,117 imported in 1922, for instance—were American. And most of those were Fords, which came in a variety of models and were more affordable than competing brands. Havana's first taxis were Fords, and for decades Cubans referred to taking taxis as "catching a Ford."[4]

The cars, the gleaming appliances, the extensive railway, trolley, and highway systems; the lavish movie theaters, some even with sound; the tall, elegant hotels with extravagant lobbies and the newest elevators, all gave Havana—which doubled its population between 1919 and 1931—a distinctly modern feel. But modernity, of course, does not preclude poverty or inequality. Not far from where modern cars and trolleys plied their routes and where containers full of modern products vied for space at the docks, shantytowns grew—with unpaved streets, insalubrious conditions, families crowded in vulnerable structures. Disparities also appeared between Havana and the rest of the island. Provincial capitals enjoyed many of the same perks of modernization that Havana did, but smaller cities and, especially, the countryside fell further behind.

As US economic penetration advanced, American political influence, already outsized, became further entrenched, too. In 1917, just three years before sugar's boom and crash, the United States had intervened after a disputed election resulted in rebellions in several provinces. In December 1920, amidst a generalized economic crisis and rumors of unrest following another contested election, President Woodrow Wilson dispatched Enoch Crowder to Havana as his special representative. Crowder, a Missourian and author of the Selective Service Act that drafted generations of American men into the military, arrived in Havana on January 6, 1921, and quickly made his intentions clear. He stated unequivocally that US power in Cuba under the Platt Amendment extended to "each and every provision whose authority could be invoked in the maintenance of a Government adequate for the protection of life, property and individual liberty." He proceeded to dictate policy to the Cuban government, telling the new president, Alfredo Zayas, that Cuba would not receive loans from the United States unless it accepted his reforms. Using what he called his "coercive influence" and "insistent advice, recommendations, and finally virtual demands," he forced Zayas to dismantle his cabinet. Then Crowder chose a new one. Perhaps at no time since the US military occupations of 1899–1902 and 1906–09 had US political power in Cuba been so uninhibited.[5]

POSTWAR CHANGES ALSO ACCELERATED A different kind of US power in Cuba—the power of travel. Americans who would have normally traveled to Europe for vacation were prevented by the war from doing so. They went to Cuba instead, and they liked it. After the war, the pace of Americans visiting the island for pleasure escalated almost as exponentially as the price of sugar. Between World War I and the stock market crash of 1929, the number of tourists visiting Cuba tripled, with Americans flocking to Cuba in ever-greater numbers: 33,000 in 1914; 90,000 by 1928; 178,000 by 1937. Tourism so boomed that some Cubans began to see it as a potential "second crop" for the island—after sugar, of course.[6]

The growth of tourism in Cuba derived from a particular kind of postwar prosperity in the United States. According to one calculation, the number of American millionaires increased fifteen-fold in the long turn of the twentieth century—from about one thousand in 1875 to fifteen thousand by 1927. In the 1920s, many of those millionaires loved traveling to Cuba. Havana, according to one popular travel book, was fast "becoming a second home for that section of the smart set which formerly spent its winters on the Riviera." The pillars of American aristocracy went there: the Vanderbilts, the Whitneys, the Astors. So did celebrities of all kinds: Amelia Earhart, Irving Berlin, Charles Lindbergh, Gary Cooper, Gloria Swanson, Langston Hughes, Albert Einstein, New York City mayor Jimmy Walker, the presidents of Coca-Cola and Chase National Bank. John Bowman, owner of the Biltmore chain of hotels, who already owned one posh hotel in Havana, built the Havana-Biltmore Yacht and Country Club. He advertised it as the "Greatest Place on Earth." It was so great that the ads for it required that every letter be capitalized: "SOME DAY BILTMORE-HAVANA WILL BE PRESCRIBED BY PHYSICIANS." Another ad featured a young, "handsome, smiling John Jacob Astor V . . . stretched out on Cuba's white sands and ready for a game of dominos while on his school's winter holiday."[7]

Postwar growth in the United States also expanded the ranks of the middle class. More people had more disposable income. At the same time, the rise of the five-day workweek and paid vacation days created another valuable commodity: leisure time. Advances in technology further popularized travel to Cuba. In the 1910s, a trip from New York, first by rail to Key West and then by steamer to Havana, took 56 hours; by the late 1920s, the trip was under 40 hours—to a destination much closer and, in winter, warmer and sunnier than Europe. The advent of commercial air travel that same decade shortened the distance even more dramatically. American companies began organizing work trips to the island, choosing it as the site of annual conventions. Generations of American newlyweds honeymooned there, too.[8]

Money, time, climate, and proximity all contributed to Cuba's popularity as a tourist destination for Americans. But so did something entirely different: American morality—more precisely, the decision of Congress to heed the call of militant teetotalers and pass the Eighteenth Amendment banning the production, transport, and sale of alcoholic beverages. Popularly known as Prohibition, it remained the law of the land from 1919 to 1933, precisely the heyday of Cuban's first tourist boom. That explains the title of the most popular Cuban travel book of the period: Basil Woon's *It's Cocktail Time in Cuba*.

In the 1920s, Havana boasted about seven thousand bars. Some were American-owned bars that had relocated during Prohibition. Ed Donovan, packed up his bar in Newark, New Jersey—the tables, chairs, mirrors, signs, even the bar itself—and opened up on Prado, the boulevard that led to the city's Central Park and the newly completed Capitol Building, very similar to the US Capitol in Washington. American drinkers followed—"fun-loving conventioneers, widows on a fling, thousands of cruise-ship excursionists." They disembarked from their ships, and their first stop was usually one of the many bars beckoning from across the landing dock. "Gray-haired ladies clung to the rail at Sloppy Joe's Bar," a popular tourist bar that Cubans called simply "the American Bar." Ninety percent of its clientele hailed from the United States, there to drink any (or many) of its more than eighty cocktails or its own brand of aged rum. Tourist pamphlets called Havana a "paradise of cocktails" and Cuba "seven hundred miles of playground."[9]

Drinking was only one part of the seduction. Havana was also known for another pastime, likewise illegal in the United States: gambling. In 1919, the Cuban Congress, with urging from President Menocal, legalized casino gambling. When the Casino de la Playa opened, the president's family boasted exclusive access to run (and profit from) the jai alai games. In 1920, when Babe Ruth played baseball in Havana for ten days (US major leaguers routinely played "winter ball" in Cuba), he charged a fee of two thousand dollars a game and blew most of his earnings at the jai alai games. Not too far away was Oriental Park, a massive race track that held some ten thousand spectators and boasted a famously large purse. At the season opening in 1925, newly inaugurated president Gerardo Machado, who also happened to be a horse breeder, had his own viewing box, draped with a Cuban flag.[10]

Gambling, drinking, everything seemed to be legal in Cuba. And that became an important part of how Americans understood Cuba. US travelers extolled the island as a place where anything was possible. One reporter in 1921 called it the "ideal country of personal liberty. . . . When we come here again next year"—because the island was worth a repeat visit, after all—"we should bring with us the Statue of Liberty, to place in the port of Havana, where it properly belongs." Another writer suggested that more and more Americans were traveling to Cuba because they wanted "to pursue life, liberty, and happiness according to the twentieth-century version." Cubans, she said, referred to their country as "Cuba Libre." And to her that made sense. For US tourists, that freedom might mean drinking or gambling without having to break the law. It might even mean access to no-fault divorce, legalized in Cuba more than fifty years before the first US state adopted it.[11]

The feeling of freedom for American visitors came not only from not having to worry about the law; it came also from the opportunity to act unlike the versions of themselves they knew in snowbound Pittsburgh or Boston. They could dress more revealingly. They could dance more suggestively, to more suggestive rhythms. The more reserved among them could simply ogle while others danced and swayed. The arrival of so many foreign tourists in search of exotic entertainment fed a nightclub craze. The open-air Château Madrid offered dining, dancing, and elaborate floor shows that mixed rumba dancers, American roller skaters, Cuban singers, American jazz musicians, and even a movie star idol from American westerns. Dozens of new nightclubs advertised their offerings: nights of pleasure, Havana's best floor shows, hot sweet music, and, of course, "beautiful girls."[12]

Cuba, though close, felt foreign and romantic, perhaps a little bit dangerous. Waldo Frank, writer for the *New Yorker* and the *New Republic*, described it this way:

> This Habana, then—this Habana of the Cubans—is not real. . . . I have this sense so vividly, and of myself awake within a sultry slumber which only half enfolds me, that I am in considerable danger. Why should I dodge this motor-car, since it is but a dream? . . . Many worlds, mingled as in a dream . . . Spain and Caribbean, Africa, Mongolia, the tree-choked ruins of near Yucatan peer together through a single shutter of flesh, through glaze of one pair of eyes. As a real yesterday breaks with the night into the crazy facets of a dream, so Habana of the Cubans. The unreality is everywhere. Bacardi rum . . . is a perfume evanescing: when you have drained your glass it is as if a dream lingered in your mouth. The fruits of Cuba are a vague delirium of flavors. Mango, mamey, papaya, avocado, guava . . . each of them is a subtle recollection of other fruits, of other climes. . . . Even the landscape dreams. . . . You know the traits of revery: how what the eye sees fuses with the clouding fancy. This is the trait of Cuba.[13]

Ernest Hemingway expressed his attraction to Cuba more crudely. He liked it, recalled a friend, because it had "both fishing and fucking." The streets of Havana, the beaches on its outskirts, even the streets of poor, working-class (but "interesting") Regla across the harbor drew American visitors eager for the feeling of being in a special place where "you could do anything you want, and know nothing is wrong."[14]

WHAT DID CUBANS MAKE OF all this? To profit, some catered to it. The owner of the famous Sloppy Joe's Bar transformed his establishment from one selling mostly food to one that offered mostly drink. He had no problem with people referring to his business as "the American bar." Many others happily used English to name their businesses and to advertise things in their windows. They catered to American tastes because the tourists were largely American, and they were the ones spending money. But other Cubans, not in the tourist trades, worried. Was the tourism of game and drink turning the island into an American "toilet," queried one politician? Did the new dominance of tourism herald a creeping Americanization, the dilution of national culture? It might have been that very unease that prompted some Cubans to note the ways in which the visitors carried themselves, "bolstered by a sense of supreme power that authorizes [them] to speak overbearingly and give orders."[15]

Of course, not all tourists acted the part of the "ugly American." In fact, the majority probably did not. They were salesmen traveling with their wives, earnest honeymooners, church groups, lonely widows and widowers, and just plain, well-meaning vacationers. Some may have seen risqué floor shows, but they also flocked to more sedate diversions, to sunny beaches and first-rate jazz shows, perhaps even to the 1921 World Chess Championship, held in Havana and won by Cuban chess genius José Raúl Capablanca, who retained the title until 1927. Albert Einstein, who visited Havana in 1930 to speak before the National Academy of Sciences, knew that the city had to be more than the sleek hotels and shows and insisted on visiting poor neighborhoods and shantytowns. Other Americans came to fish, to recover their health, to watch winter baseball, or to play it. Many members of the segregated US Negro Leagues loved playing baseball in Cuba for reasons beyond the weather. They could play all their games in first-rate, integrated stadiums, in a beautiful, fascinating city, and not have to suffer the humiliations they were subject to in Jim Crow–era United States. While many Cuban teams had American players (both Black and white), Cuban baseball promoters sometimes brought in whole major-league teams to play against Cuban ones. Those games drew the largest crowds. From this golden age of Cuban baseball, the game that many would remember years later was one in which Babe Ruth did not get one hit, Cuban star Cristóbal Torriente (who also played in the US Negro Leagues) hit three home runs, and the Cubans defeated the New York Giants 11–4.[16] It was the best possible outcome of a rivalry vigorously pursued, but—mostly—in good fun.

CUBA

AMONG THE TENS OF THOUSANDS of American visitors to Cuba in this period, the most high profile was President Calvin Coolidge in January 1928. The trip was Coolidge's only foreign trip during his presidency and the first and—until Barack Obama's trip in March 2016—the only one to Cuba by a sitting US president. Coolidge was lavishly feted; a wing of the Presidential Palace was renovated to receive him and his wife. When he was inadvertently offered rum, he observed US Prohibition and gracefully declined. Coolidge, of course, was not there as a tourist. He was there on an official state visit to open the sixth Pan-American Conference, the regular meeting of Western Hemisphere states. At the first Pan-American meeting in 1826, US delegates had opposed any effort by newly Latin American nations to free Cuba from Spanish rule.

To welcome the US president a century later, the Cuban government inaugurated an elaborate plaza around the recently completed memorial to the *Maine*, the ship whose explosion had launched the Spanish-American War. The new plaza boasted esplanades, gardens, and busts of Presidents William McKinley and Theodore Roosevelt, and another of Leonard Wood, former military governor of Cuba. Both the occasion (the Pan-American Conference) and the venue (the Maine Plaza) served as distinct reminders of the United States' long and troubled relationship to Cuban independence. But neither the Cuban hosts nor the American visitor wanted to call attention to any of that. The conference also managed to avoid explicit condemnation of US policy at a moment when the United States was engaged in military occupations in Haiti, the Dominican Republic, and Nicaragua.[17]

When Coolidge rose to address the delegates, he spoke as if that history never happened. "In the spirit of Christopher Columbus," he began, "all of the Americas have an eternal bond of unity, a common heritage bequeathed to us alone." Speaking to those other Americans of "all of the Americas," he insisted that they were equals: "All nations here represented stand on an exact footing of equality. The smallest and the weakest speaks here with the same authority as the largest and the most powerful." The delegates rose to their feet in applause, an act that signaled less a belief in the truth of that statement than a fervent desire that it be so. Gazing out at the assembly, Coolidge also addressed the history and present of Cuba. "Thirty years ago Cuba ranked as a foreign possession, torn by revolution and devastated by hostile forces. . . . Today Cuba is her own sovereign. Her people . . . have reached a position in the stability of their government, in the

224

genuine expression of their public opinion at the ballot box ... [that] has commanded universal respect and admiration."[18]

What Coolidge knew but did not say was that, in 1928, the government of Cuba was in the process of turning the ballot box into a sham. Elected with a significant majority in 1924, Gerardo Machado, a veteran of the final war of independence, had assumed the presidency as a progressive reform candidate, committed to massive investment in infrastructure and an end to the infamous Platt Amendment. From the start, he had promised not to run for reelection. Less than two years into his term, however, he knew he wanted more. Rather than break his no-reelection pledge, he tried to prolong his presidency by pushing constitutional amendments that prohibited reelection but extended presidential terms to six years, thus giving him two more years in office. Cuba's Supreme Court rejected the amendments, arguing that reelection could not be forbidden nor the presidential term extended after the fact. The current term would remain a four-year one, with reelection legal. But subsequent presidential terms would be for six years without the possibility of reelection. Under the new rules Machado could finish his four-year term and run again for a new term of six years. If he won, he would remain president for a total of ten years, until 1935. Through a series of untoward acts involving intimidation and bribery, Machado also managed to run for his second term unopposed and as the only candidate representing every major political party. When Coolidge arrived in Havana, he was aware of these machinations. Yet he praised the Cuban elections as eminently democratic, an ideal representation of public opinion.[19]

If Coolidge misrepresented the state of the island's electoral system, many also thought he misspoke when he used the term *sovereign* to describe Cuba. In fact, Cubans were talking about sovereignty all the time, and when they did, they generally decried US power on their island. A recently formed association of Cuban jurists published legal arguments against the Platt Amendment. Labor unions formed a national umbrella organization of workers; feminists founded their own organizations and convened national congresses of women. All supported an end to the Platt Amendment. With good reason, historians sometimes refer to the late 1920s in Cuba as a moment of "nationalist awakening."[20]

Finally, neither the Cuban government nor the American visitor called attention to the rise of antigovernment sentiment and to the government's increasingly extralegal campaigns against its opponents. On the eve of Coolidge's visit, the government made mass arrests of potential troublemakers. Among them were two labor leaders and two student activists arrested for putting up anti-imperialist posters.

Shortly after Coolidge left, the body of one washed up by the piers, decomposing and still weighed down by prison chains. The remains of another were allegedly found undigested in the belly of a shark. The government's sudden ban on shark fishing after the incident led wary Cubans to speculate that the prisoners were being fed to sharks through an old trapdoor in the dungeons of the Cabaña fortress.[21]

AMONG THE GROUPS CONCERTEDLY CHALLENGING Machado and speaking out against US power in Cuba were students at the University of Havana. Located on a hill that connected central Havana with burgeoning Vedado, its principal entrance was a grand staircase, as wide as it was tall, at the top a statue of a seated woman built by a Czech-born American sculptor. As a model for the face of the woman, he had used the white Feliciana Villalón, the sixteen-year-old daughter of a mathematics professor and independence war veteran. As a model for the body, the sculptor used an older, mixed-race woman. Her name, unlike Feliciana's, is unknown—another reminder of the silent biases of the archives that historians use to reconstruct history.

This serene spot was a place of learning, but in the 1920s it emerged also as a principal site of opposition politics. In 1921, students demonstrated when they learned that university officials were considering giving an honorary degree to Enoch Crowder—the US special representative who claimed the right to exercise "coercive influence" over internal Cuban affairs. The students won that battle, and the honorary degree was not granted. In 1923, they established a federation that demanded the university's autonomy from the government. When, in response to student unrest, authorities announced the suspension of classes for three days, the student federation occupied the university. They announced the names of professors who would continue teaching and of advanced students who would replace those who didn't. They opened the university not just to students, but to the Cuban public as a whole.[22]

The president of the student federation—the young man designated "interim provost" during the students' occupation of the university—was Julio Antonio Mella. His father was Dominican, his mother Irish, and because the couple was not married, the son technically bore his mother's last name, McPartland. But everyone knew him as Mella. He was not the most applied student, but he was a champion rower, a good basketball player, and one of the most important student politicians in a country that produced many. Mella was the mastermind of the occupation of the university and its brief opening to the public in 1923. He used that exercise to spearhead another: the establishment that same year of the José

Martí Popular University, which offered workers free evening classes on Cuban history, labor rights, and international politics. In that endeavor and others, Mella and his companions spoke and met and wrote with a sense of urgency and vitality. But this was the kind of activity nearly imperceptible to the throngs of tourists in search of other things.[23]

Mella had his sights set well beyond the university. In 1925, he cofounded the Cuban Communist Party (which in 1944 would change its name to the Popular Socialist Party). Mella was especially interested in the Russian Revolution, though he also argued for what one historian has called a "truly Cuban Marxism." In an article about Vladimir Lenin's death, he wrote, "we do not [aspire] to implement in our situation simplistic copies of revolutions made by other peoples . . . people [must] act according to their own thinking. . . . We want people, not sheep." In 1925, he was among the most important leaders of a wave of strikes and protests that shook the capital. Arrested for what authorities called inciting terrorism against the government, he went on an eighteen-day hunger strike, which mobilized more opposition to the government and won him public sympathy. One of Mella's collaborators met with President Machado to negotiate Mella's release, but talks broke down when the visitor allegedly called Machado "an ass with claws." Members of the feminist Club Femenino took a different approach. They visited Machado's mother in Santa Clara, and their descriptions of Mella's dire physical condition moved her to send a telegram to her son in the Presidential Palace.[24]

Julio Antonio Mella, student activist and founder of Cuba's Communist Party, in Mexico City in 1928. The photograph was taken by his lover, the famous Italian photographer and communist, Tina Modotti.

Whether it was one of those attempts or a more general clamor for Mella's release, Machado complied. Shortly after, Mella left Cuba clandestinely. Posing as a businessman and carrying false papers under the name Juan López, he boarded a banana boat bound for Honduras. He soon settled in Mexico City, where he moved among local communists, intellectuals, and artists, among them muralist Diego Rivera, artist Frida Kahlo, and Soviet ambassador Stanislav Pestkovsky. Mella organized and traveled actively in this period, to the founding meeting of the League Against Imperialism in Brussels, for instance, and to the Soviet Union. From the pages of the Mexican Communist Party's official newspaper, *El Machete*, Mella inveighed against Machado's rule and Coolidge's power, against what he saw as the twin tyrannies of capitalism and imperialism.[25]

Mella was a critical figure in Cuba's nationalist awakening of the 1920s, a leader of a vibrant group of activist intellectuals who were transforming Cuban politics. In an age of mass consumption, they championed a new kind of "mass politics" in which workers and students protested, lobbied, and organized en masse. They knew that for a majority of Cubans the kind of modern Cuba vaunted in tourist pamphlets and magazine advertisements existed only as an illusion. They sought to organize around issues of social and economic justice, and to link them explicitly with the question of national sovereignty. For them, achieving a just Cuban society required a very different relationship with the United States—a kind of relationship to which the Americans would not easily accede. Mella and like-minded compatriots thus identified two political enemies: "Yankee imperialism" and Cuban governments unable or unwilling to defend Cuban sovereignty. Here were the origins of a current of Cuban radicalism that would have enormous power for the rest of the century—in an imminent revolution in 1933 and a much more famous one in 1959.

But if Mella and his companions identified the current Cuban state as an enemy, the Cuban state reciprocated with much greater force. On the night of January 10, 1929, while Mella was walking home with his lover, the Italian photographer, actress, and communist Tina Modotti, someone shot him to death. The Mexican government tried to pin the assassination on fellow communists, though it was widely believed that Machado's agents were the culprits.[26]

AT THE TIME OF MELLA'S assassination in January 1929, the Cuban economy was suffering the effects of declining sugar prices. Then came the crash of the New York Stock Exchange in October, followed by cascading crashes elsewhere.

Cuba was plunged into the worst economic crisis it had ever experienced. The price of sugar plummeted to little over half a cent a pound by 1932. Sugar producers laid off workers, reduced wages, and shortened the harvest to about two and a half months. In 1930, mills were paying workers 80 cents a day for cutting, lifting, and hauling cane, while early in the century the average wage for that work had been $1.80–2.50 daily. Wages, said one report, were "the lowest since the days of slavery," which had ended more than forty years earlier. Observers wrote about the appearance of poverty everywhere. In parts of eastern Cuba—hub of the new US-dominated sugar economy—people were said to be subsisting on sugarcane and yams. In the public sector, the government cut salaries and laid off workers, closing hospitals, post offices, and other state institutions in an effort to weather the crisis. Public employees were going months without a paycheck.[27]

The economic crisis exacerbated the already existing political one. The government tried forbidding public demonstrations, but students and labor unions kept organizing them. In March 1930, some two hundred thousand workers staged a general strike. May Day demonstrations the same year resulted in violence in at least one city, with clashes elsewhere soon after. When schoolteachers, who had gone unpaid for six months, threatened to go on strike, Machado announced he would deploy the army against them. By the end of 1930, he had shut down Havana's principal newspaper (a conservative daily), the University of Havana, and even the Havana Yacht Club—the storied haunt of wealthy American vacationers and Havana high society—on the charge that it was harboring terrorists and other enemies of the state. With no money to pay teachers and concerned about student opposition to his government, Machado closed all schools. In October 1930, he suspended constitutional guarantees in Havana and then across the rest of the island the following month.[28]

Still, the downward spiral continued. One shuttered newspaper soon became fifteen; every member of the university's Student Directorate was arrested; eighty-five professors were indicted on charges of sedition and conspiracy to overthrow the government. Former presidents tried negotiation and then open revolt; neither worked. At every turn, Machado expanded the government's repressive capacity, adding a new Sección de Expertos, torture specialists, and the Partida de la Porra, a government death squad. The opposition escalated its tactics. A new group that called itself the ABC organized secret cells and pledged to respond to government violence with violence. The head of Machado's repressive "experts" was shot and killed from a passing car. The chief of police was assassinated, as was the president of the Senate. There were several attempts on Machado's life as well. Rumors swirled about full-blown revolution and, of course, about whether or not the United States would invoke the Platt Amendment and land troops in Cuba. One rumor suggested that Machado was about to step down and that Jimmy Walker, New York City's famously flamboyant (and corrupt) mayor, was about to become president of Cuba. Machado, however, had no intention of stepping down.[29]

In the United States, newspapers reported on the troubles in Cuba; deeper in those papers were ads that diverted readers' eyes to other, more pleasant things. They advertised holiday cruise packages to "gay Havana"; they recounted nail-biting horse races at Oriental Park; they even noted that Machado and his wife had donated the beautiful trophy for one of the races. And as 1931 came to a close, they predicted that the new year would be Havana's "Best Tourist Year."[30] In Havana, Machado celebrated the holidays lavishly. The day before Christmas Eve 1931, he addressed the Cuban public as if he could will away his problems. He rose to speak and, behind his thickly rimmed glasses, fixed eyes of steel on his audience. He would remain president of Cuba, he said, until noon on May 20, 1935, "not a minute more, not a minute less."[31]

IN POLITICS, "SMALL THINGS SOMETIMES grow into big things," wrote US journalist Ruby Hart Phillips from Havana in her diary on August 3, 1933. The "small thing" she was referring to was a labor strike that had begun little over a week earlier with Havana bus drivers protesting fare hikes and new gasoline regulations. Within days, the city was completely paralyzed. Railway workers, taxi and truck drivers, streetcar operators, and garbage collectors called sympathy strikes. Stores closed their doors; even newspapers went on strike. Soon the "little" bus drivers' strike was a general strike, active in every province of the island and nearly every sector of the economy. Police with machine guns set up camp in the city's Central Park. But the universal cry in the streets was "Machado, resign!" No president could weather this, everyone said.[32]

Late in the afternoon of August 7, when people heard the news that Machado had fled the island, they believed it and rejoiced. In front of the Capitol Building, perhaps five thousand gathered. Across the street and a block away, someone climbed the statue of José Martí in Central Park. People were shouting that Machado has resigned. But it was not true. And as people marched to the Presidential Palace, the police began firing on them. In front of the famous Sloppy Joe's Bar the police rained bullets into "the packed mass of humanity." The *New York Times* put the toll of that and other clashes that day at a minimum of 20 dead and 123 wounded, including many not expected to survive.[33]

The violent confrontation was the point of no return. Sumner Welles, assistant secretary of state for Latin America, had been in Havana for months trying to negotiate a settlement between Machado and the opposition. On August 7, he told Machado frankly that if things continued as they were, the United States would have no choice but to intervene in Cuba under the provisions of the Platt Amendment. Machado was defiant. That night he took to the airwaves to lambast US meddling in Cuban affairs and to call on Cubans to defend the island in case of US intervention. Machado was well aware that Franklin D. Roosevelt had been president for only five months and had no desire to intervene militarily in Cuba. Knowing that, Machado essentially called the ambassador's bluff. The next morning in another private meeting with Welles, Machado told him to "inform the President of the United States that he would prefer armed intervention" to acceptance of any US proposal that required him to leave office ahead of the 1935 date he had so often lorded over the public. Intervene, he implied, and the Cubans will fight you.[34]

The Cuban public, by and large, deeply resented US intervention in Cuban politics. In that moment, however, they hated Machado at least as much. And while he may have relished the idea of rousing Cubans to repel a US intervention, the Cuban army did not. It now issued its own ultimatum to Machado: leave or we will remove you from power by force. It was only then, without an ally anywhere beyond his own small circle, that Machado faced the stark reality before him. Late on the night of August 12–13, 1933, he and a few companions—some still in pajamas—headed for the airport. Desi Arnaz Sr., former mayor of Santiago and father of the famous musician and actor of the same name, helped carry bags of gold to the waiting plane. "Things came to quite a beautiful movie climax," mused New York Times writer Ruby Hart Phillips. "As the plane roared down the field, a crowd of vengeance seekers dashed up madly in automobiles screaming for the blood of the tyrant, but had to content themselves with firing at the rapidly disappearing plane." Sitting in the plane, Machado looked out his window through the gray drizzle. He could see smoke rising from below, as chaos engulfed the Cuban capital.[35] A dictator's desire, he surely realized by then, is but one force in the political life of nations. The mighty Machado had fallen.

From the late 1920s to the 1950s, Cuban workers and students became a major force in politics. Pictured here is a labor rally in 1940, the same year that Cubans enthusiastically approved a new Constitution.

Part VII

REPUBLIC, TAKE TWO

Chapter 19

AUTHENTIC MASSES

A t 8 a.m. on August 13, 1933, the US consul in Nassau, Bahamas, sent a telegram to his bosses in Washington: "Ex-President Machado arrived here at daylight this morning." Pressure from three sources had transformed Machado from a president with unparalleled powers to an "Ex-President" fleeing his country under a rain of bullets. The Cuban army's decision to withdraw support sealed his fate in his last days as president. The US ambassador's efforts to drive Machado from office, once it became clear that he could not maintain order, were likewise insurmountable. The third force that drove Machado from power was a highly mobilized public that made its voice and its power known. Labor unions, students, and unemployed workers organized strikes; they protested and rallied; they spoke, wrote, and challenged Machado at every turn. Even as the president sent his secret police for them, other Cubans joined the cause of the protestors. Sumner Welles and the Cuban army may have issued the final strikes against Machado, but the force of mass politics had served as the constant and irresistible drumbeat for years. It was the general strike that ultimately defeated the president. The fact that the public played so pivotal a role in forcing out the old regime is why Cubans—and historians—refer to the events of 1933 not as a coup, but as a revolution.

WITH MACHADO GONE, IT WAS anyone's guess how those three forces— the army, the US government, and the Cuban public—would shape not only the future but also the immediate present. First, there was mayhem. Crowds attacked Machado's old officials and sacked their homes. The head of Machado's secret police was shot to death at a drugstore on Prado Avenue, his body "riddled with bullets, his corpse paraded triumphantly through the streets." The chief of police committed suicide when he realized he was trapped. By some estimates, more than one thousand people were killed, and some three hundred houses belonging to members of the government were targeted in the immediate aftermath of Machado's fall. The British ambassador reported that "well-dressed families drove up in Packards and Cadillacs, [and] seized Louis XV cabinets and gilded chairs." People even broke into the Presidential Palace, shouting that it was their house now. One woman walked away with a tall houseplant.[1]

Amidst the chaos, an improvised government took power. The new president was US-born and educated Carlos Manuel de Céspedes—son and namesake of Cuba's first independence hero, the man who had freed his slaves to declare independence against Spain. The junior Céspedes was a neutral figure; his name entitled him to respect. But even by temperament, he seemed unfit for the revolutionary moment. He was indecisive and overly humble before the legacy of his father. Some claimed he carried a picture of the patriarch Céspedes in his wallet and consulted it whenever he was confused about what course of action to follow.[2]

Céspedes consulted a flesh-and-bone advisor as well: US ambassador Sumner Welles. Many Cubans believed that Welles had handpicked Céspedes for the job, and, in fact, Welles held enormous power over him. He selected some of the members of the presidential cabinet and weighed in on decisions big and small. Less than a week into the new government, Welles was complaining about the burden: "My personal situation is becoming increasingly difficult. Owing to my intimate personal friendship with President Céspedes and the very close relationship which I have formed during these past months with all the members of his Cabinet I am now daily being requested for decisions on all matters affecting the Government of Cuba." Within the week, he was lamenting the "general process of disintegration" unfolding all around him. Unrest continued, and rumored plots were everywhere.[3]

One thing, however, became eminently clear: Machado's fall had solved only the problem of Machado. The new government had little support and no legitimacy. The economic depression that had fed the crisis continued unabated. Most important, the people whose mobilization had ousted Machado were still clamoring for change. Sugar workers were still on strike, demanding higher wages and taking over sugar mills. Port workers, shoemakers, textile workers, hatmakers, cardboard workers, bakers, all continued to strike. A demonstration in Havana on August 20 attracted ten thousand protestors making economic demands and calling for the prosecution of Machado's henchmen. On August 24, students issued a manifesto denouncing the new government, which they said did not represent the interests of Cuba or the desires of the people who had toppled Machado. They demanded a new government, one that would resist the interference of the United States and restore order. They wanted other things, too: the expropriation of large landholdings, the distribution of land among the landless, the right of women to vote. They even wanted a new constitution—one not written under the supervision and pressure of the United States, as the 1901 one had been. Machado's removal was but a first step, they said; now the real revolution would begin.[4]

In their efforts to make that revolution, the students found an unlikely ally—the army, specifically its sergeants and corporals. A group of noncommissioned officers had been meeting for weeks to discuss grievances large and small. They sought guarantees against rumors that soldiers would lose posts and that salaries would be cut. They wanted the army purged of former Machado stalwarts, and they demanded that those directly implicated in the dictator's repression be brought to justice. They complained of meager pay and equally meager opportunities for advancement. At a meeting on the afternoon of September 4, they prepared demands to present later that night to their superiors at Camp Columbia, the largest military installation on the island, located in the Havana suburb of Marianao. By 8 p.m., most of the higher officers were gone for the night. The few who remained refused to hear the sergeants' complaints, told them to take the matter up with the provisional head of the army, and walked away, not expecting much to come from it. But with no one to stop them and without firing a shot, the sergeants took command of the base. Then they called every base on the island. The sergeants are in command, they announced. And the sergeants who answered the phones welcomed the news. Word spread like wildfire. A well-informed soldier walking through Havana's Central Park approached a corporal and asked if he had heard the news that enlisted men had taken over Camp Columbia. Who is in charge? asked the other. Batista, came the reply. And who is Batista? "The stenographer," said the soldier.[5]

The stenographer was the thirty-two-year-old Fulgencio Batista. Born near Banes, which was home to major US sugar mills, he had briefly attended night classes at a Quaker school and began working at an early age. He served as a brakeman on an American-owned railroad; he cut cane; he was the water boy and then timekeeper in a work gang on a plantation. At the age of twenty, he joined the army, later served in the Rural Guard, and eventually returned to the army, where by 1928 he was a sergeant stenographer, regularly sitting in on high-level meetings to transcribe discussions. As he entered the political stage in 1933, observers remarked that he "smiled readily and often," and that he was handsome and charming. He was "plausible in the superlative degree," wrote a *New York Times* correspondent. Not everyone saw him that way, of course, but one thing was evident: Batista had significant political skills. He had been just one of several leaders of the conspiracy, but circumstance, alliances, and cunning combined to give him center stage during the events of September 4. That night, he became the spokesman for the disgruntled soldiers and lower officers of the Cuban army. From there Batista would come to dominate Cuban politics—not just in that moment but for another twenty-five years, until Fidel Castro arrived to dethrone him. [6]

As word of the Sergeants' Revolt spread in Havana, the university students rushed to the barracks. They wanted an alliance with the mutineers. Actually, they wanted more than that. Did the soldiers not realize that by seizing the army, they now controlled the fate of the country? They could achieve much more than a modest increase in pay; they could topple a government widely viewed as illegitimate. The students, in short, wanted to make the soldiers revolutionaries. And it worked, at least for the short run. [7]

President Céspedes and his cabinet stepped down. On September 5, a newspaper headline proclaimed that the reins of government had passed to the "authentic revolution." At first, the revolutionaries attempted governing as a group, establishing a five-man ruling caucus known as the Pentarchy. Batista became commander in chief of the army. Appropriately, perhaps, the five-man government lasted just five days before it abandoned the experiment and appointed a single—provisional—president: Ramón Grau San Martín. [8]

A favorite of the students and a professor of physiology at the University of Havana, Grau had supported student activists since the 1920s and had served time in prison for his anti-Machado activities. Now, on September 10, 1933, he stepped out on the North Terrace of the Presidential Palace before a large audience to take his oath of office. He refused to swear on the Cuban Constitution, which would have been inappropriate, he said, because of its inclusion of the Platt Amendment. So he reached his arm out over the crowd gathered below the balcony and explained that he was taking his oath by vowing allegiance to the people. Someone on the balcony approached him and said Washington was on the phone. In a loud voice, for the crowd to hear, Grau intoned, "Tell Washington to wait. I am with my people now. It is time I attend to them." A big cheer went up. (In fact, it was Cuba's ambassador to the United States who was on the line.) [9]

Thus began the rule of the first government of the Republic of Cuba installed without either the express or tacit approval of the United States. Immediately Grau declared his intention to abolish the Platt Amendment. He made the announcement without any prior discussion with the United States, without even a warning. Many Cubans, of course, had spoken eloquently about the need to eliminate the Platt Amendment. Until that moment, however, none had done so like this, from the balcony of the Presidential Palace.

AMONG THE MOST PRESSING QUESTIONS of the day was what would the US government do. Would it intervene to restore the power of the Céspedes government that it had helped usher in? Many predicted just that. In fact, the army officers unseated by the Sergeants' Revolt holed up in the luxurious, American-owned Hotel Nacional in Vedado, where US ambassador Sumner Welles resided, to await a US military intervention. Welles was asking his bosses in Washington for the same thing. On the day after the Sergeants' Revolt, he requested the landing of a "certain number of troops." Forty-five minutes later, he asked for a thousand men. Two days later, he recommended the "landing of a considerable force at Habana and lesser forces in certain of the most important ports of the Republic." On September 7, the US battleship *Indianapolis* entered Havana Harbor, accompanied by the destroyers *Golff* and *Twigs*. On board the battleship was the US secretary of the navy himself.[10]

Havana, long-ago "key to the Indies," is, of course, a city on the water. From the breezy seaside promenade of the Malecón and from the shady boulevards and narrow streets that began (or ended) at the seawall, it was impossible to miss the entrance of US warships in the harbor. Massive crowds came out to witness their arrival that noonday. People lined all of Prado Avenue, from the seawall inward almost to Central Park, and along the Malecón all the way to the customs house. The crowd, of perhaps over one hundred thousand, booed and heckled the vessels. At the fortress of La Cabaña, Cuban soldiers repositioned cannons to point in the direction of the American warships.[11] Washington—for that matter, Havana—had never seen anything like this. Britain's ambassador to Cuba described the tense situation:

> Usually the United States Ambassador in Cuba acts as a Governor ... and his wishes as regards the Government and appointments are accepted as decrees. The new revolutionary Government, however, has been set up without any consultation with Mr. Welles, almost in opposition to his wishes. ... Thus we end the week in Cuba under a de facto Government which

has not been recognized, under an army led by sergeants, with
the United States Ambassador living in a hotel surrounded
by soldiers and machine guns, and the island surrounded by
United States men-of-war.

Soon there would be twenty-nine US government vessels patrolling Cuban waters, "just in case."[12]

WHILE THE US GOVERNMENT PONDERED what to do, the "authentic" revolution proceeded. The new government set about enacting one reform after another. People referred to it as the hundred days, akin to those of that other progressive politician, Franklin Delano Roosevelt. In the three months following Grau's inauguration, Cuban women won the right to vote; the university secured autonomy from the government. Peasants were promised the right to stay on the land they worked, as well as a yoke of oxen, a cow, some seed, and scientific advice. Workers—including sugarcane cutters—won rights such as a minimum wage, workers' compensation, and compulsory arbitration. When the Cuban American Sugar Company refused to negotiate with workers at its two largest sugar mills—the famous Chaparra and neighboring Delicias—the new government nationalized the mills. The nationalizations made clear that meaningful social and economic change, even when it started as a domestic concern, inevitably clashed with the reality of US power in Cuba.[13]

In international relations, as well, the government charted a new course. In October, it announced that the Cuban army would no longer train with the US military, but with Mexico, where a revolutionary government held power. In December, Cuba's new government sent a delegation to the Pan American Congress in Uruguay. When the head of the Cuban group rose to speak, he defended the sovereignty of Latin American nations, condemned foreign intervention, and denounced the Platt Amendment. It was a dramatic contrast from the previous Pan American meeting, formally opened by Calvin Coolidge in Havana in 1928 under Machado's repressive power.[14] Maybe this time, in Cuba, the revolution would be for real.

Those who sought to consolidate that revolution, however, faced enormous obstacles. From the start, US ambassador Sumner Welles had warned Washington that a far-reaching revolution could well take root in Cuba. A week after Grau's inauguration, Welles shared his worst fears: "It is . . . within the bounds of possibility . . . that the social revolution which is underway cannot be checked. American properties and interests are being gravely prejudiced and the material damage . . . will in all probability be very great." The new government, he said, was "frankly communistic." Its "confiscatory" policies revealed that it wanted to limit "any form of American influence in Cuba."[15]

Initially, Welles had argued that the best solution was intervention. The deposed officers who were holed up in the Hotel Nacional (and doing their own cooking and cleaning since the staff all went on strike) took solace in Welles's position, hopeful that he might convince Washington to restore them to power. But they all misjudged. On October 2, the new army led by Batista stormed the fancy hotel (Welles had moved out by that point), arrested the officers, and killed fourteen of them. The move eliminated a potential threat to the new government, just as it cemented Batista's role as a critical figure.[16]

Meanwhile, in the United States, a new administration led by Franklin Roosevelt was bent on changing its relationship with Latin America. The first three decades of the century had produced more than two dozen US military interventions in the region. While some were brief—Mexico in 1914—others, such as the occupations of Haiti and Nicaragua, lasted for decades. Roosevelt wanted to set that history aside. Military intervention was simply too blunt and expensive a tool. It was also counterproductive, eliciting powerful anti-American sentiment across the region. There would be no US military intervention this time.

With intervention off the table, Welles continued his campaign by other means—working to withhold US recognition of Grau's government. He cabled Washington: "If our Government recognized the existing Cuban government," he wrote on October 5, it would "imply our lending official support to a regime which is opposed by all business and financial interests in Cuba." Recognition, he continued, would "incur the antipathy of those classes in Cuba which . . . once these abnormal conditions have passed, will govern the country."[17] Washington agreed, and recognition was withheld. That refusal contributed to the grave sense of uncertainty and instability. It made it difficult for other nations to offer Cuba their own recognition. At that point, only Mexico and Uruguay had done so. More important, it motivated Cubans who opposed the government to keep undermining the new regime.

"At all the street corners groups are busy at all times, arranging for the new order. . . . Everybody talks *política, política* at all times. It seems exactly as if we were living in a madhouse," said one American observer.[18] What may have looked like political madness on the surface was but a sign of revolutionary turmoil. As Welles had predicted, the social revolution could not be contained. Cubans—in particular, the poor and working class buffeted by the Great Depression—kept making demands: higher wages, land to the tiller, food to stave off hunger. Students seconded those demands and made others: nonpayment of foreign debt, for example, and a more robust rejection of US interference. Protestors, strikers, and activists were not seeking to oust the new government. Rather, they were pushing it to rise to the revolutionary occasion. Grau's administration may have enacted laws increasing workers' wages and such, but business owners—keenly aware that the United States had not yet recognized the new government—refused to comply. So workers understood that their pressure was necessary to make the government—beset by pressure to return to business as usual—follow through on its promise of real change.

SUGAR WAS THE BACKBONE OF the Cuban economy, as well as a critical arena of US investment on the island. It was that sector that saw the most radical and insistent demands from workers. Labor unrest in the industry was not new, and cause for it was ample. Since 1925, the government had been dealing with crises in the sugar market by cutting production and limiting the length of the harvest, in a futile effort to drive up the price of sugar. The traditional harvest of 120 days had been reduced by 1933 to a paltry 66. Wages for those days were also drastically lower than before. The vacuum created by Machado's ouster—the weakening of the state and its repressive institutions—opened up more space for sugar workers to press their demands. One historian calls what happened in Cuban sugar mills in the aftermath of Machado's exit "a revolutionary avalanche."[19]

It was an avalanche that continued, indeed intensified, even after the sergeants and students staged their coup and launched their "authentic revolution." The Sergeants' Revolt occurred on September 4. On September 5, workers at the American behemoth of Chaparra seized the mill from the managers and forced them to seek refuge aboard a British freighter in the harbor. Two days later, the Lugareño mill in Camagüey was occupied by more than five hundred workers brandishing machetes and sticks. By the end of September, workers had taken control of thirty-six sugar mills.[20]

In eight of those, workers established "soviets," or workers' councils, to run the mills. In some areas, they established "flying brigades," which went from mill to mill, helping other workers organize successfully. Thousands of workers from Tacajo, near Holguín, commandeered a train and rode to the neighboring mill to confront management. From there a brigade that combined workers from both mills marched on a third. When they arrived, a Rural Guardsman advised them to elect a fifteen-person committee to negotiate with management. But when the guard climbed a tree to gauge the size of the group and saw an endless sea of strikers, he just opened the gates and let them in. They marched to the towers—the tall, imposing symbols of the sugar mill's might—and posted two new flags. One was the Cuban. The second was the red flag of the Paris Commune and the Russian Revolution, an international symbol of the labor movement and socialism. On taking the mills, in this case and in others, workers sang the Cuban national anthem, followed by the communist Internationale.[21]

When workers occupied the mills, they seized control from management and exercised it themselves. They determined work assignments and schedules. They sold sugar to buyers and used the money to pay workers. They set up soup kitchens and distributed food, as well as tools and even land. In one mill, workers established a school, a court, and a self-defense force. In many, they expelled the Rural Guard and took over company stores. They arrested mill managers (even American ones) and organized leisure activities such as baseball games. They also engaged in symbolic inversions of power, forcing management to live in the workers' quarters or to eat workers' food, or to iron their own clothes.[22]

It was this continued mobilization from below that pressured the new government to act on the progressive agenda that had emerged over the last few years. The government figure most responsive to those demands was Antonio Guiteras. When he was named to Grau's cabinet as the new secretary of the interior on September 10, 1933, he was just twenty-six going on twenty-seven. He wore his short hair parted in the middle and slicked down behind large ears. He owned only one suit; he wore it so often that some called him "the man of one suit." Mostly people called him Toni or Tony. Born just outside Philadelphia to an American mother and a Cuban father, Guiteras had spent most of his life in Cuba, taking a PhD in pharmacy at the University of Havana and, like many in his generation, becoming involved in student politics. He had spent about four months in prison for anti-Machado activities and was released as part of a general amnesty, only to return to those activities once freed. In fact, he was in eastern Cuba plotting revolution when Machado fled the island. In the program he wrote for that movement in 1932, he advocated the elimination of large landholdings and the nationalization of private monopolies in public services (such as transportation and electricity). Now as a member of a revolutionary cabinet, he would begin putting his program into practice. One journalist who interviewed him at the time referred to him as the John Brown of Cuba, after the radical abolitionist and would-be revolutionary of the pre–Civil War United States.[23]

As soon as Guiteras began enacting his policies—a minimum wage, reductions in utility rates, the nationalization of three major US-owned entities—a major obstacle reared its head: opposition from the owners of the businesses affected by the changes. They declined to pay taxes to the new government; they outspokenly disobeyed the government's new laws; they refused to pay the new minimum wage or to negotiate with striking workers—new government be damned. Their refusal was also a function of the fact that the United States had not recognized the Grau administration, fueling speculation about its likely imminent demise.[24]

Throughout, Guiteras attempted to use his power to mediate between workers and employers, and to ensure that new legislation favoring the former be respected by the latter. When in November, Cuban telephone workers went on strike because the company rejected their demands, Guiteras intervened. He personally officiated meetings between the two sides and ultimately persuaded the company to comply with the workers' demands. He did something similar in a conflict between railroad workers and the railroad company. In fact, labor strife across different transport industries convinced Guiteras to begin exploring the creation of a state transport system. In December, after months of conflicts at the famous US-owned Chaparra sugar mill, Guiteras nationalized it and another owned by the same company. The following month, he nationalized the US-owned Cuban Electric Company. Even when the businesses were American, he did not hesitate to nationalize them. Indeed, he may have relished action more in those particular cases. As Guiteras later explained, "A movement that was not anti-imperialist could not be revolutionary."[25] And Guiteras was a revolutionary. Yet as Guiteras faced down the resistance from powerful property holders, another major problem became obvious: a cavernous divide within the revolutionary government itself. In fact, it had been there all along, at the heart of the new revolutionary regime.

THE GOVERNMENT CHARGED WITH MAKING "the authentic revolution" was fundamentally fractured. Guiteras represented the left wing. In the center was President Grau himself, a reformist at heart, whose first priority was a new constitution without the Platt Amendment. He was committed to much of the social legislation, but as its passage led to growing confrontation, Grau worried and advocated a slower, more conciliatory approach. Too much confrontation might mean the United States would never recognize the government, and that would make it hard for the government to survive. Their focus should be on political independence and reestablishing republican norms, Grau believed, so that later a duly elected government, working on the basis of a new constitution, might implement more far-reaching economic changes. For Guiteras, the distinction was without meaning: "It is well known that political independence cannot exist without economic independence."[26]

Whatever doubts Grau expressed, the obstacles Guiteras faced from another quarter of the government were more menacing. The revolutionary government had come to power as the result of the Sergeants' Revolt. But, as US ambassador Sumner Welles insisted, that mutiny did "not take place in order to put [this government] in power." As Guiteras made revolutionary policy with one hand, the army—and Batista, specifically—undid it with the other.[27] Guiteras granted concessions to workers; Batista always backed their employers. The gaping divide at the heart of the new government boded ill for the longevity of the revolution. One leader was too radical for the other; the other much too conservative for the first.

The United States paid careful attention to those internal divisions and used them, above all, to advance American interests. US ambassador Welles cultivated Batista, meeting with him privately and secretly. He flattered him with assurances that he "was the only individual in Cuba today who represented authority," the only one who had the "support [of] the very great majority of the commercial and financial interests in Cuba." With lines of communication opened on those grounds and with Batista receptive to the man who seemed to hold his power in such high esteem, Welles was free with his advice. He asked Batista "whether he intended to permit a continuance of the intolerable conditions which had now existed for at least five weeks on the sugar plantations," referring of course to the numerous workers' strikes and mill occupations. As phrased, the question implied the answer Welles wanted to hear. Batista complied: the army would expel foreign agitators, imprison Cuban communists, guarantee the rights of owners and administrators, and use "troops to restore order wherever it was necessary." True to his word, Batista's army attacked the occupied sugar mills. As Batista explained in the island's principal newspaper, "Order in the sugar mills will be maintained at all costs." Elsewhere, he was even blunter: "There will be a harvest, or there will be blood."[28] In October, at US-owned Jaronú in Camagüey, then the largest sugar mill in the world, Batista's soldiers opened fire on workers who had controlled the mill since September 8, killing at least ten. Likewise at the oldest mill in the country, soldiers violently detained all the members of the strike committee. In nearby

Cortaderas, the Rural Guard killed twenty-two workers and left dozens wounded, the majority of them seasonal cane cutters from Haiti.[29]

BUT FOR WELLES THE PROBLEM was greater than that, more than a question of any particular conflict at any particular mill. Convinced that Grau's government was too radical, he wanted a new government. Welles left Havana in November (his departure had been planned from before), and still there was no new government. His replacement was Jefferson Caffery, who had been the US ambassador in Colombia during the strike and massacre of banana workers on United Fruit property in 1928—the massacre that Gabriel García Márquez famously portrayed in *One Hundred Years of Solitude*. Almost from the moment of his arrival, Caffery began repeating lines long rehearsed by his predecessor. No, the United States would not recognize the current Cuban government. It bore "communistic tendencies;" its measures were "confiscatory;" it acted with "lack of preparation," and its supporters were "ignorant masses who have been misled by Utopian promises."[30]

Like Welles, Caffery saw a potential source of security in Batista. The two men met and talked regularly. On January 10, Batista asked him frankly what the United States "wanted done for recognition." What would it take for the United States to recognize a government in Cuba? Caffery's answer was diplomatic: "I will lay down no specific terms; the matter of your government is a Cuban matter and it is for you to decide what you will do about it." "Having in mind our reiterated declarations as to our position on recognition," he added. What were those declarations? For months, the embassy had been saying that "the present government of Cuba did not fill any of the conditions . . . making possible recognition by us." So, on January 10, when Batista asked the US ambassador what it would take to win US recognition, the ambassador might as well have said, "a new government."[31]

On January 13, Batista met with President Grau and told him that he should resign; the Americans would never recognize him. For two days ministers, officers, and students met, debated, and even came to blows. But amidst the rancor, everyone accepted the obvious. Without US recognition, Grau's presidency was over. He resigned two days later. The administration that inaugurated its rule with 100 days of ambitious and far-reaching decrees and proposals would see only 127 days of rule in all. The aspiring authentic revolution was finished. On January 18, Carlos Mendieta, Batista's favorite and also amenable to the US ambassador, was sworn in as president. Just five days later, on January 23, the US embassy received the telegram that had never come during Grau's tenure: "Under authorization of the President you will please extend immediately to the Government of Cuba on behalf of the United States a formal and cordial recognition."[32] It hadn't taken much, just a new government.

Four months after Batista's coup against Grau, what, by all rights, should have been a major event in Cuban history took place. On May 29, 1934, about a week after the thirty-second anniversary of the inauguration of the Cuban Republic, the governments of Cuba and the United States abolished the Platt Amendment, that reviled piece of legislation forced on Cuba by the United States in 1901 and routinely used to threaten or justify intervention. Progressive forces in Cuba had long fought for its eradication. Ironically, that end came only after their own defeat.

Chapter 20

NEW CHARTER

So ended Fulgencio Batista's machinations: with the removal of the reformist president and of the revolutionary minister who nationalized US companies. Deposed President Grau resettled in Miami, accelerating a long history of Cuban political exile in that city. There he established a new political party and called it the Auténtico, or Authentic, Party, a gesture of commitment to the idea of the "authentic revolution." Its name notwithstanding, the party was, as Grau himself had been in office, reformist. Antonio Guiteras, the recent minister of the interior and the most radical member of Grau's government, regrouped as well. He founded another political group, Joven Cuba, or Young Cuba, a name that embraced what the United States and the old political class had scorned—the revolutionaries' youth, their imputed unpreparedness, their desire to undo what preceding political generations had done.

As for Batista, even without the title of President of the Republic, he became the most powerful figure in Cuban politics. Everyone knew that the presidents in office from the 1934 coup to the elections of 1940 were largely figureheads. All of them answered ultimately to Batista, in command of Cuba's armed forces. It was in that capacity that he tried to quash every radical vestige of the 1933 revolution. The army assassinated Guiteras and other opposition leaders; the police jailed hundreds of students and workers; the state dissolved labor unions, suspended civil rights, and proclaimed martial law. Many of those who survived the onslaught left the island—to organize in Florida, to soak up the political climate of revolutionary Mexico, to join the republican side of the Spanish Civil War. With his opposition thoroughly defeated, Batista—the former stenographer turned general in chief of the Cuban army—reigned supreme. From a radical opponent came a perceptive observation: Batista "has the imagination of a stenographer." And from that derived both his power and his method. Like any good stenographer, he had "the capacity to quickly interpret a confusing sign, a senseless paragraph or, if applied to politics, a difficult situation. . . . In Cuba today he is perhaps the man with the best political skills, . . . [a man who] when measuring his forces . . . never forgets to also measure those of his enemies."[1]

Batista understood that his enemies' power came largely from popular support for meaningful reform. Since the late 1920s, significant sectors of society had clamored for higher wages, access to land, better schools, a new constitution, and more independence from the United States. Having crushed Grau's government in 1934 and the remaining opposition in the two years that followed, in 1936 Batista began pursuing the policies of his enemies as if they had been his all along.

That change was driven less by ideology than by pragmatic considerations. Batista realized that lasting stability required some concessions to the popular demands of the last two decades. He understood that the popularity that would come from addressing those demands would give him even greater power against potential enemies. So Batista assumed the mantle of populist reformer, a man of the people working for the disinherited and the unprivileged. He was not alone in doing that. Leaders across Latin America—right and left, from Argentina to Mexico, Brazil to the Dominican Republic—were speaking in the name of the people and, in the process, changing political culture, the relationship between state and society, as well as the future of the region.

Batista followed one initiative with another. In 1936, he created a program that sent soldiers into the countryside to participate in educational and social programs. In 1937, he released a "Three Year Plan" that included health and old-age insurance, the abolition of large landed estates, profit sharing between sugar workers and mill owners, new schools, crop diversification, and a literacy campaign. Batista's Three Year Plan was so ambitious that skeptics dubbed it the three-hundred-year plan. In April 1938, he began granting small parcels of state lands to peasants. In 1939, he enacted national rent control and lowered mortgage rates. Increasingly popular, Batista moved to expand his base further, legalizing the Communist Party and removing restrictions on union organizing. Henceforth, trade union leadership would be dominated by members of the Cuban Communist Party, working closely with Batista. Historians often refer to these years as the Pax Batistiana. Batista had already nullified the opposition and made alliances with a sector of elite reformers. He knew the US embassy in Havana had his back. So Batista was free to address long-standing popular demands on his own terms.[2]

NEW CHARTER

BATISTA WAS NOTHING IF NOT ambitious. He wanted to succeed where others had failed. And for that, he could think of no better avenue than a new constitution for the Republic of Cuba. The existing Constitution of 1901 had been written under US occupation, and delegates to that convention had been forced to accept the Platt Amendment granting the United States the right to intervene in Cuba. The amendment had been abrogated in 1934, yet it still existed as an appendix to the constitution. During the revolution of 1933, an embattled President Grau had promised to convene elections for a new Constitutional Convention, though he fell from power before he could do that. Now the man who had deposed him would do it himself.

To pave the way for a new constitution, Batista granted amnesty to his former opponents, allowing the return of people who had fled or been exiled following Grau's removal. Batista legalized new or previously outlawed parties, creating the potential for broad participation in the constitutional process. Most important, the government scheduled elections by which the Cuban people would elect the delegates to a constitutional assembly.[3]

The public was swept up in all the preparations. Newspapers and magazines published proposals for constitutional articles. Public lectures and meetings were devoted to the same topic. Perhaps the most important of these events was held at Club Atenas, an elite Black social club in Havana. Starting in February 1939 and for four months after, Club Atenas hosted representatives from every political party—large and small—to present their party's proposals for the new constitution. The idea was twofold: to make the convention candidates and their programs known to the voters who would elect the delegates, and to create a space in which the voting public and potential delegates to the convention could consider the content of Cuba's foundational law together.[4]

The enthusiasm and intensive preparations for the Constitutional Convention meant that the election to select its delegates produced a 57 percent turnout among eligible voters, perhaps one of the highest voter turnouts in the history of the Cuban Republic. Voters elected seventy-seven delegates representing nine political parties across the ideological spectrum. The delegates fell into two major voting blocks: one allied to the government and Batista, the other representing the opposition and headed by former revolutionary president Ramón Grau San Martín, who received more votes than any other candidate for the convention. The communists, who had six delegates, initially declined to join either block but later joined the government coalition. Even so, the opposition block retained a slim majority.[5]

The delegates came from every region and from many walks of life. Among them were the customary lawyers, professors, bankers, and intellectuals. Tellingly, in a society where US control of the sugar industry had put obstacles to large-scale Cuban landownership, there were only a handful of *hacendados*, ranchers, and independent cane farmers. Delegates included a suffragette, a metalsmith, a bricklayer, a labor leader, a peasant activist, a sugar worker, and a shoemaker. There was a descendant of patriotic hero Antonio Maceo (José Maceo); a Black woman communist and pharmacist (Esperanza Sánchez Mastrapa); a Black communist educator inclined to oratory (Salvador García Agüero); a decidedly anticommunist journalist and radio personality (Eduardo Chibás); and a former president (Ramón Grau San Martín).[6]

AT ABOUT 2 P.M. ON February 9, 1940, the elected delegates to the Constitutional Convention began arriving at the Capitol to begin their deliberations. They found a massive crowd surrounding the building and lining the grand fifty-five-step staircase. People crammed into the corridors. Inside the chamber, people took seats in the galleries, the boxes, and even in areas normally reserved for legislators. Some five thousand people had shown up to witness the historic event.[7]

At 3:20 p.m., a bell called everyone to order. It was the same bell that had opened the Constitutional Convention in 1901. The first delegate to speak was sixty-six years old and the only one among them who had also served in that first convention. Then came a roll call and three speeches. The first, by Jorge Mañach, a major intellectual of the twentieth century, represented the opposition coalition. "If we are here it is because the people wanted it, and we are here for what the people want," he said. Next came Manuel Cortina, speaking for the progovernment coalition. He invoked José Martí—"Martí's Patria must be of all, with all, and for the good of all." He received a hearty ovation. Third came Juan Marinello, representing the communists. He, too, invoked the people, or, more specifically, "the popular masses." Their "principal yearning in recent years has been a Constitutional Charter equal to its time and to their needs." Someone read a note from the Boy Scouts of Regla (the town across the harbor from Havana), respectfully donating a Cuban flag, that it might protect and inspire the men and women gathered there to draft a constitution. From the beginning and at every session after, professional stenographers meticulously recorded the proceedings, which were published daily in the *Diario de Sesiones*, available for sale everywhere newspapers were sold.[8]

Even the most careful reading of that record, however, would have missed one of the most important elements of the Constitutional Convention: a highly mobilized and enthusiastic public. Every day, people gathered outside the building and watched from the galleries. When on February 24, the president of the convention noted the anniversary of the start of Cuba's final war of independence, they rose to their feet to applaud and chant "Long Live Cuba!" The Constitutional Convention reverberated far outside the legislative chamber, too. People listened to the proceedings live on radio broadcasts. Cuba had one of the highest rates of radio ownership in Latin America. But even those who did not own radios had access to the broadcasts. In cities, hotels allowed people to enter and listen to the debates in the lobby. Others went to hear the broadcasts in the homes of friends or families. In the countryside, small villages sometimes mounted speakers in modest central squares, and people walked for miles to listen.[9]

The public did much more than listen to or read about the constitutional debates. They also actively weighed in. Those who stood outside the Capitol greeted arriving delegates with cheers or chants. They distributed flyers and pamphlets to delegates and took positions on the things the delegates were discussing and deciding. Labor unions, social clubs, and individual citizens addressed letters and appeals to the delegates, sometimes publishing them for others to read. Associations organized postcard campaigns and inundated the Capitol with appeals for or against particular proposals. Some letters to the delegates were read aloud during the proceedings, ensuring that citizens' voices reached a large radio audience across the island.[10]

The fact that the debates were broadcast and that many of the delegates were also running for office in elections scheduled for later in the year meant that every delegate in the room suddenly had a bully pulpit if he or she wanted it. Yet for the most part, the tone of the discussion was polite and considered. The debates were often lively, sometimes unexpected. A discussion about whether or not to invoke God in the preamble to the constitution, for example, elicited heated disagreements, as did a proposal to send a message of solidarity to Finland following the Soviet invasion of the country a few months earlier. A proposal to limit the amount of time delegates could speak was swiftly approved, if not generally observed. Above all, the debate was genuine. The delegates took with utmost seriousness the charge of writing the country's fundamental law, which—given that the first constitution was written under US occupation—some saw as the first true constitution for the Republic of Cuba.

CUBA

ONE OF THE MOST IMPASSIONED debates of the convention accompanied the discussion of Article 20, which established the equality of Cubans before the law. To understand why a seemingly self-evident principle produced so much controversy, we must return to one of the thorniest problems in Cuban history: race.

The proposed article began with the same wording used in the 1901 constitution: "All Cubans are equal before the law. The Republic does not recognize exemptions or privileges." But the 1940 proposal went further: "All discrimination due to sex, race, class or any other motive harmful to human dignity is declared illegal and punishable. The law will establish sanctions for those who violate these norms." The article thus went beyond an abstract principle of equality to criminalize discrimination explicitly.

The most vocal champion of that innovation was Salvador García Agüero, a Black communist educator and intellectual. Black Cubans, he said, faced discrimination everywhere—in the labor market, in public space. In religious schools, even God discriminated, he said wryly. Clearly, the 1901 constitution's strictly abstract principle of equality before the law had not guaranteed that equality. He supported the proposal for an explicit prohibition against discrimination. But he wanted the law to go further still. To prohibit discrimination without actually defining it, he argued, made the prohibition ineffectual. He wanted the constitution to specify explicitly the behaviors it was declaring illegal and punishable. Only that way could the article be effective.[11]

García Agüero and other Communist Party delegates thus moved to amend the proposal as follows: "All behavior or action that prevents any citizen from full access to public services or public places, the right to work and culture in all its aspects, or the full enjoyment of all his civil and political activities, due to his race, color, sex, class or any other discriminatory reason, shall be declared illegal and publishable. Within six months . . . the law will establish the sanctions incurred by those who violate these norms." The forms of discrimination mentioned in the article were common in Cuba, yet a majority of white Cubans insisted that discrimination did not exist and that they, certainly, did not practice it themselves. By giving discrimination a more concrete meaning, the article sought to make it more identifiable and, therefore, more easily punishable.[12]

The communist amendment adhered to principles voiced by many Black social clubs on the island. The National Federation of Cuban Societies of the Race of Color published a manifesto calling on the convention to clearly penalize discrimination, so that "lyrical declarations" of equality did not become simply "juridical fictions." Individuals sent postcards favoring the passage of an antidiscrimination article. One such postcard writer was named José Antonio Aponte—perhaps a descendant of the man by the same name who had created the mysterious, later lost book of paintings and masterminded the 1812 antislavery conspiracy in Havana.[13]

Despite that support, on April 27, the communist amendment failed to pass by a slim margin. As opponents rose to explain their votes, they inadvertently revealed why its authors had felt it so necessary to define discrimination in the first place. One vocal conservative delegate, Delio Núñez Mesa, denied that racism or discrimination existed at all, and what might appear as such, he insisted, was not the fault of the state, nor even of white Cubans: "Blacks simply do not claim their constitutional rights. They do not know how to claim [them]. . . . neither a constitution nor any law of the land can make it so that these citizens can understand how to defend themselves like dignified men." We can almost hear the uneasy, low-grade hum before the uproar. Then the session ended.[14]

But 1940 was an election year; the convention sessions were all broadcast on radio, and the public galleries of the Capitol were full of citizens closely following the debates. When the delegates returned on May 2 to continue the discussion of Article 20, they were greeted by citizens outside the Capitol, distributing pamphlets to the delegates as they entered the building. To some of the delegates it felt like a gauntlet.[15]

At stake in the May 2 discussion was not the communist amendment, which had already been defeated. Debate now centered on the original article declaring Cubans equal before the law and discrimination (undefined) punishable by law. García Agüero, author of the just-defeated amendment, now introduced a modification, adding "color"—and not just race—to the forms of discrimination outlawed by the constitution. If the addition seems minor, its proponent insisted that it wasn't. "[In] a country such as ours, of such profound and intricate mixture, it is very difficult to distinguish any clear lines separating one race from another. It is a cyclopean task. Here it is color that separates men. . . . [And] it is based on a person's lighter or darker coloring, that people discriminate."[16]

While that change was accepted without much controversy, the underlying issue—whether or not to criminalize discrimination—was still under intense debate. The same conservative delegate whose words had touched off the controversy on Friday rose to speak: "I continue to believe that discrimination does not exist in Cuba." Incredulous, other delegates asked if he could really honestly say that no discrimination existed. Only "when they themselves allow it," he replied, referring to Afro-Cubans. Again, the temperature in the room rose.[17]

The debate echoed a broader tension around race long present in Cuban history. Throughout the colonial period, racial slavery had represented the most brutal form of exploitation. During the independence wars, Black Cubans who joined the struggle in large numbers had always had to prove that their loyalty to Cuba was greater than their loyalty to their race. In the early republic, when Black veterans of that war had condemned racism and mobilized against it, white Cubans cast that campaign as itself racist and as a dangerous affront to the Cuban nation. Now, in 1940, when delegates—especially Black delegates—publicly decried racial discrimination from the most exalted podium in the land, the same old arguments and accusations resurfaced.

The conservative delegate continued: "It is anti-Cuban and antipatriotic to deal with this question of racism in Cuba; I think that everyone, without exception, must be very careful with this because it could become very dangerous." Another conservative delegate saw a harbinger of that danger in the enormous crowd gathered outside the Capitol. "Upon entering . . . someone put in my hands accusatory pamphlets, written in harsh and rude language, angrily attacking the delegates who voted against the amendment. This issue has gotten out of hand . . . and in the process a problem was created where none existed before." At one point, the discussion grew so heated it became personal. A conservative delegate accused the Black communist delegate, Salvador García Agüero, of trying to intimidate him into silence. García denied the accusation. Thereupon followed a brief, intense back-and-forth; liar, each angrily accused the other. In the standoff, a conservative delegate rose and invoked an old, reliable practice: the secret session. The public was cleared, and for two hours the debate continued, with nothing recorded in the official minutes.[18]

However familiar and timeworn the arguments, times had, in fact, changed. And when the public debate resumed later that night, the article's opponents had ceded. One conservative publicly announced his vote in favor of the article; he did not think it would be effective, but voted for it anyway, hoping his skepticism would be proved wrong. In the end, the vote was unanimous. Article 20 of the country's new foundational charter would read: "All Cubans are equal before the law. The Republic does not recognize exemptions or privileges. Any discrimination by reason of sex, race, color, or class, and any other kind of discrimination destructive of human dignity, is declared illegal and punishable. The law shall establish the penalties that violators of this provision shall incur." Despite the unanimous vote, the debate over race and equality had been among the most passionate and contentious of the whole convention.[19]

The deliberations continued until the delegates finished drafting the constitution on June 21. Soon after, all the delegates—Black, white, communist, liberal, conservative—boarded a train to a tiny place in eastern Cuba called Guáimaro, the place where Cuba's very first constitution—the constitution of the rebel republic in arms—had been signed in 1869. On July 1, 1940, in a small rural schoolhouse, one by one, the delegates picked up a fancy gold, enamel, and diamond pen purchased with funds donated by the schoolchildren of Cuba, and signed the new Constitution of the Republic. Massive crowds waved flags and shouted "¡Viva Cuba Libre!" Four days later, the constitution was formally promulgated from the portico of the Capitol before "an immense crowd that filled the tall flight of steps and overflowed into the sidewalks, streets, balconies, and even the rooftops of surrounding buildings."[20]

THE 1940 CONSTITUTION, WITH 286 articles in 19 sections, was clearly a progressive charter. It enshrined in the fundamental law of the land a host of social rights pursued over decades of popular mobilization. Many of those rights pertained to labor. Article 61 established a national minimum wage; Article 62 mandated equal pay for equal work; Article 64 prohibited the long-held practice of paying workers in tokens or scrip. Articles 65–67 established workers' social insurance, an eight-hour day, and paid vacation. Article 68, meanwhile, granted women paid maternity leave, and Articles 70–72 guaranteed the right to unionization and to strike. Other measures focused on rural society. Article 90 aimed to restructure patterns of landholding. It outlawed *latifundio* (very large landholdings) and stipulated a maximum size for rural private property, a measure that on its own would have severely impacted US investment in Cuba. In fact, the article went further: "The law shall restrictively limit acquisition and possession of land by foreign persons and companies, and shall adopt measures tending to revert the land to Cuban ownership." Article 271 was much broader. It stipulated that "[t]he State shall direct the course of the national economy for the benefit of the people in order to assure a proper existence for each individual." The constitution also recognized traditional individual rights—the vote, freedoms of religion, speech, assembly, property, as well as freedom from arbitrary seizure. It introduced measures associated with direct democracy, giving citizens the right to propose a law to the legislature if they could collect the signatures of ten thousand voters on their proposal.[21]

Historian Rafael Rojas gives the final balance of the constitution by noting that the articles dealing with "individual rights" numbered twenty, while the articles addressing "social rights"—related to work, education, family, culture, and education—numbered more than forty. Overall, the new charter represented an ideological shift away from the tenets of classic liberalism to "the repertory of moderate lefts." It recognized the traditional liberal right to property, but balanced it against attention to its social function. Its closest analogue was probably Mexico's revolutionary constitution of 1917, which Greg Grandin calls "the world's first fully conceived social-democratic charter." In the quarter century after the Mexican document, fourteen Latin American nations rewrote their constitutions, most of them, like Cuba, adding new social rights to traditional political and individual rights. Finally, while the new Cuban charter's provisions might have echoed the tenor of the Roosevelt administration's New Deal, such policies were never written into the constitution of the United States.[22] In Cuba, the Constitution of 1940 represented the culmination of the revolution of 1933, and it revealed that many of the revolutionary ideas of the early 1930s had become part of the mainstream of Cuban political life.

The constitution went into effect on October 10, 1940, the first day of the presidency of Fulgencio Batista. For the first time in its history, Cuba would be ruled by a constitution drafted and signed without the presence of an outside governor, be he Spanish or American. On its promulgation, it was already clear that the document was both boldly progressive and immensely popular, as evidenced by the many articles addressing labor and social rights, and by the rapt attention and enthusiastic mobilization its drafting had generated.

Not long after its promulgation, however, something else became self-evident: namely, that on its own it would be unenforceable. To make the constitution a reality, "complementary laws" needed to be enacted. For those laws, the Cuban public waited and waited. "For all its enlightened clauses," writes historian Louis Pérez, "the constitution of 1940 remained substantially a statement of goals, an agenda for future achievement."[23] Yet the whole process had mobilized the Cuban public and given them a stake in the constitution. So, enforceable or not, the document became an outsized presence in Cuban politics. Everyone invoked it. Politicians based their calls for support on their allegiance to it and on their commitment to making it real. And twelve years after its signing, it became the first rallying cry of a young politician named Fidel Castro.

Chapter 21

SUITCASES

It may have been the worst inauguration in the country's history. Five days earlier, on October 5, 1948, a hurricane—the second in as many weeks—made landfall on Cuba's southwestern coast with sustained winds of up to 132 miles an hour, killing at least eleven people and wounding another two hundred. In Havana, the sea penetrated old defenses, damaging hundreds of buildings. It even sank the yacht of the president-elect, Carlos Prío Socorrás. Not everyone had their power restored in time to turn on their radios to hear the new president give his inauguration speech or take his oath on the Constitution of 1940. From the balcony of the Presidential Palace, Prío addressed the people gathered below. A military parade followed the customary route. It was an ordinary, unspectacular inauguration. But what made it arguably the worst in Cuba's history was not the ceremony itself, but rather what was happening just a few blocks away while everyone focused on the ritual transfer of executive power.[1]

At the nearby treasury building a very different event unfolded without a hitch. Four green GM trucks pulled into the garage. All appeared to be government trucks from the ministry of education. The outgoing minister himself, José Manuel Alemán, was at the head of a group of men carrying suitcases. The guard knew him and joked, "You're not going to rob the treasury, are you?" "Who knows?" was the playful response from the minister. Then he ushered his companions into the interior vault; they opened the suitcases and began filling them with cash: Cuban pesos, British pounds, French francs, Soviet rubles, Italian lire, and a fortune in US dollars. Alemán took the suitcases with the American money, headed straight to the airport, boarded a DC-3, and landed in Miami about an hour later. When customs agents asked him what he carried, the thief was honest: about $19 million. When the officers gave him a hard time, he instructed them to call Washington to confirm what he already knew: no law prohibited entering the United States with large amounts of US currency. Thus, on Cuba's inauguration day did an outgoing government minister arrive in the United States with a fortune literally raided from Cuba's treasury.[2]

With that money—and other suspicious sums pilfered by collecting the salary of thousands of ghost workers in his ministry of education—Alemán built a bicoastal empire in Florida and Havana. He owned a mansion, apartment buildings, and hotels scattered throughout Miami Beach and parts of southwest Miami that would later be known as Little Havana. He bought a palatial estate once owned by Al Capone, and he purchased Key Biscayne—all of it. Back home in Cuba, he owned a sugar mill, a freight company, a baseball team, and large tracts of land in Habana del Este, across the bay from the old city. He died less than two years later, having amassed a fortune of between $70 million and $200 million.[3]

The inauguration day heist occured during the period of Cuban history often recognized as the pinnacle of formal democracy from 1940 to 1952. The period had begun under the sign of a new constitution. The charter seemed to promise a revitalized republic, a vibrant democracy founded on social justice. Every candidate for president ran on making that promise real. Yet the three presidents elected and inaugurated under its aegis all betrayed its promise, spectacularly.

FIRST THERE WAS FULGENCIO BATISTA. In 1940, after years of maneuvering, Batista swept into the presidency in a fair and free election. He ruled over a relatively stable country. Sugar harvests were the largest in decades, and the United States was purchasing most of the island's harvest. Yet corruption scandals plagued his administration. In 1942, one lawsuit revealed that of almost two million pesos allotted for public works projects, only a minuscule $1,623 was used for the purchase of supplies. Much of the rest went to what everyone called *botellas*, the term used for the hiring of ghost workers, people whose votes and allegiance were bought with salaries for jobs for which they were never expected to report.[4]

In 1944, adhering to the principle of no-reelection enshrined in the new constitution, Batista stepped aside, expecting his prime minister to become his elected successor. A majority of Cubans, however, preferred a different candidate: Ramón Grau San Martín, the civilian, revolutionary president of a hundred days in 1933. He was elected largely on the mystique of the "authentic revolution." The generation of students who had propelled him to the presidency in 1933 had come into its own. In 1934, they had had their revolution stolen by Batista. It was their turn now. So, in 1944, their generation gave Grau the presidency once more. The outcome was more than disappointing. British historian Hugh Thomas minced no words when summarizing Grau's four years in office: "An orgy of theft, ill-disguised by emotional nationalistic speeches. He did more than any other single man to kill the hope of democratic practice in Cuba."[5]

Prío, who served as Grau's prime minister, was elected to the presidency in 1948 and lived up to his mentor's example. As president, he built "one of the hemisphere's most fabulous mansions." Situated just outside Havana, it boasted a pool, waterfall, a zoo, a stable of Arabian horses, and an air-conditioned barbershop. How was that possible, asked his fiercest critic, when there was never any money for schools, or public works, or to pay the veterans of the War of Independence?[6]

Corruption plagued the three presidencies: Batista's (1940–44), Grau's (1944–48), and Prío's (1948–52). If corruption was a moral failing, it was also a structural one. The economic power of the United States continued to constrain avenues to economic advancement for Cubans. Foreign and US capital dominated the sugar industry, the railroad, the utilities, and more. As one American journalist had observed a decade earlier, "Cubans really have little they can call their own on the island with the exception of government." Cynically, some said that "bureaucracy"—with its opportunities for graft and corruption—was the island's second crop or second harvest. To a greater or lesser extent, high government officials skimmed money from budgets for private gain—to buy a country manor, to travel, to shop in Miami, or even to buy real estate there. Every presidential administration from this period purchased votes with cash or with salaried appointments to no-show jobs; they granted government contracts to friends or relatives who often failed to deliver, and they put gunmen on the government payroll.[7] Finally, all three presidential administrations of the 1940s collaborated with one of the world's most effective purveyors of graft and illegality: the American mob.

THE AMERICAN MOB HAD FIRST set its sights on Cuba during Prohibition, using the island as a trans-shipment point for alcohol. But Meyer Lansky, famously known as the mob's accountant, saw potential for a much bigger empire there. The island could be the answer to so many things. With the end of Prohibition, it could provide a means to diversify the mob's enterprises. Money invested in casinos would grow and fund other investments, which by the late 1940s prominently included narcotics. And all the profits would remain out of reach of the US government.

CUBA

Meyer first proposed the plan to expand into Cuba to mob leader and associate Lucky Luciano, "boss of bosses." Luciano saw the merits of the scheme immediately. In order to expand into Cuba, however, Lansky and Luciano also needed Cuban buy-in. Specifically, they needed Cuban politicians amenable to the scheme, surely for a price. In late 1933, Lansky and a colleague flew down to Havana with suitcases full of cash. Allegedly, they met Fulgencio Batista at their hotel. The story of the meeting has never been confirmed, but according to mob lore, Lansky opened the suitcases, Batista stared at the money, and the two men shook hands.[8]

Between the depression, political unrest in Cuba, and the fact that Lucky Luciano was jailed in 1936, it took some time to set the collaboration in motion. But by the end of that decade, a firmly ensconced Batista was ready. Lansky began traveling to Havana regularly and received a contract to operate several casinos. Then, with a new postwar boom in full swing, Lansky's plan to expand into Cuba really took off. Lucky Luciano was released from prison in 1946 (as a reward for having helped the Allied war effort against Italy and Germany), on the condition that he remain in Italy and out of the United States. He had barely settled into his new home in Europe when he received a cryptic note from his old friend Lansky: "December—Hotel Nacional." Following a circuitous route that began in Naples and looped through Rio de Janeiro, Caracas, and Mexico City, Luciano landed in Cuba on October 29, 1946, and reunited with Lansky. When he arrived at his room in the Hotel Nacional, the bellhop opened the curtains draped over the large windows, and Luciano felt free. "When I looked down over the Caribbean from my window, I realized somethin' else; the water was just as pretty as the Bay of Naples, but it was only ninety miles from the United States. That meant I was practically back in America." Lucky Luciano had found a new home.[9]

Lansky had called Luciano to Havana's Hotel Nacional for a meeting of all the major US mob families. It was the first meeting of its kind in fourteen years. For three months, Luciano and Lansky laid the groundwork for the gathering. A few weeks before it was scheduled to start, workers at the hotel threatened to strike over wage disputes, thereby imperiling the whole meeting. The president of Cuba himself stepped in and forced the parties to negotiate so that the unlikely summit could proceed unhampered.[10]

The December 1946 meeting is notorious in mob history. About two dozen representatives were said to have descended on the Hotel Nacional, which was closed to the public and the press. For four days, the visitors lived even more lavishly than usual. According to some accounts, they feasted on grilled manatee, roast breast of flamingo, and venison supplied by Cuba's own minister of agriculture. They had their own private security and a fleet of fifty chauffeured luxury cars. At appropriate (and inappropriate) hours they brought in showgirls from the major Havana nightclubs, the Tropicana, the Sans Souci, the Montmartre, as well as prostitutes from Havana's most famous high-end bordello. Frank Sinatra performed. Leisure and decadence aside, everyone was also there to work. And one of the things on their agenda was Cuba. They pondered turning the Isle of Pines, off the island's southwestern coast, into a magnificent, tropical Monte Carlo, bigger than Las Vegas. But the most ambitious proposal made by Luciano was a plan to make Cuba "the center of all international narcotics operations," in the words of the head of the US Bureau of Narcotics and Dangerous Drugs.[11]

The elaborate plan to expand the mob's presence in Cuba required the participation of Cubans, in particular powerful Cubans willing to avert their eyes when necessary. Meyer, who was already running several casinos in Cuba, had those connections. And Lucky Luciano—newly resident in Havana—cultivated them with singular energy. Following the December meeting, Luciano rented a sprawling home in Havana's posh Miramar suburb, not too far from the private home of President Grau, whose administration had already provided Luciano with the visa that had brought him to Cuba. Luciano entertained and socialized with prominent Cuban politicians; he invited them to drink and dine; he shared cocktails by the pool, at gaming tables, sitting before risqué floor shows. He even offered a brand-new car to the wife of a senator. The list of Luciano's political friends was eye-opening. Eduardo Suárez Rivas was a senator whom US agents classified as a narco-trafficker dealing in cocaine. Francisco (Paco) Prío Socorrás, the brother of the future Cuban president, was another senator engaged in drug trafficking, according to US agents. Indalecio (or Neno) Pertierra was a congressman and manager of the Jockey Club at Oriental Race Park. US narcotics agents described him as "the axle" of Cuban and American gangsters. He was co-owner of a new airline called Aerovías Q. With President Grau's blessing, the airline operated out of military airports and made regular flights to Colombia for cocaine. Unsurprisingly, the notorious José Manuel Alemán—later mastermind of the 1948 inauguration day treasury building heist—was another of Lucky Luciano's cronies in Havana.[12]

By February 1947, everyone—even the US government—knew Luciano was hiding out in Havana. In fact, he had not really been hiding; he had been wheeling and dealing and partying publicly. One time, after Frank Sinatra arrived allegedly carrying $2 million in cash for him, a particularly raucous party was inadvertently crashed by a nun and a Girl Scout troop wanting to meet the famous crooner. Luciano's presence in Havana made for spectacular, scandalous copy in Cuba and across the United States. Washington pressured Havana to deport Luciano; in response, President Grau appealed to the ready outcry of "foreign interference." But when the United States threatened to withhold all its pharmaceutical exports to Cuba (presumably because of the possibility that Luciano would be able to divert them to the vibrant black market), Grau conceded. On March 29, 1947, Luciano was put on a ship leaving Havana. Senator Paco Prío and other Cubans friends saw him off at the port.[13]

Luciano's exit was a setback, but the US mob never relinquished its plans for Cuba. Meyer Lansky remained in close contact with his Cuban connections. Mob figures continued to invest in Havana, to winter there, to manage casinos, run drugs, and generally make and hide money, all with the approval of Cuban politicians. The mob did not control Cuba, but it was clearly "a part of institutionalized corruption, paying regular kickbacks to Cuban government officials," in the words of one historian.[14] One hand always washed the other.

The relationship was so close that at times aspects of the Cuban state itself began to resemble the mob. Increasingly, political factions employed their own private security teams who engaged in gangster-style violence. Some spectacular mob-style executions highlighted the resemblances for the Cuban public. People coined a new term for the style of politics of the period: an American word with a Spanish suffix: *gangsterismo*.[15]

Gangsterismo was perhaps the most powerful example of how much public and civic morale had changed over the 1940s. The decade had started with the hopefulness and principle exemplified by the Constitutional Convention. How abstract and innocent seemed those debates as the decade came to close, amidst a corruption so rampant it included pacts with the mob and inauguration-day raids on the national treasury.

NO COUNTRY IS EVER JUST one thing. The political malpractice of the 1940s notwithstanding, the cultural realm was vibrant and alive. New music genres like the mambo took off; new literary movements launched new publications; Cuban artists exhibited at the Museum of Modern Art in New York, in Rome, Port-au-Prince, London, Caracas. Even in politics, transformations are rarely total, and the corruption of presidential administrations never the whole story. Governments of the period devoted increasing attention to economic diversification, creating a new development bank designed to make Cuba less reliant on sugar and imported foodstuffs. From 1946 to 1948, Cuban jurists helped draft the Universal

SUITCASES

Declaration of Human Rights at the United Nations. That same decade, veterans mobilized to make the government remember Black leaders like José Antonio Aponte (of the book of paintings), Plácido (antislavery poet), and General Quintín Bandera (assassinated by his own government in 1906). If the revolutionary fervor of the early 1930s had dissipated, people continued to make claims on their government. Indeed, the popular mobilization that had helped defeat Machado in 1933 and that had rallied around the new constitution in 1940 had morphed by the end of the decade into a civic activism with considerable power. And more and more Cubans were engaging in it to demand an end to corruption.

Perhaps the principal figure in the battles to make the government clean was Eduardo Chibás. Young, bespectacled, often in a white suit, he had entered politics, as so many others had, as a student at the University of Havana. In the early 1930s, he had fought against Machado's dictatorship and had supported President Grau during his hundred-day progressive government. In 1940, Chibás was elected to the Constitutional Convention as part of Grau's new Auténtico political party. In fact, he received more votes than any other delegate save Grau himself. In 1944, when Grau won the presidency, Chibás supported him and won a Senate seat as a member of the same party.[16]

To say that Chibás became disillusioned with Grau's 1944 presidency is the greatest of understatements. "Never has a government defrauded the faith of Cubans so rapidly and radically," Chibás was known to argue. Unfortunately for Grau, Chibás was more than a politician. He was also the most popular radio personality in all of Cuba, and Cuba had a lot of radios. Every Sunday at 8 p.m., hundreds of thousands of people tuned in to hear Chibás. People who owned radios hosted those who didn't. In the small rural village of Cortés in Pinar del Río, some eight hundred walked to the house of Filiberto Porvén to listen. When they heard something they liked they applauded "as if [Chibás] were there in person." More people listened to Chibás than to any other politician on the radio. He had many more listeners than did the Auténtico Party's official radio program. In second place among political offerings, after Chibás, was the show hosted by Salvador García Agüero, the Black communist delegate to the 1940 Constitutional Convention who became senator for Havana in 1944. Still, Chibás's numbers were much greater. He rivaled even the soap operas.[17]

With rousing oratory and biting condemnations, he excoriated the abuses of Cuban government officials. His show was so familiar and his method so effective that when people wanted to scold others for any kind of improper behavior, they threatened simply "to tell Chibás." In January 1947, he sent a twelve-page open letter to President Grau urging him to fire corrupt ministers and bring them to justice. Grau ignored him. But Chibás kept publicly calling him to task. A few months later, during his May 11 show, he "signaled his readiness to found a new party based on the original Auténtico ideals of economic independence, political liberty, and social justice." The following Thursday, Chibás presided over a meeting of like-minded citizens. Among those present was a twenty-year-old law student at the University of Havana named Fidel Castro. The principal item on the agenda was splitting with the Auténticos. Chibás decided to give Grau seventy-two hours to convene a meeting of the party. But again Grau ignored him.[18]

So, on Sunday, May 18, two hours after the deadline, Chibás announced on the radio that he was forming a new party. It would be called the Partido del Pueblo Cubano—the Party of the Cuban People, more commonly known as the Ortodoxo (or Orthodox) Party. The new party opened its headquarters in the old gym of former world boxing champion Eligio Sardiñas, better known as Kid Chocolate. They called it a place to use their "revolutionary muscle to knock out corruption and sleazy politicking." As a slogan, the party selected "Vergüenza contra dinero"—best translated as "honor against money." Because the party proposed to sweep out corruption, it adopted as its symbol a broom—a modest, familiar item associated with the kind of politics the party wanted: clean. Supporters began placing brooms at their front doors or on their porches as a sign of support and a statement against government corruption. The party won enough support immediately to field candidates in the 1948 elections. Chibás himself ran for president. To launch his campaign, he flew to eastern Cuba and from there, he traveled with a large caravan, speaking and meeting voters all the way back to Havana. One rally in Santiago attracted some sixty thousand souls, thousands of them carrying brooms.[19]

Across the island, Chibás advocated a new kind of politics. But people, even supporters, often assumed that the old style of politics still ruled. His secretary later explained that people would come to see him and ask for help—a scholarship for a child, a hospital bed for a sick parent. In exchange, some offered money; others offered their identity cards, presumably so that someone could use it to vote for the party. When Chibás refused to accept the offerings, "people didn't understand, and it was necessary to explain himself many times."[20] Chibás also sought to dismantle traditional barriers between politicians and voters. According to one biographer, he routinely flung "himself off truck beds and into the arms of admirers." He walked to and from the studio for his weekly show chatting with throngs of supporters along the way. Chibás was a political star. A rumor circulated that the presumptive winner of the

Supporters of Eduardo Chibás raising brooms to symbolize the clean-government stance of the Ortodoxo Party.

election, Prío, was so worried that he offered the post of prime minister to Chibás and half the cabinet positions to his party. Never, replied the maverick.[21]

Chibás's showing at the polls was impressive. But it was not enough to win. Every other party on the ballot secured significantly fewer votes than its membership. The Ortodoxo Party, meanwhile, earned about double the number of its registered members. For that reason, despite the loss, everyone marveled. An American election observer called it "a great moral victory." A columnist for *Bohemia*, the island's most popular magazine, classified it as a miracle, a harbinger of good things to come: "The votes earned by [Chibás], who didn't offer jobs, bribes or anything else of that sort, can be utilized as a lever by which he can raise a great party, one that could become the undisputed leader of the opposition in the coming years."[22]

Having lost the election and no longer in the Senate, Chibás devoted himself full-time to building the party and to denouncing corruption wherever he saw it. He leveled accusations against judges, against the president's brother, against the president himself. "Tell me, Carlos Prío, how you can buy so many farms . . . while at the same time you say that there is no money and no material to build roads. . . . Tell me why you suddenly put at liberty the famous international drug trafficker whom you arrested in the Hotel Nacional with a cargo of drugs for the head of the secret police." More than once, his show was temporarily suspended as a result of such denunciations. But Chibás had so popularized and normalized the genre of impas-

267

sioned accusation, that whenever Chibás was jailed, a flourishing media stepped in to amplify his message and counter the government's attempt to silence him.[23] Ordinary citizens, as well, sought to follow Chibás's example, penning their own denunciations of government corruption. Sometimes press and citizenry mobilized against things other than venality. For example, in March 1949, a drunken US marine climbed to the top of the José Martí monument in Havana's Central Park and urinated on the head of the statue. Students and communists organized protests in front of the US embassy; the outcry reached far beyond those two groups, however, and the US ambassador was forced to issue a nationally televised apology and another at the foot of the monument. The apology was less effective than it might have been, because the ambassador forgot Martí's name as he was speaking. But without the public engagement and activism, there might have been no contrition at all.[24]

Chibás pioneered a new style, and young reformers followed suit. His genre of accusatory speeches, often repeating the phrase "*yo acuso*" (I accuse)—soon became a staple of Cuban politics. Fidel Castro used Chibás's "yo acuso" refrain in a campaign speech during a 1952 Senate run that helped mark him as a political and oratorical talent. Other politicians followed Chibás's example with more than speech. One brought a case before Cuban criminal courts accusing former and current government officials with the theft of $174,241,840.14. Known as Lawsuit 82, it detailed rampant embezzlement and fraud, much of it by José Manuel Alemán, the minister of education who masterminded the inauguration day heist of the treasury in 1948.

The author of the thirty-three-page accusation that launched Lawsuit 82 was Senator Pelayo Cuervo Navarro. When he began gathering evidence to make the case, his friends advised him to desist. You will end up being fed to the sharks around the Morro, they warned. But using his sons as round-the-clock bodyguards, he persisted. Soon evidence in support of his case began arriving by mysterious means: anonymous phone calls, notes left in unexpected places telling him that documents would be waiting, say, "on the third shelf of room 64 in the Treasury building." He filled a whole room in his Vedado house with documents pertaining to the case. While several judges initially declined to hear it, one judge acceded. The cache of documents—numbering over five thousand—was transferred to the judge's chambers, and a trial date was set. But at 2 a.m. on July 22, 1950, a green GM truck pulled up in front of the courthouse. Five men carrying suitcases walked into the judge's chambers, packed every last bit of paper, and left. It took the senator almost a year to reassemble the evidence. The judge handed down an indictment that named, among others, Cuba's previous president (Grau) and ten of his former ministers, including the corrupt education minister Alemán. By the time the guilty verdict came, it was for a smaller amount ($40 million instead of $174 million), and Alemán had already died a wealthy man.[25]

In many ways, Lawsuit 82 is an apt proxy for this moment in Cuban history. It exposes, on the one hand, the depth of corruption that marked Cuban politics of the period. On the other, it highlights the power and persistence of civic activism—the work of journalists, politicians, students, and citizens in challenging the routine perversion of politics by venality and crude theft.

TWO MORE UNEXPECTED KINDS OF theft close off the period. The first was perpetrated, perhaps inadvertently, by Chibás himself, then the favorite to win the presidency in the upcoming election of 1952. Engaged in a radio battle against the new minister of education, whom he accused of purloining school breakfast funds to purchase real estate abroad, Chibás promised to present incontrovertible proof of the theft on his weekly Sunday broadcast of August 5, 1951. He appeared at the station with a small suitcase, which people assumed held the evidence. But for reasons that remain unclear, he presented none. He spoke passionately, repeating general accusations against current and past presidents and against present and former education ministers. Then his voice rose further: "For economic independence, political freedom, and social justice!" he shouted. "Let's sweep away the government crooks! People of Cuba, rise up and move! People of Cuba, awaken! This is my last knock on the door!" Then he opened his briefcase, took out a gun, and shot himself on-air. But he spoke for too long, and just before the shot rang out, the program cut to a commercial for Café Pilón. I have friends not then alive or too young to remember the episode who do remember what their mothers and grandmothers told them they were were doing the moment Chibás shot himself at the end of his show.[26]

No one knows if Chibás really meant to kill himself. The bullet entered his stomach; he lingered for more than a week, wanting to live, and then died on August 16, 1951. Chibás had stolen the election from himself. At the time, he was the most popular politician in Cuba; he might have become Cuba's next president. His funeral was the largest the country had ever seen. Some three hundred thousand people accompanied the coffin from the University of Havana's Aula Magna, where it was displayed, to Colón Cemetery.[27] Everything felt different after that. His party tried to keep up the momentum. New election slogans used his name and image. It was his memory and his example, said coreligionists, that would carry them to victory on election day. That did not happen. Still, Chibás and his party left a lasting legacy. He linked the widespread and long-standing commitment to social democracy that had begun to emerge in the late 1920s with a new kind of political militancy. That connection would persist throughout the 1950s; indeed, it helps explain the rise and the appeal of Fidel Castro.

ON MARCH 10, 1952, THE greatest theft of the whole period quietly unfolded. Fulgencio Batista was running for president. His campaign billboard was a gigantic cutout picture of him standing in a suit, under him the phrase "Este es el Hombre." This is the man. But a December magazine poll placed him third in the contest. Everyone suspected that he was the man about to lose.[28]

In the very early hours of the morning, before the sun had fully risen, my mother was on her way to work and saw Batista in the lead jeep of a convoy, driving into Camp Columbia. He was there to steal the presidency. And he succeeded. Batista's coup that morning lasted one hour and seventeen minutes—a sign, say some, of the general indifference and deep cynicism with politics that limited Cubans' capacity to respond. But Batista took no chances, and he plotted the details of the coup in a way that made resistance futile. His men seized army posts across the city and set up commands at all strategic locations. Military roadblocks made entering and leaving Havana impossible. The army took over bus and train depots, banks and government offices, radio and television stations. When residents awoke and turned on news to assess rampant rumors of a coup, they could find only uninterrupted music. Tanks rolled on downtown Havana. Prío left the Presidential Palace, soon fled to Mexico, and then to Miami. Batista immediately dissolved the Congress and placed military guards around the Capitol to prevent congressmen and their staffs from gathering. A day after the coup, Batista addressed the public and canceled the elections he was about to lose. With less fanfare, he raised his presidential salary from $2,000 to $12,000 a month.[29]

Initially, even the brutal efficiency of Batista's coup did not silence widespread opposition. Students, as usual, marched and wrote. They staged a symbolic burial of the 1940 constitution before a bust of José Martí on the corner of 25th and Hospital Streets. Older politicians sought the assistance of the United Nations and the Organization of American States. Younger members of Chibás's Ortodoxo Party tried to organize boycotts; women resolved not to purchase makeup or clothes. From the balconies at movie theaters, anonymous activists showered the crowds below with flyers that exhorted, "Cubans, take your place of honor!"

SUITCASES

Less than a week after the coup, students gathered at the tomb of Eduardo Chibás to condemn the coup. Among those present was Fidel Castro, who climbed atop a crypt and, with flailing arms, called the public to overthrow Batista by force. A week later, perhaps unconvinced that armed rebellion would succeed or that enough people were willing to pursue it, Castro brought a lawsuit against Batista. The case detailed each of Batista's violations of the 1940 constitution and asked for the maximum sentence for each, or a total of more than one hundred years in prison. The case went nowhere.[30]

Batista's coup had succeeded. But it was by dint of surgical repression, not because of Cuban indifference. A little over two weeks after the coup, US president Harry S. Truman extended Batista's government official recognition. In New York City, Meyer Lansky packed his suitcase, booked a flight, and headed to the Hotel Nacional. Things, he thought, were looking up.[31]

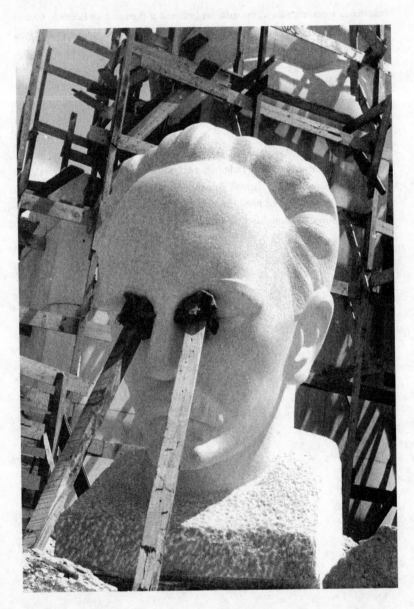

In 1953, Cubans celebrated the centennial of the birth of national hero José Martí. That year workers broke ground on a monument for the city's new Civic Plaza, later renamed Plaza of the Revolution.

Part VIII

ORIGIN STORIES

Top Left: Wooden statue of the dog-shaped deity that the Taíno called Opiyelguobirán, who carried spirits to the world of the dead.

Top Right: The Taíno leader Hatuey, who resisted the Spanish conquest, was burned at the stake in 1512. Given the chance to convert to Christianity right before his death, he refused, allegedly saying that if the Spanish went to heaven, he would prefer hell.

Below: In 1762, British naval forces attacked and captured the well-fortified city of Havana. For a time, Havana became part of the same imperial system as the thirteen colonies of North America.

4

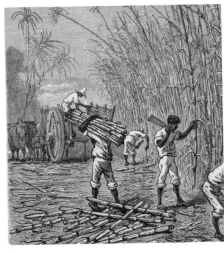

5

Top Left: Havana's free Black militia fought the British during the siege of 1762 and participated in battles linked to the American Revolution. This painting, by Black artist José Nicolás de la Escalera, shows the militia's uniform in 1763.

Top Right: Sugar, which came to dominate the Cuban economy in the early nineteenth century, had the most grueling labor regime of any tropical crop, almost all of it performed by enslaved Africans and their descendants.

Below: Nineteenth-century Cuban sugar plantations were among the largest and most advanced in the world. This 1857 Eduardo Laplante engraving shows the sugar estate Trinidad, one of the sites of the 1843–1844 antislavery conspiracies in the province of Matanzas.

6

7

8

Top Left: Carlos Manuel de Céspedes, a sugar planter from eastern Cuba, launched the island's first war of independence, the Ten Years' War, by granting freedom to the men and women he held in slavery.

Top Right: Beginning in 1847, the Spanish government in Cuba allowed the importation of Chinese men to work on eight-year contracts. Systematic abuses led the Chinese government to close the trade in 1874. Shown here is an identification document for José Chuen, a Chinese contract worker in Matanzas in 1871.

Below: A group of formerly enslaved men and women shown here shortly after emancipation in 1886. The photograph was taken by José Gómez de la Carrera, the island's first major photographer.

9

10

11

Top Left: Cuban patriot and intellectual José Martí spent most of his adult life living in New York City, writing and organizing for Cuban independence. This 1891 photograph was taken during his first trip to Key West, where he gave speeches and raised funds among Cuban cigar workers.

Top Right: Rosa Castellanos, commonly known as Rosa la Bayamesa, was a soldier and nurse in Cuba's two major wars of independence. She earned the rank of captain and was celebrated by General Máximo Gómez, the highest commander of Cuba's Liberation Army. This photograph was published in 1899 in the magazine *El Fígaro*.

Below: Afro-Cuban General Antonio Maceo (back row, center) was one of the most important figures in the struggle for Cuban independence. He is shown here in 1892 in Costa Rica with fellow members of the movement. Maceo's dog, which he named Cuba Libre, appears in the foreground.

12

13

LEFT: The USS *Maine* entered Havana harbor in January 1898, after Spanish citizens attacked US-owned establishments. The explosion of the ship on February 15, 1898, led the United States to declare war on Spain and to intervene in Cuba's final war of independence.

14

RIGHT: Theodore Roosevelt and his Rough Riders photographed after their important victory at the top of San Juan Hill in Santiago de Cuba in July 1898.

BELOW: The Governor's Palace in Havana, the seat of the Spanish colonial government, is shown here guarded by US troops and flying an American flag at the beginning of the US military occupation of 1899–1902.

15

ABOVE: During the first US occupation of Cuba, more than twelve hundred Cuban teachers traveled to the United States to spend the summer of 1900 studying at Harvard University. Architects of the program wanted the teachers to learn that capacity for self-government was slow to develop. The Cuban teachers generally rejected the lesson and stressed the need for immediate independence.

BOTTOM LEFT & BOTTOM RIGHT: The US military occupation ended only after the Cuban Constitutional Convention agreed to include the Platt Amendment as an appendix to the new republic's constitution. The Platt Amendment granted the right of intervention in Cuban affairs to the US government. In the United States, the amendment was generally regarded as precautionary and benign, while in Cuba, it was seen as the equivalent of assault and robbery. Contemporary cartoons convey the difference in US and Cuban sentiment.

A PRECAUTIONARY AMENDMENT
Yes, sonny, you can have the fire works for your celebration; but I must insist on your wearin this extinguisher.

From the Minneapolis Journal, April 22.

19

LEFT: An image of a modern Cuban sugar mill printed on a US-produced postcard, 1904.

BELOW: American companies dominated the Cuban sugar industry, controlling nineteen of the top twenty sugar-producing establishments in the early 1920s. Pictured here are workers at the US-owned Sugar Central Cunagua in 1918, posing in front of some of the expensive and modern technology required to process sugar.

20

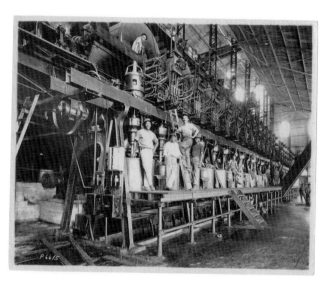

P 6615

TOWN SITE OF LA GLORIA
LOOKING NORTH.

21

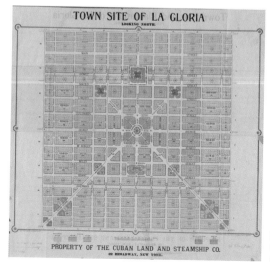

PROPERTY OF THE CUBAN LAND AND STEAMSHIP CO.
32 BROADWAY, NEW YORK.

LEFT: In the first two decades of the twentieth century, US companies bought land in Cuba and established "American colonies." La Gloria was one of the most prominent. This official map designates the blue and pink blocks as residential, the yellow as commercial, the purple structures as public buildings and churches, and the green as parks and plazas.

22

ABOVE: President Calvin Coolidge visited Havana in January 1928 to open the meeting of the Pan-American Conference. He poses here with President Gerardo Machado, a once popular president who was in the process of unconstitutionally extending his presidential term and viciously targeting his opposition.

BELOW: Machado was removed from office by a popular revolution in 1933. News of his flight on August 12, 1933, was greeted with street celebrations, and later violence, in Havana and across the country.

23

Pan American's first passenger flight
Key West, Florida, to Havana, Cuba, January 16, 1928
(Fokker F-7)

1

Above: In January 1928, Pan American's first passenger flight traveled between Key West and Havana. Advances in technology contributed to the rise of American tourism to Cuba.

Below: Prohibition in the United States (1920–1933) spurred Americans' interest in travel to Cuba. Sloppy Joe's Bar in Havana, popularly known as the American Bar, was a favorite destination for visiting Americans.

2

3

LEFT: The Revolution of 1933 resulted in the rise of a progressive government that sought the expansion of workers' and peasants' rights, closer ties to Latin America, and a more equal relationship with the United States. Led by President Ramón Grau San Martín (right), it lasted just 127 days. Once its most important military figure, Fulgencio Batista (left) was instrumental in defeating the new government.

BELOW: Workers, students, and other civic groups pressed the revolutionary government of 1933 to follow through on its promises. Crowds at a demonstration carried signs with slogans such as "Cuba for the Cubans," and "Grau: The Hope of Cuba." One sign printed in English read, "We want the Platt Amendment rescinded."

4

ABOVE: Eduardo Chibás was a popular and maverick politician. He condemned government corruption and created a new political party to combat it. He was expected to do well in a run for the presidency in 1952, but committed suicide during his Sunday evening radio broadcast in August 1951.

BOTTOM LEFT: On March 10, 1952, Fulgencio Batista, who had been running third in the race for the presidency, staged a military coup and installed himself as president. He is shown here celebrating in Camp Columbia, the island's largest military installation, a portrait of José Martí behind him.

BOTTOM RIGHT: On July 26, 1953, Fidel Castro tried to bring down Batista's government by staging an attack on the Moncada Camp in Santiago, the island's second largest army base. Though the attempt was quickly defeated, Castro would later use the date of the attack, July 26, as the name for his revolutionary movement. Castro is shown here immediately after his arrest, standing in front of a portrait of Martí.

LEFT: Student leader José Antonio Echeverría was one of the most prominent leaders of the revolution against Batista. He was killed during the attack on the Presidential Palace in March 1957. He is shown here giving a speech in 1956 or 1957 standing in front of a bust of Martí.

BELOW: Mothers protest peacefully against Batista's government in Santiago in 1957, carrying a sign that reads "Stop Assassinating Our Sons, Cuban Mothers." Civic protests of this kind were an important part of the movement to defeat Batista.

LEFT: In December 1956, Fidel Castro ensconced himself in the mountains of eastern Cuba to wage guerrilla war against Batista's army. He is shown here with his brother, Raúl, in late 1958, shortly before Batista's defeat.

11

12

ABOVE: Fidel Castro entered Havana victorious on January 8, 1959. He was greeted by enormous and enthusiastic crowds. This photo by Burt Glinn shows a rapt audience listening to him speak at the Presidential Palace.

RIGHT: The revolutionary government tried, sentenced, and executed hundreds of old Batistiano officials in its first months in power. A priest ministers last rites to a condemned man in Matanzas. Photographer Andrew López won a Pulitzer for the photo.

13

LEFT: On July 26, 1959, the new government staged a massive rally to celebrate the passage of an agrarian reform law. Hundreds of thousands of peasants traveled to Havana from across the country to celebrate. The government gave them the white shirts and hats seen in this famous photograph by Alberto Korda.

14

Top: Fidel Castro, shown here giving a speech on April 16, the eve of the Bay of Pigs invasion. It was during this speech that he first publicly identified the Cuban Revolution as socialist.

Below: After 1962, the Soviet military buildup turned the island into the world's second most militarized state (per capita), trailing only North Korea. Soviet tanks parade in Havana, a portrait of Vladimir Lenin and Cuban revolutionary Camilo Cienfuegos in the background.

15

16

ABOVE: A Cuban family reunites in Miami in 1967. The man had left Cuba by boat and reached the Texas coast. The woman and son arrived via the Freedom Flights that brought almost 300,000 Cubans to the United States from 1965 to 1973.

BELOW: Fifteen thousand Cubans march from Little Havana to downtown Miami during a political rally in 1977.

17

18

RIGHT: The Mariel boatlift brought approximately 125,000 Cubans to the United States between April and October 1980, most of them arriving in Key West, pictured here. The Cuban government designated the port of Mariel as the embarkation point, allowing Cuban Americans to pick up relatives there, provided they board other Cubans at the discretion of the government.

19

Top: In March 2016, during a brief thaw in US-Cuban relations, the result of complex and extended negotiations between the two governments, President Barack Obama visited Havana. He is shown here entering a privately owned restaurant in the neighborhood of Centro Habana waving to onlookers leaning out their balconies and windows.

Below: Havana street scene, November 17, 2017. Policies adopted by the Cuban government naturally have enormous repercussions in the daily lives of Cuban people. US policy on Cuba does as well.

20

Chapter 22

CENTENNIAL SPIRIT

In 1953, Cubans celebrated the centennial of the birth of José Martí, Cuban New Yorker and intellectual author of the island's independence from Spain. Scheduled to last for a full year, the commemoration had a projected price tag of $10 million. A congressional act in 1945 had stipulated that workers would contribute one day's salary a year toward its cost. When the hundredth anniversary of Martí's birth arrived on January 28, 1953, all of Cuba was ready. Great crowds gathered in Havana's Central Park to watch the ritual laying of wreaths at his monument. Some blocks away, Berta Singerman, renowned practitioner of literary declamation, read Martí's poetry from atop a platform erected in front of Havana's cathedral, illuminated behind her. Famed pianists gave concerts; international scholars gave lectures. Workers broke ground for a monument on a hill—a white marble statue of a seated Martí, arm draped over his knee, deep in thought; behind him a gray marble, five-pointed tower rose to more than three hundred fifty feet. The government issued new coins in many denominations, all featuring Martí's profile and the words "Centenario de Martí, 1953." They were minted in the United States.[1]

As the country celebrated Martí's centennial, Fulgencio Batista's recent coup was a year old. Batista knew that even those who hated him could not protest or boycott the man Cubans called "the Apostle." Yet even in official acts, people registered the irony of honoring the nation's symbol of freedom under the rule of Batista. On the first night of the official centennial, University of Havana students staged a torchlight procession and paid tribute to Martí by shouting "Liberty" at a dictator. To protect themselves from police retribution, they added sharp nails to their torches.

A very different commemoration occurred across the island, near the mountains where Martí had died in war in 1895. A young teacher had proposed that a monument to Martí be erected at the island's highest point: Pico Turquino, which rose 6,476 feet above sea level in the lush mountains of the Sierra Maestra, where Native Cubans escaping the Spanish, men and women running away from slavery, miners watching over the Virgin of Charity, and rebels battling against the Spanish army had all found shelter long ago. Artist Jilma Madera sculpted the bust in bronze. No one paid her, so she sold medallions and miniatures to raise funds for the project.[2]

In eastern Cuba, the sculptor counted on the intellectual and logistical support of a country doctor. He was president of the regional chapter of the national committee of the centennial, a member of the island's archeological society, the founder of the local chapter of the Ortodoxo Party, and a fierce critic of Batista. Because he was that kind of man, he asked the artist's permission to invite one of his four daughters on the expedition to Pico Turquino. "She is dying to meet you," he said, and "would like to accompany me on the trek."[3]

The daughter's name was Celia Sánchez. At thirty-three, she was tall and thin, with dark hair and long fingers and limbs. She had begun her education at a small public school, where all the grades learned together in one room; when it rained, "the teacher wrote on the board with her right hand, and with the left held up an umbrella." A little later, when her father accepted a position as doctor at a sugar *central*, the family's situation improved. By then Celia was in private school, and the family moved into one of the pretty yellow houses generally reserved for American administrators and personnel of the company. As the daughter of the only doctor in the area, she knew the families of local workers and peasants. Like her father, she was an Ortodoxo Party organizer; in fact she had stood on the dais next to Eduardo Chibás when he spoke in town during the campaign of 1948, a few years before his dramatic radio suicide. Now she trekked with her father, the sculptor, and other Martí devotées on the most romantic commemoration of the centennial—the placing of a bust of Martí at the very top of the island of Cuba. From there, they said, the Apostle would stand watch over the country's moral destiny.[4]

On May 19, the anniversary of Martí's death, the group gathered at his mausoleum in the main cemetery of Santiago. The next day, they headed into the mountains, marching single file, the men taking turns shouldering the weight of the statue and equipment. When they arrived at Pico Turquino on the morning of May 21, they built a base for the sculpture from local rock, which had saved them the task of lugging more materials. Then they carefully placed the 163-pound bust at the top. The bronze Martí faced east toward the rising sun and Haiti. On one side of the base, they secured the Martí quotation that the artist had selected for the monument: "Scarce as the mountains are the men who can look down from them and feel with the soul of a nation and of humanity." On the back of the

Orthodox Party activist Celia Sánchez in 1948

pedestal, they placed a plaque with the names of the people who had made the whole endeavor possible. On the list was Celia Sánchez, civic-minded daughter of a country doctor. Pictures taken that day show the narrow-faced Celia, smiling before a monument at once grandiose—it was, after all, at the island's very highest point—and humble—elaborated for free by a young woman and erected and dedicated by civilians on their own initiative and on their own terms.[5]

IN 1953, AS CELIA SÁNCHEZ was scaling the Sierra Maestra with Martí's bust, Fidel Castro was in Havana, a strapping, sometimes impetuous young man, twenty-six years old going on twenty-seven, and plotting something much more improbable and much more dangerous than a statue of Martí at the top of a mountain.

Fidel had been in Havana eleven years by then. But he was in a fundamental sense a man of eastern Cuba. Born in 1926 to a Spanish father who had fought for Spain during Cuba's War of Independence and to a Cuban woman (his father's second wife) who had worked as a cook in his house, Fidel spent the first years of his life on a 25,000-acre plantation near the village of Birán, near Banes. It was not too far from the bay where the Virgin of Charity had first appeared to Black and Native fishermen, and a little farther from the shores where Christopher Columbus first landed in Cuba. It was also land that had remained mostly undeveloped until the onslaught of US sugar investment and expansion in the early twentieth century. Few landscapes in Cuba were as dominated by US capital as the countryside of Fidel's youth. There Castro remained until his parents sent him to the eastern capital of Santiago to attend a Jesuit school. In 1942, he left for Havana and enrolled in the country's most prestigious school, the Jesuit Colegio de Belén, earning a prize for the best all-around student athlete in the country. In 1945, he entered the University of Havana as a law student and quickly became involved in the turbulent student politics that had been a mainstay of the institution for decades and the *gangsterismo* that had come to dominate it more recently. In 1948, two days after Prío's presidential inauguration and the education minister's notorious heist, Castro married Mirta Díaz Balart, daughter of a Cuban politician (and later aunt of two die-hard anti-Castro members of the US House of Representatives). Batista, a friend of her family, sent a wedding present, and the couple honeymooned in New York. By the time Batista staged his coup in 1952, Castro was a practicing lawyer and an aspiring politician in the Ortodoxo Party. Immediately after the coup, he brought an unsuccessful lawsuit against Batista for usurpation of power and violation of the Cuban Constitution. Increasingly frustrated by what he saw as complacency before Batista, Castro became convinced that it was time for something new, perhaps even something monumental.[6]

Castro soon settled on the idea of an armed attack on the island's second-largest army installation, the Moncada barracks in Santiago. Working with his brother, Raúl, Fidel raised funds for weapons and cars, and he recruited young men, many from the youth wing of the Ortodoxo Party. He knew their chances of success were slim. With only 135 insurgents for the attack, they would be severely outnumbered. Yet they had a few things in their favor. They timed their attack to coincide with carnival in Santiago, the liveliest anywhere on the island. The festivities would mean that many soldiers and police would be drunk or hungover. The busy, crowded carnival would also help camouflage the presence of strangers. The attackers themselves would be disguised in regular army uniforms in order to gain entry into the installation and surprise the soldiers from within. Finally, the rebels expected that once they achieved nominal control at the barracks, the soldiers would join the fight against Batista. Castro drafted a manifesto to be read on the radio immediately after the initial victory. Addressed to "the nation" and signed "the Cuban Revolution," it purported to speak "in the name of the sacred rights of the fatherland, for the honor of [Martí's] centennial."[7]

For the assault on the barracks, Fidel divided his forces into groups. Raúl and his men would attack the Palace of Justice; from its roof they would be able to control access to the adjacent barracks. Abel Santamaría, a twenty-four-year-old bookkeeper at a Pontiac dealership in Havana and a member of the Ortodoxo Party, would take control of the military hospital next door to oversee attention to any wounded. Fidel himself would lead the attack on the barracks, at the head of a group of ninety-five men, the majority wearing army uniforms and arriving in separate vehicles. That was the plan.[8]

Early on the morning of July 26, 1953, the first four assailants approached Gate 3 of the barracks, saluted the guards, and entered without mishap. Almost immediately, however, someone recognized the men as outsiders and sounded the alarm. Army troops began firing. Of Fidel's group of ninety-five, only forty-five are known to have arrived at the barracks. Some of the cars had gotten lost in the city; many of the rebels were from out of town and they found their intended routes blocked by the carnival. Meanwhile, many of the fighters with Santamaría at the hospital and Raúl Castro at the Palace of Justice were killed or captured. Fidel's car was fired on, and he never made it inside the barracks. He escaped into the nearby mountains, only to be caught a few days later.[9] The attack was a spectacular and undisputed failure.

LATER, HOWEVER, FIDEL CASTRO'S ASSAULT on the Moncada barracks would become a gripping origin story: the tale of a handful of idealistic young men (and two women) who in the spirit of Martí launched themselves at a dictatorship. The Moncada assault became the initial defeat that in hindsight proceeded inexorably to triumph. In 1955, Fidel would use the date of the Moncada attack to name his revolutionary project, calling it the 26th of July Movement. After he came to power in 1959, the anniversary of the attack would become the island's most important national holiday, celebrated with gargantuan political rallies at the Plaza of the Revolution, under the gaze of a marble Martí.[10]

But even before all that, in the days and weeks after the botched assault, Castro triumphed in the battle of public opinion. In this, he had the inadvertent help of Batista's government. The army, which lost thirty-three soldiers in the attack, viciously retaliated. It killed more than fifty of the rebels after having taken them prisoner. In some cases, they tossed assailants' cadavers in places where it might look like the men had died in combat. Many of the dead were buried without their eyes or teeth. The two women who participated in the attack were burned with cigarettes. Other tortures they suffered were worse. Authorities presented one of the women, Haydée Santamaría, with a tray holding her brother's eyes and her boyfriend's testicles. Journalists, and later historians, called the government's response to the Moncada assault "the largest mass killing of prisoners since the War of Independence."[11]

That fact turned a failed, militarily insignificant attack into a political victory for Fidel Castro. It was not that a majority of Cubans supported the attack on the barracks, nor that they even knew anything about the attackers and their specific goals. It was, rather, that the response of an already unpopular government was so intemperate and brutal that public sympathy immediately gravitated to the young rebels. Across the island, judges, journalists, university officials, priests, even the island's two archbishops condemned the army's actions, demanding fair trials for the accused and respect for constitutional guarantees (suspended by Batista in the immediate aftermath of the attack).[12]

So, when the trial for the surviving rebels of the Moncada assault began in late September, many were paying attention. Castro's trial opened on September 21, 1953. He entered the overcrowded courtroom, center stage, with everyone watching. "There he is," murmured onlookers, pointing to Fidel, standing over six feet tall, wearing his favorite navy wool suit, his wavy hair slicked into place, his new mustache trimmed. Brought to the front of the courtroom, Castro immediately lifted his arms above his head to reveal the manacles around his hands and addressed the judge, "Mr. President, . . . What guarantees can there be in this trial? Not even the worst criminals are held this way in a hall that calls itself a hall of justice. . . . You cannot judge people who are handcuffed. . . ." Total silence followed, and then the judge ordered the handcuffs removed. The accused had become the accuser. And the state's trial against Fidel Castro was about to become Fidel Castro's trial against the state.[13]

Within minutes, Castro surprised everyone a second time by claiming his right as a lawyer to assume his own defense. Again, the judge agreed, and ordered that Castro be given a black robe, like the other lawyers. For the rest of the trial, Fidel would don it when he assumed the role of lawyer, and shed it when he reverted to that of defendant. The first question put to Fidel was simple: Did you participate in the assault on the Moncada barracks? Yes, he replied. What about these other young men, asked the lawyer, pointing to some of his fellow rebels. Fidel's reply was longer: "Those young men, like me, love the liberty of their country. They have committed no crime, unless it is a crime to want the best for our country. Isn't that what they taught us in school?" The judge interrupted, advising him to just answer the questions. When the lawyers asked where he had gotten the money for the assault, Fidel compared himself to José Martí. Just as Martí had not accepted ill-gotten money, neither had he accepted money from corrupt politicians. With what political standing was he expecting to mobilize a whole people? asked an attorney. Fidel responded by comparing himself to the independence heroes every Cuban knew: with the same standing relied on by the young lawyer Carlos Manuel de Céspedes when he began the first independence war and with the same standing with which a muleteer named Antonio Maceo rose up against Spain. Neither of those patriots was well known in the beginning. Asked about the intellectual author of the assault on Moncada, Fidel replied, "only José Martí, the Apostle of our independence." People in the courtroom applauded, and the judge had to intervene.

On the last day of the trial, before the judge delivered his sentence, in a courtroom strategically closed to the public, Castro delivered one of the most important speeches of his life. At over fifty single-spaced pages, the speech was a major, if meandering, pronouncement. It detailed the crimes committed against the young revolutionaries, including the torture and murder of people who had surrendered or been captured. It rejected the very premise of the main charge against him—an assault on the constitutional powers of the state. "In what country is the prosecutor living," he asked rhetorically. "First of all, the dictatorship that oppresses the nation is not a constitutional power, but an unconstitutional one: it was established against the Constitution, over the head of the Constitution, violating the legitimate Constitution of the Republic." As during the trial, he invoked the heroes of Cuban history: Martí, Maceo, Gómez, Céspedes. But he reached well beyond them as well: to the English Revolution of 1688, the American of 1776, the French of 1789. He cited Thomas Paine and Jean-Jacques Rousseau, as well as many others whose names are less familiar: Reformation philosophers, Scottish reformers, German and Spanish jurists, a Virginia clergyman. He spoke about the Cuban people and clarified at length when he meant by the term.

> We're talking about the six hundred thousand Cubans without work, who want to earn their daily bread honestly without having to emigrate from their homeland in search of a livelihood; the five hundred thousand farm laborers who live in miserable shacks, who work four months of the year and starve the rest . . . ; the four hundred thousand industrial workers and laborers whose retirement funds have been embezzled . . . ; the one hundred thousand small farmers who live and die working land that is not theirs. . . .

And the list continued: teachers, small businessmen, young professionals, artists. All of them, he said, were the people.[14]

Finally, Castro spoke about his own revolution. He explained the five revolutionary laws that were to have been read over the radio following their victory at the Moncada barracks. The first law restored the 1940 constitution, recognizing it as "the true supreme law of the State." Another promised land to peasants; one ordered the confiscation of all ill-gotten gains. The proposed laws would have sounded familiar; they had been part of Cuba's political landscape since the late 1920s, through the revolution of 1933, and the drafting of the 1940 constitution. If the brash attack on the military barracks was unusual, the goals of the movement did not seem to be. By different means, Fidel Castro preached a political program thoroughly familiar and appealing to a wide swath of Cuban society. And that program reflected a consensus in favor of democratic principles and social justice.

Consensus, however, did not save him. Fidel ended what became arguably his most famous speech with certainly his most famous line: "Condemn me. It does not matter. History will absolve me." The judge sentenced him to fifteen years in prison. It was the outcome he had expected. Elsewhere in the speech, he revealed something else he expected: "I know that imprisonment will be harder for me than it has ever been for anyone."[15]

CASTRO SERVED HIS PRISON TERM in Cuba's most modern jail: the Presidio Modelo in the Isle of Pines. Built during the rule of Gerardo Machado in the late 1920s, it consisted of round buildings, with cells along the circumference and a watchtower in the center. Erected as a panopticon—a design named after the many-eyed monster of Greek mythology and invented in the eighteenth century by British jurist Jeremy Bentham—the modern prison allowed a single guard to watch any cell in the prison at any time without the inmates knowing they were being watched.

One of the things Fidel most hated about being imprisoned was how hard it was to speak. "To be imprisoned," he mused in a letter from jail to a friend, "is to be condemned to silence, to hear and read everything spoken and written and not be able to speak out...."[16] He was held in solitary confinement for the first four months of his sentence. There, certainly, he suffered the worst feelings of isolation and enforced silence. But after that period, he was permitted to share a cell with his brother, Raúl, and to socialize extensively with the other Moncada assailants condemned alongside him. Fidel was allowed to cook for himself and the group. He made calamari and experimented with sauces for spaghetti. The men were given ample time outside in the courtyard. Fidel often sat outside in his shorts, feeling the sun and sea breeze. "What would Karl Marx say of such revolutionaries?" he wondered.[17]

Castro imposed a routine on his men that resembled that of a school, a practical school of politics, history, and ideology. Every morning Fidel gathered his companions and delivered a lecture—philosophy one day, world history the next. Other members of his group gave lectures on other topics: Cuban history, grammar, arithmetic, geography, and even English. At night they gathered again, and Fidel delivered his second lecture of the day. Three nights a week he lectured on political economy. The other two, he taught them public speaking, "if you can call it that," he wrote to a friend. In that class, he would read aloud for a half hour "either a full description of a battle, for example, the attack of Napoleon Bonaparte's infantry at Waterloo," or "an ideological text like Martí's address to the Spanish Republic, or something along that line." Then the pupils gave three-minute talks on the subject, and prizes were awarded by judges. The 26th of every month, to commemorate their July 26 attack on Moncada, he canceled classes, and they held a party; every 27th they remembered the companions they had lost. Castro called his improvised school the Abel Santamaría Ideological Academy, after the Pontiac bookkeeper and Moncada assailant who was killed and brutally tortured.[18]

Fidel also assembled a prison library of about three hundred volumes, mostly sent by friends. In fact, he spent most of his time in jail reading voraciously. He read ten, twelve, or fourteen hours a day—"till I can't keep my eyes open," he wrote to a friend. He read Cuban authors, especially Martí. He dozed off immediately on finishing Kant's *Transcendental Aesthetic of Space and Time*. Among the great French novelists, he especially loved Honoré Balzac (whose style, Castro speculated, had greatly influenced Karl Marx's *Communist Manifesto*). Victor Hugo's *Les Miserables* made him so excited that "it is impossible to put into words," even if he found the author's "excessive romanticism, his wordiness, and his erudition" sometimes "tiresome and exaggerated." He seemed to prefer Dostoevsky's novels and read several: *The Idiot, The Insulted and Injured, Poor Folk, The House of the Dead, Crime and Punishment*. He read four volumes of Sigmund Freud's collected works and asked a friend to send the other fourteen, because he wanted to "understand for [himself] their importance, and apply them to some of the characters in Dostoevski."[19]

Castro was reading not just for fun or to help pass the many hours in his fifteen-year sentence. He was reading to learn and think—about Cuba, about history, about human nature, about contemporary politics. He imagined applying those lessons once freed. He read about Franklin Delano Roosevelt, who had interested him since the age of fourteen, when he wrote him a letter, addressed to "My good friend Roosevelt," apologized for his broken English, and asked for a "ten dollars bill green American." In jail, reading about FDR's New Deal, he allowed himself to be surprised: "Given the character, the mentality, the history of the people of the United States, Roosevelt actually did some wonderful things, and some of his countrymen have never forgiven him for doing them."[20]

From the start, however, and given how he'd gotten to prison in the first place, Fidel was less interested in reform than in revolution. He confided to a friend: "I would honestly love to revolutionize this country from one end to the other! I am sure this would bring happiness to the Cuban people. I would not be stopped by the hatred and ill will of a few thousand people, including some of my relatives, half the people I know, two-thirds of my fellow professionals, and four-fifths of my ex-schoolmates." As a young man, Castro had loved reading about the Latin American liberator Simón Bolívar. Now he devoured epic histories of the French and Russian revolutions. As he read them, he pondered questions about what made revolutions succeed or fail or even happen at all. Was it the particular man who led them? The specific moment and circumstances in which they occurred? Or the underlying structural conditions? In the time of Catherine the Great, Castro mused, Vladimir Lenin "might have been a staunch supporter of the bourgeoisie." In the Seven Years' War, José Martí would have defended Spain against the British. The specific context was always key. But Fidel also liked to consider the logic inherent to *all* revolutions. And his readings led him to the conclusion that the climax of every revolution was the "moment the radicals carried the flag." After that, the revolutionary tide began to ebb. In France, that revolutionary apex was represented by Robespierre, the leader of the revolution's most radical and bloody phase. Castro explained his affinity with the Frenchman: "The Revolution was in danger, the frontiers surrounded by enemies on all sides, traitors ready to plunge a dagger into one's back, the fence sitters were blocking the way—one had to be harsh, inflexible, tough—it was better to go too far than not to go far enough. . . ." Cuba, Fidel concluded, "needs more Robespierres."[21]

What Castro read on revolution helped him think about his own tactics. Reading obscure texts on the "revolutionary personality" and the "technique" of revolution, he became convinced of the singular importance of propaganda, by which he meant the constant and consistent projection of the revolution's presence and voice in public. In a letter to an ally, he called such propaganda their movement's first order of business: "It is the soul of every struggle," he wrote. Fidel's prison syllabus also included general texts in political theory. He found Vladimir Lenin's *State and Revolution* so enthralling he read it for six hours straight without a break. He read Karl Marx's *The Class Struggles in France* and *The Eighteenth Brumaire of Louis Bonaparte*. He "thoroughly studied" Marx's *Capital*, which he referred to as "five huge volumes on economics, researched and explained with scientific exactness." In fact, of everything he read on revolution, he seems to have been especially drawn to Karl Marx.[22]

FIDEL CASTRO WOULD IN TIME be released from his panopticon prison, and we will soon examine those circumstances. But it may be worth pausing briefly over the perennial question of Castro's relationship to Marxism. Almost from the beginning, his detractors accused him of being a communist. For a long time, Fidel emphatically rejected that characterization. His denials continued even after he came to power. "Democracy is my ideal . . . I am not a communist," he proclaimed in New York City in April 1959. It was not until two years later, on the eve of the US Bay of Pigs invasion, that he publicly proclaimed that he and his revolution were socialist. We will always be socialists; we will always be Marxists-Leninists, he pronounced in another speech later that year.[23]

Castro's initial denials and the relative lateness of his public embrace of Marxism opened the space for a veritable cottage industry of academic and popular work on the question of when exactly he became a communist. The right, and especially what would become the Cuban American right, has tended to see him as a communist who concealed that fact in order to seize power. Liberals, meanwhile, have tended to see his communism as something that evolved in the context of the revolution itself, as the confrontation with the United States spiraled out of control and as the Cuban public—frustrated with frustrated revolutions—pushed him forward and leftward. With that pressure from abroad and that support from below, perhaps Fidel decided, as Robespierre had, that "it was better to go too far than not to go far enough."

Over the years, Castro himself gave different answers to the question of when he became a Marxist—from vehement denials during his first years in power to official pronouncements in the 1970s that Marxism-Leninism had guided the revolution from the very beginning in 1953. Late in life, his interpretation, ironically perhaps, approximated the arguments long made on the right: He had been a communist all along. In 2005, in one of his last extended interviews with his only authorized biographer, Ignacio Ramonet, Fidel explained that he was "an utopian Communist" even *before* reading Marx or Lenin. Reading and studying those things in prison had simply put him on firmer ground. Marxism, he said, was for him as the compass had been for Christopher Columbus or the songs of the sirens had been for Ulysses—an indispensable guide on a long journey in one case, captivating and irresistible in the other. Before the revolution, he had never been a member of Cuba's Communist Party. No, he said to Ramonet, "And that was well calculated and thought out. But that's another story. That moment may come, and I'll tell you about it."[24]

With much less mystery and circumspection—in the revolutionary moment and for decades later—Fidel embraced the influence of José Martí, in whose centennial memory he had waged his ill-fated attack on the Moncada barracks. On many other occasions, Castro would say that the essence of his political philosophy was his particular fusion of Martí and Marx. During the interview with Ramonet, Fidel quoted—verbatim and at length—from the last letter that Martí wrote, the one he left unfinished shortly before he was killed in battle on May 19, 1895. Here is Fidel quoting Martí:

> Martí confesses: "Every day now I am in danger of giving my life for my country . . . in order to prevent, by the timely independence of Cuba, the United States from extending its hold across the Antilles and falling with all the greater force on the lands of our America. All that I have done up to now, and all I will do is for that." And then he adds: "It has to be done in silence, and indirectly, for there are things that must be concealed in order to be attained: proclaiming them for what they are would give rise to obstacles too formidable to overcome." That's verbatim. [Martí] says that in his last, unfinished, letter. . . . It's wonderful, what he says: to prevent, with the independence of Cuba, and Puerto Rico, the United States from falling with all the greater force on the lands of America. "All that I have done up to now, and all I will do . . ." he says, and then adds, "It must be done in silence," and he explains why. That is the incredible legacy left by this man [Martí] to us Cuban revolutionaries.

All that, Fidel said to his biographer. Struck perhaps by the fact that Fidel had quoted Martí's letter, at length, verbatim, and parts of it twice, Ramonet remarked: "Those are phrases that seem to have left their mark on you. Have you adopted them as your own, as your political programme?" Castro's answer was emphatic: "I have, yes. It was from those words that I began to acquire political awareness. . . ."[25]

Fidel was clearly drawn to Martí's admission of the political value of operating in secret, of hiding true intentions in order to achieve victory. Had Fidel done the same with his Marxism? He certainly seemed to hint that during the 2005 interview. But we cannot know if that interpretation emerged later, as part of the process of narrative self-fashioning and refashioning that political leaders—and all human beings—engage in after the fact. So, while we can determine the precise moment in which Fidel publicly announced the socialist and Marxist character of his revolution, we may never know with clarity the moment in which Fidel Castro decided that for himself.

Still, Castro's attachment to Martí's last letter is unexpectedly revealing. Left unfinished right before a dramatic death in battle, the letter surely fed Fidel's attraction to the idea of martyrdom. More important, perhaps, is the fact that Fidel identified with the aversion to US imperialism evident in Martí's letter, an antipathy so deep, Martí had written, that everything he did or would do was designed to thwart it. Perhaps Fidel had Martí's words in mind when in 1958 he penned his own war-time letter from the mountains of eastern Cuba. He wrote the letter to his friend Celia Sánchez, the woman who in 1953 had helped place the monument to Martí on the highest mountain in Cuba. Having witnessed US-supplied rockets hit the house of a friend, Fidel wrote, "I have sworn to myself that the Americans are going to pay dearly for what they are doing. When this war ends, another, much longer and bigger war will begin for me: the war I will wage against them. I realize that will be my true destiny."[26] His true destiny—or, to paraphrase Martí, the object of everything he would do.

Chapter 23

INSURRECTIONARY LINE

P eople interested in Cuba often make the mistake of thinking too much about Fidel Castro. It is an understandable mistake. Tall, solid, confident, he often seemed larger than life, as if preordained for victory and power. But in early 1955, as he sat in jail reading Karl Marx and Victor Hugo, he was but one revolutionary among many. Since Batista's coup in 1952, Cuban women and men had been engaging in all manner of protest against an unconstitutional regime. They protested police violence outside major department stores; they carried flyers in pleated, pocketed skirts and threw them from the balconies in theaters; they showed up at rallies decked in Cuban flag dresses; they staged "patriotic street theater" and "collective stay-at-home days." All this they did to protest Batista's rule.[1]

In November 1954, Batista won the presidency in a sham election boycotted by the opposition and in which he was the only candidate. If he hoped that that dubious victory would lead people to see him as the elected president rather than as the architect of a military coup, Cubans continually proved him wrong. They still wanted him out of power. Realizing the magnitude of that task, however, they sometimes focused on more immediate demands. After Batista's election, activists launched a massive campaign for a general amnesty of political prisoners. Chances of success in that particular campaign were high, for such pardons were a familiar feature of Cuban politics. Especially following elections, victors often granted amnesty to jailed or exiled opponents as a nod to national unity. Eager to gain legitimacy and to create a sense of normalcy after the election, Batista decided to do the thing that so many people were petitioning for and that elected presidents before him had done routinely. He approved a general amnesty for political prisoners. Those pardoned by the May 1955 amnesty included opposition figures who had left the country under pressure from the government, among them former president Carlos Prío (unseated by Batista's coup in 1952). Other dissidents, who had left the island and reentered secretly, living and organizing clandestinely, came out of hiding. When rumors circulated that Fidel Castro and his fellow Moncada assailants would not be included in the general amnesty, activists protested once more. Student leader José Antonio Echeverría published a rousing appeal in *Bohemia*: "Any attempt to exclude the Moncada combatants from the amnesty will be widely repudiated by public opinion. . . . Let no combatant against the dictatorship remain imprisoned." Batista acquiesced. Fidel received his freedom, thanks to civic activists, many of whose names have been lost to history.[2]

Historians have sometimes considered Castro's amnesty to be Batista's "greatest error of judgment."[3] But hindsight is the purview of historians, not politicians. In 1955, there was nothing noteworthy about Batista's decision. He was merely seeking legitimacy by making a routine concession to public demands and democratic practice. Other presidents had pardoned greater foes. If anything, Fidel's pardon suggests how little observers at the time, Batista included, made of Castro's threat to the state. He was the author of a spectacularly unsuccessful attack on the army, and his men had suffered brutal repression in response. But on his release from prison, Fidel Castro was not the leading figure of the opposition. In 1955, the movement against Batista was not a singular one; no one figure clearly dominated. In the few years that followed Castro's release, it would come to have multiple theaters: among them almost every city on the island, the mountains of the east, even Mexico. It would encompass most sectors of Cuban society: students, sugar workers, middle-class housewives, peasants, Catholics, lawyers, even American college students. And for more than three years, the movements made in those places and by those people proceeded on multiple tracks, at times converging, at times not. Simply put, the story of how Cubans ousted dictator Fulgencio Batista from power on January 1, 1959, is always a story in the plural. Only if we read history backward can we imagine that the revolution was Fidel Castro's from the start.

WHEN CASTRO AND HIS COMPANIONS walked out of prison as free men, the most active and powerful opponents of Batista were the students of the University of Havana. They had been marching and protesting and engaging in civic opposition since the coup of 1952. Their nationwide student group—the FEU, or the Federation of University Students—arguably enjoyed more visibility and support than Fidel Castro and his Moncada assailants. In fact, students had been the most effective lobbyists for the pardon that released Castro from prison.

And in 1955, their activism was intensifying. That year, student leaders decided to create a new organization called the Revolutionary Directorate. Led by José Antonio Echevarría, the new organization would operate clandestinely, with members organized in secret cells. Their purpose, as before, was to oust Batista. But the means would no longer be peaceful civic protest. It would be armed resistance. When the police attacked them, they would fire back. In fact, they wanted to provoke the police into attacking them. In that way, they would escalate the struggle and radicalize the public. This was what Cubans were increasingly calling "the insurrectionary line."[4]

Cuban revolutionaries love anniversaries. So, the student-dominated Revolutionary Directorate chose to debut their new strategy on November 27, 1955, the anniversary of the execution of medical students by Spanish authorities in 1871. In 1955, the students prepared themselves with bottles, pipes, and rocks; nursing students brought bottles of alcohol; medical students bottles of acid. Some four hundred descended the grand staircase of the University of Havana toward the police barricades. When the police told them to stop, they pushed forward. The police began retreating under a torrent of objects thrown by the students, before charging again in pursuit of the protestors. Student snipers fired from a rooftop. Several police were injured, and a host of students were beaten and arrested.[5]

A week later, on December 4, students staged a dramatic protest during a nationally televised baseball game. Right after the third out in the third inning of the second game of a doubleheader, twenty-two students rushed onto the field chanting "Down with Batista!" and unfurled a banner that read "Down with the dictatorship!" Police stormed the field and began beating the students with clubs. The crowd booed the police and began chanting "Down with the police!" A sportscaster on the radio narrated the scene in horror: "The students are defenseless; they are not armed. . . . They are sitting; they are on their knees. They are beating them, they are kicking them! It is a shameful demonstration! There is no name for this!" The next day, newspapers condemned the government's actions, comparing the students to those executed by the Spanish in 1871.[6]

With most of the country paying attention, the Revolutionary Directorate accelerated its protests. On December 7, 1955, the fifty-ninth anniversary of the death in battle of the legendary Afro-Cuban general and independence hero Antonio Maceo, hundreds of students and workers gathered at the Havana park that bore his name. A student leader scaled the equestrian statue of Maceo, delivered a fiery speech, and asked the crowd to follow him to the university. As the group of hundreds marched, others joined. The police tried blocking the marchers, and when that didn't work, they opened fire. About twenty students were injured, among them was a still clean-shaven Camilo Cienfuegos, later to become an important revolutionary figure. People watching from their windows and balconies shouted in outrage, launching flowerpots, frying pans, and hand tools at the police from above. Again, the press almost universally condemned the government's actions.[7]

Three days later, the students marched from the university carrying a fake coffin in a symbolic wake and funeral for a student recently shot to death by police. But plainclothes government agents joined the march undetected. They hid clubs in rolled-up newspapers and let them loose on the students. People watched, as they had from their balconies a few days earlier and at the baseball stadium a few days before that. And they wondered, horrified, is this really us? Is this what we have come to? That sentiment of disbelief and indignation helped fuel support for the students' cause and generated a visceral repudiation of Batista's tactics.[8]

Student activists knew that by continuing to demonstrate, they were risking brutal retaliation, but they also sensed that as the government's response hardened, the Cuban public increasingly turned against Batista. The Revolutionary Directorate took advantage of the momentum and expanded their repertoire of resistance. Its president, José Antonio Echeverría, called for a work stoppage in solidarity with the students and against the brutality of Batista's police. Bus drivers stopped their buses mid-route; many private vehicles did the same. Waiters stopped serving; radio announcers stopped broadcasting. Factory workers walked out; so did drugstore employees, telephone workers, stevedores at the port, workers at the Goodrich Tire Company. A list of the workplaces that participated in the walkout took up a whole page in one newspaper. The walkouts occurred not only in Havana, but also in Santiago, Matanzas, and other cities across the island. This was the first mass mobilization since Batista's coup. Its success and broad reach exceeded the expectations of the planners and demonstrated that the students' cause was now the cause of many others, too.[9]

Indeed, as the students planned their protests, sugar workers—always a major sector of Cuban labor—were staging their own resistance. Since the beginning of the year, they had organized labor actions in at least fourteen mills to protest various kinds of job and wage losses. In December 1955, after the government announced that it would reduce the traditional year-end bonus given to sugar workers, five hundred thousand of them went on strike. Workers abandoned some mills en masse. Police or Rural Guard shot at strikers, and protestors turned to the time-worn strategy of burning the cane. Strikes and other protest actions spread across the island. In Matanzas, textile workers and printers staged a solidarity strike;

in the town of Ranchuelo in Las Villas province, construction workers, tobacco workers, and others also struck in support of the sugar workers. In Marianao, a municipality that blended into the city of Havana, the employees of the legendary Tropicana Night Club did as well. About twenty cities and towns saw "dead city" protests, a kind of general civic strike in which most businesses closed their doors and people cleared the streets and refrained from outdoor activities, as if all of Cuba was in mourning.[10] The extent of these solidarity actions in support of the sugar workers hints at a wellspring of broader discontent and frustration.

As the cycle of protest and state violence intensified, many people became increasingly convinced that peaceful change was unlikely. Civic opposition groups, such as the Society of Friends of the Republic, which had favored more conciliatory approaches to Batista, lost their appeal and the confidence of the public in their solution. And as the opposition increasingly pursued insurrectionary, confrontational tactics, the more radical and popular it became. It was then, early in 1956, that the Revolutionary Directorate issued its first public statement. Dated February 24, the anniversary of the start of the War of Independence, it made the case for fighting Batista with fire. "In the face of four years of harassment, humiliation, and ruin imposed on us by a petty, traitorous tyrant, in the face of the failure of every attempt at a peaceful solution, the Cuban people, by sovereign right, declares its resolute decision to struggle and sacrifice." Only "revolutionary insurrection" could defeat Batista.[11] The Directorate was not the only group with that goal, but in early 1956, it was showing itself to be the most effective and prominent. "For the Cuban Revolution," ended the document.

Yet by fall 1956, the Revolutionary Directorate had revised its thinking—not about their goal of toppling Batista, but about the most effective means to do so. To create the conditions for a generalized insurrection from below, they decided they needed to strike at the top. In Havana, the Directorate hatched assassination plots against cabinet ministers, police chiefs, and Batista himself. They shot and killed the chief of the bureau of investigations at the Montmartre nightclub. In a firefight soon after, they killed the chief of police. The police retaliated by executing ten of the revolutionaries. The Directorate "answered in kind," and then so did the police. "Everyday students were found shot to death.... At night, action cells of the [Revolutionary Directorate] exploded bombs."[12] And the cycle continued.

AS ALL THIS UNFOLDED, FIDEL Castro was far away—not forgotten, but neither the person most Cubans would have identified as the leader of the revolution against Batista. A month after his release from jail, he arrived in Mexico with his brother, Raúl, and other Moncada prisoners. Early in his Mexican exile, Fidel met Che Guevara, Argentine doctor turned global revolutionary. The first time they met, the two spoke all night, and by the end of it Che "was already the physician of the future expedition" to Cuba. What most struck him that night was Fidel's optimism: "He had an unshakeable faith that once he left he would arrive in Cuba, that once he arrived he would fight, that once he began fighting he would win."[13]

From Mexico, Fidel kept his eyes on Cuba, and he sought to keep the Cuban public's eyes and ears on him. He wrote letters and essays for publication in the Cuban press; he toured US and Caribbean cities with large émigré communities and gave rousing speeches. On August 8, 1955, having been in Mexico a little over a month, Fidel Castro put pen to paper and wrote "Manifesto No. 1 to the People of Cuba." A long, wordy document, it summarized the goals of the revolution in fifteen points that included the classic progressive goals of past Cuban revolutions. The first was land reform, outlawing *latifundio* (very large landholdings) and distributing land among peasants. Others included confiscation of the assets of embezzlers from past Cuban administrations, nationalization of public services (such as electricity and telephone utilities), expansion of public education, and the restoration of workers' rights undone by Batista. At the very end of the manifesto, he signed off: "On behalf of the 26th of July Revolutionary Movement, Fidel Castro." His revolution now had a name.[14]

Names matter, of course. In this case, Castro named his movement after a date—the date of his assault on the Mocada barracks on July 26, 1953. The unusual name did several things. First, because so many had died in the July 26 attack, the name gave the group ready martyrs. It also set Castro's group apart from others that had taken a stance against Batista. It was infinitely more specific than "the generation of the centennial," which Fidel had used in 1953 and which defined, in effect, an entire generation hostile to Batista. Finally, the name associated the group with an event far away from the capital city of Havana and its traditional parties with their traditional party leaders. The newly christened 26th of July Movement was something else entirely, and it had one leader, Fidel Castro.

THE WHOLE WHILE, FIDEL CASTRO knew that to topple Batista he would have to return to Cuba to fight. And he knew that would require money—for weapons and supplies, for a vessel capable of transporting his men and equipment. Castro raised funds among Cuban immigrants in US cities and Cuban-born businessmen in Mexico and Latin America. He even turned to an old nemesis, former president Carlos Prío, the man he had so zealously accused of corruption. One night in August 1956, Fidel and a few companions drove hours to the US-Mexico border, supposedly swam across the Rio Grande, and arrived at a motel in McAllen, Texas, for a meeting with the former president. Prío agreed to send Fidel $50,000 in support of an armed expedition to Cuba. He sent more money later. By the time Castro assumed power in January 1959, Prío had contributed almost a quarter of a million dollars.[15]

In addition to raising funds, Castro sought organizational assistance and alliances within Cuba. He communicated with the Revolutionary Directorate and met with its leader, José Antonio Echevarría, twice in Mexico. They signed a unity pledge to support each other in their common goal of defeating Batista, though they did not necessarily agree about the best means to do so. Castro sought other alliances beyond the Revolutionary Directorate. One new ally was a young activist named Frank País. The son of the pastor of Santiago's First Baptist Church, País was an aspiring schoolteacher already active in local anti-Batista struggles. He was a leading member of a clandestine group that was quickly accumulating revolutionary bona fides, including attacks on local arms depots and some bombings in Santiago. In 1955, Fidel sent País a proposal: merge his group with the 26th of July Movement and in return assume the post of Chief of Action and Sabotage for eastern Cuba. País accepted, traveling twice to Mexico in the summer and fall 1956. Castro entrusted País with the momentous responsibility of preparing a popular uprising to occur in Santiago on November 30, 1956, the same day that Fidel and his men planned to land in Cuba, armed and ready to fight.[16]

Back in Santiago, País laid the groundwork for the insurrection. He met with workers and union members to discuss a general strike. He also identified possible landing sites for Fidel's expedition, somewhere on the long coast between the city of Santiago and the port of Manzanillo, which sat on the expansive bay of Guacanayabo. It was the same coast that had harbored and repelled pirates and maritime renegades of all kinds in centuries past. It was also the same coast that had served as home to Celia Sánchez, of the 1953 hiking expedition that had put a bust of José Martí on Cuba's highest mountain. Now in 1956, she was active in the clandestine struggle against Batista in eastern Cuba.[17]

It was to Celia that País turned for help in organizing the landing of Fidel and his men. She knew the coast and nearby countryside; she knew the people; she could identify potential allies and potential enemies. Near the Cape Cruz sugar mill, where her father had been doctor and where she had spent much of her young life, she obtained detailed maps of the surrounding countryside and mountains. She spoke to workers and their families, many of whom still thought of her as their old doctor's daughter. She sought out a notorious peasant patriarch named Crescencio Pérez, an old acquaintance of her father's who had spent decades battling the Rural Guard. Pérez hesitated not at all. He was on board, an eager new member of Celia's expanding anti-Batista network, ready to mobilize local people to receive and assist Castro's expedition. Pérez hiked into the mountains he knew well, making contacts along the way with people willing to help. A few days before the scheduled landing, local peasants began patrolling the stretch of coast where they had been told the expedition would arrive. As planned, they had trucks ready to take the arriving fighters wherever they needed to go.[18] In the countryside as in Santiago, would-be revolutionaries awaited the arrival of Fidel Castro and his men from Mexico.

Fidel Castro set sail in the early hours of Sunday, November 25, with eighty-two men aboard the *Granma*, a yacht designed perhaps for twenty. That night, Mexican authorities had issued a storm warning and asked captains to keep their vessels docked. But Fidel was either unaware of the warning or thought the risk of staying put (and getting arrested) was greater. In the Gulf of Mexico, the *Granma* encountered towering waves and punishing winds. They made little headway, and the men grew seasick. Loaded down with too many passengers, with extra fuel, and with weapons, the vessel began taking on water. At least some of the men considered trying to swim back to the Mexican coast, though they seemed to be nowhere near it. But, in the words of one passenger, "forces other than purely physical ones resisted the storm and were driving the ship to her destination."[19]

Meanwhile, in Santiago, a telegram arrived at the home of a local representative of the 26th of July Movement. "Requested book out of print. Dissemination Press." The message was the agreed-upon sign. Sent from Mexico, it secretly announced that the expedition would be landing in Cuba within forty-eight hours. Because the landing was to coincide with a general insurrection in Santiago, the message was also a call to rebellion. Every local conspirator went into action, and early on Friday, November 30, they donned, for the first time, the now well-known red and black armbands with the number 26 stitched on in white cloth. Then, everything went wrong. The man who was to operate the mortar was recognized by a policeman. A map in his pocket titled "Operation Mortar" implicated him immediately, though it is unclear whether the officer would have required proof to arrest him anyway. Insurgents engaged officers near the police headquarters, but they were repelled. Authorities were now on high alert. Rebels took off their armbands and did their best to blend into the population, but at least thirty were captured and imprisoned. The Santiago insurrection failed almost the instant it started.[20]

In Havana, it didn't even start. The Havana branch of the 26th of July Movement had not been alerted in time to take any effective action. The Revolutionary Directorate, meanwhile, had weapons for only about thirty men. It was a fool's errand to attempt an insurrection with so little. In any case, they had their own method—targeted strikes at the top—and their own plan—to assassinate Batista. And as Fidel Castro sailed toward Cuba, that scheme probably had a greater chance of success than Fidel's plan to ignite a general rebellion with his arrival.[21]

THE LANDING OF CASTRO'S MEN—LIKE the urban insurrection that failed to greet them—was all mishap. The ship carrying the expeditionaries arrived two days late and at the wrong place. Almost a hundred yards offshore at Playa Colorada, they lowered a lifeboat that immediately began to sink under the weight of too many men. They had to wade through the muddy sea bottom, but the sea seemed never to end. It gave way only to more water and then to mud and mangroves. By the time the men reached solid ground, most of their supplies were gone, their feet blistered, their spirits sunk. From above, they heard the whir of government planes. The whole area was being searched by Batista's military, and the peasants who had been waiting for them earlier had had to retreat. Fidel's men were alone, hungry, thirsty, practically unarmed, and already weary. "We were an army of shadows," recalled Che Guevara.[22]

Early in the morning of their fourth day in Cuba, unable to march any farther, the men set up camp at a place called Alegría de Pío, on the edge of a sugarcane field. Had they been able to connect with any of the peasant guides sent to meet them, they would have known that it was not a good place for a camp. By noon, the men heard the sound of airplanes. Batista's army was upon them. Three of Fidel's men died in the attack; the rest were dispersed. Fidel found himself with just two men and two rifles; his brother Raúl's group consisted of eight men with seven rifles.[23]

In Havana, the government triumphantly announced the death of Fidel Castro. Batista phoned the US ambassador, a close friend with whom he and his wife often played canasta, to inform him that a vessel trying to land in eastern Cuba had been hit by the Cuban air force, only a few men had survived, all those had been arrested, and Fidel was among the dead. A United Press correspondent in Havana reported the story, and on December 3, the *New York Times* put it on its front page. "Cuba Wipes Out Invaders; Leader Is Among 40 Dead," read the headline. People in Havana and other cities took up collections for the families of the fallen. But, of course, Fidel Castro was not dead. The revolution now had a new theater: the Sierra Maestra. And it had a new strategy: guerrilla warfare. Two weeks after the New York paper printed its story, the Castro brothers had already reunited. Now with fifteen men and fewer rifles than that, they headed higher into the mountains. Thus began the guerrilla war that changed the fate of Cuba.

Chapter 24

THE MOUNTAINS RISE

On January 17, 1957, at a tiny place called La Plata, more than nine hundred feet above sea level, Fidel Castro's mountain rebels won their first victory. Che Guevara's account of the episode reads almost like a movie script. The rebels staked out a small army outpost and then captured two peasants, who informed them that the army garrison had only about fifteen soldiers and that an unpopular foreman from a nearby plantation was due momentarily. When the rebels saw the man approaching, looking a little drunk atop his mule, one of them shouted "Halt, in the name of the Rural Guard!" The foreman replied with the password, which meant that the rebels now had it as well. Pretending to be an army officer returning from a reconnaissance mission in the mountains, Castro approached the man and railed against the ineptness of the army for not being able to rout the guerrillas. The rebels asked him about area residents to find out which ones were trustworthy. When the foreman said someone was trustworthy, Fidel knew that was someone to avoid. Those the man said were trouble, Fidel knew might be allies or recruits. Che later recalled how Fidel convinced the man to accompany him to the garrison and to take it by surprise, ostensibly to show the soldiers how vulnerable the post was. On the way, the foreman bragged to Fidel that he was wearing the shoes of a rebel he had killed, that he had killed two peasants without suffering any consequences, and that he loved "his" General Batista. The man was signing his own death sentence. When they reached the garrison, the rebels executed the unwitting guide and opened fire on the soldiers, killing two, wounding another five, and confiscating guns, ammunition, food, fuel, and clothing. The rebels lost no one in the attack.[1]

With that victory and a second that followed just five days later, Castro's mountain guerrillas got their first taste of success since the botched landing more than a month earlier. The war against Batista's army had begun, and perhaps for the first time the men were feeling ready for the fight.

CASTRO HAD IMAGINED HIMSELF READY long before those victories. He had played out the war in his head from his days in prison. And even back then he had understood that in a revolution, military strategy is just one part of the battle. The other, he had said, was propaganda—the public face of every revolution. From the moment his troops won their first military victory, he was thinking about how to pursue the battle for hearts and minds. His first task, he decided, was simple: to let Cubans know that he was alive and fighting in the mountains. To counter false reports of his death, activists from the urban wing of the 26th of July Movement were already organizing phone chains. One person would call ten other people, and then those ten another ten each, to spread the word that Fidel was alive and had just fought and won at such-and-such a place. But Castro knew that was not enough. He wanted something with more reach. And for that he did what Cubans often did: he looked to the United States.

Roughly a week after the rebel army's second victory, Fidel sent an emissary to Havana with a weighty charge and few instructions: find a foreign journalist willing to come to the mountains of eastern Cuba and interview him in person. The emissary enlisted the help of leading 26th of July activists in Havana and through them of Felipe Pazos, the former director of Cuba's National Bank and a known Batista foe. The well-connected Pazos immediately reached out to Ruby Hart Phillips, a *New York Times*' correspondent in Havana since the 1930s. Pazos later recalled the meeting at her house. "There were three or four more people and a relatively heavy traffic of persons entering and leaving—boys from the grocery and drugstore, maids, friends, etc. At my request for a private talk, she took me to an adjoining room without any door to separate it from the hall, where the other people were, five yards apart at most. I told her in a whisper that Fidel Castro wanted a foreign correspondent to visit him at the Sierra, and she answered in a loud and most penetrating voice that could be heard one block away—'So, you have contact with Fidel Castro! I cannot believe it! Please, tell me all you know.'" She could not contain her appetite for what she knew would be a major, major story. But those were other times, and the two decided that an American woman hiking up the mountains of the Sierra Maestra would be too conspicuous and dangerous. Another journalist would score the scoop: *New York Times* reporter and editorial page writer Herbert Matthews.[2]

Matthews and his wife arrived in Havana on February 9, 1957, and waited for instructions. Late in the afternoon on February 15, they received word that they would leave for eastern Cuba by car within hours. Posing as an American couple shopping for real estate, they arrived in the eastern coastal town of Manzanillo, where under the leadership of Celia Sánchez, the urban underground was thriving. Celia met the couple and, with other activists, escorted the journalist up into the mountains to meet Fidel. It would be Celia's first meeting with him, too. [3]

On February 17, when Castro heard that the journalist had arrived at his camp, he turned to his soldiers and said "look sharp, like soldiers." He donned a fresh uniform and a cap like Charles de Gaulle's. He opened a new box of cigars and gave Matthews first pick. For three hours the men talked, Matthews scribbling seven pages of notes, each folded horizontally in three. The notes documented snippets of conversation, captured in a rushed, sloppy hand, written in different directions. Matthews abbreviated words and used little punctuation. Some things he wrote down using quotation marks meant to signify they were Fidel's words: "'We are fighting for a democ Cuba + an end to the dictship.'" Fidel showed him what looked like several thousand dollars wrapped in brown cloth and said, "'We get all the money we want.'" Matthews also documented his own impressions—about the landscape ("the ghostly palms" and "the mud underfoot"), about the rebels ("How young! A motley array of arms and uniforms"), and, of course, about Fidel Castro. "Pale—powerful—telescopic gun," scribbled Matthews. Elsewhere: "A born leader." On the last page: "An enormous faith and self confidence." "All are with him," Matthews surmised. [4]

Sometime in the middle of the hours-long conversation, a rebel soldier interrupted them with a message for Fidel: "We've succeeded in reaching the second column," he said breathlessly. Castro reprimanded him for interrupting and then explained that there were other columns of rebel soldiers elsewhere in the Sierra and that the man had just returned from one of those. It was pure theater, of a piece with Fidel's later policy of giving his units nonsequential numbers, so that it seemed like he had more forces than he did. In this case it worked. Matthews jotted down that the rebels worked "in groups or cells of 7 or 10, a few of 30 or 40." At the time, Fidel's rebel army had just one column, numbering more than ten, but less than forty. [5]

When the interview was over, Matthews asked Fidel to sign and date his interview notes to authenticate them. On the end of the last page, written with ink in a different direction than everything else on the page, is the eye-catching signature, not too different than the one he had used many years before to ask

FDR for a "ten dollars bill green American." With that, Matthews left Cuba, the Fidel-autographed notes hidden in his wife's girdle. Eager to put what he had seen and heard to paper, he began drafting the story on the flight home.[6]

THE TIMING OF THE *New York Times* story could not have been more perfect for Fidel Castro. Batista's government was again circulating false news that the rebels had been routed and that the army had just killed every last one of them. Nothing would put the rumors to rest more effectively than a front-page *New York Times* interview with the rebel leader himself. Fidel had hinted as much during the interview. Asked why he didn't make his presence more known, he replied that he would do so "at the opportune moment. It will have more effect for the delay." Matthews's interview was the opportune means at the opportune time, and infinitely more effective than any military battle the rebels were then capable of winning.

Matthews's article, which appeared on Sunday, February 24, 1957, as the first of a three-part series, began with a one-sentence paragraph that conveyed perfectly the main thing that Castro himself wanted conveyed. "Fidel Castro, the rebel leader of Cuba's youth, is alive and fighting hard and successfully in the rugged, almost impenetrable fastnesses of the Sierra Maestra." The word *fastnesses*—perhaps obscure for the opening of a newspaper article—referred to a secure refuge, a place well protected by natural features. The picture alongside the piece delivered the message more dramatically: Fidel Castro, very much alive, bearded, in uniform, carrying his favorite telescopic rifle, a dense jungle behind him, and under his photograph, a picture of his own signature on the notes: "Fidel Castro Ruz. Sierra Maestra, Febrero 17 de 1957." This was, wrote Matthews, "the first sure news" that Castro was alive. "No one connected with the outside world . . . has seen Señor Castro except this writer. No one in Havana, not even the United States Embassy with all its resources for getting information, will know until this report is published that Fidel Castro is really in the Sierra Maestra."[7]

In the three articles, readers of the *New York Times* encountered a tall, confident, gracious Fidel. The veteran reporter described the way Castro welcomed him to the meeting, offered food, drink, cigars. Matthews shared the things the leader had told him. Fidel had nothing against the American people, though, yes, he considered himself an anti-imperialist. He complained that the US government provided the weapons that Batista used against his own people. Though he was fighting against Batista's army, Cuban soldiers were not his enemy. Matthews speculated about what the Cuban people thought of Fidel. They were, he wrote, "heart and soul with Fidel Castro," and increasingly "against President Batista." But what the *New York Times* journalist stressed above all—other than the simple fact that Fidel was not dead—was that Castro had "strong ideas of liberty, democracy, social justice, the need to restore the Constitution, to hold elections." While Castro's program was "vague," it represented "a new deal for Cuba, radical, democratic and therefore anti-Communist."[8]

Cuban authorities denied the story immediately and categorically. One government official told the *Times* correspondent in Havana that the interview was full of "imaginary information," embellished by "[Matthews's] imagination." Batista's defense minister sent an official cable to the *Times* declaring that "the opinion of the Government, and, I am sure, of the Cuban public also, is that the interview and the adventures described by Correspondent Matthews can be considered as a chapter in a fantastic novel. Mr. Matthews has not interviewed the pro-Communist insurgent, Fidel Castro. . . ." The *Times* published the Cuban government's accusation, followed by a statement by Matthews and a large photo of Matthews and Castro sitting side by side, Matthews scribbling notes, Castro lighting a cigar.[9] There was no denying it now.

The Cuban opposition used its own method to circulate the story and expose the government's lies. Activists traveled to the United States in anticipation of the story's publication to purchase copies. They reproduced the article and stuffed some three thousand copies in the mail to Cuba. In Miami, the Sunday *Times* ran out almost immediately; copies were being sold on the black market for $1.50 each. When those ran out, people sold photostatic copies of the original. Newspapers and copies were smuggled to Cuba by travelers, or they arrived by mail. Even up against government censorship, Matthews's gripping portrait circulated on the island.[10]

The publication of the interview in the hemisphere's most important newspaper was a major public relations victory for Castro. Once the world found out that he was alive and fighting, others wanted to see for themselves, especially since Batista kept insisting that there were no guerrilla encampments in the Sierra Maestra. US-based journalist Andrew St. George made the trek about a month after Matthews. With little Spanish to speak of, he interviewed Castro in person by writing down his questions in English. Fidel supplied written responses in Spanish. To St. George's question about whether he was "procommunist," he responded, "[that] is as absurd as telling the people of Cuba that I have died more than twenty times." The following month, Robert Taber and cameraman Wendell Hoffman arrived in Castro's camp to conduct live interviews for a CBS documentary. Airing across the United States in May 1957, it showed uniformed soldiers trekking up mountains, drinking water from tree branches, and resting on hammocks. Americans saw rebel women Celia Sánchez and Haydée Santamaría hiking alongside the men. They also saw and heard directly from three young Americans, ages fifteen, seventeen, and twenty, the sons of US citizens stationed at the Guantánamo naval base. On camera for an American audience, one of them explained that they had joined the revolution in order "to do [their] part for the freedom of the world, really." Taber followed the rebels up the mountains, all the way to Pico Turquino, the summit of Cuba's highest mountain. There, in front of the monument to José Martí, dedicated in the year of the centennial in 1953, Fidel sat down with Taber for an on-camera interview. "Contrary to rumors from the capital, we both seem to be here in the Sierra Maestra," began Taber. "Fidel, I believe you're here." In halting, but clear schoolbook English, Fidel explained that they were fighting for liberty against "the *tirano* Batista," leaving tyrant in his native Spanish. He looked straight into the camera and continued, "This is only the beginning; the last battle will be fought in the capital. [Of that] you can be sure." Fidel and his soldiers surrounded the monument to Martí and loudly sang the Cuban national anthem. Then they raised their rifles and fists in defiance of Batista. The widely watched documentary gave American viewers a live glimpse of the same Fidel whom Matthews had written about, now even more confident than before.[11]

To Taber in late April, Castro said something he couldn't have said to Herbert Matthews in February because it hadn't then been true, namely that residents of those mountains were arriving at his camp every day to volunteer their services. Frank País, the son of the Baptist minister who was organizing the urban wing of the movement, sent reinforcements from Santiago and other cities. Money and shipments of arms and ammunition arrived as well. By the time the CBS documentary aired in the United States, Fidel's star was on the rise. The prospect of victory may have still been dim, but things certainly looked different than they had six months earlier. And Castro believed—as he had told Che Guevara in Mexico in 1955 and as he had just told Taber and every American who watched him on CBS—that his revolution would win.

The *New York Times* interview and the CBS documentary inaugurated a honeymoon between the US press and Fidel Castro. Everyone wanted an interview. In 1957 and 1958, *Time* magazine, the most influential publication of its kind in the United States, ran thirty-one articles about Castro's revolution in the mountains. Its writers referred to Fidel as a "swashbuckling young lawyer," a "well-to-do daredevil of 29," and "the strapping, bearded leader of the never-say-die band of anti-Batista rebels." US college students set out to join him on their summer vacations. Even President Dwight D. Eisenhower's own brother referred to Castro as "a symbol of a noble revolution." More than a household name, he had become a romantic, irresistible hero. As a young man in prison after the Moncada barracks attack, he had ruminated on the critical importance of propaganda, on the immeasurable value of shaping public images and narratives. As Americans began to speak his name with awe, Fidel might have suspected that he was succeeding beyond his once-wildest dreams.[12]

AS CASTRO AND HIS 26TH of July Movement gained ground, Batista's other opponents lost theirs. The most dramatic loss was suffered by the Revolutionary Directorate, led by José Antonio Echeverría. In 1956, it had been the most important and influential group working against Batista. The group's goal was to defeat the government by striking at the top. And they developed an elaborate plot to do just that by assassinating Batista himself. Hatched at the University of Havana, the assassination plot called for three groups. One composed of fifty men would enter the Presidential Palace and attack Batista in his second-floor office. A second, larger group would storm the palace once the first group had breached its defenses. A third group, led by Echeverría, was to storm the studio of Radio Reloj, a popular national news station, to read a statement over the airwaves announcing Batista's death and calling on all Cubans to rise up against the government.

On March 13, 1957, the students put their plan into action. At around 3:30 p.m., Echeverría shot his way into the radio booth at Radio Reloj and seized the microphone: "The dictator, Fulgencio Batista," he announced, "has just met revolutionary justice. The gunfire that extinguished the bloody life of the tyrant may still be heard around the presidential palace." He continued, "It is we the Revolutionary Directorate, the armed hand of the Cuban Revolution, who have accomplished this final blow against this shameful regime still twisting in its own agony." As Echeverría read his statement over the airwaves, gunfire did in fact surround the Presidential Palace. His companions had made it inside the building and up to Batista's second-floor office. But, unbeknownst to the revolutionaries, the president happened to be working in a third-floor office they hadn't known existed. Unable to reach him, the men began retreating. But by then army reinforcements had arrived, and the students were slaughtered. Announcing Batista's assassination over the airwaves, Echeverria was not aware of any of that. As he left the radio station minutes after his announcement, a policeman recognized him and shot him three times at point-blank range. His companions ran away, knowing they would be shot if they tried to help him. Echeverría lay there alone, in a pool of blood, a grenade hanging from a belt loop, perhaps twisting in his own agony, as he had said minutes earlier of Batista's dictatorship. None but a group of nuns dared approach to offer help, and he died on the street about an hour after being shot.[13]

The failed attack on the Presidential Palace decimated the Revolutionary Directorate. The police assassinated the few remaining student leaders a month later in the building where they had been hiding since the attack, Humboldt Street, no. 7, between the university and the Malecón. The Directorate, which at the time of Fidel's landing in the east had been the most important opposition group, was destroyed by the failed attack on the Presidential Palace. And from that point forward, youthful, progressive opposition to Batista would flow primarily to Fidel's 26th of July Movement.

At the time, however, the 26th of July Movement was not entirely synonymous with Castro's mountain guerrillas. The guerrilla operation in the Sierra was just one part of that movement, and it was not always the most numerous nor the most prominent. The 26th of July was also an urban movement, with members in Havana, Santiago, and provincial capitals and smaller cities and towns across the island. These local branches acted more or less independently, though they were ostensibly directed by a national coordinator. That person was Frank País, who had met with Fidel in Mexico, helped organize the landing of the *Granma*, and mustered recruits, arms, and money for the struggle in the mountains. As the head of national strategy for the movement, País traveled across the country, organizing and fundraising. He ordered local branches to attack bridges, electrical generators, phone lines, and highways. País was, without question, the most important figure of the urban wing of the 26th of July Movement, the face of what people then and historians now call simply the "urban underground."[14]

In the summer of 1957, País was spearheading two initiatives. The first was a massive general strike that would paralyze the island from one end to the other. Recall that it was a general strike that had toppled Cuba's last dictator, Gerardo Machado, in 1933. From their very first meetings in Mexico, Fidel and País agreed that the task of organizing the strike would fall to País. And both conceived of the general strike, to use Che Guevara's words, as "the definitive weapon." Batista would not be able to survive it.[15]

Frank País's second task was more nebulous, and it was undertaken on his own—rather than Fidel's—initiative. With Castro ensconced and fighting in the mountains, it was País who had the better read on the state of the opposition and the dictatorship. And his sense was that the rebel leadership needed to show the country that the opposition was up to governing. As he explained in a letter to Fidel, "Nobody doubts any longer the fall of the regime, but [the people] are concerned about the quality of [our] engineers to reconstruct the building." Without consulting with his leader, País began recruiting "a series of highly representative and valuable men from national public life" to bring them into the 26th of July Movement, inviting them to a meeting with Castro in the Sierra Maestra.[16]

Perhaps the most immediate result of the meeting was a joint statement, signed by Fidel and the two most prominent attendees: Raúl Chibás (brother of Eduardo, Ortodoxo Party founder and radio announcer who committed suicide on-air) and Felipe Pazos (founding director of Cuba's National Bank). Known as the Sierra Maestra Manifesto and published in *Bohemia* on July 28, 1957, it promised that once Batista was out of power, the opposition groups would appoint a provisional government and not a military junta. That government would rule for one year, at which point democratic elections would be held. It would pursue a program that adhered to the long-standing demands of progressive Cuban politics: freedom for political prisoners, freedom of information and the press, recognition of all political and individual rights granted by the 1940 constitution, an intensive campaign against illiteracy, and a program of agrarian reform. It also explicitly rejected the mediation or intervention of foreign nations in Cuba, and called on the United States to suspend arms shipments to Batista.[17]

Pictures of Castro warmly embracing his visitors appeared in *Bohemia* for all the country to see. This is what Frank País had wanted when he set up the meeting: to show the public that Fidel and his mountain guerrillas were part of a broader movement that included men with the prestige and experience necessary to run a new government. Bringing the more traditional opposition to Fidel and the Sierra accomplished two things. It took the rousing, rustic, romantic image of Fidel as guerrilla leader and rendered it a little less quixotic, a touch more statesmanlike. Second, while the meeting and manifesto associated Fidel with more traditional opposition figures, it also associated them with him, on his ground, even on his terms. The statement professed unity, but the whole episode gave Fidel's 26th of July guerrilla movement pride of place—in the title, as the host of the meeting that produced the document, and in the text itself. "The Sierra Maestra is already an indestructible bulwark of freedom that has taken root in the hearts of our compatriots," it averred. Thus, just a few months after the legendary interviews with US journalists that allowed Fidel to begin to sway hearts and minds on the international stage, Fidel received an important boost to his already soaring reputation on Cuban soil.

Two days after *Bohemia* published the Sierra Manifesto, Frank País, the man who had orchestrated the meeting that produced it, was shot and killed by police in Santiago. Sixty thousand people—more than a third of the population of the city—attended his funeral. Stores, restaurants, and theaters remained closed; buses stopped running. País was a Baptist, but Catholic women dressed in black walked behind his mother in the funeral procession, praying the rosary for the whole route. Members of civic groups and Masonic lodges marched; there were women and men, teenagers and elders, Black and white Cubans. Marchers sang the national anthem, occasionally shouting "Death to Batista!" And as the procession wound its way through the narrow streets of the old city, people threw flowers from their balconies. This was more than a funeral; it was a whole city condemning a dictatorship.[18]

BY LATE SUMMER 1957, THEN, two things were clear. First, opposition to Batista was pervasive. One observer in Santiago estimated that 95 percent of the city's population was now against Batista. US consular officials on the island informed their Washington bosses that it would be hard for Batista to restore order. The brutality of his police and army was only serving "to aggravate this situation by driving into the ranks of the rebels many Cubans hitherto apathetically opposed to Batista."[19] The other thing that was clear was that while opposition was pervasive and growing, the number of prominent leaders was narrowing. By August 1957, the two principal leaders of the island's urban opposition to Batista— José Antonio Echeverría of the Revolutionary Directorate and Frank País of the urban wing of the 26th of July Movement—were gone. As had been happening already for months, the momentum shifted—now decisively—to Fidel Castro and the guerrilla war in the mountains. Already immensely popular, Fidel Castro was now easily the most prominent symbol and leader of the opposition.

Of course, not every other opposition figure died. The old politicians continued to conspire. Former president Prío, in exile in Miami, provided tens of thousands of dollars for the struggle against Batista. He even launched an armed expedition of his own. It crashed and got him indicted by a federal grand jury in New York for violation of US neutrality laws. For its part, the Revolutionary

Directorate, decimated after the failed attack on the Presidential Palace and the death of much of its leadership, was trying to reconstitute itself as another branch of the opposition, separate from the 26th of July Movement. But now instead of attacking at the top, they pursued Fidel's strategy for revolution and established their own guerrilla front in the Escambray mountains of central Cuba. Meanwhile, Pazos and Chibás, who had signed the Sierra Maestra Manifesto with Fidel, continued their activities, largely from Miami. In October 1957, the opposition forces met there to hammer out a new unity agreement.

Like the Sierra Manifesto, the Miami Pact, as it came to be known, pledged to unify the opposition's "moral and material forces" in order to establish a "constitutional and democratic order" after Batista's fall. Unlike the Sierra Maestra Manifesto, however, it said nothing against foreign intervention in Cuban affairs. Because it assumed that Batista's demise was more or less imminent, the negotiations for the new agreement revolved much more around the details of the provisional government and the question of who would serve as interim president after Batista's fall. The room was dominated by moderate suit-and-tie politicians. By then, Fidel saw his position as much stronger than that of the other negotiators—the old political parties and struggling newer groups. Why concede power to them at this critical juncture, when he was probably strong enough to call the shots? In a long letter signed December 14, 1957, and published in *Bohemia* on February 2, 1958, Fidel withdrew the 26th of July Movement from the Miami Pact. He argued that by its very nature the provisional government being prepared in Miami could "neither have a revolutionary character nor avail itself of the strength we will need for the enormous social and political transformations the country requires."[20] Already, the revolution he imagined was looking different than the one moderate leaders wanted. His was a revolution that would not end with Batista's departure.

BY THE TIME THE MIAMI Pact was published in early 1958, no one else had the name recognition, the standing, or, for that matter, the longevity of Fidel Castro and his mountain guerrillas. And in 1958, his army was only gaining in numbers. In the spring, it had some four hundred soldiers, with more joining all the time. By late summer, the rebel army numbered close to three thousand, about three-quarters of whom were local peasants. Young people in Santiago and its environs left by the day to join Castro's forces. Catholic priests blessed religious medallions and sent them to the fighters in the mountain. The movement's power was such that Fidel's men opened new theaters of war, among them the Second Oriental Front, commanded by Raúl Castro and located in the Sierra Cristal, north of Guantánamo (March 1958), and a new front in the Escambray mountains, in central Cuba, commanded by Che Guevara (October 1958). Other groups had pockets of guerrilla activity, but none had the power or experience of Fidel's rebel army.[21]

Certainly, no other group had the revolutionary infrastructure that Fidel had established in the mountains of eastern Cuba. One visitor called it "a veritable military-agrarian state." Makeshift camps had become a full-blown headquarters in the Sierra Maestra. Called the La Plata Command, it was high and remote in the mountains, boasting sixteen balsa wood huts camouflaged so as to be undetectable by air. Fidel's house had multiple secret escape routes in case Batista's soldiers ever came upon them. One of the huts housed the Civil Administration for Liberated Territories, which encompassed departments of Justice, Sanitation, Agrarian Issues, Public Works, Finance, Education, and so on. In the Sierra Cristal, east and north of the rebel's main headquarters, Raúl Castro created a police force and intelligence service that recruited from the local peasantry. He also established schools to teach both soldiers and local children to read. The schools even taught public speaking, insisting (unsuccessfully) that students use the correct, two-syllable pronunciation of *para* (for) rather than the shortened (and still ubiquitous) *pa'*.[22]

To do all this, the rebels established their own taxation system; indeed, thirty-six of forty-one sugar mills in the region were paying taxes to the rebel state in 1958. It also officiated marriage ceremonies, legalized divorces, and registered births. It administered justice, punishing—either by execution or imprisonment—those it deemed guilty. As the highest authority on land they called liberated, the rebel state wrote its own laws. Early rebel decrees outlawed the cultivation and sale of marijuana, for instance, and set prices for the coffee harvest. Later laws were grander in scope. The most important was Law No. 3, which gave land to the tiller. A law on paper, however, was not enough for local peasants. And immediately after the law was signed, they began clamoring for its immediate implementation.[23] In this ever-expanding mountain kingdom, it was almost as if the revolution was already in power.

Of course, there was another, actual state in Havana, with Fulgencio Batista at its helm. Desperate to retain power and eager to give his security forces greater advantage against his enemies, he routinely issued temporary suspensions of constitutional guarantees. In March 1958, he closed schools across the country for fear of violence. But nothing he did could keep the peace, because there was no peace possible with him in power. In Havana, more than a hundred bombs exploded across the city in just one night in March. Every day, the resistance engaged in acts of sabotage and demonstrations. Every day, resistors were killed by police. Santiago had the feel of an occupied city, the occupying force not a foreign army, but the Cuban police and army. News of bombs, explosions, sabotage, cane fires, murders, beatings, and tortures filled the dispatches of US consuls. The situation had become so volatile and unsustainable that on March 15, 1958, civic institutions representing two hundred thousand people publicly called for Batista's resignation. The Sugar Mill Owners and Sugar Cane Growers associations withdrew support for Batista. The Catholic Church was now in the opposition. Cuba's communist party—officially called the Popular Socialist Party and erstwhile ally of Batista—came out officially in support of Castro's 26th of July Movement. And in a major blow to Batista's power, the United States announced in March that it would cease all arms shipments to Cuba.[24]

Still, Batista would not let go. He met the revolutionaries' persistence with ever-greater force, which only nourished the revolutionaries' resolve and their numbers. In May, Batista turned wholehearted to the one pursuit he thought might solve all his problems: a major military offensive he called Operation End Fidel. It failed. On Christmas Eve, 1958, perhaps appealing to a different kind of power, Batista dedicated a huge sculpture of Jesus Christ on a hilltop overlooking Havana Harbor (by Jilma Madera, the same sculptor who created Martí's bust for a mountain peak). That didn't save him, either. A week later, at noon on New Year's Eve, he retrieved his passport and ordered a plane readied. Then shortly after midnight, to start the new year, Batista left Cuba for the last time.

The defeat of Fulgencio Batista and the coming to power of the revolution led by Fidel Castro was greeted with great enthusiasm by the Cuban people in January 1959. Here, crowds swarm the Malecón, Havana's iconic seawall promenade, early in the revolution.

Part IX

THE REVOLUTION
BEGINS NOW!

Chapter 25

FIRST TIME

It was about 10 a.m. on the first day of 1959 when Cuban media began report-ing the news that Fulgencio Batista had fled. People took to the streets and danced without music. Cars blasted their horns; churches rang their bells. Batista's police stayed inside, and urban revolutionaries occupied government buildings. In some places, Boy Scouts came out to direct traffic.[1]

Many people tuned to clandestine Rebel Radio to hear directly from the dictator's greatest remaining nemesis. "The tyrant Batista has fled," Fidel Castro began triumphantly. But the fight was not over. On his way out, Batista had left one of his generals in control of the army and the head of the Supreme Court in charge of the government. So Castro was ordering rebel advances on Santiago and Havana and proclaiming a general strike. "We . . . will not brook any outcome other than the triumph of the Revolution," he vowed. Then, as if waiting for the world to catch up with him—perhaps imagining that listeners were frantically summoning friends and neighbors, yelling "Hurry, Batista left! Fidel is on the radio!"—he slowed down, repeating his point again in different words:

> A military junta, in connivance with the tyrant, has taken power to secure his flight and that of the country's assassins, and to halt the revolutionary tide and snatch away our victory. The people and the workers of Cuba must immediately prepare for a general strike tomorrow, January 2, all over the country, as a way of supporting the armed revolutionaries and thereby guaranteeing total victory for the Revolution.

He ordered Che Guevara and Camilo Cienfuegos, his commanders in central Cuba, to advance on Havana, his brother Raúl to march on Guantánamo. Finally, he announced his own advance on the city of Santiago, near the foot of the mountains where for two years his men had waged guerrilla war against Batista's army.[2]

It was almost nightfall when they arrived. "Columns of bearded rebels," wrote one bearded rebel, "were literally swept off their feet by overjoyed people." At the city's central square, Fidel addressed a crowd of hundreds of thousands. As would become his custom, he spoke for hours. Transcribed, his speech surpasses twelve thousand words and thirty single-spaced pages, though he had not one page before him as he spoke.[3]

"We have arrived," Castro said to thunderous cheers. Then he made an announcement that took everyone by surprise and that has long since been forgotten. He declared that the city of Havana was no longer the nation's capital. As of that moment, that role would fall to Santiago, the island's capital in the days of the Spanish Conquest and the capital of Fidel's own home province. More than a matter of local pride, however, the measure was a question of expediency. In Havana that night, the general named by Batista was still in control. The rebels had Santiago, so Santiago would be the capital.

The announcement was moot almost from the moment of its enunciation. The next day, Che Guevara and Camilo Cienfuegos arrived in Havana and took control of its main military installations. With that, Havana retained its status as national capital. Yet, as Fidel Castro stood before the multitudes giving his first victory speech and making an almost immediately irrelevant announcement, he inadvertently revealed something much more fundamental about this new Cuban Revolution. "This measure," he said, referring to his statement about the nation's capital, "may surprise some people. Admittedly, it is new. But the revolution is characterized precisely by its newness, by the fact that it will do things that have never been done before." In the moment of victory, on the cusp of power, that was Fidel Castro's first promise: the revolution would be unprecedented, it would do many things for the very first time.

TO UNDERSTAND THE IMPORT OF that statement, to grasp it as Castro said it and as the crowd heard it, means understanding all the revolutions, or the attempts at revolution, that had come before. It was in relation to those that Fidel ascribed meaning and purpose to the present. "The Revolution begins now!" he shouted. But it would not be like before. It would not be like the War of Independence in 1895, when the United States swept in at the end and seized victory, preventing Cuban troops from entering the city of Santiago. This time, under his orders, the revolutionaries entered the city, and Santiago roared its approval. This revolution would not be like 1933, when students and workers rose up and a new government decreed revolutionary measures, only to have Batista and his army unravel them all. It would not be like 1944, when hopeful Cubans under a new constitution elected a once-revolutionary president and he turned out to be a paragon of corruption and graft. "Neither thieves nor traitors nor interventionists. This time it really is the Revolution." *Esta vez sí que es la Revolución.*[4]

But if Cubans had never had a real revolution, how would they know what one looked and felt like? Figuring that out was what the present was for, and what a present it was. A heady sense of energy and euphoria swept the country in those first days. People exulted not only in the extraordinary moment, but also in the consensus that appeared to be on display all around them. Department stores, Masonic lodges, insurance companies, even banks and corporations issued statements in support of the revolution. Members of the old regular army stood at attention and saluted bearded rebels as they walked by. Young people slapped on red and black armbands identifying themselves as followers of the 26th of July Movement, and when those weren't available they donned red T-shirts as a sign of their support. Young city men immediately started growing beards, and exiles began returning from Miami to rejoice and contribute. In February 1959, a public opinion poll conducted by the thoroughly mainstream, resolutely middle-class magazine *Bohemia* put the percentage of the population that believed the revolutionary government was "doing everything perfectly well" at an astounding 92 percent. An American official at a US-owned sugar company seemed to agree: "This revolution so far has been the most pleasant surprise in years," he said. Even the US government was falling in line. On January 7, the administration of Dwight D. Eisenhower formally recognized the new government.[5]

As in most revolutions, a distinctive rhythm took hold. One Havana newspaper exhorted its readers, "Be quick, we have lost 50 years," referring to formal independence a little more than half a century earlier. Time itself ceased to be a given and became instead something Cubans could master. Fidel Castro routinely spoke for hours on end as if he could bend time to his will, condensing it in a way that made a late hour in an hours-long speech no longer late at all. The new government, meanwhile, seemed to stretch time to the maximum, as if it could accomplish months' worth of change in days, years' in months, decades' in years. The government issued decree after decree in rapid-fire succession. Today's law revoked last month's or extended yesterday's. On one day alone, January 6, 1959, it passed fourteen new laws, including one that suspended all existing age requirements for public office. Young revolutionaries could now occupy government positions. In its first nine months, the new government enacted some fifteen hundred laws, decrees, and edicts. It raised wages, cut telephone and electricity rates, reduced urban rents, seized property of past government officials, and, as its defining act, passed a long-awaited agrarian reform. In just months the revolution accomplished things promised sometimes decades earlier. As Fidel Castro had said on January 1 in Santiago, this time the revolution was for real.[6]

FIDEL CASTRO'S TRIUMPHANT ARRIVAL IN the capital city of Havana on January 8 gave Cubans some sense of just how different this revolution might be. He entered the capital from the east riding on a tank. It seemed that all Havana came out to greet him. Signs reading "Thank you, Fidel" hung from windshield wipers on bus windows and from balcony railings on fancy buildings. Castro's first stop was the Presidential Palace. Fidel—Celia Sánchez beside him—was there to meet with the newly appointed president, Manuel Urrutia. A well-respected judge and vocal Batista critic, he had been the agreed-upon choice of Fidel Castro and other revolutionaries in the months leading up to their victory. From the balcony of the palace, Urrutia thanked and welcomed Fidel, and the crowd went wild. When he came forward to speak, however, he had uncharacteristically little to say: he hated the Presidential Palace and preferred to address the Cuban people elsewhere, at the large military installation on the outskirts of Havana. "I want the people to go to Columbia," he said, "because Columbia now belongs to the people. Let the tanks, which now belong to the people, go in the vanguard of the people, opening up a path. No one will be there to stop their entry now. And we will meet there." Castro said this to hundreds of thousands in the crowd, as if meeting up again at a location about seven miles away presented no logistical hurdle at all. He wasn't asking people just to listen to his words; he was asking them to follow him literally, with their feet. Fidel continued:

> And now I want the people of Havana to give me proof of something. Someone up here just told me that a thousand soldiers would be necessary to get through this crowd. And I disagreed. I am going to pass through the crowd alone. . . . Without one soldier

preceding me to open the way. I am going to call upon the people to open a wide aisle, and I will pass through it together with the President of the Republic. Thus, my fellow countrymen, we will prove to the whole world, to the newspapermen who are present here, that there is discipline and civic feeling among the people of Cuba. Open up an aisle, and we will walk through it so that they will see that we do not need a single soldier to get through the crowd.[7]

And so it happened. Well after sunset, Castro arrived at Camp Columbia at the head of a caravan of tanks and jeeps, followed by a massive procession. No one impeded their entrance. Seeing the event from an analytical distance, it is clear that Fidel was redirecting a popular outpouring of support for the revolution from a site of civic power, the Presidential Palace, to a parallel and competing site of power, the island's principle military installation. But in the moment, it was less that than the palpable sense of liberation and possibility that people felt most keenly.

Fidel began his speech at Columbia at about 8 p.m. At 1:30 in the morning, he was still talking. He wasn't even tired, he said, but he understood that people might have to travel far to get home. People shouted, "It doesn't matter! Keep going!" It was as if time, distance, even sleep were no impediment to the new revolution. During that long, meandering speech, one extended moment perfectly prefigured how much Castro was about to disrupt traditional political norms. He explained that to guarantee the revolution's success, the new government's first task was to ensure peace, to avoid the mayhem and violence that had followed the removal of other dictators in the past. A traditional politician might have left the discussion there. Fidel did not. He explained that in that very moment some revolutionary groups were amassing weapons. He didn't mention anyone by name, but he was referring to the Revolutionary Directorate, the student-dominated group that had been a major force against Batista. At times it had worked with Fidel's 26th of July Movement, but the two groups had also had conflicts and rivalries. One seemed to be brewing now, and Fidel was pressing his advantage. In signature form, he appealed to the crowd directly: "I want to ask the people a question the answer to which interests me greatly. . . . Weapons for what? To fight against whom? Against the revolutionary government, which has popular support? Weapons for what? To fight against the revolution? . . . To threaten peace?"[8]

As Fidel spoke of peace, the sun long gone, a white dove circled above him and landed on his shoulder. It was, said one witness, as if the dove was the Holy

Ghost descending on Jesus Christ, as if the Father himself had come to Havana to announce, "This is my beloved Son." The crowd grew silent; some might have made the sign of the cross. The next day, members of the Revolutionary Director-ate began surrendering weapons.[9] On January 1, Fidel had promised something new. If we judge by the tenor of political discourse one week in, everything seemed to indicate that he would deliver.

POLITICS, OF COURSE, IS NECESSARILY more than speech, more than spectacle. And a revolution—just like history itself—is always more than the pronouncements of its leaders. To avoid the familiar outcomes of other Cuban revolutions—US intervention or Cuban military coups, for instance—the new revolution had to consolidate its hold on power in practical, concrete ways. In the first instance that meant establishing a government. The president's cabinet was named in the very first days after victory. It was the kind of cabinet that would have been established, say, if the progressive, anti-corruption Ortodoxo Party had won elections. *Time* magazine characterized its members as "mostly responsible, moderate men, ready to get to work." They were lawyers, judges, and US-educated economists. The prime minister, José Miro Cardona, was president of the Havana Bar Association. Years before he had defended former president Grau San Martín when he was indicted for having stolen 84 million pesos while in office. Osvaldo Dorticós, a wealthy lawyer who served as commodore of the Cienfuegos Yacht Club, became head of a new ministry charged with studying and advising on revolutionary laws. The minister of the interior, who had joined Castro's rebels in the mountains, had presided over the university's anticommunist student group. The new finance minister and the new president of the National Bank had both held high posts in the administrations of Presidents Grau and Prío. There were also younger folks, many from the urban wing of the 26th of July Movement. Castro had one official post, an important one: commander and chief of the army. A twenty-third-floor suite in the recently opened, US-owned Havana Hilton served as his new headquarters and home.[10]

Once established, the new government began purging the old regime. The first revolutionary laws dissolved Congress, removed all existing elected officials from their posts, dismantled existing political parties, disbanded the old army, and abolished Batista's secret police and other repressive institutions. With these de-crees, one newspaper confidently announced, "we finish with all the vices of the past, all the old political games." Less than two weeks into power, the new cabinet revised two constitutional articles to allow both the confiscation of property without trial and the application of the death penalty. These measures cleared the way for the government to eliminate not only the old political games, but also the old political class. Practically everyone cheered.[11]

In fact, in terms of serving justice on the men who had done Batista's dirty work, the public sometimes seemed to lead the charge. Across the island, people demanded retribution against the Batistianos who had terrorized their communities in the preceding years. In one village near Santiago, residents had recently discovered a secret mass grave of victims killed by Batista's forces and clamored for punishment of the perpetrators. People in some towns organized strikes and protests against what they saw as inadequate punishment. Fearing an outpouring of popular revenge, as had happened immediately after the fall of Machado in 1933, the new government created Revolutionary Tribunals to try former Batista officials. For each trial, juries composed of rebel army veterans and members of the local community heard testimony of witnesses before the public. Mothers confronted the killers of their sons; children accused the murderers of their fathers. Sometimes former soldiers in Batista's army detailed the criminal actions of their superiors. In many cases, the person standing trial confessed. Often, they resorted to the famous defense of other more famous trials, "I acted under orders."[12]

In Santiago on one January morning, seventy-one prisoners were executed, all members of a private militia headed by a Batista ally. The executions reverberated far and wide. Reporters and photographers were present to document them, and footage was provided to news programs in Havana and New York. Viewers watched one accused after another face the firing squad; they heard the command to fire, saw the bodies react to the bullets, double over onto the ground, and then lie still. News photographers captured images of a priest hearing the confession of a condemned man, bodies of others already executed lined up behind them. Some photos showed the ditch, forty feet long, ten feet wide, and ten feet deep, where the corpses were placed after execution.[13]

By the end of January, the trials had resulted in the execution of more than 250 people across the island. By March, the number exceeded 500, most of them former army, police, and state intelligence members accused of multiple counts of torture or murder of prisoners.[14] The new revolutionary state—like all states—had established a monopoly on violence. It and no one else would mete out punishment and administer justice.

As news of the executions circulated, American politicians and journalists began raising their voices in opposition. Members of Congress issued outraged denunciations. One Oregon Republican denounced "the blood bath" from the Senate floor. *Time* published a long article condemning the trials. The details were graphic, the photographs—stills taken from film footage—stirring.[15]

In Cuba, however, the trials and executions had support from much of the public, who saw them as justice served swiftly and rightly on murderers. The same February *Bohemia* survey that put the new government's support at over 90 percent revealed that of all the things that government had started doing, "revolutionary justice" was the single most popular. Professional associations, students, even Catholic priests and their parishioners wrote to Eisenhower to show their support for the trials. The Havana chapter of the international Lions' Club, for instance, believed that Americans were misinterpreting the trials. The Revolutionary Tribunals, it insisted, had been established to judge men who had committed savage acts of torture. The government's measures, and the actions of the Revolutionary Tribunals, were designed "to avoid greater bloodshed."[16]

While the public spoke out in favor of the trials, their most powerful defender was Fidel Castro. In a speech on January 17, he accused the United States of trying to thwart the revolution and its legitimate application of justice. By what right, he asked, did the United States presume to command a self-governing people. To prove to the United States and the world that the trials were a rightful demand of the Cuban public, Castro invited a delegation of reporters and government officials from Canada, Latin America, Great Britain, and the United States to witness the trials for themselves. Then, to show that the trials were the people's will, he announced a rally at the Presidential Palace on January 21.[17]

The US embassy said five hundred thousand Cubans attended; the Cuban government put the number at a million. Whatever the final count, many agreed that there were more people present at this rally than there had been even at the rally welcoming Fidel to Havana on January 8. Banners in English and Spanish made the crowd's stance clear: "For revolutionary justice!" "Extradite the lackeys of imperialism!" "Cuban women demand execution of murderers!"[18]

Fidel's speech that day was a fiery one. It provided an early taste of the anti-American invective that would soon emerge as his signature theme. "I do not have to give an account to any US Congressman," he told the rapt, assenting crowd. "[They] have nothing to do with Cuban affairs." He did, however, give account, just not the one US politicians expected. Based on his estimates, for every one person executed in Cuba, one thousand men, women, and children had been killed by American bombs in Hiroshima and Nagasaki just fourteen years earlier. The much-celebrated Nuremberg Trials had condemned people under laws written after the fact, while in Cuba, the accused had violated already existing laws. Finally, he compared the indignation of Cuba's critics in the present with their silence in the past. Where were those critics, he asked, while Batista's regime was killing people? Did they raise their voices in protest then? No. He concluded that the only explanation for the condemnations now was not the trials themselves, but rather a concerted campaign against the revolution—against all the Cubans gathered there listening to his words.

As during his speech on entering Havana a few weeks earlier, Fidel called directly on the audience and asked a favor. "I am going to ask the people something: Those who agree with the justice that is being carried out, those who agree that the henchmen should be shot raise your hands." "A sea of Cubans raised their hands in unanimous consent," writes one historian. Some raised two hands. Fidel then turned to his three hundred invited guests and said, "Gentlemen of the diplomatic corps, reporters of the entire continent: The jury of a million Cubans representing all views and social classes has voted. To those who are democrats, or those who call themselves democrats I say: This is democracy...."[19]

NOT EVERYONE IN CUBA WAS happy with the trials, however. In mid-February, in part because of concerns over their form, as well as frustration with Castro's emerging political style, the first prime minister of the revolutionary government, José Miro Cardona, resigned. Fidel became the new prime minister. At about the same time, a new law gave the post of prime minister significantly more power and that of president significantly less. With the change, Fidel became institutionally what he already was in practice: the undisputed leader of a new political order.

The pace of government action accelerated even further. In the first month and a half of the revolutionary government, the deluge of laws had dealt mostly with the dismantling of the old regime, and they had largely affected people directly tied to it. With Castro as prime minister, the government decreed a host of more far-reaching policies. The first major one came in March. Called the Urban Reform Law, it cut rents by as much as 50 percent. Batista had enacted his own urban reform, but not on this scale and not in the context of such widescale popular mobilization. With 63 percent of Cubans renting their homes in 1959, many landlords suddenly saw drastic reductions in their income, and a much larger group suddenly became beneficiaries of revolutionary policy—in both cases irrespective of their relationship to Batista's government or to the revolution. The new regime followed that law with a host of other changes: increases in salaries, reductions in utility rates, measures against racial discrimination. In a few months, writes historian Louis Pérez, "hundreds of thousands of Cubans developed an immediate and lasting stake in the success of the revolution."[20]

It would be wrong, however, to characterize such changes simply as gifts bestowed by the new government on an expectant public. The public was expectant, yes. But it was also mobilized. As soon as the revolutionaries took power, citizen demands swelled. Afro-Cuban activists demanded antidiscrimination measures. Women formed new groups and called for the establishment of day care centers and cafeterias and grocery stores open at night to serve working-class women.[21] Peasants, meanwhile, demanded payment on promises made to them over decades. They wanted land, and chafed at calls for patience. Even before Fidel reached Havana on January 8, people in some areas had begun implementing their own de facto agrarian reform, distributing titles to small plots of land. This improvised agrarian reform from below was prevalent enough that the revolutionary government passed a law on February 20 stating that anyone occupying land without waiting for the Agrarian Reform Law would lose all rights to the benefits that would later be conferred by that law.[22]

Workers and labor unions pressed the government, as well, calling for 20 percent wage increases across the board, improved working conditions, the renegotiation of labor contracts, the reinstatement of workers dismissed for political reasons, and more. Facing the possibility of labor unrest during its first months in power, the government stepped in to mediate. The practice of state mediation in labor disputes was not new to the revolution, but no government (save perhaps the brief revolutionary one of 1933) did so like this—more than five thousand mediations in early 1959 alone. The state did not implement a universal wage increase, as labor unions were demanding, but it used the individual mediations, for the most part, in favor of workers. In this manner, in its first ten months alone, the government decreed 66 million pesos in wage increases to sugar workers and 20 million to workers in other areas. Overall, wages rose 14.3 percent in the first year of the revolution, compared to an average of 4.2 percent annually in the two preceding years.[23]

These actions—like many of the fifteen hundred decrees of the first ten months of the revolution in power—responded to and were inseparable from the insistent mobilizations and demands that burst forth from street corners, newspaper columns, radio broadcasts, and church sermons. The affluent mobilized, too, flooding government offices to pay back taxes. By June 1959, even with all the government spending, the national treasury boasted a surplus of $34 million. The funds, noted Havana's communist paper, freed the new government from US purse strings.[24]

AMERICANS, OF COURSE, WATCHED CLOSELY. Beyond studying the laws to understand their impact on US interests, they closely observed Fidel Castro himself. They recorded his words, listened for his tone, took note of who surrounded him when and where, decoded his ministerial and army appointments, estimated the size of his crowds, timed how long he spoke. They even kept track of how fast he spoke—up to three hundred words per minute, by one count. The US embassy in Havana advised Washington "to get used to the feeling of walking gently around the edges of a volcano that is liable to burst forth with sulphurous fumes at the slightest provocation."[25]

Yet for all the observation, there was no consensus in the United States about Fidel Castro and the Cuban Revolution. One observer declared him a closet communist; another insisted on the opposite. The latter was the conclusion of the CIA's top expert on Latin America: "Castro is not only not a Communist, he is a strong anti-Communist fighter." The same uncertainty surrounded American appraisals of Castro's attitude toward the United States. Some took Fidel at his word when he said that he was not anti-American; others disagreed. "Castro hates this Government like the Devil hates holy water," said one southern Democrat.[26]

Part of the confusion originated with Fidel himself, with contradictory signals and statements that made it hard to decipher what exactly was unfolding. Take, for example, the issue of elections. Arriving in Havana on January 8, 1959, Fidel announced that elections would occur in eighteen months. A few days later, it was fifteen months. A month later, he said it would be unfair to have elections right away, as he would get a "crushing majority." Then he said that elections would occur when political parties were organized, no date specified. He returned over and over to the question, noting that when he mentioned elections, crowds booed and hissed. At one speech, he asked members of the audience to raise their hands if they wanted elections; few or none did. Then he asked to see who did not want elections. A multitude of hands went up in seemingly unanimous consent. In another speech, he asked if people wanted elections within a year or within ten. A chorus of "ten!" rang out. In April, he coined a new motto: revolution first, elections later. He shouted, "Land first, elections later; work for every Cuban first, elections later; schools and teachers for all children first, elections later; hospitals and medicine first, elections later; justice first, elections later; national sovereignty first, elections later." The applause was raucous.[27]

American officials and the American public soon got their chance to see and question Castro up close. Invited to the United States by the American Society of Newspaper Editors, Castro's trip began on April 15, 1959. He arrived at the airport in Havana two hours late, in a rumpled uniform, and seeming more nervous than usual. More anxious were the clean-shaven, suit-and-tie ministers who joined him on the trip, the president of the National Bank and the finance minister. They fretted over Castro's aversion to protocol, his unpredictability, and his emerging penchant for anti-American polemic. They accompanied him understanding that the principal purpose of the trip was to request financial assistance from the United States, and they had shared proposals for that aid with him in preparation for the visit. So they were understandably surprised when Fidel announced at his first press conference in Washington that he was not there to ask for money. The next day, as Castro delivered a speech in English before the American Society of Newspaper Editors, he noticed his finance minister getting up to leave for a meeting with the US Treasury secretary. Fidel paused his speech midsentence and switched to Spanish to tell the minister, "Remember, Rufo, I don't want you to ask for money." Then he continued his speech in English, finishing to prolonged applause, according to the *New York Times*.[28]

In fact, the applause was prolonged and the crowds huge everywhere he went: Mount Vernon, the Jefferson Memorial, New York's Penn Station, Central Park, Princeton University, Harvard Yard. At one venue, he turned to his finance minister and said, "They're Americans, and they like me, Rufo!" In Queens, New York, he posed for photos with Cuban American boys and girls wearing green caps and beards. (An American toy manufacturer had recently released one hundred thousand Fidel cap-and-beard sets.) At the Lincoln Memorial, he read the Gettysburg Address aloud in English and laid a wreath at Lincoln's feet. The *New York Times* said Castro seemed to have swept into Washington not just from another world, but also "out of another century—the century of Sam Adams and Patrick Henry and Tom Paine and Thomas Jefferson." The reporter continued, "Perhaps because he stirred memories, long dimmed, of a revolutionary past and recalled a revolutionary ardor once deeply felt . . . Fidel Castro succeeded in achieving a suspension of disbelief, at least partial and temporary."[29]

While the American public received Fidel as a hero, the US government was less swayed and perhaps even more confused than before his arrival. Castro's was not an official state visit, which made it hard for everyone to know how to act. Eisenhower decided to leave town to play golf during the visit and left Vice President Richard Nixon to meet with the Cuban leader. Only the two men and their interpreters attended the meeting. Fidel arrived "nervous and tense," worried that he had blown his *Meet the Press* appearance earlier that day. Nixon reassured him: it was the toughest show any politician could do, and Fidel had had the courage to do it in English. Impressive, conceded the vice president. But quickly, Nixon turned to advice and censure. Why was it taking so long to call elections? He advised Castro to specify that he wanted elections as soon as feasibly possible, and certainly no longer than four years. Nixon reproached him also for the executions. Toward the end of the meeting, Nixon suggested that Fidel follow the economic example of the governor of Puerto Rico—then, as now, US territory. Perhaps nothing reveals how little the US government understood Fidel Castro than that freely offered advice. "He took a very dim view of this suggestion," wrote Nixon after the meeting. Castro had told him that "the Cuban people were 'very nationalistic' and would look with suspicion on any program initiated in what they would consider to be a 'colony' of the United States."[30]

While Nixon counseled, Castro countered with advice of his own. Nixon paraphrased some of it: "You in America"—though Fidel surely said United States and not America—"should not be talking so much about your fear of what the Communists may do in Cuba or in some other country in Latin America, Asia or Africa. You should be talking more about your own strengths and the reasons why your system is superior to Communism or any other kind of dictatorship." A State Department official waiting outside the office reported that Nixon emerged from the meeting looking "very tired," needing to unwind from "a pretty grueling 2½ hours."

By the time Nixon prepared his report on the meeting a few days later, he was less tired but no less ambivalent: "My own appraisal of [Castro] as a man is somewhat mixed. The one fact we can be sure of is that he has those indefinable qualities which make him a leader of men. Whatever we may think of him, he is going to be a great factor in the development of Cuba and very possibly in Latin American affairs generally." In that judgment, certainly, Nixon was right and not alone. The US State Department came to the same conclusion. "It would be a serious mistake to underestimate this man." Eisenhower read that sentence and scribbled in the margins, "File. We will check in a year!"[31]

EISENHOWER'S EXCLAMATION POINT SERVED AS an inadvertent portent of how dramatically and rapidly things would change in that one year. Castro returned to Havana from his trip and announced an impending, momentous change. He called it "the fundamental law of our Revolution, the defining law of our Revolution."[32] He was talking, of course, about agrarian reform. Because agrarian reform had been a centerpiece of political struggles for much of the twentieth century, many Cubans saw its enactment as a symbol of all that had been missing in the republic. If this time, as Fidel had said on January 1, the revolution was for real, nothing would demonstrate that more irrefutably than distributing land to the landless.

The country was more than ready for it. In some areas, peasants and their allies had already begun to parcel out land without waiting for the government's law. It wasn't just people in the countryside who were eager for agrarian reform. People in cities and towns across the country stepped up in support. On March 1, the magazine *Bohemia* started a fundraising drive—Operation Liberty—for the benefit of an agrarian reform program. Cubans of all classes showed up in person, mailed cash and checks, and phoned in contributions in support of the cause. Three days into the fundraiser, the magazine had collected over a quarter of a million pesos. In regular installments, it published the names of contributors with the amounts contributed. Companies participated: Hatuey Beer (a subsidiary of Bacardí Rum), 25,000; the owners of the pharmacy in Havana's main bus station, 136; American International Life Insurance, 1,000. Sometimes, people made donations collectively: teachers of the School No. 87 in Pinar del Río, 8 pesos; Cubans in the city of Chicago, 15.50; workers of the Cherry Coffee Shop, 20. Most often, though, people gave what they could as individuals or as families: Ramón Reynaldo, veteran of the independence war, 1 peso; Alina Saúl, 4 pesos; Leonardo Estévez and family, 2.25; A. Macias, 25 cents. All told, the pledged contributions amounted to over 13 million. This, too, was a mass demonstration. It had not been called forth by Fidel Castro, nor was it anonymous like the crowds who cheered his words, though one woman humbly offered five pesos to the cause simply as "Una señora agradecida"—a grateful woman.[33]

A vast majority of Cubans supported the 1959 Agrarian Reform, and many donated funds to assist in its implementation. Here, a group of customs workers donates a tractor for the campaign. The 1959 queen of Havana's carnival, Esperanza Bustamante, appears to the right of center.

The agrarian reform was signed into law on May 17, 1959, in a ceremony in the Sierra Maestra, where the revolution had passed its first agrarian reform before assuming power. In 1958, Law No. 3 of the Sierra Maestra had given land to peasants in rebel territory. The 1959 law now made agrarian reform the law of the land in all Cuba. In some ways the new law hewed closely to its 1958 predecessor. It proscribed *latifundio*, restricting all landholdings to thirty caballerías (about four hundred hectares or one thousand acres), though certain kinds of farms—sugar plantations and cattle ranches—were allowed larger limits. Anything over the established limits would be expropriated by the state, with owners receiving compensation in twenty-year bonds payable at 4.5 percent annual interest. The law established three possible uses for the land expropriated by the government: small land grants to the landless; agricultural cooperatives; and state farms to be staffed by agricultural workers employed by the state. These last two forms—the agricultural cooperative and the state farm—surprised many, for they had not been part of the 1958 Sierra Maestra law. The new law also prohibited any further eviction of peasants from land they worked, just as it prohibited further acquisition of Cuban land by foreigners—a limitation present also in the 1940 constitution, though never enforced. Finally, the new law created a National Institute of Agrarian Reform to oversee the whole process.[34]

Overall, the law was fairly moderate and well within the mainstream of the era's economic thinking. Its proscription against large landholding was present not only in the Cuban constitution of 1940, but also in recommendations for agrarian reform made by such international bodies as the United Nations. Cuba's new law was also a far cry from Soviet-style collectivization. But even a moderate law, enthusiastically supported by a majority of the population, created enemies, especially among landowners who suffered losses. Cattle ranchers in Camagüey, for instance, and tobacco growers in Pinar del Río publicly voiced their opposition to the law.[35]

The most powerful enemies of the reform, however, were in the United States. Some policy makers and economists in Washington understood that moderate agrarian reform was increasingly viewed as a cornerstone of development policy. The problem, however, was that in Cuba, much of the land directly affected by the Agrarian Reform Law was US-owned. On June 11, the United States sent a formal diplomatic note protesting the law. It requested that compensation be effective (that is, in cash rather than the bonds offered by the law), prompt (within six months rather than twenty years), and at market value (rather than at tax value). The Cuban government responded just four days later, justifying and explaining its choices. The interest rates offered were more generous than those offered by the United States in Japan after World War II. Cuba had no cash to offer as recompense, because Batista had raided the national coffers. Most important, the agrarian reform was the essence of the revolution, and the government could not wait to have cash on hand to carry it out. Though each country made its position clearly known, the exchange, for the time being, was a measured one.[36]

When the first expropriations under the new law were carried out in June, among the properties seized by the government was a forty-thousand-acre estate held by the same company that owned the King Ranch in Texas, then the largest private landholding anywhere in the United States. The president of the company immediately wrote to Eisenhower asking him to seize all Cuban assets in the United States and to send navy vessels to the Caribbean. He said the president should also remind the Cubans "that in 1898 we fought to free Cuba from [Spanish] tyranny—we will not stand by now and allow Communism to permanently destroy this freedom."[37]

In 1959, the Spanish-American War of 1898 was not yet distant, forgotten history. And in the context of the revolution, some Americans began invoking it every time Fidel Castro did something that challenged US interests. "We who in living memory rescued the island from medieval bondage; we who have given order, vitality, technical wisdom and wealth are now being damned for our civilizing and cooperative virtues!" roared one senator in 1960. Even President Eisenhower, who had been seven years old at the time of the Spanish-American War, voiced the same sentiment. "We were the ones who set them free. And when they got in trouble, we had an occupation . . . and again we set them on their feet, and set them free." By what right did Cuba now challenge the United States?[38]

Such sentiments exemplified the long-standing impasse in Cubans' and Americans' understanding of their shared history. And the two interpretations could not have been more at odds. What Americans saw as an act of selfless benevolence, Cubans saw as an act of colonial imposition. That antagonism mattered now more than ever, for it was precisely the colonial relationship between the United States and Cuba that the revolution was beginning to challenge. Unable to perceive that relationship as a colonial one, Americans were at a loss to understand what was happening in Cuba and quick to perceive all of it as naïve ingratitude, at best, and outright communism, at worst.

AS THE EXPROPRIATIONS UNDER THE agrarian reform began, accusations of communism intensified markedly. Before the agrarian reform, *Time* and *Newsweek* magazines had published only one article suggesting that the Cuban Revolution was communist; after the law was passed, such articles proliferated in those magazines and across other US media. In Cuba, even within the government, the expropriations sharpened internal divisions over the role of communism in the revolution. June 1959 saw a major shakeup in the cabinet. The agriculture minister, who had written the Agrarian Reform Law in the Sierra Maestra (but had been excluded from the drafting of the May 1959 law), resigned to protest what he saw as communist infiltration in the National Institute of Agrarian Reform, which he said was operating as a kind of shadow government. Other moderate and anticommunist ministers resigned or were forced out by Fidel Castro that same month.[39]

Cuban president Manuel Urrutia was among the last moderates standing. In June he took to the airwaves repeatedly to decry the growing influence of communism in the revolution. He did not accuse Castro himself. "In the . . . Council of Ministers I know of no Communists. Dr. Fidel Castro, you may be sure, is no communist." Even so, Castro was not pleased. For weeks, the two men issued dueling public statements over the question. But Fidel was a lot more popular than the president. And he knew it. The evening of July 16, 1959, Castro went on television to announce his resignation as prime minister. He explained that he had decided to resign due to differences with the president. He argued that raising the specter of communism, as Urrutia had done, encouraged the powerful interests—domestic and international—that were lining up against the revolution. As Castro addressed the nation, messages in his support poured into the station. Crowds gathered outside the Presidential Palace to demand Urrutia's resignation instead of Fidel's. By 11 p.m. that night, the president resigned, too.[40]

The country was left with no president and no prime minister. The cabinet refused to accept Castro's resignation, and some union leaders began calling for a general strike. People made banners and signs expressing utmost loyalty to Fidel: "Revolution without Fidel is Treason." "We are with you, Fidel," read one sign at the University of Havana. "Fidel or Death!" read another on a city bus.[41]

As the country watched and waited to see if Castro would return to power, it mobilized for the biggest party in recent memory. July 26, 1959, was the anniversary of the assault on the Moncada barracks in Santiago in 1953, and the first one celebrated since the revolution had come to power. At midnight on July 25, church bells rang. Havana's cathedral offered a ceremonial mass in honor of those who had fallen in the 1953 assault. A baseball game featured the team called "Los Barbudos" (the bearded ones); Fidel Castro pitched.[42]

But the celebration was not just a celebration of an anniversary, or even of the revolution. It was, by design, a tribute to the agrarian reform, and perhaps half a million peasants arrived in Havana to participate. Bus companies offered them transportation; Havana residents volunteered their homes, and hotels offered deeply discounted rooms. "Welcome to Havana" and "Havana is yours" read signs and ads everywhere. Textile factories manufactured white guayabera shirts and traditional *yarey* hats for them to wear. The famous Cuban (and later Cuban American) diva Celia Cruz composed and performed a song for the occasion.[43]

The highlight of the events was the mammoth rally at the Civic Plaza—not yet renamed Plaza de la Revolución, but already boasting the massive marble monument to José Martí begun for the centennial of his birth. Some estimate that a million people were in attendance, including the peasants who had traveled to Havana for the celebration. Photos of the crowd show a sea of white guayaberas and straw hats adorned with signs saying "I am with Fidel." Men wielded machetes and twirled their straw hats on the points of their blades.

Castro was seated at the dais, but not as prime minister, for he had renounced that post. He felt the energy of the crowd. He heard the chants clamoring for his return. He stood up, approached the new president, Osvaldo Dorticós, and whispered something in his ear. Then, Dorticós spoke: "As President of the Republic I can announce to you that in the face of the public's demand, Dr. Fidel Castro has agreed to return to the position of Prime Minister."[44] The crowd went wild with cheers; peasants threw their hats high in the air; they banged the blades of their machetes together to make the most boisterous applause possible. The noise was deafening.

This was acclamation in its purest form. That same euphoria that had greeted news of Batista's flight on the first day of the year was palpable once more. But it had something of a different quality the afternoon and evening of July 26, 1959. It was surer and steadier. The revolution was doing what it said; the people counted; the future was theirs. Fidel stood at the dais and looked out at the immense crowd, cheering his return. The people were with him, and the rapture of the crowd became wonder in his eyes.

It may be a mistake to single out one moment in which a future becomes clear, because the future never is and no moment can ever fully anticipate it. But in *that* moment, everything seemed possible. A real revolution was within reach. And in July 1959, the vast majority of Cuban people seemed to have little problem with that. After all, this real revolution had been their doing, too.

Chapter 26

RADICAL NONSTOP

(Or a Visit and Three Funerals)

If 1959 began as a feeling, it quickly became a question. The question was deceptively simple: What would this new Cuban Revolution be? To answer it, however, Cubans could not pause the clock or will away the world. They had to make and define their revolution in real time, on concrete ground. Had they had a choice, they might have preferred a different moment in global history as context for their revolution. Instead, they were stuck with the Cold War at one of its hottest junctures.

In the decade before the Cuban Revolution, the Cold War had split the world into two hostile camps led respectively by the Soviet Union and the United States. In 1959, the outcome of that conflict was far from certain; in fact, the United States was on the defensive. In 1956, Soviet leader Nikita Khrushchev had famously promised to "bury" the capitalist states of the West. In 1957, the Soviet Union had unexpectedly upstaged the United States by launching the world's first satellite into space. In 1960, the Soviets shocked Americans by shooting down a US spy plane. In addition, the escalating conflict between the two superpowers was unfolding as colonies across Africa and Asia gained political independence and sought new allies in an increasingly bipolar world. Because the outcome of the Cold War was not at all clear, what every new government decided mattered greatly.

Whether for philosophical reasons or strategic ones, Fidel Castro initially sought to evade the stark schism of a cold war that divided the world in two. The revolution, he said time and again, represented a middle path between capitalism

335

and communism, between the hunger of the former and the unfreedom of the latter. Why argue over communism, he asked, when Cuba was charting a third way for the world? The only "ism" that could properly be attached to the Cuban Revolution, he averred, was "humanism." "Liberty with bread, bread without terror," Castro had said in New York in April 1959. "That is humanism."[1] Yet however much Castro may have wanted to avoid the question of communism, the question could simply not be dodged—not in that world, in that moment, in a country with such an entangled relationship with a Cold War superpower expecting allegiance.

In Cuba, the question of communism seemed to be on everyone's lips. Sometimes the question even dropped from the skies, as airplanes piloted by Cubans newly exiled in the United States dropped thousands of leaflets urging Cubans to fight against "the communist dictatorship." They also dropped bombs on sugar mills and cane fields in the name of combating communism. The issue invaded Sunday sermons and sometimes resulted in shouting and fighting outside churches. It dominated classroom discussion and meetings in university halls. In Havana's Central Park, young people debated the matter ad nauseam. They all considered themselves revolutionaries, but while some vehemently rejected communism, others concluded, "If Fidel's a communist, sign me up!" Each side had its own bench in the park. Catholic student groups, who had participated actively in the struggle against Batista and rejoiced when he fell, called the Cubans on the other bench Moscow's lackeys. These called the Catholics the Vatican's minions. It was more than name-calling and posturing; people pondered the revolution's character seriously, earnestly. They knew how much was at stake.[2]

At the highest levels of government, the question of communism was explosive. It had already resulted in the resignation of the revolution's first president earlier in 1959. In October, when a former 26th of July member, Huber Matos, resigned a government post to protest what he believed was communist influence, Castro had him arrested as a traitor. Part of the cabinet was indignant. If Matos had been arrested for opposing communism, said one member, then so, too, should some of them be arrested, for they opposed it as well. More ministers resigned in the months that followed. By late 1959 and early 1960, then, communism was not primarily a theoretical question. It relegated other issues to the margins and became an argument signifying everything.

For some, perhaps especially for those who had fought against Batista and now began resigning from the revolutionary government, warning against communism was a way to emphasize and protect the original goals of the revolution. That revolution had resulted from the most broad-based coalition in Cuban history. It had included Catholics and students, exiles and peasants, traditional political parties and nontraditional secret organizations, the middle class and the working class. The revolution most of those people had fought for was socially progressive and politically democratic. But it was also emphatically not communist. While individual communists participated in the revolution, the Popular Socialist Party had not supported it until almost the very end. None of the public proclamations of the revolution—from Castro's "History Will Absolve Me" speech in 1953 to the manifestos issued from the mountains in 1957 and 1958—had countenanced the establishment of a communist state or socialist economy. Equally important, before the seizure of power, many revolutionaries were explicitly anticommunist. Now with the revolution in power, some of those same people believed that taking a stand against communist influence at this defining moment was to defend the revolution for which they had all fought.

For Fidel Castro and another sector of the revolutionary coalition, however, the exact opposite was true. The revolution was always in danger of being undone before it could deliver on its promises. For them, raising the specter of communism was to weaken the revolutionary government—not because the revolution was communist, they insisted, but because, in the context of the Cold War and in the shadow of the United States, that charge made the new government particularly vulnerable to attack. A model for what could happen was close at hand in Guatemala. There, just a few years earlier, a legitimately elected government enacted a progressive agrarian reform; the United States called it communist and orchestrated a coup that deposed the government and ended the agrarian reform. To raise the specter of communism in Cuba, especially in the aftermath of its own agrarian reform, was to invite a similar outcome. In this view, anticommunism was, simply put, counterrevolution.[3]

It was in this context—with moderate government officials resigning, with leaflets and bombs falling from the sky, and with the example of Guatemala readily available—that arguments about the role of communism in the revolution proliferated and intensified. One controversy followed another; each built on earlier ones and generated new ones in its wake. And as the controversies accumulated, one trend became palpable: an intensifying, unremitting radicalization that fundamentally redefined the character of Cuba's most famous revolution.

THE FIRST CONTROVERSY OF 1960 derived from an unexpected and risky embrace. On February 4, the deputy prime minister of the Soviet Union,

Anastas Mikoyan, arrived in Havana for a visit. He was there to open a new exhibition on Soviet science, technology, and culture. The exhibit had already traveled to Mexico City and New York, and Castro had invited Mikoyan to bring it to Havana. At the time, Cuba and the Soviet Union did not have diplomatic relations. Historically, Cuba had followed the lead of the United States in matters of international affairs, voting with it in the United Nations, recognizing governments it recognized, and shunning those it didn't. Mikoyan's visit, then, represented the arrival on Cuban soil of the United States' archenemy—at the invitation of Cuba's government, at the height of the Cold War.

The Cuban government hosted the Soviet visitor with all the fanfare it could muster. It offered his forty-person delegation lodgings at the lavish estate of a former Batista ally, long since ensconced in Miami. Mikoyan gave Castro a personal tour of the exhibit, praising the technological and cultural achievements of the Soviet Union, as photographers snapped pictures. Wearing a straw, peasant-style hat with the word *Cuba* painted on the front, Mikoyan joined Fidel for a tour of the island. At Havana's Central Park he laid the obligatory wreath at the old monument to national hero José Martí. In a private meeting with President Dorticós, Mikoyan expressed his astonishment that some were calling Cuba's agrarian reform communist. In a public speech, he urged the government to go further and to pursue "confiscation—without any compensation—of all means of production."[4]

No one was especially surprised when on the last day of the Soviet exhibition, the Cuban press published news of a trade agreement between the two countries. The Soviets agreed to purchase 20 percent of the annual Cuban sugar harvest for the next five years. They would pay only a fraction of what the United States was paying, and payment would be in cash, machinery, petroleum, and the services of Soviet technicians on the island. Mikoyan, it seemed, would be only the first Soviet citizen to spend time in revolutionary Cuba.[5]

News of Mikoyan's visit and the Cuban-Soviet trade agreement sent shock waves through Washington. One closed-door meeting followed another, the conclusion of each grimmer than the one before. A State Department staffer prepared a long memo titled "Possibilities of Salvaging Cuba." His assessment was pessimistic in the extreme. "We have never in our national history experienced anything quite like [the Cuban Revolution] in magnitudes of anti-US venom, claims for expropriation, or Soviet threats to the hemisphere," he wrote. "There is not a clear enough realization among our own people that pre-Castro Cuba will not return, or that, if we are to reestablish influence within Cuba, it must be in a context different from that which obtained in the past." Humility was in order, he counseled his superiors.[6]

For their part, Cubans appear to have responded to the high-profile Soviet visit and trade deal with support, even enthusiasm. When Mikoyan gave speeches in public, he had to stop repeatedly for extended applause. When he mentioned the trade deal, crowds chanted "and guns and planes, too!" "Whether out of conviction or caution," writes historian Lillian Guerra, "most opted to treat Mikoyan's presence as testament to Cuba's newfound national sovereignty."[7] What clearer way to demonstrate Cuba's independence from the United States than to trade with its enemy?

Not everyone cheered, however. Those who had already been warning about the growing influence of communism were among the first to raise objections to the Soviet visit. Catholic students protested Mikoyan's appearance at the monument to Martí. They removed the wreath left by the visitor and put another in its place. It read, "To you, Apostle, to make amends for the visit of the assassin Mikoyan." They chanted, "Cuba, Yes; Russians, No!" The *Diario de la Marina*, the oldest newspaper on the island, published headlines that read "Democracy, Yes; Communism, No!"; "Sacrifice for Cuba, Yes; For Moscow, No!" "Thank you, Mr. Mikoyan, your visit has . . . defined the camps," read one editorial.[8]

Heated debates on the visit flooded Cuban media. But those debates were never just about the visit. They were fundamentally about that other question, the question that the press had already been asking, the question that just wouldn't go away: What was the Cuban Revolution's relationship to communism? But because one thing always quickly led to another, media debates about Mikoyan and communism soon triggered another major controversy—one about the role of a free press in revolutionary Cuba.

FOR DECADES, CUBAN NEWSPAPERS HAD reprinted stories from international wire sources such as the Associated Press (AP) and United Press International (UPI). As the revolution took root—as it confiscated US-owned property and hosted Soviet officials—those stories became increasingly critical of the Cuban government. They made charges of communism, spoke disparagingly of Cuban leaders, and took a pro-US stance regarding disputes between the two countries. Such positions, by then, were increasingly identified with counterrevolution. So, professional associations of journalists and typographic workers announced that whenever a newspaper printed an international cable story, workers at that paper had the right to print a note of clarification stating their disagreement with the story. One example read, "The information above is published by will of this company in legitimate use of the freedom of the press that exists in Cuba. But the journalists and the typographic workers of this workplace, relying on that same right, state that the content of this article does not conform to the truth nor to the most elementary journalistic ethics." These clarifications, which came to be nicknamed *coletillas* (little tails), soon began appearing everywhere.[9]

On January 16, 1960, the newspaper *Información* chose to print two stories by AP and UPI, and its workers insisted on adding a *coletilla*. The owner of the paper, however, refused to let them. The workers went to the police, and with its intervention managed to print the stories as they wanted, that is, with their clarifying notes included. The next day, much of the liberal (and conservative) press published defenses of the owners of *Información* and repudiations of the new *coletillas*. But many of those defenses were followed by the very clarification notes now under heated discussion, which were in turn followed by publishers' clarifications of the workers' clarifications, and then by a final clarification by the workers. Sometimes the space occupied by the *coletillas* rivaled that dedicated to the texts of the articles themselves. The collage-like effect of different fonts and inset boxes on single pages of newspaper conveyed visually the cacophony of dissent, and maybe also the gathering drumbeat of compulsory consensus.[10]

The *coletillas* were here to stay. Most of the traditional newspapers were not. Just two days after the confrontation at *Información*, the publisher of *Avance*, unwilling to print *coletillas*, suspended publication of the newspaper. Within the week, he was in the United States, writing for the *Miami Herald*.[11] February saw the government seizure of other newspapers, including *El Mundo* and *El País*, the latter of which had avoided having to print *coletillas* by not publishing international wire stories at all. But the paper ran into trouble when it decided to print a prominent priest's denunciation of Mikoyan's visit to Cuba. Workers rushed to add their dissenting notes, and the publisher resigned. When the workers met in his absence to decide what to do next, Castro appeared at the meeting and announced that the newspaper's offices would be converted into the headquarters of a newly established National Press. Its first book, published just two months later, was a new Cuban edition of *Don Quixote*, that "immortal book" about a "universal hero"—a hero, pointed out one review, alive, well, and still bearded in the Cuba of 1960.[12]

Then, in May, the oldest newspaper in Cuba folded. *Diario de la Marina*, a conservative paper established in 1832, had defended Spanish colonialism, US intervention, and the dictatorships of Gerardo Machado and Fulgencio Batista. In

January 1959, its pages had welcomed Fidel Castro and his bearded revolutionaries to Havana. But the honeymoon was short-lived. In its editorial page, the ardor of antigovernment positions intensified by the day. Everything came to a head in May when a group of the paper's employees signed a letter in defense of its embattled editor. Another group of workers at the paper refused to print it and broke the plates. Soon after, the publisher asked for asylum in a foreign embassy and left Cuba.[13]

The last issue of the paper was published on May 12, 1960. Emblazoned across the top was the headline "One Day with the People; 128 Years at the Service of Reaction." The front page included a letter addressed to "The People of Cuba and the Revolutionary Government." Written by members of the newspaper's staff, it announced their takeover of the paper and their decision to shutter the publication for good. A phrase in Latin ended their missive: "*Requiescat In Pace*, DIARIO DE LA MARINA." Rest in Peace. Appropriately, just up and to the right of those words was a funeral announcement—a funeral for the newspaper itself. "Cubans! Today we will bury 128 years of ignominy." The funeral procession began in Old Havana outside the offices of the newspaper and proceeded, coffin and all, to the university. One participant later wrote that a hundred thousand people turned out for the funeral; the US embassy estimated the crowd at several thousand. The speaker pointed out that there were three more tombs ready—presumably for the three remaining papers not yet linked to the government. Four days after the funeral, another one of those papers (*Prensa Libre*) folded. Its publisher left the country, and the government took over its offices.[14]

The whole controversy with the *Diario de la Marina*, though in part a dispute over the role of the press in Cuba, was at its core a confrontation over the very nature and reach of the revolution. To what extent would it uphold traditional political rights guaranteed in the much-vaunted 1940 constitution and trampled under Batista's rule? The publishers of leading independent newspapers called vocally for the restitution and protection of those rights. Many workers in those establishments, like the new government, countered that to make such demands publicly at that moment was to embolden the opposition—both domestic and foreign. As the speakers at the funeral for the *Diario de la Marina* argued, only two roads were possible in Cuba now: revolution or counterrevolution. The former was the path of Cuba; the latter was the path of old Batistianos and US intervention. "To defend the Revolution," proclaimed the newspaper's workers, "was nothing other than to defend Cuba."[15]

If to defend the revolution was to defend Cuba, then by default, to attack the revolution was to attack Cuba. Even to question it might open the door to potential attack. The revolution seemed to be following through on long-made and long-frustrated promises (agrarian reform, most notably), and many prioritized those achievements over other potential sources of discomfort. Perhaps because every revolution before this had been thwarted, there was no popular notion of a total, permanent revolution, and perhaps no way, so early in the process, to know how different this one would be. As the rapid-fire succession of events chipped away at the press or at independent labor unions, some surely worried. But the focus remained on ends justifying means. So, for the time being, people buried newspapers in makeshift coffins and stuck by the project of social revolution and the man at its helm. But what would happen if they changed their minds? What newspaper would express that opinion?

THERE WAS ANOTHER MAJOR REASON that support for the government remained strong in 1960: the United States. Fidel Castro made repeated references to a hostile US government eager to punish Cuba for its popular revolution. And at every turn, the United States seemed to prove his point. He quoted trigger-happy legislators threatening to send a few marines to take care of Cuba, and then those same legislators gave him more statements to quote. He warned an attack might come from the United States, and planes appeared overhead dropping leaflets and bombs. People in Cuba readily—and plausibly—believed that the US government relentlessly opposed their revolution. And that conviction had the power to unify and mobilize many Cubans behind their new government.

Nowhere did such unified militancy become more evident than immediately following the explosion of the French ship *Le Coubre*. Loaded with munitions from Belgium and docked at the busy port of Old Havana, it exploded without warning at 3:10 p.m. on March 4, 1960. The upper structure of the ship was almost completely destroyed; the stern sank; fires immediately broke out in the surrounding piers and buildings. Forty-five minutes later, with everyone rushing to put out the flames and to save the wounded, a second explosion rocked the area. All told, seventy-five people were killed and more than two hundred wounded, among them Cuban dockworkers, the French crew of the ship, and soldiers, first responders, and civilians who had rushed to help and were killed in the second blast.[16]

To this day, no one knows the true cause of the explosion. American officials in Cuba blamed inexperienced workers unused to unloading such dangerous material. The French company that owned the ship, meanwhile, saw no reason to blame "unsatisfactory unloading" and was "at a complete loss" as to the cause of the explosion. Dockworkers interviewed by *New York Times* reporter Herbert Matthews believed to a man that it was sabotage. The Cuban government said the same thing and laid the blame on the United States. In the face of what appeared to be a deadly attack on Cuban soil, Cubans answered the calls for unity and resolve. Even those—like the Catholic youth groups—who had excoriated Mikoyan's visit and the revolution's seeming openness to communism stood behind their government in the immediate aftermath of the *Coubre* explosion.[17]

The country was in mourning, and there was a real funeral to attend. Restaurants, bars, and businesses closed, and huge crowds turned out to honor the victims. Fidel Castro, President Dorticós, Che Guevara, and Raúl Castro led the somber procession. Fidel delivered the main speech, a fierce oration that mentioned the United States more than thirty times. Investigations were ongoing, he said, but the perpetrators of the crime *had* to be those who wanted to keep Cuba defenseless, those who did not want the Cuban government to get its hands on the war material on the ship. Who was that? The answer was obvious: the United States, which for months had been pressuring other governments not to sell arms to Cuba. Castro mentioned, unsurprisingly, the explosion of the *Maine* in the same harbor in 1898. The United States had blamed that explosion on Spain, used it as a pretext for war, and then intervened in Cuba. But he warned the United States that the Cubans of today were not the Cubans of 1898. This generation of Cubans, he said, would fight to the last person and to the last drop of blood.

> Here in this act, among these dead . . . let us say once and for all . . . the Cuban people—its workers, its peasants, its students, its women, its youth, its elderly, even its children—will not hesitate in occupying their posts calmly, without flinching, without even blinking, the day that any foreign force dares to disembark on our shores, whether they come by boat, or they come by parachute or they come by airplane, however they might come or however many there might be.[18]

The people cheered; his government ministers looked on approvingly. A famous Cuban photographer snapped a picture of Che Guevara, long hair grazing the collar of his zippered jacket, his starred beret perfectly placed, his gaze intent. The photograph, titled *The Heroic Guerrilla*, later became the iconic image of Che, worn on T-shirts all over the world. Another icon was born at that funeral-cum-political rally when Castro, his voice cracking and raspy, uttered the words that became the revolution's new motto: "Patria o Muerte." Fatherland or Death.[19]

Ernesto Che Guevara photographed by Alberto Korda during the funeral for victims of the explosion of the *Coubre*, as its crew began unloading its cargo of weapons. Fidel Castro attributed the explosion to sabotage by the United States.

As always, US officials were listening closely. The embassy in Havana, which had initially counseled a wait-and-see attitude, reluctantly yielded. "There is no hope that US will ever be able to establish a satisfactory relationship with Cuban Government as long as it is dominated by Fidel Castro, Raúl Castro, Che Guevara, and like-minded associates." Referring to the *Coubre* explosion and Castro's accusations, the State Department's Cuba Desk officer in Washington wrote, "From then on, there really was no talking."[20]

IN FACT, AUTHORITIES IN WASHINGTON had been thinking that for a while. In November 1959, Eisenhower had signed off on a new State Department policy on Cuba. Its main recommendation was that "all actions and policies of the United States Government should be designed to encourage within Cuba and elsewhere in Latin America opposition to the extremist, anti-American course of the Castro regime." At that point, however, the policy represented a general orientation rather than a concrete plan. A more specific policy was formulated over the first months of 1960. By the time the *Coubre* exploded and Fidel patented "Patria o Muerte," the nature of the policy had become crystal clear. Titled "A Program of Covert Action against the Castro Regime," the project was approved by President Eisenhower at a March 17, 1960, meeting of his National Security Council. The policy expressly aimed "to bring about the replacement of the Castro regime with one more devoted to the true interests of the Cuban people and more acceptable to the US." Regime change, however, was to happen "in such a manner as to avoid any appearance of US intervention."[21]

The "Program of Covert Action" consisted of four policy recommendations. First, the CIA was to create "a responsible, appealing and unified opposition to the Castro regime, publicly declared as such and therefore necessarily located outside of Cuba." The CIA was already in touch with several external opposition groups and hoped to merge them into a coherent front. Second, "so that the opposition may be heard [in Cuba] and Castro's basis of popular support undermined," the project would develop "the means for mass communication to the Cuban people so that a powerful propaganda offensive can be initiated in the name of the declared opposition." Consequently, the CIA purchased air time on US and Latin American radio stations that reached Cuba, and it established an undercover station on Swan Island off the coast of Honduras. Third, the United States would continue and expand work already in progress to create "a covert intelligence and action organization *within* Cuba that will be responsive to the orders and directions of the 'exile' opposition." Finally, the United States would expand efforts to develop a paramilitary force outside of Cuba that would be available for immediate deployment into Cuba to train and lead resistance forces once the latter had developed an active base of operations. Importantly, in each of these four endeavors, the hand of the United States was to remain invisible. As President Eisenhower said at the March 17 meeting, "Everyone must be prepared to swear that he has not heard of it."[22]

The American officials who devised the policy of covert action against the Cuban government understood—reluctantly, to be sure—that the Cuban Revolution had massive support. So, the CIA concluded that for their US-backed opposition to be successful against Castro's government, it had to bear some resemblance to the revolution itself. It could have no connection to Batista, and it had to espouse some of the same principles championed during the revolutionary struggle. It should even advocate for a "realistic agrarian reform program" and incorporate men who had been "for the revolution as originally conceived." Accordingly, US officials looked for former revolutionaries who had broken with Fidel "because of his failure to live up to the original 26th of July platform and his apparent willingness to sell out to Communist domination."[23]

The CIA did not manufacture some Cubans' sense of betrayal, but it did seek to capitalize on and weaponize that sentiment. The American script was really quite simple: Fidel Castro had betrayed the revolution. Then, everyone—from the leadership to rank and file of the opposition, to the US president himself—stuck to the script. "In all candor," said President Eisenhower, "I must state that many longtime friends of Cuba . . . who were heartened by the ideals expressed by the present leaders of Cuba when they assumed control have been gravely disillusioned by what is coming to be considered a betrayal of those ideals. . . ." Hence the motto of this US-designed counterrevolution would be "Restore the Revolution."[24] No one yet knew when the confrontation would come, but both governments were increasingly convinced that it would.

THE FIRST REALLY HEATED DISPUTE between the Cuban and US governments ended in another funeral. It was a few months in coming, as each government tried to outmaneuver the other, each side's action upping the ante and daring the other to do the same. The dispute began as a result of the Cuban-Soviet trade agreement, under which the Soviets would provide Cuba with six million barrels a year of crude oil. Crude oil, of course, needs to be refined, and in Cuba all three existing refineries were owned by US companies: Esso, Shell, and Texaco. Che Guevara, as head of Cuba's National Bank, instructed the companies, first, to accept the Soviet oil as payment for debts owed them by the Cuban government and, second, to refine the oil. After consulting with Washington, however, the companies refused. Fidel stepped in, himself ordering the companies to refine the oil. Again they said no. The Cuban government's next move was more forceful: Castro ordered that all three refineries be "intervened." That meant the refineries remained the property of their respective US companies, but their day-to-day operations now reverted to the Cuban government. The Americans called it yet another instance in Cuba's "relentless economic aggression" and yet more proof that it sought to destroy the island's "traditional investment and trade relations with the free world." On July 6, Washington responded by cutting the sugar quota—the US government's long-standing agreement to buy a set amount of the Cuban sugar harvest at a guaranteed price. The sugar quota had been a cornerstone of the Cuban economy throughout the twentieth century. To cut it was to leave the island holding a major part of its sugar harvest without a buyer. As one might expect, officials in Havana then turned to the Soviet government, which agreed to purchase what the United States would no longer buy.[25]

The conflict did not end there, however. On Friday, August 5, Raúl Castro gave only the vaguest of hints. "Tomorrow, in the Stadium of El Cerro, Fidel will make very important declarations. Now you know: tomorrow, everyone with Fidel." The next evening, each of the thirty-five thousand seats in the baseball stadium was occupied; thousands more gathered in the field below. The occasion was not a sporting event, but the closing ceremony of the first-ever Congress of Latin American Youth. Fidel arrived late, at 10:25 p.m. Everyone not already standing stood to cheer; people threw berets and hats in the air; handkerchiefs waving in the air resembled the flutter of hummingbirds. When he stepped up to the podium at 11:40 p.m., handlers released perhaps two hundred white doves. He caught one and let it go; the applause and chants were deafening. Fifteen minutes later, at 11:55, he finally began to speak. Twenty-five minutes after that, he lost his voice.[26]

People chanted for him to rest. Raúl Castro took the microphone and addressed the crowd. Some minutes later, whether by inspiration or design, he looked back at Fidel. The brothers conferred, and then Raúl announced, "I have bad news for Yankee imperialism. Fidel's voice is back!" When loud cheers erupted, Raúl called for quiet. "Let us make an effort together, Fidel speaking softly and you observing silence." Back at the podium, his voice gravelly, Fidel Castro read every word of Law 851, which authorized the government to nationalize by means of expropriation US-owned or controlled property. The government identified the first twenty-six US corporations to which the law would be applied. The US oil refineries were only the beginning. Also included were the US-owned telephone and electric companies, as well as thirty-six sugar mills, valued by the Cuban government at $829 million. In theory, owners would be compensated in fifty-year bonds at 2 percent interest, drawn from funds set aside from the sale of Cuban sugar to the United States. Of course, the United States had just canceled its agreement to purchase Cuban sugar. Everyone guessed the obvious: no compensation would be paid.

As the hoarse Castro read the name of each company, the crowd cheered and chanted. Twenty-fourth on the list was the United Fruit Company. Fidel struggled with the pronunciation of the word "fruit," but everyone knew what he meant. Jacobo Arbenz, former president of Guatemala, who had been removed by the 1954 coup engineered by the US government and the United Fruit Company, was in the platform party. When Fidel said United Fruit, Arbenz stood up and embraced the Cuban leader. The crowd's roars grew louder. It was almost 4 a.m. by the time everything ended. One journalist observed that as people filed out, "they looked as if resurrected." "A Second Independence," wrote another.[27]

The public announcement of the law launched what the government called the Week of Popular Jubilation. In public ceremonies, the old American names of companies were removed from buildings and replaced with banners bearing new Cuban names. At a rally in front of the Capitol, Cubans repeated an oath "to defend the Revolution with the greatest effort and sacrifice, since it incarnates the most vital desires" of the nation. Then everyone went to a funeral— a great, symbolic funeral for the US companies just confiscated by the Cuban government. It was festive and irreverent. Women dressed in black and carried signs identifying them as widows of this or that US company. Men served as pallbearers for empty coffins representing the remains of Esso, Shell, United Fruit, and the like. Together, sometimes dancing, the crowd marched to the Malecón and ceremoniously hoisted the coffins over the seawall and into the ocean, where the current that Ben Franklin had long ago named the Gulf Stream might sweep them up toward Florida.[28]

With less fanfare, the expropriation of US property continued. Indeed, it became a cornerstone of revolutionary policy. In September, the government nationalized every US bank branch in Cuba, including Chase Manhattan, First National City Bank of New York, and others. In October, the government—now also targeting Cuban-owned property—expropriated 105 sugar mills, 18 distilleries, 8 railroad companies, department stores, hotels, casinos, pharmacies, and more. By the end of that month, the government had seized approximately 550 US and domestic properties, including nearly all remaining nonresidential US property in Cuba.[29] Expropriations on this scale had not been part of the revolutionary program before coming to power. Now they seemed unstoppable, self-evident.

The expropriations further intensified the enmity between Washington and Havana. That fall, in one of the longest speeches ever delivered before the UN General Assembly, Castro excoriated the United States as no one ever had before. At every opportunity, the Cuban delegation voted against the United States and with the Soviet Union. When Fidel returned to Havana, he announced the establishment of a new organization: the Committees for the Defense of the Revolution (CDRs). He called them "a system of revolutionary collective vigilance" designed to defeat any would-be "lackey of imperialism." To raucous cheers, he explained that "everyone will know everyone else on his block, what they do . . . what they believe in, what people they meet." As Fidel spoke, two bombs went off, and the crowd chanted, "¡Paredón!" (To the execution wall) and "¡Venceremos!" (We will triumph). On January 3, 1961, Washington announced that it would close its embassy in Havana. "There is a limit to what the United States in self respect can endure. That limit has now been reached," said Eisenhower. For the first time since Cuban independence, the two countries broke off all diplomatic relations.[30]

HOW HAD SO MUCH HAPPENED so quickly? How had a multiclass revolution with goals squarely in the mold of long-standing progressive demands in Cuban politics produced something so seemingly unexpected? The answer to that question lies not in any single moment, but rather in the frenzied day-to-day accumulation of events over the first two years of revolution. For all the uncertainty of that period, some patterns became obvious in the maelstrom. Most apparent was a potent radicalization that transformed progressive social and economic goals into something much more far-reaching. In this first phase of the revolution, powerful people lost property and prerogative. But in the process, many more gained land, literacy, and wage increases; masses of people developed a profound stake in the revolution. As radicalization won adherents among a majority, that majority then helped further consolidate and propel that leftward turn. Popular support was thus both cause and effect of the revolution's growing radicalism.

Apace with that radicalization, another process unfolded that was perhaps its inverse. As the revolution's social and economic aims expanded, its more traditional political goals contracted. Before coming to power, revolutionaries had promised things like elections and freedom of the press. But as the revolution unfolded in practice, these goals, unlike the others, receded from view. The growing hostility of powerful—especially, external—enemies helped the government justify the deferral of traditional political rights. In fact, invoking those rights now became increasingly associated with counterrevolution. Despite the plurality of actors and goals that comprised the revolutionary struggles against Batista, by late 1960, the Cuban leadership had succeeded in giving them a singular form: *The Revolution*. And that revolution—always with a definite article and a capital R—was coming to mean one thing, the power to define it devolving to one person. Even as that happened, a majority expressed support above all, seeming to consent even to the closing of other means by which to express anything other than that support.

There were other sources of radicalization beyond any immediate material benefits the revolution might offer and beyond whatever charisma and authority Fidel Castro might project. These other sources came from outside, from the exigencies of the global Cold War and, perhaps above all, from Cubans' relation-

CUBA

ship to the weighty, ever-present history of US power on their island. Americans owned so much in Cuba, and Washington was so accustomed to wielding power there, that for the revolution to follow through on its promises necessarily threatened US interests. As US hostility grew increasingly apparent, it was easier for the Cuban government to defend radical measures not only on the basis of any inherent merit, but also on the basis of sovereignty and patriotism. Never before—except possibly for the 127-day interlude of the 1933 revolution—had both the state and the people voiced such a militant anti-imperialism together. Perhaps the United States could have responded differently to that threat; perhaps Castro could have assumed a slower pace of change; each side might have pursued a more conciliatory approach. But the outlines of a major conflict were present almost from the start and becoming clearer by the day. Historians are loath to regard anything as inevitable. But given the history of the two countries—the shared and uneven intimacy of more than a century—a confrontation of one kind or another may have been as inevitable as anything could ever be.

Part X

CONFRONTATION

Cuban soldiers standing by antiaircraft artillery on Havana's Malecón on January 1, 1962, in the midst of warnings of a possible US invasion.

Chapter 27

BATTLE

Geography has given the place a remarkable resistance to change. Located about eighty-five miles southeast and worlds away from Havana, the vast Zapata Peninsula houses living species as old as the brontosaurus and the pterodactyl. Reeds rise up from a vast expanse of thick water, underneath which lies a dense, tangled forest of hardwood timber many thousands of years old. In the rivers and lakes of the peninsula still swims the Cuban gar, a species so old and unchanged that scientists categorize it as a living fossil. Atop the trees, a rare species of nightingale sings the same melody its predecessors sang an eternity ago. Much of the swamp extends into the Caribbean Sea, but in a few places it gives way to a strip of solid, sandy ground. Along part of the coast is a large shelf of dog-teeth rock, so named for the hard, jagged limestone that made the area inhospitable even after humans had begun to put shoes on draft animals. Near the eastern end of the vast wetlands is a deep, wide inlet. Like the swamp, it boasts ancient species, among them the reef dweller that probably gave the bay its name: the queen triggerfish, known in Cuba as *cochinos*, or pigs.

Humans arrived much later to give names to those places and those species. Generations of Taínos made their home in this unusual terrain, burying their dead, feet always to the west, under mounds that alternated black earth and snail shells. In 1493, Columbus hugged this coast on his second voyage. A century later, pirates were said to hide their treasure there. And two centuries after that, slave traders sometimes used the unwelcoming coast to land illegal cargoes of Africans, forced after their long, grueling voyage across the Atlantic to trek over the dog-teeth limestone in bare feet. But these illicit uses aside, the place was so unwelcoming, so isolated from the rest of the island, that it was settled but sparsely, whether by Native Taínos, or Spaniards, or Africans, or the descendants of any or all these.

CUBA

The wetlands were hardly arable, and there were no towns to speak of. So the people who did settle there worked hard to make a living. They harvested the swamp, using rudimentary tools and the weight of their own bodies to loosen heavy, gnarled roots from under a foot or more of thick water. They excavated small patches of earth, built fires in them, and burned the wood to make charcoal. That was their occupation, and charcoal was the area's only industry. There was one route in and out of the swamp, a narrow-gauge railroad track. Often covered with water and unusable, it left the people who lived there cut off from the rest of the island for weeks at a time.[1]

It was here, in this swamp, that Fidel Castro arrived by helicopter on December 24, 1959, to celebrate his first Christmas in power. He arrived with soda, beer, and a pig and a half, and invited himself and his thirteen companions to Christmas Eve dinner at the home of a resident charcoal worker. "I remember," recalled the man later, "[Fidel] said to me, 'You are all going to see how buses from Havana are going to come here.' I thought he was nuts." Yet, by the following Christmas, a newly built highway into the swamp was facilitating the transformation of the whole area. There was a new and fully staffed general hospital, an aqueduct, an electric plant, and a telegraph. A new commercial center had clothing and crafts stores, a pharmacy, a butcher, a barbershop, and a post office. Thirty literacy workers were in the immediate area teaching people to read and write, and more were expected to arrive soon. The charcoal workers, having received title to land under the 1959 Agrarian Reform Law, no longer paid rent. And on the beautiful beach called Girón, surrounded by some of the poorest, most unusual countryside on the island, the new government was building a seaside resort: 153 fully furnished, one- and two-bedroom cabins in a complex that boasted a swimming pool, cabaret, cafeteria, game room, and more. Construction on the resort started just a few weeks after Fidel showed up for Christmas dinner, and the opening date was set for May 20, 1961, the fifty-ninth anniversary of both Cuban independence and the end of the first US military occupation.[2]

ON A MOONLESS NIGHT, ALMOST exactly one month before the scheduled opening of the resort, some fourteen hundred men sat on vessels off that coast, unaware of all this activity. The men belonged to the US-trained and funded Brigade 2506, made up of Cuban exiles returning to topple Fidel Castro. Their plan was to secure a beachhead, spur internal resistance movements, and spark a general rebellion. Three days in, a new provisional government for Cuba was to arrive from Miami. Once that happened, the brigade would proceed north from the beachhead, turn left, and march on Havana. Some expected things to go well enough that Fidel's government might fall even before their arrival in the capital. If things went more slowly, or the men ran into trouble, they would fade into the mountains, link up with insurgents there, and wage the kind of guerrilla war against the Cuban government that Fidel himself had waged against Batista just a few years earlier.

Among the first to realize that things would not go as planned were the men of the underwater demolition team motoring a small launch toward their landing site at Playa Girón. Their job was to set up marker lights that would guide the large vessels and their landing gear onto shore to disembark brigade members and their materials. But as the frogmen approached on their rubber raft, they looked up and saw the beach coming into view ahead. One of the men later recalled that it was "lit up like Coney Island." Fifty yards from where they had intended to land, people were having a party, and floodlights "were lighting up [their] landing point like daylight."[3]

In war, soldiers are used to improvising. Off the coast of Cuba that night, the men quickly adjusted their landing site to avoid the revelers. But everything unraveled anyway. The dark shadows that their Washington bosses had seen on reconnaissance photos were not seaweed, as they had been told, but jagged coral reefs. Now the men had to walk over them, their raft hoisted over their heads. In the midst of this awkward struggle against nature, one of the lights inside the raft shorted and lit up, announcing their arrival to two people on shore, a thirteen-year-old literacy worker and a militia commander. The two Cubans did not jump to the worst conclusion; they thought the raft was a fishing boat looking for a way around the reefs. The team on the raft didn't know that, of course. So when the Cubans trained their jeep's lights on the small vessel to guide it onto shore, the men in the water started shooting. Now everyone for miles around would know they were there. They had lost the element of surprise, and in very little time, they would be facing truckloads of Cuban forces on the ground. Meanwhile, at the secondary landing site of Playa Larga, the landing was proceeding with all the grace of a "drunken ballerina." The winches lowering the small landing boats onto the water were so rusty and loud that they announced their arrival for miles around. Some of the boats wouldn't start; on one, the motor fell off and sank. Soon those forces would be under fire, too.

Yet even with so much going wrong in the first few hours, the men of Brigade 2506 were eager to fight, and they still expected to win. As they reached the beaches, they cheered, and some knelt down to kiss the ground.[4]

Just before 1 a.m., the USS *Blagar*, the command ship for the operation, received a message from Washington: "Castro still has operational aircraft. Expect you will be under attack at first light. Unload all men and supplies and take the ships to sea." Working against time to unload everything before daybreak, the smaller landing vessels hit the jagged coral at full throttle. One sank before getting its men ashore; another landed men and then sank. Then, as warned, at daybreak Cuban government planes began an aerial assault. For brigade member Alfredo Durán, it was looking up and seeing he was being shot at by a Cuban Sea Fury "that was not supposed to be there" that made him realize that things would not go as planned. By midmorning, Cuban planes had sunk the US munitions ship.[5]

On the beach, brigade commander José (Pepe) San Román sent one radio message after another: "Must have jet air support in next few hours or will be wiped out." Moments later: "Request jet support or cannot hold. Situation critical." Then: "Have no ammo left for tanks and very little for troops." Before midnight on day two, he sent a longer message, frantic and angry: "Do you people realize how desperate the situation is? Do you back us up or quit? All we want is low jet cover and jet close support. Enemy has this support. I need it badly or cannot survive. Please don't desert us." A final message came on day three: "Am destroying all equipment and communications. Tanks are in sight. I have nothing left to fight with. Am taking to the woods. I cannot wait for you." It did not take long for the men to realize that the mountains the CIA had touted as their escape hatch were much, much too far. Years later a brigade veteran explained, "After walking I suddenly realized, well, I looked at a map and I said that there is no way that we are going to make it." Soon after the last radio message from the brigade, a navy admiral radioed the Pentagon: "Castro is waiting on the beach."[6]

OVER THE COURSE OF SEVENTY-TWO hours, a US-sponsored invasion of Cuba to overthrow Fidel Castro was revealed as "one of those rare events in history—a perfect failure." In 1996, two scholars convened a group of men who had participated in the event in different capacities—Cuban veterans of the brigade, participants in the short-lived urban resistance against Castro, and former members of Kennedy's White House, State Department, CIA, and Department of Defense—to read then recently declassified documents and together reconstruct and understand what had happened. It was a fascinating exercise and, for many of the participants, acutely painful. But another overpowering sentiment emerged from their discussions—a kind of stupefied incredulity. Jacob Esterline, the Bay of Pigs project's first CIA director (and Washington director of the Guatemala coup operation in 1954), summed it up like this: "I have thought back so many times I have lost count: how did this thing start to steamroller and get away from us? ... How did it happen? More to the point: how did we *let* it happen?"[7]

In the beginning, the event Americans now know as the Bay of Pigs invasion was conceived neither as an invasion nor as happening at the Bay of Pigs. The project's origin lay in Eisenhower's approval of the March 1960 "Plan for Covert Action Against the Castro Regime," which sought to overthrow Fidel Castro without the US role being visible. That plan had advocated the creation of a moderate exile opposition, a covert intelligence and action network inside Cuba (responsive to the exile leadership), and a paramilitary force of Cuban exiles trained outside Cuba for guerrilla action inside Cuba. That force, however, was not initially imagined as anything like an invasion force. Instead, it would consist of "a number of paramilitary cadres" who would be trained by the US government and deployed in Cuba covertly "to organize, train and lead resistance forces recruited there." The primary focus of this first plan was on guerrilla warfare within Cuba—supported materially and logistically by the United States. This emphasis was not all wishful thinking on Washington's part. There were pockets of armed resistance against Castro's government, the most significant of which was in the Escambray mountains of central Cuba. The CIA envisioned a modest exile force joining and leading that resistance and other smaller ones around the island.[8]

The first major change to that plan appears to have come in August 1960, as the CIA began to question whether guerrilla warfare and rebellion inside Cuba would be sufficient to topple Castro anytime soon. The August version of the plan expanded to address that concern. Like its predecessor, it envisioned the development and support of guerrilla groups on the island. But it added new features: a combined air-sea assault by exile forces, timed to coincide with a march on the capital by the combined guerrilla-exile forces. At one meeting on August 18, there was a discussion of whether it might be advisable to land a larger force, or even some US military. But people disagreed heartily on that point and decided to postpone deciding.[9]

It was over the course of fall 1960 that a new concept for the operation took shape. US officials were increasingly worried about Castro's growing strength and his access to weapons from Eastern Bloc nations. They were also running into logistical issues with their plans to infiltrate men and materials into Cuba as part of the effort to support internal resistance. During a clandestine airdrop on September 28 in the Escambray mountains, for example, the crew missed its target by seven miles and dropped the weapons on a dam, where they were quickly recovered by Cuban government forces. During another drop two days later, the parachutes carried the weapons to a recently created agricultural cooperative, whose members quickly turned them over to authorities.[10] The sense that the guerrilla part of the operation might be too difficult for them to control and the sense that they were running out of time nudged planners in another direction. Maybe, some began to think, a conventional infantry landing from the sea would stand a better chance of success. So, on October 31, CIA headquarters cabled the camp in Guatemala where the exile recruits were being trained: the infiltration teams were to be reduced to just sixty men; all the others were to receive conventional training for an amphibious and airborne assault. That plan required more men: "Do not plan strike with less than about 1500 men. Smaller force has little chance success in view situation in target."[11]

By mid-November, the Special Group, a secret committee with representatives from the CIA, State, Defense, and the President's National Security Council, was meeting at least weekly to discuss Cuba plans. With each meeting, the shape of the plan seemed to become clearer. Sort of. The idea of guerrilla warfare and covert infiltrations gradually receded from view; the seaborne landing and air assaults, meanwhile, began occupying more attention. The operation was beginning to resemble an invasion, but no one seemed ready to call it that. Take, for example, the Special Group's meeting with President Eisenhower on November 29, 1960. Some government investigators later stated that Eisenhower gave his approval for the plan that day. Yet the official record of the meeting does not convey that sense. First, no one at the meeting clearly discussed the changes taking shape; no one mentioned the drastic reduction of the forces being trained in guerrilla warfare; and there was no discussion of what a conventional air and sea assault might look like in practice. Rather than approval, what Eisenhower expressed, above all, was a sense of unease. He queried: Are we doing enough? Are we doing what we're doing effectively? He wondered "whether the situation did not have the appearance of beginning to get out of hand." On four separate occasions, he returned to a simple question: Wouldn't it make sense to have someone in charge? "One individual who would have the situation always at his fingertips," "an individual executive to pull the whole Cuban situation together who would know precisely at all times what State, CIA, and the military were doing." A "coordinating chief" was what the president called the person he was craving. But no one appointed such a leader. Throughout the meeting, the discussion seemed meandering and circular. Decisions were deferred, major questions left unresolved.[12]

As the men of Washington considered what to do about Cuba, they were also preparing for the inauguration of John F. Kennedy. That fact, too, contributed to the unsettled sense of the room during that November 29 meeting. Eisenhower said he hoped that the new president "would follow the general line" of his administration's Cuba plan. Left unsaid was that he hesitated to give any kind of definitive approval to any particular version of the plan, because his days in the White House and as commander in chief were just about over.

On December 8, exactly one month after the election, the Special Group met to consider the revised plan. By then, the centerpiece of the operation was the landing of an amphibious force of 600–750 men equipped with "weapons of extraordinarily heavy fire power." The landing would be preceded by air strikes against Cuban military targets. The transformation of the operation was now complete; guerrilla infiltration had become an invasion. Someone expressed doubts about whether the Cuban people would really rise up when the invasion arrived, but no one fully addressed the concern. Ironically, a CIA National Intelligence Estimate issued on the same day as that meeting concluded that Castro "remain[ed] firmly in control." His popularity had diminished since 1959, but he still enjoyed "widespread support among the poorer classes, particularly in the countryside." That judgment, however, seems not to have informed the plans being formulated at the top.[13]

Indeed, the next major summary of the plan ignored that judgment altogether. "It is expected," read the CIA report of January 4, 1961, "that these operations will precipitate a general uprising throughout Cuba and cause the revolt of large segments of the Cuban Army and Militia." The beachhead established by the exile brigade, "it is hoped, will serve as a rallying point for the thousands who are ready for overt resistance to Castro but who hesitate to act until they can feel some assurance of success." The report then ventured that "a general revolt in Cuba, if one is successfully triggered by our operation, could serve to topple the Castro regime within a period of weeks."[14] It was optimism bordering on lunacy.

SUCH WAS THE PLAN THAT welcomed John F. Kennedy to the White House in January 1961. Though Kennedy had been briefed before taking office, his briefers, CIA Director Allen Dulles and CIA Deputy Director of Plans Richard Bissell, stressed the guerrilla aspect of the plan and referred to US military intervention as a "contingency plan."Without yet having taken office and without all the relevant information, however, Kennedy viewed the whole operation as a "contingency plan.""He did not yet realize," wrote advisor Arthur M. Schlesinger, "how contingency planning could generate its own momentum and create its own reality."[15]

The gears of government ground both fast and slow following the presidential transition, as Kennedy ordered his own evaluations of the plan. Agency heads wrote memos outlining everything that remained to be done: selecting a landing site, analyzing the likelihood of an internal revolt, assembling a new government for Cuba. Some in the State Department began to refer to the project as "the Cuban adventure." Throughout, the CIA acted as the operation's most eager advocate. It won others to its side—the Joint Chiefs of Staff, State, and the president himself. But in reality, it was less that it won people over than that it neutralized their objections.

One of the most important meetings occurred on March 11, 1961. By then, the invasion force was at 850 and growing. Analysts had selected a landing site: a beach named Casilda, near the town of Trinidad and close to the Escambray mountains. According to March's version of the plan, that detail was critical for two reasons. First, the Escambray mountains were the epicenter of resistance to Fidel Castro, with perhaps some 700–800 guerrillas already fighting and organizing there. The exile expeditionaries would thus have willing allies and troops. Second, should the exile brigade not be able to secure a beachhead, they could easily retreat to the mountains to regroup and continue fighting. That safety valve satisfied some of the skeptics.[16]

But Kennedy hated the plan. It was too spectacular, more like a World War II landing than the covert operation he had been promised. "Reduce the noise level," he instructed. He wanted something quiet, unspectacular; something in which his government's hand would be imperceptible. The last request was nothing if not chimerical. People in Guatemala saw the training camp with their own eyes, and communists there informed the Soviet embassy, which passed word on to Havana. Cuban newspapers began reporting on the exile training camp and coming invasion seven months before it happened. In Miami, the invasion was a subject of rumor and chatter over almost every thimble-sized cup of strong coffee. In Washington, one senator called the project "an open secret."[17] The CIA could not quiet the chatter, but it could try to reduce the operation's noise level, as the new president had requested.

After several more attempts, the CIA presented a quieter version of the plan.

By then, the operation had been nicknamed Bumpy Road. Operation Bumpy Road reduced the number of prelanding air strikes; the landing itself would now happen at night; the ships transporting the men would be gone by dawn, and no one would see them arrive. Another very significant change was the landing site for the invasion. The original site near the populous city of Trinidad carried the risk of civilian casualties. Its airfield, said the CIA, would not work for the B-26s they wanted the Cuban exile pilots to use. (A government report after the invasion showed that to be untrue.) Instead, the CIA now proposed landing at the Bay of Pigs, sparsely populated and set in the millennia-old swamplands where generations of Cuban charcoal workers had made their homes.[18]

KENNEDY CALLED A MEETING ON April 4 to come to a decision on the operation. Skeptics still abounded. The Joint Chiefs of Staff had concluded that of all the recently proposed versions, this new plan had the likeliest chance of success, but also judged that, even so, it was not likely to accomplish the objective. The undersecretary of state wrote a memo to his boss in anticipation of the meeting, and asked him to share it with the president. As "now planned," it read, "the chances of success are not greater than one out of three." It is not clear that Kennedy ever saw the memo.[19]

At the meeting itself, several asked questions that revealed their disquiet. What if the men cannot establish a beachhead, asked one official present. The CIA's Richard Bissell replied that they could retreat to the mountains, pointing in the general vicinity of the Escambray range on the map. Perhaps the map was missing topographical information. Or perhaps it was missing a scale indicating distances. Or maybe with momentum so clearly propelling the plan forward, people hesitated to press the point. What if the Cubans do not rise up in revolt? asked another Washington insider. Bissell turned to an assistant and asked, "We have an NIE on that, don't we?" They did, in fact, have National Intelligence Estimates on that. But what they said would not have allayed the doubts of anyone present. Castro was securely in power, with significant (if declining) support and firm control of all the institutions on the island. What resistance existed did not "portend any serious threat" to Castro, read one March report. In any case, the intelligence reports ignored critical information: namely, that the new landing site in the Bay of Pigs was squarely in the middle of the same area where Fidel Castro had celebrated his first revolutionary Christmas and where his government had been distributing land and building infrastructure.[20]

Almost satisfied that the plan was unspectacular enough, the president went around the room to hear each person's verdict on the project. All gave their assent but one. It is unlikely that the discussion at the meeting would have truly satisfied the doubts many had expressed or felt. So momentum and maybe a sense of inevitability carried the moment. The meeting lasted less than an hour, and the verdict was a go. At the end of the meeting, however, Kennedy asked what the final deadline was for killing the project. Noon on the fourteenth for the air strikes and noon on the sixteenth for the landing, replied Bissell.[21]

In a private conversation between Kennedy and Bissell on April 14, Kennedy gave the go-ahead for the air strikes the next day. "Almost as an afterthought," Kennedy asked about the number of planes in that first air strike, less than twenty-four hours away. When Bissell replied, sixteen, Kennedy directed him to reduce the scale, to make it "minimal." Without consultation by either of them with anyone else, Bissell on the spot cut the number of air strikes in half, to eight. Around noon on April 16, Kennedy called Bissell to give the final okay for the landing. But at about 9:30 p.m., as the ships carrying the brigade were nearing Cuba, Kennedy, at the State Department's urging, approved a major, eleventh-hour change to the plan: he canceled the air strikes scheduled for days two and three of the operation. There would be no further air strikes until the brigade secured an airstrip and made it possible for the air strikes to originate on Cuban soil, the better to hide US involvement. CIA protests against the cancellation had little effect, and the operation proceeded without them.

So, after months of erratic planning, in the early morning hours of April 17, the men of Brigade 2506 arrived at their destination determined to depose Fidel Castro and free Cuba. They landed having to avoid obstacles no one told them would be there—coral reefs, late-night parties of construction workers, fire from Cuban militia members on the ground and from Cuban Sea Furies in the air. They were attacked by Cuban planes that easily survived the minimal air strikes ultimately approved in Washington. They confronted Cuban army and militia members who, despite the predictions of the CIA, remained loyal to Fidel Castro. There was no rebellion by Cubans on the ground, just as there was no conceivable way to fade into the mountains. Less than seventy-two hours after their landing, they were defeated—114 of them killed in battle, 1,189 captured by Castro's forces. And again the same question rears its head: How had the United States failed as badly, as blindly as it did?

BATTLE

THE ANSWER, AS WITH MOST important questions, depends on who you ask. For the men of Brigade 2506, the answer can be summarized in a single word: betrayal. They had been promised air assaults that would neutralize the Cuban air force. That did not happen, and, for the men, that failure, among others, doomed the entire operation. For decades after the events, that sense of betrayal was commonplace in exile circles in the United States and helps explain part of Cuban Americans' disdain toward Kennedy and one source of their antipathy to the Democratic Party more generally.

Historians have tended to downplay the brigade members' interpretation. They counter that "Kennedy never promised US military support to anyone, under any circumstances, at the Bay of Pigs." That may be true, yet even the quiet version of the plan approved on April 4 included air strikes that would neutralize the Cuban air force. The men of the brigade were not privy to the discussions that eroded that part of the plan. Throughout, their commanders in Guatemala had given wholehearted, unambiguous indications that they would have all the support they needed. Some commanders in Guatemala may have even led the men to believe that, should they need it, there would be land support as well. In fact, there were two thousand marines off the coast of Cuba, ordered there apparently without the president's authority and with the impression that they would be part of a "follow-on wave." As one of the brigade members later said in frustration, without US military support, the plan never made sense. Given all that, the men's sense of betrayal, their despair on the beach—and long after—makes sense.[22]

If the Cuban expeditionaries felt the sting of betrayal acutely, in one fashion or another, so, too, did almost everyone else involved. Kennedy felt betrayed, or at least misled, by the CIA, which never gave him a clear sense of the likelihood of failure, exaggerated the levels of internal opposition to Castro, and failed to clarify how unlikely it was that the men would ever make it to the mountains. He blamed the CIA, above all, for not having believed him when he said the operation had to be covert, that air strikes would be minimal, and that there would never be a US troop presence. Not surprisingly, some months after the debacle, Kennedy dismissed CIA director Allen Dulles and Richard Bissell, the head CIA man on the project.[23]

The CIA, meanwhile, regarded Kennedy as insufficiently committed to the operation from the start. For them, Kennedy's ultimate betrayal was allowing the operation to fail when the time came. Then CIA director Allen Dulles wrote after the fact that many operations started out the way the Bay of Pigs had, but that the limitations and problems tended "to disappear as the needs of the operation became clarified. [We] felt that when the chips were down, when the crisis arose in reality, any action required for success would be authorized, rather than permit the enterprise to fail." The CIA simply had not taken Kennedy at his word when he insisted that the US military would not become directly involved. Much to the CIA's surprise, he had meant it.[24]

Almost immediately after the operation's failure, the CIA inspector general conducted an investigation. Over seven months, he reviewed hundreds of documents and interviewed 125 participants. The ensuing report, and others that followed, pointed to one mistake after another, to bad judgments superseded by worse ones: the change of landing site, the possibility that the invasion was premature or that it was too late, the fact that most of the Cubans trained for infiltration so as to be there when the invaders arrived were never sent back to Cuba. The list goes on: rampant security leaks made the operation known to the world before it happened; an operation designed as covert became a substantive military campaign beyond the capacity of the CIA to orchestrate. The CIA's assertion that Cubans would support the invasion was mistaken and had no basis in the evidence available at the time. The agency handlers treated the Cuban exile political leaders "like puppets" and the brigade members "like dirt." Then, at the last minute, the president reduced the number of air strikes. But the president's decision had been made without adequate briefing from the CIA and without a frank appraisal of the likelihood of success, said the report. In the end, most assessments placed the lion's share of the blame on the CIA. "The fundamental cause of the disaster," concluded the IG's report, "was the Agency's failure to give the project, notwithstanding its importance and its immense potentiality for damage to the United States, the top-flight handling which it required" in organization, staffing, and oversight. The result was a host of "serious operational mistakes and omissions" and a "lack of awareness of developing dangers." To paraphrase Dwight D. Eisenhower, hadn't there been someone really in charge?[25]

In 1971, a Yale psychologist invented a whole theory to explain what happened at the Bay of Pigs. He called it groupthink, a phenomenon in which there are too many people in a room, uncomfortable disagreeing, reluctant to raise sometimes obvious questions, unwilling to change course even when, objectively, all facts clearly point in that direction. The Bay of Pigs, he said, perfectly encapsulated the process by which groupthink results in dysfunctional decision-making.[26]

BATTLE

YET, EVEN AS GOVERNMENT AND scholarly studies pointed to all these insufficiencies and errors, they failed to consider a much more fundamental question: Would it have been possible for an exile invasion to succeed at all? And that question cloaks a more fundamental truth: no invasion lands on empty ground; no intervention unfolds on a blank slate.

As two presidents and countless agency officials prepared the invasion in Washington, time had not stood still in Cuba. The US government had decided secretly to pursue a program opposing Castro in November 1959, before the revolution was even a year old; concerted planning to topple Castro began in March 1960. That whole time, Fidel Castro had been decrying US aggression and warning of a possible invasion. And his government had been preparing. In late 1959, Castro ordered the creation of a civilian militia, composed of men and women receiving part-time military training to help guard potential targets. In early 1960, with US-Cuban relations deteriorating rapidly, Fidel expanded the size and role of those militias. Convinced of the likelihood of a US invasion and suspecting that it might arrive near the Escambray mountains, where antigovernment guerrillas were active, Castro ordered a massive military operation in the area, carried out jointly by the regular army and the civilian militias. During that operation, government forces imprisoned or executed local guerrillas, confiscated weapons arriving from abroad, and captured twenty-five of the agents infiltrated into the area by the United States. In the months preceding the US invasion, Cuban government forces in the area numbered perhaps sixty thousand. As one historian notes, the agents being infiltrated into Cuba by the CIA probably had a greater chance of running into a Cuban militia member than any of the anti-Castro guerrillas.[27]

It was precisely at the beach closest to these mountains that US planners first envisioned the arrival of the Cuban expeditionary forces. They had originally chosen that site because the mountainous terrain offered refuge should the expeditionaries need it, and because there was a local guerrilla movement with which they could join forces and then command. Some, to this day, consider that for those reasons, it may have been a better landing spot than the one ultimately chosen. But that view fails to take account of the very significant presence of Cuban troops there. To be sure, the operation would have played out differently in the mountains than in the swamps, but, with some sixty thousand Cuban soldiers in the area, a victory there was far from guaranteed.[28]

On the beaches where the Cuban brigade did land, there was significant government activity, as well. Though not as large as in the Escambray, the civilian militia was active, protecting infrastructure and patrolling the beaches. There were at least thirty literacy workers teaching locals how to read. Recall that the first two people to spot the invaders were a thirteen-year-old literacy worker and a militia commander, and that militia army units had arrived quickly thereafter. Even a relatively desolate beach is not a blank slate onto which invaders can simply impose their designs. Everything being built there, everything already built—the hospital, the roads, the telephone park—attested to that. Fidel had celebrated Christmas there; the agrarian reform had confiscated large holdings and formed cooperatives of charcoal workers. Inadvertently, Washington sent Brigade 2506 to a timeless place that in two years of revolution had probably changed more than in the whole century before. Of all places in western Cuba, the revolution may well have made it one of the least likely to support a US-sponsored invasion.[29]

In the immediate lead-up to the attack, Castro took other measures to guard against the imminent invasion. He positioned sentries and troops along the coast and ordered them to dig trenches and intensify patrols. He ordered the air force to move its planes to other locations and to camouflage them, so as to make them undetectable to US reconnaissance flights. The tactic worked. On April 15, a few minutes before 6 a.m., US planes camouflaged to look like Cuban ones attacked three Cuban air bases. These were the strikes that were to have incapacitated the Cuban air force, limiting their ability to fire on Brigade 2506. But the operation destroyed just 22 percent of Cuba's air force.[30]

Not only did the air strikes announce the imminence of the invasion, but one of them managed to kill seven Cubans and injure fifty-three as it dropped its bombs. Fidel Castro addressed the nation and called on Cubans to "occupy their posts." The Committees for the Defense of the Revolution rounded up people who they suspected might support the US invasion. According to one estimate, perhaps fifty thousand people were detained in Havana alone. There were no jails big enough, so theaters and stadiums were turned into temporary detention centers. Family members went from place to place looking for husbands, sisters, fathers. At Havana's Blanquita theater, then the largest in the world and soon to be renamed Karl Marx, my mother found my father, who was among the five thousand held there for days. While most of those detained were released, members of the antigovernment underground who were to have seconded the invasion were arrested, swiftly tried, and executed.[31]

On April 16, with the invasion expected at any moment, people gathered for the funeral of the victims of those killed at the airfield the day before. Fidel Castro's speech on that occasion remains one of the most important of his very long career. This is a socialist revolution, he said for the first time. And for that, he continued, the United States will never forgive us. They will never forgive "that we are here right under their noses and that we have made a socialist revolution right under the very noses of the United States!"[32] Then in the middle of the night, in the earliest hours of April 17, the invasion came, just as he had said that it would. And it failed spectacularly.

FOR THE UNITED STATES, THE military failure of the Bay of Pigs paled in comparison to the depth of the political failure it heralded. New billboards in Cuba announced that the Bay of Pigs was the "first defeat of Yankee imperialism." Others would follow, implied the motto. The failed invasion also severely weakened the already vulnerable internal opposition in Cuba. The US operation had taken opposition members out of Cuba to train them as guerrilla fighters and covert operators. Some were never sent back into Cuba. Others who returned as covert agents were discovered and jailed or executed by the government. Those who joined the brigade were killed or captured during the invasion. Rather than defeat Castro, the US operation helped Fidel purge many of his most committed opponents. Even the CIA admitted that the failed invasion greatly strengthened Castro's hand. Ten days after the invasion, it reported that "Castro's position is stronger than before the invasion attempt." Four months after the invasion, sometime after 2 a.m. on August 17, 1961, at a diplomat's birthday party in Montevideo, Uruguay, Kennedy advisor Richard Goodwin met secretly with Che Guevara. Che was triumphant. The Cuban Revolution, he said, was irreversible. It would now formally establish a single-party system with Fidel Castro as head of the Communist Party and head of state. Cubans overwhelmingly supported the government, and the government would continue to expand its ties to the Eastern Bloc. Che was content to share another message with the US official. "He wanted to thank us very much for the invasion—that it had been a great political victory for them—enabled them to consolidate—and transformed them from an aggrieved little country to an equal." Goodwin was almost speechless: "I said he was welcome."[33]

Castro drew another conclusion from his victory at the Bay of Pigs: that the US government would not let its defeat stand. The first invasion had failed, but another would surely come—a bigger, better-organized invasion. Kennedy's political future depended on that, surmised Fidel. So, in the aftermath of the Bay of Pigs invasion, Castro drew closer to the Soviet Union not just by publicly declaring the revolution socialist, but also by actively seeking massive military assistance. The Soviets exceeded Cuban expectations and set the stage for a major global crisis eighteen months later.[34]

Chapter 28

BRINK

In the fall of year three of the Cuban Revolution, the world's eyes trained on the sleepy, rural town of Santa Cruz de los Pinos, about sixty-five miles west of Havana. Men there wore traditional peasant hats; their families cultivated small plots of land, tending pigs, chickens, and the occasional cow. Residents began to get suspicious when their little town was suddenly overrun with young Soviet soldiers. Earnest, homesick, and with minimal Spanish, they traded watches, soap, shoes, and belts for something called *alcohilitis*, a 90-proof rum that Cubans considered too strong to drink. They sought out Cuban girls and Cuban food; they carved their names in the Cyrillic alphabet into trees and rocks to document their presence in this unremarkable hamlet in western Cuba.

Rumors about their purpose grew more ominous when the town—where most people still got around on foot, horse, carriage, and station wagon taxis—suddenly began having traffic jams in the middle of the night. The ground shook with the passing of mammoth trucks too large to maneuver around corners. A building that housed a shoe shop was partially demolished on the spot to allow for the trucks' wide turns; at another corner, the column of a portico disappeared. Cuban soldiers motioned for residents to stay inside. But people peered through the wooden slats of their louvered windows. What they saw puzzled them: trucks with long beds covered with tarps, and under the tarps objects that looked like the trunks of very large palm trees.[1]

Residents of Santa Cruz de los Pinos soon had something else to puzzle over: American airplanes flying low and loud over their town and neighboring countryside. Years later, people remembered those flights as vividly as they remembered the Soviet trucks and the Soviet soldiers. People cowered, assuming the planes would drop bombs. Even though they didn't, the flights confirmed the

CUBA

townspeople's sense that something sinister and threatening was afoot. They could feel the danger as a physical sensation—the ground vibrating under the weight of heavy trucks, the wind kicking up below low-flying planes, feelings of pins and needles up and down their spines.[2]

On October 14, 1962, a plane flying south to north over Santa Cruz de los Pinos revealed to the world what the villagers craning for views between the slats of their windows had not yet learned: that the tree-shaped items on the backs of the trucks were Soviet missiles. Known as R-12 missiles by the Soviets and SS-4 by NATO, they had a range of fourteen hundred miles, enabling them to strike Miami, Washington, and New York. A nuclear warhead on each could pack seventy-five times more power than the US atomic bomb detonated over Hiroshima. Subsequent flights spotted dozens of missiles scattered over six sites across the island, all pointing north in the direction of the United States. The people of Santa Cruz de los Pinos were both the first and last to know.

PUTTING NUCLEAR MISSILES IN CUBA had been Nikita Khrushchev's idea. "I [have] some thoughts to air on the subject of Cuba," he announced at a meeting of his Defense Council on May 21, 1962. "It would be foolish to expect the inevitable second invasion to be as badly planned as the first," he explained, referring to the Bay of Pigs. Like Fidel, the Soviet leader was convinced that one failure would not deter the Americans from trying to invade Cuba again, But Khrushchev had other, ultimately more decisive reasons to countenance the risky move of arming Cuba with nuclear weapons. The United States had its own missiles in Turkey and Italy capable of striking Soviet territory within ten minutes of being launched. Soviet missiles ninety miles from the United States would neutralize that threat. "Now they would learn just what it feels like to have enemy missiles pointing at [them]," said Khrushchev.[3]

Hardly a week passed before a Soviet delegation arrived in Havana with the stated purpose of studying irrigation problems. American intelligence did not appear to note the presence of key figures whose work had nothing to do with water and everything to do with rocketry. On arrival, a delegate quietly told Raúl Castro that one of the rocket engineers needed to talk to Fidel directly. At the meeting three hours later, the Soviets offered to place nuclear missiles in Cuba. "It was the only time," recalled one of the visitors, that he ever saw "the Cubans writing things down."[4]

Raúl Castro visited the Soviet Union for two weeks in July to work out the details. Then, on July 13, he put pen to paper to sign the new Cuban-Soviet defense agreement, its front page stamped "strictly secret."

He returned from his Moscow trip in time to celebrate July 26, the national holiday commemorating the revolutionary attack on the Moncada barracks in 1953. When Fidel spoke that day, he was as confident as usual. We are unvanquished and invincible, he announced. But he could not resist hinting at something new: Those who think they can defeat us "forget that our people, who began with a few little rifles now have weapons of all kinds; modern weapons, powerful weapons." As he said this, the Soviet ships were already on their way to Cuba.[5]

Khrushchev called the project to arm Cuba with nuclear missiles Anadyr, an attempt at misdirection, since that was the name of a strategic air base in Siberia. To sustain the ruse, the government told the people being deployed to pack for extremely cold weather. To hide the purpose of those voyages from US reconnaissance aircraft, passengers were allowed aboveboard only at night and in small groups. During the day, crews turned hoses on them to provide some respite from the extreme heat below deck. Clearly, there would be no need for the cold weather gear the passengers had been instructed to pack.[6]

Operation Anadyr promised many things for Cuba. Chief among them were forty medium- and intermediate-range ballistic missiles: twenty-four of the former (R-12) with a range of 1,050 miles and sixteen of the latter (R-14), able to travel twice as far. Both types of missiles could carry nuclear warheads with the firepower of one megaton of TNT. Because the missiles could not install or operate themselves, Anadyr included other things, too: four motorized regiments, two tank battalions, a MiG-21 fighter wing, forty-two light bombers, two cruise missile regiments, antiaircraft gun batteries, surface-to-air missiles, two of the Soviets' newest tanks, and more than fifty thousand military personnel (including advisors, technicians, engineers, soldiers, sailors, pilots, and nurses).[7]

By the time the ships began arriving on the island in early September 1962, US officials had already grown suspicious. On September 4, President Kennedy issued a public statement announcing that the United States had incontrovertible evidence of the arrival in Cuba of antiaircraft defensive missiles, torpedo boats armed with ship-to-ship missiles, extensive radar and other electronic equipment, as well as Soviet military technicians presumably to assist in installation and training. But Kennedy also assured the American people that these were only defensive weaponry and that there was no evidence of any "significant offensive capability." "Were it to be otherwise," he warned, "the gravest issues would arise."[8]

The Soviet Union responded with denials. Its ambassador in Washington reassured administration officials that only defensive weapons were being sent to Cuba. The official Soviet news agency, TASS, released a ten-page statement to the same effect and announced that a US attack on Cuba would be the "unleashing [of] war." Before the UN General Assembly, the Soviet foreign minister issued a similar warning.[9]

In fact, war seemed to be on the minds of everyone involved. In Washington, DC, the Senate passed a resolution on Cuba authorizing the use of force, if necessary. In early October, the Atlantic Command ordered military units to increase readiness for Operation Plans 312 for an air strike on Cuba and 314 and 316 for a full invasion. Cuban president Osvaldo Dorticós, meanwhile, told the UN that Cuba stood ready to repel the United States, vaguely hinting at new means to do so. "We have sufficient means with which to defend ourselves; we have ... weapons which we would have preferred not to acquire and which we do not wish to employ."[10]

Though a few officials harbored suspicions, the US government had as yet no knowledge of the presence of Soviet nuclear or offensive weapons in Cuba. At the time, then, the saber-rattling invocations of war, on the US side at least, assumed only conventional military operations with conventional weapons. But the steady talk of war in September and early October set the stage for a very different and unprecedented kind of hysteria once the United States and the world discovered the truth about all those weapons.

KENNEDY LEARNED OF THE EXISTENCE of Soviet missiles in Cuba early on the morning of October 16. From that moment, the deliberations were virtually nonstop. But this Kennedy was different than the Bay of Pigs Kennedy. That earlier debacle made his focus ironclad in the present. He convened a Cuba crisis group that came to be known as the Executive Committee of the National Security Council (ExComm), which pored over reconnaissance information, consulted with missile experts, and meticulously studied scenarios and plans developed by the appropriate agencies. At a meeting on the evening of October 16, members learned that the Soviet missiles would be "fully operational within two weeks," though individual ones could be ready "much sooner." On October 18, they learned that the medium-range missiles could "probably be launched within eighteen hours." For five days, the president took in the information, participated in ExComm deliberations, and considered the feasibility of two principal responses. The first was a naval blockade of the island to prevent the further introduction of offensive weaponry; the second consisted of air strikes against the missile bases. Both options had massive drawbacks. Proponents of air strikes pointed out that a blockade would do nothing against weapons already in Cuba. Proponents of the blockade pointed out that attacking without warning was immoral, tantamount to Japan's attack on Pearl Harbor. Furthermore, a direct attack on Cuba would likely result in Soviet military retaliation and possibly "escalate to general war." Everyone present knew that, in this case, "general war" was a refined euphemism for nuclear war.[11]

Kennedy set a deadline of October 22 for a decision. That day, for the first time ever, all aircraft belonging to the Air Defense Command were armed with nuclear weapons. US military forces worldwide went on DEFCON 3 (the same state of military readiness declared following the attacks of September 11, 2001). The US fleet of long-range B-52 bombers began round-the-clock flights. By October 24, there would be one taking off from a US Air Force base every twenty minutes. So large and menacing that they would later earn the nickname BUFF, for Big Ugly Fat Fucker, each B-52 was armed for the crisis with enough nuclear firepower to destroy multiple Soviet targets. Almost two hundred of the medium-range B-47 nuclear bombers were dispersed to thirty-three airfields, some ready to obliterate Cuba with 20-megaton weapons. All this was prepared quietly. When details of the crisis began to leak to the press, Kennedy called the *New York Times* and *Washington Post* personally to request that the stories be held for the sake of national security.[12]

Then, at 7 p.m. on October 22, President Kennedy addressed the nation. He came to the point immediately: "This Government, as promised, has maintained the closest surveillance of the Soviet Military buildup on the island of Cuba. Within the past week, unmistakable evidence has established the fact that a series of offensive missile sites is now in preparation on that imprisoned island." Lest anyone wonder what exactly that meant, he continued, "The purpose of these bases can be none other than to provide a nuclear strike capability against the Western Hemisphere." Medium-range ballistic missiles, he said, were capable of carrying nuclear warheads as far as Washington, DC, Mexico City, or the Panama Canal. A second type of installation, not yet completed, was designed for intermediate-range missiles capable of going twice as far, to Hudson Bay, Canada, or to Lima, Peru, in the other direction. To counter the threat, the United States was establishing a strict quarantine on all offensive military equipment being shipped to Cuba. Gravely, he warned that the United States would "regard any nuclear missile launched from Cuba against any nation in the Western Hemisphere as an attack by the Soviet Union on the United States, requiring a full retaliatory response upon the Soviet Union." By full retaliatory response, the president meant simultaneous nuclear attacks on the Soviet Union, China, and the Eastern Bloc nations of Poland, East Germany, Albania, Bulgaria, Yugoslavia, Romania, Czechoslovakia, and Hungary. The Soviets would have then responded in kind. Combined, attacks launched by the two superpowers would have meant the end of most life on earth. Kennedy implored Khrushchev: "move the world back from the abyss of destruction."[13]

Millions of Americans watched or heard Kennedy's speech that night. At military bases, service members gathered around single radios intent on every word. At department stores, people surrounded the television displays all tuned to the speech. Across the country, everyone's attention was riveted on the unfolding, deadly drama.[14]

Khrushchev, too, was listening intently. And first indications were that Kennedy's strongly worded address had not changed his mind about anything. TASS issued a statement on October 23, warning that Soviet ships had orders to sink American vessels if they were attacked. Khrushchev himself delivered a combative message to the president of Westinghouse Electric, then on a visit to Moscow. It was wrong, he said, to view the Soviet missiles in Cuba as offensive. He demonstrated his point by analogy: "If I point a pistol at you like this in order to attack you, the pistol is an offensive weapon. But if I aim to keep you from shooting me, it is defensive, no?" If the United States really wanted to ascertain what kind of Soviet weapons were in Cuba, all it had to do was invade. Guantánamo naval base, he promised, "would disappear on the first day."[15]

IN CUBA, FIDEL CASTRO PUT his military on highest alert and mobilized and expanded the civilian militia. Across the island, large red banners implored, "¡A las armas!" (To arms!) In a speech, seventy-three minutes longer than Kennedy's the night before, Castro was defiant. As a sovereign nation, Cuba had the right "to obtain the arms we want for our defense, and we take the measures we deem necessary for our defense. And this is what we have done." To disarm now, he added, was to relinquish Cuban sovereignty, and for Cuba to do that "it will be necessary to wipe us off the face of the earth." That outcome was now entirely plausible.[16]

By Friday, October 26, all twenty-four medium-range missile sites in Cuba were operational, and construction on other weaponry was continuing at an accelerated pace. Clearly, the blockade was not enough, thought the men assembled around Kennedy. As the group debated options, two clear camps emerged. One camp wanted to negotiate with Khrushchev and find a political solution. Another camp, more vocal, advocated a military solution in the form of an air strike followed by an all-out invasion. Some among the hawks saw their chance finally to remove Fidel Castro from power. Kennedy was undecided. In the meantime, to increase the pressure on Khrushchev and to obtain information for potential air strikes, he increased the frequency of reconnaissance flights over Cuba to every two hours. Air strike plans expanded to include three massive strikes per day and 1,190 bombing sorties for day one of the operation, if things came to that.[17]

In Cuba, Castro stared up at the low-flying U-2 planes and fumed. This was a preamble to an air strike, he was convinced. And, as during the Bay of Pigs, an air strike would surely be the preamble to an invasion. On the afternoon of October 26, he drafted an angry letter to the secretary general of the UN. "Cuba does not accept the vandalistic and piratical privilege of any warplane to violate our airspace....Any warplane that invades Cuban airspace does so at the risk of meeting our defensive fire."[18]

Castro's conviction that a US attack was imminent made complete sense in that moment. Kennedy had not yet decided what to do, and military action was very much on the table. A public statement by one US State Department official that day made ominous reference "to further action" beyond the blockade. In Florida, hundreds of attack planes had already converged, and tens of thousands of troops were loading onto amphibious vessels. On October 26, Castro also received word from the president of Brazil that the United States was planning to destroy the missile sites unless construction on them was halted within forty-eight hours. The Cuban press agency in New York informed him of rampant rumors that Kennedy had given the UN a deadline by which the dismantling of the nuclear installations must begin in order to avoid US military action. Castro expected a US attack. He had been predicting one since the US failure at the Bay of Pigs. The time had now come, he thought.[19]

From the bomb shelter in the Soviet embassy in Havana where he had spent the night, Fidel Castro penned a letter to Moscow. He dictated in Spanish while the ambassador and an assistant translated to Russian as they transcribed. For that reason, no Spanish version of the letter—the one that would have best captured Castro's thinking that night—ever existed, much less survived. Fidel started and stopped and then started again many times. He wanted to convey his thoughts clearly and coolly, and the ambassador was struggling to understand his sometimes intricate Spanish. Castro began by expressing his certainty that a US attack within twenty-four to seventy-two hours was inevitable. That attack might take the form of air strikes against missile installations or all-out invasion of the island. Should the United States invade Cuba, Castro went on to say, "the Soviet Union must never allow circumstances in which the imperialists could carry out a nuclear first strike against it." A US invasion of Cuba "would be the moment to eliminate this danger forever, in an act of the most legitimate defense. However harsh and terrible the solution, there would be no other." The ambassador—trying to transcribe and translate simultaneously in the stressful environment of a nuclear bunker—pressed for clarification: "Do you mean to say that we should be the first ones to strike a nuclear blow against the enemy?" Castro quickly answered, "No. I do not want to say this directly. But under certain circumstances." What was the circumstance and what was Fidel's recommendation? "If they attack Cuba, we should wipe them off the face of the earth."[20]

IN MOSCOW AND UNBEKNOWNST TO Castro, Khrushchev was pursuing other options. The Soviet leader had written to Kennedy on October 26 offering to withdraw the missiles from Cuba in exchange for a pledge from Kennedy never to invade the island. While Khrushchev had expected a US attack on Cuba from the start, by this point he had begun to question that view. If the United States was going to invade, wouldn't they have done so already? The fact that they were responding to feelers suggested to him that Kennedy favored a peaceful solution. It was at this moment that Khrushchev raised his price for removing the missiles. He drafted a second letter to Kennedy and offered to remove the weapons from Cuba, with independent confirmation by UN inspections teams. In exchange he asked for two things. The first, once more, was a public pledge of noninvasion of Cuba. The second condition was new. "You are disturbed over Cuba . . . because it is 90 miles by sea from [your] coast. . . . But Turkey adjoins us; our sentries patrol back and forth and see each other. Do you consider, then, that you have the right to demand security for your own country . . . but do not accord the same right to us?" Khrushchev proposed a simple trade. The Soviet Union would withdraw missiles from Cuba if the United States withdrew theirs from Turkey.[21]

Khrushchev's letter arrived at the White House during yet another tense ExComm meeting on October 27, the day historians sometimes refer to as Black Saturday. Kennedy seemed to favor Khrushchev's proposal, but the hawks in the room wanted to ignore the new Soviet offer and attack Cuba. That position gained momentum when in the middle of the meeting word came that a US reconnaissance plane had been shot down over eastern Cuba, its pilot killed. The shooting amplified the calls for war. The Washington consensus now seemed to be that if Cuba continued to fire on American planes, the United States would have to retaliate by taking out all the surface-to-air missile sites. Everyone in the room knew that once that happened, events would accelerate quickly, leading to an invasion of Cuba and a nuclear war with the Soviet Union.[22]

President Kennedy did not want that invasion or that war. Meeting with a few advisors, he asked his brother, Bobby Kennedy, to set up a secret meeting with the Soviet ambassador. They met at the Justice Department at 7:45 p.m. that night. The younger Kennedy began with a dire prediction: After the shooting of the U-2 plane the president was under extreme pressure to fire if fired upon, and that would start "a chain reaction" that "will be very hard to stop." Bobby offered to guarantee no invasion of Cuba if the missiles were withdrawn. "What about Turkey?" asked the ambassador. Kennedy replied "if that is the only obstacle" to achieving a resolution, "then the president doesn't see any insurmountable difficulties in resolving this issue." But, he added, there could be no public discussion of the trade.[23]

The meeting lasted only fifteen minutes, and Bobby returned to the White House in time for the last ExComm meeting of the night. Only a few people in the room knew about the meeting he had just attended, and even those who did had no idea if it would yield the response they wanted. So, preparations continued for a war that still seemed very likely. If US planes were fired upon, US forces would take out the surface-to-air-missile sites, the president said. The president also approved an order calling twenty-four squadrons of Air Force Reserve, involving fourteen thousand personnel and three hundred troop carriers. At the end of the meeting, Defense Secretary Robert McNamara turned to Bobby Kennedy and said, "We need to have two things ready, a government for Cuba, because we're going to need one . . . and, secondly, plans for how to respond to the Soviet Union in Europe, because sure as hell they're going to do something there." Someone joked about naming Bobby mayor of Havana.[24]

IN HAVANA, ACTUALLY EXISTING OFFICIALS were preparing for war. The army and militias had been mobilized for days. They erected sandbag barriers around machine guns on the Malecón seawall. Even civilian officials helped dig trenches and barbwire the shore. Civil defense operations were accelerated, hos-

pitals readied, blood drives organized, stretchers constructed from sheets and bur-
lap. Castro set up headquarters at the famed Hotel Nacional. Once the haunt of
American mobsters, its towering grounds overlooking the Malecón now housed
an underground bunker. Instructions over Cuban radio told listeners to collect
buckets of sand to use in case of fires, to not hoard food, and to "keep a small piece
of wood handy to place between teeth when bombing begins." Foreigners commented on how calm everything seemed. The streets were emptier than usual in
Havana, but it was October, and seasonal rains may have also kept people inside.
One Havana resident running errands on Black Saturday overheard two militiamen talking in an elevator. One complained that everything was so frantic that he
had not had time to shave that morning. You will have to wait till after the war,
replied the other. The attack will come this afternoon between three and four,
someone told him. Yet as he walked around majestic Havana—the ocean's spray
curling over the seawall, red flamboyant trees abloom, a beautiful woman walking
under their canopy—he suddenly thought, "What a shame that all this will disappear between 3 and 4 this afternoon." A young soldier later told two US scholars
that everyone in his unit had fully expected total destruction, and they hoped that
the Soviets would place a floating monument in the Caribbean Sea, where Cuba
"used to be."[25]

As the preparations unfolded, no one—certainly not Fidel Castro—knew
that Kennedy and Khrushchev were negotiating secretly. Then, on Sunday morning, October 28, a Moscow radio announcer read a letter from Khrushchev to
Kennedy. It announced: "In order to eliminate as rapidly as possible the conflict
which endangers the cause of peace . . . the Soviet Government, in addition to
earlier instructions on the discontinuation of further work on weapons construction sites, has given a new order to dismantle the arms which you described as
offensive, and to crate and return them to the Soviet Union." Heeding Bobby
Kennedy's request not to mention the Turkey missiles publicly, Khrushchev's letter referred only to the noninvasion pledge. "I regard with respect and trust the
statement you made in your message of October 27, 1962, that there would be
no attack, no invasion of Cuba." In another part of the statement, Khrushchev
presumed to speak for Cuba, "The Cuban people want to build their life in their
own interests without external interference. This is their right, and they cannot be
blamed for wanting to be masters of their own country and disposing of the fruits
of their own labor."[26]

When the message arrived in Washington, some of the hawks in the Ex-
Comm doubted its sincerity. But Kennedy was swayed. At 11:10 a.m., he approved

a public statement. "I welcome Chairman Khrushchev's statesmanlike decision." "It is my earnest hope," he continued, "that the governments of the world can, with a solution of the Cuban crisis, turn their urgent attention to the compelling necessity for ending the arms race and reducing world tensions." Early that afternoon, Soviet commanders in Cuba received instructions to dismantle the missiles and bases, and by 5 p.m. the work had already begun. The next day, a large headline across the front page of the *New York Times* announced: "US and Soviet Reach Accord on Cuba; Kennedy Accepts Khrushchev Pledge to Remove Missiles Under UN Watch." Everyone, or almost everyone, breathed a deep sigh of relief.[27]

BUT NO ONE HAD BOTHERED to ask Fidel Castro for an opinion on the matter. He heard about Khrushchev's decision to withdraw the missiles only after it was broadcast on Moscow radio. He was said to have flown into a rage; "son of a bitch, bastard, asshole," he reportedly yelled. The missiles were in Cuba, and a deal was worked out and announced not only without his consultation, but without even bothering to inform the Cuban government. The historical comparison was easy to see. It was like 1898, at the end of the Cuban War of Independence and the Spanish-American War, when the independence army and rebel government were prohibited from taking part in negotiations for the final peace treaty. It was, said Fidel to one of his companions, utterly humiliating and wrong. And he would not accept it. He drafted a public letter to the UN rejecting the agreement between Kennedy and Khrushchev. Kennedy's pledge to not invade Cuba was inadequate if not accompanied by five other measures. Among them were the end of the US economic embargo and the closing of the US naval base at Guantánamo.[28]

Khrushchev might have realized he had a problem. His agreement with Kennedy hinged on UN inspections in Cuba, which meant that it depended, in part, on Fidel accepting it. Khrushchev addressed a letter to Fidel: "We would like to recommend to you now, at this critical moment, not to yield to your emotions, to show restraint." He warned that "unbridled militarists" in the Pentagon were looking to undermine the agreement by provoking Castro. "For this reason we would like to offer the following friendly advice to you: show patience, restraint, and more restraint." Castro's reply to Khrushchev was cold. "Our government's position on the issues you raised is laid out in our declaration made today," referring to Cuba's public statement to the UN with its five demands. The letter ended ominously: "I want to inform you as well that we are generally opposed to the inspection of our territory."[29]

The weapons were to be removed from Cuba under UN supervision and only on UN confirmation of that withdrawal would the US pledge not to invade Cuba. Now, after the public announcement of that deal by the two superpowers, Castro was saying there would be no such inspections of Cuban territory—not unless the United States conceded to having its own territory inspected.[30] Perhaps this was the kind of emotion Khrushchev had warned Castro against. Or maybe it was just cool, defiant logic.

Power is in part about the right to speak; it is, even more so, about who gets to be heard. And in that moment, Kennedy and Khrushchev had little intention of hearing Fidel Castro. For most people in the United States, the Soviet Union, and the world, the Cuban Missile Crisis ended on Sunday, October 28, when Khrushchev and Kennedy agreed to the terms for the withdrawal of nuclear weapons from Cuba. Long narrated as a crisis of "thirteen days," that Sunday was day 13. But as long as Castro refused international inspections of Cuban territory, the predicament was not resolved.

More muted but still tense, the crisis continued well into November. The United States kept insisting on the inspections as a precondition for the deal, and they kept sending twenty to thirty planes a day to photograph the nuclear sites. For his part, Castro kept insisting on his five points, including an end to US violations of Cuban airspace. On November 15, he even reauthorized the shooting of US planes flying over Cuban territory. Consistently, he rejected the possibility of international inspections in Cuba, which in the end never occurred. On November 20, realizing that Castro would never agree and again without consultation, Khrushchev and Kennedy arrived at a second deal. The Soviets now agreed to remove not only the missiles but also the light bombers from Cuba; the United States gave up on on-site inspections—which Castro would never allow—and settled for reconnaissance flights over Soviet ships on open waters.[31]

THE CUBAN MISSILE CRISIS WAS a strange and unexpected affair. Thousands of pages have been written on it. Had nuclear war ensued, its import would be painfully obvious to the descendants of survivors. The fact that nuclear war did not happen had lasting effects. It accelerated the installation of a direct White House–Kremlin communication link—"the hotline" or "red phone"—so present in our collective Cold War imagination. More important, the Missile Crisis slowed the momentum in the nuclear arms race and led eventually to the signing of a limited nuclear test ban treaty.[32]

BRINK

Assessing the impact of the Missile Crisis in Cuba itself is more difficult. Kennedy vowed never to invade Cuba. In that sense, the Missile Crisis (coupled with Cuba's victory at the Bay of Pigs) might be interpreted as strengthening Cuba's hand internationally. It had defeated the United States in 1961; now in 1962, the Americans promised never to invade again.

But Castro never put any stock in Kennedy's pledge; indeed, it was only ever made orally. At a press conference on November 20, Kennedy stated again "that once these adequate arrangements for verification had been established, we would remove our naval quarantine and give assurances against invasion of Cuba." Asked by a reporter if by adequate verification he meant the on-site inspections, Kennedy answered ambiguously: "Well, we have thought that to provide adequate inspection, it should be on-site. As you know, Mr. Castro has not agreed to that, so we have had to use our own resources." Were these other, less ideal means of verification adequate to guarantee noninvasion? Kennedy's final letter to Khrushchev was not categorical on the issue: "I regret that you have been unable to persuade Mr. Castro to accept a suitable form of inspection . . . and that in consequence we must continue to rely on our means of information. But . . . there need be no fear of an invasion of Cuba while matters take their present favorable course." The last phrase was hardly a guarantee. In fact, in 1963, US secretary of state Dean Rusk testified before a closed hearing of the Senate Foreign Relations Committee that if Castro were to do something that from the US government's perspective justified an invasion, the noninvasion pledge would not be considered binding.[33]

In the meantime, covert activities against the Cuban government that had been suspended briefly during the crisis resumed full force. The CIA continued to explore assassination plots with poison pens, mafia hit men, exploding cigars, and toxic diving suits. It experimented with a substance derived from LSD and planned to somehow spray it on Fidel before a speech so as to make him seem insane. They used thallium salts to create a depilatory substance that would make Fidel lose his beard and with it, perhaps, his charismatic appeal. All of it was to no avail.[34]

The strange resolution of the Missile Crisis and Khrushchev's failure to consult with Fidel Castro almost caused a break between Cuba and the Soviet Union. But the alliance continued. In fact, it strengthened. After 1962, the Soviet military buildup accelerated (without nuclear weapons) and turned the island into the world's second most militarized state (per capita), trailing only North Korea. Little over a decade later, Cuba would use that Soviet weaponry and Soviet economic support to project its power internationally, in support of like-minded causes around the world.

CUBA

Yet most Cubans came back from the brink of nuclear holocaust to a reality almost identical to what had preceded it. By late 1962, the island was already suffering from the combined effects of the US economic embargo and inefficient centralized planning. A widespread system of rationing had been instituted in March of that year, and shortages by then were well known. Back in the little town of Santa Cruz de los Pinos, where young Cubans had forged friendships with young Soviets, people were shocked at how quickly the soldiers disappeared. A decade after the Missile Crisis, the Cuban government repurposed the empty Soviet base to train Cuban soldiers for a massive and daring military intervention in Africa—not only in defiance of the United States, but also, fittingly, without bothering to inform the Soviets. Castro could return superpower arrogance with some of his own. But the Cubans of Santa Cruz de los Pinos repurposed the base in their own way. When the Soviets evacuated the camps, they quietly entered the sites and took things left behind: perforated steel mats, steel wires, and concrete barriers. Then they recycled them for their own ends, incorporating them into the pens that housed their favorite source of meat: pigs. Life in revolutionary Cuba went on.[35]

Part XI

HEARTS AND MINDS

Che Guevara and, for a time, Fidel Castro believed that the Cuban Revolution would make "new people"—men, women, and children who would work and volunteer for the greater good. A young man volunteers in the sugar harvest, possibly the Ten Million Ton Harvest of 1970.

Chapter 29

NEW PEOPLE?

Real revolutions aim to sweep away the time of the past—to pulverize it, in the words of one historian of the French Revolution.[1] In many ways, the Cuban Revolution appeared to be doing just that. The old army, the legislature, political parties, so many of the institutions of the old Cuba had disappeared. Feeling increasingly unwelcome and soon barred by their own government from traveling to the island, American tourists disappeared. The US embassy was shuttered. Cuba's once-seemingly immovable relationship to that government had fundamentally changed. Large private enterprises—whether landed estates or corporations, whether foreign or domestic—vanished. The revolution also disrupted the signs of old class relations. Rationing theoretically gave everyone access to the same goods in the same amounts for the same prices. Former maids went to school and now interacted with their former employers as accountants and bank tellers. White-collar professionals volunteered to cut sugarcane in the hot sun, usually underperforming people they might have looked down on before the revolution. Middle-class girls and boys trekked into remote mountains to teach people to read, learning to live without toilets and with the responsibility of manual labor. The government moved working people into stately homes, their former owners now in Miami or New York, living in tenements and working in garment factories. Gone, too, were the days of *señor* and *señora*. Often translated as Mister and Mrs., *señor*'s historical meaning was closer to master or lord. In the new Cuba, there was ostensibly no more use for that. Men and women became *compañeros* and *compañeras*. A waiter was *compañero*; so was the customer he served. Even Fidel Castro, who had always been identified as Dr. at the beginning of the revolution, became simply Fidel, or sometimes *compañero* Fidel. Of course, no past simply vanishes; no change is ever total. Still, so much that happened in the crucible of revolution pointed to the obvious. Cuba was different now.

CUBA

Having won at the Bay of Pigs and survived the Missile Crisis, Fidel Castro tried to implement a more systematic, more purposeful change than what the country had yet seen. Scholars sometimes refer to the period from 1963 to 1970 as the "push for communism." Extrapolating from Marx's idea that history unfolded in stages, Cuban leaders posited that, with the right policies, Cuba could accelerate time, speed through socialism (a transitional stage between capitalism and communism), and make a great leap forward to communism. To hasten the transition to communism, the state eliminated virtually all private property. Already, the 1959 Agrarian Reform Law had confiscated large landholdings, and the nationalizations of 1960 had confiscated large and medium private companies. In 1963, the revolutionary government went further. That year, a second agrarian reform set much smaller limits on the size of private lands, bringing a total of two-thirds of the Cuban countryside under direct state control by mid-decade. In 1968, a campaign called the Revolutionary Offensive transferred as many as fifty-eight thousand businesses from private hands to the state—everything from bars and restaurants to retail stores and street vendors' carts.[2] The push for communism between 1963 and 1970 aimed to defeat the past once and for all, to make change total and irreversible.

But there was more. The revolutionaries believed that the rupture with the past would occur not only at the level of society but also at the level of the individual. As the revolution changed the fundamental structures of society, people themselves would change, too. Social relations would be completely transformed, and individuals would develop different relationships to work, to money, to each other, and to themselves. In the Cuban Revolution, the principal proponent of this view was Che Guevara, the Argentine doctor who had joined Fidel Castro's revolution in Mexico, followed it to the mountains of the Sierra Maestra, to Havana to serve as minister of industry and president of the National Bank, and eventually to far corners of the world to spur other Cuban revolutions. In perhaps his most famous essay, "Socialism and Man in Cuba," written in newly independent Algeria in 1965, Guevara elaborated on the means of achieving true communism. "The new society in formation," he wrote, "has to compete fiercely with the past." During the transition to this new future society, the past was not yet dead. And that made it deadly. For Guevara, the battle against the past occurred everywhere, even within individuals. To achieve communism people had to defeat the past in themselves and adopt a whole "new scale of values." People had to be reborn, figuratively, as new men and new women.[3]

Guevara wrote that essay based on his deep knowledge and experience of the

Cuban Revolution. And that raises the question: Did what he described actually happen in Cuba? As the country around them changed, did Cubans change with it? Did they change to their core? Did they become new men and new women? Revolutions have a strange relationship to the most intimate areas of human existence; they insinuate themselves into the most unlikely areas of day-to-day life. Whatever the resistance of property holders, the old regime, or the US government to the Cuban Revolution, it may have been in the home, in the seclusion of the bedroom and the familiarity of the dining table that the past most valiantly resisted passing. There, even those who applauded the revolution writ large sometimes struggled mightily against a change in themselves.

TO MAKE NEW PEOPLE, THE revolution began with the children. The new government knew that to create a new society with new values, children were the key. They were, in Che Guevara's words, "malleable clay from which the new person can be built with none of the old defects." The government thus focused considerable attention on creating new institutions for children and youth. In 1960, it announced the establishment of free state-run nursery schools, an effort meant to give women more opportunities outside the home and also to create "a more advanced youth"—a revolutionary youth. The next year, the Communist Party established a children's auxiliary club, known as the Pioneers, to instill in children between the ages of six and fourteen a love of country and revolution. That same year, Castro nationalized education, closing all private schools. Every child would now be educated by the state. The government also established boarding schools in the countryside that combined traditional academic subjects, immersion in social-ist values, and agricultural labor. By 1967, about 85 percent of high school students attended those boarding schools.[4]

All this was new to Cuban parents, and some worried by using formulas from the past. Parents, not the government, traditionally taught their children values; families, not the government, decided when children would leave the household. Now, mothers and fathers sensed that the government was establishing a cultural and moral monopoly over their children. The new schools and programs, they said, were evidence of the state's eagerness to intervene in private relations between parents and children. Some even said that the government would turn children into spies against their own parents. Rampant rumors that children would be taken away from parents and shipped to the Soviet Union for indoctrination led some parents to send their children out of the country without them. Between

1960 and 1962, fourteen thousand school-aged children left Cuba for the United States in Operation Peter Pan, then the largest organized migration of unaccompanied minors in the history of the Western Hemisphere.[5]

Tensions over the government's relation to Cuban children also emerged during a very different educational project, the Literacy Campaign of 1961. Designed to rid the country of illiteracy (which stood at over 20 percent of the population), the campaign enjoyed enormous popularity. Literacy had been part of progressive political platforms in Cuba for decades; Batista himself had spearheaded a literacy campaign in the late 1930s. But if the goal of universal literacy was a long-standing one, the revolutionary government pursued it by new means and on an entirely different scale. The teachers' manuals and the early readers for students imparted lessons by teaching revolutionary content. In these books, M was for Martí, R for Raúl. F was for Faith, Fusil (rifle), Fidel, or all three. Simple declarative sentences told the story of agrarian reform. The literacy campaign, then, was more than a means to eradicate illiteracy. It was also a political project. It taught peasants new political lessons. It mobilized and incorporated young people en masse, not only as teachers but as living embodiments of the revolution.

Of Cuba's roughly 7 million inhabitants, approximately 1.25 million took part directly, either as teachers or students. In one year, approximately 700,000 Cubans learned to read and write. Close to 300,000 volunteered to teach peasants to read and write, many traveling to the island's remotest corners. So many young people volunteered for the campaign that the government organized them in special youth brigades boasting over 105,000 members. Approximately 48 percent of them were fifteen to nineteen years old; another 40 percent were between ten and fourteen. Slightly more than half were girls; one teacher was eight years old. Cubans who did not volunteer to teach or study were swept up in other ways. To make teachers available for the campaign, most schools closed for eight months. Mothers who couldn't go teach volunteered to watch children suddenly free all day. Others filled in at work for those who left to teach. Crowds gave raucous sendoffs to literacy workers; the volunteer teachers marched with giant pencils, their own version of Fidel's *fusil*. Newly literate peasants were honored at festive and public graduation ceremonies.[6]

Yet for all the mobilization around the literacy campaign, its impact was perhaps most keenly felt in private. Peasants opened their homes to teachers—gave them food and lodging, washed their clothes, forged relationships. The teachers, overwhelmingly young and urban, were suddenly living in close quarters with strangers, under completely unfamiliar and sometimes uncomfortable conditions. For each departure by a hopeful, idealistic young teacher, there were numerous conversations at home with family. Many parents were proud to see their children participate in such a noble project. But Cuban parents also tended to be strict with children, particularly when those children were girls. Mothers and fathers withheld permission, forcing determined teenagers to forge signatures on paperwork and to conceal their plans until the last moment. One young woman who joined the literacy brigades when she was fifteen later remembered how her relatives objected: How could her mother allow her "to go alone to God knows where, to live among God knows who, in the countryside where there was no running water or electricity?" Eager young women heard over and over that girls their age could not leave home. Parents wondered who would protect their daughters from the sexual advances of either peasants or other teachers. Detractors joked that if 1961 was the Year of Education, then the literacy campaign would make 1962 the Year of Maternity. Cuban revolutionaries could make uptight parents, especially when it came to their daughters and sex.[7]

Ironically, as urban adolescents clashed with parents over going to the countryside, young country women tussled with theirs over going to the city. The government brought rural girls to Havana to attend the Ana Betancourt School for peasant girls, where they would learn sewing and reading and receive political instruction. The school was part of a broader project that sought to educate (or reeducate) women. Other schools retrained maids and prostitutes as chauffeurs, accountants, and typists. Peasant girls attending the new schools stayed in Miramar mansions recently vacated by Miami-bound Cubans and took their classes in the meeting rooms of the famed and luxurious Hotel Nacional, which once welcomed such luminaries as John Wayne, Winston Churchill, and Simone de Beauvoir. Now it would serve to help the government reinvent peasant girls and for the girls to reinvent themselves away from their parents. It was easier to make new people at a distance from parents who had been formed in an earlier, prerevolutionary time.[8]

JUST AS THE REVOLUTION TRIED to mold relationships between parents and children, it aspired to do the same in relations between husbands and wives. Everything that the revolution expected of Cuban men—to serve on the Committees for the Defense of the Revolution, join the militia, or volunteer their labor—it also expected of Cuban women. But as women did more outside the home, traditional roles inside the home buckled under the weight of new obligations and expectations.

The Federation of Cuban Women, created in 1960, oversaw a major campaign to bring more women into the labor force. Its goal was to recruit a hundred thousand new women workers every year. And, indeed, between 1969 and 1974, more than seven hundred thousand women entered the workforce. But old norms hindered their incorporation. Of the seven hundred thousand who began working outside the home in that period, only about two hundred thousand continued to work after the first year. For the majority who left the workforce, the single most important factor was the perceived conflict with family obligations at home. It was a familiar struggle: women's much-discussed double shift of paid work outside the home and unpaid work in the home. But in revolutionary Cuba, women had to contend with what some have called the "triple shift" to encompass also the obligations of political work. This "triple shift" became a major theme in revolutionary cinema and the press, often prompting heated discussions about the struggle between emerging revolutionary realities and stubborn old attitudes about gender roles.[9]

Maybe this was the kind of conflict that Che Guevara had foreseen, a by-product of a transitional period in which a new order had already begun to emerge but in which the past was not yet dead. Here, as in the case of children, the state intervened. It instituted an eighteen-week paid maternity leave, followed by a year-long unpaid one. Free day care centers were designed in part to free up women to work. Working women received other perks, including the right to skip lines at stores.[10] Still, the government knew that these kinds of institutional changes would not be sufficient. Cuban men had to change, too.

The revolutionary state did not shy away from trying to make that happen. The most notable example of how it did that was the Family Code, which became law in 1975. The purpose of the code was to strengthen the family on the basis of "absolute equality of rights between men and women." It defined marriage as "established with equal rights and duties for both partners." That meant both had the right to work (or study) outside the home and the duty to support each other in that endeavor. Work outside the home, it clarified, did not exempt either partner from work inside the home. Both would participate in running the household and raising children. "According to the principles of socialist morality," it added.[11]

To ensure that this equality would be more than a paper one, the state called for prolific discussion on the Family Code in the months before it became law. At meeting after meeting, at workplaces and block associations, few people felt comfortable coming out openly against the principle of equality in marriage or openly questioning the government's prerogative to legislate their personal relationships. But many expressed ambivalence. Women asserted skeptically that the law could never succeed: the state would never be able to enforce it; their husbands would never change. Cuban men, they prophesied, would not share equally the burdens of homemaking and child-rearing. The objections raised by men at the meetings surely fed those doubts. Some said that while they were willing to "help with" dishes and other household chores, they did not want to do things like hang laundry in their yards or balconies, where neighbors could see them doing housework. Socialist morality notwithstanding, men tended to view doing "women's work" in public as emasculating and embarrassing.[12]

Such sentiments revealed how formidable the challenge really was. In an effort to give the law more power, the state decreed that the Family Code's "Rights and Duties between Husband and Wife" (Articles 24–28) be incorporated into state wedding ceremonies. (Hardly anyone was having church weddings by then.) At every legal marriage ceremony on the island, each partner vowed aloud to share equally in the duties of home, family, and socialism. Thanks to the state, then, the very last thing individuals said and heard as single people entering matrimony was a vow to perfect equality in the home.[13]

The state's incursion into gender relations did not always fall on the side of liberation, however. Concern with creating the ideal communist individual—the new man or the new woman—sometimes carried the presumption that some people would require more rehabilitation than others. In particular, gay Cubans became the targets of one of the most notorious revolutionary attempts to remake individuals. Traditional beliefs about gender roles and masculinity fused with rigid notions of socialist morality to condemn gay men (and, to a lesser extent, women) as socially deviant, as unwanted remnants of old bourgeois decadence. They were purged from the university and other institutions, barred membership in the Communist Party, and generally condemned as standing outside the revolution. In 1965, the government opened camps in the countryside where gays—and others deemed "antisocial"—would be rehabilitated as "new men." The principal means of rehabilitation was labor, hence the name of the camps: Military Units to Aid Production, or UMAP. Run by the military, with social workers and psychologists on staff, they combined forced labor with such practices as hormone and talk therapy. This was compulsory conversion therapy purportedly in the service of socialist revolution. International condemnation and domestic pressure eventually resulted in their closure in 1967.[14]

CUBA

EAGER AS IT WAS ABOUT intervening in family and gender relations, the revolutionary state trod more gingerly in another arena of human relations: race. Historically, segregation was not nearly as rampant and rigid in prerevolutionary Cuba as in the United States. Still, there were episodes of lynching; there was a small Ku Klux Klan, and public spaces sometimes bore physical signs of attempts to separate people by race. In the small rural town where my mother grew up, people used a rope to divide the only dance hall into Black and white sections, though white men exercised the privilege of disregarding the barrier at their pleasure, to dance with women of color or to ensure that their nonwhite daughters danced with white men. In the provincial capital of Santa Clara, the central park had promenades divided into white and Black sections. Racial discrimination was also structural. Private schools denied admission to Black children. Job centers advertised for workers of "good appearance," a euphemism for white. And almost every sociological indicator—education, earnings, life expectancy—showed that Afro-Cubans suffered the effects of institutionalized racism.[15]

When the revolution came to power in 1959, Black activists and intellectuals insisted that the revolution would not solve the "race problem" simply by existing. It needed bold and explicit policies of antidiscrimination. Many of their demands were long-standing ones, but Black activists in 1959 had hope that the revolutionary government, unlike earlier ones, would deliver. At first the revolutionary leadership seemed to agree. In March 1959, still new to power, Fidel Castro addressed the question directly at a labor rally. He spoke at length against the practice of racial discrimination in employment, which he identified as the cruelest form, since it denied people the right to make a living. But as the speech went on, Fidel began to elaborate on discrimination in social life. His solution was the same one Che Guevara would propose as a general antidote to outdated, capitalist values: education. If all Cuban children were educated together in good public schools, then they would play together after school. In fact, the state wanted all people to play together, to interact socially. So it would also build social clubs, recreation centers, and other spaces that Cubans—no matter their race—would enjoy together. It looked like everyone applauded.[16]

After the rally, however, many white Cubans dissented. Few defended the practice of job discrimination, but many questioned why Fidel had gone beyond that to talk about integrating other more private or social spaces. Social clubs were private affairs; determining whom a child would play with was a parent's business. In the private sphere, critics seemed to imply, racial barriers were fine and, certainly, no concern of the state. The distress occasioned by his speech was so strong that Castro was forced to backtrack. Just three days later, he appeared on national television to assuage some of the unease. While he denounced racial discrimination, he now seemed to accept the distinction invoked by his critics between a public and a private sphere. "I did not say that we were going to open the exclusive clubs for blacks to go there to dance or to entertain themselves. I did not say that. People dance with whomever they want and . . . socialize with whomever they want." Three months after taking power, it was more important to maintain unity than to insist too explicitly on what had always been a heated topic in Cuban society.[17]

That moment helped determine the government's approach to race for decades to come. Throughout, the state avoided questions of race in the so-called private sphere. With regard to economic and social policy, it pursued race-blind policies that would benefit the poor. Because the poor were disproportionately Black, such policies would benefit Afro-Cubans without the state needing to call attention to race. To tackle workplace discrimination, it rejected the idea of racial quotas and, in 1960, created instead a national registry of job seekers. The registry included information not only about the skills of potential workers, but also about their family income, economic needs, and so on. Rather than hire directly, employers with job vacancies would notify the Ministry of Labor, which would then fill those posts according to the information provided for the registry and without knowledge of the candidate's race, or even name. To target racial segregation in public settings, the government redesigned spaces to eliminate physical dividers. So the planters that separated the white and Black paths on the promenade of Santa Clara's main park, for example, were just removed. Changing physical spaces would change people's habits, and changing people's habits would ultimately change their attitudes and values.[18]

By 1961, Castro deemed that two years of government action on the issue had successfully eliminated racial prejudice and discrimination. Once the state declared the problem solved, talking about discrimination became more difficult. To point it out was ostensibly to threaten national unity and implicitly to accuse the state of lying or failing.[19]

Importantly, there was a stark contrast between the way the revolutionary government approached race domestically and the way it approached race internationally. The Cuban Revolution unfolded in the midst of the civil rights struggle in the United States, and Cuban media prominently featured news of that struggle and of the racist violence deployed against it. Havana offered asylum to prominent Black radicals. Robert Williams, NAACP leader and author of the influential book *Negroes with Guns*, lived in Cuba from 1961 to 1965, and from there broadcast Radio Free Dixie, which decried US racism and called on Black Americans to rise up in rebellion. Eldridge Cleaver, an early Black Panther leader and the author of another influential book, *Soul on Ice*, spent time in Cuba in 1968 after he fled the United States while out on bail for a charge of attempted murder of two police officers. The welcome and support Cuba offered these and other Black radicals from the United States, however, was not extended to its own Black activists. In fact, the government sometimes strove to keep prominent Black visitors from talking to Afro-Cuban intellectuals about race in Cuba. The government had declared the problem solved, and that left little room for Afro-Cubans to publicly discuss, much less decry, racism.[20]

There was another obvious contrast between the way the revolutionary state approached race and the way it approached gender. In the latter case, the state was more than willing to intervene in private space to shape behavior inside the home, between husbands and wives and between parents and children. It also encouraged sustained public discussions about discrimination against women. It didn't do that with the question of racism. Perhaps the leadership did not view racism as a major problem. Or perhaps it viewed a frontal attack on racism as potentially divisive at a moment when it wanted unity. So the government ceded that ground. It set aside the private sphere and targeted other things (like job discrimination) in other ways (using a language of class and nation rather than of race). It hoped by these means to will away the problem of racism. It was, ultimately, a classically Marxist position: because racial discrimination derived from the very structure and relations of capitalist society, once capitalism was dismantled, racism itself would eventually cease to exist. For some time, the view went, there would be residual, individual racism, but that, too, would disappear once the structural causes were gone. Put another way, the government decided it was easier to eradicate capitalism *tout court* than to dismantle old racial attitudes and assumptions.

CUBANS, IT SEEMED, WERE STUCK in the middle of an extended moment of transition in which the past was not yet dead. It wasn't even really past, as William Faulkner once famously said. To do the things it wanted to do, the revolutionary state needed Cubans to do things differently than they had before.

NEW PEOPLE?

But here was the conundrum: In order to become a true revolution, the revolution needed new people. And in order to become new people, individuals needed a true revolution. Revolution would make new people; new people would make the revolution. Would those things happen at the same time? Would one precede the other? How exactly would this radical change within people really happen?

Considerations such as these informed a major debate among the revolutionary leadership. On one level it was an abstract debate about human nature itself. On another level, it shaped concrete government policies on labor, education, and the economy. Part of that debate centered on the question of whether people in a revolution were motivated by moral or material incentives. On one side of that debate, Che Guevara championed the idea of moral incentives and the new man for whom they always sufficed. Against that view, other officials argued that moral incentives would not suffice to mobilize a labor force—not in the long run and not before true communism had been achieved. Rising worker absenteeism gave credence to that position. In some regions of the country, 20–29 percent of the labor force was absent from work on any given day. The state was the only employer, and labor unions were government run. Foot-dragging, tardiness, and absenteeism were among the few ways workers could independently express discontent over things like wages or working conditions. One study conducted in 1968 estimated that between one-quarter to one-half of the workday was wasted owing in part to such strategies.[21]

For years, Fidel Castro favored the idea of moral incentives, until harsh reality intruded and changed his mind. That shift was the result of an extraordinary campaign called the *zafra de los 10 millones*, or the Ten Million Ton Harvest. It was, as the name suggests, a gargantuan drive to produce a 10 million ton sugar harvest in 1970, by far the largest in the nation's history. The idea of the campaign was a temporary and intensive focus on sugar in order to produce the means to carry out industrialization. Castro said that its success would constitute the defeat of underdevelopment, the ultimate triumph of the Cuban Revolution.

There was a problem, however. Nowhere were there near the number of sugar workers necessary to produce a harvest of that size. Under the revolution, sugar workers had been moving to cities for expanding opportunities for education and work. Many of the formerly underemployed workers who had migrated to plantations in the harvest season before the revolution no longer needed to do that. They had jobs or went to school or had their own plots of land. They had no desire to return to the drudgery of the sugar harvest. To produce a 10 million ton harvest, then, the state would have to rely on an extraordinary campaign of voluntary labor from cities and towns. It would require Herculean effort and sacrifice, something worthy of new men and new women.[22]

The government named 1969 the "Year of the Decisive Effort." On January 1, Fidel announced: "We begin a year of great effort. We begin a year of eighteen months!" People applauded; some looked puzzled. The harvest would be extended by months, beginning for the first time ever in the dead heat of summer, when, with excellent reason, "no one ever dreamed of cutting cane in the past." Christmas and New Year's would be postponed until the harvest ended in July 1970. A diplomat in the audience turned to a friend and asked, "Have you ever heard anything so screwy?" As in 1959, time itself would have to bend to the will of the revolution.[23]

The 10 million ton harvest was a massive, unprecedented mobilization even for a revolution that produced many. State radio stations provided regular updates on the harvest; the island's main newspaper published a table on the front page every day showing progress toward the 10 million tons. Signs everywhere asked, "What are you doing for the 10 million," because everyone was supposed to be doing something. Schools shut down; so did restaurants and theaters. The ranks of city denizens thinned as in Paris in August, though no one was on vacation. Special buses and express trains carried volunteers to the countryside to cut cane; work centers sent contingents of men and women to the fields. All told, some 1.6 million Cubans worked in the harvest that long year. They were men and women and teenagers as young as fourteen. They included teachers, bankers, students, factory workers, government ministers, even ballet dancers and novelists, all now cutting cane together.[24]

People who participated in the legendary *zafra* would remember it for the rest of their lives. One young man named David, seventeen at the time of the harvest, later recalled the feeling of brotherhood. "All of us made sure that everyone's quota [of cane] was cut," even if that meant covering for a companion who was late or sick or just unwilling to work. "One really felt inspired every time they announced that a million *arrobas* had been cut somewhere in Cuba over the radio because there was less to cut, plus you saw that your work produced something that all the world would see and there was tremendous hope because . . . it was going to benefit Cuba, the economy, and everything." But the work was grueling, and many would remember other things. Novelist Reinaldo Arenas later compared the intensity of the labor to Dante's last circle of hell. The cane cutters woke up at 4 a.m. and headed to the fields with their machetes for the entire day, under a blistering sun, amidst cane leaves so sharp they cut. To accelerate the pace in the final months, administrators ordered controlled fires in the fields to burn away the leaves and make it easier to fell the stalks. The cane cutters set the fires at night and, after a brief rest in the barracks, entered the sometimes still-smoldering fields to begin working again in the morning, their heads covered with helmets and mesh to keep the burnt spears away from their eyes. Castro likened the work to slavery. "Until we are willing to do as free men what they had to do as slaves, the Revolution will not have reached its highest moral standard," he warned.[25]

A French agronomist observing the harvest noted the obvious: poets, stenographers, barbers, and the like harvested a lot less cane than seasoned sugar workers. He estimated that city dwellers cut about 500 kilograms of cane daily; in the case of "bureaucrats or intellectuals unused to physical effort," that figure might be as low as 250–300 kilograms a day. A sugar worker accustomed to harvesting cane, by contrast, averaged 3.5 to 4 metric tons of sugarcane daily. Unfortunately for those whose eyes were trained on the 10 million ton goal, the vast majority of those working the harvest were inexperienced. For every two hundred volunteers, only about a half dozen were experienced field hands. Alma Guillermoprieto, a Mexican dancer, trained in New York and then teaching ballet in Havana, came to a similar conclusion born of different experience. "Any dancer could have told Fidel that the movements of the dance of the *zafra*—elastic when stooping to the base of the stalk, where most of the sugar is stored, forceful when cutting the bundle of stalks with a single stroke of the machete, and precise when stripping each cane of its leaves—can't be learned in a single day, or even in several." Years later, the dancer still remembered by name a piano student who lost a finger to an unfortunate stroke of his machete.[26]

Because so much energy was devoted to the enterprise and because everything else was put in a state of suspension, people were surprised when suddenly one Thursday in May 1970, the newspaper did not run its usual front-page table showing the status of the harvest. On Friday, there was no table, either. On Saturday, the front page, with no sugar harvest chart, was devoted to a story about two African American students killed during a demonstration in Jackson, Mississippi. Sunday's front page featured a rally against the United States in Havana; photos showed protestors carrying signs with Nixon's name spelled Ni⇊on.[27]

It was another Cuban story, however, that drew everyone's attention that day: the sinking of two Cuban fishing boats by a Cuban American paramilitary group and the kidnapping of the men aboard the vessels. When the men were released a week later, the government organized a great rally to welcome them. The fishermen spoke; Fidel spoke. There were threats to occupy the former US embassy building and comparisons between Nixon and Hitler. Speaking from the podium, near the end of his speech and already late into the night, Castro made a pained announcement. There would be no 10 million ton harvest. There was just no way around that reality, he confessed—the rhythm of his words slower, his voice more tentative, his hands fidgeting with the microphones before him.[28]

The government had tried to recuperate the same sense of purpose as in the early days. And it had not been enough. In the end, the harvest amounted to 8.5 million tons of sugar, the largest harvest in Cuban history. But it came at a time when the world price for sugar was less than half of what it had been earlier in the decade. That severely limited what the country could earn from its historic yield.[29] The harvest had also come at a great cost. Other areas of the economy were neglected; machinery was run into the ground in a race against time. Land suitable for crops like rice had been turned over to sugar and would now produce neither well. Workers had lost months of work, students months of school. In short, the economy was in complete disarray. And everyone wondered: If the 10 million ton harvest was supposed to signal the end of underdevelopment, did the failure signify its persistence for the foreseeable future?

THE CAMPAIGN TO PRODUCE THE harvest was the largest mobilization of the revolution, larger than the literacy campaign, larger even than the mobilization that had accompanied the Bay of Pigs invasion of 1961 or the Missile Crisis in 1962. In both those conflicts, Cuba had faced off against the United States. In the first, Cuba won; in the second, Cuba survived. Now, in 1970, in a campaign against underdevelopment, against time and nature, against the limits of their own bodies, victory eluded them. People later recalled their shock. In 2010, a famous science fiction writer remembered it as the moment when the vision many Cubans had of the revolution as victorious had to confront a different reality.[30]

The failure of the 10 million ton harvest marked a turning point in the history of the Cuban Revolution. Early revolutionaries had hoped—even assumed—that they could make people anew. But after that failure, Castro maintained time and again that the revolutionary leadership had been too idealistic. For now and for a long time still, Cuba would remain in a period of transition; the "really new man . . . is still relatively far off," he mused on December 31, 1971.[31] Though still ideologically significant, the idea of the new man ceded ground to a different conception of work and personhood, as the government began to prioritize other, more material kinds of incentives for people to work. Exemplary workers would receive not only commendations in the forms of medals or diplomas. They would also receive bonus pay or the chance to purchase Soviet consumer goods or a vacation at a state-owned resort. The state's new emphasis on material incentives, like the Cuban economy itself, was subsidized by stronger ties to the Soviet Union and Eastern Europe. Those ties were institutionalized in 1972, with Cuba's entry into the Council for Mutual Economic Assistance (COMECON), the Soviet-led economic alliance of communist states.

But the 10 million ton harvest was a strange turning point. If it signaled a change in the revolutionary state's approach to labor and the economy, it also revealed the persistence of entrenched patterns that had marked Cuban history since long before the revolution. With the 10 million ton harvest unachieved, dreams of industrialization waned. The strengthened economic ties with the East—premised on the exchange of sugar for much more valuable things like oil—meant the survival of two longtime features of Cuban economy and society: monoculture and dependency. The future of the Cuban economy now looked like the past: sugar and more sugar. Before economic dependence had been on the United States; now the island became wholly dependent on the Soviet Union and the Eastern Bloc. So much had changed, but, still, the past—or parts of it, anyway—proved intractable.

Chapter 30

NEW AMERICANS?

A long-ago historian of other revolutions once suggested that the intensity of a revolution could be calculated objectively, dispassionately. How? By counting the number of people who fled it. In Cuba, a lot of people left. The first year, more than 25,000 did; another 60,000 did the second. By late 1960, 1,500 Cubans were arriving in the United States every week, and by late 1961, with the embassy in Havana already closed, an astounding 1,200 people per working day were applying to the US Immigration and Naturalization Service for entry. Between the start of the Cuban Revolution in January 1959 and the Missile Crisis of October 1962, nearly a quarter of a million people left.[1] Other waves followed, some of them even more concentrated. Numbers, in the end, give quantitative credence to a qualitative impression: the Cuban Revolution was nothing if not intense.

For a majority of those who quit the island, the destination of choice was the city of Miami, the southernmost major city in the continental United States. Anyone who travels to Miami today sees a city transformed by Cuba's presence. Yet Cuban migration to that city transformed Cuba as well. In fact, migration has served as a central force in the history of the Cuban Revolution writ large. In revolutionary Cuba, the possibility of leaving—or of being left—became part of everyday life. Weighty decisions about whether to stay or go shaped individual and collective experiences of revolution. Loved ones applied for passports; neighbors left valuables with neighbors to safeguard; people tired of all the good-byes. "Today, Monday," wrote one Havana resident to a friend already in the United States, "I've stayed home waiting for the customary visits where people tell you everything they're leaving behind." A month later, he complained that he could write letters only in snatches of time, as he was continually interrupted by the visits of people leaving. "Here even the cat is leaving," he joked.[2]

But leaving Cuba was not always easy. Plane tickets had to be purchased in US dollars; there were waiting lists for flights, and, after 1961, people were allowed to leave with only five dollars and thirty pounds of luggage each.[3] In addition to all these practical hurdles were the emotional ones. Could they really leave their country? When would they see their family again? Would they ever be able to return? For many who left, the moment of departure remained vividly etched in memory. Everyone remembers the airport. After saying good-bye to family, travelers waited in a glass-enclosed room dubbed the *pecera*, or the fishbowl. From inside they could see their relatives on the other side, pushing up against the glass, communicating by signs. Women wore sunglasses to hide puffy, red eyes. A teenager later recalled seeing grown men cry for the first time. A six-year-old boy watched customs officials tear up his father's graduation diploma from the University of Havana. A young grandmother remembered the humiliation of being searched too thoroughly, having personal items rifled through, being made to disrobe, seeing babies in diapers checked for hidden jewelry. A mother, my mother, recalls a young woman in uniform feeling the soft skin of her baby's earlobes, trying to decide whether to confiscate the tiny gold posts, and then leaving them be. When travelers boarded the planes, the silence was heavy and somber. Some cried quietly, and as the planes took off, sometimes the passengers applauded.[4]

AT THE VERY BEGINNING, THE people leaving were those most closely allied to Batista. Then, as the new government began expropriating property and reducing rent income, many of those who were adversely affected bought tickets to Miami. As the revolution radicalized, others opted to leave as well. By the time they arrived in Florida, most hated Fidel Castro. But many had not started out that way. In a 1962 survey conducted in Miami, 22 percent of respondents confessed to having originally viewed Fidel as Cuba's savior. The number was likely higher, as few would have been eager to admit that view in Miami then. In fact, the city was full of people who had participated in one way or another in the struggle against Batista, whether in Castro's 26th of July Movement or in other groups. The revolutionary government's first prime minister moved to Miami when he resigned, as did its first finance minister, among others.

Professionals and businessmen also left in droves. Of 6,000 doctors in Cuba in 1959, about half left for the United States. So did over 700 dentists out of almost 2,000, and 270 agronomists out of 300. In 1961, more than two-thirds of the 1959 faculty at the University of Havana was living in Miami, and the senior medical faculty had shrunk from 200 to 17. These early Cuban exiles generally had much higher education levels than the Cuban population as a whole; 36 percent had at least some college education, while only about 4 percent had that among the Cuban population generally. Only 4 percent of early exiles had less than a fourth-grade education, whereas 52 percent of the Cuban population did. In Cuba, their departure helped create massive opportunities for upward mobility for those who stayed and who were trained for those jobs by the new government. In the United States, meanwhile, the exiles could rely on their significant cultural capital—education, connections, sometimes even English. Little wonder, then, that these early transplants were later dubbed the "golden exiles."

On arriving in Miami, however, they could not usually exercise their professions. To survive, medical doctors took jobs as hospital orderlies; architects worked as gardeners, teachers as janitors, pharmacists as milkmen. People who had lived in palatial homes in posh Vedado or Miramar (in Havana) or Vista Alegre (in Santiago) now squeezed into small apartments in a down-and-out neighborhood soon to be known as Little Havana. It was there that the changes wrought by Cubans in Miami were first felt. The neighborhood had been declining for years, which made it affordable for Cubans arriving with little. Rents were cheap, and it was close to downtown and its job opportunities. School enrollments soared, and the neighborhood high school became the largest in the state almost overnight. "Alphabetizing 300 Gonzaleses can be tedious," complained the Anglo editor of its yearbook. Small Cuban-owned businesses gradually began opening—cafeterias, photography studios, jewelry stores, usually with the same names they had had in Cuba.[5]

Not everyone welcomed Cubans to Miami. Anglo Miamians wrote letters to editors complaining about their new neighbors. Apartment buildings began posting signs that read, "No Children, No Pets, No Cubans." Merchants complained that Cubans only wanted to do business with other Cubans. "It's unbelievable how the Cubans could push out the Americans" so quickly, remarked one. That phenomenon was not limited to business. The garment sector's labor force went from 94 percent to just 18 percent non-Hispanic white in less than ten years, the difference due almost entirely to newly arrived Cubans.[6]

Perhaps no one felt as pushed out by the Cuban arrivals as brusquely as Black Miamians. Little Havana sat across the Miami River from Overtown, the city's historic Black neighborhood since the 1890s. Miami belonged to the Jim

Crow South. And as African Americans watched Cubans ensconce themselves there, they noted all kinds of contradictions. At a time and place in which racial segregation was rampant, they observed how almost all Cubans—often no matter their skin color—became white. Sometimes it happened at the very moment of arrival. When they registered at the refugee center downtown, people received hotel vouchers if they needed them. Almost all but the very darkest refugees received vouchers for white hotels. Miami beaches were just as segregated. Some were restricted to whites, others to Blacks, "but Cubans may use either beach," reported *Look* magazine in April 1959. Cuban children—almost no matter their complexion—were allowed to go to white public schools, which were invariably better resourced than their Black counterparts. In 1961, a local Black minister speculated that African Americans in Miami could solve the problem of school segregation simply by teaching their children to speak only Spanish. Such observations aside, Black leaders consistently emphasized that their problem was not with the new arrivals themselves, but with the preferential treatment given them by the government. As the head of Miami's Urban League insisted, "We're not angry at the Cubans, but at a system that will do more for outsiders than for its own citizens."[7]

The Cubans, however, were not just any outsiders. They were outsiders fleeing communism at the height of the Cold War. And that made the refugees an asset. They might be willing recruits for Washington's anti-Castro projects; at the very least, their arrival in large numbers helped tarnish the image of the revolution before the world. Accordingly, the Immigration and Naturalization Service gave Cubans temporary legal status. Then, near the end of his term, Eisenhower established the Cuban Refugee Emergency Center to coordinate relief to Cuban arrivals. The program, renamed and expanded by Kennedy, gave Cubans access to all kinds of resources: work permits, job training, English classes, small loans, subsidized child care, housing assistance, and job referrals.[8]

Access to those benefits allowed Cubans to work for lower wages than others—sometimes for as little as half the wage garnered by their Black counterparts. One report estimated that between 1959 and 1962, twelve thousand African Americans lost jobs to Cubans. Sometimes it was the US government itself that gave the Cubans employment. In the early 1960s, the CIA had twelve thousand Cubans on its payroll, making it one of the largest employers in the state of Florida. In fact, the CIA's largest station in the world (outside its headquarters in Langley, Virginia) was located in Miami. The agency also controlled more than fifty front businesses, a large number of them in Little Havana. These were CIA-owned, Cuban-exile-run travel agencies, gun shops, real estate offices, and the like. Such ventures "helped exiles hone their entrepreneurial skills and boosted them economically," though they did nothing to topple Castro.[9] It was assistance from the US government, not only cultural capital or up-by-the-bootstraps determination, that made the early exiles golden.

JUST A FEW YEARS INTO the revolution, Cubans—with their yearning for return, their hatred of Fidel Castro, and the support of the US government—were on their way to completely transforming a major American city. Miami, however, could not have become what it became without another, lesser-known influx of Cubans. This new wave of refugees followed a relative dry spell after the Missile Crisis, when commercial flights between the two countries were permanently suspended. After the Missile Crisis, Cubans who wished to travel to the United States had to do so by other means. Some left through third countries such as Mexico or Spain. Others—more every year—undertook risky, illegal sea voyages to Florida. In 1964 and 1965, US newspapers routinely carried stories about Cubans leaving by boat. The *New York Times*, for instance, reported the dramatic escape of a Castro family chauffeur, who left with almost one hundred others.[10]

The departures and the negative publicity they garnered irked Castro. But his response was completely unexpected. During a speech on September 28, 1965, he announced that his government would allow Cubans in the United States to sail to the port of Camarioca, a small fishing village on the island's northern coast, and pick up relatives who wanted to leave Cuba for the United States. "Now let us see what the imperialists do or say."[11]

Castro's announcement coincided with passage of the Immigration and Nationality Act of 1965, which phased out the system of national quotas for immigration to the United States and which Lyndon Johnson signed into law at the foot of the Statue of Liberty on October 3. In his speech for the occasion, Johnson gave Castro his answer: "I declare this afternoon to the people of Cuba that those who seek refuge here in America will find it." Cubans in Miami went into action even before Johnson's announcement, withdrawing their savings, renting boats, cabling relatives in Cuba. By late November, the Camarioca boatlift had brought some three thousand Cubans to Florida's shores, and more were waiting to be picked up.[12]

Neither government was happy with the arrangement. Fidel was embarrassed by the publicity. The Americans worried that the unorthodox and disorderly means of migration made it difficult to control who was coming into the United States. The boatlift also posed obvious dangers to the migrants: the Coast Guard had already rescued dozens of vessels in distress. For those reasons, the two governments agreed to suspend the boatlift and begin an airlift in its stead. The Freedom Flights, as they were called in the United States, began on December 1, 1965. Two flights a day made the quick trip from the beach resort of Varadero, Matanzas, to Miami. Every day, Cuban radio in Miami broadcast the names of arrivals. By 1973, 3,048 flights had brought almost 300,000 Cubans to the United States. For decades it would remain the largest wave of Cuban migration to the United States.[13]

The Freedom Flight migrants were significantly different than the "golden exiles" who had come before. The US government granted entry primarily to relatives of Cubans already living in the United States. The Cuban government, meanwhile, refused exit visas to men of military age; it also expedited those visas for the elderly. These two things together meant that the new wave of migrants was significantly more female and significantly older than the first wave. Many were the parents of the young professionals who had left in the first three years of the revolution. If the earlier arrivals were christened golden exiles, we might call these the silver ones.

The character of this exile wave was shaped, too, by other policies pursued by the Cuban government. In 1968, Castro's Revolutionary Offensive targeted small-scale urban commercial property, and many of their former owners left soon after. Small entrepreneurs were thus well represented among the Freedom Flight arrivals. It was also in this wave that the island lost a substantial proportion of its Chinese and Jewish communities, who were well represented among small business owners in Cuba.[14]

With so many Cubans once more arriving in Miami and taxing the city's resources, the federal government provided incentives for them to settle elsewhere. Many Cuban-Chinese refugees settled in New York, explaining why the 1970s saw a proliferation of Cuban-Chinese restaurants in that city and not in Miami. It was also in this period that Cuban immigrant communities in northern New Jersey grew most dramatically. Yet despite the government's efforts at resettlement, roughly half of the new Cuban arrivals stayed in Miami, and others returned to the city after experiencing winter up north.[15]

In many ways, the Freedom Flight migrants guaranteed that Miami would become a Cuban city. Indeed, it was in this period that Little Havana became Little Havana, with 85 percent of its residents hailing from the island. It became a classic "stepping-stone" neighborhood. Cubans who had arrived earlier moved away, dispersing Cuba to other parts of the city. And the newly arrived took their place in Little Havana. Many of Miami's famous Cuban businesses—iconic places like the Versailles restaurant, where Cuban exiles have for decades protested visits by island Cubans or celebrated events like the death of Fidel Castro—opened precisely in this period. In 1968, WMIE radio became WQBA. If the letters—Q-B-A—didn't alert one to its programing focus, its other name did: "La Cubanísima." It broadcast in Cuban Spanish all day, and by 1976, its signature news show boasted the largest audience of any Miami radio program, English or Spanish.[16]

Together, the Freedom Flight migrants and the earlier golden exiles made Miami of the 1960s and early 1970s not only a Cuban American city, but also a kind of alternate universe. It was an enclave of legal permanent residents and citizens yearning to return home, a haven for conformists to a world that no longer existed, a politically riven place where arguments from Havana in 1959 never ended, an antirevolutionary community strewn with onetime revolutionaries, a place steeped in counterrevolution rather than counterculture, an abstrusely triracial city in a stubbornly biracial nation, a world where a minority was the de facto majority and where clerks always asked in Spanish if customers preferred English.

The US government, meanwhile, continued to confer favors on Cubans leaving Cuba. In 1966, it adjusted their immigration status, so that they could apply for legal residency after just two years. Thus were Cubans fast-tracked to citizenship and voting rights—at a time when the struggle of African Americans for that same right had only just resulted in the 1965 Voting Rights Act. Though the Cuban Adjustment Act passed in 1966, its provisions applied to all Cubans who had arrived in the United States after January 1, 1959, and it would be applied indefinitely going forward. Later amendments further exempted Cubans from having to show that they had jobs or family waiting in the United States or that they would not become public charges. The government also reduced by half the amount of time Cubans had to wait to apply for residency (to a year and a day). No other immigrants from Latin America had these advantages conferred on them on arrival. Clearly, immigration policy continued to be Cold War policy.[17]

Yet the relationship between US-government Cold Warriors and Cuban American hawks was never straightforward. In the case of the Bay of Pigs, Cuban exiles had done the US government's bidding. But they had done so in large part because the goal of removing Castro from power was their goal as well. That failure soured the relationship between Washington and exile militants; Kennedy's 1962 promise to Khrushchev not to invade Cuba angered them as well. By 1970, the exile community was becoming increasingly allied with the Republican Party. Conservative Cuban Americans, among them a Bay of Pigs veteran, were even among the Watergate burglars doing Nixon's dirty work.

By the mid-1970s, however, a subset of Cuban American conservatives was pursuing anti-Castro projects by purposefully defying the US government. As Washington and Moscow pursued détente, conservative exiles worried that Cuba policy, too, would begin to focus on coexistence. In fact, President Jimmy Carter issued a directive to his National Security Council to begin confidential talks with Cuba for the purpose of "normalizing" relations between the two governments. Even without knowledge of that move, militant sectors of the exile community were permanently mobilized against any kind of rapprochement with Cuba. In 1974, some veterans of the Bay of Pigs founded a new group, Omega-7, willing to use violence and to assassinate Cuban communists and those in the United States who negotiated with them. While it was not the only anti-Castro group, the FBI considered it "the top domestic terrorist organization operating in the United States." It was active in Miami, New York, and New Jersey. Omega-7 and other like-minded groups appear to have been responsible for more than one hundred bombings in Miami alone in 1974–75. In New York, anti-Castro exiles set bombs at the Cuban mission to the UN, the TWA terminal at JFK, and Avery Fisher Hall, all associated with overtures of one kind or another to the Cuban government.[18] Even as many Cuban exiles were becoming American immigrants, the first impetus for the community's existence—the Cuban Revolution—was never far from view.

AND, IF IN THE COURSE of trying to make it in America, Cubans forgot what had brought them there to begin with, Fidel Castro could always be counted on to remind them. He did that in the most unforeseen manner in September 1978, when he publicly invited Cubans in the United States to travel to Cuba to meet and talk with him personally. If they came, he would free as many as three thousand political prisoners. He would also consider allowing Cuban Americans to return to the island to visit their families—something they had not been allowed to do since they left. When someone asked him what accounted for his change of heart toward the exiles, he responded, "The revolution will be twenty years old soon. From our point of view, it is absolutely consolidated and irreversible. We know it, the government of the United States knows it, and I think that the Cuban community abroad knows it, too." The passage of a socialist constitution in

1976 (to replace the 1940 one) and the creation of a legislature called the National Assembly of People's Power the same year had given the revolution and the one-party state a stability difficult to deny. And from that position of power, Castro extended an invitation to his habitual foes. [19]

The invitation stunned Miami. Many insisted that it was some kind of trap and that negotiating with Castro was to recognize his legitimacy, to grant him even more authority. Thirty exile organizations, including the veterans of the Bay of Pigs, publicly and vehemently repudiated the meetings. But that was far from the only view. In fact, Cuban Americans flooded Cuban government offices with telegrams volunteering for the meetings in Havana. Castro had final say on who participated. Some were academics; some were young Cuban Americans who had already been traveling to Cuba and building ties to the Cuban government for years; a few were Bay of Pigs veterans who had renounced their old position and now favored negotiation with Castro. Seventy-five Cuban exiles traveled to Havana that fall to meet with Fidel and participate in what everyone was referring to as "the dialogue." A larger group returned for a second set of meetings. The hard-liners fumed. One exile paper (published in Puerto Rico, but widely circulated in Miami) printed the names and home addresses of those who had traveled to Cuba and urged readers to harass them. Critics of the talks bombed Miami's Continental Bank, because its president, Bernardo Benes, was a big proponent of the dialogue, having traveled to Cuba fourteen times in 1978. They also boycotted Miami's main cigar company because its owner was photographed offering Castro one of his cigars. Still, while almost the entire community loved to lambaste Fidel, most cheered when political prisoners began arriving in Miami as a result of the negotiations. And while most cursed Castro, when he announced that Cubans abroad could visit the island, throngs rushed to take advantage of the opportunity to return home for the first time since their exile began. Political ideology was one thing, family devotion another. [20]

The family reunification visits that began in 1979 constitute one of the most consequential yet overlooked events in the history of the Cuban Revolution. Over a hundred thousand Cubans living in the United States made trips back to the island in the first year, laden with gifts, cash, and affection. Travelers paid heftily to renew their Cuban passports; they rushed to complete their US residency paperwork so they could reenter the United States without any trouble. They were going to Cuba, but whatever fantasies they might have once harbored about a return, they knew their stays would last just a week, the limit imposed on the visits by the Cuban government. [21]

They filled those one-week stays with as much as possible. They walked around their old neighborhoods, giving little gifts to old acquaintances, five dollars here, a bottle of nail polish there. They won over grandchildren with new blue jeans and daughters-in-law with modern Hitachi rice cookers. (The Family Code notwithstanding, it was women who did most of the cooking in Cuba.) Families made outings to special stores opened just for the visitors, stores with shelves full of food unavailable in Cuban bodegas or in Cuban currency. But mostly, the visitors soaked up the nearness of loved ones. So, too, did their Cuban family.[22]

Cubans then resident on the island remember the visits vividly. For almost two decades, Castro had referred to those who left Cuba in the most derogatory terms imaginable—scum, worms, traitors, mobsters, lackeys of imperialism. Now the government welcomed those people back as members of the "Cuban community abroad." For younger people—those who had come of age with the revolution—the encounters were initially perplexing. The confusion derived less from the government's sudden change in tone than from the fact that the people now before them seemed so normal, so Cuban. A fifteen-year-old at the time recalled her neighbor's visiting cousins. "They weren't at all what I expected . . . they were people just like us." For the parents of those teenagers, the reencounters with relatives who had left were joyful and poignant. People embraced and cried on seeing loved ones after separations of one or two decades. But the doctor who belonged to the Cuban Communist Party likely chafed a little at his Miami sister's purchasing power, as he pondered the overflowing bags of groceries laid out in his spare kitchen. He might have wondered, too, about friends without family abroad—a demographic that would have skewed Black—and the fact that they would have no access to this infusion of cash and goods.[23]

In the loaded encounters between Cubans from abroad and Cubans from the island, the latter were often left wondering. Why was the government offering those who had left what they who had stayed—and done voluntary labor, or cheered at rallies, or joined CDRs—had never had? Cubans played with words to make sense of the conundrum. The *gusanos* (worms) had returned as butterflies, they joked. The *traidores* (traitors) were really just *traedolares* (dollar bringers). It wasn't just that those who left seemed to be leading more prosperous lives than those who stayed. It was also that the government showed itself publicly in a light no one had ever seen. Either the government had lied when it called the exiles traitors, or the government was subordinating that belief to the need for hard cash. In fact, the trips were a great moneymaker for the Cuban state. Between the special stores and the fees charged for passports and visas and the requirement that returnees purchase all-inclusive tourist packages (even though they were staying with and eating with family), the government stood to make almost $150 million in the first year of the visits, predicted analysts.[24]

Yet the Cuban government paid a huge and unexpected price for family reunification. The visits raised issues and comparisons that the government would have preferred to avoid. It didn't help that the visitors' "demonstration effect" coincided with an economic downturn. During a speech in late 1979, Fidel ruminated that the country was in a sea of difficulties and that it would continue to be for some time. "The shore is far away," he lamented.[25] It was not the first time Fidel had said something like that, nor would it be the last. In the context of the family reunification visits, however, the words raised more doubts. Why was it that those who had left seemed untroubled by the storms? When would they, who had stayed, get to glimpse the shore? Could it be that they should leave, too?

THEN ON APRIL 1, 1980, a full-fledged crisis brought those difficult questions to the fore. That day, six Cubans stole a city bus, crashed it through the gates of the Peruvian embassy, and requested asylum. Located on embassy row in Havana's toney Miramar district, Peru's embassy, like all the embassies there, had Cuban guards around the perimeter. When the bus crashed the gates, the guards opened fire, and one guard accidentally killed another. The Cuban government demanded that the embassy return the gate crashers to its authority, but the ambassador refused, citing the rule of inviolability. That was when Fidel surprised everyone. He announced that the Cuban government would no longer protect foreign embassies that did not cooperate with it. The next morning, the Peruvian embassy staff awoke to the sound of bulldozers demolishing the sentry boxes at the main gate and removing the large boulders blocking the driveway. Then the Cuban guards abandoned their posts. The embassy now stood completely open and unprotected. The ambassador was sure that Cuban forces were about to storm the embassy and remove the Cuban asylum seekers by force. He was mistaken. Instead, the Cuban government did nothing.[26]

As people learned that the government would not prevent people from entering the grounds, hundreds began heading there. Buses whose routes went by the embassy became fuller and fuller at each stop. Riders did not chat and joke as usual; they rode in silence. Then at the stop closest to the embassy, everyone got off and began walking in the same direction. Some bus drivers left their hats and credentials on the steering wheel and followed the subdued procession of passengers. By nightfall, there were thousands of Cubans on embassy grounds, all seeking asylum, all wanting to leave Cuba.[27]

Now it was Fidel's turn to be surprised. He had expected some to respond to the opening of the embassy, but not so many in so little time. Embarrassed at how very quickly the embassy filled to capacity, he ordered its perimeter sealed to prevent anyone else from entering. But by that point, just forty-eight hours after the embassy had been left unprotected, about 10,800 Cubans had already entered. There were so many people that some sat on tree branches and the roofs of buildings in the compound. There were not enough bathrooms, not enough food, not enough room to lie down to sleep. Two babies were born, and an old woman died. The situation was so precarious that the Cuban government started issuing safe-conduct passes. People who took them were promised that they would be able to leave the country, but they could wait at home until a means of exit was resolved. Some were desperate for food or peace and accepted the offer; others worried that leaving the embassy diminished their chances of leaving Cuba and opted to hunker down in place.

By then, the question on many minds was how 10,800 people would ever get out of the Peruvian embassy and out of the country. Several nations offered to take some of the refugees; Jimmy Carter decided that the United States would accept 3,500 of them. Costa Rica agreed to serve as a staging ground for screening the US-bound migrants, and on April 16 began sending planes to pick up asylum seekers. But when footage showed Cubans landing in Costa Rica, kissing the ground, shouting liberty, and cursing Fidel, the Cuban government suspended the flights. On April 19, it organized a million-person march down Miramar's Fifth Avenue, and crowds outside the Peruvian embassy yelled epithets at the people inside, shouting at them to leave the country. But no one had any idea how that departure would actually happen.[28]

In Miami, Cubans mobilized. They collected food, clothes, and other supplies for the people in the embassy. Some—a smaller group—cleaned out army supply stores, imagining that the crisis spelled the end of Castro's rule and that they might get to go back and fight against him. A man named Napoleón Vilaboa mobilized differently. A onetime Havana radio show host who had denounced Fulgencio Batista every week on-air, he had eagerly supported Fidel's revolution. But in 1960, horrified by what he saw as the burgeoning influence of communism, he left. In 1961, he participated in the Bay of Pigs invasion. By the time the embassy crisis began in April 1980, Vilaboa was a car salesman in Miami and had abandoned the hard, combative line he had followed body and soul in the early 1960s. He was part of the Miami delegation that traveled to Havana in 1978 for the dialogue with Fidel. He also happened to be in Havana when Cubans stormed the Peruvian embassy. He visited them there and confirmed what many suspected: the asylum seekers did not want to go to Peru. They wanted to go to Miami.[29]

By Vilaboa's own account, he made a proposal to the Cuban government. Allow Cuban Americans to sail to a designated port to pick up their relatives, provided they also took some of the people from the embassy. Castro liked the idea and settled on the port of Mariel, about 25 miles west of Havana and roughly 125 miles almost directly south of Key West. Vilaboa returned to Miami determined to set the boatlift in motion. On April 17, he spoke on a popular news show on WQBA and explained the plan. Some thought he was playing right into Fidel's hands. But a sizable group, eager to bring their relatives from Cuba, set all qualms aside and began preparations. Within hours, they were withdrawing savings, borrowing money, and looking for boats and captains to take them to Cuba to pick up their people. Many did not know how to swim, but that was no obstacle. Vilaboa himself was the first to go, as captain of his forty-one-foot yacht named *Ochún*, the Afro-Cuban deity of love and fresh water, syncretized always with Cuba's patron saint, the Caridad del Cobre. The first to make the journey, *Ochún* was also among the first to return to Florida with Cuban refugees on April 21, 1980. The Coast Guard captain on duty barely noted the arrival. After all, occasional boats with people leaving Cuba had been arriving in Key West for years. It would not take long for him to realize that *Ochún's* arrival was the beginning of something quite out of the ordinary.[30]

More boats came every day, almost every hour. Within days, there were thousands of boats between Key West and the port of Mariel in Cuba. One observer remarked that if someone could line up all the boats one behind the other, their relatives would be able to walk to Florida. Two months after that first arrival on April 21, the number of Cubans who had disembarked on Florida shores—113,969—roughly equaled one-third of the city of Miami's total population at the time.[31]

MOVEMENT ON THAT SCALE IS necessarily disruptive; in this case, it was chaotic and often heart-wrenching. That this was a seaborne migration at the start of a tempestuous season did not help. Tornados and storms hit the Florida Keys multiple times during the operation. On one stormy day (April 27), between ten and fifteen boats sank, but just ten refugees were rescued from the water.

On May 17, of fifty-two people aboard a yacht named the *Olo Yumi*, fourteen drowned, among them the entire family—mother, father, grandmother, and two sisters—of a young girl named Ibis Guerrero, who refused to shed a tear at the funeral in Key West. "So many people have already died," she told a *Miami Herald* reporter.[32]

In Mariel, Cuban Americans who arrived to pick up their relatives saw a scene almost beyond belief. In the harbor, hundreds of boats jockeyed for position. New arrivals tied their vessels to others already there. Cuban government boats patrolled the waters, and every hundred yards on the shore, a Cuban guard trained an AK-47 on the boats in the harbor. At night, floodlights illuminated everything, the evening air alive with sounds from the floating nightclub opened by the government to entice the waiting captains and crew. In this unnerving setting, each captain handed authorities a list of the Cubans he sought to pick up. When Cuban authorities received the lists, they checked to make sure there were no especially prominent people or others with highly technical skills. Officials then notified the relatives claimed by the captains.[33]

Officials, however, did more than notify the people who were leaving. They also informed the local Committees for the Defense of the Revolution. The CDRs then organized public repudiations of those seeking to depart. Crowds would show up in front of their houses, hurling epithets, stones, and eggs at those leaving. They called them scum, traitors, criminals, worms, and worse, all of it with the government's encouragement and approval. On the surface, the island seemed to divide between those leaving and those staying, but almost everyone in each category knew—and sometimes loved—people in the other. Many Cubans who publicly repudiated departing neighbors themselves left later. In fact, Miami is full of people who participated in acts of repudiation. One Miamian who left through Mariel recalled years later running into the person who had organized the act of repudiation against him and who now asked for his forgiveness. He granted it. Whether in Cuba or Miami, real life was too messy for the labels deployed in that moment.[34]

Part of what made everything so chaotic was that many more Cubans were leaving than either the Cuban or US governments ever expected. Very shortly after it started, the boatlift began to include people who had never been in the Peruvian embassy and who did not have family picking them up on boats. That was evident at the port. The *Sundance II*, a sixty-five-foot boat arrived at Mariel on April 24 with fewer than one hundred Cuban Americans going to pick up family;

it departed almost a month later with about three hundred passengers. Only about ten of those passengers were the relatives it had come to retrieve.[35]

Who were all those passengers? From the first days of the boatlift, the Cuban government labeled people seeking to leave as "social misfits."[36] Soon Cubans began appearing at police stations calling themselves that and requesting permission to leave the country on that basis. Social misfit, however, could be a capacious category. And the means by which authorities made the judgment of who qualified was not at all transparent. Living in Miami years later, a former police officer remembered how people showed up at his station asking for permission to leave. Few had proof of anything, so he just let the "bad ones" leave. Years later, more familiar with such concepts as implicit bias, he was evasive on how exactly he made those decisions. Sometimes people went to the police and pretended to be gay, which also served as a reason for the granting of an exit visa. In fact, many Cuban gays left during the boatlift, among them the renowned Cuban writer Reinaldo Arenas. At the police station, an officer asked if he was "homosexual." When he answered in the affirmative, he was asked to elaborate: Was he "active or passive?" Having heard that responding "active" could be grounds for denial, he answered "passive." The officers also made him walk in front of them. "I passed the test," he recalled. He left aboard the *San Lázaro* on May 4. Ten years later, dying of AIDS in New York, he committed suicide.[37]

The Cuban government also forced people to leave. One man, on parole in Havana, was picked up by police, put on a departing boat, and later relayed the story over Miami radio. Meanwhile, a *Miami News* photographer who had traveled to Mariel to cover the story reported that Cuban passengers on his return voyage had told him that the government was taking prisoners out of jail and putting them aboard the vessels heading to Miami from Mariel. Other rumors suggested that the Cuban government was expelling psychiatric patients. The truth was more complicated than that. An estimated 1,500 people (of a total migration of about 125,000) had mental health or cognition problems. One scholar estimates that perhaps 26,000 had criminal records. But Cuban law criminalized alcoholism, homosexuality, drug addiction, vagrancy, political dissidence, and participation in an ever-present black market.[38]

That the Cuban government was eager to let such people leave was no guarantee that the United States would allow them to stay. Having any kind of criminal record—violent or not, petty or grand—was grounds for exclusion from the United States. So was having "mental defect" of any kind. Because the US government considered homosexuality to be evidence of psychopathic personality, that, too, was grounds for exclusion. Ultimately, 2,746 Mariel arrivals were deemed to be "excludable" from the United States by virtue of either criminal records or mental health issues. They were never released, and many were returned to Cuba, but, in most cases, after decades of detention in the United States.[39]

However small those numbers, observers were correct that the Mariel exodus was unlike the earlier waves of migration from revolutionary Cuba. This wave of refugees was neither overwhelmingly white nor mostly upper and middle class, as the first wave had been. It was not overwhelmingly white, female, and aged, as the Freedom Flights wave was. This new Cuban exodus was poorer than any that had come before. It was also blacker—between 15 and 40 percent Afro-Cuban, compared to just 3 percent among Cubans who had arrived between 1959 and 1973. One former resident of Little Havana later recalled one way in which the Mariel exodus recalibrated his sense of self and place: "We had invented a Cuba in which everyone was white. When the Marielitos came, we were forcibly reminded that Cuba is not a white island but largely a black one."[40] The new arrivals were, simply put, a cross section of Cuban society.

But that seemed not to matter to those seeing and judging the Marielitos. Increasingly, people in the United States talked about them in terms that echoed those used by the Cuban government: incorrigibles, criminals, failures, undesirables, and so on. "Retarded People and Criminals Are Included in the Cuban Exodus," blared the front page of the New York Times on May 11. The hometown Miami Herald was even more critical. By the middle of May, about 90 percent of its coverage cast a negative light on the new Cuban arrivals.[41]

And the more Marielitos arrived, the more negative the coverage became. In one hour on one night (April 29–30), three thousand Cubans arrived in Key West. Improvising on the edge of calamity, a state official gave the National Guard $10,000 in vouchers to purchase every candy bar and carton of cigarettes on the island. May 11—the same day that the New York Times published its story about "retarded people and criminals"—broke all previous records, depositing just under five thousand Cubans in Key West. As many as seven hundred arrived in just one boat—the three-deck, 120-foot catamaran called America.[42]

Key West was overwhelmed; Miami was as well. Monroe and Dade Counties were under a state of emergency order. Unable to process all the arrivals in Key West, the government opened multiple processing centers in Miami. Krome, a defunct missile base on the edge of the Everglades built in 1965 to protect the United States from a Cuban attack, was repurposed to process the arrivals. (It remains today an immigrant detention center.) But even that was not enough.

Eventually, arrivals not yet claimed by family members or other sponsors were housed in a makeshift camp at the bleachers and parking lots of the Orange Bowl. Others were placed in a tent city, hastily erected on an old baseball field under the Interstate 95 overpass, between Little Havana and Overtown, where it remained for many months. And still, that was insufficient.[43]

Unable to handle all the arrivals in Key West and Miami, the federal government established processing centers in military bases as far away as Wisconsin and Arkansas. More than sixty thousand of the Mariel immigrants were housed at these camps while the government determined what to do with them. Some were there for just days, as they waited to be cleared for entry and for family to find them. Many others—without family or of uncertain admissability—waited for much longer. It was quite a welcome to America. Outside the Eglin Air Force Base, on the Florida panhandle, the Ku Klux Klan staged a protest and hired a plane to circle the base flying their banner. As the base quickly reached maximum capacity, even residents not associated with the KKK protested against the presence of Cubans in their area. Frustrated by delays in processing and by curfews imposed on them, Cuban detainees staged a hunger strike, jumped the fences, and threw bricks and stones.[44]

In Fort Chaffee in Arkansas, the situation grew even more desperate. As processing continued to drag on, some of the Cubans managed to escape from the base. On May 29, a large group advanced on the gate, and guards forced them back in a tense confrontation. Three days later, about one thousand Cubans rose up. They burned several buildings, and forty Cubans and fourteen policemen were injured. The citizens of Barling, home to the base, began arming themselves in anticipation of a Cuban refugee invasion. The beleaguered governor, Bill Clinton, secured a promise from Washington to not send any more Cubans to his state. But it was too little too late. Clinton, then running for reelection, later blamed the Cuban crisis at Fort Chaffee for his defeat in that fall's race. Across the country, officeholders announced their refusal to accept any Mariel migrants. The Cubans had outworn their welcome.[45]

As the boatlift wore on—as the numbers soared, as grossly exaggerated stories of the arrivals' provenance in Cuban jails and mental hospitals took flight, as tent cities teemed and violence erupted—even Miami rescinded its welcome. In Dade County, which had been officially designated as bilingual in 1973, a group of Anglo citizens introduced a successful ballot measure in county elections prohibiting "the expenditure of county funds for the purpose of utilizing any language other than English, or promoting any culture other than that of the United States."

All county meetings, the ordinance read, "shall be in the English language only." It was about this time that bumper stickers appeared reading, "Will the last American to leave Miami please take the flag?"[46]

Resentment among African Americans in Miami, present since the early 1960s, escalated, too. When on May 17, an all-white jury in Tampa acquitted four Dade County police officers in the fatal shooting of Arthur McDuffie, an unarmed, thirty-three-year-old, Black insurance agent, residents of Overtown and Liberty City, the city's historic Black neighborhoods, rose up in repudiation of the verdict. The unrest lasted for four days and left eighteen dead or fatally injured. At the time, the incident was also seen as an expression of African American frustration and discontent over the favorable treatment proffered to Cubans and never to them.[47]

Among Cuban Miamians, too, the exodus created a backlash. Even the name used to identify the refugees—*marielitos*—was coined as pejorative. These new Cubans, the old exiles said, were different than them. They had lived and chosen to stay in communist Cuba for many years before this. That alone made them suspect. They would change Miami; they would change the community. In that, they were correct. The Mariel migration did change Miami and its Cuban community. For a time, it divided Miami into old Cubans and new Cubans, defined not by age, but by year of arrival. It made the Cuban community more diverse in terms of race and class, closer to—if still whiter than—the demographic makeup of the island itself. If by 1980, with migration stalled for years, the community had become more Cuban American, more immigrant than exile, the new exodus provided an infusion of Cuban Cubans, children of Castro's revolution, tired of politics and its obligatory slogans, and eager to make new lives unconstrained by them.

The problem was that Cuban American Miami was not ready to give up its slogans. If anything, the boatlift occurred at the exact moment that Cuban Americans were beginning to flex their political muscle. By the time the Mariel refugees arrived, the earlier waves of Cuban Americans were already citizens, and they voted. In 1981, with encouragement from the administration of newly elected president Ronald Reagan, they even created a powerful lobbying group called the Cuban American National Foundation. Thus began the pattern by which aspiring presidents railed against Fidel Castro to win Cuban votes in the inevitable swing state of Florida.[48]

NEW AMERICANS?

BEFORE THE MARIEL BOATLIFT, AS after, Miami continued to be defined as much by its intense relation to Cuba as its relation to the rest of the United States. As many people who know Cuba and Miami well have observed, each is a peculiar mirror of the other. Pulitzer Prize–winning journalist Mirta Ojito, who arrived in Key West as a teenager on May 11, 1980, aboard the *Mañana*, remembers coming above deck and getting her first view of the United States: "I began to hear familiar loud cheers of 'Viva Cuba Libre.' Men and women stood behind a wire fence shouting 'Long live Cuba' until they were hoarse. Another group sang the Cuban national anthem in an endless loop. Yet others hurled slogans aimed at Fidel Castro: '!Abajo Fidel! Death to the tyrant!' I wanted to cry. This is why I had left Cuba, I thought, so that I would never again have to hear another slogan. . . ."[49] She was listening to an uncanny echo, peering through a distorted looking glass.

But that feeling—Miami's cognitive dissonance, as Joan Didion once called it—was not always sinister. Sometimes it was just about family and survival, longing and attachment. So, a young girl in Cuba grows up in a home with a special drawer filled with nice clothes given to her family by relatives in the United States. They were clothes, pressed and never worn, waiting for the day the family would fly to its exile abroad. A young girl in Miami grows up in a home with another special drawer, also filled with nice clothes, pressed and saved, waiting to be sent to family in Cuba. In so many ways, big and small, each place depends on the other. But two facts are clear: it is impossible to understand the Cuban Revolution without understanding Miami, and it is impossible to understand Miami without understanding the Cuban Revolution.

Chapter 31

OTHER CUBAS?

In Lisbon, capital of the empire that at the dawn of the sixteenth century launched the world's transatlantic slave trade, young men from Portugal's African colonies made their home at a boardinghouse aptly called the Imperial Students' House. They gathered regularly to talk about the future of Africa. In the northern part of the continent, many former European colonies had recently gained their independence. In sub-Saharan Africa, too, independence was gaining ground. Beginning with Ghana in 1957, one colony after another saw the end of rule by England, France, and Belgium. But so far, independence had eluded Portuguese Africa. As the students in Lisbon pondered history's strange unfolding, they read widely, debated heatedly, and dreamed—sometimes cautiously, sometimes grandly—about their own independence. Among other things, they read Fidel Castro's "History Will Absolve Me," the speech he had given in his own defense during the Moncada trial in 1953. In 1959, the students followed from afar as Castro defeated Batista. In 1961, they watched as Castro's army roundly defeated a US-backed invasion. By 1962, they were secretly meeting with Cuban agents in Lisbon.[1]

Like the students in Lisbon, many around the Third World trained their eyes on Cuba and saw something noteworthy: a young government—bearded, informal, irreverent—challenging the greatest power on earth. Just as remarkable was what new Cuban leaders were saying to people such as themselves: there would be other Cubas, and Cuba would help bring them into being. In 1966, five hundred delegates from eighty-two countries gathered in Havana for the Tricontinental Conference of African, Asian, and Latin American Peoples. US officials called it "the most powerful gathering of pro-Communist, anti-American forces in the history of the Western hemisphere." At the closing session, Castro promised that revolutionary movements "in every corner of the world" would be able to count on Cuba. He also announced the creation of the Organization of Solidarity with the People of Asia, Africa, and Latin America (OSPAAAL) to serve as a bridge between revolutionary movements across the three continents.[2]

It was more than talk. Almost from the moment of taking power, Castro's government sought to encourage like-minded revolutions abroad. In 1959, it sponsored an unsuccessful invasion against Dominican dictator Rafael Trujillo. In 1961, it sent weapons to anticolonial rebels in Algeria; the ship that carried that equipment returned to Cuba with seventy-six wounded Algerian rebels and twenty children, most of them war orphans. In 1962, Cubans set up a military mission in newly independent Algeria, which, according to the US State Department, soon became "a congenial second home for traveling Cubans, and an all-important base for extending Cuban influence in Africa."[3]

In fact, Algeria, for a time, became Cuba's global base. US surveillance made it difficult for Havana directly to support revolution in Latin America, to send weapons or to infiltrate Cuban-trained military cadres back into Latin America. Algeria agreed to serve as a bridge between the island and South America. Cubans and Algerians jointly trained Argentine and Venezuelan recruits for guerrilla warfare. Argentines and Venezuelans training in Cuba, meanwhile, were sent back home circuitously through Algeria to avoid detection. Algeria thus helped Cuba extend its influence back across the Atlantic to Latin America.[4]

For Cuba, the decision to pursue such a foreign policy had several motivations. One was ideological. Decolonization in Africa was unfolding precisely as the Cuban Revolution gained strength, creating fertile ground for anticolonial and anti-imperialist solidarity. That some of Africa's newly independent governments were also leftist was another source of ideological kinship. In fact, two-thirds of African states had some kind of socialist government at some point between 1950 and 1990. In Latin America, Cuba pursued solidarity even more forcefully initially. Che Guevara, of course, was himself Argentinean. He had traveled extensively throughout the continent and developed a strong affinity for social revolution long before ever laying eyes on Fidel Castro in Mexico in 1955. His experience waging a successful guerrilla war in the mountains of Cuba had convinced him that revolution was possible in Latin America. Rather than wait for the conditions for revolution to emerge, he argued, revolutionary leaders could create those conditions by organizing rural guerrilla insurgency. Che's commitment—and the Cuban government's for much of the 1960s—was to create "a transcontinental, anti-imperialist revolutionary theater in Latin America." Indeed, Castro created an entity called the Americas Department to train and provide material support to Latin American revolutionaries. The Cuban Revolution was replicable and exportable. The Andes could be South America's Sierra Maestra.[5]

Whatever its ideological motivations, Cuban foreign policy was also another arena in which to challenge US interests. An activist foreign policy signaled Cuba's new international prestige, won in part by its defeat of the United States at the Bay of Pigs. A hostile United States pressured other countries to heed its stance on Cuba by, for example, prohibiting US-based transnational companies from doing business in Cuba or threatening to cut off aid to countries that traded with Cuba. But the more the United States tried to isolate Cuba internationally, the more Cuba sought connections with the rest of the world—and not just any connections. Fomenting revolution abroad—usually on the side opposite the Americans—was a powerful way to give substance to both its newfound role in the world and its deep-seated enmity with the United States. "They internationalized the blockade," recalled Castro years later. "We internationalized guerrilla warfare."[6]

Officials in Washington presumed that Cuba's international role was that of a Soviet proxy. But Cuban foreign policy was actually often at odds with Soviet wishes. "This Revolution," Castro said, "will follow its own line." Che publicly questioned Moscow's trade policies with the West, and Havana broke openly with the Soviets on the nuclear test ban treaty. Cuba's most significant dispute with the Soviets, however, was a broad, ideological one: the question of whether to promote revolution abroad. Moscow's position was one of peaceful coexistence with the West. Cuba's position begged to differ. Recall Che's famous dictum: "Two, three, many Vietnams."[7]

Still, Cuba was a small country, and there were all kinds of obstacles to pursuing the foreign policy of a big one. In the late 1960s, its internationalist stance suffered important setbacks. With the fall of Algerian president Ben Bella in 1965, Cuba lost an important ally. In 1967, Che Guevara was killed trying to make another Cuba in the mountains of Bolivia. Castro made the announcement on national television and declared three days of national mourning. With Guevara's death, Cuba lost its main proponent of a hemispheric revolution. As the island grew increasingly dependent on the Soviet Union, moreover, it lost some room to maneuver. When the Soviets invaded Czechoslovakia in 1968, Castro shocked everyone by publicly offering his approval. "Some of the things we are about to say are in some cases in conflict with the emotions of many," he conceded. "We accept the bitter necessity that required sending those troops into Czechoslovakia." Crucial economic support from the Soviets made it difficult for Cuba to actively pursue a foreign policy that openly contradicted that of its benefactor.[8]

At the same time, however, Soviet support gave Cuba the means to project its power abroad. It was in the 1970s, as that dependence grew stronger than ever, that Cuba pursued its most ambitious foreign interventions. One kind of intervention involved civilians. Cuba sent engineers, doctors, teachers, and other professionals to nearly forty countries around the world to take part in development projects of various kinds, to countries as close to Cuba as Jamaica and as far as Vietnam. The scale of this civilian internationalism was unprecedented. By the end of the 1980s, more than 110,000 Cubans served on international civilian missions. In the mid-1980s, Cuba had one government aid worker for every 625 inhabitants; the United States had one for almost every 35,000 inhabitants. Cuba's participation also dwarfed that of other countries in the socialist bloc. Cuba had only 2.5 percent of the bloc's population, yet it accounted for almost 20 percent of its aid workers. In a secret conversation with a prominent Cuban American in 1978–79, Fidel Castro kept returning to the subject of Cuba's international missions. He wanted to fill the world with Cuban doctors and nurses, he said; he wanted to leave Kennedy's Peace Corps in the dust. He wanted to charge ten dollars a head for the doctors, Castro mused. In fact, Cuba was already charging for the services of their civilians on a sliding scale, and by 1977, civilian internationalists generated an estimated $50 million in hard currency for the government.[9]

Cuba's civilian commitments abroad, however important, paled alongside its military ones. Its most consequential military intervention on foreign soil involved almost half a million Cubans. It fundamentally challenged Soviet foreign policy, put the country on a collision path with the United States, and helped change the course of history in Southern Africa.

TO TRACE THE ADVENTURE TO its immediate origins takes us briefly back to the Imperial Students' House in Lisbon, where young activists read Fidel Castro with delight. Many of those students belonged to the recently formed People's Movement for the Liberation of Angola, a Marxist group advocating Angolan independence. When the MPLA launched a guerrilla movement against Portugal in 1961, they saw Havana as a natural ally. Che met with the MPLA leaders to discuss support, and in 1966, when Havana hosted the Tricontinental Conference, the MPLA was the only Angolan organization invited.[10]

OTHER CUBAS?

The alliance would grow much stronger in the 1970s. In January 1975, Portugal agreed to end its rule of Angola officially on November 11. In the intervening months, the territory would be governed by a coalition composed of the three parties that had fought against Portuguese rule: the National Union for the Total Independence of Angola (UNITA), the National Liberation Front of Angola (FNLA), and the Cuban-allied MPLA. The coalition broke down almost immediately, and fighting resumed among the three contenders for power. According to one historian, more than thirty countries became indirectly involved in the Angolan conflict at that point, providing weapons, advisors, and funds to the different groups. Castro committed to sending 480 advisors for six months. The MPLA's rivals for power (UNITA and FNLA), meanwhile, had the support of South Africa. Indeed, South Africa committed part of its regular army to the fight against the MPLA. Before the date set for Portugal's withdrawal, the South African army invaded Angola, occupied the country's second-largest city, and began marching north on the capital of Luanda.[11]

The independence ceremony in Luanda on November 11, 1975, was a strange affair. The city was almost abandoned; everyone who remained feared the South African army might arrive at any moment. The night was even more humid than usual, clouds obscured the light of the moon, and the air, like time itself, stood still. When the cathedral clock struck midnight, the new president, the MPLA's Agostinho Neto, rose and proclaimed Angola's independence. His speech was short; people cheered, and everyone dispersed quickly. They had been warned to avoid large crowds, in order to avert a massacre when the South Africans arrived. Some of the MPLA soldiers, perhaps thinking that it was wrong for the moment of independence to be so somber, began firing shots of celebration into the air. "There was a chaotic uproar and the night came alive," remembered a Polish journalist who had been covering the war for months.[12]

Unbeknownst to the anxious people celebrating independence that night, the Cuban government had already committed major military support to the new Angolan president. In a famous 1977 interview with Barbara Walters, Castro later explained that decision. "Either we would sit idle, and South Africa would take over Angola, or we would make an effort to help. That was the moment. On November 5, we made the decision to send the first military unit to Angola to fight against the South African troops."[13]

November 5, the day Castro decided to intervene in Angola, was the anniversary of the famous Escalera slave rebellions of 1843, in which an African woman named Carlota took the lead and was killed in the effort. Castro named the Angolan mobilization Operation Carlota in her honor. The invocation was fitting in more ways than one. Angola had been home to a significant number of the men and women forcibly taken to Cuba in chains more than a century earlier. Cuban troops—many of them descended from those nineteenth-century Angolan captives—would now return to Africa to fight against the army of apartheid South Africa. Cuban leaders saw the power of the symbolism. When Raúl Castro visited Angola in 1977, he remarked that Cuban slaves, many born in Africa, had fought for Cuban independence in the late nineteenth century. "Only the reactionaries and the imperialists are surprised by the fact that the descendants of the slaves who gave their lives for the freedom of our country have shed their blood for the freedom of their ancestors' homeland." Fidel Castro observed, "those who once sent enslaved Africans to America," referring to the Americas as a whole, "perhaps never imagined that one of those places that received the slaves would send soldiers to fight for the liberation of black Africa."[14]

The Cuban mobilization began immediately after that decision was taken. Planes carrying troops and weapons flew at over 100 percent capacity. Pilots who usually flew seventy-five hours a month logged more than two hundred. One recalled being at his seat fifty hours uninterrupted, save for a few short breaks. The Luanda airport was mostly abandoned; it hadn't even been cleaned since the evacuation of half a million mostly white refugees between August and October. Then one night, headlights suddenly appeared above the runways. In minutes, four Cuban planes landed and began unloading armed and uniformed soldiers. The airlift of soldiers was matched by a massive sea lift. President Neto looked out a window at the bay of Luanda, and watching the arrival of one Cuban ship after another, said to a friend, "It's not fair. At this rate, Cuba will be ruined."[15]

The Cubans sent thirty-six thousand combat troops to Angola in just a few months. On one level, the Cubans intervened to back the MPLA. On another level, they intervened against two greater powers: South Africa and the United States. Throughout the war the United States had materially supported South Africa and other MPLA rivals. That support was indirect and discreet. After all, the United States had just extricated itself from Vietnam and Watergate; an unelected president sat in the White House; the Republicans were heading into a raucous primary season; and Americans were marking the bicentennial of independence. Neither Congress nor public opinion was inclined to let the administration become embroiled in another foreign war, especially on the side of apartheid South Africa against the government of a newly independent African nation. Yet the United States remained deeply involved. Secretary of State Henry Kissinger later dated the start of US involvement to April 1975. Acting against the advice of his own Africa Desk, he convinced President Gerald Ford to support the MPLA's rivals and arranged for the first million to be sent in a suitcase to Mobutu Sese Seko in Zaire, who would get it to Angola. Even before the Cuban troops arrived, President Gerald Ford had approved $35 million to assist the two groups fighting against the MPLA.[16]

The United States knew Cuba was getting involved in the conflict. A National Intelligence Estimate, a few weeks before Cuba's full-scale intervention in November, suggested that Castro was in a strong position to project his prestige internationally. The revolution was stable and institutionalized; his popularity and power were on the rise; the economy was "better than at any time since 1959." With all that in his favor, Castro was successfully becoming the spokesman for the Third World and for revolutionary causes the world over. A week later, the CIA reported that Cubans had begun sending military personnel to Angola. Kissinger's Working Group on Angola, meanwhile, reported that Cuban involvement was increasing significantly. But nowhere did US officials envision a full-scale Cuban intervention.[17]

Even after that intervention happened, the US government seemed unwilling or unable to realize what it was. "It is absurd that a country of eight million that has no resources should send expeditionary forces halfway around the globe," opined Kissinger. And because he deemed it absurd, he assumed it was impossible. The only explanation US officials could countenance was that the Cubans intervened in Angola on behalf of the Soviet Union. Therefore, they assumed that the Cubans, as Soviet proxies, could be called off by Moscow. But when Kissinger told the Soviet ambassador in Washington to withdraw the Cuban army, the ambassador told him to talk to the Cubans himself. The Cubans, wrote the ambassador later, intervened "on their own initiative and without consulting us." In fact, Moscow first heard about the Cuban intervention from their ambassador to Guinea, who himself learned of it when the Cuban ambassador there happened to mention that "some planes with Cuban troops" would land there for refueling on their way to Angola. After the Cold War ended and having consulted some of those very documents, Kissinger admitted his mistake. "We could not imagine that [Castro] would act so provocatively so far from home unless he was pressured by Moscow to repay the Soviet Union for its military and economic support. Evidence now available suggests that the opposite was the case." The Cubans were leading the Soviets in Angola.[18]

Cuba's presence in Angola turned the tide of the war. On November 13,

1975, Cubans blew up bridges to stop the advance of enemy troops; on November 23, they ambushed South African troops and issued them a setback they would not survive. Just a few months after Cuba's intervention, South Africa withdrew its army, and immediately the MPLA's two rival groups collapsed. Other African countries formally recognized the MPLA as the legitimate government of independent Angola. Thus, without Soviet supervision—and fighting against US-backed and nuclear-armed South Africa—the Cuban side won.[19]

NOVELIST GABRIEL GARCÍA MÁRQUEZ, AUTHOR of the famous magical realist work *One Hundred Years of Solitude*, had just arrived in Havana as the victorious troops began returning from Angola.

> From arriving at the airport, I had the definite impression that something very profound had happened in Cuba since I was last there, a year earlier. There was an indefinable, but very noticeable change not only in the spirit of the people, but even in the very nature of things, of the animals and the sea, in the very essence of Cuban life. There were new men's fashions . . . smatterings of new Portuguese words in the talk of the street, new accents in the old African accents of popular music.[20]

A novelist, he surely overstated the depth of change—did the animals and the sea really seem different? But he undoubtedly picked up on something. Cubans had just engaged in a massive military intervention across the Atlantic Ocean, in a place deeply connected to Cuba historically. They had defeated the side supported by the United States and apartheid South Africa. Cuba was a powerful country, indeed. For Fidel Castro, it may have been the peak of his political career.

Castro did not imagine in that moment of victory that Cuban forces would remain in Angola for another fifteen years. It is a lesson that victors are often reluctant to accept: maintaining a victory in practice is often more costly than winning it in the first place. Fighting resumed immediately, almost as if it had never stopped. Cuban troops kept arriving and fighting. Angolan antigovernment forces, supported by South Africa and the United States, continued to threaten MPLA rule. Time and again, peace negotiations failed. And ten years after the initial Cuban victory, full-scale war and intervention continued. By then, the conflict was motivated not just by the desire to protect MPLA rule, but above all to defeat South Africa's apartheid regime, which held sway not only in South Africa itself, but in neighboring Namibia, which it had occupied since the end of World War I. Losing to South Africa in Angola would have extended apartheid's reach further still.

The war came to a head in a long and famous battle named after the village where it happened: Cuito Cuanavale. The village was contested ground between South African and Cuban-dominated territory. To lose it, thought Castro, would be to lose the war. Bent on achieving victory and without informing Moscow, he sent a new contingent of fifteen thousand soldiers across the ocean. Castro later said that he was spending 80 percent of his time planning Cuban moves at Cuito Cuanavale. It has been called the biggest battle on African soil since World War II. The Cuban and MPLA forces won it decisively.[21]

The victory at Cuito Cuanavale allowed the Angolan government to negotiate peace from a position of strength. Peace talks had been ongoing for some time, mostly among the United States, Angola, and South Africa. Cuba—though a pivotal player on the ground—had been kept from the negotiating table by the Americans. With the Cuito Cuanavale victory and momentum now pointing to a political solution, the United States had little choice but to accept Cuba's presence. In the new round of peace talks, Cuba agreed to withdraw all its forces from Angola within twenty-seven months. South Africa agreed to do the same. South Africa also agreed to grant independence to neighboring Namibia, thus ending the apartheid regime there.[22]

UNRAVELING THE LEGACIES OF THE Cuban intervention in Angola depends, in part, on where one looks, and whom one asks. In Cuba, the impact was momentous. Between 1975 and the final withdrawal in 1991, some 430,000 Cubans spent time in Angola, the vast majority (377,000) as soldiers. Tens of thousands of civilians served as teachers, engineers, construction workers, doctors, even artists. By one estimate, about five percent of Cuba's population served there during the war in one capacity or another. If we account for those left behind in Cuba—parents and children, brothers and sisters, lovers and friends, husbands and wives—we can say that Angola swept up a whole generation of Cubans, either directly or indirectly. Cubans witnessed firsthand a brutal civil war—battles, massacres, rapes, torture. They saw it; they took part it in. To this day, no one knows for sure how many Cubans died there. The government has never been forthright about the numbers, and estimates range from two thousand to twelve thousand.[23]

Those who made it back sometimes returned with keepsakes—a photo, a necklace, a musical instrument. Some had experiences of religious conversion and returned with artifacts such as bones and soil to make altars to the saints in Cuba. Some brought back porcupine spines and presented them as gifts to loved ones, even to relatives visiting from the United States. But they rarely talked about the war itself and what they saw. While some were proud of their role in Africa, others questioned the very nature of the internationalist project. It was one thing to risk one's life on Cuban soil in defense of one's country, but quite another to go halfway around the world for someone else's, said some veterans and nonveterans, questioning both the personal and economic toll of the intervention. The war was far from uniformly popular.[24]

Some Angolans might have shared that ambivalence. Few, if any, would have preferred to suffer occupation by South Africa's apartheid state. But neither was postcolonial freedom what it was supposed to be. Indeed, just sixteen months after the Cubans left, fighting broke out again after a contested election, and it continued until 1994. Another war between the MPLA and UNITA killed thousands between 1998 and 2002. War's destructive power casts a long shadow. So does colonialism's.

Cuba's victory over the South African army has meant that the Cuban role in Angola has been viewed in postapartheid South Africa in emphatically positive terms. Years later, Nelson Mandela—famed antiapartheid fighter turned president and Nobel Peace Prize winner—acknowledged Cuba's critical role in Southern Africa. When he visited the island in 1991, he spoke at the annual July 26 rally commemorating Castro's assault on the Moncada barracks. Referring to Cuba's victory over South Africa in the battle of Cuito Cuanavale, Mandela explained, "The decisive defeat of the aggressive apartheid forces destroyed the myth of the invincibility of the white oppressor . . . [and it] served as an inspiration to the struggling people of South Africa. . . . Cuito Cuanavale marks an important step in the struggle to free the continent and our country of the scourge of apartheid." Clearly, the end of apartheid was a complicated affair; it went well beyond the role of Cuba. But for Mandela, Cuba's victory over South Africa ended apartheid in Namibia and accelerated negotiations with antiapartheid forces in his own country, contributing to the dismantling of the apartheid regime there as well. For those reasons, Mandela felt a strong bond with the Cuban leader.[25]

For Fidel Castro, Cuba's involvement in Angola was a clear source of pride. He had supported a kindred cause and projected Cuba's power and legitimacy on multiple fronts—military, political, moral. He had faced off against South Africa, the region's greatest and most despised power, and won. Revolutionary Cuba had embraced its role as a world player. It had helped defeat apartheid. In the process, it had also contested US power, and that pleased him, too.

Many years later, when Mandela died in 2013, Fidel Castro was too sick to travel to the funeral. As then president of Cuba, Raúl Castro attended and sat in the platform party. Also present was the second-term US president, Barack Obama, who stunned the world by casually and warmly shaking Castro's hand. No US president had publicly recognized a Cuban president since before Obama was born. He knew the world—and his Republican opponents—would be scrutinizing the move. But to his advisors he said there was no question that he would greet Castro. "The Cubans," he said, "were on the right side of apartheid. We were on the wrong side." Cuba had earned the right to be on the platform at Mandela's funeral. Later, during the negotiations between the Cuban and US governments that ended with the most important shift in relations in more than half a century, advisor Ben Rhodes repeated Obama's private sentiment to his Cuban counterparts, and something in the room seemed to shift. The knowledge of what Obama had said about Cuba's role in Angola helped persuade the Cubans of his administration's seriousness. For a time, it even helped soften Fidel Castro's antipathy to rapprochement, but that is a story for a little later.[26]

More than 1.3 million Cubans left the island between 1959 and 2015. In 1994, during a deep economic crisis called the Special Period, tens of thousands left on skimpy rafts and headed to Florida. People crowded the Malecón to see off friends, relatives, and strangers. Nobody knows how many perished in the crossing.

Part XII

DEPARTURES

Chapter 32

SPECIAL YEARS

In some cultures a birthmark on the forehead is said to signal a person's inability to foresee the consequences of his or her actions. If there was ever an example to give credence to this superstition it might be the large, port-wine-stain birthmark on the forehead of Mikhail Gorbachev, the half-Russian, half-Ukrainian son of peasants who became leader of the Soviet Union in 1985. The young, tall Gorbachev convinced much of his country that ambitious reform would usher in brighter times, and he began to do things no other Soviet leader had done before. He took high-profile, televised trips across the country. He freed dissidents and allowed the screening and publication of films and novels previously banned. He began planning an end to the Soviet war in Afghanistan and surprised Ronald Reagan by proposing reductions in nuclear weapons. Most important, he adopted two new approaches to governance. The first, *glasnost*, was a campaign for greater openness and transparency in government and public life. The second, *perestroika*, was a restructuring of the economy, the party, and politics. On the economic front, Gorbachev ushered in an era of rapid decentralization. On the political front, he legalized associations outside the Communist Party and convinced party leaders to allow contested elections to a newly founded Congress of People's Deputies.

Gorbachev's campaign to make the Soviet Union anew ended Christmas Day, 1991, with something he likely never foresaw on taking office: his own resignation and the dissolution of the nation he ruled. Seventy-four years after the Russian Revolution and sixty-nine years after its founding, the Soviet Union ceased to exist. Fidel Castro's Cuba almost disappeared with it.

CUBA

WHEN GORBACHEV BEGAN HIS REFORMS, Castro was pursuing his own changes. Like Gorbachev, he gave them a name—the Campaign of Rectification of Errors and Negative Tendencies—or Rectification, for short. Initiated in 1986, Rectification sought to return to a more idealistic form of socialism, reminiscent of Che Guevara with his faith in the new man. As in the 1960s, the government would privilege moral over material incentives, expand its role in the economy, and call for more voluntary collective labor. One economist called the campaign an "economic counter reform." And it was the opposite of what Gorbachev was doing.[1]

Yet Cuba's economy was completely dependent on the Soviet Union. The island's reliance on Moscow and the Eastern Bloc had increased significantly after Cuba joined COMECON in 1972. By the time perestroika began, about 85 percent of Cuban exports went to the Soviet Union and Eastern Bloc, often, as in the case of sugar, paid for at prices well above market rate. The Soviet Union, meanwhile, provided all manner of essential material. In 1987, it supplied 100 percent of Cuba's oil and oil products, 91 percent of its fertilizer, 94 percent of its grain, 70 percent of its iron, and 70 percent of its trucks. Almost all that trade, moreover, was conducted in soft currency. Finally, because Cuba was not paying back its debt to the Soviet Union, that trade functioned essentially as grants-in-aid. One report published in 1990 put the island's debt to the Soviet Union at 15 billion rubles, or by that year's official exchange rate, almost 28 billion US dollars.[2]

During glasnost, details of the subsidies to Cuba became public knowledge, and they were not popular. An informal survey by an American economist in April 1991 showed that nine out of ten "ordinary Soviet citizens"—"taxi drivers, students, shoppers, workers, housewives, and others on the street"—opposed Soviet aid to Cuba.[3] Many were convinced that because the island was the country's largest recipient of foreign assistance, cutting that aid would improve a flailing domestic economy.

Before Gorbachev, the Cuban and Soviet governments had usually negotiated economic agreements for terms of five years. A new one was due in 1990. Signed on the last day of the year, the new agreement was guided by a novel principle, namely, that trade between the two countries had to be mutually beneficial. The new requirement put Cuba at a significant disadvantage. The agreement cut oil deliveries from 13 million to 10 million tons, and the Soviets reserved the right to send less if necessary. Moscow would no longer pay for sugar at above-market prices. Neither would it supply consumer durables, such as refrigerators and televisions. The Cuban government would also have to change the way it conducted its trade with the Soviet Union. Whereas before, Cuba had bought and sold goods through agreements made with the central state, now it would have to deal with hundreds of separate entities, most uninterested in buying what Cuba had to sell. Because Gorbachev's reforms allowed enterprises to keep a part of their profits from foreign sales in hard currency, no one wanted to sell to Cuba.[4]

The 1990 economic agreement, moreover, had validity for just one year, rather than the usual five. In the current climate, that could only mean the next one would be even worse. Indeed, two developments in 1990–91 sealed the fate of Soviet support for Cuba. One was the shrinking of the Soviet Union, as its constituent republics began to break away and proclaim independence. Among them was the largest republic of the union, Russia, now ruled by Boris Yeltsin, who resigned from the Communist Party and openly opposed aid to Cuba. The other development that boded ill for Castro was a failed coup attempt by the old communist guard. Four of the eight plotters had been part of the "Cuba lobby" in Moscow, strongly supporting assistance to the island. With the coup defeated and some of its leaders arrested, there were few, if any, left in the Soviet government willing to make the case for Cuban aid.[5]

Another major source of strain on Soviet-Cuban relations was external—the US government. Amidst the deepening crisis and uncertainty in the Soviet Union, the United States suddenly had considerable leverage over its old Cold War rival. In 1990, Washington suggested to Moscow that loans and economic aid would be more likely if assistance to Cuba ended. Gorbachev complied and promised to end Soviet trade subsidies within the year. In 1991, US secretary of state James Baker traveled to Moscow. Meeting with Gorbachev, he requested that the Soviet Union withdraw all its troops from Cuba. Gorbachev surprised him by agreeing and then publicly announcing the withdrawal during the news conference that followed.[6]

In Havana, Fidel Castro learned the news only when it was publicly announced. He was livid—at the withdrawal, certainly, but also about not having been consulted or even informed before it was announced. This was just like the Missile Crisis, when the Soviets had agreed to US demands without consulting Cuba. Two days after the news broke, Castro published a scathing editorial in *Granma*, the island's principal newspaper. The Soviets' withdrawal of the troops, he wrote, was tantamount to giving the United States "a green light to carry out its plans of aggression against Cuba." Moscow had succumbed to Washington's "hegemonic delirium." Castro insisted that he would not accept the withdrawal—not until the United States agreed to withdraw its own troops from Guantánamo.[7]

Fidel could say what he wanted, but he knew what was coming. Many of his allies in Eastern Europe had already renounced the path of state socialism; the Berlin Wall was no more; the republics were abandoning the Soviet Union. "We are alone—all alone—here, in this ocean of capitalism that surrounds us," he said in 1991.[8] This was a new world, and its emergence challenged everything he had made—and failed to make—in Cuba.

At every opportunity, Castro criticized the changes sweeping the East, expressing his disapproval in characteristic style. "Nowadays the advocates of capitalist reforms are called progressive [while] the defenders of Marxism-Leninism . . . [and] of Communism are called rigid. Long live rigidity!" Castro cast his former allies' abandonment of socialism as betrayal. To make his point he turned to history, equating Soviet reformers to Cuba's lukewarm patriots of 1878, who had abandoned the Cuban cause and surrendered to Spain. Today's Cubans, meanwhile, were the die-hard patriots who refused to surrender. Billboards across the country read, "Cuba: An Eternal Baraguá"—Antonio Maceo's famous last stand in the Ten Years' War. Another source of moral capital in Fidel's efforts to discredit the Soviets came from the most unlikely place: the catastrophic nuclear accident at Chernobyl in 1986. In 1990, as Soviet aid to Cuba was disappearing, Castro opened a center to treat Soviet children affected by the disaster. Against the Soviet abandonment of socialist solidarity, Castro relished touting its antithesis.[9]

Whether treating Soviet children or invoking nineteenth-century patriots, the message was clear: Cuba would stay the course of socialism. In December 1989, Castro began ending his speeches with a fresh slogan, adding to the old "Fatherland or Death!" a new "Socialism or Death!" As changes in the East completely battered the Cuban economy, a new joke started making the rounds on the island. Three heads of states—which ones matters less than the fact that Fidel was the third—are invited to take part in a bullfight. The first two presidents fail miserably. Then Fidel enters the arena, approaches the bull, whispers something in its ear, and the bull immediately falls dead. The other two leaders marvel and ask for his secret. Easy, Fidel replies. I just said, "Socialism or death!"[10]

BETWEEN SOCIALISM AND DEATH WAS something called the Special Period. The habitual hostility of the United States meant that the Cuban government had been preparing for war—"for a special period in time of war"—for decades. The drastic changes unfolding in the Eastern Bloc now meant that Cuba had to repurpose those measures absent a war. Castro first used the phrase "the special period in times of peace" publicly in January 1990 to refer to an unprecedented austerity program that the government had developed to deal with an imminent economic crisis. Special Period would be the label for Cubans' pain. On December 30, 1990, *Granma* announced that the Special Period was no longer imminent; it had arrived. And a year later, on Christmas Day 1991, the Soviet Union dissolved, and things got even worse.[11]

Numbers offer one way of apprehending the level of crisis that racked the Cuban economy during the Special Period. Over three years, the state lost 70 percent of its buying power. In 1992, the Soviet bloc trade, which had until recently accounted for more than 80 percent of all Cuban trade, plummeted. Trade with the Soviets dropped by more than half; trade with Eastern Europe all but vanished. Without fuel to power machinery, the sugar harvest dropped almost by half in two years. To save fuel, the government ordered the closing of at least half of its enterprises, displacing (with unemployment insurance) a substantial part of the labor force.[12]

Those numbers, however, cannot convey how Cubans experienced the Special Period day-to-day. In all aspects of life, Cubans lived the collapse of the Soviet Union with every cell in their being. The daily consumption of calories dropped on average by a third. Dietary staples for thirty years—Russian canned meat, Bulgarian canned vegetables, German sausage—all disappeared. Two hundred consumer products were added to lists of rationed items, and allowances of rationed goods were drastically cut. The new quota of fish was now two servings a month; of coffee, four ounces. Milk, which had been allotted to everyone, was now reserved only for children under seven. That was what people were now guaranteed in theory, but in practice, ostensibly guaranteed products were not always available. In 1993, a shortage of imported feed for chickens resulted in the almost total disappearance of eggs. People began calling them *americanos*, "because no one knows when they are coming or how many they will be." One month's allotment of ground "beef" (now mostly soy bean mash flavored with animal blood) or coffee (doctored with fillers) arrived a month or four late. When they arrived, supplies were often gone before the end of the line made it to the counter. On average, families—mostly women—spent fifteen hours a week on line waiting to buy food, reducing time for leisure. But book publishing and television programing had been reduced by half to conserve paper and fuel, so there was less to do in that regard anyway. Many workplaces closed their dining rooms and stopped serving subsidized lunches. "The Revolution has only three problems," went a popular joke at the time: "breakfast, lunch, and dinner." By June 1993, nutritional deficiencies (perhaps combined with toxins from the home-brewed alcohol that had replaced beverages no longer available in stores) had left some forty thousand without their eyesight. (The government stopped the epidemic by distributing vitamins.)[13]

Cubans were eating less of necessity, but they were also having to exert much more energy. The lack of gasoline and drastic cutbacks in public transportation made commuting a daily tribulation. Lines for infrequent buses were massive conglomerations of people. Buses traveled with their doors wide open, tangled clusters of riders spilling out, hoping that those among them most firmly clinging to the bus frame would not let go. People with access to bikes invented extra seats for them so that one could carry two, or three, or four people. But many just walked with weary feet and little energy, sometimes many miles to get to work. In the early 1990s, the average Cuban adult lost an estimated twenty pounds. In three months in Havana in 1992, even with access to hard currency, I lost about ten.[14]

To survive, Cubans were also having to spend a lot more money. At government stores, prices soared—150 percent for potatoes, 125 percent for tomatoes; 75 percent for plantains. But it was the black market where activity most intensified and prices most skyrocketed. For example, the official price for chicken was 70 cents (pesos) a pound, but on the black market—increasingly the only place they were available to Cubans—a two-pound chicken that should have cost 1.40 pesos was going for 20–30 instead. For a pensioner, the cost of one chicken on the black market was the equivalent of about a third of her monthly salary of 90 pesos. And the black market value of the Cuban peso dropped as low as 150 to the dollar.[15]

People had to make do as best they could. They ate less and ate differently. They sautéed grapefruit peels and called it steak. In the countryside, they made soap out of pork fat; in the city, they raised pigs in bathtubs. They cooked with firewood; they brushed their teeth without toothpaste. With so little food at home, some cast their dogs into the street. I saw the tail of a cat next to the dumpster of a tourist restaurant specializing in rabbit. Women complained that their hair had gone gray almost overnight, from the stress of all the shortages and the disappearance of hair dye from the marketplace.[16]

The lack of petroleum meant also that the country grew dark. At first the state rationed electricity and water and gas, staggering outages for certain hours in certain places. But soon neighborhoods were going without one or another or all three for days at a time. A doctor suddenly found herself with water, electricity, and gas available simultaneously for the first time in weeks, and invited friends for an improvised meal—bring your own food and drink. Power outages were so constant that Cubans joked that they had *alumbrones* (light-ins) rather than *apagones* (blackouts).

Indeed, Cubans developed a whole vocabulary for the country's state of crisis. *No es fácil*—it's not easy—took on the character of a verbal tic, used to start conversations, to end them, to transition from one topic to another, to fill an awkward pause. Cubans used *inventar*, literally to invent, to denote everything they had to do to survive. But they did not talk about surviving the crisis, they talked about *resolviendo*, solving something, finding a solution not to a general problem, but to every big and little thing they had to deal with day-by-day—replacing a pair of shoes, finding medicine or a birthday cake, replenishing an empty water tank. Surviving, living, became the accumulation of all those acts of inventing and resolving. And, as Cubans liked to say, it wasn't easy. Yet even with the island plunged into darkness and Cubans completely consumed by the daily grind of life in severe austerity, Fidel's speeches always closed on the same note: Socialism or Death!

FOR EVERY SLOGAN IN HAVANA there is usually another one in Miami. Bumper stickers there announced "Next Year in Havana!" *Miami Herald* reporter Andrés Oppenheimer published a popular book with a prediction for a title: *Castro's Final Hour*. The conservative and powerful Cuban American National Foundation wrote a constitution for a post-Castro Cuba, for surely such a Cuba was now only a matter of very little time. With one socialist state after another falling like dominoes, with economic support to Cuba reduced virtually to zero and the Cuban economy in tatters, surely Fidel Castro was "a dead man walking."[17]

In Washington, politicians rushed to the same conclusion. Castro's fall was both inevitable and imminent, they thought. But in any case, a little shove could be opportune. That push came in the form of the Cuban Democracy Act, which tightened the US embargo on Cuba just as the country was reeling from the Soviet collapse. Among other things, the law banned vessels that had traveled to Cuba from landing in the United States for 180 days. It also gave the US president the right to cut foreign aid to any country that aided Cuba. Its sponsor, Congressman Bob Torricelli, Democrat from New Jersey, stated the bill's purpose bluntly: "Castro must be brought to his knees." As the United States geared up for the 1992 presidential election, both candidates—Bill Clinton and sitting president George H. W. Bush—supported the legislation. In Miami, before members of the Cuban American National Foundation, Bush signed it into law on October 24, 1992, two weeks prior to his electoral defeat.[18]

Draconian legislation and jubilant predictions in the United States notwithstanding, Castro did not fall. Despite the very real experience of deprivation among Cubans in the early 1990s, there was no final hour for Fidel, at least not then. A lion in winter, *Time* magazine called him.[19] By then he had sworn off his habitual cigars but not his evening martini. He was nearing seventy, still in uniform, some pounds heavier, his beard grayer, the crows'-feet wrinkles around his eyes visible from a distance. He continued to write and give long speeches, and in them to excoriate the United States, capitalism, and now also the perfidy of the former communist states.

WHAT EXPLAINS THE SURVIVAL OF Cuba's communist government in that unprecedented crossroads? In 1959, when the island had to confront the crisis of losing its main trading partner—the United States—Castro had been able to rely on two things: the strong, energetic support of a newly revolutionary people and the emergence of an alternative market in the Soviet Union. Now in the early 1990s, the people were thirty years wearier of sacrifice, and nowhere in the world was there an obvious replacement for the Soviet Union.

So, to ensure his government's survival, Fidel Castro essentially did what individual Cubans did to survive—he made do; he improvised; he resolved immediate issues, hoping ultimately to invent a way out of the vise-like grip of total crisis. But to do that, he could count on a lot of things: command of Cuba's command economy, a powerful state security apparatus, the commitment of Cuban Americans to their families, and the predictable behavior of the United States.

Castro's first recourse, as we have seen, was severe austerity measures. But he knew that those would not be enough. The government needed to do something more proactive. It had to create something to make up for everything lost in the collapse of the communist bloc. And for this, he invented a return of sorts—a selective, calculated, strategic return to a prerevolutionary Cuba.

He turned to international tourism and foreign investment. Initially viewed as a temporary strategy to alleviate the immediate crisis, tourism became a major lifeline for the Cuban economy. New hotels were built, old ones renovated. Beach resorts opened in isolated keys. Restaurants, nightclubs, and special stores catering to tourists and accessible only with dollars sprouted up everywhere, at first their windows curtained so that Cubans could not see inside. The efforts yielded results almost immediately. In 1990, Cuba hosted 340,000 tourists; five years later, that number had grown by almost 120 percent to 745,500. By 2000, standing at about 1.75 million, it had grown by another 138 percent. Accordingly, the state's gross income from tourism had grown from just $243 million in 1990 to approximately

$1.9 billion ten years later. Tourism became the country's biggest source of revenue, surpassing the shrinking return on sugar and the growing share generated by family remittances. Tourism had become a permanent development priority.[20]

To facilitate the growth of tourism, the government also legalized—and eagerly sought—foreign investment. Some had existed before, but on an exceedingly modest scale and with restrictions that allowed foreign companies to hold only up to 49 percent of the investment in any given entity. Now all that was up for reconsideration. In 1992, the socialist constitution was revised, and three years later, the government enacted the Foreign Investment Act. Together, these changes made it easier and more appealing for foreign companies to do business in Cuba. They could own a majority of shares in their investments; they could repatriate all their profits; they received a moratorium on tax payments; they could hire and fire workers on their own, without approval from any Cuban ministry. By 1992, Cuban officials reported that thirty new joint ventures were already operational, another twenty imminently so, and another hundred then being negotiated. Many of the new joint ventures were in tourism, as foreign (mostly Spanish) companies built new hotels across the country. Chilean, Canadian, Mexican, British, Italian, Israeli, French, Australian, and Dutch companies entered the fray, investing in such capital-intensive projects as bottling plants, nickel mines, detergent and toiletry factories, textiles, telecommunications, and more. Importantly, much of this investment was funneled through the Cuban military, headed by Raúl Castro.[21]

In 1993, the government introduced another major innovation: it legalized the US dollar. The symbolism of Castro, who had railed against the United States and its embargo for decades, welcoming US currency might seem jarring, but it was a concession to the world as it was, and to Cuba as it was. The government knew that citizens were acquiring dollars already—by working in the growing tourist sector and, in particular, from relatives and friends living in the United States. For the most part, those dollars were being funneled into the black market. By legalizing the dollar, the government recaptured part of that important revenue stream. Cubans could now use that currency to shop at the state-run dollar stores. The name, of course, referred not to the price of items, but to the currency accepted at the establishments. The same year, the government legalized self-employment in 117 occupations and then expanded that number to 157 in 1997. It also allowed individuals to operate very small-scale bed-and-breakfasts and twelve-seat restaurants in their homes—all heavily taxed. These measures, too, created more income for the state.[22]

Experts would later agree that such changes averted a total collapse of the

Cuban economy. New enterprises generated much-needed revenue and created jobs for people who'd recently lost them to the government's austerity measures. The government was even able to keep up its provision of social services. Health care and education continued to be provided as before. And Cuba retained its status as the Latin American country with the lowest infant mortality rate and the highest doctor-population ratio, even as food for students and medicines for patients began to disappear.[23]

Despite all this, no one at the time was certain that all these measures would work. Sometimes it even seemed as if the government's efforts to adapt economically made the government more vulnerable politically. Indeed, the government's solutions introduced all manner of new problems.

EARLY IN ITS HISTORY, THE revolutionary government had reveled in opening up beaches and country clubs. Cuba for the Cubans, the revolution had proclaimed. The tourism of the 1990s seemed like an obvious reversal. Beaches and hotels were open to foreigners with dollars. It wasn't just that tourists got to stay in nice hotels; it was that all manner of resources were diverted to serve them. In a city perpetually darkened by blackouts, *habaneros* walked by brightly lit hotel lobbies and heard the hum of window air conditioners above. Returning to homes without water for days at a time, they saw trucks piping it into hotels. Waiting for buses that never came, they stared at foreign passengers in modern taxis, windows closed for the AC inside. A 1992 song by Pedro Luis Ferrer captured the public sense of frustration. It began: "Because my Cuba is 100 percent Cuban, tomorrow I'll make a reservation in Havana's best hotel. Then I'll go to Varadero and reserve a house with my money that I earned in the harvest." That was, of course, impossible.[24]

The revolution had traditionally prided itself on equal access to education. The Special Period didn't change that, but it did change people's relationship to education. Scrambling furiously to make ends meet, knowing that hard currency was increasingly necessary for black-market and dollar-store purchases, people began to value even menial jobs with access to dollars over professional jobs and the education necessary to secure them. With tips and small percentages of their salaries distributed in hard currency, waiters, bellhops, and hotel maids often made more than teachers, architects, and doctors. As people migrated to jobs with access to dollars and many students lost interest in some of the traditional professions, the government soon had to contend with a shortage of teachers. Meanwhile, many of the professionals who remained in their jobs had to do other things on the side to ensure a livelihood. One Havana radiologist, for instance, pilfered X-ray film and used it to make headbands to sell.[25]

Others without access to tourist jobs or to work-related side gigs or to remittances from family abroad turned to what Cubans called *jineterismo*. Literally the act of jockeying, but closer to hustling, the word referred to a broad range of activities, from selling black-market cigars in dollars, granting access to Santería rituals for goods, serving as informal tour guides for a free meal in a tourist restaurant, and selling sexual favors in exchange for any of the above. In fact, it was this last form of exchange that became most associated with Cuba's Special Period. The revolution had touted the elimination of prostitution. Now Fidel tried to explain away the reemergence of sex tourism by suggesting, among other things, that Cuban *jineteras* were the healthiest and most educated in the world. Political and patriotic posters that plastered cities and highways remained. But now they shared space with posters promoting Cuban tourism, many featuring bikini-clad women in poses not that different from those that appeared in *Playboy* magazine's government-approved Cuban photo shoot in 1990.[26]

The early revolution had also prided itself on eliminating—or at least, reducing—institutional discrimination. And even as racial prejudice clearly persisted, the government succeeded in reducing racial inequality in key areas. The gaps between whites and Blacks in measures such as infant mortality and life expectancy disappeared. In 1981, Black Cubans had a life expectancy one year shorter than whites; the gap in the United States at the same time was 6.3 years. In education as well, under the revolution, Blacks and whites graduated from high school and college in roughly equal numbers. Because the state was the main employer, racial discrimination in employment declined. The revolution's promise of racial equality was captured eloquently in the 1964 poem "Tengo," by Cuban poet Nicolás Guillén. "I have, let's see / that being Black / I can be stopped by no one at / the door of a dancing hall or bar. / Or even at the desk of a hotel. . . ." It continues with a long list of things he could now do and ends with a line that is difficult to translate into English as beautifully as it reads in Spanish. "Tengo lo que tenía que tener." I have what I had to have.[27]

The Special Period threatened to reverse, or at least undo, that promise. Overtures to foreign investors diminished government oversight of hiring and firing practices, so nothing prevented foreign hotel owners from discriminating. Because hotel and other tourist jobs were now among the most lucrative and coveted, bribes were sometimes required to get one's foot in the door. Because

Cubans with family abroad had the greatest opportunities to accumulate cash, and because those Cubans were still overwhelmingly white, Black Cubans found themselves once more at a disadvantage. They could not enter the new private hotel and restaurant sector because those had to be operated out of one's homes, and while the revolution had eliminated racial disparity in many areas, it had not done so in housing. The houses in the best condition and the families most able to undertake the renovations required to make them tourist-friendly tended to be white. A rap song from the late 1990s rendered Guillén's 1964 "Tengo" subversive. Using the same title, it listed the things Blacks had (and didn't have) in the Special Period: "I have so many things I can't even touch / So many places I can't even go / I have liberty in parentheses of iron."[28]

The Special Period cleaved time itself. There was a before and an after. For many, the before was simpler to grasp. There was no luxury, but there was a kind of parity, even a basic well-being. In the present of the Special Period, both were gone. There was nostalgia among some for the relative and relatively equal plenty of the 1970s and early 1980s. A friend remembered wistfully how in the 1970s, Christmas toys were sold by lottery. People drew a number randomly; that number determined the order in which customers were allowed in the store. If you were lucky and drew a low number, you had access to almost any toy in the store; if you drew a high number, it was slim pickings for the children of the house that year. In the 1990s, when any toy worth buying was available only in dollar stores at prices that rivaled a month's salary, some missed the counterintuitive fairness of the old system.

Amidst the deep uncertainty, it sometimes felt like people were just waiting—waiting for the situation to improve, to become clearer, for something to change. Time was suspended over and over again, while waiting in line, or for May's allotment of meat in June, or for the water or lights to come back on, or for a bus that never arrived. The Special Period was a time the government portrayed as temporary, but no one knew when it would end. In theory, it was a time of transition, but no one was sure to what. So, if the present was uncertain, the future was unfathomable.

FOR SOME, THE FUTURE BECAME—literally—another country. As the economic situation deteriorated, illegal departures to the United States accelerated. Unable to attain visas, many began leaving by sea. In 1990, the US Coast Guard intercepted 467 Cuban rafters. In 1993, a new record was set at 3,656.

Whether one's vantage point was a shore in Florida or Cuba, everything suggested that 1994 would see even greater numbers.[29]

Havana's iconic Malecón, always busy, became busier still, as people gathered to share news and rumors about the gathering exodus. Passersby could see rafts launching from the rocks below. Unlike the Mariel exodus, where neighbors had thrown sticks and eggs at the would-be migrants, this time neighbors, families, even strangers gathered to send off departing rafters and wish them well. On August 5, with the Malecón bustling, police officers tried to deter a group from launching their raft. The rafters resisted; then others joined. Some people said the protestors numbered in the hundreds, others in the thousands. They attacked the symbols of the new Cuba. They broke the windows of the Hotel Deauville, entered its dollar store, and began seizing merchandise. Some began shouting, "Down with Fidel!" In the end, two police were killed, and another was wounded. In Castro's Cuba, street demonstrations and protests were organized by the government. This protest was something else entirely. Confronted with an obvious example of discontent, Castro blamed the United States. If Washington would grant the twenty thousand visas it had promised to grant annually, people would not be taking to sea on unseaworthy crafts. But Fidel did something else, too. On August 11, 1994, he announced that the Cuban government would not stop people from leaving the island.[30]

A rafter crisis was now in full swing. Cubans left on all manner of vessels, if one could call them that. There were rafts, small boats, car tops attached to floats, pine boards fastened on tractor tires, inner tubes tied together or alone. That the strange vessels floated at all, that they made it to Florida, seemed a miracle. In fact, many did not make it. In one month alone, the Coast Guard rescued thirty-seven thousand people. Many others—between 25 and 50 percent of the migrants— were not rescued at all and perished.[31]

To Bill Clinton, in the White House for less than two years, all this seemed uncannily familiar. He blamed an earlier Cuban sea exodus for having cost him the governorship of Arkansas in 1980. "No new Mariel," became the watchword of Clinton's White House. Eager to put an end to the rafter crisis, he modified US policy on Cuban immigration. The Johnson-era law that granted Cubans automatic asylum remained, but Clinton applied a stricter definition of what it meant to arrive in the United States. The wet foot/dry foot principle, as it came to be known, distinguished between Cubans rescued at sea and those who reached US soil. The latter, if not excludable, would be granted asylum. Those picked up at sea, on the other hand, would be returned to Cuba. In the meantime, while the government figured out how to make that happen, intercepted rafters would be taken to the US naval base at Guantánamo (where tens of thousands of Haitian rafters had previously been held between 1991 and 1993).[32]

As Cubans realized that the Coast Guard was really taking people to Guantánamo, the flow dwindled. In addition, the Cuban government began preventing the departures as a result of agreements with the United States reached secretly (and with the mediation of Jimmy Carter, novelist Gabriel García Márquez, the president of Mexico, and others). The United States promised to abide by its agreement to grant 20,000 immigrant visas a year to Cubans. In the first year (1995), 189,000 Cubans applied for a US visa, but just under 8,000 were approved. Most Cubans called the visa lottery *el bombo*; some called it a plebiscite. People were voting with their feet.[33]

OTHER DISCONTENTED PEOPLE, HOWEVER, PREFERRED to stay and give voice to their dissent at home rather than abroad. Gorbachev's reforms had created the expectation among some in Cuba that Fidel might pursue a similar opening on the island, and a few independent groups began to form and advocate such policies. More than a dozen small dissident groups existed by 1991. Some had ties to conservative and powerful Cuban Americans in Miami; some did not. Many advocated a free market; a few identified as socialist. The number of Cubans involved was never large. That was due to many factors: genuine support for the government, uncertainty about the kind of change that might occur, the all-consuming nature of their daily struggle to survive the economic crisis, a sense that a visa application had a higher probability of success than trying to launch a peaceful revolution.

Undoubtedly, there was also trepidation in the face of repression, for to deal with these dissenters, Fidel mobilized a powerful security state. With the economic situation worsening and examples of dissent and revolution shaking Eastern Europe, the Cuban state resolved to neutralize any threat. It created rapid-response brigades, composed of members of mass organizations such as the CDRs, who could be called on quickly to publicly counteract any moves by dissidents. In 1991, when several writers and intellectuals jointly crafted an open letter to the government calling for open national debate on the country's future, many of its authors were fired from their jobs, targeted by rapid-response brigades, or arrested. Repression followed the 1995 establishment of Concilio Cubano (Cuban Conciliation), an umbrella organization for dissident groups. It launched with roughly forty groups; within two months, another sixty joined. Six months after its founding, the government detained about two hundred members for short periods and sentenced the most important leaders to fourteen and fifteen months in prison on charges of resistance, disobedience, and disrespect for the government.

In 1996, dissident leader Oswaldo Payá organized the Varela Project (named after the early nineteenth-century pro-independence Cuban priest in New York). The Cuban Constitution allowed citizens to propose measures to the National Assembly if they presented a petition with a minimum of ten thousand signatures in support. Payá drafted a petition calling for political and economic reforms, including multiparty elections and the right to start private businesses. In 2002, having gathered the requisite number of signatures, Payá presented it to the National Assembly two days before the arrival of President Jimmy Carter in Havana. The petition drive became known to the Cuban public at large only when Carter referred to it in public on live television. Shortly after Carter's departure, the government organized a referendum on a constitutional amendment making Cuban socialism untouchable, irrevocable. The culmination of the government's crackdown on dissidents would come a year later, on the eve of the Iraq War in 2003, when it jailed seventy-five dissidents and independent journalists in what came to be known as Black Spring.[34]

Some observers invoke such waves of repression—and the absence of meaningful rights of association, a free press, and so on—to explain the survival of Castro's state even in the midst of the severe economic crisis of the 1990s. While these factors were certainly important, they cannot be considered in isolation from other measures taken by the government to overcome the dislocation of the Special Period—the turn to tourism, the emergence of foreign direct investment, modest measures of internal economic reform (legalization of the dollar, self-employment, and so on). After 1999, a key factor was the Cuban state's relationship with newly elected Hugo Chávez in Venezuela, who was soon providing Cuba with much of the oil it needed—fifty-three thousand barrels a day—without requiring payment in hard currency.[35] All these factors allowed the Cuban state to survive, predictions to the contrary notwithstanding.

JUST AS THE WORLD EXPECTED Cuban communism to fall in the early 1990s, so did many people expect the long cold war between the United States and Cuba to end. The actual Cold War was over. The United States had prevailed over the Soviet Union. The Soviet Union did not even exist anymore. What was the point of prolonging a war against its onetime ally? In his first term, President Clinton had normalized relations with Vietnam—a communist, one-party state that was also a onetime war enemy. If the United States could do that, surely there was no rational reason for the standoff between the United States and Cuba to continue. Yet, rather than abate, the Cuban-US enmity intensified. The dynamic resembled in a minor key the one that had taken hold back in 1959–61, when each action by one party produced a more extreme reaction by the other. Take the Helms-Burton Act of 1996. The law hardened existing sanctions on Cuba. It also sought to make the embargo against Castro's Cuba as permanent as Castro himself. It gave Congress the right to override the president if he or she ended the embargo. It also authorized financial support to dissident groups within Cuba.[36]

All this served Fidel Castro just fine. Now, when he inveighed against dissidents for being in the service of the United States, he simply had to point to US law as written. Beyond that, he took the Helms-Burton Act as an invitation to respond in kind. Before the year was out, the Cuban National Assembly passed Law No. 80, or Law Reaffirming Cuban Dignity and Sovereignty. Article 1 was unequivocal: "The Helms-Burton Act is declared illegal, inapplicable, and without any legal value or effect." Just as Helms-Burton could punish any individual or company dealing with Cuba, Cuba could now punish anyone who directly or indirectly collaborated with the application of the Helms-Burton law. In 1999, the government also issued Law 88 for the Protection of Cuban National Independence and the Economy, which expanded the 1996 law. It established penalties of up to twenty years in prison for acts such as collaborating with US radio stations or distributing subversive material from the United States. Because Helms-Burton authorized money for Cuban dissidents, the law also criminalized receipt of such funds.[37]

Meanwhile, every time there was a glimmer of a possible thaw, Fidel acted so as to prevent one. In 1996, it was not initially clear that Republicans had the votes to pass Helms-Burton, or that Clinton would sign it if passed. Castro effectively guaranteed its passage by cracking down on the dissidents of Concilio Cubano and by shooting down two planes belonging to Brothers to the Rescue (an anti-Castro exile group that rescued Cuban rafters at sea) when they allegedly entered Cuban airspace.[38]

Why did Fidel Castro seem so intent on sabotaging any potential rapprochement? For that matter, why did the United States act so differently in Cuba than it did elsewhere? Both sides seemed to relish the never-ending face-off. Even as they were intermittently willing to negotiate through back channels on matters like migration, they were unwilling to relinquish the bigger fight. With no more Soviet Union and easily able to cite aggressive US discourse, Fidel Castro warned Cubans that a US invasion was now more likely than it had ever been since the early 1960s. In 1992, doing research at the Cuban National Archives in Havana, I heard recurrent explosions outside. The government was building underground bunkers for use in the event of just such an invasion. (By the end of the decade, in a typically Cuban twist, the dark, dank tunnels were being used to grow gourmet mushrooms for the international and high-end tourist market.) The Cuban government built huge defensive ditches in the most unlikely of places, in small rural towns in the middle of the island. A decade later, when I asked residents in a small town on the south-central coast about a ditch in their main square, people explained, "in case of a US invasion." The response is so automatic, so conditioned that it makes for perfect cinematic fodder. The award-winning 2011 Cuban film *Juan of the Dead* hit a flawless note when in one scene Cuban government radio announces that a zombie invasion of Havana was the work of dissidents on the payroll of the US government. To some, Fidel himself might have seemed like something of a zombie—always there, undying. When he fainted in the hot sun while giving a speech one morning in June 2001, he walked himself back to the podium and declared cheerfully, "I am whole!"[39] He hadn't broken, and he was not changing.

THE COLD WAR WRIT LARGE had ended years earlier, but the war between Cuba and the United States continued. Though that may at first appear surprising, a deeper understanding of Cuban-US relations renders it not surprising at all. The cold war between these two American republics was never only about the Cold War, never only about communism. It was also—indeed, primarily—about something that long preceded the existence of the Cold War or even, for that matter, the Soviet Union. The long and fraught encounter between Cuba and the United States was instead a struggle between American power and Cuban sovereignty, and about what the character and limits of each would be. But for Cubans to assert their sovereignty as they did—in opposition to their northern neighbor's long presumption of direct and indirect rule—was not just to press their right to self-rule. It was also fundamentally to challenge Americans' very notion of themselves as a nation. Cuban history can have many meanings, and many functions. One of the many things it can do, as I've said before, is to serve as a mirror for the history of the United States. And in that mirror, the American empire for liberty—whether in Jefferson's time, or in Roosevelt's, or in Reagan's—is revealed differently. Not as an empire for liberty at all, but just an empire. It may have been that that US government was least willing to forgive, end of the Cold War be damned.

Chapter 33

OPEN AND SHUT

On July 31, 2006, a surprise announcement on Cuban television provoked joy and anticipation from many quarters in Cuban American Miami. That day, a presenter read a statement by Fidel Castro. Castro was ill, required intestinal surgery, and was handing provisional power to his younger brother, Raúl. After the announcement, however, the younger Castro, now interim president, seemed to be missing in action. Neither was Fidel anywhere to be seen or heard. Details about his illness were secrets of state, and rumors swirled. Observers wondered if maybe Fidel was already dead, if Raúl was fighting off internal challenges and thus unable to make public appearances. Could it be that the end of the forty-seven-year-old Cuban regime was really at hand?

Yes, believed officials in Washington. The United States broadcast radio messages into the island, announcing Washington's support for a democratic Cuba. Expecting Cubans to take to the streets to bring down the government or to the seas to escape it, the State Department set up a "war room" to deal with the imminent Cuban collapse. It cabled its ambassadors across Europe and the Americas, asking them to speak to their host governments at the highest levels and remind them that a transition from Fidel to Raúl Castro was no transition at all. Now was the time for the United States and its allies to push for multiparty elections and for a new Cuban government without a Castro at its helm.[1]

Events, however, did not play out as US officials predicted. With few exceptions, other governments did not join the US campaign for regime change. Instead, foreign governments sent telegrams to Havana congratulating the new interim president and wishing the elder Castro a speedy recovery. Neither did Cubans follow the script written in Washington. They did not pour into the streets in spontaneous revolution, nor did they launch another exodus by sea. For the most part, Cubans just continued their normal routines. Of course, the government took no chances. It stepped up its surveillance of known dissidents and aggressively targeted owners of illegal satellite antennas in an attempt to limit the reach of messages broadcast from Miami.[2]

Two weeks after the initial announcement of Fidel Castro's illness, on August 13, which was also his eightieth birthday, a state newspaper published a message in which he urged Cubans to be both optimistic and "ready always to face adverse news." In the photographs that accompanied the piece, he wore an Adidas track suit. In one, he held up a newspaper dated August 12, ostensibly to show that, rumors notwithstanding, he was alive and alert.[3]

In the end, Castro's exit from power was surprisingly anticlimactic. Raúl Castro remained acting president until 2008, when he formally assumed the presidency. Fidel remained president of the Communist Party. For years, he welcomed visiting dignitaries wearing his signature track suits, always red, white, or blue. Rather than give speeches, he wrote "reflections" that were published in *Granma* and that continued, as always, to rebuke US power. The cold war between the United States and Cuba, it seemed, had outlived even the reign of Fidel Castro.

On assuming power, Raúl Castro began instituting modest economic reforms that expanded a nascent and very modest private sector. New measures allowed Cubans to acquire cell phones, to leave the country without an exit permission, to lease state lands, to sell or purchase a primary residence, and to pursue self-employment in hundreds of occupations. Raúl even proposed restricting the number of years a person could serve as head of state. Still, Cuba's economic and political system remained fundamentally unchanged. Government control of media and communications meant that the country still had one of the lowest rates of internet penetration in the world. And the permanence of revolution and socialism remained the cornerstone of political discourse. There were, however, some important differences of style. Raúl Castro's speeches were a lot shorter than Fidel's, and the younger brother spent significantly less time lambasting the United States. He signaled, publicly and privately, that he was willing to work with Washington in areas of mutual interest—disaster response, drug trafficking, migration. He had given those signals before, when Fidel Castro first became ill. Washington had brushed them off as the same old thing, nothing meaningful.

BUT IN POLITICS, AS IN history, timing matters. Raúl Castro became president of Cuba in 2008. That same year, Americans elected their nation's first Black president: Barack Obama. And regarding Cuba, Obama seemed to offer something new. He insisted that a fifty-year strategy of hostility had not resulted in any positive change within Cuba. Instead, it had given the Cuban government a ready excuse for its failures, just as it had served to isolate the United States from its allies in Europe and, especially, Latin America, where summits with leaders were often dominated by complaints about US Cuba policy. Obama stated the obvious: Washington's Cuba policy had never worked; there was no logical reason to continue it. He also broadcast his willingness to enter into bilateral talks with Cuba—without any preconditions.

Perhaps for that reason, Obama was immensely popular in Cuba from the start. During his campaign in 2008, Cubans had suspected what much of the world did: that a Black man could not be elected president of the United States. Everything they thought they knew about their neighbor to the north led them to predict his loss. When he won, many were pleased. In one Havana neighborhood, predominantly Black, people came out of their houses smiling in wonder to consider what if anything might now change. "I listen to Barack Obama," wrote one Afro-Cuban intellectual, "I look at my skin, my children's, I cry, and I smile." *Our* president, some said, not without emotion.[4] Two and a half months later, I watched Obama's inauguration with friends in Havana, and I could observe the obvious: Obama was popular not just because of what he said, but also because of who he was.

If many Cubans were still marveling at the fact of a Black president in the United States, Fidel Castro was not. From retirement, Fidel continued to weigh in on all kinds of national and international issues—from Middle East peace, to climate change, to US elections. He reserved for Obama compliments he did not usually bestow on US presidents; Obama, he said, was intelligent, even-tempered, sincere. But what would the well-meaning Obama do, Castro asked after watching the inauguration, once he realized that all the power he had just assumed was useless in the face of what he called the very great contradictions of the US system? Inveterate Marxist, he likely meant the contradictions of capitalism. But he might as well have referred to Washington politics more generally, from its intense bipartisanship to the power of vested interests. Obama, Castro concluded, would not be able to change things much.[5]

Obama and Washington quickly provided proof of Fidel's hypothesis. In his second full day in office, having promised to do so throughout his campaign, Obama issued an executive order calling for the closure of the US detention center at Guantánamo. The administration of George W. Bush had been using the base to hold "enemy combatants" in the War on Terror that followed the September 11, 2001, attacks on US soil. As the Bush administration placed Cuba on its infamous axis of evil list, it was transfering prisoners from the US war in Afghanistan (and later Iraq) to Guantánamo. At the base that Americans called Gitmo, US law would not reign. That was precisely the point. Prisoners did not have to be charged; they could be held preemptively, indefinitely, and generally hidden from view. Some were subjected to what the administration in Washington euphemistically titled "aggressive interrogation techniques." More than two hundred FBI agents reported abusive treatment of detainees there. Alberto Mora, Cuban American general counsel for the US Navy, called Guantánamo one of the greatest causes of combat deaths in Iraq—"as judged by [its] effectiveness in recruiting insurgent fighters into combat." By the time Obama took office, nearly eight hundred so-called enemy combatants, ranging in age from thirteen to eighty-nine, had been transported there; most had not been charged, and just three had been convicted. The Supreme Court had already ruled the whole endeavor unconstitutional. It was time to close Guantánamo for good, Obama had said during his campaign. On election night, detainees at the base chanted "Obama, Obama, Obama," confident in the new president's promise. Obama's executive order, issued on day two of his presidency, signaled that he intended to deliver on his promise. Henceforth, there would be no US jurisdiction above the law.[6]

At the end of Obama's second term—and still today—the US prison on Cuban soil remains open. A combination of Republican hostility, hesitation on Obama's part, the unwillingness of states to take detainees, Defense and Pentagon opposition—in short, Washington—derailed the new president's promise to close Gitmo. As Obama himself later explained to a seventh grader who asked him about the biggest regret of his presidency, the politics of closing Guantánamo got difficult, and "the path of least resistance was just to leave it open."[7] Fidel Castro might have thought something like "I told you so."

YET, IN ANOTHER REGARD, OBAMA surprised Castro. Candidate Obama had promised a new Cuba policy. In his second term, he delivered. The policy was three years in the making. Its principal architect was Ben Rhodes, the high-ranking White House advisor whom Obama came to call "our man in Havana." Rhodes's Cuban counterpart was Alejandro Castro, son of Raúl Castro and a veteran of the war in Angola. The negotiations were dauntingly complex. They involved secret meetings in airport hotels in Ottawa; visitors' names kept off White House logs;

aggressive lobbying by a few wealthy Cuban Americans; a Cuban American social media campaign called #CubaNow; the insistence of a handful of senators, congressmen, and their staff on both sides of the aisle; lengthy lectures on history imparted by Cuban statesmen; the mediation of church officials in Havana, Boston, and Washington; the intervention of the pope; and even two attempts at artificial insemination for a US-held Cuban prisoner and his forty-year-old wife in Cuba. The process was propelled as well by both leaders' willingness, in a sense, to suspend their disbelief, to act as if reversing a policy of more than fifty years was just a matter of will, which it actually turned out to be. Obama told Rhodes that he wasn't worried about the politics of pursuing a new Cuba policy. It was simply the right thing to do. "The politics will catch up to what we're doing."[8]

At exactly noon on December 17, 2014, Barack Obama addressed the nation and announced that the United States was embarking on a new path with Cuba. At the last minute, his staff realized he was set to make the announcement before a large portrait of Teddy Roosevelt charging up San Juan Hill. They moved the event to another room. "There's a complicated history between the United States and Cuba," Obama professed. "We can never erase that history." But it was time to move forward unshackled by it. Prisoners had just been exchanged; collaboration on public health, disaster response, and migration would continue more robustly; restrictions on travel and flows of information and money would be substantially eased; telecommunications links would be expanded. Further, the United States promised to review its designation of Cuba as a state sponsor of terrorism. In short, the two countries were on the path to normalizing relations. For the first time in more than half a century, each country would have a fully functioning embassy in the other. All this Obama explained.[9]

For decades, US politicians had acted on the principle that negotiations with Cuba had to be incremental—if Cuba did x, the United States would respond with y, and so on until meaningful change was achieved. Obama abandoned that course. What he announced on December 17 was not incremental change; it was the beginning of a new relationship with a postrevolutionary Cuba. Against critics, he argued preemptively that one could not keep doing the same thing for more than fifty years and expect a different result. He intoned Cubans' Special Period refrain "no es fácil." He quoted José Martí. And in the spirit of Martí perhaps, he said—in Spanish—"todos somos Americanos." We are all American. Here was a modern US president using the word "American" as something other than a synonym for the United States.

At the exact same hour as Obama, Raúl Castro addressed his own nation. His speech was shorter, more circumspect, less grandiose. He began by conveying the news that five Cubans, held as spies by the United States, would now be returned to Cuba. Just after the halfway mark, he said, "We have also agreed to renew diplomatic relations." He elaborated but briefly. Obama had not ended the embargo against Cuba; only Congress could do that, Raúl reminded his listeners, calling on Obama to use what executive authority he had in order to modify its application. Finally, he stated Cuba's willingness to pursue bilateral measures aimed at normalizing relations between the two countries.[10] The announcement, if a little sparse, felt historic. Going forward, Cubans would refer to it—and the new opening it represented—as 17-D. The last time they had referred to something simply by its date was 9-11; the time before that was July 26. Something momentous was clearly on the horizon. And Cubans welcomed the prospect hungrily.

In fact, almost everyone, everywhere—with a few exceptions such as the Russian state and sectors of Cuban American Miami—celebrated. Several Latin American presidents were attending a summit in Argentina when the news broke; they responded with spontaneous applause. European Union officials regarded the change as the falling of "another Wall." In the United States, the public responded to the news with overwhelming support. More than 60 percent of Americans supported the normalization of relations, and more than two-thirds favored the easing of travel restrictions. Even among Cuban Americans, support was significant. Forty-four percent agreed with the announcement; 48 percent disagreed. Among those born in the United States and those under sixty-five, however, a majority favored the change. Older exiles—and their representatives in Washington—were the ones most likely to disagree.[11] But even there, opinions sometimes surprised. My own elderly parents—in the United States since the early 1960s, Republican and anticommunist by default, once working class, then poor in old age—cheered the announcement. It had been too long; it was time for something more normal, they opined.

Signs of change appeared quickly. The parade of potential US investors began almost immediately. Representatives from JetBlue, Google Ideas, Amazon, Marriott Hotels, Carnival Cruise Lines, John Deere, the National Basketball Association, North Dakota barley farmers, and many others traveled to the island to explore new opportunities for investment and collaboration. As in the 1920s, high-profile celebrities descended on the island to see it "before it changed": Beyoncé and Jay-Z, Ludacris and Usher, Paris Hilton and Naomi Campbell. Comedian Conan O'Brien filmed an episode of his late-night comedy show there. Standing before ruins of old Havana buildings, he imagined each as a subsidiary of a US chain store—Baby Gap, Lululemon, Foot Locker. Direct mail between the two countries resumed for the first time in over fifty years. For the first time in over fifty years, so, too, did direct commercial flights. The official sign of the new relationship was the opening—for the first time in over fifty years—of a full-fledged US embassy in Havana and a full-fledged Cuban embassy in Washington. There were so many historic firsts in the months after 17-D that *New York Times* journalist Damien Cave joked that he craved some kind of keyboard shortcut for the phrase "for the first time in over fifty years."[12]

THEN, FOR THE FIRST TIME in more than eighty-eight years, a US president arrived in Cuba. As in 1928, with Coolidge's visit, Havana prepared. The more combative, anti-imperialist billboards gave way to innocuous ones: *haz el bien sin mirar a quien* (roughly, do what's right no matter what people think). Roads were repaved, buildings repainted, windows replaced. Outside the Capitol Building, new sidewalks were poured and a flower garden planted. Cubans joked that if Obama visited regularly, the city would look new in no time.[13]

Obama arrived the afternoon of Palm Sunday, March 20, 2016, "to bury the last remnant of the Cold War in the Americas," he said. A few hours before his plane touched down at José Martí International Airport, I was standing in Havana's cathedral. People crowded every pew, and many others stood in the side aisles and at the back of the church. A priest read the biblical tale of Jesus's triumphant arrival in Jerusalem. During the universal prayer, the priest asked the congregants to pray for the reconciliation of all Cubans. He prayed that the imminent meetings between Presidents Obama and Castro be guided by the Holy Spirit, for the good of the Cuban and American people. He raised his arms to call for the response, and it was the most enthusiastic of any given that morning. Minutes later, the traditional sign of peace was animated and joyful. Outside the church, as morning became afternoon and the hour of Obama's arrival drew near, the mood seemed to grow ominous. State security officers in civilian dress were everywhere, their eyes very obviously combing the crowds for signs of something potentially less obvious. Then, for the first time in more than two weeks, clouds descended on Havana, and it poured.

The rain served Obama well. He climbed down the steps of Air Force One, opened his umbrella, and immediately covered First Lady Michelle, standing next to him. A friend, who watched Obama's arrival on TV at a bar in Centro Habana, told me that a man sitting near him broke out in applause at that moment. Across the city, along the routes of Obama's motorcades, Cubans gathered, hoping to get a glimpse of him, his family, or even just his cars, which Cubans knew to call "the beast"—*la bestia*. Along Linea, in Vedado, an elderly white woman relished the chance, in front of a uniformed Cuban policeman, to see the man she called "*mi presidente.*" From balconies above street level, people cheered and filmed Obama's arrival at the Black-owned private restaurant San Cristóbal. In one recording, the voice of a woman, overcome by emotion, cries in English, "Oh my God."[14]

Cubans knew from their own government about Obama's drone wars and deportations, about his failure to close the notorious prison at Guantánamo, and more. But in that moment those things mattered much less to them than what Obama's trip seemed to herald: that with renewed engagement would come opportunity. In a place and time where the average monthly salary was the equivalent of about $22, where the ration book got a family meager allotments such as five eggs per month, and where an hour of slow internet access cost a tenth of the average monthly salary, that hope was urgent and palpable. Obama's visit fed it like nothing else in recent (and not so recent) memory. The fact that the government had cast the US embargo as the main impediment to economic progress, and that an American president now seemed interested in ending it, nurtured a new sense of possibility.

The public highlight of the visit was, without a doubt, a nationally televised speech on his third day in Havana. It was a surprising, remarkable speech. Obama jettisoned US platitudes on Cuba; gone were the references to Cuba as "the imprisoned island"—a formulation standard since John F. Kennedy uttered it in 1962. Instead Obama spoke of Cuba as one would speak of a normal nation, of the Cuban Revolution as one would any major historical event. He surprised Cubans by stating clearly his opposition to the US embargo and explicitly admitting that the embargo had harmed the Cuban people. Thus, a sitting American president openly criticized US policy in Cuba.

But what was perhaps most interesting about the speech was the way it approached the history of Cuba. Two moments stood out. The first came early, when the United States' first Black president began outlining the bonds between the two countries by declaring: "We share the same blood. . . . We both live in a new world, colonized by Europeans. Cuba, like the United States, was built in part by slaves brought here from Africa. Like the United States, the Cuban people can trace their heritage to both slaves and slave-owners." Obama represented a shared history of slavery and a shared sense of racial identity as common ground between Cuba and the United States. A visitor in a country in which political discourse rarely mentioned race explicitly, Obama seemed to be saying to Cubans of African descent, I see you, and I understand your centrality in the past and future of your country. Toward the end of the speech, Obama returned to the question of race. "We both realize we have more work to do to promote equality in our own countries—to reduce discrimination based on race in our own countries. And in Cuba, we want our engagement to help lift up the Cubans who are of African descent." An elderly Black woman listened to Obama and later described her first thought by quoting the title of a 1959 essay by Black intellectual Juan René Betancourt, "Negro, ciudadano del futuro"—citizen of the future. It was almost as if in that moment Obama became America's first Afro-Cuban president, wrote Cuban American cultural critic Ana Dopico.[15]

The second surprise in Obama's speech was his portrayal of Cuba's historical relationship with the United States. Obama spoke of prerevolutionary Cuba in terms not entirely unlike those used by the Cuban government itself. He spoke of a republic that the United States treated "as something to exploit, ignor[ing] poverty and enabl[ing] corruption." Before 1959, he seemed to imply, Cuba was a country that needed a revolution, or at least a new kind of relationship with the United States. Of the revolution the Cubans made, Obama spoke in respectful terms, treating the revolution, at least in its origins, as a popular and principled movement for national sovereignty. He referred to "the ideals that are the starting point for every revolution—America's revolution, Cuba's revolution, the liberation movements around the world." The comparison cast the Cuban Revolution as a war of liberation. From whom? The United States itself. Remarkably, an American president spoke about the Cuban Revolution of 1959 and the American Revolution of 1776 in the same breath. More than half a century after it started, the cold war between the United States and Cuba seemed to be at its end.

BUT IN HISTORY, ENDINGS—LIKE BEGINNINGS and middles—are usually discernible only in hindsight. Obama left Havana the day after his speech. On his departure, the embargo was still US policy, and almost every obstacle that Cubans had faced beforehand—those due to US policy and those due to Cuban—remained. But Cubans overwhelmingly believed that some change for the better was now likely. I left Havana the same day as Obama. My host—a woman who rented a room in her house to make ends meet, a devout Catholic, the mother of two adult children in Miami—hugged me good-bye and saw me off with these words: "Remember, vote for Hillary," referring, of course, to the likely Democratic candidate in the upcoming presidential election.

Meanwhile, Fidel Castro, soon to turn ninety, followed Obama's visit closely, and he was not happy. By then, Fidel was too old for speeches, but he was still weighing in with written reflections in *Granma*. "Brother Obama," he titled his 1,500-word response to Obama's speech. Fidel quoted Obama's "sweetened words" about the two countries leaving the past behind and looking to the future hopefully. "We can make this journey as friends, and as neighbors, and as family—together," Obama had said. Americans might detect in Obama's statement a conciliatory, even optimistic gesture. Fidel, however, heard it as preposterous enough to provoke bodily harm. "Each one of us ran the risk of a heart attack on hearing these words spoken by the President of the United States," he wrote. Above all, Fidel's long essay—which began with the arrival of the Spanish conquistadores, encompassed the revolution's struggle for racial justice, lingered on Cuba's decisive role in Angola, and ended with Obama's visit—was skeptical. It did not question Obama's goodwill necessarily, but it questioned his—or perhaps any one president's or any one person's—ability to rise above history. Sounding like a man close to the end of his life, Fidel wrote: "The first thing to consider is that our lives are but a fraction of a historical second and that humans tend to over-value their role [in history]."[16]

EIGHT MONTHS AFTER PENNING THOSE words, at 10:29 p.m. on November 25, 2016, Fidel Castro died. The public announcement went out at midnight, and everything came to a halt. At music clubs, performers stopped mid-number; TV and radio programming was interrupted. The government announced nine days of mourning, with no music and no alcohol sales. Cubans signed funeral registry books across the island; they lined streets and roads to watch the solemn procession that wound its way from Havana to the eastern city of Santiago, where his ashes would be buried in the city's main cemetery. Castro's tomb is a simple monument, a large boulder-like sculpture with a plaque that says only FIDEL. It stands a few yards from the imposing mausoleum for José Martí. By the time of his death, Castro had more than amply proved Richard Nixon's 1959 prediction: without a doubt, he had been "a great factor in the development of Cuba" and beyond. But as Fidel himself had said after Obama's visit, human lives are but a fraction of a historical second. He had wielded great power for a very long time.

But he did not have the power to stop the rapprochement between Cuba and the United States launched by Barack Obama.

Unfortunately, someone else did. Less than eight months after Obama's historic visit and just two and a half weeks before Fidel Castro's death, Hillary Clinton won the popular vote but lost the race for the White House to Donald Trump. Fidel Castro had outlived the terms of ten US presidents whose rule overlapped with his. But he did not live to see the country's strangest modern president assume office. Cubans, like people around the world, have jokes for just about everything. After Trump's election and Castro's death, one joke went something like this: Fidel had always said he could not rest until America was destroyed. Believing that Trump's victory guaranteed that outcome, he went ahead and died. A Canadian cartoon conveyed the same sentiment. It depicted an ailing Fidel being pushed in his wheelchair by Che Guevara, the bubble above the latter reading, "Congratulations, Fidel, you outlived American democracy."[17]

In Cuba, the death of Fidel Castro in 2016, though meaningful for many people, was almost as anticlimactic as his exit from power a decade earlier. Raúl Castro remained in office until April 2018, when he was succeeded by his vice president, Miguel Díaz-Canel, longtime Communist Party cadre and former minister of higher education. For the first time in almost sixty years, a Castro did not rule Cuba. The new president had not even been born when the Cuban Revolution came to power in 1959. The same was true for the vast majority of people on the island, where the median age in 2019 was forty-two, and where almost 79 percent were born after 1959. In fact, about one-third of the population was born after the fall of the Soviet Union.[18]

In 2019, the country adopted a new constitution. As expected, it renewed the government's commitment to socialism. But compared to the 1976 socialist constitution, this one accorded a greater role to private property and promoted foreign investment as fundamental to the country's economic development. Other reforms followed the passage of the constitution. Private business owners were allowed to hold bank accounts in foreign currency, as well as to import and export directly, rather than through a government entity. In effect, the new constitution and subsequent economic reforms envisioned a modestly mixed economy. Yet critics argued that the mix the government wanted was capitalism for the state and socialism for the people. And, in fact, under Raúl Castro, the Cuban military, through a conglomerate called GAESA, greatly expanded its reach in the economy, coming to control about 60 percent of the total and a much higher percentage in sectors such as tourism. Other critics said the pace of reform was too slow. A new government motto—and, for a time, a routine Twitter hashtag of the new president—seemed to give credence to that charge: *Somos continuidad*. We are continuity.[19]

Cubans, however, seemed to be more interested in change than in continuity. It wasn't necessarily a political position, simply an overriding sense that they wanted improvement—in their earnings, their diets, their daily commutes, their choices and opportunities, their lives. Perhaps in response to that, the government increased its surveillance of dissidents and broadened its definition of who constituted the opposition. One of the first laws issued under Díaz-Canel was Decree 349. The law required that artists performing or exhibiting in public do so only with permission from the Ministry of Culture, effectively closing the door to all art not explicitly approved by the government. Other laws restricted the use of Cuban patriotic symbols by artists and prohibited the dissemination of information that the government deemed as contrary to the social interests or public morality. Government enforcement of the laws stepped up harassment of artists, journalists, and activists. The San Isidro Movement—a growing collective that includes many young Afro-Cuban artists and writers—was targeted by the new policies, and its members recorded and broadcast their own harassment and arrests over social media. Meanwhile, international human rights organizations documented an increase in arbitrary detentions. Even as the government sent doctors around the world to help other countries handle the Covid-19 crisis and as it organized a robust public health response on the island, it also used the pandemic to increase surveillance and to suppress protests, including one in June 2020 against police violence.[20]

WHILE THE DEATH OF FIDEL Castro did not seem to change much in Cuba, the election of Donald Trump and the ensuing change in US Cuba policy had a substantial impact. Representatives from Trump's business organization had traveled to Cuba to explore investment opportunities only months before he assumed the presidency. While in office, however, he closed off all such opportunities for other Americans. He reversed Obama's thaw, reviving and strengthening the failed policies of the past. He eradicated new travel opportunities that Obama had opened for US residents and citizens. He banned American cruise ships from docking in Cuba; in 2018 alone, cruises had taken eight hundred thousand travelers to the island. Trump limited the amount of money Cuban Americans could send to their relatives on the island and also illegalized the sending of money via any transfer company that worked through the Cuban military, which most have to do to operate in Cuba. His administration ended all US flights to cities other than Havana. Trump cast these moves as efforts to promote democracy in Cuba, even though his own autocratic proclivities made him the strangest of champions for democracy. Often, Trump announced the new policies in Miami, and he announced them with increasing frequency as the election of 2020 neared. For him, Cuba was always a gambit.[21]

Without a doubt, the government in Havana felt the sting of Trump's policies. By targeting remittances, the Trump administration threatened to dry up an income stream of more than $3.6 billion a year. By shutting down opportunities for travel, it deprived the Cuban government of billions in revenue. But the Cuban government had options to mitigate, at least in part, the challenges presented by Trump's tightening of the embargo. Russia and Venezuela still provided oil imports, managing to evade US sanctions and pressure; new Chinese investments made that country Cuba's second largest trading partner after Canada. The Cuban government, working with a Canadian enterprise, even began to imagine it might hit gold literally, in a new mining venture in the western part of the island. The levels of such investments and the proceeds from all these endeavors were not nearly sufficient to overcome the crisis, but they helped.

The vast majority of Cuban people, however, had no escape valves. Those who had opened small businesses hoping to capitalize on the rise of US tourism shut their doors and parked their carts. The decline in travel and remittances meant that people could no longer count on help from family and friends abroad. Reductions in oil supply made transportation more difficult. Food supplies dwindled, lines grew longer, prices climbed higher. People woke up at 5 a.m. to get in line for chicken; bread prices increased by 20 percent; electricity rates tripled. Everywhere people began to talk about another Special Period, like the one that had followed the fall of the Soviet Union. The new crisis, said some, was even worse than that. It was not all Trump's doing—there was the Covid-19 pandemic and a long history of low domestic productivity and inefficient central planning. After delaying for a long time, the government embarked on a policy to eliminate its long-standing dual currency system and unify the currency, a very painful process felt more acutely by people without access to hard currency, a group that grew in size during the Trump presidency. As one Cuban schoolteacher said in 2020, "Trump wanted to bury us alive." He made a bad situation even worse.[22]

For that reason, the election of Joseph Biden—who during his campaign promised to reverse the Trump policies that hurt the Cuban people—was received with great enthusiasm on the island. On November 7, 2020, Cubans didn't dance in the streets as Americans had in Atlanta and Philadelphia. But, for the moment at least, they felt like they might soon be able to breathe a little easier.

Of course, the future is far from clear. What Biden will actually do in office remains an open question. In any case, improvement in the day-to-day lives of Cuban people depends on more than the occupant of the White House. It depends, also, on how their own government responds to the crisis and how it charts—or doesn't chart—a path forward. But it might be worth recalling Howard Zinn's warning about history. It can never be understood only as the memory of states. Perhaps the same holds for the future. For, surely, it has to be something more than the sum of the actions of the two governments in question. The real question, then, is how much space the Cuban people will have to carve out the futures they want and deserve.

Epilogue

IF MONUMENTS COULD SPEAK

Teodoro Ramos Blanco was born in Havana in December 1902, the same year as the Cuban republic. A few months after his second birthday, on March 18, 1905, he arrived in Key West, a city that was home to many Cuban cigar workers. He was there with his mother and infant brother to visit his father. At that young age, Ramos Blanco was already part of long-standing networks of travel and migration that linked Cuba and the United States. At fifteen, he enrolled in Havana's professional art school, San Alejandro, which had been established in 1818 expressly to limit the influence of Black men such as himself in the arts, which they had come to dominate. To pay for school and support himself, he worked as a policeman for eleven years. As a young man, then, he was already familiar with institutions and structures of exclusion born of slavery and colonialism and re-created in a different form after emancipation and independence. Then success and international acclaim rained down on him. In 1928, he won a contest for the design of a major national monument to Mariana Grajales, the mother of the famed Afro-Cuban general Antonio Maceo, the man in whose honor so many African Americans named their sons. As depicted in the statue, the mother towers over her son, pointing toward the distance ahead, as if imploring him to march on.

In the decades that followed that early achievement, Ramos Blanco would envision the history of Cuba and give it solid form in marble and bronze. In fact, he created monuments to many people who have appeared in the pages of this book: Plácido, the poet and man of color executed for his alleged role in the antislavery conspiracies of 1843 and 1844; Juan Gualberto Gómez, son of enslaved parents, civil rights activist, and fierce critic of the Platt Amendment; Antonio Guiteras, the radical government minister, born in Pennsylvania to an American mother and Cuban father, who nationalized several US properties during the

Revolution of 1933. Sometimes Ramos Blanco sculpted Black figures from other countries: Langston Hughes, trailblazer of the Harlem Renaissance who visited Havana more than once; Henri Christophe and Jean-Jacques Dessalines, leaders of the Haitian Revolution, so pivotal to the history of Cuba. Not surprisingly, Ramos Blanco also fashioned multiple monuments to Cuba's two most famous heroes: Antonio Maceo and José Martí. He made busts of both men and donated them to people and institutions in the United States—Howard University, Eleanor Roosevelt, the city of Baltimore. He created the monument to Maceo that sits at the spot in western Cuba where the general was killed in battle by Spanish forces on December 7, 1896. He built a bust of Martí at the site of the old stone quarry where the seventeen-year-old had been forced to labor in chains by the Spanish government. After it was built, the monument, which is not far from the University of Havana, became a site of political pilgrimage. Students began and ended marches there. When Fulgencio Batista staged his coup in 1952, student activists staged a funeral for the Constitution of 1940 there to make a weighty symbolic statement. Over his career, Ramos Blanco fashioned history with his hands, modeling monuments to some of the greatest figures of Cuban history. And then history continued to unfold under the shadow of those very monuments, which stood like silent, unmoving witnesses.[1]

The written history of a country or an epoch is sometimes a tale propelled by the kinds of heroes to whom sculptors build monuments. Sometimes, it is an account moved not by exceptional individuals but by more abstract forces—social classes or groundbreaking ideas or economic structures. At times, history proceeds as a contest between sweeping transformations and stubborn continuities. Events accumulate one on top of the other like palimpsests, layer upon layer, each leaving its trace for ones yet to come.

But if history is all those things, it is also the countless lives that are nested in its sway. Consider all the people who may have lived at some point during Cuba's long history, from before the arrival of Christopher Columbus to the present. Every one of those lives embodies and condenses the history that made it. The large-scale events of history—conquest, enslavement, revolution, war—ripple through individual lives, shaping them like so much stone or clay. As history makes people, so do people make history, reworking it, day by day, creating meaning of the world around them, often acting in ways that tend to fit but awkwardly in the categories of epic history.

Perhaps that is why Teodoro Ramos Blanco, renowned creator of monuments to heroes, also loved to carve anonymous people, the kind of people who might have walked by his monuments every day. In wood and bronze and marble, he carved beautiful statues to them, too. One, titled simply *The Slave*, won first place at the World's Fair in Sevilla in 1929; another called *Negra Vieja* (*Old Black Woman*) sits in the permanent collection of the Museum of Modern Art in New York City. One of his most famous pieces shows the head and face of a Black woman sculpted in white marble. He gave the piece, which is on permanent display in Havana's National Museum of Art, an evocative title: *Interior Life*. The woman's face is serene, contemplative; her eyes are closed. She could be one woman thinking about something that happened the night before. She could be any of the many millions of women whose lives overlapped with the more than five centuries of Cuban history in this book. She might be remembering the feel of the sharp coral as she walked onto Cuban shores when she first arrived on the island in chains, or wondering at how glowworms could light the interior of a slave hut. She could be a woman mourning the brutal murder of a lover during the racial violence of 1912, or a young activist in 1933 or 1957, worrying about police brutality at a rally she had just helped to plan. She could be a new reader sounding out words in her head, or a sugar worker feeling the pain of the harvest in her bones, in the eighteenth century or the twentieth. She could be a doctor getting ready to travel to Africa to help battle Ebola, or a would-be migrant pondering a plan to make it to US soil. She could be a daughter recalling her mother's deathbed in the midst of a pandemic, or an expectant mother praying to a Madonna for a safe childbirth. Ramos Blanco made several of those, too, including the towering statue of mother and child that graces the entrance of Workers' Maternity in Marianao, the Madonna my own mother saw as she entered the hospital alone to give birth to me amidst the maelstrom of revolution, ten months before we left Cuba.

As we ponder the sweep of centuries, it is important to pause at those lives, not just to invoke them, but to endeavor to grasp history through their eyes, as if walking among them, to paraphrase the nineteenth-century Haitian historian Émile Nau. It is an impossible endeavor in many ways—we cannot simply slip into someone else's place. But the attempt itself is essential. It has the potential to disrupt, if fleetingly, our assumptions about people, places, and pasts. It nudges us to glimpse the world differently, to grasp history on a more human scale, perhaps even to see ourselves through the eyes of others.

That effort might allow us to understand the present and future differently, too. If every present is a kind of crossroads, then that seems especially true now, when so much—from the fate of the planet to the possibilities for racial and economic justice—seems to be on the line. This particular present may contain within it the possibility for a new relationship between Cuba and the United States, a chance to move beyond enmity of the last sixty years and the unequal impositions long before that. But that future—like the past—will harbor the lives of billions. To construct it ethically requires knowledge of what has come before, awareness that actions taken in one place reverberate in others, and generosity and humility in the face of the many challenges ahead. It requires, ultimately, the mutual recognition without which there can be no justice or reconciliation. If the monuments of Teodoro Ramos Blanco could bear witness and speak, I imagine they might say something like that.

ACKNOWLEDGMENTS

I started writing this book in 2015, but I began my journey to understand Cuba and its history decades before that. To thank everyone who has helped in that endeavor—as teachers, mentors, companions, allies, and interlocutors—would result in acknowledgments as long as the longest chapter in this book. I will do my best to be brief. My thanks to the many historians and scholars of Cuba on whose work I have drawn and from whose work I have learned enormously. Among them are María del Carmen Barcia, Samuel Farber, Tomás Fernández Robaina, Reinaldo Funes, César García Ayala, Julio César Guanche, Lillian Guerra, Oilda Hevia Lenier, María de los Angeles Meriño, Consuelo Naranjo, Aisnara Perera, Louis Pérez, José Antonio Piqueras, Antonio José Ponte, Rafael Rojas, Zuleica Romay, Eduardo Torres Cuevas, Carlos Venegas, Oscar Zanetti, Michael Zeuske, and Roberto Zurbano. I am fortunate to count them also as my friends. Several of my original Cuban guides in its history have passed away since I began working on this book: Jorge Ibarra, Enrique López Mesa, and Fernando Martínez Heredia. But their work and memory are present here.

I was fortunate to have a host of friends and colleagues read chapters of the book and offer their insights and suggestions: Esther Allen, Betty Banks, Manuel Barcia, David Bell, Tom Bender, James Blight, Michael Bustamante, Michelle Chase, Robyn d'Avignon, María Elena Díaz, Ana Dopico, Laurent Dubois, Anne Eller, Nicole Eustace, Aisha Finch, Becky Goetz, Faith Hillis, Martha Hodes, Marial Iglesias, Sara Johnson, janet Lang, Benedicto Machava, Jennifer Morgan, Elena Schneider, Rebecca Scott, Franny Sullivan, Sinclair Thomson, and Barbara Weinstein. A few brave souls offered to read the whole manuscript, and I jumped at the chance. My sincere gratitude to Alejandro de la Fuente, Steven Hahn, and Lisandro Pérez for doing that and for providing their invaluable insights. I benefitted over the years from research assistance and fact-checking by wonderful gradu-

ACKNOWLEDGMENTS

ate students, many of them now former students: Joan Flores, Anasa Hicks, Sara Kozameh, Keyanah Nurse, Amilcar Ortiz, Miriam Pensack, Katherine Platz, and Tony Wood. Any errors, of course, are mine.

Several institutions provided critical support for this project. My gratitude goes to the Guggenheim Foundation and the Provost's Global Research Initiative at New York University. Early in the project, I made great progress during a summer visiting professorship at the École des Hautes Études en Sciences Sociales in Paris; my thanks to Jean-Frédéric Schaub for the invitation and to Romy Sánchez, Martha Jones, and Jean Hébrard for their engagement during my time there. I drafted a significant part of this book as a Fellow at the Dorothy and Lewis B. Cullman Center for Scholars and Writers at the New York Public Library. I could hardly imagine a more fantastic place to do that. My deep gratitude to the program, its director, Salvatore Scibona, and its staff, Lauren Goldenberg and Paul Delaverdac, for their generosity and welcome. My fellow fellows were a constant source of inspiration and comradery: David Bell, Jennifer Croft, Mary Dearborn, Vona Groarke, francine j. harris, Faith Hillis, Martha Hodes, Brooke Holmes, Karan Mahajan, Corey Robin, Marisa Silver, Kirmen Uribe, Amanda Vaill, and Frances Wilson. Thanks, too, to the wonderful librarians there for all their help during my Cullman year: Paloma Celis Carbajal, Ian Fowler, Melissa Gasparotto, Denise Hibay, and Tom Lannon. The staff of the Cuban Heritage Collection at the University of Miami was helpful in so many ways; my thanks, in particular, to Amanda Moreno and Martin Tsang, who graciously helped with my photo research. Ramiro A. Fernández gave me access to his unparalleled collection of more than forty thousand Cuban photographs and was a model of generosity and patience.

I feel very fortunate to have landed at Scribner for this book. My thanks to Nan Graham, Liese Mayer, and Daniel Loedel for their support, and to Emily Polson, Sarah Goldberg, and Jason Chappell for all their work on the book. My brilliant editor, Colin Harrison, offered his generous enthusiasm and made this a better book. My agent, Gail Ross, title whisperer and nudge, helped make it all possible. My old friends Elisa Shokoff at Simon & Schuster and Tracy Behar at Little, Brown offered invaluable insights along the way, as well as their unflagging friendship.

The family I made—my husband, Gregg, and my daughters, Alina and Lucía—have lived with this book for years. Decades before I could ever imagine writing it, Gregg was giving me title ideas and all his love and support. Alina and Lucía sometimes think I work too much. But I think they know that they are my world and my joy. To the three of them, I offer acknowledgments that can never adequately express all that I owe them and how much they mean to me.

The family I was born into in Cuba is present all over this book. My mother died at ninety-three, as I was finishing; I drafted and revised parts of it at her bedside. My father, holding on, turned one hundred shortly before its publication. My beautiful sister, Aixa, who lives and works in Miami, shouldered the greater part of the burden of caring for my parents, yet always managed to be there for me, too. My parents will never read this book; neither will my two half brothers, no longer living. So I will never know if they might have recognized themselves or their ancestors in its pages. I will never know if I have succeeded in making room for them in my history of Cuba. I hope I have. I hope also that by finally writing this history—a history that made them, as well as me—I might be able to shoulder its burden, and its blessing, more lightly.

NOTES

Prologue: There and Here

1. Howard Zinn, *A People's History of the United States* (New York: Harper Classics, 2005), 9–10; Leo Tolstoy, *War and Peace* (London: Wordsworth Classics, 1997), 939.

2. Louis A. Pérez, *The War of 1898: The United States and Cuba in History and Historiography* (Chapel Hill: University of North Carolina Press, 1998); Emilio Roig de Leuschenring, *Cuba no debe su independencia a los Estados Unidos* (Havana, 1950).

Chapter 1: Heaven and Hell

1. A classic formulation of this distinction is Michel-Rolph Trouillot, *Silencing the Past: Power and the Production of History* (Boston: Beacon Press, 1995).

2. Christopher Columbus, *The Journal of Christopher Columbus (During His First Voyage, 1492–1493)*, trans. Clements R. Markham (London: Hakluyt Society, 1893), 15; Felipe Fernández-Armesto, *Columbus on Himself* (Indianapolis: Hackett, 2010), 32; Tony Horwitz, *A Voyage Long and Strange* (New York: Picador, 2008), 51.

3. Columbus, *Journal*, 37.

4. Horwitz, *A Voyage*, 3.

5. David Ramsay, *History of the United States* (Philadelphia: M. Carey, 1817); George Bancroft, *History of the United States* (Boston: Charles Bowen, 1834); Jill Lepore, *These Truths: A History of the United States* (New York: Norton, 2018).

6. Lepore, *These Truths*, 9–10. A project created by *New York Times* writer Nikole Hannah-Jones advocates reimagining the narrative of US history as beginning in 1619, with the arrival of the first enslaved Africans to English North America. See "The 1619 Project," *New York Times Magazine*, August 14, 2019.

7. Thomas Jefferson to Archibald Stuart, January 25, 1786, in *Founders Online*, National Archives (hereafter FONA), https://founders.archives.gov/documents /Jefferson/01-09-02-0192.

8. Columbus, *Journal*, 38–39, 43.

9. Columbus, *Journal*, 60–63.

NOTES

10. Columbus, *Journal*, 74.

11. Horwitz, *A Voyage*, 68–69; Irving Rouse, *The Taínos: Rise and Decline of the People Who Greeted Columbus* (New Haven, CT: Yale University Press, 1992), 145–47.

12. Samuel Wilson, *Hispaniola: Caribbean Chiefdoms* (Tuscaloosa: University of Alabama Press, 1990), 92; Noble David Cook, *Born to Die: Disease and New World Conquest, 1492–1650* (Cambridge: Cambridge University Press, 1998), 58. A much lower estimate has recently provoked controversy on the question. See David Reich and Orlando Patterson, "Ancient DNA is Changing How We Think About the Caribbean," *New York Times*, December 23, 2020.

13. Lepore, *These Truths*, 25.

14. Bartolomé de Las Casas, *A Short Account of the Destruction of the Indies*, ed. and trans. Nigel Griffin (New York: Penguin, 2004), 27–28.

15. Las Casas, *Short Account*, 28–29.

16. William Keegan and Corinne Hofman, *The Caribbean Before Columbus* (New York: Oxford University Press, 2017), 13; Luis Martínez-Fernández, *Key to the New World: A History of Early Colonial Cuba* (Gainesville: University of Florida Press, 2018), 29–34; Sidney Mintz, *Caribbean Transformations* (New York: Routledge, 2017), 188.

17. Charles C. Mann, *1493: Uncovering the New World Columbus Created* (New York: Knopf, 2011), 308–9; Antonio M. Stevens Arroyo, *Cave of the Jagua: The Mythological World of the Taínos* (Scranton: University of Scranton Press, 2006), 224.

18. Irene Wright, *Early History of Cuba, 1492–1586* (New York: Macmillan, 1916), 102–3.

19. Vicente Murga Sanz, ed., *Cedulario Puertorriqueño: Compilación, estudio y notas* (Rio Piedras: Universidad de Puerto Rico, 1961).

20. Arthur Helps, *The Spanish Conquest in America and Its Relation to the History of Slavery and to the Government of Colonies*, 4 vols., ed. M. Oppenheim (London: John Lane, 1900), 1:264–67.

21. Murga Sanz, *Cedulario Puertorriqueño*, 157.

22. Wright, *Early History of Cuba*, 64, 81.

23. Wright, *Early History of Cuba*, 136.

24. Juan Pérez de la Riva, "A World Destroyed," in *The Cuba Reader: History, Culture, Politics*, eds. Aviva Chomsky, Barry Carr, Alfredo Prieto, and Pamela María Smorkaloff (Durham, NC: Duke University Press, 2003), 22–24.

25. Wright, *Early History of Cuba*, 72.

26. Bernal Díaz del Castillo, *The History and Conquest of New Spain*, ed. David Carrasco (Albuquerque: University of New Mexico Press, 2008), 19.

27. Wright, *Early History of Cuba*, 190; Alejandro de la Fuente, *Havana and the Atlantic in the Sixteenth Century* (Chapel Hill: University of North Carolina Press, 2008), 3.

28. Wright, *Early History of Cuba*, 63–64; Levi Marrero, *Cuba: Economía y sociedad*, vol. 1, *Siglo XVI: La presencia europea* (Madrid: Editorial Playor, 1978), 220.

29. José Barreiro, "Indigenous Cuba: Hidden in Plain Sight," *American Indian* 18, no. 4 (Winter 2017); interview with Beatriz Marcheco Teruel, director of Cuba's National Center of Medical Genetics, Cubahora, August 16, 2018, http://www.cubahora.cu /ciencia-y-tecnologia/de-donde-venimos-los-cubanos-segun-estudios-de-adn.

Chapter 2: Key to the Indies

1. Louise Chipley Slavicek, *Ponce de León* (Philadelphia: Chelsea House, 2003), 45.

2. Robert S. Weddle, *Spanish Sea: The Gulf of Mexico in North American Discovery, 1500–1685* (College Station: Texas A&M Press, 1985), 42; Vicente Murga Sanz, *Ponce de León* (Ponce: Pontificia Universidad Católica de Puerto Rico, 2015), 109.

3. Marrero, *Cuba*, 1:139.

4. De la Fuente estimates about forty Spanish households later that decade. See de la Fuente, *Havana and the Atlantic*, 5, 82–83.

5. Sherry Johnson, "Introduction," *Cuban Studies* 34 (2003): 1–10.

6. Marrero, *Cuba: Economía y sociedad*, vol. 2, *Siglo XVI, La economía*, 139–42.

7. Marrero, *Cuba*, 2:156; Oscar Zanetti, *Historia mínima de Cuba* (Mexico City: Colegio de Mexico, 2013), 45–47; de la Fuente, *Havana and the Atlantic*, 51–53.

8. Marrero, *Cuba*, 2:143.

9. The description of Sores's attack is based on the reports of Havana officials in *Colección de documentos inéditos relativos al descubrimiento . . . de las antiguas posesiones españolas de ultramar*, Series II (hereafter *CODOIN* II) (Madrid: Sucesores de la Rivadeneyra, 1885–1932), 6:364–437; quote appears on 365. Wright, *Early History of Cuba*, 235–41.

10. *CODOIN* II, 6:368–69.

11. *CODOIN* II, 6:372–74, 378, 436.

12. Wright, *Early History of Cuba*, 346.

13. Karen Kupperman, *Roanoke: The Abandoned Colony* (Lanham, MD: Rowman & Littlefield, 2007), 5.

14. De la Fuente, *Havana and the Atlantic*, 77–78.

15. De la Fuente, *Havana and the Atlantic*, 69.

16. David Wheat, *Atlantic Africa and the Spanish Caribbean, 1570–1640* (Chapel Hill: University of North Carolina Press, 2018), 274–75; de la Fuente, *Havana and the Atlantic*, 107; The website slavevoyages.org has three databases: the Transatlantic Slave Trade Database (hereafter TSTD), the Transatlantic Slave Trade Estimates

Database (TSTD-E), and the Intra-American Slave Trade Database (IASTD). TSTD, https://slavevoyages.org/voyages/mPTF8byb.

17. De la Fuente, *Havana and the Atlantic*, 136–46.

18. Alejandro de la Fuente, "Slaves and the Creation of Legal Rights in Cuba," in *Hispanic American Historical Review* 87 (2007): 659–92; Wheat, *Atlantic Africa*, 280; Kenneth Kiple, *Blacks in Colonial Cuba, 1774–1899* (Gainesville: University of Florida Press, 1976).

19. Frank Tannenbaum, *Slave and Citizen: The Negro in the Americas* (New York: Knopf, 1947). A fascinating and recent work on the comparative law of slavery is Alejandro de la Fuente and Ariela Gross, *Becoming Free, Becoming Black: Race, Freedom, and Law in Cuba, Virginia, and Louisiana* (New York: Cambridge University Press, 2020).

20. "Ordenanzas de Alonso de Cáceres," in *Documentos para la historia de Cuba*, ed. Hortensia Pichardo (Havana: Editorial de Ciencias Sociales), 1:114.

21. "Ordenanzas de Alonso de Cáceres," 1:114.

22. Louis A. Pérez, *Cuba: Between Reform and Revolution*, 3rd ed. (New York: Oxford University Press, 2006), 31.

Chapter 3: Copper Virgin

1. Olga Portuondo Zúñiga, *La Virgen de la Caridad del Cobre: Símbolo de la cubanía* (Santiago de Cuba: Editorial Oriente, 2001), 37–86; Salvador Larrua-Guedes, *Historia de Nuestra Señora la Virgen de la Caridad del Cobre* (Miami: Ediciones Universal, 2011), 1:125–29; José Luciano Franco, *Las minas de Santiago del Prado y la rebelión de los cobreros, 1530–1800* (Havana: Editorial de Ciencias Sociales, 1975); Levi Marrero, *Los esclavos y la Virgen del Cobre: Dos siglos de lucha por la libertad de Cuba* (Miami: Ediciones Universal, 1980).

2. The account on which I base my description of the apparition was given by Juan Moreno in a deposition taken in 1687. For the original document in facsimile, Spanish transcription, and English translation, see El Cobre, Cuba, University of California, Santa Cruz, http://humwp.ucsc.edu/elcobre/voices_apparition.html. This 1687 testimony is the only known surviving account by one of the witnesses of the apparition. María Elena Díaz, *The Virgin, the King and the Royal Slaves of El Cobre* (Stanford, CA: Stanford University Press, 2000), ch. 5.

3. Larrua-Guedes, *Historia*, 1:140–41.

4. Larrua-Guedes, *Historia*, 1:142–50, and Jalane Schmidt, *Cachita's Streets: The Virgin of Charity, Race, and Revolution in Cuba* (Durham, NC: Duke University Press, 2015), 27.

5. Larrua-Guedes, *Historia*, 1:163, 173–75.

6. Portuondo, *Virgen*, 130; Franco, *Minas*, 30–33.

7. Díaz, *Virgin*, 70–71; Franco, *Minas*, 36–37.

NOTES

8. Díaz, *Virgin*, 60, 79–83, 339–40; an English translation of the petition is available at El Cobre, Cuba, University of California, Santa Cruz, http://humwp.ucsc.edu /elcobre/voices_petition.html.

9. Díaz, *Virgin*, 92, 147; Larrua Guedes, *Historia*, 1:228.

10. Portuondo, *Virgen*, 153–54; Díaz, *Virgin*, ch. 6; Franco, *Minas*, 39–41.

11. María Elena Díaz, "To Live as a *Pueblo*: A Contentious Endeavor, El Cobre, Cuba," in *Afro-Latino Voices*, ed. Kathryn Joy McKnight and Leo Garofolo (Indianapolis: Hackett, 2009), 137–40.

12. Larrua Guedes, *Historia*, 1:295–96. The letter also refers to San Antonio, whom the town council (cabildo) of Santiago had named patron saint of the fields and garden plots in 1782 in response to repeated droughts.

13. Larrua Guedes, *Historia*, 1:301–2; the Royal Cédula is reprinted in Franco, *Minas*, 133–45.

14. Portuondo, *Virgen*, 218–27; Schmidt, *Cachita's Streets*, 54–58.

15. Ada Ferrer, *Freedom's Mirror: Cuba and Haiti in the Age of Revolution* (New York: Cambridge University Press, 2014), 233; Julio Corbea, "Autógrafos en los libros de visita de la Virgen de la Caridad del Cobre," *Del Caribe*, 57–58: 73–82. The monument was created by Cuban sculptor Alberto Lescay.

Chapter 4: Havana for Florida

1. Robert Burton, "The Siege and Capture of Havana in 1762," *Maryland Historical Magazine* 4 (1909), 326.

2. Elena Schneider, *The Occupation of Havana: War, Trade, and Slavery in the Atlantic World* (Chapel Hill: University of North Carolina Press, 2018), 68; Nelson Vance Russell, "The Reaction in England and America to the Capture of Havana, 1762," *Hispanic American Historical Review* 9 (1929), 303.

3. Robert Burton, "Siege," 321.

4. Schneider, *Occupation of Havana*, 63–65.

5. Amalia Rodríguez, ed., *Cinco diarios del sitio de la Habana* (Havana: Archivo Nacional de Cuba, 1963), 46; Guillermo de Blanck, ed., *Papeles sobre la toma de La Habana por los ingleses en 1762* (Havana: Archivo Nacional de Cuba, 1948), 199–201; Sonia Keppel, *Three Brothers at Havana, 1762* (Salisbury, UK: M. Russell, 1981), 32.

6. Schneider, *Occupation of Havana*, 138.

7. Blanck, *Papeles*, 199–201; A. Rodríguez, *Cinco diarios*, 70–72; Burton, "Siege," 327.

8. Burton, "Siege," 327–28; Patrick MacKellar, *A Correct Journal of the Landing of His Majesty's Forces on the Island of Cuba, and the Siege and Surrender of the Havannah, August 13, 1762*, 2nd ed. (Boston: Green & Russell, 1762), 4–5; Antonio Bachiller y

NOTES

Morales, *Cuba: Monografía histórica que comprende desde la pérdida de La Habana hasta la restauración española* (1883; repr., Havana: Oficina del Historiador, 1962), 40–41.

9. *An Authentic Journal of the Siege of Havana* (London: Jeffries, 1762), 11, 13; Bachiller y Morales, *Cuba*, 38–40; MacKellar, *Correct Journal*, 4; Schneider, *Occupation of Havana*, 138; Allan Kuethe, *Cuba, 1753–1815: Crown Military and Society* (Knoxville: University of Tennessee Press, 1986), 17.

10. Schneider, *Occupation of Havana*, 17; Kuethe, *Cuba*, 16–17.

11. *Authentic Journal*, 22–23.

12. Bachiller y Morales, *Cuba*, 52–54; Blanck, *Papeles*, 181–82; A. Rodríguez, *Cinco diarios*, 25, 29, 33–35; 102; MacKellar, *Correct Journal*, 5–6. On the role of Black soldiers, see Schneider, *Occupation of Havana*, ch. 3; César García del Pino, *Toma de La Habana por los ingleses y sus antecedentes* (Havana: Cienias Sociales, 2002), 94.

13. Bachiller y Morales, *Cuba*, 84–85; Ferrer, *Freedom's Mirror*, ch. 7.

14. Thomas Mante, *The History of the Late War in North-America* (London: Strahan & Cadell, 1772), 461; Burton, "Siege," 328–29; MacKellar, *Correct Journal*, 7.

15. *Authentic Journal*, 22–23.

16. A. Rodríguez, *Cinco diarios*, 31–35, 48, 99–100; Mante, *Late War*, 461; Burton, "Siege," 329; Keppel, *Three Brothers*, 65; David Syrett, ed., *The Siege and Capture of Havana: 1762* (London: Navy Records Society, 1970), 323–24.

17. Syrett, *Siege*, xxv.

18. Schneider, *Occupation of Havana*, 69, 121.

19. A. Rodríguez, *Cinco diarios*, 25, 27, 32, 49, 50–59.

20. Asa B. Gardiner, *The Havana Expedition of 1762 in the War with Spain* (Providence: Rhode Island Historical Society, 1898), 172; Blanck, *Papeles*, 73–77.

21. Gardiner, *Havana Expedition*, 174–76.

22. Levi Redfield, *A Succinct Account of Some Memorable Events and Remarkable Occurrences in the Life of Levi Redfield* (Brattleborough, VT: B. Smead, 1798), 2–3; and certificate issued by the Connecticut Adjutant General's Office, Jan. 25, 1901, in Ancestry.com, "U.S., Sons of the American Revolution Membership Applications, 1889–1970."

23. Burton, "Siege," 329; MacKellar, *Correct Journal*.

24. *Authentic Journal*, 33–35; MacKellar, *Correct Journal*, 13; Burton, "Siege," 332; Bachiller y Morales, *Cuba*, 64–66; A. Rodríguez, *Cinco diarios*, 59.

25. Bachiller y Morales, *Cuba*, 66; MacKellar, *Correct Journal*, 15–16; *Authentic Journal*, 38–39; Gardiner, *Havana Expedition*, 184; A. Rodríguez, *Cinco diarios*, 62, 117–18.

26. Fred Anderson, *A People's Army: Massachusetts Soldiers and Society in the Seven Years' War* (Chapel Hill: University of North Carolina Press, 1984), 22–23; Russell, "Reaction,"

312–13; Hugh Thomas, *Cuba: The Pursuit of Freedom* (New York: Harper & Row, 1971), 42–43; Rev. Joseph Treat, *A Thanksgiving Sermon, Occasion'd by the Glorious News of the Reduction of the Havannah* (New York: H. Gaine, 1762).

27. Bishop of Havana, May 7, 1763, in Archivo General de Indias (hereafter AGI), Estado, leg. 7, exp. 9.

28. Thomas, *Cuba: The Pursuit of Freedom*, 43; Keppel, *Three Brothers*, 78–79; Gardiner, *Havana Expedition*, 185.

29. Blanck, *Papeles*, 92–93; *The Papers of Henry Laurens* (hereafter PHL), (Columbia: South Carolina Historical Society, 1970), 2:115n; Redfield, *Succinct Account*, 8; *The Two Putnams, Israel and Rufus, in the Havana Expedition, 1762* (Hartford: Connecticut Historical Society, 1931), 9; Schneider, *Occupation of Havana*, 181.

30. Schneider, *Occupation of Havana*, 197.

31. Sidney Mintz, *Sweetness and Power: The Place of Sugar in Modern History* (New York: Penguin, 1986).

32. TSTD-E, https://www.slavevoyages.org/estimates/gPw1xOTE and https://www.slavevoyages.org/estimates/PyPGntzn.

33. Manuel Moreno Fraginals, *El ingenio: Complejo económico social Cubano del azúcar* (Havana: Editorial de Ciencias Sociales, 1978), 1:36.

34. Schneider, *Occupation of Havana*, 199; Thomas, *Cuba: The Pursuit of Freedom*, 51; Marrero, *Cuba: Economía y sociedad*, vol. 12, *Azúcar, ilustración y conciencia (1763–1868)*, 4.

35. Moreno Fraginals, *El ingenio*, 1:27–36; Schneider, *Occupation of Havana*, 205–14; Thomas, *Cuba: The Pursuit of Freedom*, 3–4, 49–51; Peggy Liss, *Atlantic Empires: The Network of Trade and Revolution, 1713–1826* (Baltimore: Johns Hopkins University Press, 1982), 79–80.

36. Francis Thackeray, *History of the Right Honorable William Pitt* (London: Rivington, 1827), vol. 2, ch. 19, p. 14.

37. José María de la Torre, *Lo que fuimos y lo que somos, o La Habana antigua y moderna* (Havana: Spencer y Cía, 1857), 170; David Narrett, *Adventurism and Empire: The Struggle for Mastery in the Louisiana-Florida Borderlands* (Chapel Hill: University of North Carolina Press, 2015), 65–68.

38. Schneider, *Occupation of Havana*, 243–44; Blanck, *Papeles*, 181–82. "Testimonio de las diligencias practicadas sobre el pago hecho a diferentes dueños de esclavos a quienes en nombre de su Magestad se dió libertad . . ." in AGI, Santo Domingo, 2209. I am grateful to Elena Schneider for sharing this document with me.

39. Gustavo Placer Cervera, *Ejército y milicias en la Cuba colonial* (Havana: Embajada de España en Cuba, 2009), 55–63.

40. Thomas, *Cuba: The Pursuit of Freedom*, 61; Marrero, *Cuba*, 12:36.

NOTES

Chapter 5: Most Favored Nation

1. Rafael de la Luz, Havana, January 14, 1776, in AGI, Cuba, 1221, ff. 316–17, available in English with other correspondence on the Uchiz visits to Havana, at Florida History Online, http://www.unf.edu/floridahistoryonline/Projects /uchize/index.html. *Uchiz* was the term the Spanish used for people referred to as Ochese Creeks by the British. See James L. Hill, "'Bring them what they lack': Spanish-Creek Exchange and Alliance Making in a Maritime Borderland, 1763–1783," *Early American Studies* 12 (2014), 36–67.

2. *Morning Post* (London), January 12, 1779, in New-York Historical Society, *Collections of the New-York Historical Society for the Year, 1888* (New York: NYHS, 1889), 277; John Adams to Samuel Adams, December 7, 1778, and Arthur Lee to Benjamin Franklin, March 5, 1777, FONA; Robert W. Smith, *Amid a Warring World: American Foreign Relations, 1775–1815* (Washington, DC: Potomac Books, 2012), 8–9.

3. L. T. Cummins, *Spanish Observers and the American Revolution, 1775–1783* (Baton Rouge: Louisiana State University Press, 1991), 55–59.

4. American Commissioners to the Committee of Secret Correspondence, March 12, 1777, and A. Lee to Franklin and Deane, March 16, 1777, FONA; Cummins, *Spanish Observers*, 60; Stanley Stein and Barbara Stein, *Apogee of Empire: Spain and New Spain in the Age of Charles III, 1759–1789* (Baltimore: Johns Hopkins University Press, 2003), 256.

5. Helen Matzke McCadden, "Juan de Miralles and the American Revolution," *Americas* 29 (1973): 360; Nikolaus Böttcher, "Juan de Miralles; Un comerciante cubano en la guerra de independencia norteamericana," *Anuario de Estudios Americanos* 57 (2000): 178–79; Cummins, *Spanish Observers*, 105–8.

6. Cummins, *Spanish Observers*, 108–10, 125; J. Rutledge, April 18, 1778, in *PHL*, 13:146.

7. McCadden, "Juan de Miralles," 361; Andrew Mellick, *The Story of an Old Farm, or Life in New Jersey in the Eighteenth Century* (Somerville, NJ: Unionist Gazette, 1889), 485–86; Cummins, *Spanish Observers*, 115–16, 124–25.

8. Martin, *Catholics and the American Revolution* (Ridley Park, PA, 1907), 1:298–301; Charles Rappleye, *Robert Morris, Financier of the American Revolution* (New York: Simon & Schuster, 2010), 206; McCadden, "Juan de Miralles," 362; H. Laurens to Governor Navarro, Havana, October 27, 1778; and H. Laurens to John Laurens, July 26, 1778, in *PHL*, 14:455 and 14:80–81. See also *PHL*, 14:196n; Cummins, *Spanish Observers*, 130; General Orders, December 25, 1778, FONA.

9. Archivo Nacional de Cuba (hereafter ANC), Asuntos Políticos (hereafter AP), leg. 99, exp. 67; Cummins, *Spanish Observers*, 126–27; Rappleye, *Robert Morris*, 207.

10. Library of Congress, *Journals of the Continental Congress, 1774–1789* (Washing-

NOTES

ton, DC: US Government Printing Office, 1909), 15:1082–84; McCadden, "Juan de Miralles," 362–64; Washington to Morris, October 4, 1778, and Miralles to Washington, October 2, 1779, FONA.

11. Washington to Lafayette, September 30, 1779; Miralles to Washington, October 2, 1779; Washington to John Sullivan, September 3, 1779, FONA.

12. James Thacher, *Military Journal during the American Revolutionary War* (Boston: Cottons & Barnard, 1827), 181.

13. Rappleye, *Robert Morris*, 208; Thacher, *Military Journal*, 188–89; Griffin, *Catholics*, 1:303–4; Washington to Navarro, April 30, 1780, FONA; Rendón to Navarro, May 5, 1780, in Library of Congress, Manuscripts Division (hereafter LCMD), Aileen Moore Topping Papers, Box 1, Folder 4.

14. James A. Lewis, "Anglo-American Entrepreneurs in Havana: The Background and Significance of the Expulsion of 1784–1785," in *The North American Role in the Spanish Imperial Economy*, ed. Jacques Barbier and Allan Kuethe (Manchester: Manchester University Press, 1984), Table 38; *The Papers of Robert Morris* (hereafter *PRM*), (Pittsburgh: University of Pittsburgh Press, 1996), 8:63, 67.

15. Stephen Bonsal, *When the French Were Here: A Narrative of the Sojourn of the French Forces in America and Their Contribution to the Yorktown Campaign* (Port Washington, NY: Kennikat Press, 1965), 119.

16. Francisco Saavedra, *Journal of Don Francisco Saavedra* (Gainesville: University of Florida Press, 1989), 200–11. Some dispute the story of the women offering their jewels. See James Lewis, "Las Damas de la Habana, el Precursor, and Francisco de Saavedra: Some Notes on Spanish Participation in the Battle of Yorktown," *Americas* 37 (1980), 83–99.

17. J. J. Jusserand, *With Americans of Past and Present Days* (New York: Charles Scribner's Sons, 1916), 78–79; *The Journal of Claude Blanchard* (Albany, NY: J. Munsell, 1876), 143; Eduardo Tejera, *Ayuda de España y Cuba a la independencia norteamericana* (Editorial Luz de Luna, 2009), 231, 233; Bonsal, *When the French*, 119–20; Washington to Lafayette, September 2, 1781, and General Orders, September 6, 1781, both FONA.

18. Conde de Aranda in *La revolución americana de 1776 y el mundo hispano: Ensayos y documentos*, ed. Mario Rodríguez (Madrid: Editorial Tecnos, 1976), 63–66; Stein and Stein, *Apogee*, 345–46.

19. Lewis, "Anglo-American Entrepreneurs," 121.

20. Among the newspapers that printed the decree were: *Pennsylvania Evening Post* (Philadelphia), May 19, 1783; *Freeman's Journal* (Philadelphia), May 21, 1783; *Maryland Gazette* (Annapolis), May 22, 1783; *Newport Mercury* (Newport, RI), May 24, 1783; and *South Carolina Gazette* (Charleston), June 3, 1783. Rendón to Uznaga, June 15, 1783, in LCMD, Topping Papers, Box 2, Folder 3.

21. *PRM*, 8:475–6.

22. Lewis, "Anglo-American Entrepreneurs," 122–23.

23. Linda Salvucci, "Atlantic Intersections: Early American Commerce and the Rise of the Spanish West Indies (Cuba)," *Business History Review* 79 (2005).

Chapter 6: Sugar's Revolution

1. Thomas, *Cuba: The Pursuit of Freedom*, 82.

2. TSTD, https://slavevoyages.org/voyages/FjxKjHRo.

3. Ferrer, *Freedom's Mirror*, 29–31.

4. Ferrer, *Freedom's Mirror*, 33–35.

5. Ferrer, *Freedom's Mirror*, 22, 35–36.

6. TSTD, https://www.slavevoyages.org/voyages/IfiSVxkc and https://www.slave voyages.org/voyages/HAVSASzB. Ferrer, *Freedom's Mirror*, 37.

7. Ferrer, *Freedom's Mirror*, 283.

8. Mary Gardner Lowell, *New Year in Cuba: Mary Gardner Lowell's Travel Diary, 1831–1832* (Boston: Northeastern University Press, 2003), 89.

9. Daniel Rood, *The Reinvention of Atlantic Slavery: Technology, Labor, Race, and Capitalism in the Greater Caribbean* (New York: Oxford University Press, 2017), 19–20.

10. Frederika Bremer, *Cartas desde Cuba* (Havana: Editorial Arte y Literatura, 1981), 78–99; Richard Henry Dana, *To Cuba and Back* (Boston: Ticknor & Fields, 1859), 112–42; Letter from Mrs. Wilson to "My dear little friend," Camarioca, April 18, 1819, in Bristol Historical and Preservation Society (hereafter BHPS), DeWolf Family Papers, Box 10, Folder 77.

11. "Expediente criminal contra Francisco Fuertes," in ANC, AP, leg. 9, exp. 27; Ferrer, *Freedom's Mirror*, 213–23.

12. Gertrudis Gómez de Avellaneda, *Autobiografía y epistolarios de amor*, ed. Alexander Roselló-Selimov (Newark, DE: Juan de la Cuesta, 1999), 51.

13. Peter Fregent to Duque de Infantado, June 29, 1826, in AGI, Estado, leg. 86B, exp. 78.

14. Ada Ferrer, "Speaking of Haiti: Slavery, Revolution, and Freedom in Cuban Slave Testimony," in *The World of the Haitian Revolution*, eds. David Geggus and Norman Fiering (Bloomington: Indiana University Press, 2009), 223–47; David Geggus, "Slavery, War, and Revolution in the Greater Caribbean," in *A Turbulent Time: The French Revolution and the Greater Caribbean*, eds. David Geggus and David Barry Gaspar (Bloomington: Indiana University Press, 1997), 46–49.

NOTES

15. "Autos sobre el incendio de Peñas Altas," in ANC, AP, leg. 13, exp. 1; Las Casas to Príncipe de la Paz, December 16, 1795, in AGI, Estado, leg. 5B, exp. 176.

16. Ferrer, *Freedom's Mirror*, ch. 7, and Digital Aponte, http://aponte.hosting.nyu.edu/.

17. Ferrer, *Freedom's Mirror*, 325.

7: Adams's Apple

1. Stephen Chambers, *No God but Gain: The Untold Story of Cuban Slavery, the Monroe Doctrine, and the Making of the United States* (New York: Verso, 2015), 3, 7–8, 99, 107, 145–48; TSTD, https://www.slavevoyages.org/voyage/data base#searchId=agomJNP5; Cynthia Mestad Johnson, *James DeWolf and the Rhode Island Slave Trade* (Charleston, SC: History Press, 2014), 50–51, 64; John Quincy Adams, *Memoirs of John Quincy Adams, Comprising Portions of his Diary from 1795 to 1848* (Philadelphia: J. B. Lippincott, 1875), 5:486; Leonardo Marques, *The United States and the Transatlantic Slave Trade* (New Haven, CT: Yale University Press, 2016), 28–32; Marcus Rediker, *The Slave Ship: A Human History* (New York: Penguin, 2007), 343–46; Lowell, *New Year*, 176.

2. Rafael Rojas, *Cuba Mexicana: La historia de una anexión imposible* (Mexico City: Secretaría de Relaciones Exteriores, 2001), 112.

3. Jefferson to Madison, April 27, 1809, FONA.

4. José Luciano Franco, *Política continental americana de España en Cuba, 1812–1830* (Havana: Archivo Nacional de Cuba, 1947), 16; Philip Foner, *A History of Cuba and Its Relations with the United States* (New York: International, 1962), 1:130.

5. J. Q. Adams to Hugh Nelson, April 28, 1823, in *Writings of John Quincy Adams*, ed. Worthington Chauncey Ford (New York: Macmillan, 1913–17), 7:372–73; Herminio Portell Vilá, *Historia de Cuba en sus relaciones con los Estados Unidos y España* (Miami: Mnemosyne, 1969), 1:226.

6. Ari Kelman, *A River and Its City: The Nature of Landscape in New Orleans* (Berkeley: University of California Press, 2003), 2; Walter Johnson, *River of Dark Dreams: Slavery and Empire in the Cotton Kingdom* (Cambridge, MA: Harvard University Press, 2013), 84.

7. J. Q. Adams to Hugh Nelson, April 28, 1823, *Writings of John Quincy Adams*, 7:373.

8. Francisco Dionisio Vives to Juan Antonio Gómez, May 14 and May 20, 1825, AGI, Estado, leg. 17, exp. 101.

9. Chambers, *No God but Gain*, 93, 96; Portell Vilá, *Historia de Cuba*, 1:207.

10. Foner, *A History of Cuba*, 1:141.

11. J. Q. Adams, *Memoirs*, 6:70; Foner, *A History of Cuba*, 1:141–42; Ernest May, *The*

Making of the Monroe Doctrine (Cambridge, MA: Harvard University Press, 1974), 43.

12. J. Q. Adams, *Memoirs*, 6:70–73. See also Foner, *A History of Cuba*, 1:141–43; Portell Vilá, *Historia de Cuba*, 1:214–15.

13. Portell Vilá, *Historia de Cuba*, 1:217–18; Chambers, *No God but Gain*, 108; Louis A. Pérez, *Cuba: Between Reform and Revolution*, 64.

14. J. Q. Adams, *Memoirs*, 6:137–39; Foner, *A History of Cuba*, 1:103–5.

15. F. E. Chadwick, *Relations of the United States and Spain* (New York: Charles Scribner's Sons, 1909), 224–25; Vidal Morales y Morales, *Iniciadores y primeros mártires de la revolución cubana* (Havana: Cultural, 1931), 55; Foner, *A History of Cuba*, 1:104, 120; Andres Pletch, "Isles of Exception: Slavery, Law, and Counterrevolutionary Governance in Cuba" (PhD diss., University of Michigan, 1997).

16. Zanetti, *Historia mínima*, 130; Manuel Barcia, *The Great African Slave Revolt of 1825: Cuba and the Fight for Freedom in Matanzas* (Baton Rouge: Louisiana State University Press, 2012).

17. Jorge Ibarra: *Varela, el precursor: Un estudio de época* (Havana: Ciencias Sociales, 2004); Enrique López Mesa, *Algunos aspectos culturales de la comunidad cubana de New York durante el siglo xix* (Havana: Centro de Estudios Martianos, 2002), 14; J. J. McCadden, "The New York to Cuba Axis of Father Varela," *Americas* 20 (1964), 376–92. In 2002, Varela's name was used for a dissident project that sought to use a clause of the 1976 Cuban constitution to mobilize for democratic reforms.

18. Chambers, *No God but Gain*, 122.

19. Jefferson to Monroe, June 23, 1823, and October 24, 1823, FONA; Adams, *Memoirs*, 6:185–87; Caitlin Fitz, *Our Sister Republics: The United States in an Age of American Revolutions* (New York: Liveright, 2016), 156–58.

20. Adams, *Memoirs*, 6:177–78, 186.

21. Monroe Doctrine, www.ourdocuments.gov; Jay Sexton, *The Monroe Doctrine: Empire and Nation in Nineteenth-Century America* (New York: Hill & Wang, 2011), 51–53; R. Rojas, *Cuba Mexicana*, 113, 162–67, 234–35.

22. Roland T. Ely, "The Old Cuba Trade: Highlights and Case Studies of Cuban-American Interdependence during the Nineteenth Century," *Business History Review* 38 (1964), 458n9; Dana, *To Cuba and Back*, 127–30; Robert Albion, *The Rise of New York Port, 1815–1860* (New York: Scribner, 1970), 178; Gerald Horne, *Race to Revolution: The United States and Cuba during Slavery and Jim Crow* (New York: Monthly Review Press, 2014), 69.

23. According to the estimates on Slave Voyages, 778,541 African captives disembarked in Cuba over the course of the entire transatlantic trade; 551,913 of those arrived after the trade became illegal in 1820. In addition to those numbers, which account for captives taken to Cuba directly from Africa, another

117,941 Africans arrived in Cuba from other locations in the Americas over the course of the trade; see IASTD, https://www.slavevoyages.org/voyages /HAVSASzB.

24. Horne, *Race to Revolution*, 62; C. M. Johnson, *James DeWolf*, ch. 9, and Thomas DeWolf, *Inheriting the Trade: A Northern Family Confronts Its Legacy* (Boston: Beacon Press, 2008).

25. Lisandro Pérez, *Sugar, Cigars, and Revolution: The Making of Cuban New York* (New York: New York University Press, 2018), 27–28; Chambers, *No God but Gain*, 18; DeWolf, *Inheriting the Trade*, 42.

26. BHPS, "Nueva Esperanza Account Book."

27. Ely, "Old Cuba Trade," 458–59; Lisandro Pérez, *Sugar, Cigars, and Revolution*, 29–30.

28. DeWolf, *Inheriting the Trade*. Also BHPS, Benson Research Files, Box 4; "Nueva Esperanza Account Book," "Misc. Notes on Cuba," and Joseph Seymour's Journal of New Hope Estate, 1834–39. See also Rafael Ocasio, *A Bristol, Rhode Island and Matanzas, Cuba Slavery Connection: The Diary of George Howe* (Lanham, MD: Lexington Books, 2019).

29. Joseph Goodwin diary, excerpted in DeWolf, *Inheriting the Trade*, 186; "Diary of George Howe, Esq. 1832–1834," entry for January 5, 1833, in BHPS.

30. Horne, *Race to Revolution*, 52; Louis A. Pérez, "Cuba and the United States," *Cuban Studies* 21 (1991); Laird Bergad, *Cuban Rural Society in the Nineteenth Century: The Social and Economic History of Monoculture in Matanzas* (Princeton, NJ: Princeton University Press, 1990); Moreno Fraginals, *Ingenio*, 1:141.

Chapter 8: Torture Plots

1. Rita Llanes Miqueli, *Víctimas del año del cuero* (Havana: Ciencias Sociales, 1984), 46–53; Enildo García, *Cuba: Plácido, poeta mulato de la emancipación* (New York: Senda Nueva Ediciones, 1986), ch. 1; Matthew Pettway, *Cuban Literature in the Age of Black Insurrection: Manzano, Plácido, and Afro-Latino Religion* (Jackson: University Press of Mississippi, 2020), 14–15, 93.

2. Aisha Finch, *Rethinking Slave Rebellion in Cuba: La Escalera and the Insurgencies of 1841–1844* (Chapel Hill: University of North Carolina Press, 2016), 119–21; Robert Paquette, *Sugar Is Made with Blood: The Conspiracy of La Escalera and the Conflict Between Empires over Slavery in Cuba* (Middletown, CT: Wesleyan University Press, 1988), 259–60.

3. Finch, *Rethinking Slave Rebellion*, 126–27; Paquette, *Sugar Is Made with Blood*, 258–63.

4. Thomas, *Cuba: The Pursuit of Freedom*, 122, 146–48, 154, 203, 207; Dick Cluster and Rafael Hernández, *The History of Havana* (New York: Palgrave Macmillan, 2006),

NOTES

77; Expediente reservado sobre un motín de negros en la propiedad de Domingo Aldama, Archivo Historico Nacional (Madrid), Ultramar, leg. 8, exp. 10.

5. Paquette, *Sugar Is Made with Blood*, 152–56.

6. Paquette, *Sugar Is Made with Blood*, 156–66; Finch, *Rethinking Slave Rebellion*, 115–29.

7. Finch, *Rethinking Slave Rebellion*, 128–29.

8. Paquette, *Sugar Is Made with Blood*, 192.

9. Finch, *Rethinking Slave Rebellion*, 128; Paquette, *Sugar Is Made with Blood*, 201.

10. Finch, *Rethinking Slave Rebellion*, 82–85; Paquette, *Sugar Is Made with Blood*, 177–78.

11. John Wurdemann, *Notes on Cuba* (Boston: J. Munroe, 1844), 271–72; Jane Landers, *Atlantic Creoles in the Age of Revolutions* (Cambridge, MA: Harvard University Press, 2010), 223.

12. Finch, *Rethinking Slave Rebellion*, 148.

13. Paquette, *Sugar Is Made with Blood*, 214; Alberto Perret Ballester, *El azúcar en Matanzas y sus dueños en La Habana: Apuntes y iconografía* (Havana: Ciencias Sociales, 2007), 331–32; María del Carmen Barcia Zequeira and Manuel Barcia Paz, "La conspiración de la Escalera: El precio de una traición," *Catauro* 2, no. 3 (2001), 199–204; E. García, *Cuba*, 54; Lisandro Pérez, *Sugar, Cigars, and Revolution*, 95–99.

14. In addition to Finch and Paquette, the major works on this extended episode are Gloria García, *Conspiraciones y revueltas: La actitud política de los negros (1790–1845)* (Santiago de Cuba: Editorial Oriente, 2003); Manuel Barcia, *Seeds of Insurrection: Domination and Resistance on Western Cuban Plantations, 1808–1848* (Baton Rouge: Louisiana State University Press, 2000); Michele Reid-Vazquez, *The Year of the Lash: Free People of Color in Cuba and the Nineteenth-Century Atlantic World* (Athens: University of Georgia Press, 2011); José Luciano Franco, *La gesta heroica del triunvirato* (Havana: Editorial de Ciencias Sociales, 2012).

15. Paquette, *Sugar Is Made with Blood*, 220–22.

16. Matthew Karp, *This Vast Southern Empire* (Cambridge, MA: Harvard University Press, 2016), 61–67; *Daily Picayune* (New Orleans), May 28, 1843.

17. Maria Gowen Brooks to W. B. Force, September 3, 1844, Maria Gowen Brooks Papers, New York Public Library, Berg Division; William C. Van Norman, *Shade Grown Slavery: Life and Labor on Coffee Plantations in Western Cuba, 1790–1845* (Chapel Hill: University of North Carolina Press, 2005), 77.

18. Paquette, *Sugar Is Made with Blood*, 225–26; Rodolfo Bofill Phinney, "Los naúfragos cubanos del Mayflower," June 25, 2014, www.cubaencuentro.com.

19. Paquette, *Sugar Is Made with Blood*, 221–23, 228–29, 258–59; Landers, *Atlantic Creoles*, 224–25; Gregory Downs, *The Second American Revolution: The Civil War–Era*

Struggle over Cuba and the Rebirth of the American Republic (Chapel Hill: University of North Carolina Press, 2019), 63.

20. Paquette, *Sugar Is Made with Blood*, 232, 259–61; E. García, *Cuba*, 55, 59; Finch, *Rethinking Slave Rebellion*, 119; *Daily Picayune* (New Orleans), April 20, 1844.

21. Reid-Vazquez, *Year of the Lash*, 65–67; Paquette, *Sugar Is Made with Blood*, 232.

9: Dreams of Dominion

1. Felice Belman, "Worst Inauguration Ever? That Would Probably Be Franklin Pierce's in 1853," *Boston Globe*, January 18, 2017; Daniel Fate Brooks, "The Faces of William Rufus King," *Alabama Heritage* 69 (Summer 2003), 14–23. Franklin Pierce Inaugural Address, March 4, 1853, University of Virginia, Miller Center, http://millercenter.org/president/pierce/speeches/speech-3553. On the significance of Cuba in the election of 1852, see Gregory Downs, *Second American Revolution*, 55, 72–74.

2. Mrs. Frank Leslie, "Scenes in Sun-Lands," *Frank Leslie's Popular Monthly* 6, no. 1 (July 1878), 417.

3. Wurdeman, *Notes on Cuba*, 7, 137; William H. Hurlbert, *Gan-Eden: Or Pictures of Cuba* (Boston: John Jewett, 1854), 134; Bremer, *Cartas desde Cuba*, 81–82, 90; Dana, *To Cuba and Back*, 123.

4. Thomas Balcerski, *Bosom Friends: The Intimate World of James Buchanan and William Rufus King* (New York: Oxford University Press, 2019), 165–66.

5. The description of King's visit and swearing in comes from "The Week," *Pen and Pencil: Weekly Journal of Literature, Science, Art and News* (Cincinnati, OH), 1, 17 (April 23, 1853), 543–44; "Vice President King," South Carolina Historical Society, Barbot Family Papers, file 11/67/24; Balcerski, *Bosom Friends*, 166; Brooks, "The Faces"; Perret Ballester, *El azúcar*, 193.

6. Warren Howard, *American Slavers and the Federal Law, 1837–1862* (Berkeley: University of California Press, 1963), 192–93, 201, 269; José Luciano Franco, *Comercio clandestino de esclavos* (Havana: Ciencias Sociales, 1980), 231–32; Arthur Corwin, *Spain and the Abolition of Slavery in Cuba* (Austin: University of Texas Press, 1967), 62–63; David R. Murray, *Odious Commerce: Britain, Spain, and the Abolition of the Cuban Slave Trade* (New York: Cambridge University Press, 1980), 185; María del Carmen Barcia Zequeira, Miriam Herrera Jerez, Adrián Camacho Domínguez, and Oilda Hevia Lanier, eds., *Una sociedad distinta: Espacios del comercio negrero en el occidente de Cuba (1836–1866)* (Havana: Universidad de la Habana, 2017); John Harris, *The Last Slave Ships: New York and the End of the Middle Passage* (New Haven, CT: Yale University Press, 2020).

7. Barcia, *Una sociedad distinta*, 17–35; Alfred J. López, *José Martí: A Revolutionary Life* (Austin: University of Texas Press, 2014), 20–23; José Martí, "Verso Sencillo XXX,"

NOTES

in *José Martí Obras Completas: Edición Crítica* (Havana: Centro de Estudios Martianos, 2007), 14:335.

8. Frederick Douglass, "Cuba and the United States," *Frederick Douglass' Paper*, September 4, 1851; Foner, *A History of Cuba*, 2:21–23; Robert E. May, "Lobbyists for Commercial Empire: Jane Cazneau, William Cazneau, and US Caribbean Policy, 1846–1878," *Pacific Historical Review* 48 (1979), 383–412; James Polk, *Diary of James K. Polk During His Presidency* (Chicago: A. C. McClurg, 1910), 3:476–80; W. Johnson, *River*, 330.

9. Foner, *A History of Cuba*, 2:23.

10. Foner, *A History of Cuba*, 2:10–12, 21–22, 28, 32.

11. Foner, *A History of Cuba*, 2:43.

12. Foner, *A History of Cuba*, 2:43–55; W. Johnson, *River*, 331–32.

13. Foner, *A History of Cuba*, 2:55–56; Douglass, "Cuba and the United States."

14. W. Johnson, *River*, 359–60; Foner, *A History of Cuba*, 2:60.

15. Foner, *A History of Cuba*, 2:61; "Jordan is a Hard Road to Travel, as written and sung by Phil Rice, the celebrated banjoist," https://www.loc.gov/resource/amss .sb20241a.0/?st=text.

16. Foner, *A History of Cuba*, 2:76–78; Karp, *Vast Southern Empire*, 192; Corwin, *Spain*, 117.

17. Ambrosio José Gonzales, "Cuba—The Turning Point," *Washington Daily Union*, April 25, 1854, 3.

18. Foner, *A History of Cuba*, 2:83, 87; Robert E. May, *The Southern Dream of a Caribbean Empire, 1854–1861* (Baton Rouge: Louisiana State University Press, 1973), 46; Downs, *Second American Revolution*, 76; Stanley Urban, "The Africanization of Cuba Scare, 1853–1855," *Hispanic American Historical Review* 37 (1957), 37.

19. Foner, *A History of Cuba*, 98; W. Johnson, *River*, 322; Downs, *Second American Revolution*, 74–75; Ostend Manifesto, reprinted in James Buchanan, *James Buchanan, His Doctrines and Policy as Exhibited by Himself and Friends* (N.P.: Greeley & McElrath, 1856), 5–7.

20. Edward Baptist, *The Half Has Never Been Told: Slavery and the Making of American Capitalism* (New York: Basic Books, 2014), 373–74; Karp, *Vast Southern Empire*, 197; Downs, *Second American Revolution*, 77–87.

21. Buchanan, Inaugural Address, Presidency Project, http://www.presidency.ucsb .edu/ws/?pid=25817; Robert E. May, *John A. Quitman: Old South Crusader* (Baton Rouge: Louisiana State University Press, 1985), 328–29.

NOTES

Chapter 10: Civil War Journeys

1. Rafael de la Cova, *Cuban Confederate Colonel: The Life of Ambrosio José Gonzales* (Columbia: University of South Carolina Press, 2008); Michel Wendell Stephens, "Two Flags, One Cause—A Cuban Patriot in Gray: Ambrosio José Gonzales," in *Cubans in the Confederacy: José Agustín Quintero, Ambrosio José Gonzales, and Loreta Janeta Velázquez*, ed. Phillip Tucker (London: McFarland, 2002), 143–224.

2. Richard Hall, "Loreta Janeta Velazquez: Civil War Soldier and Spy," in *Cubans in the Confederacy*, 225–39; Loreta Janeta Velazquez, *A Woman in Battle: A Narrative of the Exploits, Adventures, and Travels of Madame Loreta Janeta Velázquez* (Richmond, VA: Dustin, Gilman, 1876). Some scholars have questioned the veracity of Velázquez's account, but military historian Phillip Tucker argues that some inconsistencies notwithstanding "in general, and in many small particulars, historical evidence supports her story." Tucker, *Cubans in the Confederacy*, 230, 237.

3. Matthew Pratt Guterl, *American Mediterranean: Southern Slaveholders in the Age of Emancipation* (Cambridge, MA: Harvard University Press, 2008), 58; Tucker, *Cubans in the Confederacy*, 5–6.

4. Portell Vilá, *Historia de Cuba*, 2:170–71; Emeterio Santovenia, *Lincoln en Martí* (Havana: Editorial Trópico, 1948), 3; Foner, *A History of Cuba*, 2:133–34; A. López, *José Martí*, 30.

5. Adam Rothman, *Beyond Freedom's Reach: Kidnapping in the Twilight of Slavery* (Cambridge, MA: Harvard University Press, 2015), 98–99; *Compilation of the Messages*, 111, 133.

6. *Compilation of the Messages*, 2:111–13, 125; Portell Vilá, *Historia de Cuba*, 145–46; Horne, *Race to Revolution*, 349n28.

7. Horne, *Race to Revolution*, 103–4.

8. Rothman, *Beyond Freedom's Reach*; Horne, *Race to Revolution*, 111; Guterl, *American Mediterranean*, 88, 147, 221n2.

9. *A Compilation of Messages and Papers of the Confederacy*, ed. James D. Richardson (Nashville: United States Publishing Company, 1905), 2:204.

10. Portell Vilá, *Historia de Cuba*, 2:155.

11. William Davis, *Breckinridge: Statesman, Soldier, Symbol* (Lexington: University Press of Kentucky, 2015), 536–47; Guterl, *American Mediterranean*, 76.

12. Davis, *Breckinridge*, 536–47; Trusten Polk Diary, January 1–October 28, 1865, p. 44, Trustan Polk Papers, Southern Historical Collection, UNC; Guterl, *American Mediterranean*, 76; Eliza McHatton-Ripley, *From Flag to Flag: A Woman's Adventures and Experiences in the South During the War, in Mexico, and in Cuba* (New York: Appleton, 1889), 132; Eli N. Evans, *Judah P. Benjamin: The Jewish Confederate* (New York: Free Press, 1989), 41; Ulrich. B. Phillips, ed., *Annual Report of the American Historical Association for the Year 1911*, vol. 2, *The Correspondence of Robert Toombs, Alexander*

H. *Stephens, and Howell Cobb* (Washington, DC: American Historical Association, 1913), 675–76; Lynda Lasswell Crist, Suzanne Scott Gibbs, Brady L. Hutchison, and Elizabeth Henson Smith, eds., *The Papers of Jefferson Davis*, vol. 12, *June 1865–December 1870* (Baton Rouge: Louisiana State University Press, 2008), 270–71; Joseph H. Parks, *General Edmund Kirby Smith, C.S.A.* (Baton Rouge: Louisiana State University Press, 1992), 482–83; *Compilation of Messages*, 2:74, 105, 133.

13.   McHatton-Ripley, *From Flag to Flag*, 59–60, 122–26, 155, 170; Guterl, *American Mediterranean*, 88–92.

14.   Kathleen López, *Chinese Cubans: A Transnational History* (Chapel Hill: University of North Carolina Press, 2013), 23; McHatton-Ripley, *From Flag to Flag*, 174; Guterl, *American Mediterranean*, 104.

15.   *The Cuba Commission Report: A Hidden History of the Chinese in Cuba* (Baltimore: Johns Hopkins University Press, 1993); Guterl, *American Mediterranean*, 105–8.

16.   McHatton-Ripley, *From Flag to Flag*, 293–95.

Chapter 11: Slave, Soldier, Citizen

1.   Ada Ferrer, *Insurgent Cuba: Race, Nation, and Revolution, 1868–1898* (Chapel Hill: University of North Carolina Press, 1999), 15, 37; Schmidt, *Cachita's Streets*, 54–56; Foner, *A History of Cuba*, 2:50.

2.   Ferrer, *Insurgent Cuba*, 15.

3.   Ferrer, *Insurgent Cuba*, 62.

4.   Ferrer, *Insurgent Cuba*, 24.

5.   Ferrer, *Insurgent Cuba*, 24–25; Teresa Prados-Torreira, *Mambisas: Rebel Women in Nineteenth-Century Cuba* (Gainesville: University Press of Florida, 2005); Rosa Castellanos Castellanos, 3er Cuerpo, 1a División, ANC, Fondo Ejército Libertador.

6.   Ferrer, *Insurgent Cuba*, 26; Carlos Manuel de Céspedes, *Escritos* (Havana: Ciencias Sociales, 1982), 1:142–46.

7.   Ferrer, *Insurgent Cuba*, 26–27; Constitución de Guáimaro, in Pichardo, *Documentos para la historia de Cuba*, 1:376–79.

8.   Ferrer, *Insurgent Cuba*, 38–42, 68. The taking of Cuba as a last name on winning freedom is something I have observed in church records of baptisms of parishioners of color during the last three decades of the nineteenth century.

9.   Ferrer, *Insurgent Cuba*, 58; José Luciano Franco, *Antonio Maceo: apuntes para una historia de su vida* (Havana: Ciencias Sociales, 1989), 1:45.

10.   Ferrer, *Insurgent Cuba*, 21.

11.   Ferrer, *Insurgent Cuba*, 58–59.

12. Ferrer, *Insurgent Cuba*, 61.

13. Ferrer, *Insurgent Cuba*, 62–63.

14. Ferrer, *Insurgent Cuba*, 63–67.

15. Ferrer, *Insurgent Cuba*, 73.

16. Ferrer, *Insurgent Cuba*, 74, 77.

17. Ferrer, *Insurgent Cuba*, 78–79.

18. Ferrer, *Insurgent Cuba*, 86–87.

19. Ferrer, *Insurgent Cuba*, 79.

20. Rebecca Scott, *Slave Emancipation in Cuba: The Transition to Free Labor* (Princeton, NJ: Princeton University Press, 1985), 194.

Chapter 12: A Revolution for the World

1. *New York Herald*, November 1, 1880, 9.

2. A. López, *José Martí*, 58–59; José Martí, "Presidio Político," in *José Martí Obras Completas: Edición Crítica*, 3rd ed. (hereafter *JMOC* 3), (Havana: Centro de Estudios Martianos, 2010), 1:63. There are many editions of Martí's collected works. When possible, I have used the twenty-eight-volume edition published by the Centro de Estudios Martianos in Havana, which is available digitally at http://www.josemarti.cu/obras-edicion-critica/.

3. A. López, *José Martí*, 93–191.

4. José Martí, "Del viejo al nuevo mundo, escenas neoyorquinas," in *JMOC* 3, 17:154–56; Laura Lomas, *Translating Empire: José Martí, Migrant Latino Subjects, and American Modernities* (Durham, NC: Duke University Press, 2009), 58; López Mesa, *Algunos aspectos culturales de la comunidad cubana de New York durante el siglo xix*, 36–37.

5. José Martí, "A Town Sets a Black Man on Fire," in *José Martí: Selected Writings* (hereafter *JMSW*), trans. and ed. Esther Allen (New York: Penguin, 2002), 310–13; see also A. López, *José Martí*, 212–14.

6. Martí notebook fragments cited or translated in *JMSW*, 287, and Lomas, *Translating Empire*, 2.

7. José Martí, "Our America," in *JMSW*, 288–96.

8. Jesse Hoffung-Garskof, *Racial Migrations: New York City and the Revolutionary Politics of the Spanish Caribbean* (Princeton, NJ: Princeton University Press, 2019).

9. Ferrer, *Insurgent Cuba*, 126, 123; Hoffnung-Garskof, *Racial Migrations*, 155–62.

10. Montecristi Manifesto in *JMSW*, 337–45.

NOTES

11. Chronicling America, LOC; Martí, *Diario,* entries for May 2–4, in *JMOC* 3; *New York Herald*, May 19, 1895, 1.

12. Martí to Manuel Mercado, May 18, 1895, *JMSW*, 346–49. Emphasis mine.

13. Ferrer, *Insurgent Cuba*, 148–49.

14. Ferrer, *Insurgent Cuba*, 147–48.

15. Ricardo Batrell, *Para la historia: Apuntes autobiográficos de la vida de Ricardo Batrell Oviedo* (Havana: Seoane y Alvarez, 1912); José Isabel Herrera (Mangoché), *Impresiones de la Guerra de Independencia* (Havana: Editorial Nuevos Rumbos, 1948).

16. Ferrer, *Insurgent Cuba*, 151–53.

17. Ferrer, *Insurgent Cuba*, 142–43; Violet Asquith Bonham-Carter, *Winston Churchill: An Intimate Portrait* (New York: Harcourt, Brace & World, 1965), 2:18.

18. John Tone, *War and Genocide in Cuba, 1895–1898* (Chapel Hill: University of North Carolina Press, 2006), 8; Francisco Pérez Guzmán, *Herida profunda* (Havana: Ediciones Unión, 1998); Emilio Roig de Leuchsenring, *Weyler en Cuba: Un precursor de la barbarie fascista* (Havana: Páginas, 1947), 175; Louis A. Pérez, *The War of 1898*, 28, 72–73.

19. Ferrer, *Insurgent Cuba*, 165–67; Philip S. Foner, *The Spanish-Cuban-American War and the Birth of American Imperialism*, vol. 1, *1895–1898* (New York: Monthly Review Press, 1972), 84–85.

20. Foner, *Spanish-Cuban-American War*, 1:85–88; José Miró y Argenter, *Cuba: Crónicas de la guerra* (Havana: Instituto del Libro, 1970) 3:240–44.

21. Franco, *Antonio Maceo*, 3:214; Foner, *Spanish-Cuban-American War*, 1:90–92; Miró y Argenter, *Cuba*, 3:267–312, 328.

22. Franco, *Antonio Maceo*, 3:375; Foner, *Spanish-Cuban-American War*, 1:97; López Mesa, *La comunidad*, 51; *New York Sun*, December 13, 14, and 16, 1896; *Congressional Record*, December 14, 1896. A sense of the popularity of Maceo as a name for African American boys can be gleaned by searching www.ancestry.com birth and military service records.

23. Foner, *Spanish-Cuban-American War*, 1:127–29.

24. Foner, *Spanish-Cuban-American War*, 1:135.

25. Louis A. Pérez, *Cuba and the United States: Ties of Singular Intimacy* (Athens: University of Georgia Press, 1990), 84, 89.

26. Martí to Manuel Mercado, May 18, 1895, *JMSW*, 346–49. Emphasis mine.

27. Ferrer, *Insurgent Cuba*, 171; Louis A. Pérez, *Cuba and the United States*, 90.

28. Headlines quoted are from the *New York Sun*, February 24 and March 3, 1898; *Washington Evening Times*, quoted in Mark Lee Gardner, *Rough Riders: Theodore Roosevelt, His Cowboy Regiment, and the Immortal Charge up San Juan Hill* (New York: HarperCollins, 2016), 13.

29.   Louis A. Pérez, *Cuba and the United States*, 93.

30.   Louis A. Pérez, *Cuba and the United States*, 96.

Chapter 13: A War Renamed

1.   Greg Grandin, *The End of the Myth: From the Frontier to the Border Wall in the Mind of America* (New York: Metropolitan Books, 2019), 136–37.

2.   Gardner, *Rough Riders*, 10, 17; Theodore Roosevelt, *The Rough Riders* (New York: Charles Scribner's Sons, 1899), 1.

3.   Gardner, *Rough Riders*, 25, 29; Roosevelt, *Rough Riders*, 47. Matthew Frye Jacobson, *Special Sorrows: The Diasporic Imagination of Irish, Polish, and Jewish Immigrants in the United States* (Berkeley: University of California Press, 2002), ch. 4.

4.   Roosevelt, *Rough Riders*, 57; Gardner, *Rough Riders*, 17, 22, 25, 29. Luna's service record from the Spanish American War is available online, NARA, https://catalog.archives.gov/id/301062.

5.   Roosevelt, *Rough Riders*, 47.

6.   Rebecca Scott, *Degrees of Freedom: Louisiana and Cuba After Slavery* (Cambridge, MA: Harvard University Press, 2005), 42–47, 155, 190.

7.   Jerome Tucille, *The Roughest Riders: The Untold Story of the Black Soldiers in the Spanish-American War* (Chicago: Chicago Review Press, 2015), 29–31.

8.   Nancy Hewitt, *Southern Discomfort: Women's Activism in Tampa, Florida, 1880s–1920s* (Urbana: University of Illinois Press, 2001); Willard Gatewood, *"Smoked Yankees" and the Struggle for Empire: Letters from Negro Soldiers, 1898–1902* (Fayetteville: University of Arkansas Press, 1987), 22–24.

9.   Gatewood, *Smoked Yankees*, 27–29.

10.   Gatewood, *Smoked Yankees*, 5.

11.   Ferrer, *Insurgent Cuba*, 177; Martí to Manuel Mercado, May 18, 1895, in *JMSW*, 346–49.

12.   Ferrer, *Insurgent Cuba*, 185–86; Louis A. Pérez, *Cuba Between Empires, 1878–1902* (Pittsburgh: University of Pittsburgh Press, 1983), 290–92.

13.   Louis A. Pérez, *Cuba Between Empires*, 106; Ferrer, *Insurgent Cuba*, 179–80.

14.   Ferrer, *Insurgent Cuba*, 180–83.

15.   Ferrer, *Insurgent Cuba*, 182–84.

16.   Ferrer, *Insurgent Cuba*, 192, 187–88.

17.   Ferrer, *Insurgent Cuba*, 189.

18.   Ferrer, *Insurgent Cuba*, 187, 192; Marial Iglesias, *A Cultural History of Cuba during the U.S. Occupation, 1898–1902* (Chapel Hill: University of North Carolina Press, 2011), 40–42.

NOTES

19. Foner, *Spanish-Cuban-American War*, vol. 2, *1898–1902*, 369–70, 372.

20. Foner, *Spanish-Cuban-American War*, 2:423.

21. Albert G. Robinson, *Cuba and the Intervention* (New York: Longmans, Green, 1905), 87; José M. Hernández, *Cuba and the United States: Intervention and Militarism, 1868–1933* (Austin: University of Texas Press, 1993), 76.

Chapter 14: Island Occupied

1. Archivo Nacional de Cuba, *Guía breve de los fondos procesados del Archivo Nacional* (Havana: Editorial Academia, 1990), 46; Joaquín Llaverías, *Historia de los Archivos de Cuba* (Havana: Archivo Nacional de Cuba, 1949), 278.

2. Iglesias, *Cultural History*, 11, 23–24; *El Fígaro*, vol. 15, no. 16, April 30, 1899.

3. Foner, *Spanish-Cuban-American War*, 2:433–43; Louis A. Pérez, *Army Politics in Cuba, 1898–1958* (Pittsburgh: University of Pittsburgh Press, 1976), ch. 1; "Cuban Republic's Army," *New York Times*, June 26, 1902, 3.

4. Foner, *Spanish-Cuban-American War*, 2:452–53.

5. Foner, *Spanish-Cuban-American War*, 2:453, 519–27.

6. Hermann Hagedorn, *Leonard Wood: A Biography*, 2 vols. (New York: Kraus Reprint, 1969); Leonard Wood, "The Military Government of Cuba," *Annals of the American Academy of Political Science* 21 (1903), 1, 5.

7. Hagedorn, *Leonard Wood*, 1:288, 261–62.

8. Ada Ferrer, "Education and the Military Occupation of Cuba: American Hegemony and Cuban Responses" (MA thesis, University of Texas, Austin, 1988), 7, 28, 35.

9. Ferrer, "Education," 30–34; Iglesias, *Cultural History*.

10. Charter Appendix, quoted in Ferrer, "Education," 30–31.

11. Ferrer, "Education," 41–42, 49.

12. Iglesias, *Cultural History*, 75; Ferrer, "Education," 42–44, 51–55.

13. Ferrer, "Education," 46–49, 65.

14. Ferrer, "Education," 66.

15. Louis A. Pérez, *Cuba: Between Reform and Revolution*, 147–49; Gillian McGillivray, *Blazing Cane: Sugar Communities, Class, and State Formation in Cuba* (Durham, NC: Duke University Press, 2009), 76.

16. Louis A. Pérez, *Lords of the Mountain: Banditry and Peasant Protest in Cuba, 1878–1918* (Pittsburgh: University of Pittsburgh Press, 1989), 95–96.

17. Louis A. Pérez, *Lords of the Mountain*, 96–98; McGillivray, *Blazing Cane*, 76; Carmen Diana Deere, "'Ahí vienen los yanquis': El auge y la declinación de las colonias

NOTES

norteamericanas en Cuba (1898–1930)," in *Mirar el Niágara: Huellas culturales entre Cuba y los Estados Unidos*, ed. Rafael Hernández (Havana: Centro de Investigación y Desarrollo de la Cultura Cubana Juan Marinello, 2000), 131–34.

18. Louis A. Pérez, *Lords of the Mountain*, 100.

19. McGillivray, *Blazing Cane*, 76, 91; Oscar Zanetti, "United Fruit Company: Politics in Cuba," in *Diplomatic Claims: Latin American Historians View the United States*, ed. Warren Dean (Lanham, MD: University Press of America, 1985), 165.

20. Foner, *Spanish-Cuban-American War*, 2:528–34.

21. Foner, *Spanish-Cuban-American War*, 2:540–42.

22. Foner, *Spanish-Cuban-American War*, 2:543–44; Ferrer, *Insurgent Cuba*, 121.

23. Foner, *Spanish-Cuban-American War*, 2:545.

24. Foner, *Spanish-Cuban-American War*, 2:546.

25. Foner, *Spanish-Cuban-American War*, 2:557; "Annual Report of the Secretary of War, 1901," 57th Congress, 1st Sess., House Document 2, vol. 4269, 49.

26. Foner, *Spanish-Cuban-American War*, 2:563–64; "A Symposium on Cuba," *The State*, February 4, 1901, 4.

27. Foner, *Spanish-Cuban-American War*, 2:547–56, 567–69.

28. Foner, *Spanish-Cuban-American War*, 2:572–73.

29. Gómez to Convention, March 26, 1901, in Juan Gualberto Gómez, *Por Cuba Libre*, 2nd ed. (Havana: Ciencias Sociales, 1974), 486–88.

30. Foner, *Spanish-Cuban-American War*, 2:594, 613–15.

31. J. G. Gómez, *Por Cuba Libre*, 132, 486–88; Wood to Roosevelt, October 28, 1901, p. 3, in Library of Congress, Teddy Roosevelt Papers, available online, http://www.theodorerooseveltcenter.org/Research/Digital-Library/Record/?libID=o35547.

Chapter 15: Empire of Sugar

1. Emeterio S. Santovenia and Raúl M. Shelton, *Cuba y su historia* (Miami: Rema Press, 1965), 2:385–87.

2. Louis A. Pérez, *Cuba: Between Reform and Revolution*, 149–50; Louis A. Pérez, *Cuba Between Empires*, 363; Ramiro Guerra y Sánchez, *Sugar and Society in the Caribbean: An Economic History of Cuban Agriculture* (New Haven, CT: Yale University Press, 1964), 80, 159; Thomas, *Cuba: The Pursuit of Freedom*, 469.

3. Louis A. Pérez, *Cuba Under the Platt Amendment, 1902–1934* (Pittsburgh: University of Pittsburgh Press, 1986), 72; Louis A. Pérez, *Cuba: Between Reform and Revolution*, 157; McGillivray, *Blazing Cane*, 77; Guerra y Sánchez, *Sugar and Society*, 168–69; Deere, "'Ahí vienen los yanquis,'" 140.

NOTES

4. Deere, "'Ahí vienen los yanquis,'" 130, 136–45, 147–52; Louis A. Pérez, *Cuba: Between Reform and Revolution*, 150–51.

5. Guerra y Sánchez, *Sugar and Society*, 63, 77; Alan Dye, *Cuban Sugar in the Age of Mass Production: Technology and the Economics of the Sugar Central, 1899–1929* (Stanford, CA: Stanford University Press, 1998), 11; Susan Schroeder, *Cuba: A Handbook of Historical Statistics* (Boston: G. K. Hall, 1982), 258.

6. Louis A. Pérez, *Cuba: Between Reform and Revolution*, 156; Thomas, *Cuba: The Pursuit of Freedom*, 467.

7. Dye, *Cuban Sugar*, 82; Reinaldo Funes Monzote, *From Rainforest to Cane Field in Cuba: An Environmental History since 1492* (Chapel Hill: University of North Carolina Press, 2008), 181–82, 193; Jorge L. Giovannetti-Torres, *Black British Migrants in Cuba: Race, Labor, and Empire in the Twentieth-Century Caribbean, 1898–1948* (New York: Cambridge University Press, 2018), 72; Matthew Casey, *Empire's Guestworkers: Haitian Migrants in Cuba during the Age of US Occupation* (New York: Cambridge University Press, 2017), 20.

8. Muriel McAvoy, *Sugar Baron: Manuel Rionda and the Fortunes of Pre-Castro Cuba* (Gainesville: University Press of Florida, 2003), 37–40; Mary Speck, "Prosperity, Progress, and Wealth: Cuban Enterprise during the Early Republic, 1902–1927," *Cuban Studies* 36 (2005), 70–71; Louis A. Pérez, *Intervention, Revolution, and Politics in Cuba* (Pittsburgh: University of Pittsburgh Press, 1979), 4.

9. In 1906, it would be reorganized as the Cuban American Sugar Company. McAvoy, *Sugar Baron*, 40; César Ayala, *American Sugar Kingdom: The Plantation Economy of the Spanish Caribbean, 1898–1934* (Chapel Hill: University of North Carolina Press, 1999), 80; Foreign Policy Association Commission on Cuban Affairs, *Problems of the New Cuba* (New York: Foreign Policy Association, 1935), 226.

10. Foner, *Spanish-Cuban-American War*, 2:476–77; Ayala, *Sugar Kingdom*, 80; McGillivray, *Blazing Cane*, 89–90; *Planter and Sugar Manufacturer*, vol. 28; *Montgomery Advertiser*, October 21, 1906, 2.

11. Louis A. Pérez Jr., *On Becoming Cuban: Identity, Nationality, and Culture* (Chapel Hill: University of North Carolina Press, 1999), 222; McGillivray, *Blazing Cane*, 95–106; Imilcy Balboa, "Steeds, Cocks, and Guayaberas: The Social Impact of Agrarian Reorganization in the Republic," in *State of Ambiguity: Civic Life and Culture in Cuba's First Republic*, eds. Steven Palmer, José Antonio Piqueras, and Amparo Sánchez Cobos (Durham, NC: Duke University Press, 2014), 213; Guerra y Sánchez, *Sugar and Society*, 194–208.

12. McGillivray, *Blazing Cane*, 92–93.

13. Eva Canel, *Lo que ví en Cuba* (1916; repr., Santiago: Editorial Oriente, 2006), 278; Louis A. Pérez, *On Becoming Cuban*, 222.

14. Louis A. Pérez, *On Becoming Cuban*, 219.

15. Louis A. Pérez, *On Becoming Cuban*, 221; Cluster and Hernández, *History of Havana*, 118.

16. Zanetti, *Historia mínima*, 203; Louis A. Pérez, *On Becoming Cuban*, 221; Louis A. Pérez, *Cuba Under the Platt Amendment*, 77.

17. Cluster and Hernández, *History of Havana*, 116–18, Louis A. Pérez, *On Becoming Cuban*, 137.

18. Louis A. Pérez, *On Becoming Cuban*, 235–37.

Chapter 16: City of Dreams

1. Renée Méndez Capote, *Memorias de una cubanita que nació con el siglo* (Barcelona: Argos Vergara, 1984), 10–11, 126–29.

2. Cluster and Hernández, *History of Havana*, 113–5; "Relación de las calles ... cuyos nombres han sido cambiados desde 1899 hasta la fecha," in *Jurisprudencia en materia de policía urbana* (Havana, 1924), 382–85; Iglesias, *Cultural History*, ch. 4.

3. Méndez Capote, *Memorias*, 42–43, 127.

4. Mayra Beers, "Murder in San Isidro: Crime and Culture during the Second Cuban Republic," *Cuban Studies* 34 (2003), 103; Cluster and Hernández, *History of Havana*, 125; Leonardo Padura, *Siempre la memoria, mejor que el olvido: Entrevistas, crónicas y reportajes selectos* (Miami: Editorial Verbum, 2016), 52–53; Tiffany Sippial, *Prostitution, Modernity, and the Making of the Cuban Republic, 1840–1920* (Chapel Hill: University of North Carolina Press, 2013), 13, 139–44.

5. Dulcila Cañizares, *San Isidro, 1910: Alberto Yarini y su época* (Havana: Editorial Letras Cubanas, 2000), 12–15.

6. Padura, *Siempre la memoria*, 50–51.

7. Two different (and somewhat conflicting) accounts of the confrontation appear in Cañizares, *San Isidro*, 90–93, and Beers, "Murder," 108.

8. Beers, "Murder," 98–99; Tomás Fernández Robaina, *Recuerdos secretos de dos mujeres públicas* (Havana: Editorial Letras Cubanas, 1984), 36.

9. "The Degradation of Cuba," *Daily Oklahoman*, November 29, 1910, 6. The article dates the incident to 1906, but it occurred in 1908. Yarini's funeral was covered in newspapers in Florida, Louisiana, Georgia, Massachusetts, Idaho, Oregon, South Carolina, and Texas.

10. Méndez Capote, *Memorias*, 16, 47–48; Cluster and Hernández, *History of Havana*, 140.

11. Méndez Capote, *Memorias*, 15–17, 39–40; Zanetti, *Historia mínima*, 205–8; Louis A. Pérez, *Cuba: Between Reform and Revolution*, 155; Ned Sublette, *Cuba and Its Music: From the First Drums to the Mambo* (Chicago: Chicago Review Press, 2004), 293–94; Aline Helg, *Our Rightful Share: The Afro-Cuban Struggle for Equality, 1886–1912* (Chapel Hill: University of North Carolina Press, 1995), 101–2.

NOTES

12. Méndez Capote, *Memorias*, 15; Renée Méndez Capote, *Por el ojo de la cerradura* (Havana: Editorial Letras Cubanas, 1981), 102–3.

13. Lillian Guerra, *The Myth of José Martí: Conflicting Nationalisms in Early Twentieth-Century Cuba* (Chapel Hill: University of North Carolina Press, 2005), 110, 130–32, 139; Helg, *Our Rightful Share*, 124–26.

14. Méndez Capote, *Por el ojo*, 103; Raúl Ramos Cárdenas, "'Previsión' en la memoria histórica de la nación cubana," published online September 29, 2014, http://www .arnac.cu/index.php/documentos-en-el-tiempo/prevision-en-la-memoria-histor ica-de-la-nacion-cubana/2212.html.

15. Arthur Schomburg, "General Evaristo Estenoz," *Crisis* 4, no. 3 (July 1912), 143–44; Jesse Hoffnung-Garskof, "The Migrations of Arturo Schomburg," *Journal of American Ethnic History* 21 (Fall 2001), 20–21, 25.

16. L. Guerra, *Myth of José Martí*, 178–81.

17. David A. Lockmiller, *Magoon in Cuba: A History of the Second Intervention, 1906–1909* (New York: Greenwood Press, 1969), 48.

18. Helg, *Our Rightful Share*, 137–81; L. Guerra, *Myth of José Martí*, 133, 181–83; Alejandro de la Fuente, *A Nation for All: Race, Inequality, and Politics in Twentieth-Century Cuba* (Chapel Hill: University of North Carolina Press, 2001), 65.

19. Ada Ferrer, "Rustic Men, Civilized Nation: Race, Culture, and Contention on the Eve of Cuban Independence" *Hispanic American Historical Review* 78 (1998), 663–86; "The Killing of Bandera: Negro General and Two Companions Shot and Slashed to Death," *New York Times*, August 24, 1906, 2; Manuel Cuellar Vizcaíno, *12 muertes famosas* ([Havana]: n.p., 1950), 44.

20. Cuellar Vizcaíno, *12 muertes*, 39–40, 45–48; "The Killing of Bandera," *New York Times*, August 24, 1906, 2; L. Guerra, *Myth of José Martí*, 185. Author's communication with Heriberto Feraudy and Ida Bandera, Havana, May 2015.

21. Lockmiller, *Magoon in Cuba*, 46, 57, 68–71.

Chapter 17: Fratricide

1. Miguel Barnet, *Rachel's Song: A Novel*, trans. Nick Hill (New York: Curbstone Press, 1991), 33; Helg, *Our Rightful Share*, 106.

2. "Nuestro Programa," *Previsión*, August 30, 1908. I am grateful to Raúl Ramos Cárdenas of the Cuban National Archives for sharing his transcription of the article.

3. Helg, *Our Rightful Share*, 154–55, 165; Scott, *Degrees*, 233; de la Fuente, *A Nation for All*, 64, 72–73.

4. Helg, *Our Rightful Share*, 167–68.

NOTES

5. Silvio Castro Fernández, *La masacre de los independientes de color en 1912* (Havana: Ciencias Sociales, 2002), 67; Helg, *Our Rightful Share*, 169, 174–79, 185; Scott, *Degrees*, 237.

6. Scott, *Degrees*, 236, 239; Helg, *Our Rightful Share*, 191.

7. Helg, *Our Rightful Share*, 194–97; Castro Fernández, *La masacre*, 103.

8. Helg, *Our Rightful Share*, 194, 203–4; Castro Fernández, *La masacre*, 100, 140; McGillivray, *Blazing Cane*, 88; de la Fuente, *A Nation for All*, 74.

9. Some historians have argued that Estenoz himself appealed to the Americans to intervene, basing that assertion on a letter dated June 15, 1912. New evidence recently found suggests that the letter may have been written by others who forged Estenoz's signature. See Julio César Guanche, "Una replica documental sobre el 'anexionismo' de Evaristo Estenoz: Una propuesta sobre su testamento político," manuscript under preparation; my thanks to the author for sharing it with me.

10. Helg, *Our Rightful Share*, 204–5, 219; Castro Fernández, *La Masacre*, 105–7.

11. Helg, *Our Rightful Share*, 205, 219; *Index to Dates of Current Events Occurring or Reported During the Year 1912* (New York: R. R. Bowker, 1913).

12. Helg, *Our Rightful Share*, 204, 210–11, 221.

13. Helg, *Our Rightful Share*, 199, 205, 210–11.

14. Scott, *Degrees*, 242–43.

15. Helg, *Our Rightful Share*, 203–4, 210–11; de la Fuente, *A Nation for All*, 75.

16. José Miguel Gómez, "Proclama del Presidente al Pueblo de Cuba," quoted in Guanche, "Replica," 18. See also Helg, *Our Rightful Share*, 211.

17. "El manifiesto de Estenoz," in Guanche, "Replica," 18–21.

18. *El Cubano Libre* (Santiago), June 18, 1912; *La Discusión* (Havana), June 21, 1912; L. Guerra, *Myth of José Martí*, 231; Helg, *Our Rightful Share*, 224; Castro Fernández, *La Masacre*, 205.

19. Helg, *Our Rightful Share*, 225; Castro Fernández, *La Masacre*, 3, 100, 142.

20. Portuondo, *La Virgen*, 245.

Chapter 18: Boom, Crash, Awake

1. Thomas, *Cuba: The Pursuit of Freedom*, 530; "Cuban Aero Squadron for France," *Aviation Week and Space Technology*, September 15, 1917, 254.

2. Thomas, *Cuba: The Pursuit of Freedom*, 543; Louis A. Pérez, *Cuba Under the Platt Amendment*, 186–94; Luis Aguilar, *Cuba 1933: Prologue to Revolution* (Ithaca, NY: Cornell University Press, 1972), 43.

NOTES

3. Zanetti, *Historia mínima*, 203–6; Peter Hudson, *Bankers and Empire: How Wall Street Colonized the Caribbean* (Chicago: University of Chicago Press, 2018), 147, 201–2; Robin Blackburn, "Prologue to the Cuban Revolution," *New Left Review*, 21 (October 1963), 59.

4. Louis A. Pérez, *Cuba Under the Platt Amendment*, 230; Schroeder, *Cuba*, 432; Louis A. Pérez, *On Becoming Cuban*, 336–39; Cluster and Hernández, *History of Havana*, 136.

5. Louis A. Pérez, *Cuba Under the Platt Amendment*, 169–70, 190, 195–96, 205–11.

6. Louis A. Pérez, *On Becoming Cuban*, 167; Rosalie Schwartz, *Pleasure Island: Tourism and Temptation in Cuba* (Lincoln: University of Nebraska Press, 1997), 4.

7. Schwartz, *Pleasure Island*, 5, 50, 56–60, 89; Basil Woon, *When It's Cocktail Time in Cuba* (New York: Horace Liveright, 1928); Louis A. Pérez, *On Becoming Cuban*, 168.

8. Louis A. Pérez, *On Becoming Cuban*, 166–68; Schwartz, *Pleasure Island*, 55, 89.

9. Louis A. Pérez, *On Becoming Cuban*, 169, 183–84; Schwartz, *Pleasure Island*, 82; Peter Moruzzi, *Havana Before Castro: When Cuba Was a Tropical Playground* (Salt Lake City, UT: Gibbs Mith, 2008), 42, 83–84; Roberto González Echevarría, *The Pride of Havana: A History of Cuban Baseball* (New York: Oxford University Press, 1999), 164.

10. Schwartz, *Pleasure Island*, 1–2, 30–33; González Echevarría, *Pride of Havana*, 162.

11. Louis A. Pérez, *On Becoming Cuban*, 184–87.

12. Schwartz, *Pleasure Island*, 85–86.

13. Waldo Frank, "Habana of the Cubans," *New Republic*, June 23, 1926, 140.

14. Louis A. Pérez, *On Becoming Cuban*, 167, 187, 194; Schwartz, *Pleasure Island*, 81.

15. Schwartz, *Pleasure Island*, 31–32; Louis A. Pérez, *On Becoming Cuban*, 167, 187.

16. Sublette, *Cuba and Its Music*, 349; González Echevarría, *Pride of Havana*, 127, 160–61; Walter Isaacson, *Einstein: His Life and Universe* (New York: Simon & Schuster, 2007), 371; José Altshuler, *Las 30 horas de Einstein en Cuba* (Havana: Centro Felix Varela, 2005), 5.

17. Marial Iglesias, "A Sunken Ship, a Bronze Eagle, and the Politics of Memory," in *State of Ambiguity*, 44–45; Fernando Martínez Heredia, "Coolidge en La Habana: La visita anterior," www.cubadebate.cu, March 8, 2016, at http://www.cubadebate.cu/opinion/2016/03/08/coodlige-en-la-habana-la-visita-anterior/#.XpPPYC2ZNBw.

18. Calvin Coolidge, Address Before the Pan-American Conference in Havana, Cuba, January 16, 1828, http://www.presidency.ucsb.edu/ws/?pid=443.

19. Louis A. Pérez, *Cuba Under the Platt Amendment*, 269–72; Coolidge, Address Before the Pan-American Conference.

20. Zanetti, *Historia mínima*, 215–26.

21. Carleton Beals, *The Crime of Cuba* (Philadelphia: J. B. Lippincott, 1933), 270.

22. Louis A. Pérez, *Cuba Under the Platt Amendment*, 196–210; Jaime Suchlicki, *University Students and Revolution in Cuba, 1920–1968* (Coral Gables, FL: University of Miami Press, 1969), 20; "Los estudiantes proclaman la universidad libre," *Pensamiento Crítico* 39 (April 1970), 20–22.

23. Robert Whitney, *State and Revolution in Cuba: Mass Mobilization and Political Change* (Chapel Hill: University of North Carolina Press, 2001), 44–45; "Relato de Fernando Sirgo," *Pensamiento Crítico* 39 (April 1970), 28–29.

24. Whitney, *State and Revolution*, 49; Thomas, *Cuba: The Pursuit of Freedom*, 580; Lynn Stoner, *From the House to the Streets: The Cuban Women's Movement for Legal Reform, 1898–1940* (Durham, NC: Duke University Press, 1991), 70–71.

25. *Pensamiento Crítico* 39 (April 1970), 36–47; Christine Hatzky, *Julio Antonio Mella (1903–1929): Una biografía* (Santiago de Cuba: Editorial Oriente, 2008); Tony Wood, "The Problem of the Nation in Latin America's Second Age of Revolution: Radical Transnational Debates on Sovereignty, Race, and Class, 1923–1941" (PhD diss., New York University, September 2020), pp. 96–99.

26. Gabriela Pulido Llano and Laura Beatriz Moreno Rodríguez, *El asesinato de Julio Antonio Mella: Informes cruzados entre México y Cuba* (Mexico: Instituto Nacional de Antropología e Historia, 2018); Letizia Argenteri, *Tina Modotti: Between Art and Revolution* (New Haven, CT: Yale University Press, 2003), 113–14.

27. McGillivray, *Blazing Cane*, 200; Aguilar, *Cuba 1933*, 98–100; Louis A. Pérez, *Cuba Under the Platt Amendment*, 266, 280–81.

28. Aguilar, *Cuba 1933*, 98–107; Beals, *The Crime of Cuba*, 249–50; Louis A. Pérez, *Cuba Under the Platt Amendment*, 283.

29. Louis A. Pérez, *Cuba Under the Platt Amendment*, 283, 292; Aguilar, *Cuba 1933*, 107, 121.

30. See, for example, *San Diego Union*, December 24, 1931, 3, and December 26, 1931, 13; *San Francisco Chronicle*, December 26, 1931, 5, 8; December 28, 1931, 24.

31. Newton Briones Montoto, *Esperanzas y desilusiones: Una historia de los años 30* (Havana: Ciencias Sociales, 2008), 17.

32. Ruby Hart Phillips, *Cuban Sideshow* (Havana: Cuban Press, 1935), 44–46; "Walkouts in Cuba," *New York Times*, August 6, 1933, 9; "Troops Are Called Out," *New York Times*, August 8, 1933, 1. See also *Bohemia*, August 6, 1933.

33. Phillips, *Cuban Sideshow*, 51–54; "Havana Police Kill Score in Crowd Outside Capitol; Machado Expected to Quit," *New York Times*, August 8, 1933, 1.

34. Welles to Secretary of State, Havana, August 7, 1933 (noon), and Welles to Secretary of State, Havana, August 8, 1933 (9 p.m.), in *Foreign Relations of the United*

NOTES

States, Diplomatic Papers (hereafter *FRUS, DP*), 1933, vol. 5, doc. 129; Louis A. Pérez, *Cuba and the United States*, 190–91.

35. Sublette, *Cuba and Its Music*, 413–14; Welles to Secretary of State, August 11, 1933 (8 p.m.), in *FRUS, DP*, 1933, vol. 5, doc. 150; Louis A. Pérez, *Cuba and the United States*, 192; Phillips, *Cuban Sideshow*, 74.

Chapter 19: Authentic Masses

1. Consul Hurley to Secretary of State, August 13, 1933, in *FRUS, DP*, vol. 5, doc. 319; Sublette, *Cuba and Its Music*, 413–14; Thomas, *Cuba: The Pursuit of Freedom*, 628; Phillips, *Cuban Sideshow*, 65, 68, 100.

2. Phillips, *Cuban Sideshow*, 72.

3. Welles to Hull, August 19, 1933, *FRUS, DP*, vol. 5, doc. 327; Phillips, *Cuban Sideshow*, 84; Louis A. Pérez, *Cuba Under the Platt Amendment*, 319; Welles to Secretary of State, August 24, 1933, *FRUS, DP*, vol. 5, doc. 331; Aguilar, *Cuba 1933*, 157.

4. Aguilar, *Cuba 1933*, 157–59; Whitney, *State and Revolution*, 100; Thomas, *Cuba: The Pursuit of Freedom*, 632.

5. Newton Briones Montoto, *Aquella decisión callada* (Havana: Ciencias Sociales, 1998), 153–66; Rolando Rodríguez, *La revolución que no se fue a bolina* (Havana: Ciencias Sociales, 2013), 124.

6. Scholars disagree about Batista's role in the conspiracy, with some identifying him as its principal leader, and others insisting that he seized that role from the first leader, who was out of Havana that night. Briones Montoto, *Aquella decisión callada*, 153–64; Frank Argote-Freyre, *Fulgencio Batista: From Revolutionary to Strongman* (New Brunswick, NJ: Rutgers University Press, 2006), 57–63; "Entrevista a Pablo Rodríguez," *Pensamiento Crítico* 39 (April 1970), 220–26; Lionel Soto, *La Revolución del 33* (Havana: Editorial Pueblo y Educación, 1985), 3:15–40, 73–74; Ricardo Adán y Silva, *La gran mentira, 4 de septiembre de 1933* (Havana: Editorial Lex, 1947), 100–103; Thomas, *Cuba: The Pursuit of Freedom*, 635–37.

7. R. Rodríguez, *La revolución*, 132.

8. Aguilar, *Cuba 1933*, 161–62.

9. Briones Montoto, *Aquella decisión callada*, 172, 182; R. Rodríguez, *La revolución*, 212; Fernando Martínez, *La revolución cubana del 30: Ensayos* (Havana: Ciencias Sociales, 2007), 30, 68.

10. Welles to Secretary of State, September 10, 1933, *FRUS, DP*, vol. 5, doc. 376; Louis A. Pérez, *Cuba Under the Platt Amendment*, 323–25: R. Rodríguez, *La revolución*, 153, 186; Phillips, *Cuban Sideshow*, 126.

11. R. Rodríguez, *La revolución*, 186.

NOTES

12. Whitney, *State and Revolution*, 105; McGillivray, *Blazing Cane*, 207.

13. José A. Tabares, *Guiteras* (Havana: Instituto Cubano del Libro, 1973), 261–3; McGillivray, *Blazing Cane*, 207–8, 211; Whitney, *State and Revolution*, 113.

14. Louis A. Pérez, *Cuba Under the Platt Amendment*, 324; Tabares, *Guiteras*, 262–63.

15. Welles quoted in Louis A. Pérez, *Cuba Under the Platt Amendment*, 323–25. R. Rodríguez, *La revolución*, 153.

16. Welles to Secretary of State, September 12, 1933, in *FRUS, DP*, 1933, vol. 5, doc. 385; Aguilar, *Cuba 1933*, 188.

17. Welles to Secretary of State, October 5, 1933 (midnight), in *FRUS, DP*, 1933, vol. 5, doc. 430.

18. Grant Watson, September 26, 1933, quoted in Barry Carr, "Mill Occupations and Soviets: The Mobilisation of Sugar Workers in Cuba, 1917–1933," *Journal of Latin American Studies* 28 (1996), 143.

19. Julio LeRiverend, *La República: Dependencia y revolución* (Havana: Editorial de Ciencias Sociales, 1973), 246; Barry Carr, "Mill Occupations," 131; McGillivray, *Blazing Cane*, 211.

20. Carr, "Mill Occupations," 140.

21. McGillivray, *Blazing Cane*, 212–13; Carr, "Mill Occupations," 140.

22. McGillivray, *Blazing Cane*, 211–13; Carr, "Mill Occupations," 152–56; Thomas, *Cuba: The Pursuit of Freedom*, 657.

23. Tabares, *Guiteras*, 40–46, 70–72, 101, 121–24, 135–40, 275; Thomas, *Cuba: The Pursuit of Freedom*, 650; Cluster and Hernández, *History of Havana*, 169.

24. Thomas, *Cuba: The Pursuit of Freedom*, 654; Tabares, *Guiteras*, 188, 282–93.

25. Tabares, *Guiteras*, 188, 262, 271, 288–89, 297, 331.

26. Tabares, *Guiteras*, 176, 257–60, 277–79.

27. Welles to Secretary of State, October 5, 1933 (midnight), in *FRUS, DP*, 1933, vol. 5, doc. 430; Whitney, *State and Revolution*, 106–7.

28. Welles to Secretary of State, September 16, 1933 (1 p.m.), *FRUS, DP*, 1933, vol. 5, doc. 400; Welles to Secretary of State, October 5, 1933 (midnight), *FRUS, DP*, 1933, vol. 5, doc. 430; Welles to Secretary of State, October 4, 1933 (7 p.m.), *FRUS, DP*, vol. 5, doc. 428; Welles to Secretary of State, October 7, 1933 (midnight), vol. 5, doc. 436; McGillivray, *Blazing Cane*, 235.

29. Welles to Secretary of State, October 4, 1933, *FRUS, DP*, 1933, vol. 5, doc. 428; Welles to Secretary of State, October 7, 1933, *FRUS, DP*, 1933, vol. 5, doc. 436; Tabares, *Guiteras*; Paco I. Taibo, *Tony Guiteras* (Mexico City: Planeta Editorial, 2008), 239, 315; Barry Carr, "Identity, Class, and Nation: Black Immigrant Workers, Cuban Communism, and the Sugar Insurgency, 1925–1934," *Hispanic Ameri-*

can Historical Review 78 (1998), 113; *San Francisco Chronicle*, October 27, 1933, 2, and October 28, 1933, 1; *New York Times*, October 27, 1933, 12, and October 28, 1933, 17; Efraín Morciego, *El crimen de Cortaderas* (Havana: Unión de Escritores y Artistas de Cuba, 1982), 11–13.

30. Jefferson Caffery to Acting Secretary of State, December 21, 1933, *FRUS, DP*, 1933, vol. 5, doc. 530; Caffery to Acting Secretary of State, January 10, 1934, *FRUS, DP*, 1934, vol. 5, doc.77.

31. Caffery to Acting Secretary of State, January 10, 1934, *FRUS, DP*, 1934, vol. 5, doc.77; Caffery to Acting Secretary of State, January 13, 1934 (5 p.m.), *FRUS, DP*, 1934, vol. 5, doc.79; Welles to Secretary of State, October 4, 1933, *FRUS, DP*, 1933, vol. 5, doc.428.

32. Secretary of State to Caffery, January 23, 1934, *FRUS, DP*, 1934, vol. 5, doc.103. Thomas, *Cuba: The Pursuit of Freedom*, 674–77.

Chapter 20: New Charter

1. Aguilar, *Cuba 1933*, 173; Ariel Mae Lambe, *No Barrier Can Contain It: Cuban Antifascism and the Spanish Civil War* (Chapel Hill: University of North Carolina Press, 2019, 76–100.

2. See Whitney, *State and Revolution*, ch. 7; Thomas, *Cuba: The Pursuit of Freedom*, 707–14; Argote-Freyre, *Fulgencio Batista*, 214–33; Louis A. Pérez, *Cuba: Between Reform and Revolution*, 212; Joanna Swanger, *Rebel Lands of Cuba: The Campesino Struggles of Oriente and Escambray, 1934–1974* (Lanham, MD: Lexington Books, 2015), 62; Julio César Guanche, "Disputas entre populismo, democracia y régimen representativo: un análisis desde el corporativismo en la Cuba de los 1930," in *Las izquierdas latinoamericanas: Multiplicidad y experiencias durante el siglo xx*, ed. Caridad Massón (Santiago de Chile: Ariadne, 2017), 153–64.

3. Zanetti, *Historia mínima*, 235–38; Louis A. Pérez, *Cuba: Between Reform and Revolution*, 217–18.

4. Club Atenas, *Conferencias de orientación ciudadana: los partidos políticos y la Asamblea Constituyente* (Havana: Club Atenas, 1939).

5. Nestor Carbonell, *Grandes debates de la Constituyente cubana de 1940* (Miami: Ediciones Universal, 2001), 48–50; Mario Riera, *Cuba política, 1899–1955* (Havana: n.p., 1955), 475–76.

6. Carbonell, *Grandes debates*, 17–20, 358; Stoner, *From the House*, 190.

7. Carbonell, *Grandes debates*, 50–51; *Álbúm histórico fotográfico: Constituciones de Cuba, 1868–1901–1940* (Havana: Cárdenas y Compañía, 1940), 155.

8. *Álbúm histórico fotográfico*, 155–66; *Diario de sesiones de la Convención Constitutente* (Havana: [P. Fernández], 1940).

NOTES

9. Ana Suarez, ed., *Retrospección crítica de la Asamblea Constituyente de 1940* (Havana: Centro Juan Marinello, 2011), 24; Alejandra Bronfman, *Isles of Noise: Sonic Media in the Caribbean* (Chapel Hill: University of North Carolina Press, 2016), 59, 104; John Gronbeck-Tedesco, *Cuba, the United States, and Cultures of the Transnational Left, 1930–1975* (New York: Cambridge University Press, 2015), 106; "Manolo Manuscript," New York University Archives, Carl Withers Collection, Box 12.

10. Carbonell, *Grandes debates*, 75, 85; Alejandra Bronfman, *Measures of Equality: Social Science, Citizenship, and Race in Cuba, 1902–1940* (Chapel Hill: University of North Carolina Press, 2004), 172–77; Tomás Fernández Robaina, *El negro en cuba: Apuntes para la historia de la lucha contra la discriminación racial* (Havana: Ciencias Sociales, 1990), 143–44.

11. Carbonell, *Grandes debates*, 77.

12. *Diario de sesiones*, April 27 and May 2, 1940; Bronfman, *Measures of Equality*, 174–78.

13. Bronfman, *Measures of Equality*, 173, 177; Melina Pappademos, *Black Political Activism and the Cuban Republic* (Chapel Hill: University of North Carolina Press, 2011), ch. 6.

14. Andres M. Lazcano, *Las constituciones de Cuba* (Madrid: Ediciones Cultura Hispánica, 1952), 1:257–84; Carbonell, *Grandes debates*, 74–86; *Diario de sesiones*, April 27 and May 2, 1940.

15. Carbonell, *Grandes debates*, 84–85.

16. Carbonell, *Grandes debates*, 82–84.

17. Lazcano, *Las constituciones*, 1:257–84; Carbonell, *Grandes debates*, 85–86; *Diario de sesiones*, May 2, 1940.

18. Carbonell, *Grandes debates*, 85; *Diario de sesiones*, May 2, 1940.

19. Lazcano, *Las constituciones*, 1:257–84; Carbonell, *Grandes debates*, 74–86; *Diario de sesiones*, May 2, 1940; Stoner, *From the House*, 191; Bronfman, *Measures of Equality*, 177–78.

20. *Album histórico fotográfico*, 251; Gustavo Gutiérrez, *La Constitución de la República de Cuba* (Havana: Editorial Lex, 1941), 2: 86; Timothy Hyde, *Constitutional Modernism: Architecture and Civil Society in Cuba, 1933–1959* (Minneapolis: University of Minnesota Press, 2012), 21–22.

21. Constitución de la República de Cuba, 1940, https://pdba.georgetown.edu /Constitutions/Cuba/cuba1940.html.

22. Rafael Rojas, "La tradición constitucional hispanoamericana y el excepcionalismo cubano," in *El cambio constitucional en Cuba*, eds. Rafael Rojas, Velia Cecilia Bobes, and Armando Chaguaceda (Mexico City: Centro de Estudios Constitucionales Iberoamericanos, A.C., 2017), 64–66; Greg Grandin, "Liberal Traditions in the Americas: Rights, Sovereignty, and the Origins of Liberal Multilateralism," *American Historical Review* 117 (February 2012), 68–91; Roberto Gargarella, *Latin American*

NOTES

Constitutionalism, 1810–2010: The Engine Room of the Constitution (Oxford: Oxford University Press, 2013).

23.   Louis A. Pérez, *Cuba: Between Reform and Revolution*, 214.

Chapter 21: Suitcases

1.   *Diario de la Marina* (Havana), October 6, 1948, 1 and October 12, 1948, 1.

2.   *Time*, April 21, 1952; *New York Times*, March 19, 1951; Sam Boal and Serge Fliegers, "The Biggest Theft in History," *American Mercury*, April 1952, 26–35; *Alerta*, October 25, 1948; *Bohemia*, April 2, 1950; Humberto Vázquez García, *El gobierno de la Kubanidad* (Santiago: Editorial Oriente, 2005), 438–39; Enrique Vignier, *La corrupción política administrativa en Cuba, 1944–1952* (Havana: Ciencias Sociales, 1973), 119–29; Ilan Ehrlich, *Eduardo Chibás: The Incorrigible Man of Cuban Politics* (Lanham, MD: Rowman & Littlefield, 2015), 83.

3.   Vázquez García, *El gobierno*, 125–29; 438–39; Vignier, *La corrupción*, 119–29; Cluster and Hernández, *History of Havana*, 178, 183; Sublette, *Cuba and Its Music*, 558; *New York Times*, March 26, 1950, 92.

4.   Zanetti, *Historia mínima*, 239; Thomas, *Cuba: The Pursuit of Freedom*, 729; Ehrlich, *Eduardo Chibás*, 58; Sublette, *Cuba and Its Music*, 504.

5.   Thomas, *Cuba: The Pursuit of Freedom*, 735–37; Louis A. Pérez, *Cuba: Between Reform and Revolution*, 216–17; Zanetti, *Historia mínima*, 240.

6.   *Time*, April 21, 1952; Chibás quoted in Thomas, *Cuba: The Pursuit of Freedom*, 763.

7.   Vignier, *La corrupción*; Phillips, *Cuban Sideshow*, 130.

8.   T. J. English, *Havana Nocturne: How the Mob Owned Cuba and Then Lost it to the Revolution* (New York: William Morrow, 2008), 16; for a critical reinterpretation of the role of the mob in Cuba, see Frank Argote-Freyre, "The Myth of Mafia Rule in 1950s Cuba: Origin, Relevance, and Legacies," *Cuban Studies* 49 (2020), 263–88.

9.   Florida passenger lists available on ancestry.com reveal dozens of trips by Meyer Lansky to Cuba, most of them from the late 1930s through 1958. English, *Havana Nocturne*, 3–6.

10.   English, *Havana Nocturne*, 31–32.

11.   English, *Havana Nocturne*, 33; Enrique Cirules, *The Mafia in Havana: A Caribbean Mob Story* (Melbourne: Ocean Press, 2016), 35–45; Vásquez García, *El gobierno*, 297; Jack Colhoun, *Gangsterismo: The United States, Cuba, and the Mafia, 1933–1966* (New York: Or Books, 2013), 11; Sublette, *Cuba and Its Music*, 516. While the story of the conference appears in many histories of the mafia, historian Frank Argote-Freyre has recently questioned the reliability of their sources; see his "Myth of Mafia Rule in 1950s Cuba."

NOTES

12. English, *Havana Nocturne*, 8, 44; Colhoun, *Gangsterismo*, 9–11.

13. English, *Havana Nocturne*, 40–42; Cirules, *Mafia in Havana*, 53.

14. Argote-Freyre, "Myth of Mafia Rule in 1950s Cuba." 265.

15. Samuel Farber, *Revolution and Reaction in Cuba, 1933–1960: A Political Sociology from Machado to Castro* (Bridgeport, CT: Wesleyan University Press, 1976), 119–22.

16. Ehrlich, *Eduardo Chibás*, 3, 10, 107.

17. Ehrlich, *Eduardo Chibás*, 10, 20–21; Bronfman, *Isles of Noise*, 54–59.

18. Ehrlich, *Eduardo Chibás*, 10, 18.

19. Lillian Guerra, *Heroes, Martyrs, and Political Messiahs in Revolutionary Cuba, 1946–1958* (New Haven, CT: Yale University Press, 2018), 57; Luis Conte Agüero, *Eduardo Chibás, el adalid de Cuba* (Miami: La Moderna Poesía, 1987), 568–69; Ehrlich, *Eduardo Chibás*, 18–22, 60–61.

20. Ehrlich, *Eduardo Chibás*, 19–20.

21. Conte Agüero, *Eduardo Chibás*, 567; Ehrlich, *Eduardo Chibás*, 78.

22. Ehrlich, *Eduardo Chibás*, 75; L. Guerra, *Heroes*, 61; Conte Agüero, *Eduardo Chibás*, 564, 571.

23. Conte Agüero, *Eduardo Chibás*, 612–19; Thomas, *Cuba: The Pursuit of Freedom*, 763.

24. Conte Agüero, *Eduardo Chibás*, 614; Thomas, *Cuba: The Pursuit of Freedom*, 763; L. Guerra, *Heroes*, 64.

25. Ehrlich, *Eduardo Chibás*, 94; Boal and Fliegers, "The Biggest Theft in History," 26, 35; Thomas, *Cuba: The Pursuit of Freedom*, 768.

26. L. Guerra, *Heroes*, 74; Ehrlich, *Eduardo Chibás*, 219, 232–33.

27. L. Guerra, *Heroes*, 33; Ehrlich, *Eduardo Chibás*, 233–37.

28. English, *Havana Nocturne*, 88; "El pueblo opina sobre el gobierno," *Bohemia*, December 16, 1951, 27.

29. Louis A. Pérez, *Cuba: Between Reform and Revolution*, 219–25; L. Guerra, *Heroes*, 83–91; Thomas, *Cuba: The Pursuit of Freedom*, 780–82.

30. Antonio R. de la Cova, *The Moncada Attack: Birth of the Cuban Revolution* (Columbia: University of South Carolina Press, 2007), 32. Michelle Chase, *Revolution Within the Revolution: Women and Gender Politics in Cuba, 1952–1962* (Chapel Hill: University of North Carolina Press, 2015), 35–37; L. Guerra, *Heroes*, 81–82.

31. Thomas, *Cuba: The Pursuit of Freedom*, 79; English, *Havana Nocturne*, 95.

NOTES

Chapter 22: Centennial Spirit

1. *Bohemia*, February 1, 1953; Willis Knapp Jones, "The Martí Centenary," *Modern Language Journal* 37 (1953), 398–402.

2. Carlos Marchante Castellanos, *De cara al sol y en lo alto de Turquino* (Havana: Consejo de Estado, 2012).

3. Roberto Rodríguez Menéndez, "Jilma Madera. Símbolo de la escultura cubana," *Somos Jóvenes*, no. 259 (October 2006), 34–36.

4. Pedro Alvarez Tabío, *Celia, ensayo para una biografía* (Havana: Consejo de Estado), 125, 135–39.

5. Marchante Castellanos, *De cara al sol*; Alvarez Tabío, *Celia*, 135–39; Tiffany Sippial, *Celia Sánchez Mandeley: The Life and Legacy of a Cuban Revolutionary* (Chapel Hill: University of North Carolina Press, 2020), 53–55.

6. Fidel Castro and Ignacio Ramonet, *My Life: A Spoken Autobiography*, trans. Andrew Hurley (New York: Scribner, 2009), 28, 631–34; Thomas, *Cuba: The Pursuit of Freedom*, 804–9; Cova, *The Moncada Attack*, 5, 27.

7. Fidel Castro, *Revolutionary Struggle, 1947–1958*, ed. Rolando Bonachea and Nelson P. Valdés (Cambridge, MA: MIT Press, 1972), 155–58. The description of the assault below draws on Rolando Bonachea and Marta San Martín, *The Cuban Insurrection, 1952–1959* (New Brunswick, NJ: Rutgers University Press, 1974), 18–22; L. Guerra, *Heroes*, 125–30; Cova, *The Moncada Attack*, xxvi–xxvii, 34–38, 68–80.

8. Cova, *The Moncada Attack*, 33–34, 68–80.

9. Bonachea and San Martín, *The Cuban Insurrection*, 22–23; Cova, *The Moncada Attack*, 82–92.

10. Carlos Franqui, *Diary of the Cuban Revolution* (New York: Viking, 1980), 68.

11. L. Guerra, *Heroes*, 123, 128–29; Cova, *The Moncada Attack*, xxvii; Margaret Randall, *Haydée Santamaría, Cuban Revolutionary: She Led by Transgression* (Durham, NC: Duke University Press, 2015), 63; Rafael Rojas, *Historia mínima de la Revolución cubana* (Mexico City: Colegio de Mexico, 2015), 37–38.

12. Jorge Eduardo Gutiérrez Bourricaudy, "La censura de prensa ante los sucesos del Moncada," in *Los Caminos del Moncada*, ed. Reina Galia Hernández Viera (Havana: Editora Historia, 2013), 169–85, 172–76.

13. My description of the trial draws on Marta Rojas, *La generación del centenario en el juicio de Moncada* (Havana: Ciencias Sociales, 1973), 15–73; Georgie Anne Geyer, *Guerrilla Prince: The Untold Story of Fidel Castro* (Boston: Little, Brown, 1991), 121–25; and Jorge Bodes Torres, José Luis Escasena Guillarón, and Rafaela Gutiérrez Valdés, *Valoración jurídico penal del juicio más trascendental de Cuba* (Havana: Ciencias Sociales, 1998).

14. Bonachea and Valdés, *Revolutionary Struggle*, 1:164–221.

NOTES

15. Thomas, *Cuba: The Pursuit of Freedom*, 843.

16. Fidel Castro to Luis Conte Aguero, March 1955, in Fidel Castro, *The Prison Letters of Fidel Castro* (New York: Nation Books, 2009), 65.

17. Franqui, *Diary*, 73–75.

18. Franqui, *Diary*, 68, 75.

19. Franqui, *Diary*, 71–72; Castro and Ramonet, *My Life*, 508.

20. Franqui, *Diary*, 76; Fidel Castro to Franklin D. Roosevelt, November 6, 1940, https://catalog.archives.gov/id/302040.

21. Franqui, *Diary*, 9, 69, 73, 76.

22. Castro and Ramonet, *My Life*, 90; Fidel Castro, *Prison Letters*, 32; Franqui, *Diary*, 66, 71, 73, 75.

23. Fidel Castro's speeches are available online in English at the Castro Speech Database (http://lanic.utexas.edu/la/cb/cuba/castro.html) and in Spanish at Cuban government websites: http://www.cuba.cu/gobierno/discursos/ and https://fidel-discursos .ipscuba.net. Unless otherwise specified all speeches cited are from one of those database. See Castro speeches of April 24, 1959, April 16, 1961, and December 20, 1961.

24. On the early denials, see chapters 25–26. For examples from the 1970s of Castro's retrospective embrace of Marxism, see Rafael Rojas, "The New Text of the Revolution," in *The Revolution from Within: Cuba, 1959–1980*, eds. Michael Bustamante and Jennifer Lambe (Durham, NC: Duke University Press, 2019), 36–37; Castro and Ramonet, *My Life*, 99, 100, 103, 112.

25. Castro and Ramonet, *My Life*, 151–52.

26. Castro to Celia Sánchez, June 5, 1958, in Bonachea and Valdés, *Revolutionary Struggle*, 379.

Chapter 23: Insurrectionary Line

1. Chase, *Revolution*, 19–20.

2. "Amnistía, presos y exiliados," *Bohemia*, May 22, 1955, 59–64; Julio Fernández León, *José Antonio Echeverría: vigencia y presencia* (Miami: Ediciones Universal, 2007), 194–95.

3. Thomas, *Cuba: The Pursuit of Freedom*, 862.

4. L. Guerra, *Heroes*, 197; Chase, *Revolution*, 41, 47; Bonachea and San Martín, *Cuban Insurrection*, 53–59.

5. Bonachea and San Martín, *Cuban Insurrection*, 58–59.

6. Bonachea and San Martín, *Cuban Insurrection*, 53–56; L. Guerra, *Heroes*, 150; Chase, *Revolution*, 40; Fernández León, *José Antonio Echeverría*, 269–73.

NOTES

7.   Fernández León, *José Antonio Echeverría*, 274–76; Bonachea and San Martín, *Cuban Insurrection*, 55.

8.   Fernández León, *José Antonio Echeverría*, 277; Bonachea and San Martín, *Cuban Insurrection*, 55.

9.   Bonachea and San Martín, *Cuban Insurrection*, 55–56; Fernández León, *José Antonio Echeverría*, 279–80; Steve Cushion, *Hidden History of the Cuban Revolution: How the Working Class Shaped the Guerrilla Victory* (New York: Monthly Review Press, 2016), 80.

10. Cushion, *Hidden History*, 88–94; Chase, *Revolution*, 28. The bonus was called the *diferencial*, the sum distributed at the beginning of the yearly harvest in accordance with increases in the cost of living.

11. José Antonio Echeverría, *Papeles del Presidente: Documentos y discursos de José Antonio Echeverría Bianchi*, ed. Hilda Natalia Berdayes García (Havana: Casa Editora Abril, 2006), 28–32, 61–63; Rolando Dávila Rodríguez, *Lucharemos hasta el final* (Havana: Consejo de Estado, 2011), 1:55; Chase, *Revolution*, 20; Bonachea and San Martín, *Cuban Insurrection*, 59–60.

12. Bonachea and San Martín, *Cuban Insurrection*, 72–73.

13. Bonachea and San Martín, *Cuban Insurrection*, 65, 68–69.

14. Bonachea and Valdés, *Revolutionary Struggle*, 1:259–71.

15. Dávila Rodríguez, *Lucharemos hasta el final*, 2:157; Bonachea and San Martín, *Cuban Insurrection*, 66; Van Gosse, *Where the Boys Are: Cuba, Cold War America, and the Making of a New Left* (New York: Verso, 1993), 65.

16. Bonachea and San Martín, *Cuban Insurrection*, 70–78; Echeverría, *Papeles del Presidente*, 84–87; Julia Sweig, *Inside the Cuban Revolution: Fidel Castro and the Urban Underground* (Cambridge, MA: Harvard University Press, 2002), 13; L. Guerra, *Heroes*, 183; José Álvarez, *Frank País y la revolución cubana* (repr., CreateSpace, 2017).

17. Bonachea and San Martín, *Cuban Insurrection*, 78.

18. Alvarez Tabío, *Celia*, 100, 156–69; Franqui, *Diary*, 127.

19. Franqui, *Diary*, 122; Dávila Rodríguez, *Lucharemos*, 2:209.

20. Dávila Rodríguez, *Lucharemos*, 2:211–12, 222; Bonachea and San Martín, *Cuban Insurrection*, 80–83; Sippial, *Celia Sánchez*, 70.

21. Bonachea and San Martín, *Cuban Insurrection*, 80–83.

22. Franqui, *Diary*, 123–24; Ernesto Che Guevara, *Episodes of the Cuban Revolutionary War, 1956–1958* (New York: Pathfinder, 1996), 87–88.

23. Franqui, *Diary*, 129.

NOTES

Chapter 24: The Mountains Rise

1. Guevara, *Episodes*, 102–14; Jon Lee Anderson, *Che Guevara: A Revolutionary Life* (New York: Grove Books, 2010), 224–28.

2. Jerry Knudson, *Herbert L. Matthews and the Cuban Story* (Lexington, KY: Association for Education in Journalism, 1978), 5–7; Sippial, *Celia Sánchez*, 75–76.

3. Knudson, *Herbert L. Matthews*, 5–7; Sippial, *Celia Sánchez*, 75–76; Herbert L. Matthews, "Cuban Rebel Is Visited in Hideout," *New York Times*, February 24, 1957.

4. Franqui, *Diary*, 139, 141; Herbert Matthews, interview with Fidel Castro in Sierra Maestra Mountains, autograph manuscript notes, February 17, 1957, Columbia University, Rare Books and Manuscripts, Herbert Matthews Papers, Miscellaneous Collections Vaults.

5. Matthews, interview with Fidel Castro in Sierra Maestra Mountains, autograph manuscript notes; Matthews, "Cuban Rebel Is Visited in Hideout." See also Anthony DePalma, *The Man Who Invented Fidel: Cuba, Castro and Herbert L. Matthews of the New York Times* (New York: PublicAffairs, 2006), 84–85; Nancy Stout, *One Day in December: Celia Sánchez and the Cuban Revolution* (New York: Monthly Review Press, 2013), 148–49.

6. Knudson, *Herbert L. Matthews*, 5–7.

7. Stout, *One Day*, 136–38; Herbert Matthews, "Cuban Rebel Is Visited in Hideout," *New York Times*, February 24, 1957, 1.

8. Matthews, "Cuban Rebel Is Visited in Hideout."

9. Phillips telegram dated Havana, February 28, 1957, in Matthews Papers, Columbia, Box 10, Folder 3; "Stories on Rebel Fiction, Cuba Says," *New York Times*, February 28, 1957, 13.

10. Bonachea and San Martín, *Cuban Insurrection*, 91–92; Knudson, *Herbert L. Matthews*, 9.

11. CBS, "Rebels of the Sierra Maestra"; L. Guerra, *Heroes*, 249–50; Dávila Rodríguez, *Lucharemos*, 3:70, 84–86.

12. Van Gosse, *Where the Boys Are*, 61, 68–71, 90–91, 102n55.

13. Bonachea and San Martín, *Cuban Insurrection*, 109, 114–20; L. Guerra, *Heroes*, 222.

14. L. Guerra, *Heroes*, 231.

15. Chase, *Revolution*, 66.

16. Bonachea and San Martín, *Cuban Insurrection*, 143; Sweig, *Inside*, 30.

17. Sweig, *Inside*, 29–34; "Al Pueblo de Cuba," *Bohemia*, July 28, 1957, 69, 96–97.

18. Stout, *One Day*, 213–14.

19. The two observations are dated May 1957 and June 12, 1957, both Department of State Central Files, Cuba, Internal Affairs, 1955–1959, Microfilm 6188, Reel 1,

frames 646–49 and 713. My thanks to Michelle Chase for sharing her notes on these sources.

20. Bonachea and San Martín, *Cuban Insurrection*, 165–66; Van Gosse, *Where the Boys Are*, 65–66; Sweig, *Inside*, 68–74; *Bohemia*, February 2, 1958.

21. "Despatch from the Consulate at Santiago de Cuba to State Department," January 21, 1958, in *FRUS, DP*, 1958–1960, Cuba, vol. 6, doc. 18; R. Rojas, *Historia mínima*, 87–89.

22. Sara Kozameh, "Guerrillas, Peasants, and Communists: Agrarian Reform in Cuba's 1958 Liberated Territories," *Americas* 76 (2019), 641–73.

23. Kozameh, "Guerrillas"; L. Guerra, *Heroes*, 264.

24. Department of State Central Files, Cuba, Internal Affairs, 1955–1959, Microfilm 6188, Reel 34, passim; secret telegram dated February 21, 1958, and March 27, 1958, memo, Reel 2, frames 710–11 and 1000–1010; despatch from US Embassy to State Department, Havana, January 10, 1958, in *FRUS, DP*, 1958–1960, Cuba, vol. 6, doc. 2; Sweig, *Inside*, 105; Earl Smith, *Fourth Floor: An Account of the Castro Communist Revolution* (New York: Random House, 1962), 77.

Chapter 25: First Time

1. Rufo López Fresquet, *My 14 Months with Castro* (Cleveland: World, 1966), 65; Hugh Thomas, *The Cuban Revolution* (New York: Harper & Row, 1977), 248.

2. Fidel Castro, January 1 broadcast, Radio Rebelde, in Franqui, *Diary*, 483–84.

3. Franqui, *Diary*, 501; Fidel Castro speech, Santiago, January 1, 1959.

4. Castro speech, Santiago, January 1, 1959.

5. Thomas, *Cuban Revolution*, 248–49, 283; Franqui, *Diary*, 504; interview, Adelaida Ferrer, December 3, 2018; *Bohemia*, February 22, 1959, 78. The poll was conducted between February 6 and 13, 1959; the 92 percent figure I use is rounded up from 91.85 percent.

6. Lynn Hunt, "Revolutionary Time and Regeneration," *Diciottesimo Secolo* 9 (2016), 62–76; María del Pilar Díaz Castañón, *Ideología y revolución: Cuba, 1959–1962* (Havana: Ciencias Sociales, 2004), 106–7; Franqui, *Diary*, 503; Louis A. Pérez, *Cuba: Between Reform and Revolution*, 242–43; Lillian Guerra, *Visions of Power: Revolution, Redemption, and Resistance, 1959–1971* (Chapel Hill: University of North Carolina Press, 2012), 57; Santovenia and Shelton, *Cuba*, 3:307.

7. Fidel Castro speech, Presidential Palace, Havana, January 8, 1959. (I use translation from English version; crowd reactions noted in Spanish version.)

8. Fidel Castro speech, Camp Columbia, Havana, January 8, 1959, http://lanic.utexas.edu/project/castro/db/1959/19590109-1.html.

NOTES

9. Ernesto Cardenal, *In Cuba* (New York: New Directions, 1974), 322; Thomas, *Cuban Revolution*, 287–88.

10. Thomas, *Cuban Revolution*, 149, 284–86, 303; Franqui, *Diary*, 503–4; "The Vengeful Visionary," *Time*, January 26, 1959.

11. Thomas, *Cuban Revolution*, 303.

12. Thomas, *Cuban Revolution*, 292–94; Michelle Chase, "The Trials: Violence and Justice in the Aftermath of the Cuban Revolution," in *A Century of Revolution: Insurgent and Counterinsurgent Violence during Latin America's Cold War*, eds. Gilbert Joseph and Greg Grandin (Durham, NC: Duke University Press, 2010).

13. Chase, "The Trials," 177–8; L. Guerra, *Visions*, 46–47; Ezer Vierba, "Image and Authority: Political Trials Captured in Cuba and Panama, 1955–1959," *Estudios Interdisciplinarios de America Latina y el Caribe* 26, no. 2 (2015), 77.

14. López Fresquet, *14 Months*, 68; Aleksandr Fursenko and Timothy Naftali, *One Hell of a Gamble: Khrushchev, Castro, and Kennedy, 1958–1964* (New York: Norton, 1995), 8; "Scolding Hero," *Time*, February 2, 1959; Jules Dubois, "Las ejecuciones en Cuba," *Bohemia*, February 1, 1959, 6; L. Guerra, *Visions*, 46–48.

15. Chase, "The Trials," 165–66; "Scolding Hero," *Time*, February 2, 1959.

16. William A. Williams, *The United States, Cuba, Castro: An Essay on the Dynamics of Revolution and the Dissolution of Empire* (New York: Monthly Review Press, 1962), 31; Chase, "The Trials," 166; L. Guerra, *Visions*, 46–47; Vierba, "Image and Authority"; *Bohemia*, February 22, 1959, 79, Table 2. "Establishing liberty" was the second most popular at 30 percent. Lions' Club letter to Eisenhower was published in *Revolución*, February 2, 1959. See Díaz Castañón, *Ideología*, 143n44.

17. Fidel Castro speech at Presidential Palace, January 17, 1959; R. Hart Phillips, "Cuba to Try 1,000 for 'War Crimes,'" *New York Times*, January 20, 1959, 1.

18. Thomas, *Cuban Revolution*, 305.

19. Fidel Castro speech, January 21, 1959; L. Guerra, *Visions*, 47.

20. Louis A. Pérez, *Cuba: Between Reform and Revolution*, 244; William Kelly, "Revolución es Reconstruir: Housing, Everyday Life, and Revolution in Cuba, 1959–1988" (PhD diss., Rutgers University, 2021); L. Guerra, 45–46.

21. De la Fuente, *A Nation for All*; Devyn Spence Benson, *Antiracism in Cuba: The Unfinished Revolution* (Chapel Hill: University of North Carolina Press, 2016); Chase, *Revolution*.

22. Sara Kozameh, "Harvest of Revolution: Agrarian Reform and the Making of Revolutionary Cuba, 1958–1970" (PhD diss., New York University, 2020); Thomas, *Cuban Revolution*, 442; Fernando Martínez, personal communication.

23. Marifeli Pérez-Stable, *The Cuban Revolution: Origins, Course, and Legacy* (New York: Oxford University Press, 1993), 67–68.

NOTES

24. L. Guerra, *Visions*, 46; Zanetti, *Historia mínima*, 268.

25. Lars Schoultz, *That Infernal Little Cuban Republic: The United States and the Cuban Revolution* (Chapel Hill: University of North Carolina Press, 2009), 91.

26. Thomas, *Cuban Revolution*, 417, 431; R. Rojas, *Historia mínima*, 99–100; Schoultz, *Infernal Little Cuban Republic*, 90–91, 101; López Fresquet, *14 Months*, 110.

27. Thomas, *Cuban Revolution*, 301, 418; Schoultz, *Infernal Little Cuban Republic*, 88; Fidel Castro speeches of April 8, April 9, and April 12, 1959.

28. Schoultz, *Infernal Little Cuban Republic*, 93; López Fresquet, *14 Months*, 106–8; Thomas, *Cuban Revolution*, 427–28.

29. Schoultz, *Infernal Little Cuban Republic*, 93; Gosse, *Where the Boys Are*, 113–16; E. W. Kenworthy, "Castro Visit Leaves Big Question Mark," *New York Times*, April 19, 1957, E7.

30. The description of the meeting between Nixon and Castro comes from two sources, both available through the Digital National Security Archive (Proquest) database (hereafter DNSA): "Rough Draft Summary of Conversation between the Vice President and Fidel Castro," April 25, 1959, and Ambassador Bonsal, "Brief Evaluation of the Castro Visit to Washington," April 22, 1959.

31. Schoultz, *Infernal Little Cuban Republic*, 93.

32. Fidel Castro speech, May 8, 1959, Plaza Cívica, Havana.

33. *Bohemia*, March 29, 1959, 4ª Relación, 76–97, passim. Castro later refused to accept funds offered by cattle ranchers and large corporations, significantly reducing the total collected by the government. María del Pilar Díaz Castañón, " 'We Demand, We Demand . . .' Cuba, 1959: The Paradoxes of Year 1," in *The Revolution from Within*, 103–7.

34. Kozameh, "Harvests;" Juan Valdés Paz, *Procesos agrarios en Cuba, 1959–1995* (Havana: Editorial de Ciencias Sociales, 1997), 58–73; Oscar Pinos Santos, "La Ley de la Reforma Agraria de 1959 y el fin de las oligarquías en Cuba," *Temas* nos. 16–17 (October 1998–June 1999), 42–60; Schoultz, *Infernal Little Cuban Republic*, 95.

35. Kozameh, "Harvest."

36. Thomas, *Cuban Revolution*, 437, 445; Schoultz, *Infernal Little Cuban Republic*, 99–100.

37. Schoultz, *Infernal Little Cuban Republic*, 95–96.

38. Schoultz, *Infernal Little Cuban Republic*, 125–26, 129.

39. Thomas, *Cuban Revolution*, 441n; Maurice Zeitlin and Robert Scheer, *Cuba: Tragedy in Our Hemisphere* (New York: Grove Press, 1963), 287–88; R. Rojas, *Historia mínima*, 105.

40. Thomas, *Cuban Revolution*, 452, 455; Luis M. Buch Rodríguez and Reinaldo

NOTES

Suárez, *Gobierno revolucionario cubano: génesis y primeros pasos* (Havana: Ciencias Sociales, 1999), 139–41; Díaz Castañón, *Ideología*, 304.

41. Díaz Castañón, *Ideología*, 120; Thomas, *Cuban Revolution*, 457; L. Guerra, *Visions*, 69; *Bohemia*, July 26, 1959, 68–69.

42. L. Guerra, *Visions*, 73; A newsreel of Castro playing in that game is available at https://www.openculture.com/2014/06/fidel-castro-plays-baseball-1959.html.

43. L. Guerra, *Visions*, 67–73; Celia Cruz, "Guajiro, ya llegó tu día," https://www.you tube.com/watch?v=aB7HNwzenv0&feature=share&fbclid=IwAR3fbaAqomGSF Nx9JT_SmQw2E3szstN4cWT11d59ducGLR6mlixoAOz4FL8.

44. L. Guerra, *Visions*, 73–74; R. H. Phillips, "Castro Resumes the Premiership," *New York Times*, July 27, 1959, 1; Footage of the rally appears in the Cuban government documentary *Caminos de la Revolución*, vol. 3, at 8:28–9:28.

Chapter 26: Radical Nonstop

1. Thomas, *Cuban Revolution*, 452; Schoultz, *Infernal Little Cuban Republic*, 101; R. Rojas, *Historia mínima*, 105; Fidel Castro speech, New York Central Park, April 24, 1959.

2. Schoultz, *Infernal Little Cuban Republic*, 111; Thomas, *Cuban Revolution*, 466–68, 473–74, 477–78; telegram from the embassy in Cuba to Department of State, October 22, 1959, and February 1, 1960, in *FRUS, DP*, 1958–1960, Cuba, VI, docs. 374 and 446; Jesús Díaz, *The Initials of the Earth*, trans. Kathleen Ross (Durham, NC: Duke University Press, 2006), 100–101, 131; Eduardo Boza Masvidal, "¿Es cristiana la revolución social que se está verificando en Cuba?" *La Quincena* (Havana), October 30, 1960; Díaz Castañón, *Ideología*, 162–67.

3. US Department of State, "Summary of Speeches Made at October 26, 1959 Mass Demonstration," Che Guevara section, in Castro Speech Database, http://lanic .utexas.edu/project/castro/db/1959/19591026-2.html.

4. "Mikoyan in Cuba," CIA Current Intelligence Weekly Review, February 11 1960, https://www.cia.gov/library/readingroom/docs/DOC_0000132448.pdf; Herbert Matthews, "Confidential Report on Trip to Cuba, March 6–13, 1960," in New York Public Library, New York Times Company Records, Foreign Desk, Box 123, Folder 4; L. Guerra, *Visions*, 110.

5. Jacqueline Loss and José Manuel Prieto, eds., *Caviar with Rum: Cuba-USSR and the Post-Soviet Experience* (New York: Palgrave Macmillan, 2012), 15; Díaz Castañón, *Ideología*, 309; Schoultz, *Infernal Little Cuban Republic*, 114.

6. "Memorandum from Henry C. Ramsey of the Policy Planning Staff, February 18, 1960; and Secretary of State Herter to Foreign Secretary Lloyd," February 21, 1960, in *FRUS, DP*, 1958–1960, Cuba, VI, docs. 458 and 461.

NOTES

7. L. Guerra, *Visions*, 109–13; Jonathan C. Brown, *Cuba's Revolutionary World* (Cambridge, MA: Harvard University Press, 2017), 111; Carlos Franqui, *Family Portrait with Fidel: A Memoir* (New York: Random House, 1984), 66; "Memorandum of Discussion at the 435th Meeting of the National Security Council, Washington, February 18, 1960"; FRUS, 1958–1960, Cuba, VI, doc. 456; "Mikoyan Lauded at Cuban Meeting," *Stanford Daily*, February 6, 1960.

8. L. Guerra, *Visions*, 111–3; Gregorio Ortega, *La coletilla: una batalla por la libertad de expresión, 1959–1962* (Havana: Editora Política, 1989), 136–7; Thomas, *Cuban Revolution*, 489.

9. Ortega, *Coletilla*, 117–8; Thomas, *Cuban Revolution*, 483, 502.

10. Ortega, *Coletilla*, 138–41; "Ampliado el 'nuevo sistema' de censura de prensa," *Diario de la Marina*, January 17, 1960, A1; "'Libertad de prensa', ¿para qué, para quiénes?" *Hoy*, January 17, 1960, 1.

11. Ortega, *Coletilla*, 143–51. In June 1960, Jorge Zayas began publishing an exile version of *Avance*, called *Avance Criollo*, sponsored by the CIA. "A Program of Covert Action against the Castro Regime," Washington, March 16, 1960, 416; FRUS, DP, 1958–1960, Cuba, VI, doc. 481 and DNSA, The Cuban Missile Crisis Revisited.

12. Ortega, *Coletilla*, 161–64; "Don Quijote llega a Cuba," *Bohemia*, August 7, 1960, 30–31.

13. Havana Embassy, 1674, confidential, May 17, 1960, in maryferrell.org; Ortega, *Coletilla*, 190–99; *Bohemia*, "En Cuba," May 22, 1960, 63. There are competing and contradictory accounts of the end of the *Diario de la Marina*. In US sources, those who take over paper are called "workers" in quotes, while those who sign the letter in support of the publisher are called workers without quotes. In Cuban sources, those who write the *coletillas* and take over papers are workers; those who sign the letter in support of the publisher are not mentioned at all. The internal dynamics at the newspapers—the ways in which the coletillas were drafted, for example—are not clear. To what degree were these actions taken on by workers independently; to what degree did by-then communist-dominated labor organizations strongly encourage those actions, we do not know. The newspaper's owner, José Ignacio Rivero, recounted his version of these events in a memoir titled *Prado y Teniente Rey* (Miami: Editorial SIBI, 1987).

14. "Un Día con el Pueblo ..." *Diario de la Marina*, May 12, 1960, A1; "¡Cubanos!" *Diario de la Marina*, May 12, 1960, A1; Havana Embassy, 1674, confidential, May 17, 1960, p. 12, in maryferrell.org; Thomas, *Cuban Revolution*, 502.

15. "¡Cubanos!" *Diario de la Marina*, May 12, 1960, A1; Havana Embassy, 1674, confidential, May 17, 1960, p. 3, in maryferrell.org.

16. Telegram from embassy to Department of State, Havana, March 4, 1960 (8:55 p.m.), in DNSA; Thomas, *Cuban Revolution*, 491; Díaz Castañón, *Ideología*, 124.

17. George Horne, "City Desk. On the attached tip from Wally Carroll," March 18,

NOTES

1960 (8 p.m.); Herbert Matthews, "Confidential Report on Trip to Cuba, March 6–13," both in New York Public Library, New York Times Company archives, Foreign Desk, Box 123, Folder 4.

18. Fidel Castro speech, March 5, 1960.

19. Díaz Castañón, *Ideología*, 124: L. Guerra, *Visions*, 125.

20. Telegram from embassy in Cuba to Department of State, March 8, 1960, *FRUS, DP*, 1958–1960, Cuba, VI, doc. 470; desk officer quoted in Schoultz, *Infernal Little Cuban Republic*, 116.

21. Christian Herter to President, November 4, 1959, DNSA, Cuban Missile Crisis Revisited; "A Program of Covert Action against the Castro Regime," Washington, DC, March 16, 1960, and Memorandum of a Conference with the President, White House, Washington, DC, March 17, 1960 (2:30 p.m.), both in *FRUS, DP*, 1958–1960, Cuba, VI, docs. 481 and 486.

22. "A Program of Covert Action against the Castro Regime," and Memorandum of a Conference with the President, White House, Washington, March 17, 1960 (2:30 p.m.). Emphasis mine.

23. "A Program of Covert Action against the Castro Regime."

24. "A Program of Covert Action against the Castro Regime"; "Ike Takes Swipe at Lost Cuban Ideals," *Daily Review* (Hayward, California), April 9, 1960, 2.

25. Schoultz, *Infernal Little Cuban Republic*, 119–25; "Big Oil Headaches Vex Hemisphere," *New York Times*, May 29, 1960, F1.

26. The description of the rally is taken from "Sucedió el 7 de Agosto de 1960," *Bohemia*, August 14, 1960, 44, and "¡Se llamaba!," *INRA* 1, no. 8 (September 1960), 4. The text of the speech, Law 851, and audience responses appear at http://www.cuba.cu/gobierno/discursos/1960/esp/f060860e.html.

27. "Sucedió el 7 de Agosto de 1960," and "La Segunda Independencia," *Bohemia*, August 14, 1960, 44–52.

28. "¡Se llamaban!," *INRA* 1, no. 8 (September 1960), 4; L. Guerra, *Visions*, 142–3.

29. Schoultz, *Infernal Little Cuban Republic*, 124–25; R. Rojas, *Historia mínima*, 112–13.

30. Schoultz, *Infernal Little Cuban Republic*, 126, 130–31, 136, 141; Richard Fagen, *The Transformation of Political Culture in Cuba* (Stanford, CA: Stanford University Press, 1969), 69.

Chapter 27: Battle

1. Willis Fletcher Johnson, *The History of Cuba* (New York: B. F. Buck, 1920), vol. 5, ch. 7; "The Charcoal Industry of Cuba," *Coal Trade Journal*, January 9, 1907, 28; Julio García Espinosa and Tomás Gutiérrez Alea, *El Mégano* (The Charcoal Worker),

NOTES

1955 (documentary short, twenty-five minutes); Samuel Feijoo, "Los Prisioneros del Mangle," *Bohemia*, June 3, 1956, 4–6; Barcia, *Una sociedad distinta*; Margaret Randall, *Cuban Women Now: Interviews with Cuban Women* (Toronto: Women's Press, 1974), 171.

2.   "Raúl Castro en la Ciénaga de Zapata," *Hoy*, August 25, 1959, 1; "En Cuba," *Bohemia*, January 3, 1960, 69; "Ya llegó la justicia a los hombres de la Ciénaga," *Bohemia*, August 7, 1960, 10–13, 109–11; "Playa Girón: Millones de pesos invertidos en el Pueblo," *Bohemia*, January 29, 1961, 28–31; J. C. Rodriguez, *Inevitable Battle: From the Bay of Pigs to Plara Girón* (Havana: Editorial Capitán San Luis, 2009), 201–2; "Ni Girón interrumpió la campaña de alfabetización en Cuba," Radio Cadena Agramonte de Camaguey, http://www.cadenagramonte.cu/articulos /ver/13476:ni-giron-interrumpio-la-campana-de-alfabetizacion-en-cuba0.

3.   Grayston Lynch, *Decision for Disaster: Betrayal at the Bay of Pigs* (Washington, DC: Brassey's, 1998), 83–84.

4.   Lynch, *Decision for Disaster*, 85–86; Peter Wyden, *Bay of Pigs: The Untold Story* (New York: Simon & Schuster, 1979), 136–37, 217–21; Jim Rasenberger, *The Brilliant Disaster: JFK, Castro, and America's Doomed Invasion of Cuba's Bay of Pigs* (New York: Scribner, 2011), 238–39.

5.   Lynch, *Decision for Disaster*, 88–9, 111; Howard Jones, *The Bay of Pigs* (New York: Oxford University Press, 2008), 102; James Blight and Peter Kornbluh, eds., *The Politics of Illusion: The Bay of Pigs Invasion Reexamined* (Boulder, CO: Lynne Reiner, 1998), 11–12; *FRUS, DP*, 1961–1963, vol. x, Cuba, Editorial Note, 112.

6.   Jones, *Bay of Pigs*, 118; Schoultz, *Infernal Little Cuban Republic*, 143; Blight and Kornbluh, *Politics of Illusion*, 110–12.

7.   Blight and Kornbluh, *Politics of Illusion*, 41.

8.   "A Program of Covert Action." See also chapter 26.

9.   Peter Kornbluh, ed., *Bay of Pigs Declassified: The Secret CIA Report on the Invasion of Cuba* (New York: Free Press, 1998), 30; Memorandum of a Meeting with the President, White House, August 18, 1960, in *FRUS, DP*, 1958–1960, vol. 6, Cuba, doc. 577.

10.   Kornbluh, *Bay of Pigs Declassified*, 75; *Verde Olivo* 1, no. 32 (October 22, 1960), 6–7.

11.   United States Central Intelligence Agency secret cable, October 31, 1960, DNSA, CIA Covert Operations III; The "Narrative of the Anti-Castro Operation Zapata," which was part of the Taylor Commission Report, gives the date of November 4, 1961, for the cable; Piero Gleijesis, "Ships in the Night: The CIA, the White House, and the Bay of Pigs," *Journal of Latin American Studies* 27 (February 1995), 11.

12.   *FRUS, DP*, 1958–1960, Cuba, v. vi, Editorial Note 612; "Memorandum of a Meeting with the President, November 29, 1960, 11 a.m.," in United States,

NOTES

Special Assistant to the President for National Security Affairs, Top Secret, Memorandum of Conversation, December 5, 1960, DNSA, Cuban Missile Crisis Revisited.

13. Arthur M. Schlesinger, *A Thousand Days: John F. Kennedy in the White House* (Boston: Houghton Mifflin, 1965), 233–34; "Memorandum No. 1. Narrative of the Anti-Castro Cuban Operation Zapata," June 13, 1961, DNSA, Cuban Missile Crisis Revisited; Gleijesis, "Ships in the Night," 11–12; Wyden, *Bay of Pigs*, 72–73; Special National Security Estimate, Number 85-3-60. Prospects for the Castro Regime, December 8, 1960, DNSA, Cuban Missile Crisis Revisited.

14. "Memorandum from the Chief of WH.4/PM, CIA (Hawkins) to the Chief of WH/4 of the Directorate of Plans (Esterline), January 4, 1961, *FRUS, DP*; "Briefing of Secretary of State Designate Rusk," January 1961, DNSA, Cuban Missile Crisis Revisited.

15. "Briefing Papers Used by Mr. Dulles and Mr. Bissell—President-Elect Kennedy," November 18, 1960, in DNSA; Schlesinger, *Thousand Days*, 226, 229, 233; "Kennedy Briefed by Allen Dulles, *New York Times*, November 19, 1960, 1.

16. Rasenberger, *The Brilliant Disaster*, 134; Brown, *Cuba's Revolutionary World*, 151.

17. Schoultz, *Infernal Little Cuban Republic*, 148; L. Guerra, *Visions*, 158; Wyden, *Bay of Pigs*, 122; Department of State, Daily Files, September 29, 1960; Weekly Interagency Summary, November 4, 1960.

18. Schoultz, *Infernal Little Cuban Republic*, 154–55; Memorandum from the Chairman of the Joint Chiefs of Staff to the Commander in Chief, Atlantic, Washington, April 1, 1961, in *FRUS, DP*, 1961–1963, vol. 10, Cuba, Doc. 76.

19. Memorandum for Secretary of Defense from Joint Chiefs, March 15, 1961, DNSA, Cuban Missile Crisis Revisited Collection; Memorandum from Under Secretary of State (Bowles) to Secretary (Rusk), March 31, 1961, in *FRUS, DP*, 1961–1962, vol. 10, Cuba, doc. 75.

20. Schoultz, *Infernal Little Cuban Republic*, 154–5; National Intelligence Estimate, December 8, 1960; "The Situation in Cuba," Department of State, Bureau of Intelligence and Research, Secret, Intelligence Memorandum, December 27, 1960, DNSA, Cuban Missile Crisis Collection; Wyden, *Bay of Pigs*, 99.

21. Rasensberger, *Brilliant Disaster*, 180–83.

22. Rasensberger, *Brilliant Disaster*, 185; Richard M. Bissell Jr., *Reflections of a Cold Warrior: From Yalta to the Bay of Pigs* (New Haven, CT: Yale University Press, 1996), 183; Wyden, *Bay of Pigs*, 170; Blight and Kornbluh, *Politics of Illusion*, 3, 92–97, 102n27.

23. Blight and Kornbluh, *Politics of Illusion*, 2–3.

24. Dulles quoted in Schoultz, *Infernal Little Cuban Republic*, 163; Arthur Schlesinger offers a similar interpretation in Blight and Kornbluh, *Politics of Illusion*, 65, 69.

25. Kornbluh, *Bay of Pigs Declassified*, 12; the IG's report and related documents are transcribed in that volume's appendix.

26. Irving Janis, *Groupthink: Psychological Studies of Foreign-Policy Decisions and Fiascos* (Boston: Houghton Mifflin, 1972), ch. 2.

27. J. R. Herrera Medina, *Operación Jaula: contragolpe en el Escambray* (Havana: Verde Olivo, 2006); J. C. Rodriguez, *The Inevitable Battle*, 52, 99; Brown, *Cuba's Revolutionary World*, 151.

28. Brown, *Cuba's Revolutionary World*, 88–100, 150–51; Juan C. Fernández, *Todo es secreto hasta un día* (Havana: Ciencias Sociales, 1976), 57–58; J. C. Rodríguez, *Inevitable Battle*, 78.

29. *Bohemia*, August 7, 1960, 10–13; "Playa Girón: Millones de pesos invertidos en el Pueblo," *Bohemia*, January 29, 1961.

30. J. C. Rodríguez, *Inevitable Battle*, 206–8, 222–23.

31. US Department of Justice, FBI, June 6, 1961, "Memo on Cuban Situation," Mary Ferrell Foundation; Rosendo Rosell, *Vida y Milagros de la farándula de Cuba* (Miami: Ediciones Universal, 1994), 3:382; conversations with Ramón and Adelaida Ferrer, January 2019; Raymond Warren, "Documentation of Castro Assassination Plots," August 11, 1975, in http://documents.theblackvault.com /documents/jfk/NARA-Oct2017/NARA-Nov9-2017/104-10310-10019.pdf.

32. Fidel Castro speech, April 16, 1961.

33. Kornbluh, *Bay of Pigs Declassified*, 3; Richard Goodwin, Memorandum to the President, August 22, 1961, in FRUS, DP, 1961-1963, vol 10, doc.257; Richard Goodwin, *Remembering America: A Voice from the Sixties* (New York: Open Road, 2014), 199.

34. James Blight and janet M. Lang, *The Armageddon Letters: Kennedy, Khrushchev, Castro in the Cuban Missile Crisis* (Lanham, MD: Rowman & Littlefield, 2012), 52–54; Fursenko and Naftali, *One Hell*, 97–98, 139–40.

Chapter 28: Brink

1. Anders Gustafsson, Javier Iglesias Camargo, Håkan Karlsson, and Gloria Miranda González, "Material Life Histories of the Missile Crisis (1962): Cuban Examples of a Soviet Missile Hangar and US Marston Mats," *Journal of Contemporary Archeology* 4 (2017), 39–58.

2. Gustafsson et al., "Material Life." On popular awareness of presence of Russian soldiers, Benito to Dr. Claudio Rodríguez, August 20, 1962, Cuban Letters Collection, New York University, Tamiment Archives, Box 1, Letter 14.

3. Fursenko and Naftali, *One Hell*, 180; Tomás Diez Acosta, *Octubre de 1962: un paso del holocausto: una mirada cubana a la crisis de los misiles* (Havana: Editora Política, 2002), 87.

4.   Fursenko and Naftali, *One Hell*, 187.

5.   Diez Acosta, *Octubre*, 100, 108; Naftali and Fursenko, *One Hell*, 191; "Secret Agreement July 13, 1962," in History and Public Policy Program Digital Archive, Wilson Center, https://digitalarchive.wilsoncenter.org/document/110878.

6.   Fursenko and Naftali, *One Hell*, 188, 192.

7.   Fursenko and Naftali, *One Hell*, 193; Fidel Castro speech, Santiago de Cuba, July 26, 1962, http://www.cuba.cu/gobierno/discursos/1962/esp/f260762e.html.

8.   Laurence Chang and Peter Kornbluh, eds, *The Cuban Missile Crisis, 1962: A National Security Archive Documents Reader* (New York: New Press, 1998).

9.   "Soviet Statement on US Provocations," September 11, 1962, CIA, FOIA Reading Room, https://www.cia.gov/readingroom/docs/CIA-RDP79T004 28A000200010014-0.pdf; Chang and Kornbluh, *Cuban Missile Crisis*, 368.

10.   Chang and Kornbluh, *Cuban Missile Crisis, 1962*, 368–70; "Excerpts from Dorticós Speech," October 8, 1962, at UNGA, in Princeton University, Adlai Stevenson Papers, Box 346, Folder 1-4, https://findingaids.princeton.edu/MC124/c01827 .pdf.

11.   Chang and Kornbluh, *Cuban Missile Crisis, 1962*, 371–75.

12.   Chang and Kornbluh, *Cuban Missile Crisis, 1962*, 376–77; Michael Dobbs, *One Minute to Midnight: Kennedy, Khrushchev, and Castro on the Brink of Nuclear War* (New York: Vintage, 2009), 38, 95, 249, 279.

13.   President John F. Kennedy "Radio and Television Report to the American People on the Soviet Arms Buildup in Cuba," October 22, 1962, https://microsites.jfk library.org/cmc/oct22/doc5.html; James Reston, "Ships Must Stop," *New York Times*, October 23, 1962, 1; Blight and Lang, *Armageddon Letters*, 42.

14.   Photograph in *Harpers*, https://www.theatlantic.com/magazine/archive/2013/01/ the-real-cuban-missile-crisis/309190/; Alexa Kapsimalis interview, Storycorps, https://archive.storycorps.org/interviews/grandpa-cuban-missile-crisis/.

15.   Chang and Kornbluh, *Cuban Missile Crisis, 1962*, 380; Dobbs, *One Minute*, 84–85.

16.   Chang and Kornbluh, *Cuban Missile Crisis, 1962*, 380; Fidel Castro speech, October 23, 1962; Adolfo Gilly, "A la luz del relámpago: Cuba en Octubre," *Viento Sur* 102 (March 2009), 82.

17.   Fursenko and Naftali, *One Hell*, 265–67; Chang and Kornbluh, *Cuban Missile Crisis, 1962*, doc. 42 and p. 387.

18.   James Blight and janet M. Lang, *Dark Beyond Darkness: The Cuban Missile Crisis as History, Warning, and Catalyst* (Lanham, MD: Rowman & Littlefield, 2018), 36; Dobbs, *One Minute*, 159.

19.   Dobbs, *One Minute*, 169–70.

20.   Fidel Castro to Khrushchev, October 26, 1962. There are multiple English translations of the Russian "original." I have used the one used by the John F. Kennedy

Library, https://microsites.jfklibrary.org/cmc/oct26/doc2.html: See also NSA, *Cuban Missile Crisis, 1962*, doc. 46, and p. 387; Wilson Digital Archive, https://digitalarchive.wilsoncenter.org/document/114501; Diez Acosta, *Octubre*, 177–78; Blight and Lang, *Dark*, 39–40.

21. Khrushchev to Kennedy, October 26, 1962 and October 27, 1962 (Chang and Kornbluh, *Cuban Missile Crisis, 1962*, docs. 45 and 49); Fursenko and Naftali, *One Hell*, 273–74.

22. Transcript of ExComm meetings, October 27, 1962, DNSA, Cuban Missile Crisis Collection; Chang and Kornbluh, *Cuban Missile Crisis, 1962*, doc. 50.

23. Fursenko and Naftali, *One Hell*, 282.

24. Transcript of ExComm meetings, October 27, 1962, Chang and Kornbluh, *Cuban Missile Crisis, 1962*, doc. 50; Dobbs, *One Minute*, 309, 312–13; Jack Raymond, "Airmen Called Up," *New York Times*, October 28, 1962.

25. Dobbs, *One Minute*, 239–40; telegram from Havana Embassy to Foreign Office, October 27, 1962 (11:35 a.m.), in British Archives on the Cuban Missile Crisis, 340; "Cable no. 328 from the Czechoslovak Embassy in Havana (Pavlíček)," October 28, 1962, History and Public Policy Program Digital Archive, National Archive, Archive of the CC CPCz (Prague); File: "Antonín Novotný, Kuba," Box 122, https://digitalarchive.wilsoncenter.org/document/115210; Gilly, "A la luz," 90; *Hoy* (Havana), October 26, 1962, 5; *Bohemia*, October 26, 1962, 69; James Blight and janet Lang, personal communication, March 3, 2020.

26. Khrushchev to Kennedy, October 28, 1962, Chang and Kornbluh, *Cuban Missile Crisis, 1962*, doc. 53, https://microsites.jfklibrary.org/cmc/oct28/doc1.html.

27. White House statement, October 28, 1962, https://microsites.jfklibrary.org/cmc/oct28/; *New York Times*, October 29, 1962, 1.

28. Franqui, *Family Portrait*, 194; Gilly, "A la luz," 91–94.

29. Permanent Representative of Cuba to the UN Secretary General, October 28, 1962, in Chang and Kornbluh, *Cuban Missile Crisis, 1962*, doc. 57.

30. Khrushchev to Castro, October 28, 1962, and Castro to Khrushchev, October 28, 1962, Chang and Kornbluh, *Cuban Missile Crisis, 1962*, docs. 55 and 56.

31. Kennedy to Khrushchev, October 27, 1962, in https://microsites.jfklibrary.org/cmc/oct27/; Khrushchev to JFK, October 27, 1962, https://microsites.jfklibrary.org/cmc/oct27/doc4.html.

32. Chang and Kornbluh, *Cuban Missile Crisis, 1962*, 402–3; Naftali and Fursenko, *One Hell*, 304–9.

33. Chang and Kornbluh, *Cuban Missile Crisis, 1962*, 405.

34. Kennedy, transcript of November 20, 1962 press conference, https://www.jfklibrary.org/archives/other-resources/john-f-kennedy-press-conferences/news

-conference-45; Kennedy to Khrushchev, November 21, 1962, in Chang and Kornbluh, *Cuban Missile Crisis, 1962*, doc. 79.

35.   Brian Latell, *Castro's Secrets: The CIA and Cuba's Intelligence Machine* (New York: Palgrave Macmillan, 2012), 159, 202–3; Naftali and Fursenko, *One Hell*, 305; Chang and Kornbluh, *Cuban Missile Crisis, 1962*, 406.

36.   Mats Burstom, Tomás Diez Acosta, et al, "Memories of a World Crisis: The Archeology of a Former Nuclear Missile Site in Cuba," *Journal of Social Archeology* 9 (2009), 295–317; Gustafsson, "Material Life."

Chapter 29: New People?

1.   Hunt, "Revolutionary Time."

2.   Juan Valdés Paz, "The Cuban Agrarian Revolution: Achievements and Challenges," *Estudios Avançados* 25 (2011), 75; Susan Eckstein, *Back from the Future: Cuba Under Castro* (Princeton, NJ: Princeton University Press, 1994), 57–58, 84; Louis A. Pérez, *Cuba: Between Reform and Revolution*, 262; Zanetti, *Historia mínima*, 290.

3.   Hunt, "Revolutionary Time"; Che Guevara, "Socialism and Man in Cuba," *The Che Guevara Reader* (Melbourne: Ocean Press, 2003), 212–28. Guevara uses the term *hombre nuevo*, or new man. Since many of the projects discussed in this chapter specifically targeted women, I use instead *new people* or *new person*.

4.   Guevara, "Socialism and Man"; Chase, *Revolution*, 183; Anita Casavantes Bradford, *The Revolution Is for the Children: The Politics of Childhood in Havana and Miami, 1959–1962* (Chapel Hill: University of North Carolina Press, 2014), 186.

5.   Chase, *Revolution*; Casavantes Bradford, *Revolution*; Victor Andres Triay, *Fleeing Castro: Operation Pedro Pan and the Cuban Children's Program* (Gainesville: University Press of Florida, 1998), 71–72.

6.   Fagen, *Transformation*, ch. 3; Jonathan Kozol, *Children of the Revolution: A Yankee Teacher in the Cuban Schools* (New York: Dell, 1980), 6; Benson, *Antiracism in Cuba*, 200–206; L. Guerra, *Visions*, 82–83; R. Rojas, *Historia mínima*, 20.

7.   Oscar Lewis, *Four Women* (Urbana: University of Illinois Press, 1977), xxx, 66–67; Chase, *Revolution*, 184–89; Rebecca Herman, "An Army of Educators: Gender, Revolution and the Cuban Literacy Program of 1961," *Gender & History* 24 (2012), 104–5; Casavantes Bradford, *Revolution*, 117.

8.   L. Guerra, *Visions*, 221–23; Anasa Hicks, "Hierarchies at Home: A History of Domestic Service in Cuba, from Abolition to Revolution" (Ph.D. diss, New York University, 2017).

9.   Lois Smith and Alfred Padula, *Sex and Revolution: Women in Socialist Cuba* (New York: Oxford University Press, 1996), chs. 8 and 9; Debra Evenson, "Women's Equality in Cuba: What Difference Does a Revolution Make," *Minnesota Journal of*

NOTES

Law & Inequality 4 (1986), 307. The classic Cuban film on the triple shift dilemma is *Portrait of Teresa*, directed by Pastor Vega, Havana, 1979.

10. Evenson, "Women's Equality," 311, 318.

11. *Cuban Family Code*, Articles 1, 26–28.

12. Elise Andaya, *Conceiving Cuba: Reproduction, Women, and the State in the Post-Soviet Era* (New Brunswick, NJ: Rutgers University Press, 2014), 37; Margaret Randall, *Women in Cuba, Twenty Years Later* (New York: Smyrna Press, 1981), 37–41.

13. *Cuban Family Code*, Article 16; Rachel Hynson, *Laboring for the State: Women, Family, and Work in Revolutionary Cuba, 1959–1971* (New York: Cambridge University Press, 2019), 108.

14. Carrie Hamilton, *Sexual Revolutions in Cuba: Passion, Politics, and Memory* (Chapel Hill: University of North Carolina Press, 2012), 39–41; Abel Sierra Madero, "'El trabajo os hará hombres': Masculinización nacional, trabajo forzado y control social en Cuba durante los años sesenta," *Cuban Studies* 44 (2016), 309–44.

15. Benson, *Antiracism*, 72–76; de la Fuente, *A Nation for All*, 157, 178–80, 259–60, 269; Adelaida Ferrer, personal communication.

16. Benson, *Antiracism*, 112–21; de la Fuente, *A Nation for All*, 263–8; Fidel Castro speech, March 22, 1959.

17. De la Fuente, *A Nation for All*, 264–65.

18. De la Fuente, *A Nation for All*, 269, 274.

19. Fidel Castro speech, January 1, 1961; he repeated the claim in the Second Declaration of Havana on February 4, 1962.

20. Henry Louis Gates and Eldridge Cleaver, "Cuban Experience: Eldridge Cleaver on Ice," *Transition* 49 (1975): 32–44; Timothy Tyson, *Radio Free Dixie: Robert F. Williams and the Roots of Black Power* (Chapel Hill: University of North Carolina Press, 2020); Andrew Salkey, *Havana Journal* (New York: Penguin, 1971); Santiago Alvarez, director, *Now!*, Havana, 1965; Amanda Perry, "The Revolution Next Door: Cuba in the Caribbean Imaginary" (PhD diss., New York University, 2019).

21. Eckstein, *Back from the Future*, 40; Carmelo Mesa Lago, *Cuba in the 1970s: Pragmatism and Institutionalization* (Albuquerque: University of New Mexico Press, 1974), 36.

22. Brian Pollitt, "Crisis and Reform in Cuba's Sugar Economy," in *The Cuban Economy*, ed. Archibald Ritter (Pittsburgh: University of Pittsburgh Press, 2009), 89; Zanetti, *Historia mínima*, 297–98.

23. Fidel Castro speech, January 1, 1969; K. S. Karol, *Guerrillas in Power: The Course of the Cuban Revolution* (London: Jonathan Cape, 1971), 410; Robert Quirk, *Fidel Castro* (New York: Norton, 1995), 620; Margaret Randall, *To Change the World: My Years in Cuba* (New Brunswick, NJ: Rutgers University Press, 2009), 74.

24. L. Guerra, *Visions*, 305–6; Thomas, *Cuban Revolution*, 659; Alma Guillermoprieto, *Dancing with Cuba: A Memoir of the Revolution* (New York: Vintage, 2006), ch. 4; Randall, *To Change*, 75; Julie M. Bunck, *Fidel Castro and the Quest for a Revolutionary Culture in Cuba* (University Park: Pennsylvania State University Press, 1994), 144; Louis A. Pérez, *Cuba: Between Reform and Revolution*, 260.

25. Reinaldo Arenas, *Before Night Falls: A Memoir* (New York: Viking, 1993), 128–32; L. Guerra, *Visions*, 311, 315; Guillermoprieto, *Dancing*, 86.

26. René Dumont, *Is Cuba Socialist?* (New York: Viking, 1974), 68–69, 74; Guillermoprieto, *Dancing*, 85, 89; Karol, *Guerrillas*, 413.

27. Guillermoprieto, *Dancing*, 107–8.

28. Guillermoprieto, *Dancing*, 106–8; Randall, *To Change*, 77; footage of the rally at https://www.youtube.com/watch?v=4BAlsoBnzlQ.

29. Eckstein, *Back from the Future*, 39–40, 64.

30. Selma Díaz, Julio Díaz Vázques, and Juan Valdés Paz, "La Zafra de los diez millones: Una mirada retrospectiva," *Temas* 72 (October–December 2012): 69–76.

31. Fidel Castro speech, December 31, 1971. He made similar statements regularly in this period; see, for example, speeches of March 1, 1971; July 26, 1971; December 31, 1971; and November 15, 1973.

Chapter 30: New Americans?

1. María Cristina García, *Havana USA: Cuban Exiles and Cuban Americans in South Florida, 1959–1994* (Berkeley: University of California Press, 1996), 13–19; María de los Angeles Torres, *In the Land of Mirrors: Cuban Exile Politics in the United States* (Ann Arbor: University of Michigan Press, 2014), 72; R. R. Palmer, *The Age of the Democratic Revolution* (Princeton, NJ: Princeton University Press, 1969), 1:188. Cuba's rate of outmigration was significantly higher than those for the American and French revolutions and lower than for the Haitian. Seymour Drescher, "The Limits of Example," in *The Impact of the Haitian Revolution in the Atlantic World*, ed. David Geggus (Columbia: University of South Carolina Press, 2001), 10.

2. [?] to Nnene (February 26, 1962) and V. to Japonesa querida (March 16, 1962), letters 7 and 8, Folder 1, Cuban Letters Collection, Tamiment Archives, New York University.

3. M. C. García, *Havana USA*, 16–17. After the US embassy closed in January 1961, Cubans could no longer acquire visas and received "visa waivers" on arrival.

4. Grupo Areíto, *Contra viento y marea* (Havana: Casa de las Américas, 1978), 16; M. C. García, *Havana USA*, 17; Michael Bustamante, personal communication, April 15, 2020. My mother and I left Havana in April 1963 via Mexico.

NOTES

5. Louis A. Pérez, *Cuba: Between Reform and Revolution*, 261; Richard R. Fagen, Richard A. Brody, and Thomas J. O'Leary, *Cubans in Exile: Disaffection and Revolution* (Stanford, CA: Stanford University Press, 1968), 19; M. C. García, *Havana USA*, 20, 28; Grupo Areíto, *Contra viento y marea*, 26; Guillermo Grenier and Corinna Moebius, *A History of Little Havana* (Charleston, SC: History Press, 2015), 14, 25–28, 36.

6. M. C. García, *Havana USA*, 29; Grenier and Moebius, *History of Little Havana*, 28, 38; Nathan Connolly, *A World More Concrete: Real Estate and the Remaking of Jim Crow South Florida* (Chicago: University of Chicago Press, 2014), 220–22.

7. Connolly, *A World*, 26, 218; M. C. García, *Havana USA*, 29; Chanelle Rose, *The Struggle for Black Freedom in Miami: Civil Rights and America's Tourist Paradise, 1896–1968* (Baton Rouge: Louisiana State University Press, 2015), 185, 219. The hotel story is my mother's description of what happened to her on arrival in Miami on July 4, 1963.

8. Guillermo Grenier and Lisandro Pérez, *Legacy of Exile: Cubans in the United States* (Boston: Pearson Higher Education, 2003), 22–23.

9. Alejandro Portés and Alex Stepick, *City on the Edge: The Transformation of Miami* (Berkeley: University of California Press, 1993), 43; Connolly, *A World*, 220–21; M. C. García, *Havana USA*, 19; Grenier and Moebius, *History of Little Havana*, 41.

10. "The Dramatic Story," *Parade*, August 30, 1964; "86 Who Fled Cuba Reach US Safely," *New York Times*, September 24, 1965, 3; Carl Bon Tempo, *Americans at the Gate: The United States and Refugees During the Cold War* (Princeton, NJ: Princeton University Press, 2015), 124.

11. Fidel Castro speech, September 28, 1965.

12. M. C. García, *Havana USA*, 38; Sidney Schanberg, "Cubans Continue to Leave by Sea," "Refugee Flow Continues," "Cubans in Miami Rush to Help Kin," *New York Times*, October 13, 1965, 18; October 14, 1965, 3; and October 24, 1965, 60.

13. M. C. García, *Havana USA*, 37–39, 43; Grenier and Pérez, *Legacy of Exile*, 24.

14. Grenier and Pérez, *Legacy of Exile*, 24; M. C. García, *Havana USA*, 43.

15. Yolanda Prieto, *The Cubans of Union City: Immigrants and Exiles in a New Jersey Community* (Philadelphia: Temple University Press, 2009); M. C. García, *Havana USA*, 39–40; "The Simple Pleasures of a Chino-Cubano Restaurant," https://cubannewyorker.wordpress.com/2012/07/01/the-simple-pleasures-of-a-chino-cubano-restaurant-2/.

16. Grenier and Moebius, *History of Little Havana*, 27, 41, 47, 62–63; Grupo Areíto, *Contra viento y marea*, 116–19; Geoffrey E. Fox, *Working-Class Emigres from Cuba* (Palo Alto, CA: R & E Research Associates, 1979), 96.

17. M. C. García, *Havana USA*, 42. See also Cuban Adjustment Act, http://uscode.house.gov/statutes/pl/89/732.pdf and https://www.uscis.gov/greencard/caa.

18. Jimmy Carter, Presidential Directive/NSC-6, in https://nsarchive2.gwu.edu

/news/20020515/cartercuba.pdf; Grenier and Moebius, *History of Little Havana*, 62–63; Joan Didion, *Miami* (New York: Simon & Schuster, 1987), 99–101.

19. M. C. García, *Havana USA*, 47–50; Mirta Ojito, *Finding Mañana: A Memoir of a Cuban Exodus* (New York: Penguin, 2005), 51.

20. M. C. García, *Havana USA*, 48–50; Ojito, *Finding Mañana*, 48–51.

21. M. C. García, *Havana USA*, 51–52; Ojito, *Finding Mañana*, 59–60.

22. Ojito, *Finding Mañana*, 59–64; José Manuel García, *Voices from Mariel: Oral Histories of the 1980 Cuban Boatlift* (Gainesville: University Press of Florida, 2018), 44; Adelaida Ferrer, personal communication, May 21, 2019.

23. Ojito, *Finding Mañana*, 59–64; M. C. García, *Havana USA*, 53–54.

24. Ojito, *Finding Mañana*, 63–64; M. C. García, *Havana USA*, 52; Jorge Duany, *Blurred Borders: Transnational Migration Between the Hispanic Caribbean and the United States* (Chapel Hill: University of North Carolina Press, 2011), 141.

25. Ojito, *Finding Mañana*, 114.

26. Grenier and Pérez, *Legacy of Exile*, 24–25; Ojito, *Finding Mañana*, 103–4; M. C. García, *Havana USA*, 54–57.

27. Mari Lauret, *La odisea del Mariel: un testimonio sobre el éxodo de la embajada de Perú en La Habana* (Madrid: Editorial Betania, 2015), chs. 2–3; Ojito, *Finding Mañana*, 106; M. C. García, *Havana USA*, 54–57.

28. Graham Hovey, "US Agrees to Admit up to 3500 Cubans from Peruvian Embassy," *New York Times*, April 15, 1980, A1; Ojito, *Finding Mañana*, 132; M. C. García, *Havana USA*, 58–59.

29. In a 1989 interview with the *Miami Herald*, Vilaboa claimed to have been a Cuban agent; in an interview with the same paper in 2010, he insisted he was not. Liz Balmaseda, "Exile: I Was Mastermind of Mariel," *Miami Herald*, July 31, 1989, 1-B; Juan Tamayo, "Napeleón Vilaboa, Father of Mariel Boatlift, Speaks," *Miami Herald*, May 15, 2010.

30. Ojito, *Finding Mañana*, 137–53; Kate Dupes Hawk, Ron Villella, and Adolfo Leyva de Varona, *Florida and the Mariel Boatlift of 1980: The First Twenty Days* (Tuscaloosa: University of Alabama Press, 2014), 49–50. Miami city population in 1980 was 346,865; see US Census Bureau, 1980 Census of Population, Florida (Volume 1, Chapter A, Part 11), Table 5.

31. By October, 125,000 had arrived. Hawk et al., *Florida and the Mariel Boatlift of 1980*, 70; M. C. García, *Havana USA*, 60–61; Ojito, *Finding Mañana*, 253.

32. Hawk et al., *Florida and the Mariel Boatlift of 1980*, 80; Grenier and Lisandro Pérez, *Legacy of Exile*, 21; Juan Tamayo, "El éxodo cobra vidas en la isla y por naufragios," *Nuevo Herald*, May 2, 2010.

33. Hawk et al., *Florida and the Mariel Boatlift of 1980*, 77; Stephen Webbe, "One Man

NOTES

Who Sailed to Cuba," *Christian Science Monitor*, May 29, 1980, B6; author interview with Matt Cartsonis, crew member aboard the *Sundance II*, September 18, 2020; Ojito, *Finding Mañana*, 184–85.

34. J. M. García, *Voices from Mariel*, 16–17, 46–48; Ojito, *Finding Mañana*, 174–74; Arenas, *Before Night Falls*, 285–86; Abel Sierra Madero, "'Here Everyone's Got *Huevos*, Mister!': Nationalism, Sexuality, and Collective Violence in Cuba during the Mariel Exodus," in *The Revolution from Within*, 244–74.

35. Author interview with Matt Cartsonis, September 18, 2020.

36. *Granma* quoted in Ojito, *Finding Mañana*, 171; Fidel Castro speech, May 1, 1980 (UT LANIC).

37. M. C. García, *Havana USA*, 64; personal communication with Onelio López, 1989; Arenas, *Before Night Falls*, 281–84.

38. Sam Verdeja and Guillermo Martínez, *Cubans: An Epic Journey: The Struggle for Truth and Freedom* (St. Louis: Reedy Press, 2012), 152; Ojito, *Finding Mañana*, 241; Hawk et al., *Florida and the Mariel Boatlift of 1980*, 31, 41, 240–41.

39. M. C. García, *Havana USA*, 64–65; Julio Capó, "Queering Mariel: Mediating Cold War Foreign Policy and US Citizenship among Cuba's Homosexual Exile Community, 1978–1994," *Journal of Ethnic History* 29 (Summer 2010): 78–106; Jennifer Lambe, *Madhouse: Psychiatry and Politics in Cuban History* (Chapel Hill: University of North Carolina Press, 2016), 200–10; Mark Hamm, *The Abandoned Ones: The Imprisonment and Uprising of the Mariel Boat People* (Boston: Northeastern University Press, 1995), 60–65, 71.

40. M. C. García, *Havana USA*, 68; Grenier and Moebius, *History of Little Havana*, 69.

41. Edward Schumacker, "Retarded People and Criminals Are Included in the Cuban Exodus," *New York Times*, May 11, 1980, 1; Ojito, *Finding Mañana*, 242; Portés and Stepick, *City on the Edge*, 27–28.

42. Hawk et al., *Florida and the Mariel Boatlift of 1980*, 112; Ojito, *Finding Mañana*, 242–43.

43. M. C. García, *Havana USA*, 62–63; Grenier and Moebius, *History of Little Havana*, 67–68; Hawk et al., *Florida and the Mariel Boatlift of 1980*, 93, 107; Didion, *Miami*, 42.

44. M. C. García, *Havana USA*, 63; Hawk et al., *Florida and the Mariel Boatlift of 1980*, 183, 218; Jenna Loyd and Alison Mountz, *Boats, Borders, and Bases: Race, the Cold War, and the Rise of Migration Detention in the United States* (Berkeley: University of California Press, 2018), 54; Tom Mason (Air Force Materiel Command History Office), "Operation Red, White, and Blue: Eglin Air Force Base and the Mariel Boatlift," https://www.afmc.af.mil/News/Article-Display/Article/1703372/operation-red-white-and-blue-eglin-afb-and-the-mariel-boatlift/.

45. M. C. García, *Havana USA*, 66, 71; "Cuban Refugee Crisis," Encyclopedia of Arkansas, https://encyclopediaofarkansas.net/entries/cuban-refugee-crisis-4248/.

46. M. C. García, *Havana USA*, 66; Hawk et al., *Florida and the Mariel Boatlift of 1980*, 235–36; Ojito, *Finding Mañana*, 241.

47. Didion, *Miami*, 40–45.

48. Grenier and Moebius, *History of Little Havana*, 78–79; Torres, *In the Land*, 115.

49. Ojito, *Finding Mañana*, 225.

Chapter 31: Other Cubas?

1. Edward George, *The Cuban Intervention in Angola, 1965–1991: From Che Guevara to Cuito Cuanavale* (London: Routledge, 2012), 22.

2. Fidel Castro speech, February 4, 1962; US Senate, *The Tricontinental Conference of African, Asian, and Latin American Peoples: A Staff Study*, Committee on the Judiciary (Washington, DC: US Government Printing Office, 1966), 135; *The Art of Revolution Will Be Internationalist*, Dossier no. 15, Tricontinental: Institute for Social Research, April 2019, https://www.thetricontinental.org/wp-content/uploads/2019/04/190408_Dossier-15_EN_Final_Web.pdf.

3. Piero Gleijeses, *Conflicting Missions: Havana, Washington, and Africa, 1959–1976* (Chapel Hill: University of North Carolina Press, 2002), 31, 50; Schoultz, *Infernal Little Cuban Republic*, 279.

4. Castro and Ramonet, *My Life*, 293; Schoultz, *Infernal Little Cuban Republic*, 279; Gleijeses, *Conflicting Missions*, 50–52.

5. Robyn d'Avignon, Elizabeth Banks, and Asif Siddiqi, "The African Soviet Modern," *Comparative Studies of South Asia, Africa, and the Middle East*, 41, no. 1 (2021); Jorge G. Castañeda, *Utopia Unarmed: The Latin American Left after the Cold War* (New York: Knopf, 1993), 57; Anderson, *Che*, 511; Fidel Castro speech, July 26, 1960.

6. Jorge Domínguez, "Cuban Foreign Policy," *Foreign Affairs* 57, no. 1 (Fall 1978): 85; Castro and Ramonet, *My Life*, 293.

7. Jorge Masetti, *In the Pirate's Den: My Life as a Secret Agent for Castro* (San Francisco: Encounter Books, 2004), 12; Jorge Domínguez, *To Make a World Safe for Revolution: Cuba's Foreign Policy* (Cambridge, MA: Harvard University Press, 1989), 70–71.

8. Quoted in Domínguez, *To Make a World Safe*, 76. On immediate response to Guevara's death, Anderson, *Che*, 714; Díaz, *Initials of the Earth*, 300–303.

9. Domínguez, *To Make a World Safe*, 36; Louis A. Pérez, *Cuba: Between Reform and Revolution*, 289; Eckstein, *Back from the Future*, 175, 189; Dick Krujit, ed., *Cuba and Revolutionary Latin America: An Oral History* (London: Zed Books, 2017), 153; interview with Bernardo Benes, in Luis Botifoll Oral History Project, University of Miami, Cuban Heritage Collection, https://merrick.library.miami.edu/cdm/ref/collection/chc5212/id/53.8.

10. George, *Cuban Intervention*, 22.

11. George, *Cuban Intervention*, 49, 65.

12. Ryszard Kapuscinski, *Another Day of Life* (New York: Vintage, 2001), 117.

13. Schoultz, *Infernal Little Cuban Republic*, 280.

14. Christabelle Peters, *Cuban Identity and the Angolan Experience* (New York: Palgrave Macmillan, 2012); Finch, *Rethinking Slave Rebellion*, 88; George, *Cuban Intervention*, 77; Raúl and Fidel Castro quoted in Schoultz, *Infernal Little Cuban Republic*, 278.

15. Kapuscinski, *Another Day of Life*, 111–2; Gabriel García Márquez, "Operación Carlota," 1977, available at https://dispensario22.files.wordpress.com/2013/05/operacion-carlota-gesta-cubana-en-angola-g-garcc3ada-mc3a1rquez.pdf.

16. Gabriel García Márquez, "Operación Carlota"; Schoultz, *Infernal Little Cuban Republic*, 281; "Memorandum of Conversation," Beijing, December 2, 1975, in *FRUS, DP*, 1969–1976, vol. 18, China, 1973–1976, doc. 134.

17. "National Intelligence Estimate, 85-1-75. Cuba's Changing International Role," October 16, 1975, in *FRUS, DP*, 1969–1976, vol. E-11, Part 1, Documents on Mexico, Central America and the Caribbean, 1973–1976, doc. 304; and "Report Prepared by the Working Group on Angola, October 22, 1975," in *FRUS, DP*, 1969–1976, vol. 28, Southern Africa, doc. 132.

18. "Memorandum of Conversation," Washington, DC, December 9, 1975 (Kissinger/Dobrynin in *FRUS, DP*); Schoultz, *Infernal Little Cuban Republic*, 286; Anatoliy Dobrynin, *In Confidence: Moscow's Ambassador to America's Six Cold War Presidents* (New York: Crown, 1995), 362; Henry Kissinger, *Years of Renewal* (New York: Simon & Schuster, 1999), 816–17.

19. George, *Cuban Intervention*, 94, 100–13; Schoultz, *Infernal Little Cuban Republic*, 284; Kapuscinski, *Another Day of Life*, 120.

20. García Márquez, "Operación Carlota."

21. Piero Gleijeses, *Visions of Freedom: Havana, Washington, Pretoria, and the Struggle for Southern Africa (1976–1991)*, (Chapel Hill: University of North Carolina Press, 2013), 407–14; Eckstein, *Back from the Future*, 172; George, *Cuban Intervention*, 213, 251.

22. William LeoGrande and Peter Kornbluh, *Back Channel to Cuba: The Hidden History of Negotiations between Washington and Havana* (Chapel Hill: University of North Carolina Press, 2015), 252–54; George, *Cuban Intervention*, 11, 253.

23. Eckstein, *Back from the Future*, 172; Marisabel Almer, "Cuban Narratives of War: Memories of Angola," in *Caribbean Military Encounters*, eds. Shalini Puri and Lara Putnam (New York: Palgrave Macmillan, 2017), 195.

24. Almer, "Cuban Narratives," 198–203; Alejandro de la Fuente, personal communication, January 2, 2021. A cousin who served in Angola gave me a porcupine

spine he had brought back from the war as a gift on my first visit back to Cuba in 1990.

25. Isaac Saney, "African Stalingrad: The Cuban Revolution, Internationalism, and the End of Apartheid," *Latin American Perspectives* 33, no. 5 (2006): 81–117; Nelson Mandela speech in Havana on July 26, 1991, in http://lanic.utexas.edu/project /castro/db/1991/19910726-1.html; Gleijeses, *Visions*, 338–40, 379.

26. Ben Rhodes, *The World as It Is: A Memoir of the Obama White House* (New York: Random House, 2018), 261, 265; Interview with Ben Rhodes, December 18, 2020.

Chapter 32: Special Years

1. Carmelo Mesa-Lago, ed., *Cuba After the Cold War* (Pittsburgh: University of Pittsburgh Press, 1993), 4; Eckstein, *Back from the Future*, 60.

2. H. Michael Erisman, *Cuba's Foreign Relations in a Post-Soviet World* (Gainesville: University Press of Florida, 2002), 108; Cole Blasier, "The End," and Carmelo Mesa-Lago, "Cuba and the Downfall," both in *Cuba After the Cold War*, 73, 88, 152; Louis A. Pérez, *Cuba: Between Reform and Revolution*, 271, 292.

3. Cole Blasier, "The End," 70; Eckstein, *Back from the Future*, 91–92.

4. Blasier, "The End," 86–89.

5. Blasier, "The End," 89–90; LeoGrande and Kornbluh, *Back Channel to Cuba*, 265.

6. LeoGrande and Kornbluh, *Back Channel to Cuba*, 265.

7. LeoGrande and Kornbluh, *Back Channel to Cuba*, 265–66; Blasier, "The End," 90; Carmelo Mesa-Lago, "Cuba and the Downfall," 150–51.

8. Quoted in Louis A. Pérez, *Cuba: Between Reform and Revolution*, 303.

9. Mesa-Lago, *Cuba After the Cold War*, 6, 219; I saw the placards during a three-month stay in Cuba in early 1992.

10. Mesa-Lago, *Cuba After the Cold War*, 3–6. Fidel's first use of "socialism or death" appears to have been on January 1, 1989, but it became standard only after December 1989, the same month the Berlin Wall fell. I heard the bullfighter joke in Havana in early 1992.

11. Fidel Castro speech, January 29, 1990; *Granma*, December 30, 1990.

12. José Bell Lara, Tania Caram, Dirk Kruijt, and Delia Luisa López, *Cuba, período especial* (Havana: Editorial UH, 2017), 21–25; Sergio Guerra and Alejo Maldonado, *Historia de la Revolución cubana* (Tafalla [Spain]: Txalaparta, 2009), 139–40; Ariana Hernández-Reguant, *Cuba in the Special Period: Culture and Ideology in the 1990s* (New York: Palgrave Macmillan, 2009), 4; Louis A. Pérez, *Cuba: Between Reform and Revolution*, 293–4.

13. Eckstein, *Back from the Future*, 99, 127–28, 169; Louis A. Pérez, *Cuba: Between Reform and Revolution*, 294;

NOTES

14. Eckstein, *Back from the Future*, 134–35; Louis A. Pérez, *Cuba: Between Reform and Revolution*, 294; Cluster and Hernandez, *History of Havana*, 255–57; observations from author trip March–June 1992.

15. Mesa-Lago, "Cuba and the Downfall," 181; Carmelo Mesa-Lago, "Economic Effects," in *Cuba After the Cold War*, 33; Cluster and Hernandez, *History of Havana*, 257.

16. Hernández-Reguant, *Cuba in the Special Period*, 1–2; author observations.

17. LeoGrande and Kornbluh, *Back Channel to Cuba*, 264.

18. LeoGrande and Kornbluh, *Back Channel to Cuba*, 269–71.

19. "Open for Business," *Time*, February 20, 1995.

20. Andrea Colantonio and Robert Potter, *Urban Tourism and Development in the Socialist State: Havana during the Special Period* (Burlington, VT: Ashgate, 2006), 38, 111.

21. Jane Franklin, "The Year 1992," in *Cuba and the US Empire: A Chronological History* (New York: New York University Press, 2016), 288–307; Louis A. Pérez, *Cuba: Between Reform and Revolution*, 307–9; Mesa Lago, "Cuba's Economic Strategies," in *Cuba After the Cold War*, 201–2.

22. Ted Henken and Gabriel Vignoli, "Entrepreneurial Reform and Political Engagement," in *A New Chapter in US-Cuba Relations*, eds. Eric Hershber and William LeoGrande (New York: Palgrave Macmillan, 2016), 165.

23. Louis A. Pérez, *Cuba: Between Reform and Revolution*, 296.

24. Pedro Luis Ferrer, "Ciento por ciento Cubano," in *Cuba: apertura y reforma económica*, ed. Bert Hoffman (Caracas: Editorial Nueva Sociedad, 1995), 129.

25. Louis A. Pérez, *Cuba: Between Reform and Revolution*, 310; author observations.

26. Valerio Simoni, *Tourism and Informal Encounters in Cuba* (New York: Berghan Books, 2016), 52; Fidel Castro speeches on April 4 and July 11, 1992; Eckstein, *Back from the Future*, 105.

27. De la Fuente, *A Nation for All*, 277.

28. De la Fuente, *A Nation*, 318–22; the song "Tengo" is by the group Orishas.

29. LeoGrande and Kornbluh, *Back Channel to Cuba*, 280.

30. According to Human Rights Watch, thousands participated, hundreds were arrested, https://www.hrw.org/legacy/reports/pdfs/c/cuba/cuba94o.pdf; LeoGrande and Kornbluh, *Back Channel to Cuba*, 281.

31. Gillian Gunn, "Death in the Florida Straits," *Washington Post*, July 14, 1991; LeoGrande and Kornbluh, *Back Channel to Cuba*, 281; Grenier and Lisandro Pérez, *Legacy*, 25.

32. LeoGrande and Kornbluh, *Back Channel to Cuba*, 299.

NOTES

33. LeoGrande and Kornbluh, *Back Channel to Cuba*, 285–92; Deborah Ramirez, "Cubans Scramble to Win Lotto," *Sun Sentinel*, April 27, 1996, https://www.sun -sentinel.com/news/fl-xpm-1996-04-26-9604250736-story.html.

34. Jimmy Carter, "President Carter's Cuba Trip Report," https://www.cartercenter .org/news/documents/doc528.html; LeoGrande and Kornbluh, *Back Channel to Cuba*, 351–55; https://cpj.org/reports/2008/03/cuba-press-crackdown.php.

35. Tom Fletcher, "La Revolución Energética: A Model for Reducing Cuba's Dependence on Venezuelan Oil," *International Journal of Cuban Studies* 9, no. 1 (2017): 91–116.

36. Text of law at https://www.congress.gov/bill/104th-congress/house-bill/927.

37. "Cuba: Reaffirmation of Cuban Dignity and Sovereignty Act," in *International Legal Materials* 36, no. 2 (1997): 472–76; Library of Congress, Law Library, "Laws Lifting Sovereign Immunity: Cuba," https://www.loc.gov/law/help/sovereign -immunity/cuba.php; Amnesty International, "Cuba: Human Rights at a Glance," September 17, 2015, https://www.amnesty.org/en/latest/news/2015/09/cuba -human-rights-at-a-glance.

38. LeoGrande and Kornbluh, *Back Channel to Cuba*, 305, 314; "Cuba Cracks Down on Dissidents," BBC, March 19, 2003, http://news.bbc.co.uk/2/hi/amer icas/2863005.stm.

39. "Castro Appears to Faint at Podium," *New York Times*, June 23, 2001.

Chapter 33: Open and Shut

1. US Department of State, Case No. F-2007-01578, Doc. No. C17731028, "Demarche Request: Democracy and Castro Succession," August 6 [2006], DNSA, Cuba and the US, 1959–2016 Collection; LeoGrande and Kornbluh, *Back Channel to Cuba*, 365–67.

2. LeoGrande and Kornbluh, *Back Channel to Cuba*, 365–67; "La disidencia interna dice que Cuba vive con 'aparente calma' pero 'cierta expectación' los últimos cambios," Europa Press, Notimérica, August 10, 2006, https://www.notimerica.com /politica/noticia-cuba-disidencia-interna-dice-cuba-vive-aparente-calma-cierta -expectacion-ultimos-cambios-20060809235800.html.

3. David Beresford, "Photographs show Castro alive," *The Guardian*, August 14, 2006; "Fotos actuales del Presidente cubano Fidel Castro," *Juventud Rebelde*, August 13, 1960.

4. Mauricio Vicent, "El 'efecto Obama' sacude la isla," *El País*, November 18, 2008.

5. Fidel Castro, "Las elecciones del 4 de noviembre" and "El undécimo presidente de Estados Unidos," *Granma*, November 3, 2008, and January 22, 2009.

6. American Civil Liberties Union, "Guantánamo by the Numbers," https://www

NOTES

.aclu.org/issues/national-security/detention/guantanamo-numbers; Obama speech, May 21, 2009, https://obamawhitehouse.archives.gov/the-press-office /remarks-president-national-security-5-21-09; Mora quoted in "Inquiry into the Treatment of Detainees in U.S. Custody," Report of the Committee on Armed Services, US Senate, November 20, 2008, p. xii; Connie Bruck, "Why Obama Has Failed to Close Guantánamo," *New Yorker*, August 1, 2016.

7. Bruck, "Why Obama Has Failed to Close Guantánamo."

8. LeoGrande and Kornbluh, *Back Channel to Cuba*, epilogue to the 2nd ed., 421–49 (earlier citations to this book are from first edition); Rhodes, *The World as It Is*, 209–17, 261–66, 283–89, 300–8 (Obama quote appears on 287).

9. Rhodes, *The World as It Is*, 307–8. Obama, "Statement by the President on Cuba Policy Changes," December 17, 2014, https://obamawhitehouse.archives.gov/the -press-office/2014/12/17/statement-president-cuba-policy-changes.

10. Raúl Castro, "Statement by the Cuban President," December 17, 2014, http:// www.cuba.cu/gobierno/rauldiscursos/2014/ing/r171214i.html.

11. LeoGrande and Kornbluh, *Back Channel to Cuba*, 448.

12. Damien Cave, personal communication, Havana, March, 2016.

13. The description of Obama's visit comes largely from my own observations, published as "Listening to Obama in Cuba," NACLA, March 28, 2016, https:// nacla.org/news/2016/03/28/listening-obama-cuba. Obama quote is from his speech in Havana on March 22, 2016, https://obamawhitehouse.archives.gov /the-press-office/2016/03/22/remarks-president-obama-people-cuba.

14. "Llegada de Obama al restaurante San Cristobal Paladar en Centro Habana," https://www.youtube.com/watch?v=xs6VrbKyXx4.

15. Author conversation with audience member at "José Antonio Aponte: Perspectivas Interdisciplinarias," Havana, November 2017; Ana Dopico, "I'll Be Your Mirror: Obama and the Cuban Afterglow," *Cuba Cargo/Cult* (blog), March 25, 2016, https://cubacar gocult.blog/2016/03/25/ill-be-your-mirror-obama-and-the-cuban-after-glow.

16. Fidel Castro, "Brother Obama," *Granma*, March 28, 2016.

17. Editorial Cartoonist Michael de Adder, November 26, 2016, http://deadder.net /?s=castro.

18. US Census Bureau, International Programs Database, Cuba, https://www.census .gov/data-tools/demo/idb/region.php?T=15&RT=0&A=both&Y=2020&C=C U&R=.

19. William M. LeoGrande, "Cuba's Economic Crisis Is Spurring Much-Needed Action on Reforms," *World Politics Review*, November 17, 2020; Marc Caputo and Daniel Ducassi, "Trump to Clamp Down on Cuba Travel and Trade," Politico, June 16, 2017.

NOTES

20.   Human Rights Watch, "Cuba: Events of 2019" and "Cuba: Events of 2020"; Congressional Research Service, "Cuba: U.S. Policy Overview," updated January 25, 2021, https://fas.org/sgp/crs/row/IF10045.pdf.

21.   Rhodes, *The World as It Is*, 411; LeoGrande, "Cuba's Economic Crisis."

22.   Nelson Acosta, "Cubans Applaud Biden Win, Hope for Easing of Sanctions," Reuters, November 8, 2020, https://www.reuters.com/article/usa-election-cuba -idINKBN27O050.

Epilogue: If Monuments Could Speak

1.   The information on Ramos Blanco's visit to Key West appears in *Florida, U.S., Arriving and Departing Passenger and Crew Lists, 1898–1963*, available on ancestry.com. Frank Guridy, *Forging Diaspora: Afro-Cubans and African Americans in a World of Empire and Jim Crow* (Chapel Hill: University of North Carolina Press, 2010), 107–8, 114–16. I am grateful to Ramón Cernuda of Cernuda Art, which holds several pieces by Ramos Blanco, for sharing a comprehensive list of the sculptor's works.

Image Credits

Interior

p. xii: M. Roy Cartography

p. 7: *De insulis nuper in mari Indico repertis* (The islands have recently been discovered in the Indian Sea), 1494. Courtesy of the John Carter Brown Library

p. 12: M. Roy Cartography

p. 29: Map of Havana, ca. 1567. Archivo General de Indias, Fondo Mapas y Planos, Santo Domingo, 4

p. 40: A view of the Franciscan Church and convent in the city of Havana, by Elias Walker Durnford, 1768. Courtesy of the Library of Congress

p. 78: Steam Sawmill on the New Hope Sugar Estate, Cuba, by George Howe, 1832–1834. Courtesy of the Bristol Historical & Preservation Society

p. 84: M. Roy Cartography

p. 126: Cuban mambises crossing a river, 1895–1898. Courtesy of the Cuban Heritage Collection, University of Miami

p. 154: Cuba Libre, 1898. Courtesy of the Library of Congress

p. 168: General Máximo Gómez in discussions about the disbandment of Cuban army, 1899. Courtesy of the Miriam and Ira D. Wallach Division of Art, Prints and Photographs, The New York Public Library

p. 182: Studebaker with passengers posing in front of the Presidential Palace, 1926. Courtesy of the Ramiro A. Fernández Collection

p. 185: President Tomás Estrada Palma and his cabinet, 1902. Courtesy of the Cuban Heritage Collection, University of Miami

p. 189: M. Roy Cartography

p. 203: General Quintín Bandera. Courtesy of the Cuban Heritage Collection, University of Miami

IMAGE CREDITS

p. 227: Julio Antonio Mella, by Tina Modotti. Wikicommons

p. 232: Workers' rally with flag, 1940. Courtesy of the Ramiro A. Fernández Collection

p. 267: Women raising brooms in support of Eduardo Chibás, by Enrique Llanos. Courtesy of the Cuban Heritage Collection, University of Miami

p. 272: Constructing the monument to José Martí, Ernesto Fernández, 1957. Courtesy of Ernesto Fernández

p. 276: Celia Sánchez. Courtesy of the Cuban Heritage Collection, University of Miami

p. 312: A crowd on the Malecón during the early Cuban Revolution. Courtesy of the Ramiro A. Fernández Collection

p. 329: Customs workers donating tractor, 1959. Courtesy of the Cuban Heritage Collection, University of Miami

p. 344: Ernesto Che Guevara, by Alberto Korda. Courtesy of ARS and Korda Estate

p. 351: Cuban soldiers next to antiaircraft artillery on the Malecón, January 1, 1962. Getty Images

p. 383: Young volunteer during the sugar harvest. Courtesy of the Ramiro A. Fernández Collection

p. 432: Rafters at Havana's Malecón, 1994. Photo A. Abbas. Magnum Photos

Photo Insert 1

1. Taíno sculpture. Courtesy of the Smithsonian Museum of Natural History
2. The execution of Hatuey. Courtesy of the John Carter Brown Library
3. British siege of Havana, 1762. Courtesy of the Library of Congress
4. Uniform of Havana's Black militia. Courtesy of Archivo General de Indias (MP-UNIFORMES, 25)
5. Enslaved workers harvesting sugarcane. Courtesy of the Ramiro A. Fernández Collection
6. Trinidad plantation, Matanzas. Wikicommons
7. Carlos Manuel de Céspedes. Wikicommons
8. Identification Document for José Chuen, 1871. Courtesy of the University of Miami, Cuban Heritage Collection
9. The Elders, photograph by José Gómez de la Carrera, 1890s. Courtesy of the Ramiro A. Fernández Collection

IMAGE CREDITS

10. José Martí, 1891. Courtesy of the University of Miami, Cuban Heritage Collection
11. Rosa la Bayamesa, *El Fígaro*, October 22, 1899.
12. Antonio Maceo with fellow conspirators, 1892. Courtesy of the Biblioteca Nacional de España
13. USS *Maine* entering Havana Harbor, 1898. Courtesy of the New York Public Library, Prints and Photographs Division
14. Teddy Roosevelt and the Rough Riders. Courtesy of the Library of Congress
15. The Governor's Palace in Havana, 1899. Courtesy of Harvard University, Houghton Library
16. Cuban Teachers at Harvard, 1900. Courtesy of the Harvard University Archives
17. "A Precautionary Amendment," *Minneapolis Journal*, April 22, 1901. Courtesy of the Hennepin County Library
18. "Asalto y Robo," *Política Cómica*, March 21, 1901
19. Modern Sugar Mill, Cuba, 1904. Wikicommons
20. Workers at Sugar Central Cunagua. Courtesy of the University of Miami, Cuban Heritage Collection
21. Map of La Gloria, an American "colony" in Cuba. Courtesy of the New York Public Library, Map Division
22. Presidents Calvin Coolidge and Gerardo Machado, 1928. Courtesy of the Library of Congress
23. Havana, 1933. Courtesy of Granger

Photo Insert 2

1. Pan American flight, 1928. Courtesy of the University of Miami, Richter Library, Special Collections
2. Sloppy Joe's Bar. Courtesy of the University of Miami, Cuban Heritage Collection
3. Ramón Grau San Martín and Fulgencio Batista, 1933. Courtesy of the University of Miami, Cuban Heritage Collection
4. Political Demonstration, Havana, December 1933. Courtesy of the University of Miami, Cuban Heritage Collection
5. Eduardo Chibás. Courtesy of the Ramiro A. Fernández Collection
6. Fulgencio Batista, March 1952. Courtesy of AP Images

IMAGE CREDITS

7. Fidel Castro, 1953. Courtesy of the University of Miami, Cuban Heritage Collection
8. José Antonio Echeverría. Photographer unknown. Author collection
9. Mothers' Protest, 1957. Courtesy of Silvia Arrom and the University of Florida, George A. Smathers Library
10. Fidel and Raúl Castro, 1958, by Dickey Chapelle. Courtesy of the Wisconsin Historical Society
11. Crowd listening to Fidel, Havana, January 8, 1959, by Burt Glinn. Courtesy of Magnum Photos
12. Last Rites, 1959, by Andrew López. Courtesy of Getty Images
13. El Quijote del Farol, July 26, 1959, by Alberto Korda. Courtesy of ARS and Korda Estate
14. Fidel Castro speech, April 16, 1961. Photo Raúl Corrales. Courtesy of Alamy
15. Military Parade. Courtesy of the Ramiro A. Fernández Collection
16. Family Reunion, 1967. Courtesy of the University of Miami, Cuban Heritage Collection
17. Miami rally, 1977. Phil Sandlin, Associated Press
18. Key West, 1980. Courtesy of Duke University Libraries, Caribbean Sea Migrations Collection
19. Obama in Cuba, March 2016. Alamy
20. Havana, 2017. Allen Brown, Alamy

Index

INDEX

INDEX

INDEX

Céspedes, Carlos Manuel de (son), 236, 238, 239

Chaparra Sugar Company, 188–90, 204, 210, 214, 240, 242, 244

Charleston (city), 60, 74, 108, 119

Chávez, Hugo, 448

Chibás, Eduardo, 252, 265–70, 271, 277

Chibás, Raúl, 307, 309

children and Cuban Revolution, 387–89

China
  contract workers from, 124–25, 133, 134
  trade with Cuba and, 465

Chinese Cubans, migration of, 406

Christianity, and Spain's colonization of Cuba, 13, 15, 16–17, 18–19, 20

Christophe, Henri, 75, 468

Churchill, Winston, 147, 389

CIA
  Bay of Pigs invasion and, 356–57, 358–61, 362, 363–64
  Cuban exiles working for, 404–5
  Eisenhower's Cuba policy and, 345–46

Cienfuegos, Camilo, 292, 316

Civil War (US), 119–25, 154, 157, 159

Cleaver, Eldridge, 394

Clinton, Bill, 417, 441, 447, 450

Clinton, Hillary, 462, 463

Cocking, Francis Ross, 99–100

Cold War, 5–6, 335–36, 337, 349, 407, 451, 459

coletillas, 339–40

Columbus, Christopher, 7, 9–15, 16, 29, 224, 353
  celebrations of discovery myth of, 10–11
  Cuba landings by, 9, 11, 13–14, 15
  first permanent settlement by, 14
  Spanish backing for, 9–10, 13, 14–15
  US origin stories and, 11–13

Committees for the Defense of the Revolution (CDRs), 348, 366, 389, 414, 448

communism
  Castro and, 285–87, 303, 325, 335–37, 367, 438
  concerns about influence on 1959 revolution of, 331–32, 336–37

concerns about influence on 1933 revolution of, 241, 246

Communist Party
  Batista's legalization of, 250
  Castro's presidency of, 454
  founding of, 227
  Mella's shooting and, 228
  1940 constitutional convention and, 251–52, 254–55
  26th of July Movement and, 311

Concilio Cubano, 448–49, 450

Confederacy (Civil War), 119–25

Conservative Party, 197, 198, 201, 210

Constitution (1869), 132, 257

Constitution (1901)
  Grau's desire for rewriting of, 238, 244
  Platt Amendment and, 179–80, 187, 192, 238, 251
  US occupation and, 176–80

Constitution (1940)
  anti-discrimination amendment debates in, 254–57
  Batista and, 251, 468
  convention for drafting of, 251–57
  rights under sections of, 257–58

Constitution (1976)
  foreign investment under, 443
  petition for political and economic reforms under, 449
  socialism affirmed in, 408–9, 449, 463

Constitution (2019), 463

Constitutional Army, 202

Continental Congress, 57, 59, 60–61

conuco system, 17–18, 70

Coolidge, Calvin, 224–26, 228, 240

copper mining, 33–39

Cortés, Hernán, 21, 24

Cortina, Manuel, 252

Cosme Osorio, Gregorio, 37–38

Coubre ship explosion, 342–43, 344

Council for Mutual Economic Assistance (COMECON), 399, 436

Covid-19 crisis, 464, 465

Crittenden, William, 113–14

Crowder, Enoch, 219, 226

Cruz, Celia, 332

INDEX

INDEX

INDEX

Franco, José Luciano, 76

Frank, Waldo, 222

Franklin, Benjamin, 23, 50, 57–58, 348

free people of color. *See also* Black Cubans
leadership in Ten Years' War by, 132–34
militias with, 46, 114
rise of population of, 30, 105
siege of Havana in Seven Years' War and
militias of, 46
slave rebellions and, 74–77, 99, 100
Spanish repression of, 103–5
Virgin of Charity cult in El Cobre and,
35–38, 39

Freedom Flight migrants, 406–7, 416

French and Indian War. *See* Seven Years'
War

GAESA, 463

Gálvez, Bernardo, 63

gangsterismo, 264

García, Calixto, 137, 139, 162, 163, 165

García Agüero, Salvador, 252, 254, 255,
256, 265

García Márquez, Gabriel, 246, 428, 448

Gardoqui, Diego de, 58

gay Cubans, Cuban Revolution and, 391

George III, King of England, 48

gold
Columbus's search for, 13, 14, 15
Cuban mining of, 465
Spain's mining of, 16, 17, 18, 20, 21, 24

Gómez, Juan Gualberto, 179–80, 467

Gómez, Máximo, 133–34, 142, 144–45,
146, 149

Gómez de Avellaneda, Gertrudis, 72

Gompers, Samuel, 169

Gonzales, Ambrosio José, 115, 119, 120

Goodwin, Richard, 367

Gorbachev, Mikhail, 435–37, 448

Gordon, Nathaniel, 110

Grajales, Mariana, 467

Grandin, Greg, 157, 258

Granma, 437, 439, 454, 462

Grau San Martín, Ramón, 238–46
Batista's ouster of, 246–47, 250
conflicts over "authentic revolution" of,
244–45, 260

as constitutional convention delegate,
251, 252
desire to abolish Platt Amendment by,
238–39, 244
first presidency (1933) of, 238, 240–42,
243–46
Miami exile of, 249
second presidency (1944) of, 260–61, 265
US fears of revolution by, 239, 241–42
workers' demands and policies of, 243–44

Great Britain. *See also* England
Cuban slave rebellion support from
abolitionists in, 99, 100–101
Monroe Doctrine and, 91
rumors of takeover of Cuba by, 81–82,
87, 88, 97, 103
siege and occupation of Havana by,
44–54
slave trade ban by, 82, 85, 87, 94, 99

Grimaldi, Marquis de, 58

groupthink, 364

Guamá (Taíno leader), 20

Guantánamo (city), 144, 161, 192, 208,
211, 310

Guantánamo naval base (Gitmo), 192–93,
374, 379, 437, 448, 455–56, 460

Guatemala, 140, 337, 347, 358, 360, 363

Guerra, Lillian, 339

Guerrero, Ibis, 414

Guevara, Che, 463
background to iconic image of, 343–44
on Bay of Pigs invasion, 367
Castro's La Plata victory and, 299
Cuban foreign policy and, 422–23, 424
death of, 423
first meeting with Castro of, 294, 304
general strike strategy and, 306
Kennedy advisor's meeting with, 367
military advances of, 310, 316
new man concept of, 386–87
US-Cuba relationship and, 344
US oil refineries dispute and, 346

Guillén, Nicolás, 445, 446

Guillermoprieto, Alma, 397

Güines, 69, 71

Guiteras, Antonio, 243–45, 249, 467–68

Gulf Stream, 23–24, 84

INDEX

INDEX

INDEX

INDEX

INDEX

INDEX

INDEX

INDEX

INDEX

About the Author

Ada Ferrer is Julius Silver Professor of History and Latin American and Caribbean Studies at New York University, where she has taught since 1995. She is the author of *Insurgent Cuba: Race, Nation, and Revolution, 1868–1898*, winner of the 2000 Berkshire Book Prize for the best first book by a woman in any field of history, and *Freedom's Mirror: Cuba and Haiti in the Age of Revolution*, which won the Frederick Douglass Prize from the Gilder Lehrman Center at Yale University, as well as multiple prizes from the American Historical Association. She has received fellowships from the Guggenheim Foundation, the Dorothy and Lewis B. Cullman Center for Scholars and Writers at the New York Public Library, the National Endowment for the Humanities, the American Council of Learned Societies, the Fulbright Commission, and the Schomburg Center for Research in Black Culture, among others. Born in Cuba and raised in the United States, she has been traveling to and conducting research on the island since 1990.